Celebrating
What Is Important to Me

South
Grades 7-12
Fall 2007

Creative Communication, Inc.

Celebrating What Is Important to Me
South
Grades 7-12
Fall 2007

An anthology compiled by Creative Communication, Inc.

Published by:

CREATIVE COMMUNICATION, INC.
1488 NORTH 200 WEST
LOGAN, UT 84341

Copyright © 2008 by Creative Communication, Inc.
Printed in the United States of America

ISBN: 978-1-60050-142-5

Foreword

A few years ago there was a series of books of photographs that recorded a day in the life of the country. It was insightful and refreshing to see how people lived, worked and experienced their world. Along the same lines, this anthology is a day in the life of our youth. The essays that are recorded between these pages reflect the perceptions of our youth as they experience their world. These essays tell a story about global warming, relationships, and hundreds of other topics that are important to students today.

We are proud to have recorded these perceptions. Without this anthology these essays from our youth would have been lost in a backpack or a locker. We hope you enjoy the enclosed essays as much as we have in recording them.

Believe in our youth. They have much to offer our world.

Thomas Worthen, Ph.D.
Editor
Creative Communication

WRITING CONTESTS!

Enter our next POETRY contest!

Enter our next ESSAY contest!

Why should I enter?

Win prizes and get published! Each year thousands of dollars in prizes are awarded in each region and tens of thousands of dollars in prizes are awarded throughout North America. The top writers in each division receive a monetary award and a free book that includes their published poem or essay. Entries of merit are also selected to be published in our anthology.

Who may enter?

There are four divisions in the poetry contest. The poetry divisions are grades K-3, 4-6, 7-9, and 10-12. There are three divisions in the essay contest. The essay division are grades 4-6, 7-9, and 10-12.

What is needed to enter the contest?

To enter the poetry contest send in one original poem, 21 lines or less. To enter the essay contest send in one original essay, 250 words or less, on any topic. Each entry must include the student's name, grade, address, city, state, and zip code, and the student's school name and school address. Students who include their teacher's name may help the teacher qualify for a free copy of the anthology.

How do I enter?

Enter a poem online at:
www.poeticpower.com
or

Mail your poem to:
Poetry Contest
1488 North 200 West
Logan, UT 84341

Enter an essay online at:
www.studentessaycontest.com
or

Mail your essay to:
Essay Contest
1488 North 200 West
Logan, UT 84341

When is the deadline?

Poetry contest deadlines are April 8th, August 14th, and December 4th. Essay contest deadlines are July 15th, October 15th, and February 17th. You can enter each contest, however, send only one poem or essay for each contest deadline.

Are there benefits for my school?

Yes. We award $15,000 each year in grants to help with Language Arts programs. Schools qualify to apply for a grant by having a large number of entries of which over fifty percent are accepted for publication. This typically tends to be about 15 accepted entries.

Are there benefits for my teacher?

Yes. Teachers with five or more students accepted to be published receive a free anthology that includes their students' writing.

For more information please go to our website at **www.poeticpower.com**, email us at editor@poeticpower.com or call 435-713-4411.

Table of Contents

States included in this edition:

Alabama
Arkansas
Florida
Georgia
Kentucky
Louisiana
Mississippi
Missouri
North Carolina
Oklahoma
South Carolina
Tennessee

Fall 2007 Writing Achievement Honor Schools

* Teachers who had fifteen or more students accepted to be published

The following schools are recognized as receiving a "Writing Achievement Award." This award is given to schools who have a large number of entries of which over fifty percent are accepted for publication. With hundreds of schools entering our contest, only a small percent of these schools are honored with this award. The purpose of this award is to recognize schools with excellent Language Arts programs. This award qualifies these schools to receive a complimentary copy of this anthology. In addition, these schools are eligible to apply for a Creative Communication Language Arts Grant. Grants of two hundred and fifty dollars each are awarded to further develop writing in our schools.

Bak Middle School of the Arts
West Palm Beach, FL
Elizabeth Bornia
Jessica Samons Kutz*

Baton Rouge Magnet High School
Baton Rouge, LA
Carrie Brumfield*

Baylor School
Chattanooga, TN
Fontaine Alison
Sally Naylor*

Bishop Verot High School
Fort Myers, FL
Mary Julia Dakin*

Chelsea Jr High School
Chelsea, OK
Ms. C. Quinton*

College Heights Christian School
Joplin, MO
Kelli Barnett*

Countryside High School
Clearwater, FL
Rosemarie Ceraolo-O'Donnell*

Deltona High School
Deltona, FL
Kesia Boother*

Dyer Elementary & Jr High School
Dyer, TN
Lee Hudson*

Eagles Landing Middle School
Boca Raton, FL
Ms. Humm*

Germantown High School
Germantown, TN
Billy M. Pullen*

Grandview Alternative School
Grandview, MO
Amy Cameron*

Greenfield Jr/Sr High School
Greenfield, MO
Renée Burton*

Greenwood High School
Bowling Green, KY
Angela Townsend*

Heritage Hall School
Oklahoma City, OK
Robert Ring*

Holy Ghost Catholic School
Hammond, LA
Marie Bernard*

Mineral Springs Middle School
Winston Salem, NC
De'Shaunda Hampton*

Mulhall-Orlando High School
Orlando, OK
Kathy McNabb*

Osceola Middle School
Loxahatchee, FL
Tracey Getson*

Owasso High School
Owasso, OK
Sallyanne H. Wallace*

Pigeon Forge Middle School
Pigeon Forge, TN
Mrs. Fowler
Laura Turner*

Providence Classical School
Huntsville, AL
Katie Fletcher
John Swanner

Sebastian River Middle School
Sebastian, FL
Rachel Sullivan*

Seminole County Middle/High School
Donalsonville, GA
Becky Shamblin*

Slater High School
Slater, MO
Randolph Niswonger*

Southside High School
Chocowinity, NC
Lynn Newman*

Southwest Jr High School
Springdale, AR
Lisa Spears*

St Charles Catholic High School
LaPlace, LA
Mrs. Lohfink*

St Gerard Majella School
Kirkwood, MO
Lorraine Behrens*

St Mary's School
Greenville, SC
Sr. John Thomas Armour*

Stanton College Preparatory School
Jacksonville, FL
Matilda Bagby*

Stroud Middle School
Stroud, OK
Justin Kana*

Trinity Christian Academy
Oxford, AL
Bobbie Morris*

Turner Middle School
Atlanta, GA
Elva B. Overton*
Ms. Word

Vero Beach High School
Vero Beach, FL
Donna Griffith*

Walker Valley High School
Cleveland, TN
Sherry Everett*

West Jr High School
Columbia, MO
Heidi Barnhouse
Jeff Fagan
Michelle Jones

White Station Middle School
Memphis, TN
Angela Davis
Helen C. Erskine*
Ruby Hubbard
Karla Varriano*

Language Arts Grant Recipients 2007-2008

After receiving a "Writing Achievement Award" schools are encouraged to apply for a Creative Communication Language Arts Grant. The following is a list of schools who received a two hundred and fifty dollar grant for the 2007-2008 school year.

Acadamie DaVinci, Dunedin, FL
Altamont Elementary School, Altamont, KS
Belle Valley South School, Belleville, IL
Bose Elementary School, Kenosha, WI
Brittany Hill Middle School, Blue Springs, MO
Carver Jr High School, Spartanburg, SC
Cave City Elementary School, Cave City, AR
Central Elementary School, Iron Mountain, MI
Challenger K8 School of Science and Mathematics, Spring Hill, FL
Columbus Middle School, Columbus, MT
Cypress Christian School, Houston, TX
Deer River High School, Deer River, MN
Deweyville Middle School, Deweyville, TX
Four Peaks Elementary School, Fountain Hills, AZ
Fox Chase School, Philadelphia, PA
Fox Creek High School, North Augusta, SC
Grandview Alternative School, Grandview, MO
Hillcrest Elementary School, Lawrence, KS
Holbrook School, Holden, ME
Houston Middle School, Germantown, TN
Independence High School, Elko, NV
International College Preparatory Academy, Cincinnati, OH
John Bowne High School, Flushing, NY
Lorain County Joint Vocational School, Oberlin, OH
Merritt Secondary School, Merritt, BC
Midway Covenant Christian School, Powder Springs, GA
Muir Middle School, Milford, MI
Northlake Christian School, Covington, LA
Northwood Elementary School, Hilton, NY
Place Middle School, Denver, CO
Public School 124, South Ozone Park, NY

Language Arts Grant Winners cont.

Public School 219 Kennedy King, Brooklyn, NY
Rolling Hills Elementary School, San Diego, CA
St Anthony's School, Streator, IL
St Joan Of Arc School, Library, PA
St Joseph Catholic School, York, NE
St Joseph School-Fullerton, Baltimore, MD
St Monica Elementary School, Mishawaka, IN
St Peter Celestine Catholic School, Cherry Hill, NJ
Strasburg High School, Strasburg, VA
Stratton Elementary School, Stratton, ME
Tom Thomson Public School, Burlington, ON
Tremont Elementary School, Tremont, IL
Warren Elementary School, Warren, OR
Webster Elementary School, Hazel Park, MI
West Woods Elementary School, Arvada, CO
West Woods Upper Elementary School, Farmington, CT
White Pine Middle School, Richmond, UT
Winona Elementary School, Winona, TX
Wissahickon Charter School, Philadelphia, PA
Wood County Christian School, Williamstown, WV
Wray High School, Wray, CO

Grades 10-11-12

Top Essay Grades 10-11-12

In Love

I sat in the chair, cold and alone. I had never felt this low in my life. Everything about these past few days had made me want to crawl under a rock and never speak to another human being again. I saw this tall, lanky, dark skinned woman gliding like a swan through the living room. It was as if she didn't even have to look at me to tell how horrible I felt. She asked, "Well, Amanda, what do you love?"

I didn't know how to respond. No one had ever asked me that before. I love the feeling of sand between my toes at the beach. I love staying up until three in the morning giggling with my friends for no good reason. I love reading to my sister and making stories come alive for her. As I started to expel my feelings, they flowed like the mighty Mississippi River. I love to sit with my mom and drink iced tea with her on the porch when the weather is just right. I love to run on cool mornings in the summer. I love the way my bed feels after being at work for a long night. And now, I love the feeling of having something important to say and someone sincerely listening.

She could feel by the way my arms wrapped around her, I was so glad to have this beautiful lady in my life. I was thankful for all the love she gave me.

Amanda Carl, Grade 12
Newnan High School, GA

Top Essay Grades 10-11-12

The Living Painting

Splashes of color dart from sight when I enter the room, but I do not fear because I know they will return. I sit gazing, resting on the leopard skin ottoman as my mind melts all of these colors into one stunning piece of art that would make a smile crawl onto even the Mona Lisa's pursed lips. I then reach for the cabinet door ever so calmly, as to not disturb these whimsical colors in their graceful acrobatic dances in pure suspension against the undulating canvas. I outstretch my arm and grasp a yellow container. I rotate the lid, lift the glass top, and peer directly into this blurred multihued painting. I pinch a handful of the orange and green flakes from this life-sustaining container and submerge these pieces directly into this living painting. Currents of color eagerly engulf these tiny flakes as they twirl through the water. Two orange, black, and white shadows in the painting swim over to snatch the larger flakes, and worm their way over to a tentacle-like phantom in the far corner, where the colors are most vibrant. The diminutive hands of some of the plants in this watercolor grasp some of the remaining particles and transport them to their tiny mouths.

Feeding my fish is one of the most enjoyable chores during the day. It is amazing to be able to mimic a natural ecosystem in my bedroom, one that is abyssal in its opportunities, variations, and discoveries.

Ryan Clark, Grade 12
Hilton Head Preparatory School, SC

Top Essay Grades 10-11-12

Hidden by the Light

Blank pages stare up like a face without features. They plead for you to form and mold a picture, a moment, a thought, a meaning. It is oppressive, the pressure to create something that amazes and captivates others and yourself. It weighs you down, like a boulder tied to your ankles.

The gaping white spaces continue to glare. The only weapon available is a pen, and even that shifts uncomfortably in your hand. It seems to know that you have nothing. Your thoughts are immobilized by the spotlights of the deadline beating down. How can anything of worth be made in these conditions you wonder.

Then the garish yellow lights of the requirement suddenly dim, and a soft breeze stirs within the murkiness. There's a rustle far off, away from the lights. You follow the sound of the wind moving a once-hidden thought through the emptiness of your mind. Without the lights, movement is easier. No one is watching anymore. You are no longer afraid to stumble and fall, because there is no one to know. You can stand back up and continue like it never happened.

Soon you see it, a paper fluttering through the air. You reach for it and read the message, and suddenly it is clear. Everything that you needed to create was there, hidden by the blinding lights from others and the weights you tie to yourself.

Kaitlyn Dela Cruz, Grade 11
Academics Plus Charter School, AR

Top Essay Grades 10-11-12

A Teenager's Freedom

What is freedom in the eyes of a sixteen year old? Do we as teenagers really stop to think of the benefits of this country? Like freedom of speech for example; this wasn't put in our Constitution to be translated into having our cell phones attached to our hands permanently, or talk during the playing of our national anthem. My dad is a retired Naval Chief and served in the military for 20 years defending our flag. That three minutes of music represents what it took to give Americans their freedom.

As a Navy brat, I have been taught growing up what freedom means. It means I can wake up every day knowing I don't have to cover my face before walking outside. It means I can practice my own religion at my own free will. But most importantly, it means I can choose my future. As teenagers, we are expected to be the next generation of leaders for our nation. So as a free citizen what can I be to help the people in America? A doctor? Teacher? First woman president? The sky is the limit and the opportunities are endless.

We have the fighting soldiers to thank for this. Without our military and the heart of this country to support them, I may not be sitting in this classroom writing about it. Soon it will be our turn to take a stand, make history, and keep our freedom for the red, white, and blue.

Katelin Maiden, Grade 11
Camden Central High School, TN

Top Essay Grades 10-11-12

Consider This

Since the beginning of time the world has started to shrink, while the mind started to expand. The Earth was once thought as this vast place where viewing all of its corners in a lifetime would be impossible. But as technology has evolved throughout the ages the Earth seemed to shrink and be incapable of housing all of our physical psychological extremities, that the possibility of suffocation became rather imminent. Now in this shrunken world, people are faced with new problems like global warming and global terrorism. It seems every problem that arises is never considered a domestic threat but somehow a global one. When everything seems so close to home we don't seem to recognize the violence, deceit and injustice and how shabby our house has become.

America in general has become accustomed to knowing everything, and if we don't then it's only a couple of clicks away on the computer. Our ignorance of our ignorance though has recently gotten us into trouble. Once being a country that relied on truth and justice, we now rely on skewed "facts" and other assumptions (we all know what assuming does, right?). And these assumptions and facts are now leading to our demise. The truth is not hard to find these days though, it's rather just picking the right source. So all I ask of my fellow Americans is to consider the source, and consider the bias, because brains that have been washed are hard to clean up. And to change them would require a much longer essay than this one.

Abe Melloh, Grade 11
Bishop Verot High School, FL

Top Essay Grades 10-11-12

Sitting with a Friend

Death — stereotypically dooming and awful. Actually, death is a teacher. I was ignorant to the lessons death can teach a life before it opened its arms to me — disguised as need for moral support.

My friend Kayla's grandmother stopped living, and I was asked to attend the funeral. Due to Kayla's adamancy, I went. I nudged the door: a creak in a room filled with murmurs.

The mourners blended as each meandered about the room. Globbing together while pushing away, they resembled cells dividing in the process of mitosis rather than the advanced systems they were. Their motions seemed manual — reflexive instead of sincere. It seemed easier for each person to go through painless steps of dealing with loss rather than to mentally exercise the emotions associated with his movements.

"Sit with me. Please." Kayla's voice: a searing beg.

I felt it rude to observe the ceremony occupying the family's section, but her panic was persuasion.

Reminiscing words trickling around me, I sat ineptly. A montage of people rose to relay cherished memories. Heads bobbed in agreement as reveries flowed. Respectful of those who dismissed their shields of no-pain and unveiled actual emotion, I smiled and nodded.

I stumbled upon a truth sitting in this dismal of life: death is peculiar. It temporarily groups many together, while permanently dismissing one. Emotions are capped because if they are physically portrayed, vulnerability results. Eventually shields deteriorate and are replaced by grief, even then mourning only employs those *in* loss — not *the* loss.

Hanna Miller, Grade 11
Mississippi School for the Arts, MS

Top Essay Grades 10-11-12

As the Rainbows Danced

It was usually Sundays that we would go for visits, walking down the halls, past doors and windows. We would work our way through the nursing home's honeycomb of halls to her room. For me, it was always standing outside her door when I would get nervous about seeing my vivacious grandmother wasting away. Nevertheless, my mom would knock and then swing the door open.

I can still remember the way the light always shone through the window; blinds open or closed. That constant light brought life into the room by means of a glass hummingbird. My grandmother, now in a nursing home, had once been a true hummingbird. She had successfully raised three daughters with her Air Force officer.

My grandparents had won dance contests and drank in life with every new day. The years had passed, taking their toll. My hummingbird, my busy bee, now lived in a diminishing world. Alzheimer's began to take her memories. I could feel her trying to break through the barrier of mixed and mingled thoughts, forgotten names and places from her past.

However, her eyes always remained, two shimmering pools, that remembered everything. Those eyes helped me to see how she shone from within; casting out more light than the rainbows from her glass counterpart. They glittered, giving me hope through it all as the disease pulled her under.

It seemed, to me, as though Grandma would be there forever, but I was wrong. My grandmother passed peacefully as the rainbows danced.

Lindsay Ogles, Grade 12
Countryside High School, FL

Top Essay Grades 10-11-12

Run for Your Love

I first learned about love through people. My relationships with people have taught me that love for someone — or something — is measured not always by the happiness it brings, but by the pain and heartache you will endure for it. Guided by this definition, I now realize that, unconsciously and even unwillingly, I have fallen hopelessly in love with running.

People who discover that I run cross country inevitably ask — "Do you actually enjoy running?" Every time, I respond affirmatively, an awkward half-smile on my face, as if making an excuse. The brave ones continue — "Why?" My response is a noncommittal shrug. Yet this nonchalance is far from the truth.

I love running for the freedom, the power of a smooth stride hitting steadily against the ground, the aimless thinking that is provoked by hours of running without a purpose. I love running for its blissful monotony, and because it makes me believe, suddenly and without justification, that I can conquer the world.

Yet in a perverse way, I love running more for the struggles it presents. I thrive on the sweat that coats my face and stings my eyes after a hard workout. I relish the excruciating ache that overtakes my legs while I attempt to overtake a hill. I live off the pain of the last 100 meters of a race, when everything in my body tells me to stop — but I keep going.

I love running because running has taught me what it means to love.

Gabriela Reed, Grade 10
East Mecklenburg High School, NC

Top Essay Grades 10-11-12

A Message to the World

Wake Up.

Just two words, and they don't offer a solution. They don't offer hope. They don't offer comfort. Yet, those two words could change our world because, quite simply, our world is sleeping, and it needs to wake up.

If we consider how many technological breakthroughs have occurred recently, the 21st century seems quite impressive. But that's perhaps the only place our world has moved forward. Crime, poverty, famine, and war devastate massive regions of the globe, unnoticed. Even when we read our newspapers and watch TV, nothing really registers in our minds. Our society is driven by selfish desires for the latest car, the trendiest clothes, and whatever it takes to look like Hollywood stars.

Despite the fact that education has more funding and literacy rates are up, the truth is that most students in first world countries really couldn't care less about their grades, nor how they could impact the world. Every man lives for himself, but as John Donne said, "No man is an island." We all share the same Earth and will share the same consequences of inaction, if we don't choose to acknowledge the bigger picture of life!

So, may the world wake up and realize the power it holds. May each of us wake up and choose to make a difference because we are the world. There is no one else. The responsibility for change lies on our shoulders. Wake up.

Rachel van der Merwe, Grade 12
Home School, TN

Top Essay Grades 10-11-12

The Power of Proximity

One of the most profound truths of our time is simply this: that one cannot survive alone, that the human being is essentially interdependent. Each person, whether consciously or not, has an effect on another. The person you pass on the street on the way into work, a waiter or waitress at dinner, the author of a favored book, or a friend or family member all have an incredible impact on who you are to become.

For years, scientists have studied this necessity of human bonding, Harry Harlow being a great example with his hotly debated monkey experiments. His experiments show the necessity of companionship and love to human survival. A simple touch can create an extraordinary bond between two individuals, and conversation even more so. Without these encounters, one would seemingly cease to be human, for who would we be without the thoughts and opinions of others? Who you are, is essentially determined by what relationships you possess. A mother's love creates softness in a person's heart, as well as a capability of compassion, just as a child creates a sense of responsibility in a parent. This is visible and usually noted by a host of people in one's environment. Karl Marx, in his theory of historical materialism, stated that "it is not the consciousness of men that determines their existence, but, on the contrary, their social existence that determines their consciousness."

As Barbara Streisand vocalized it, "people who need people are the luckiest people in the world."

Rebecca Wilken, Grade 11
Owasso High School, OK

The Civil War

The Civil War separated many families. It holds the largest death count for Americans in a war in American history. In the beginning, the war was in favor of the South. This was before the turning point of the war, Gettysburg. Soon after that became the South's downfall.

The war was started at Fort Sumter when the general of the South Carolina Militia, B.G.T. Beauregard, ordered his troops to attack the fort. Major Robert Anderson, Commander of Fort Sumter, was under orders by President Lincoln to not attack but to wait and fight only if the militia attacked. Lincoln declared war on the Confederacy after the South gained control of Fort Sumter.

Gettysburg was the turning point of the war. Robert E. Lee, the Southern General, lost this battle because he was forced to order a direct charge on the Northern lines to help free Vicksburg from the North's siege. This battle is known as Picket's Charge.

The war ended in the North's favor after Ulysses S. Grant was put in charge of the entire Union army and started the Total War plan. Eventually, Lee's troops ran out of supplies and were trapped by Grant's troops at Appomattox. Lee signed the terms of surrender at the Appomattox Courthouse on April 9, 1865.

The Civil War had the highest number of American deaths than any other war in U.S. history. It was a brutal war, but it shaped most of what we are as a country today.

Brittni Martin, Grade 11
Grove High School, OK

Changes with Each Season

The seasons: spring, summer, fall, and winter. As each period transpires, we watch the world around us change. Spring is the year's beginning, filled with new life and promises. Summer is a mile marker. It begins the downhill roll towards the end of the year. Fall arrives, where humanity slows down and lingers. When winter is finally near it serves as a celebration, for the constant progression of time will soon begin. As the world's population is caught in the rush of living life, do we really notice what makes each day worthwhile?

As each time of the year passes, I think people's mind set changes. Be it their disposition, focus, or outfit based on the weather, something alters. For me, spring is exciting. Sunlight, flowers, and fresh air lift my spirits. Summer is a break, to relax but take risks both at once. Fall comes at a perfect time each year. The color of the leaves and a slight breeze center my mind to the year's goals, yet I feel like it is possible to float up into the clear sky. Winter brings the holidays. The atmosphere is light hearted and generous. Try not to let days pass by overlooked and unimportant. Find something valuable in each. Slow down; take the time to notice the feelings that come with the changes of seasons. When we miss small details, our lives can turn into a hectic swirl of deadlines, routines, and bitterness.

Courtney Cleveland, Grade 11
Owasso High School, OK

The Twenty Dollar Bill Man

The seventh president of the United States of America has the nickname "Old Hickory." He was given this nickname because he was tough like a hickory tree. Do you know what his real name is? His name is Andrew Jackson.

Andrew Jackson was born on March 15, 1767. Jackson was the son of Scots-Irish immigrants, Andrew and Elizabeth Jackson in Lancaster County, South Carolina. He was the youngest of three sons. His father died just a few weeks before Jackson was born. Jackson moved to Tennessee in 1787; and, even though he could only read law a little, he decided to become a frontier lawyer. He was elected as Tennessee's first Congressman in the late 1790s.

Jackson was nominated for the presidency by the Tennessee legislature in 1822. In the election of 1824, Jackson ran against William H. Crawford. He lost the election, but gained many supporters. The Tennessee legislature nominated him for the presidency again in 1825. Soon after he stepped down from the United States Senate. Jackson teamed up with Vice President John C. Calhoun, Martin Van Buren, and former supporters of Crawford. They built a force so strong that they easily defeated the reelection of John Quincy Adams in 1828.

Jackson was president from 1829 to 1837. After eight years of retirement in Nashville, Jackson died on June 8, 1845 at the age of 78. He died from chronic tuberculosis, dropsy, and heart failure.

Aaron Watkins, Grade 12
Rossville Christian Academy, TN

The Strength of Survival

"What makes someone normal or beautiful?" This is dedicated to a girl who's been through a series of quandries and hardships. The truth of how she survived a world of pain and sorrow. Her family and friends supported her through everything. She had a sense of debonair. No one expected what was yet to come. The summer of 2001 changed her physically and mentally. She had recently lost her best friend from a deadly car accident and suffered a strange sickness that left her hanging on the edge of life. From love and praise, she survived what she most feared, death. The Lord gifted her with a second chance and she would never forget what she'd experienced as a 10-year old.

She had a goal to reconstruct herself, to show the world her salutary and determination. People would consistently ask her "what happened to you or I feel so sorry for you." The only thing she wanted was for people to not feel sorry but to treat her as a normal human being. Years passed and she never shared her heartfelt story to anyone. She was now thought of as a beauty, but she felt horrid; the scars that she had from her battles were boldly displayed on her body. She had faith to reveal herself, that beautiful debonair girl is me.

Daphnee Paul, Grade 11
Vero Beach High School, FL

A Gift for My Mother

Some people say that when you first hear the diagnosis you become scared, others say that you become weak. However, when I heard the verdict I became quiet. I could not hear my sisters crying; I could not even hear my own thoughts. All I could hear was my heart: I could've sworn it skipped several beats. I could not hear the doctor's words after he dared to utter that phrase to my mom: "You have breast cancer."

My mother and my sisters mourned in anguish, yet I could not seem to produce even the slightest sign of grief. My mother's new condition had petrified me and I thought about it constantly, "How could such a loving and caring individual be given such an evil and disease-ridden plague?" I never suspected my mother, of all people, to develop this disease.

My mother had always been there for me and I recognized that I could never return the debt. However, this time would be different. She did not need luxuries, nor did she need pity. She did not need favors, nor did she need charity. What she needed, I had; what she needed, I could lend her. What she needed was most important to me, in that it was what she cared for. I gave her my love, because that is what she truly wanted.

I would be, along with my two sisters, her pillar of strength. Even with a disease so detrimental to her body, my mother will always receive my love.

Sankalp Bhatnagar, Grade 11
Germantown High School, TN

What Classes Are You Taking?

Besides the core content classes that you are forced to take you can also choose four electives. These could include Band, Art, Multimedia, or Home Economics. Why not choose a class that you are interested in? It could help you later in life or help you discover a career you might want to take into consideration. The important thing is for teens to put a lot of thought into the classes they choose. They could learn a new skill or improve on one they already have!

However, not everyone agrees that the classes you choose can shape your future. Once I asked a student this question, "What classes are you taking next semester?" They replied, "Agriculture and Zoology." I asked, "Why?" The truth is that the person couldn't tell me why. I later found out that they didn't care what happened to them after high school. They didn't even want to go to college, get a job, or get a drivers license. I don't understand why someone would not want a successful future. It is a known fact that the choices you make in high school and college can shape and mold your future.

Teens should care about the classes and the grades they make in high school. You only have four years of high school. You should make every decision carefully and do the best you can do at all you do. Cherish these four years because once you graduate you can never go back.

Kaylynne Jones, Grade 10
Greenwood High School, KY

War

All through mankind's history wars have been fought. Whether over land money or some other matter. As time progressed wars became more abundant and costly as new weapons and technology were developed. Armies went from groups of militia to professional soldiers trained to kill. Along with new weapons came new desire for greed and power. Countries began seeking war and looking for battles and lands to be conquered. One such example is the holy crusades. The Pope used a letter from Constantinople to justify creating his own personal army to help fight the churches enemies through Islam. As empires expanded so did war and the fighting spread around the world. Many societies were based on war and expansion alone. Man's desire for conquest and power started the two greatest wars in the history of mankind. Wars were started purely for personal and selfish reasons. Many children orphaned and families were killed because of the mindless killing and violence. In today's society we are always at war for one reason or another. Sometimes it is because of a natural resource, to gain independence, or just to commit genocide. People seem to be drawn to the bloodshed and despair that war brings along. In man's early times of war men were sent to fight to protect their homeland and families. Now children and women are sent to fight to create havoc and bloodshed across many countries. War is not just between the nations fighting but rather everybody caught in the crossfire.

Wesley Mitchell, Grade 11
Owasso High School, OK

The Baby That Changed Everything

It was the summer of my 5th grade year when my parents sat my sister and me down. They told us something that would change our lives forever, my mom was pregnant.

That day began the rest of my life. It made me realize how important one person could be influencing another. Those 9 months with my mom were tough. We had to help her do almost everything, but it was definitely worth it.

There were late night trips to get Breyer's chocolate ice cream and early morning visits to Dunkin' Donuts, but everything seemed like fun and games back then. Then came the day my little sister was born.

It was a Saturday morning when Kaitlyn was born. I went to the hospital with my mom's best friend and both my grandmothers. I remember looking at Kaitlyn for the first time and the entire world came to a stop.

When we brought her home everything was different. I had to start being a better person, because she learned from everything she saw. I love playing games with her on the week nights and watching her cheerlead on Saturdays. She's helped me become a more responsible person and that's what I love the most.

Richard Shockley, Grade 11
Countryside High School, FL

Colt .45s Win National Championship

In July 2006, the select travel baseball team, the Colt .45s, that I was playing with won the Super Series 14-Under National Championship at the Fountain Bluff Sports Complex in Liberty, Missouri. My teammates were 14-year olds from Destrehan, Norco, Luling, Des Allemands, Montz, LaPlace, Gramercy, and Cutoff, Louisiana. Our overall 2006 season record was 45-14-2.

The Colt .45s were 2-0-1 in the pool play part of the tournament and received the 4th seed heading into the double elimination part of the tournament. We lost the first game of double elimination to the Dallas Panthers. We knew that one more loss meant we would be going home so we had a team meeting the night before the next game and decided we were not going home without a championship title. We came back to win the next six games sending home the Tahlequah Cardinals, Missouri Rebels, Lee's Summit Panthers, Keller Sabercats, Texas Bulldogs and the Grayson Gators. This secured us a shot at the undefeated Texas Jax for the championship. The Colt. 45s knew we had to beat the Texas Jax twice to win the National Championship and we did it 12-3 and 12-2.

Playing in this tournament was an experience I will never forget. I even got a championship ring and watch. According to the tournament director, in the three years that this tournament has been held at the Fountain Bluff Sports Complex, this was the first time a team had come from the loser's bracket to win the tournament.

Andrew Massa, Grade 10
St Charles Catholic High School, LA

This Is Sparta: The Road to Glory

Our team has been through a lot this year. In June we started off going to a camp to learn our state routine. We started this year with twenty people and one alternate. As this year progressed it seemed like we just kept losing girls left and right. As a captain, it was extremely stressful on me since the girls just kept saying, "God doesn't want us to win," and me having to tell them yes he does, we just needed to practice and do our best. Then time comes and a week before regionals, one of our best flyers who is a senior quits. That is when everyone including myself started to worry. At that time we all sat down and talked about what we think we should do, and as a team we decided to come together and stop just thinking about ourselves. That's where we came up with the motto, "It's not about me, it's the team."

We all finally came together and not only acting but practicing like a team as well. Which comes to show everyone that, that is what it took for each of us to stop caring about ourselves and for the team. On September 29, 2007 we all realized this all happened for a reason to show us that you can handle anything if you put your heart into it because in the end you will come out the state champs.

Karla Wallis, Grade 12

Pollyanna

One rainy Saturday afternoon two years ago, I randomly chose to read Eleanor Porter's *Pollyanna*. Little did I know, I was in for a life-changing experience. Before I selected this children's book, I was very serious about life. Rarely did I smile or laugh because I was so concentrated on my school work or extracurricular activities. However, once I finished this book, I was able to shift my concentration from being the best to enjoying each day and accepting the best I am able to be.

Pollyanna introduced me to the Glad Game. To play this game, one has to think of one positive attribute of particular event. For example, if a classmate or teacher of mine is feeling somewhat overwhelmed, I tell them it could be worse; there could be a tornado outside or our Extended Essay could be due. By playing the Glad Game, I have earned the name of Miss Sunshine by many of my teachers. I go into their classrooms and wish them an enthusiastic, "Good Morning!" even though I do not have them as a teacher.

Although considered by some to be overly optimistic and idealistic in our realistic world, I regard this game with great respect. Since my transformation from a taciturn and unsociable youth to an outspoken, happy young woman, I enjoy seeing others smile with me. Therefore, by playing the game, I bring some joy and happiness into my peers' lives. *Pollyanna* inspired me to make others' lives happier.

Charlotte Mae Kent, Grade 12
Jefferson County International Baccalaureate School, AL

The Road to Sweepstakes

Sweepstakes is the award given to bands in Oklahoma for getting superior ratings in marching, sight reading, and concert band. My band won sweepstakes this year. The road to sweepstakes is stressful, fun, and awarding.

The road to sweepstakes is stressful because it takes a lot of practice. Since marching is part of the sweepstakes, we start working for it in the fall. After we marched our show at district contest, we found that we got a superior rating. We were one step closer to sweepstakes. Once concert band started, the stress level went up, district contest is where you qualify for state. State is stressful because that's where sweepstakes is awarded. We were stressed after sight-reading because we messed up and thought that we were not going to get sweepstakes.

Though the road is stressful, it's fun. It's fun because you get to spend lots of time with your friends. You get to take long bus rides and just hang out. You also get to eat at cool places like Eskimo Joe's in Stillwater. State contest is the best part because it's held at Oklahoma State University, and you get to spend all day on campus.

The road to sweepstakes is also awarding. Though throughout the year we complain about all the work we have to do, getting sweepstakes is well worth it. Seeing the sweepstakes plaque makes you proud. Our band directors also got us T-shirts for sweepstakes. It's one fantastic time.

Stephanie Higgins, Grade 10
Grove High School, OK

Trust in Yourself

What makes a person a good one? How can a person be all they can be? Firstly you have to believe and trust in yourself. You have to do this before you can even think about having a great day because there are all kinds of depression now.

Knowing who you are can help. If you do not know who you are when you wake up in the morning you can be influenced into something you are not. You need to find out what you like to do, and how you really feel about things. Find your own style and make it your own; if you do everyone will know that it's you.

Trust in yourself. The only person you can always count on is you. If you don't trust in you or believe in you then whom can you trust if not yourself? Depression is part of everyday life; it isn't something you can run away from. If you start to feel depressed then think of something happy and make yourself feel good. You have to deal with your problems but you do not have to dwell on them.

To be a good person and be all you can be, just be yourself. Deal with all your problems and feel ecstatic. It is only hard if you make it that way. Believe and make your own style. You don't have to be the same as everyone else. Make this day your own and just live!

Alexandria Richards, Grade 11
Bob Jones High School, AL

Role Models

This past summer I received an amazing opportunity to be a staffer for a Student Life for Kids Camp. Student life is a huge Christian-based association that strives to share the message of Christ through camps of all ages; I staffed the elementary age kid's camp. As staffers, both I and a few others helped the actual staff members with ministering to the children through recreation and interaction. Over two thousand children across the south attended this camp, and I was able to sit down and talk with some of them. I learned so much from these children. They were so grateful to be at camp; some did not have much from their hometown and some were so excited to hear about the Lord.

The fact that I instantly became a role model to the kids because I was older than them amazed me. Not only that, but I was also amazed by how well the kids got along. I know that as teenagers, we are very judgmental. We gossip, lie, exclude and classify others based on what they wear, how they act, and who they hang out with. These kids at camp all came together and were friendly with everyone. Even if there was a dispute, the kids forgave each other quickly and moved on. Teenagers, however, seem to hold grudges forever. I think it is so ironic that we are considered role models to younger children when really they should be role models for us.

Emily Gray, Grade 11
Germantown High School, TN

Following Your Dream

I've always followed my own dreams because someday I would like to have a job. My dream is to find my own job. I have two choices to follow: one is my dream to work in Orlando as a travel guide. My dream is going to Orlando every year because it has so many resort hotels like Universal and Disney Theme Park.

Unfortunately, I have to use a G-tube to feed overnight. I want to get rid of the G-tube because it drives me crazy when I have had to use this for the past 11 months! If I could eat more food by mouth, the doctor said he would take it out. The biggest reason I want to get rid of this G-tube is so I can go to college and study to follow my dream career.

If everything works out all right for me then in my dream I will go straight to college and study my career. I will then work as a travel guide and be able to be a free man and travel around the world.

Noup Palacios, Grade 11
Easter Seals of South Florida School, FL

What Is Love?

Most people do not know what love is. Many people have different definitions of love. Some people think that love is based on looks and outer appearance. I think that loving someone is loving what is on the inside. Many people cannot help the way that they look, but they might have a wonderful personality. That is why one loves what is on the inside of a person. Love is unconditional, and it is never-ending. It is being happy and being unselfish. Love is a special and incredible, once-in-a-lifetime experience. Love is one of the most wonderful feelings you can have. I believe in love at first sight because of the connection you feel when you see the person. That is my definition of love.

John Paul Abernathy, Grade 11
New Covenant Christian School, SC

Work It Out

"All things work together for good to them that love God." This Biblical truth is found in Romans 8:28. It is proved in the lives of Christians. First, it is true because it is in the Bible. Second Timothy 3:16 says, "All Scripture is given by inspiration of God, and is profitable for doctrine, for reproof, for correction, for instruction in righteousness." Second, everything that happens is in God's hands. When the Christian proves his love for God, God will make sure that everything works out to be good for him. This applies even to the times when things are not going so well; eventually, everything will work out. Once the vertical relationship (the relationship between God and a Christian) is where it should be, the horizontal relationships (the relationships with other people) will all fall into place. However, the horizontal relationships will never all be perfect because all people are sinners. As long as one does his part in getting his relationship with God right, God will do His part and take care of the Christian.

Misty Brecht, Grade 12
New Covenant Christian School, SC

The Hard Teacher

Experience is a hard teacher. One day, as I was mowing the lawn, I noticed a garden hose on the ground several feet to my right. Instead of moving it right away, I carelessly chose to wait until it was directly in front of me. As I continued to mow, my mind began to drift, and before I knew it, the garden hose was wrapped around the blades, stopping the engine. Naturally, a good deal of my time was then spent repairing the now mutilated hose. Experience is certainly a hard teacher, but it is also an effectual one. That day, I learned my lesson about the harmful habit of procrastination.

Daniel Atkinson, Grade 11
New Covenant Christian School, SC

Snow

There's something about snow. A snowy day, or a fresh fall overnight. Sitting in a chair, watching the big, lacy flakes come floating gently down, with a steaming mug of hot chocolate by your side, a fire burning in the hearth, Christmas carols murmuring quietly in the background, and a good book in your hand. You feel so contented, and yet are filled with childish exuberance that gives you an irresistible urge to get up, go outside, and be silly. Something about snow releases the inner child in you. You run about, jump and play. You build snowmen, make snow angels and snow forts, and have a huge snowball fight. Then suddenly, like a child, you are tired, and ready to come back in to a roaring fire, the comfortable chair, the steaming cocoa, and the entrancing book. Meanwhile, the snow continues to come quietly down. There's something about snow. Something strange. Something wonderful. Something childlike. Something free.

Therese Spollen, Grade 11
Rock Bridge Sr High School, MO

Decision Time

So what are you going to do with the rest of your life? Are you going to be a teacher? An engineer? Choosing what you want to do with the rest of your life is a big decision. This decision can affect the rest of your life. It's a big choice, and something you have to think about very carefully.

There is a lot of pressure to choose what you want to do for the rest of your life. Remember when you were little and you wanted to be a movie star or an actress, well I'm here to tell you that probably won't happen. You're going to have to pick a job that is more realistic. If you can't sing, then you more than likely won't be a singer. Some teens already know what they are going to do with their life. You look at them and feel pressure to pick what you want to do. It's hard, but pick something that you are good at and go with the flow.

Deciding what to do with your life can be stressful. But you need to relax. You will find your perfect job. Pick something realistic that you can do. If you don't like your job, then look from something else. When one door closes another door opens.

Jennifer Grothe, Grade 10
Greenwood High School, KY

Hallelujah!

Every year many kids and their parents go all out for Halloween. My family never did that, but we did something cooler. We would go to church for Hallelujah night. Families from the church brought bags of candy to pass out. There were all kinds of games including bowling, catching fish, and treasure hunts. After each game you either got candy or dumanis dollars to spend on small prizes. Many people went all out on costumes, mostly Bible themed. Boys would be Moses, David, or Bible Man. Girls would be angels, Esther, or Mary. After all the candy and dumanis dollars were spent, the church would act out a Bible story so that the kids who didn't go to church would find out about the Bible. The goal of the night was not who got the most candy or toys but learning more about Jesus. This is one of the best outreaches a church does for kids, even if it's just a few hours. The kids will remember it for a lifetime.

Sarah Coleman, Grade 12
Bixby High School, OK

Saving Lives

Because medicine has progressed so much over the years, many lives have been saved. Anesthesia and blood transfusions are both great accomplishments of our day. Many years ago during wars, there were lives lost due to loss of blood and pain during surgery.

Anesthesia comes from the Greek word "loss of feeling," which numbs patients for operation. Enduring so much pain, before anesthetics, patients had to be strapped and held to the table. Chemists discovered that nitrous oxide and ether deaden pain; however, ether's nauseating, revolting smell made people want something else. Chloroform was quickly discovered. After this discovery James Young Simpson, a Scottish doctor, used chloroform during childbirth, but only after Queen Victoria used chloroform was it popular. Anesthetics were successfully used in numbing patients for surgery.

Blood transfusions have saved many patients that have lost excessive amounts of blood, when most of them would have died. The intelligent Dr. Richard Lower successfully performed a dog-to-dog transfusion. In 1667 Jean-Baptiste Denis performed the first transfusion to a human. Although some animal-to-human blood transfusions were successful, some were not, causing death. Dr. Karl Landsteiner studied blood and soon discovered that there are different types: A, B, O, and AB. After discovering the types of blood, physicians were able to perform transfusions successfully. Saving lives has been easier since transfused blood was discovered.

Anesthesia and transfusions have brought medical progress, and have helped save many lives. Both of these medical procedures have made surgery and blood loss easier to treat.

Hannah Grace Whitaker, Grade 10
Rossville Christian Academy, TN

Why I Choose "Them" Over Me

Walking down a high school hall is a challenge for anyone; do you add that extra strut with that special bounce to your walk or keep your head down hoping not to be noticed? For me it's my own runway, why stop and care what other people think? Unfortunately there is one thing that stops me dead in my tracks and dampers my mood, "them." We all know "them," we all see "them," and we all hate "them."

Of course I am alluding to the high school couple, the pair that are never seen separated, constantly hand in hand, cheek on cheek, and nauseating every time. I was brought into the world of love with the help of Cinderella and Snow White, a skewed view of what love truly is. Is it really just "them?" We have the tendency to settle for what is right there. They know that they're not meant for one another but stay together just for the imagery.

I would love to be in love just to be in love. The sad part is everyone has done it, faked love. The true romantics are the ones who are willing to give it time and find the one. I guess it's our jet-speed world of Match.com and speed dating that causes youth to flock to the fake and easy. Why do teenagers feel the need to constantly be reassured? Are we that vain in our idea of love and will he finally make me a "them?"

Emily Atkinson, Grade 10
Grady High School, GA

Ho, Ho, Ho, Oh My Broken Nose!

When people glance at my face, they occasionally notice something slightly wrong. Even with its well hidden appearance, my broken nose is sometimes seen. I am asked for an explanation; the injury's cause contains an odd story.

Initially, it was noticeably frigid. It was my sixth Christmas; my family and I were headed toward my paternal grandmother's annual Christmas brunch. We had loaded up my father's pewter truck with presents and food to exchange with our loved ones. The truck contained my parents, myself, a set of new golf clubs, a few dozen biscuits, a warm apple pie, and an entire plethora of other coveted gifts meant for exchanging. We were on our short trip when, all of a sudden, my mother screamed. "Hank, look out," she yelled out, warning my father of a dog that had entered the street. It was a large Great Dane, and unfortunately my father's brakes were not up to par; we collided with the large animal.

The dog was left unharmed, but my nose was another story. It was apparently broken, and Christmas brunch needed to be put on hold while I was driven to the nearest emergency room. I spent my Christmas morning in a hospital room being x-rayed and diagnosed with a broken nose.

While the nose almost reset itself, it remains slightly tilted to the right. People notice the imperfection, and ask what happened. I reply, "One Christmas morning a dog entered the street."

Daniel Wyatt, Grade 12
Rossview High School, TN

Why Don't We Understand?

While in America, people look down upon minority groups. They do not understand exactly why they've come to America to live. One can never understand the circumstances in other countries until they have experienced first hand.

Last summer my family took a vacation to Mexico. I have taken Spanish for five years, but have never understood the extent of their poverty. I knew living conditions were horrible, but one has to see with their own eyes to know how horrible. Housing is unremarkable. Think about it, could you live in a run-down shack with your whole family? One reason conditions are bad is that their income is not a fixed number like it would be in America. Their salary can vary depending on the number of tourists. Food is a hard thing to come by in Mexico. If the merchants are not making enough, they cannot purchase a sufficient amount of food for their families. Clothing is not abundant, either. Most children do not have a pair of shoes and walk around barefoot.

It is understandable why Americans are unhappy with others coming here and taking over jobs that could be taken by Americans, but how many of us actually know what it is like to live in extreme poverty? My trip to Mexico opened my eyes on how other ethnicity groups live. I am grateful and appreciative of how Americans live now. I wish that we would not be so hard on others for coming here.

Cassie Norris, Grade 11
Owasso High School, OK

Grand Nationals

It was a long and arduous Saturday night. We had marched prelims earlier that morning. Though it wasn't as good of a run as I thought, I was praying that it would be good enough. We had some time to relax after prelims; so, I sat on the bus and thought through the show. "Man, can't believe I messed up there!" was all that was going through my mind. Frantically, I had sat there thinking that I had screwed everything up. It got to be about six o' clock and we were instructed to go back into the stadium to listen for the finalists. The Colts stadium was packed! There wasn't an empty seat to be found anywhere. Bands were going crazy, doing things like the wave back and forth. It had felt like a football game was about to begin there instead of a marching contest. We sat and waited as the announcer came over the speakers. One by one he started to list off the names of the finalists. I sat there with my eyes closed just counting as each of the twelve spots filled up without our name being called. "Number eleven…Avon High School!" the announcer screamed as Avon's band jumped up and down like wild animals. Sitting there, I thought to myself that it was over. Then the announcer read, "The twelfth and final spot…Owasso High School!" I couldn't believe it; we had made finals!

Jason Troy, Grade 11
Owasso High School, OK

What Is Love

Love is something you can't see, but you can feel. It's the feeling you get when you are with a special person for a long time. Love is when you care about someone just because they are around you. It is where you can't stop thinking about someone for five minutes. Love doesn't start with the outer beauty, but the inner beauty. When you love someone, you can't imagine living life without that person because they mean the world to you. It's when that special person that you care about takes your breath away every time they are around you. Love is strong and powerful that when problems come your way, you and that special person become invincible. When you are in love, there's no way that love can end. People in the world have changed the true meaning of the word love. Girls are getting their virginity taken away because a guy is whispering in their ears "If you *love* me you will." people are losing their lives because someone is telling their spouse, "If I can't have you or love you, no one can." Love is not something that people should use in vain. Love is something special and something people should take seriously. That's what *love* means to me.

Keeonna Bobo, Grade 11
Grandview Alternative School, MO

Are We Free?

Over two hundred years ago Abraham Lincoln signed the Emancipation Proclamation which liberated black men and women from the evils of slavery. I'm posing the question now as an American woman of color, "Are we really emancipated?" The Emancipation Proclamation relieved black Americans of the physical constraints of slavery; however, the remnants of the mental aspect of slavery are still present today.

As I look around in my community, I see many oppressed people who are on welfare instead of faring well. I see slaves being raped by the educational system due to low funding and an overall unenthusiastic outlook on black students in the inner cities. I see black Americans who have become slaves to drugs, gangs, and violence, and slaves of a society that sets the standards very low for the economic and educational success of a black person.

In the 1700's, Willie Lynch wrote a letter stating how to keep a slave in bondage. In this letter, the remnants of his doctrine can be seen in the single parent household and in the fact that three hundred years later, many black people still hold negative connotations toward their race.

In essence, two hundred years after slavery has been abolished, many blacks still have not completely shaken the mental chains of slavery that keep them prisoner to failure. Many African Americans are becoming products of their environment, instead of using their minds, talents, and God given abilities as a ticket out of the "hood."

Danielle Fain, Grade 11
City University School of Liberal Arts, TN

My Mom Story

You know that story that your mom tells about you? We all have one. You laugh about it but you do not really appreciate it until you are older. My story has been told countless times by my mother, the only person who does the story justice. The story gets told at least once per theater competition. Someone asks my mom to tell the story of "Jamie's first acting experience."

The story starts off the same way every time. I was three years old. My mother was the youth director at our church. She was brainstorming one night and said it would be fun for the youth group to have a talent show. I said I would sing.

Months passed and the talent show was on. My mother was the M.C. I was going to sing, or at least, I thought I was. I was seated on the front row happily waiting to perform. My mom was at the microphone to close. It seemed that my mom had forgotten about my proposal from months ago. I stood up and wailed, "You forgot me!" My mother was speechless.

The room was chaos with my mother and I both crying. I said "Mom I don't just hurt here," pointing to my heart, "I hurt here, and here…," pointing to other parts of my body.

Fifteen minutes passed until I stepped to the microphone and started to sing. There was thunderous applause after my performance; the first of many more to come.

James Jones, Grade 11
Vero Beach High School, FL

The Club

As I walk into the dimly lit gym, I stop to look at the solemn line of bags hanging from chains, each suspended about three feet from the ground.

I study the ring. Drenched with water, reeking of years of sweat and blood, the roped-off square of about twenty feet by twenty feet is the most imposing feature of the gym. I drop my bag on one of the plastic lawn chairs lined up against the north wall and pull off my shirt. Steven follows me in, studying the club in almost the exact fashion as I did. "I'm feeling a running night, whaddya think?" he asks. "We'll see, Steve." I pull on my sleeveless shirt and my hoodie, and turn to stretch. I rotate my body left, then right, trying to work out the kinks and strains in my back and my chest. No one else is here; hardly anyone ever is. Even the coaches generally leave us be.

The smell of mold and stagnant water is in our nostrils as we pound the bags, left-left-right. At ten the lights go off, and that's when we spar. As darkness falls on the ring, my best friend and I circle each other, remembering weaknesses, exploiting pain. The first punch to the bridge of my nose wakes me up, and we begin.

Walking home, with my best friend at my shoulder, blood drips into my eye. Life is as it should be, and I smile.

Thomas Bentz, Grade 11
Owasso High School, OK

Questioning the Questions

Why do scientists try to explain the beauty of our world? Why can't they let it be? The thunder roars and clashes. The lightning lights up the sky and the heavens. The raindrops feel cool to the touch. The flowers blossom in the spring and the snowflakes of winter are never alike. Why must you find out why? Why can't you simply enjoy the colors of the sunset or the sweet songs of the mockingbird?

God imagined these beautiful things; they were not concocted in a lab. How can you think to clone the connection between mother and child or the scent of roses in a new season? Enjoy things as they are and peace will follow. The good and bad of this world should be cherished, not pulled apart and studied. The lightning bugs glow in the night so softly because they do, because they were meant to be that way.

So don't explain it, just relive it in your mind. Don't question why the redwoods grow so tall and the moss so short; only question why you question. Don't question why the stars light up the night sky or the sun's flames are so bright. So, why do scientists try to explain the cosmos? The reason is that they have simply the nature of curiosity within them, which is a natural beauty in itself. But should we question our own questioning as well? There, my friend, lies the true question worth asking.

Melissa Rosenow, Grade 10
Cypress Bay High School, FL

Ann Marie Cates

My aunt, Ann Marie Cates, is my hero. She is my hero because she is trustworthy, caring, and strong. She is only 21 and she has been through a lot of things.

She is a very trustworthy person because of the many things said and done between the two of us. I can tell her anything and I do. Of the things I have told her, which is everything, she had never told anything. If I have a problem then I can trust that she will listen and help me.

Ann has always been a very caring person. She has always been there for me whenever I needed her. She has helped me with a lot of my issues. She has also bought me stuff that she knew I needed.

She is a very strong person because of all of the events in her life that have occurred. She had made it through a C-section with her son, Lucas. After that, she had complications and pulled through amazingly. Matt and she were thinking about getting divorced for awhile. Luckily, they resolved their issues and decided that they should stay together.

Ann Marie Cates is a great hero. She is a trustworthy, caring, and a strong person. These are some qualities of a hero. Everyone's hero can have different qualities. She is my hero and will always be my hero.

Skye Smith, Grade 11
Mulhall-Orlando High School, OK

Cherishing Each Moment

One of the experiences that has impacted my life most was meeting a woman named Eagle. When I joined Mission Club I thought the service group would be a great way to get community service hours done, but I never thought that it would change my life.

The club announced that we would be going to Mississippi for a week during summer. I was at first skeptical with the thought that it would be hot and buggy, but eventually I decided to go on the trip. When I saw what the trip was really about, I realized I needed to look beyond myself. Every day we worked on hurricane-devastated homes, and with every act of service I became more aware of the gift of giving.

But, I did not know what it meant to be truly selfless until the day I met Eagle, a woman undergoing the long struggle against cancer. Even though she is being treated with chemotherapy, she still goes to work every day and gives each action her all. When she came home from work she began cleaning her house because she had friends coming over that night.

I was so moved by the effort she put forth out of appreciation for that one dinner with her friends. She cherished each moment and lived her life to the fullest. This is more than I can say for most people, including myself. I learned to stop taking things for granted and to live each moment like it was my last.

Elizabeth Adams, Grade 11
Bishop Verot High School, FL

Justification

People are dying every day, but they say it's for a good cause. Every night on the news there are more new victims of a war. Is this war justified or not? There are many good points for both sides, for the war in Iraq or against it.

Several interesting things have been said for the war in Iraq. The Iraqis are being trained in combat so that they can defend themselves. Also, the Iraqi citizens are happy to be liberated. Many people are confident that we'll soon find the weapons of mass destruction. Another great point is that the war, in a way, put an end to Saddam Hussein's power and terrorism.

Even if there were some wonderful points made for the war, many people are still against it. Most people feel that the government lied and really went to war for reasons other than what they have been telling everyone. One huge point most often made in the argument against the war is the fact that we have been looking for almost seven years and we have not found, heard, or seen any evidence that the weapons of mass destruction actually exist.

There are many phenomenal points made for the war and against it. It is excellent to know how the other side is justified in their thinking. People are at liberty to their opinions and beliefs. The war is just something everyone will have to make up their own minds about.

Kayla Capper, Grade 11
Owasso High School, OK

Regret

I started playing basketball in sixth grade. I was going to the Catholic school in Pilot Grove. First/second grades were in one classroom. Third/fourth grades were in a classroom. Fifth/sixth grades were in a classroom, and seventh/eighth grades were in one classroom. Along with being on the fifth/sixth grade team, I also played on the seventh/eighth grade team. This was because they only had five people and they had to have some backup players. Two other girls in my grade played on the team as well. I didn't get to play very much on the seventh and eighth grade team. I played a lot more on the fifth and sixth grade team.

After practicing, I acquired the skill of playing basketball fairly well. I started most games, and played for a large portion of the game. I was able to make baskets, rebounds, assists, and steal the ball from the opposing team, which I was excellent at.

Some time between sixth and seventh grade, I started smoking cigarettes, purely for the fact that I wanted to be like my sister. I developed an addiction to cigarettes, and made it hard on my lungs when it came to running. I already had bad lungs from secondhand smoke. After I finished the season my seventh grade year, I stopped playing. If I could change one thing I've ever done, it would be to have never started. The regret I live with daily was not worth giving up my passion.

Gabrielle Elizabeth Fisher, Grade 11
Slater High School, MO

I Took "The Walk"

One of the most influential days of my life was October 3, 2007. I had been waiting months to see my favorite band, Hanson, take "The Walk." I want to share this story of hope as the brothers walk the streets and explain HIV/AIDS in Africa.

For months, I had been singing along to their new indie-album, The Walk. This album spreads the word of hardships in Africa. Their main focus? HIV/AIDS. I praise them for educating people through inspirational music. My two friends and I attended the one-mile walk, along with hundreds of other fans. As we walked downtown, Taylor and Zac went barefoot and blended in with the crowd. They even talked one-on-one with fans. As we started to pick up the pace, Taylor started preaching the facts to his fans. He was explaining the concept of helping people through little things such as purchasing TOMS shoes. Each pair of shoes sold, a child in Africa would get a pair. As we reached the water fountain, Taylor told his fans that the city we were in is ranked as one of the highest HIV/AIDS registered cities. That fact really hit home for me. Finally, we finished the walk and all the fans felt inspired.

I thank Hanson for teaching the awareness of this world-sweeping disease. The fact that they would rather write about lifesaving songs than blend in with all the other artists' shows their love for helping people.

Paige Pregler, Grade 11
Owasso High School, OK

Of the Absurdities of This Essay Contest

Alas, this essay will be without my characteristically pompous language, and it shall also be lacking in the metaphors, analogies, imagery, and various allusions with which I typically soak my essays to the point of saturation. The reason this paper shall be devoid of all elements which could hope to make it in any way enjoyable is the simple, perplexing fact that I am limited to a mere two hundred and fifty words, in the short space of which I am expected to somehow express myself upon any subject which my heart may desire. It's not that I lack the capacity to seek out an interesting subject for my ramblings, but rather that I lack the space necessary to write sufficiently about any subject! I could write for volumes about the laughable inefficiency of the UN, our media's sheer lack of anything even hinting of originality, or the necessity of space travel.

However, I suppose there is one subject which I could cover in so short a composition, and that would be the confounding laziness and sheer lack of foresight which the founders of this ill-begotten contest of the written word acted in when they placed such absurd limits upon the creativity of our minds. Did they honestly think we have nothing interesting enough to say that it might take more space then a footnote in a child's encyclopedia?

Jacob Mosier, Grade 11
Owasso High School, OK

Do You Have a Good Education?

"Hey, look at her clothes. They are so cute. Yeah, but do you know how expensive that outfit must have been? If you have a good education then you wouldn't have to worry about how much something costs or if someone has a better wardrobe than you." I believe having a good education is very important. It helps you succeed in life. Receiving a good education helps you get a good paying job.

For instance, having a good education will improve your chances of getting a well paying job. If you have knowledge that will help you in the work place, then you are more likely to be hired for that job than someone who doesn't have the same variety of knowledge. If you have a well paying job then you can afford nice clothes and have a first-class lifestyle.

In order to be successful in life you are required to have a high-quality education. Being successful isn't just about having a great job, it's about teaching others, your children, that having a good education is a necessity. Succeeding in life is about having a family, taking care of them and giving your children the best that you can give them.

In conclusion, having a good education is extremely important. It allows you to receive a high paying job, and improves your life style. Helping you succeed with your life and family. Having a good education, you can provide your children with what they want.

Rebekka Wilkerson, Grade 11
Chiefland High School, FL

Riding Is

Riding is my passion. It is late nights spent in Cotton's stall with my arms wrapped around his neck, for he is my Jack-of-all-trades, my Superman. Riding is the anticipation before my next class. It is a way to soar. Riding is the smell of freshly painted jumps, ready to be conquered. It is falling off and falling off and falling off and getting back on. It is his slippery, slimy tongue licking the sugar off my hand. Riding is bumpy feel of his braided mane. It is a pat on his thick neck or a rub on his prickly nose. Riding is the sound of that diesel, transporting my precious cargo. It is the bruise on my arm from a certain someone mistaking me for carrots. Riding is the soothing sound of my trainer's whistle after a successful trip. It is my escape, it's my life.

Caroline Mescon, Grade 12
Baylor School, TN

Hamburgers 13

People can all get a little impatient sometimes, but in this case one person's eagerness turned out to create something great. In 1885 Charley Nagreen, a chef in Wisconsin, was cooking meatballs. After waiting for a meatball to cook he got anxious and decided to flatten the meatball to make it cook faster. After the patty was finished cooking Charley had another great idea. He thought if he put this patty between two pieces of bread it would make a meatball easier to carry and more portable. Charley sure was on to something because he continued to sell hamburgers for the next 66 years.

Charley Nagreen's idea was the first time the hamburger was ever brought to America, but not the first time they were created. The hamburger was first invented in Hamburge, Germany, hence the word hamburger. The people there are now know as "pork eaters."

Catherine Monica, Grade 10
St Charles Catholic High School, LA

Individuality

What makes me an individual of this society? I believe my heritage, my relationship with God, my personality, where I live, who I know, and the family and friends that are by my side are the aspects that make me…me. Whether I have good or bad moments in my life, I learn from them each day and I learn to embrace the character within me.

Many people go on with their lives trying to be like other individuals and never stop to ask themselves, "Who am I and what makes me different from everyone else?" Why would one trust the mind of someone else when God gave everyone a perfectly good one to think and make decisions of their own. I know I'm one of a kind and you won't find anyone else in the world like me…not even the best imitator in the world could understand the feelings and emotions of my everyday life. I'm perfectly content with myself because I know God made me exactly who I am and I know He made me for His purpose.

Veronica Caldwell, Grade 12
Blue Ridge Christian School, MO

Words of Wisdom

In a society ruled by trends, cliques, 'best friends', expensive shoes, and things of the sort, it's discomforting for one to be an individual. Surrounded by a cloud of arrogance, one has to climb a ladder to show who they are. Even then the cloud will consume the ladder and slowly rise from beneath them only for the person whom dared to be different feel out of place. Everybody in this world loves the company of another. If it weren't for this exigency of companionship then I doubt there would be any "social outcasts."

If we were to accept one another for who we are and not for what we wear, it's easy to think that the world would be a much better place. The majority of us practice a religion which is often a cause of contention between even the closest of brothers. We accept our religion, whatever it may be, as the one and only righteous path. However, such beliefs lead to casualties and sometimes wars.

The world is meant to live as a whole and befriend our own worst enemies. If we are to follow such religious beliefs then we need not to schlep down this path laid before us. We are only equal in a sense that we share a common land and are able to attend the same events, schools, dinners, and things of the sort. This is not equal, equal is what lies behind our pride.

William Long, Grade 11
Porter Ridge High School, NC

Reality

What is reality? Is it something you can see? Something you can feel? If that's the case then can those senses not also apply while you dream? You can see the different people or things, you can feel the sensations of falling or flying. So does this make the dream reality? Are we nothing more than prisoners of our mind watching a never-ending tape play before us while we do nothing more than desperately cling to that false notion of reality? If so there are multitudes of human drones walking about clinging to their reality and they are quick to judge what is real or what is not even though they themselves can't define it.

There are some that question the boundary and perceive the world in a different state of mind. To them their world is as real as yours is. So would you still tell these people that their reality is false while not considering that perhaps they have the greater understanding? Then would you proceed to rip that person from their normalcy and place them back among the blind? Can one blind man tell another what is so and what is not? Is it right for him to judge when he can't even see or even comprehend the truth himself? How do you know that perhaps it is your reality that is mistaken and that you your whole life have not been misled by force-fed notions of the true reality?

Becky Guin, Grade 12
Nature Coast Technical High School, FL

Jordan

My hero is my big brother, Jordan. I think Jordan has many heroic qualities including strength, intelligence, kindness and humor.

Jordan has a strong strength of character. He was active in sports while in high school, and was recruited to play college baseball. He passed on the opportunity to play college ball so that he could continue to work full-time to help with college expenses. I admire his work ethic. He carries a full load of college courses and works forty hours per week.

I admire Jordan's intelligence. He was an honor roll and National Honor Society member. He was awarded five scholarships at the end of his senior year and has been awarded two more at college. These scholarships have paid for his first two years of college. I think that is a great accomplishment.

Jordan's kindness and sense of humor are evident to anyone who knows him. He is sensitive and truly cares for others. He would make a great teacher. Jordan would never think of belittling or hurting someone. People like to be around Jordan because he also has a great sense of humor. He doesn't take himself too seriously and makes everyone around him feel comfortable. He was voted most fun to be around his senior year.

While some might pick pro-athletes or rehab-bound celebrities as their hero, I don't have to look any farther than my family for mine. Jordan Kindschi has always been and will continue to be my hero.

Karly Kindschi, Grade 12
Mulhall-Orlando High School, OK

Most Important Mentor!!!

The most important mentor I ever had was my friend, Jenea Butler. I consider her my mentor for a lot of reasons. First of all, Jenea helps me by encouraging me to do well in school. When I need help I let her know; she takes me places with her and we have talks about the important things in life. In addition, when I was transitioning from high school to another school, she told me that it would be all right and I would get to make new friends. When I was having problems with my mom, I called her and talked to her and she gave me advice. She told me everything would be ok, and she would always be there for me. She takes a place of a counselor when I have problems at school. For example, Jenea would tell me not to make bad choices, or have a bad attitude, and I would see that the good behavior would pay off in the long run. In conclusion, Jenea is a good mentor because she gives me advice. She helps me when I need help and she teaches me right from wrong. She reminds me to keep doing well in school and that I will be successful in the future.

Bethany Flowers, Grade 11
Grandview Alternative School, MO

Wanderlust

I had a bad case of wanderlust that summer. I would haphazardly take the train to one place or another, never bothering to pay attention to where I was going. I was simply only interested in the people. To me, each person had a story behind them and I would often fabricate fascinating stories of these people in my head. Once I sat next to a forty-something year old woman dressed in an atrocious pink sweater, with a trashy romance novel in her hands. "Probably going through a divorce." Another time I was squeezed in a packed compartment, up against a twenty-something year old young man who wore ripped jeans and held The Atheist Bible in hand. "Probably seeking truth." You can tell a lot about a person from the books he or she reads.

The train stops and the doors slide open. There's a strange satisfaction in standing underground, across a rusty set of rails gazing blankly at a sea of eyes, a sea full of curious people and wanderers just like you and bright young things and old dreamers who never really learned to let go of their teenage hopes. At this moment, the artificial wind blows, the wind of a hundred metal cars rushing past you with the speed of a thousand lost memories fleeing from your very soul. The doors open, and you are reunited with the eyes of someone you have never met before, but wait, yes, you remember something…just something about them reminds you…

Alisha Ramos, Grade 12
Terry Sanford High School, NC

Mistakes

Mistakes should be forgiven. No person who ever walked the earth was ever perfect, except for Jesus. All too often I find people judging other people. Should they cast the first stone? Have they looked at themselves? More than likely they have not, and this gives them no right to judge someone else.

If I could approach someone who does this, my first question would be, "Have you ever walked in their shoes?" You see them and the situations they go through for what it looks like on the outside. However, have you ever been on the inside? For example, do you know what it is like when he looks perfect, and it looks like the two of them are in a happy relationship, but it isn't? He controls your life and every single thing you do, right down to the things you say, think, the people you talk to, even the music you listen to. You feel trapped, like this is the way it is going to be for the rest of your life. Therefore you make a mistake. Then everyone looks down on you and talks about you and cuts their eyes.

You should never judge someone for what mistakes they have made. No one is perfect and more than likely neither are you. You shouldn't judge someone for something they did, when you have no clue what they went through. After all would you want someone to judge you?

Kristen McRoy, Grade 11
Southside High School, NC

Teens and Our Government

Unfortunately, today's teens know more about drugs and alcohol than they do our politics. I would bet if you asked the average teen to name 5 side-effects of drinking they could tell you 10. But, if you asked them to name you 5 political leaders running for President in 2008 they could only name one. Teens need to get more involved in our government and those who are eligible to vote need to do it.

Some adults don't think, however, that we "kids" should be involved. They think we are too young to do anything. They think we are too immature to care. But, I think they are wrong. We do care. And we should. We do have a say, they just don't want to hear it. We want to make a difference. Sure, some teens don't have an interest in politics, but we all have an opinion.

If teens were given the chance to voice their opinions, and to learn more about our leaders, then teens might become more interested. There are commercials about getting teens to vote. But, if they shut down our ideas what motive does it give us to further our interest? That's why teens need to become more involved. Then everyone can make a difference.

Ryan Shutt, Grade 10
Greenwood High School, KY

The Spinal Cord vs the Heart

We have all heard the phrase, "Listen to your heart." Joshua Porter contradicts this idea in his book *The Spinal Cord Perception*. He states, "No one can ever use his heart to listen, or touch, or feel or see or smell. It is just a lump of muscle pumping mechanically inside your ribs."

The heart is a muscle inside your chest that involuntarily pumps blood through your entire body. People have always connected their hearts to the emotions they may feel. It is associated with that because your heart rate changes when you are scared, excited, or even in love. Proverbs 15:13 says, "A happy heart makes the face cheerful, but heartache crushes the spirit." The heart is the source of emotion.

There are millions of nerve fibers connecting from your skin to your spinal cord. Those nerves tell you what you feel. Through the spinal cord one can taste, hear, smell, feel, and see things. However, it cannot tell you that you are scared, or in love. It cannot feel emotions.

I once heard that your heart cannot really feel, and that you feel things through the tube locked in a column of bone in your back. The things you feel with your spinal cord are physical. However, your heart provides emotion. Joshua Porter finally defined hearts by saying, "The lump of meat caged within our bosoms are solely responsible for sending the pain of emotional razor blades throughout our entire central nervous system, eventually finding our souls, wherever they are."

Amie Delong, Grade 11
Maranatha Christian Academy, GA

What Relationship?

"Did you hear?! Cody's dating Susanna now! I know… SUCH a shocker! They're so different. Personally, I think he's just dating her for her looks. I know, right? She's absolutely gorgeous. Bye." Look familiar? It would to many teenagers in America today, who want more to do with relationships and drama than almost anything else. They worry too much about their high school relationships instead of their future.

Many children will *not* find the love of their life in high school. They won't grow up to marry their high school sweetheart. And odds are, none of the social aspects that they stressed over so much in high school will even matter afterwards. Many people would say it's just a pastime, just a game. But then, there are still those who take the innocent little game too far. So many girls will build walls between themselves and other girls just because the others "stole" their boyfriend. Teenagers often neglect the more important things in life due to the fact that they were too busy crying over a two week relationship that ended too soon.

"I know! No way! Seriously? That's what she told you? With April? You're kidding right? Poor kid, yeah…bye." How tragic is it that so many children are made fun of for not having a "relationship" in high school when the others spend all their time worrying about it. Teens spend too much time worrying about high school drama.

Hilary Harlan, Grade 10
Greenwood High School, KY

Words to My Father

I wonder how it feels to know nothing about your daughter, except for her physical appearance. Don't you want to know anything about your own flesh and blood?

The only childhood memories I have of you aren't remotely happy. You *always* came home drunk. One time you came home, and pointed a gun in my mother's face and persisted to pull the trigger. Thankfully, it wasn't loaded! I bet you don't even remember that. I remember waiting for you in the window for days; upon arrival, you were always belligerent and ready to fight Mom.

I remember riding on your motorcycle after the rain in Grandma's backyard. We slipped and fell; you dropped the bike onto me, then ran inside. It's ok though, Grandma rescued me. In almost twenty years, you have not kept one "promise." These horrific pictures replay in my mind now and forever; I will never forget. I don't want your apologies or your excuses; they're all fake.

You never, and never will be my father; that's a foreign concept to me. I'd like to consider you a sperm donor. You did my little brother so scandalous, and I resent you for that. You are another drunken lowlife in the world, and the epitome of white trash.

I didn't write this so that you can feel sorry for yourself, you do that enough. I just thought you should know something about me, and my thoughts about you.

Katie Quinn, Grade 12
Grandview Alternative School, MO

Acknowledging Nature

In society few people care about the environment. They're too busy to realize their surroundings. Cities are cutting down trees and taking land that was home to many animals to build parking lots. People need to realize the importance of having open land where animals can graze without feeling the need to turn it into another building.

If people would appreciate natural beauty the world would be a happier place. People rarely notice the weather or that the season is changing. No one has time to go on a walk or to stop and, as the cliché goes, "smell the roses." Taking a walk through green grass and breathing fresh air can make a person more relaxed and as a result make them a happier person.

As humans we take many things in life for granted. We appreciate wind when there is none, and only wish for rain when everything is dying. People will throw their trash on the ground because they're too lazy to walk over to a trash can five feet away. Not caring about the animals that could eat the wrappers, or how ugly the trash looks on the ground.

The world would be a much cleaner place if people would notice how they affect it. The main problem is that people don't take time to realize the beauty they're destroying. If everyone would realize how pretty nature is they wouldn't want to ruin it. We need to learn to appreciate our world.

Megan Tucker, Grade 11
Owasso High School, OK

Mi Amigos

A friend is: "a person who one knows well, likes, and trusts." Friends are a really significant part of my life, and I do not know what I would do without them. Friends are important to me because they are fun, reliable, and supportive.

I love my friends because they are so much fun and cheer me up. We laugh a lot, play silly games, and make fun of each other; but we do have serious conversations sometimes. My favorite thing to do is spend time with them, and we have made some awesome memories together.

Reliability is a major quality in a friendship. I need someone who I can confide in, who will offer their shoulder and a hug when I cry, and someone I can count on. My friends are all of these; trustworthy, considerate, and solid as a rock.

If I am feeling down on myself, my friends are always there to support me. Even when I am happy, they continue to encourage me and cheer me on, whether it is band, sports, school, my faith, or just life in general. Though they tease me sometimes, I know they love me, and I love them too.

My friends are my favorite people in the whole world. They make me laugh, I can depend on them, and they never stop encouraging me. They are always there for me and never cease to amaze me. My friends are so special to me; I will never forget them.

Taylor Tate, Grade 10
Grove High School, OK

Treasured Gifts

Do you have a gift that you cherish the most? Who was it from? Was it from your mother, your pet, or your best friends? These special gifts are treasured greatly. Many of these gifts are priceless like the embedment of friendship and love from your grandmother.

Friendship is a priceless gift. It's one of the many gifts that I value. It can get me into trouble, render happiness, and bring about sadness. All my friends carry these; they get me in trouble, bring happiness upon my face, and also cloud the happiness with sadness. They console me when sadness comes to play, criticize me to excel the days that I am falling, and celebrate with me with enthusiastic energy. Friendship is all about lending a hand to one another and letting that relationship grow stronger.

I went to visit my grandmother last year. She gave me her necklace. It now hangs on my neck beautifully. I gaze at it often this time of the year because she is ill. The necklace reminds me of her, young and beautiful — full of life. She will be gone in a few years and it is sad to think about it, but I am grateful that my grandmother is such an extraordinary person.

Precious gifts resembling the embedment of friendship and love from your grandmother are priceless. Whoever these gifts were from, it has a valuable meaning.

Myshenyenne Vang, Grade 11
Owasso High School, OK

Triumph

Our red uniforms shown brilliantly underneath the stadium lights. My heart jumped around wildly as I gazed upon the full house. At the sight of our army, they welcomed us to the stage with a standing ovation. This was it! Weeks upon weeks of preparation now hinged on one single performance. Marching band, not too many people can compare with the experience. Since August 1st, The Pride of Owasso had been building a family. Countless hours of rehearsal, pain, heat, sweat, tears, and triumphs had brought us together in ways that one would find difficult to understand. The announcer introduced our band as we marched onto the field. I held my chin high and let the special power that connected myself to everyone else flow through my consciousness. One breath, and the show was in motion. We were there to convince the crowd just how awesome we knew we were. It was amazing to be able to connect with the audience on a personal level through beautiful marching drill, incredible music, and an emotional general effect. In my short lifetime and high school marching band career, I have yet to find a greater feeling than standing there out of breath after a performance, knowing we did the very best we could because we persevered towards a goal, and left it all out there on the field.

Taylor Warren, Grade 11
Owasso High School, OK

My Love

A peaceful smile upon a face, the power of God's Grace. The simple things one can share, a breeze of fresh summer air. Mom and dad encouraging me through, being myself and sharing that with you. Brother and sister to give peaceful company, for we all grow together as one family. Aunts and uncles and all relatives the same bring happiness and good fortune to represent our name. Respect and loving nature, possessed among my friends, a bond that will grow strong and never have an end. A nourishing meal after a busy day, a stable resting place for my head to lay. A gentle hand to help me cope, a single sign of uplifting hope. A giving heart that is kind and pure, for any downfall that is the cure. To love and be loved is what I strive, for from the bottom of goodness, I will derive. The good Lord guiding me on my way, my main motivation each and every day. A tender affection that may never fall, for these are the things I love most of all.

Heather Hanson, Grade 12
Newnan High School, GA

Battlefield Hero

My grandfather was a marine during WW2. He was a decorated veteran, who fought on several different campaigns, and received two purple hearts. One of the purple hearts he received was on Guadalcanal. He was in the 3rd amphibious tractor battalion of the 12th marine regiment of the 3rd marine division. He was stationed at Henderson air field to protect the CB's, which was the navy construction battalion. Almost every night there were Japanese mortar, light infantry, bonsai, and bayonet attacks trying to make the airstrip useless, and during one of those attacks, an artillery shell landed in a bunker across from the barrack and my grandfather heard screaming, so he and another man ran across the air strip. They took a few men each trip to the navy core men for medical assistance under continuous mortar fire. He was hit in the lower back with shrapnel, but was still able to bring two other men back to safety.

Stephen Brothers, Grade 11
Vero Beach High School, FL

My Little Black Dog Queenie

One night I was walking outside and I heard this constant howl that was coming from the storage room. I poked my head in the door and to my surprise I saw a little black dog.

As soon as I saw that it was a dog, I went into the house and got my mother. I told her to come outside because there was a little black dog that was in the storage room. I asked her if she knew whom the dog belonged to, she said that she didn't know. I asked her if I could keep it and she said yes.

After a couple of days I decided to name her Queenie. She was so beautiful to me. She had blue eyes and she was all black. She is a pit and lab mix. I still have her to this day. She weighs about 45-50 pounds.

I enjoy playing with her and I plan on keeping her till she either dies or until I lose her.

Milton Long, Grade 11
Southside High School, NC

A Changed Me

I am one of the few teenagers who can honestly say that I have been through a life changing experience. My adolescence was much different from those of my peers; instead of spending my Sunday afternoon throwing a ball around with my father, I was forced to clean up after him. My father was a cancer patient for as long as I could remember. He was sickened by several types of cancer. Even though the sickness limited his mobility, he didn't let himself succumb to the disease. The cancer had been in recession until September of 2005, when a cancerous tumor was found on my father's spine. From that day on I went from an unordinary young man to a permanent caretaker. I doubt in any other essay submissions that a teenager can say that after a long week of hard school work that they had to forfeit their weekend to wash, feed, and clean up after a sick parent. This job went on until the following September when my father, my hero, and my best friend passed away. I often go back to that day and think of what I could have become after my father's death and then look at what I have now. I am a successful student who has excelled in everything that I have attempted after his death. My past is what has gotten me to my future, and even though it has been painful, I am sure that it has changed me, for the better.

Zak Elfenbein, Grade 11
Miami Killian Sr High School, FL

Teen Depression from Teen Eyes

I feel that main cause of teenage depression is people at the school. When you're at school you have to worry about being judged. Those can't escape into love and happiness. Escape into drugs, alcohol, sex, suicide, eating disorders or cutting themselves. Some people make it through school without anything. Most go through that and once they start they can't stop! Some are afraid to get help fear of more people making fun of them.

Those who do escape are stronger than most can think. They should talk to others who are going through the same things. That would give them hope to overcome their problems. It would help them by letting them talk to someone and give them the support they need to help them stop. If they have more support from someone who made it out they have a better chance to stop them from doing it again.

No matter how many people say to their kids you can tell me anything they really can't. We would love to be able to but we are afraid and when you talk to a teacher they might not always have the best advice but at least you're telling someone. It never helps when people makes fun of them it hurts a million times worse. It lowers all of the confidence they had. What would you do if your family member told you that they wanted to end their life?

Jonica Smith, Grade 10
Prue High School, OK

Divorce for the Better

My parents were like most married couples, who have their ups and downs, but as time went on they could no longer resolve their issues. When I was thirteen years old, my parents got a divorce. They had been married for fourteen long years. At that time, I didn't really understand what a divorce was, so I was surprised when I found out my mother and I had to move. I couldn't believe it. Move, why? That's not how divorces happen on television and in movies. I wanted to blame somebody, but who, my mother, my father, or me? Was it my fault? I felt that maybe I could have done something to prevent my parents from getting a divorce. It took me a while to adjust to life in Louisiana, but it worked out okay. I go to one of the top schools in the state, and I have found someone that I could possibly spend the rest of my life with. It's still an everyday struggle to accept the fact that my parents are divorced and will probably never get back together. I still sometimes think that if I had spoken up, maybe just maybe, my parents would still be together and I would still be in Texas with all of my friends. I've had a little counseling and the counselor told me that everything happens for a reason, and I am okay with that.

India McDougald, Grade 12
Baton Rouge Magnet High School, LA

Don't Repeat the Lyrics — The Definition of Hip-Hop

Let me say this; I love hip-hop, but I hate rap music. There's a difference. But it's become evident to me that rap music has been sucking the life from hip-hop. This essay will display my opinion of hip-hop and where it went wrong.

Songs made 10-20 years ago had a beat and a message. What I see now is that real lyrics do not equal "real music." Music now says, "Hey, who needs talent when you've got a catchy song?" This philosophy has been the "inspiration" for many of the biggest songs today.

2007 was full of controversies, which have threatened to bury hip-hop. One of the questions raised: if Don Imus lost his job should rappers lose theirs? The main problem is inconsistency. People don't want CDs that have one or two lyrical songs and the rest talk about nothing.

Luckily, there are artists still making lyrical, catchy songs. Old school artists like Nas and KRS-ONE use their songs to reach out to fans so people could relate to their experiences. Rising artists like Lupe Fiasco bring music back by experimenting with different sounds. Music like this displays what real hip-hop is.

Finally, I will compare a rapper to a hip-hop artist. A rapper "wraps" around the wrong issues and uses a colorful "wrapping" because nothing was inside their lyrical package. A hip-hop artist is literally an artist whose music has double meanings. In conclusion, real hip-hop has to be "hip" to what's real, and "hop" past commercialism.

Kyle Dyon Gardner, Grade 10
Jefferson City High School, MO

What the Differences Are Between Public and Christian Schools

There are many differences between Christian school and Public school. Some may not know it, but Christian schools are a lot more different then what the Public schools are. And the reason is they are a lot stricter.

Most of the Public schools don't allow kids to pray while Christian schools do allow praying. The dress codes are also very different. In Public schools, students get to wear pretty much whatever they want, while students at the Christian schools usually have to wear clothes that are dressier. Rules differ a lot. While students at the Christian schools have to follow very strict rules, public schools are very lenient on their rules. The teachers at the schools are very different. The Christian school teachers care a lot about the students, and their education, while the public school teachers hardly care at all. The students at the public schools do not treat the other students the way they are supposed to be treated. While the Christian school students treat the other students the way they are supposed to be treated.

I believe that Christian schools are the best schools for students to attend. Not only because they are really good schools, but because of the Christian environment. And the teachers care very much about the students and their education. And that is what really counts.

Caiti Thompson, Grade 12
Trinity Christian Academy, AL

Cloning for Medical Reasons

More than 95,000 people are on the U.S. organ transplant waiting list, waiting for kidneys, livers, and lungs. Research in organ cloning should be supported and funded because it could save people's lives, provides another alternative to organ doning, and people would not have to wait on a list to get an organ transplant.

Cloning organs, not people or living things, should be strongly considered. A person might need a kidney, but could be unable to find a donor. He could get his other kidney cloned and would have an exact replica of his healthy kidney. This would save his life. If he had received an organ from a person that is not related to him, the kidney would fail in a couple of years and he would need a kidney transplant. When a person receives an organ transplant, the body reacts to it as if it is a foreign substance. The immune system would fight the organ and destroy it. That person would need a kidney transplant again and again. If he received a cloned kidney, the body would not destroy it because it would consider it part of the body.

There are more people that need an organ than there are organ donors.

Have you ever known a person who needed an organ transplant? Too many times the poor person waits and waits, never receives an organ transplant, and ends up dying. Something like that should never happen in a country like this!

Damir Dandic, Grade 10
Woodlee's Christian Academy, GA

R-E-S-P-E-C-T: Please Sock It to Me

Aretha Franklin's big hit, "Respect," was very popular in 1967. But now, both the song and the subject of the song are both a thing of the past.

The other day, I was sitting in American history when the teacher asked a student a yes or no question. The student answered the question first with a grunt, and when asked to repeat his answer, preceded to roll his eyes and say, "Yeah." I sat there wondering whether the student had a limited vocabulary or if he just lacked respect.

In today's society, "please and thank you's" are a very rare occurrence. Instead, you're greeted with the friendly phrase, "About time," and the ever popular sigh following with rolling of the eyes.

This lack of respect is troubling. I believe American teenagers have issues mostly with self respect. Teens do not respect their own lives anymore. They laugh in the face of death by doing drugs, sleeping around, and drinking. I've had to accept the fact that most of my classmates will be dead by age 40 by either STDs, liver cancer, lung cancer, or a car accident.

Franklin's song, "Respect," has come and gone. You still hear it every once in a while, but for the most part, it is in the past and that's where it'll stay. I'm afraid the characteristic of respect is condemned to the same fate.

Teresa Fowler, Grade 11
Camden Central High School, TN

The Great Crossing

Following a dirt path, we enter into the forest, heading towards the river. Next to the river is a large clearing with thousands of river rocks underfoot. The other horses begin to cross.

When Summer, my horse, gets to the edge of the water, she is not so sure and backs up a few steps. I urge her to the edge once more; she stops and backs up.

Again we come to the calm waters of the bank. Everyone else is on the other side waiting. I look down and see small tadpoles swimming in circles. Summer leans down and smells the water. One foot stomps down and she backs up. She neighs to the other side not wanting to be left behind. Her ears prick up, listening for an answer. I can feel her tense up beneath me as she calls out again. This time she is answered. Reaching down to pet her neck, I silently urge her into the water once more. This time she goes.

As we wade through, the cold water splashes up on me. It feels refreshing and a wave of goose bumps washes over me. In the middle of the river, my boots go under and are soaked, but I don't mind, I am proud of my horse. As I think this I reach down and pat her water-speckled neck. As we continue our ride I think back on our great crossing and enjoy the warm, sunny morning.

Kelsey Russell, Grade 10
Savannah High School, MO

Steroids and Adolescence

The dangers and risks associated with teens who decide to use steroids are phenomenal. Steroid use can lead to cardiovascular disease, including heart attacks and strokes, increased risk of contracting HIV/AIDS, male-pattern baldness, cysts, acne, severe mood swings, stunted growth and major depression that has lead to suicide in many documented cases. Other major effects steroids have on a young person's body are the development of breasts, impotence for males, and growth of facial hair and deepening of the voice for females.

The ever increasing controversy over steroid use in professional sports is staggering. These same professional athletes are role models for younger athletes. If there were stricter rules with continuous testing and harsher punishments in place to keep steroids out of professional sports, steroid use among teens would drop dramatically.

Also, more awareness on the dangers of steroids could dramatically reduce teen steroid use. Most adolescents who take steroids are uneducated about the risks involved. An increasing number of high school seniors say they don't believe the drugs are risky. A sophisticated approach in battling teen steroid use is to incorporate a mandatory steroid awareness program in the high school curriculum.

There is no place for steroids and other performance enhancing drugs in sports, especially not in youth sports. The negative effects the drugs have on the body significantly outweigh the "positive" results that they offer. Education and positive role models for adolescents are the keys to ending steroid use.

James Ray, Grade 11
Rossville Christian Academy, TN

My Last First Week of My Junior Year

I was extremely hesitant about starting my first week of junior year. I was terrified of all the new rules I had been hearing about and about having all of my classes spread throughout the new portables.

When I arrived at school I realized that my parking spot wasn't as close as I thought it was. The trek to my first class was quite long. Luckily, all of my friends parked close to me and we all walked to class together. It was difficult finding out where to go because the signs that are stuck in the ground aren't TOO specific, and they can be confusing.

I was not thrilled about receiving my "Dog Tag," as some might call it. It was a major disappointment right at the beginning of my day. In my opinion, they are pointless and ugly. As the day passed, I was a little confused on what time we get out of a certain class, and how to know which class to go to next, I was just praying that after a few days or weeks it would start coming natural.

All in all, my first week of junior year didn't turn out as bad as I had originally planned. I have a lot of friends in all my classes, and although the schedule is still undergoing changes, I think it's going to be a fun year.

Taylor Wynn, Grade 11
Vero Beach High School, FL

A Hard Decision

The Death Penalty has been and continues to be an issue of extensive discussion and argument. Two-thirds of Americans, or 68%, support the Death Penalty for people convicted of murder. Support for this side comes from a few motives. The remaining 32% believe the Death Penalty is wrong. Many have compiled plenty of reasons on why the Death Penalty should be abolished.

For the 68% of supporters the Death Penalty remains just another way of punishment for criminals. Many believe this sentence brings closure to the families of the victim. Also, the penalty is thought of as a crime deterrent. While life in prison is effective as a deterrent, crimes continue to be done. The fear of the Death Penalty apparently keeps people from committing heinous crimes.

The supporters of banning the Death Penalty support their argument vehemently. The financial cost of capital punishment remains a high concern. Because of a long court process the death sentence is 2 to 5 times more money than sentencing someone to life in prison. Many also stand by the fact that the death sentence violates the "cruel and unusual" clause in the Bill of Rights.

The United States is 1 of 43 countries currently retaining the Death Penalty, while 40 countries have abolished this punishment. Within American there are 12 states without the Death Penalty and 38 approving of it. This wide range of differences makes this argument a hard one to solve. The United States is no closer to accepting one stand.

Lauren Durling, Grade 11
Bishop Verot High School, FL

My Friends

Life is full of things that people are truly thankful for and mine is my friends. Here are two reasons whey I am thankful for my friends.

Most people would say that I'm the quiet girl that never talks but my friends know better than to believe that. One incident that happens more often than it should is when friends tell a joke and while everyone else is laughing esoterically, I'm still trying to figure out why that joke was so funny. After ten minutes, when everybody stops laughing about it, I finally realize what the joke was about and start laughing out loud. My friends know me and may pick on me but they don't disown me. I am thankful for my friends because they don't care how crazy I can be sometimes but instead they love me.

I know that if I need someone to talk to, I always have my friends. For example, you know you have a friend when you are in tears, call her, and she says she will be at your house in a few minutes. Although you may be crying over a stupid boy, she holds you tight and tells you she loves you. That's when you know you have a true friend.

These are two reasons why I'm thankful for my friends. I don't know what I would do without them. No matter what, I love them. Nothing can ever change that.

Dorothy Jones, Grade 11
Southside High School, NC

Downside of Life, Upside of Death

Why do you mourn when you lose a loved one? Why do you celebrate when a baby is born? I mourn when someone dies because they will no longer be in my presence. They will no longer be here as a friend, relative, or lover. Celebrate life; don't mourn death. It is nearly impossible not to grieve over death — everyone does it. But instead of grieving what the dead will miss out on — focus on what they accomplished.

Death is difficult to deal with, but so is life sometimes. I wonder why you don't grieve when a child is born and celebrate when someone dies. At birth, you have a life full of happiness, sadness, grief, accomplishments, and disappointments just waiting to happen. But when you die, you no longer feel pain or sadness; you don't experience grief or worry. You're simply at peace.

I believe in Heaven which is something to rejoice when you die. So, when you lose a loved one, don't lament. Instead, celebrate the life they lived. When the next baby is born, be jubilant about the new life, but feel sympathy for the long journey they have yet to encounter.

Elizabeth Hurst, Grade 10
Academics Plus Charter School, AR

Never Again! Do We Really Mean It?

For many years, almost two and a half million men, women, and children have been chased from their homes in the Darfur region of Sudan. These innocent people face the threat of starvation, disease, and rape on a daily basis. The lucky ones that remain in their homes face the threat of displacement, torture, and murder. These heinous acts sometimes seem unstoppable but I disagree; I think that this genocide can be stopped.

The obvious first step humanitarians should take is encouraging the passage of a resolution where peacekeepers could enter without the permission of the Sudanese government. The Sudanese government is the sole participant in the atrocities and laughs at the thought of allowing peacekeepers. Meanwhile, they rape and murder their citizens. Until this resolution is passed, nothing can be done to help these people.

I, and many others, believe that if we don't do something about it, this genocide in Darfur, will turn out to be a second Holocaust. After the Holocaust was over, the world spoke the two words "never again". Never again would we allow the wholesale slaughter of any group by a government. Omar Al-Bashir (the dictator of Sudan) is making a wicked mockery of this pledge by committing horrid crimes against humanity on a budget less than most U.S. states. If the rest of the world is unwilling to intervene in a genocide committed by a minor player on the world scale, how are we going to stop another Adolf Hitler?

Noah Johnson, Grade 10
Grady High School, GA

Reality Hit

I've realized…Life isn't always as it seems to be. Friends will lie, family will hurt you, and love will come and go. But, just like there's gold at the end of the long rainbow, good will always come after every bad situation. We can blame ourselves and ask questions 'bout why somethin' has happened. In the end, we can only be lucky that it did happen.

There's light at the end of every tunnel. There's a lucky charm at the end of all our heartaches. There's peace at the end of every war. Just like there's a friends shoulder to cry on after every bad word has been spoken.

None of us can choose who we are. Our friends, family, and loved ones will lie, cheat, and die just like every other person in this world. Some things may be harder to grip than others, but after hours of cryin' and thinkin', I, as well as everyone else, will notice that, in the end…it's all worth it!

Cassandra Jennings, Grade 10
Bourbon High School, MO

What Marching Band Has Done for Me

July heat turns into October chill too quickly. For four years I have watered the football field with my tears, sweat, and blood. Anyone who knows me will say I live for the half-time and competition performances. The Swansea Tiger Marching Band has honored me with pride, respect, accomplishment, and humility. The purple uniform on every member reminds me of where I come from and what I have been able to accomplish through hard work. I have learned that respect must be given if it has been earned. Every trophy I helped earn is displayed in the band room, permanently chronicled for the world to see. Every mistake I have made has left me humbled amongst my peers. I can stand proudly and announce: "I have never traded what I have wanted at the moment for what I have wanted most."

Chelsea Rhodes, Grade 12
Swansea High School, SC

Being a Team

Being part of a team can be a challenge. Everyone needs to have discipline, respect for each other, and has to want the best for the team. I talk from experience because I am part of a very large team; my high school band. There are at least one-hundred and fifty teenagers in one place at the same time. You would think it might be trouble, but we strive for excellence. During practices we must have self discipline so that we can get things done instead of talking and wasting time. We cannot waste time or else we will not achieve our goal of excellence. Another part of being a team is respect for everyone on the team. You need to respect them because they want the same thing for the team as you do and that is to be the best. Everyone must want the very best for the team too or else it will go nowhere. Wanting the best for the team is a must because it leads to self discipline and respect which are key matters of being a team.

Celeste Brown, Grade 11
Vero Beach High School, FL

An Adventure Completed

The year was 1996 and a young Jeffrey Trudeau was about to make a breakthrough. He was sitting in a back room of his Louisiana house. His eyes were focused and his mind was occupied on one thing and one thing only. He reached over for his cup of ice tea and, after taking a sip, returned to his controller. Connected to his controller was a wire that stretched across the room to the Super Nintendo placed on top the fat television.

The game was *Super Godzilla* and Jeffrey had finally reached the last level. The final showdown was against Bagan, a giant red monster created by the aliens. He appeared to be tough but Jeffrey was confident. He un-paused the game and the battle began. Fists clashed and the health bars began to fall. Each attack a monster made was matched by the other. It wasn't long before each monster was down to their final breaths. Jeffrey slammed down the directional pad and held the B button down, charging up a punch. He released the button and Godzilla released his punch. His fist made contact with Bagan's jaw and its health dropped down until it was almost gone. The end was finally near as Godzilla began to charge up his fire breath. With the release of his blue flames Bagan's health dropped to zero and its life came to an end. Jeffrey cheered as the credits began to roll. After weeks of playing the adventure was finally over.

Jeffrey Trudeau, Grade 12
Germantown High School, TN

Dinosaurs and Birds

Arguably the most magnificent creatures ever to walk the Earth were the dinosaurs. They were also one of the most mysterious. The only thing we know matter-of-factly about them is that they once existed. Everything else we know about them is strictly theory or hypothesis. One of the most illogical theories is the one that states that dinosaurs are the direct ancestors to birds. This theory makes less sense than the one that states apes are the ancestors to humans. The main reason this theory first came into being was the discovery of a group of dinosaurs called the ornithomimosaurs or "bird mimics." These dinosaurs bear a striking resemblance to ostriches. However, if you look at their skeletal structures they are nothing alike. Dinosaurs are placed into two distinct groups. The saurichians or "lizard hips" have, as their names suggest, hips very similar to modern day lizard's hips. The ornithischians or the "bird hips" have hips shaped like modern day birds. So you would expect that the direct ancestors of birds would have bird shaped hips. However, the ornithomimosaurs belong to the lizard hipped group of dinosaurs. Also, the bird-hipped dinosaurs looked nothing like birds at all. So this theory that dinosaurs are the direct ancestors to birds is completely ridiculous.

Robbie Foy, Grade 11
Rossville Christian Academy, TN

Dance

Albert Einstein called dancers "the athletes of God," because of their beauty and grace. For many centuries humans have danced all over the Earth, before music. Dance is the expression of emotions and feelings through the body. But dance is not just all emotion and spontaneous movement spawned from our feelings; it is a rigorous and tough art. Not all of a dance class is spent learning how to wave your arms in willowy motions or how to spin and pointe your toes. The majority of the class is spent in muscle and memory building. Though dance may look easy and effortless, it most certainly is not. It takes much muscle to lift one's leg up in the air and move it around while not moving one's torso the tiniest bit. This may sound easy, but there are many things a dancer must remember while doing the most basic dance steps. On top of the original dance step, a dancer must remember to hold in stomach, lift head, lengthen body, turn out legs, tuck bottom under, lift chest, and keep your body aligned. Because of its emphasis on memory, dance benefits both your body and mind. Dance is much more complicated and draining than it looks, but one of a dancer's jobs is making the dance look effortless. Many people dismiss dance as wimpy or girly and refuse to call it what it truly is — a sport.

Abby Sullivan, Grade 11
Providence Classical School, AL

Ends Always Bring New Beginnings

My PopPop has been very sick for the past three years. He just had surgery on his heart and the doctors said, "He only has a little more time to live."

We went to my Nanny and PopPop's house tonight to spend time with him. My PopPop had been fast asleep, and then out of nowhere he started singing. A couple hours later my mom said, "Get ready to leave." While I was in the bathroom everyone had already said good-bye and my PopPop had already fallen back to sleep, so I decided not to say good-bye. On the care ride home that's all I could think about.

The next morning was different. I walked into the den at the same time my sister was coming out. She was bawling her eyes out. Then I asked my parents, "What's going on?" I got an answer I really didn't want to hear. I couldn't believe that my PopPop was dead. He had died peacefully in his sleep that morning. All I could say was why didn't I tell him I loved him, and say good-bye? For a few hours all I did was cry and hug the teddy bear my PopPop had given me when I was little.

During the Mass portion of the funeral Mrs. Michelle was singing not just any song but the song he sang the night before he died. Every time I hear that song now I begin to almost cry.

Erin Carroll, Grade 10
Stanton College Preparatory School, FL

Change

In today's society, we desire stability. However, throughout my personal life I have not had this convenience. For me life has been about constant change. I have moved a total sixteen times in my seventeen years of life. To be more precise, I lived in the same house for eleven years which means that I moved fifteen times over six years.

It all started when my parents got divorced, when I was four months old. Over the next three years we lived in 6 different places. By this time my mother had married another man, so we moved into a house, where we lived for eleven years. Then at the age of fourteen after my mother and step father had divorced, the moves began again. I moved around 8 more times for various reasons.

People that have lived in the same house their entire life, or even just 3 or 4 houses, are far more fortunate than they realize most of the time. I wish I had that chance for stability that they have.

Hollie Guthrie, Grade 12
Walker Valley High School, TN

Work Ethic

As an athlete, work ethic plays a big part in my life. Every day is made or broken by the effort I put forth in everything I do. If I slack, it shows; if I work hard, it shows. On and off the field I do my best every day to put forth the effort to succeed.

I was taught since I was a small child to earn everything by working for it. Since I was little, yes, a lot of things have been handed to me, but I saw that as an open door. Just because the door was opened to me didn't mean it was going to stay open. I took lemons and made lemonade. I worked hard to earn everything I have now. Work ethic is the main characteristic of my life. My work ethic is known, and it has made me known too. I owe my accomplishments to my devoted work ethic God gave to me at such a young age. Everything I earned was given to me from the Lord my God.

Ashley Bryson, Grade 12
Walker Valley High School, TN

Courage

Courage can be defined by many words; strength, bravery or daring. But I define courage a different way; I define it with a name. My father Lyle Kamm is a strong, caring, loving man. No task is too big or too small for him, he is invincible. However, this man has a secret, a secret that he has kept to himself and his friends and family for the past year; he is suffering from prostate cancer. This blow was a heavy one; it has affected both himself and the people around him for over a year now. While it was not as serious as cancer usually is, it still required a two-day surgery and lengthy recovery time, with no time to spare for his usual activities. However, this great man managed to help out at the local soccer park, and continue to help others through his work. He is a hero to others and a hero to his loving wife. But most of all, he is a hero to his children. I am proud to call him my father.

Lauren Kamm, Grade 10

Love

Love has many definitions, but varies from one person to another. The definition of love cannot be defined as something solid but something that surrounds us forever. Love can be found in a family, in the eyes of a mother holding her child, in a husband kissing his wife, and in friendships all people share. Everyone in their lives searches for love. They either choose to accept it or turn away from it. Those who turn away may never know how true love feels, it can only be experienced. Yet the misconception of love undertakes a lot of people. Some are willing to have someone else love them and care for them unconditionally, but true love only lasts if it is secured by two people. Loving someone involves accepting someone for who they are, being there for them whenever they are in need, and never underestimating them. Unfortunately, love does not dwell in all people. Some search for it forever but never find their "soul mate." Others lose hope in themselves and believe that they don't deserve to be loved in the first place. Love is what you make of it. What you put into it is what you will get out of it in the long run. Everyone hopes that once they find that one person worth giving their heart to, they will never leave. Love in today's world is unpredictable but worth experiencing.

Lauren Kiddy, Grade 11
Bishop Verot High School, FL

The Genius of King Louis XIV

"One king, one law, one faith," the policy put into effect by the greatest ruler of Europe, King Louis XIV. He was a master of propaganda and of eliminating any potential challengers to his power. He accomplished this absolute power by putting France under one law, one faith, and one king.

First, Louis got rid of his only threat, the nobility. He did this by placing them in his court, where he could keep them preoccupied with court life and at the same time, keep them out of politics. However, that alone would not keep them down for long. That's when he used propaganda. Louis referred to himself as the "Sun King" because he believed himself to be the center of France and the center of its government. Thus, he put France under one king. Then he built France's most famous building, Versailles. With that built, he placed the nobility there, and in the process, managed to get the nobility and everyone else to grovel at his feet, thanks to his propaganda. Thus, France was put under one law. However, France's faith was still split between Catholicism and Protestantism. So, he passed the Edict of Fontainebleau, that destroyed all things Protestant, and the Protestants left France. Thus, France was under one faith.

France was finally put under the rule of one king, one law, with one faith. Of course, it was all thanks to the genius of King Louis XIV.

Jayson Kimmey, Grade 10
Stanton College Preparatory School, FL

My Third Eye

I scope out the view looking for the perfect angle. I squint and put the image into focus. With the click of the shutter and the blink of the flash, I've captured another memory.

I have a passion for photography. I've always been fascinated with the idea of freezing moments in time. Photographs can be records of celebratory events or creative mediums that make statements about the ideas and thoughts of an artist.

Portrait shots convey many ranges of emotions. People are different in their own unique way, and their personalities are expressed through a photo. A person's soul shines through and imprints itself on to the film. Their eyes tell all, and through them, a thousand stories can be told.

I love that sometimes a screw-up can be the most wonderful mistake. An accidental cover-up of the flash can create red lighting, making the photo look dark and ominous. Even a blur can cause images to show more emphasis. I never have expectations with my photographs, because I know that none of them will come out the way I had planned.

When I'm behind the camera lens, I'm in control. I decide the composition, perspective and lighting. I have the power to communicate with people through still images. Everything's in my hands.

Capturing a moment is what I love to do. My camera is always available in case I need a quick snap of an image. Whether I'm with my friends, or creating artwork, my third eye is always open.

Courtney Holtzman, Grade 11
Countryside High School, FL

Frankenstein

The search for acceptance is something that everyone goes through, whether it's trying to be accepted by a group that you consider popular at school, or it's trying to be accepted by new coworkers. Being a part of a group is a crucial part of life. If you're too fat, or your nose is too big, or your hair is too curly, you pay thousands of dollars to get it fixed just to look "normal." The truth is that nobody's "normal" and everyone has his own flaws. In *Frankenstein*, all the monster wants is to be normal and accepted by people. He begs his creator Victor to make a female like him so he wouldn't be alone.

The monster tells Victor that his actions of evil are due to his loneliness. When Victor begins to make a companion, the monster is overjoyed. But when Victor destroys the project, the monster is furious and lashes out against him. The monster only wants acceptance of someone. When we go to a new school or job, all we want is for people to like us and to not feel left out by others.

We should accept everyone for who they are, and "treat others the way that we want to be treated," or we could be unleashing a monster into society.

Tanya Dolfi, Grade 10
Miami Killian Sr High School, FL

Allegiance

There is a value which seems to become increasingly overlooked in our multicultural society, but it is the cord that binds us all together. It is called patriotism, and I love it.

I fully expect patriotism from others who claim to have American interests at heart. Times have often been difficult in the United States, where, as in the America Revolution, patriotism was sometimes the only thin thread protecting our citizens from being overtaken. In January 1776, Thomas Paine's famous pamphlet Common Sense was first published. In it, he challenged fledgling patriots when he wrote "The summer soldier and the sunshine patriot will shrink from the service of their country." Precisely because I believe so strongly in patriotism, I mean to stand by my convictions. When I visit other countries, I can be proud of the people I represent, and not feel I must make concessions for what people think of that. When I vote for the first time, I can be informed as to which candidates truly want the best for my country. True devotion requires unfaltering fealty to a cause. America commands my utmost respect.

I pledge allegiance to one flag. Whether pristinely furling on a porch or jerking violently riddled with bullet holes, the American flag is an emblem of devotion to the United States. It is fitting that whether the times are easy or hard, I should be a patriot on whom the country can count. I am an American.

Wendy Greve, Grade 12
Salem Baptist Christian School, NC

Challenges Aren't Always a Bad Thing!

This year's volleyball season was challenging. Our coach, Jeff Smith (Bro. Jeff), was ready for a season to finish what we start. He was determined to put fight and determination into his fifteen players no matter what. Whether it took bear crawls, kneel downs, or jumps. He was determined to make us into a better, faster, and smarter team.

The girls were pumped the first few weeks of practice leading up to our first game. We won that game but didn't play well. Every game leading up to the Florence Invitation Tournament was a building block for our team. At the tournament Trinity played two of the top teams in the state of Tennessee. We lost those games, but only by a few points which made our coach excited about the steps we were taking. Those games helped us, but our 15-0 loss to Covenant, a home school group, was a step we didn't need to take. After a win at Brooklane, with only three varsity girls able to play and with three junior varsity girls, we got the momentum we needed for the season. With that momentum we were able to win out our regular season with a 11-5 record. That record promised us a seat in the state tournament.

The season started with many challenges but we stayed together and were able to come so far. We worked through our difficulties and just played ball. We started as a team and ended as a team. Goal accomplished!

Amanda Sansom, Grade 11
Trinity Christian Academy, AL

My Softball Life

I have been playing softball since I was four years old. When I was younger, I would always play ball with my cousins and they would teach me things about softball. As I grew older I played for many teams. My softball years started when I played at Little Farms on a little league team my uncle coached. I played there for a year and also played in the older age groups. I played at another recreation park, Carrolton. I played there for a while and played with the All-Star team. After I left recreation I played for a travel team. I started playing for the Hurricanes when I was eleven years old and I am still playing for the team. I have participated in many tournaments in many different states. Our team went to numerous tournaments in Louisiana and in other states as well. We also traveled to Tennessee, Mississippi, Alabama, Ohio, Florida, and Texas. I had the opportunity to play softball for my high school and took that chance. I played on varsity as a freshman and pitched. I have been pitching as long as I have played the game. I love playing softball and I hope to grow as a player and to be able to play college softball. One of my goals in softball is to play for college and I have worked hard to pursue it. I look forward to the day I can say that I have accomplished my goal and enjoy every minute of it.

Courtney Western, Grade 10
St Charles Catholic High School, LA

Unseen Love

My name is Kristy Lee Parker. I am a Beta Club member, an environmentalist, and an older sister. I have a younger sister, Courtney, who sadly views me as the "perfect" one, the one that can do anything well. Little does she know, she has the potential to be the stronger, better of us.

There has always been a sort of sibling rivalry between us, but not by my doings. She has always had to live in my shadow and I can understand why I irritate her. In school, the teachers expect her to be me. In a way I've never displayed to her, I admire her for striving to be her own person and not follow my exact footsteps. It was easy for me to set the bar; what makes her stronger is that she sets her own.

Although she has always tried her best, Courtney never had much confidence in herself. It really saddens me because she never felt she could succeed or triumph over me in anything. Then she joined the Color guard. When I see her out on the football field at half time performing with the discipline of an Army general, I can tell she really feels a sense of pride.

Courtney is not me, and I realize this. I've just always wanted her to have the strong confidence I have in her own self. Although sisters never say corny things like that, we do feel it; we just show it in a different way.

Kristy Parker, Grade 11
Camden Central High School, TN

Love

Love, generally defined as a tender feeling of affection, actually has several meanings depending on the context it's used in. In the English language, "love" is really the only word used to describe such an emotion. Those who speak English use it when describing how one feels toward friends, family, as well as a significant other. The Greek language however, has a plurality of words to express "love." *Philia* means "friendship" in Greek, it is a dispassionate love which includes loyalty to friends, family and community. *Storge* means "affection" in modern Greek and is a natural love such as that felt by parents toward offspring. *Thelema* describes a desire, such as a want to be occupied. *Agape* is a modern Greek term which is loosely used to express love. It is used interchangeably to denote feelings toward children, food, fondness of an activity, or a love for Christ. *Eros* expresses a passionate love that includes a longing for another, however it does not necessarily have a sexual connotation. The philosopher Plato refined the definition noting that *eros* means "without physical attraction to," and should be used when simply describing an appreciation for one's physical appearance. Plato inspired philosophers and lovers alike for centuries to come to seek truth through *eros*. Not only does the Greek culture define love in many ways, but other cultures including Italian, Latin, and Chinese do as well. Therefore, when using "love" in English, one must be careful of the context and not be mistaken for friendship, loyalty, or even lust.

Christina LoSauro, Grade 11
Bishop Verot High School, FL

Fighter

What happens when a person gets sick? He goes to the doctor and he fixes him right up. But what happens when a person has a stroke? He can't eat, speak, move or talk, feeling almost dead. The only thing anyone can do is pray and pray. Well this happened to my grandpa. My life changed after that as well as my family's.

December 24th, 2005 was a happy day. It was a fun day. I was with just about all my family in Atlanta, Georgia where we were eating dinner. That's when the phone call came. My aunt came into the room to tell us the news. "Grandpa's had a stroke," she said as the room fell silent.

The next day I called my grandma to find out the details. He was unable to talk, walk, breathe or eat. My grandpa was always an active person. He actually shoveled snow at his house the day that he had his stroke.

Now I look up to him even more. Every day he gets up and fights. He hardly walks with a walker but still tries. Every day my grandma with her bad back picks him up from bed and helps him with his therapy.

My grandpa is my hero. It's his voice that I hear every day when I call him that pushes me to achieve my goals. He helped me be who I am today and I help him be what he will tomorrow.

Nick Mighion, Grade 11
Countryside High School, FL

Lessons of Literature

Pride. Ambition. Recklessness. These words could easily portray a horrid tyrant who killed millions, but they could just as effortlessly be used to describe the characters of modern and classical literature, characters who are frozen in time forever. Why, then, do authors choose to tell stories of girls with broken hearts after years of partying, kings who murder teenagers for nothing more than covering the body of a sibling, and old men who look upon their past with regret? Do they really believe that readers will enjoy hearing tales of people dying because of their stubbornness, or is there a bigger lesson?

I believe that authors are trying to throw our own faults in our faces. When someone reads the poem Antigone and sees her own characteristics reflected in King Creon, that person is given the opportunity to see an example of the possibilities of her life to come. Authors are trying to give people the chance to see their own future, albeit slightly more dramatized. So what should a person take from a story, like that of Antigone? Should they look upon these stories with agony and despair, believing that they too are condemned to death and destruction? No. Readers of classical and modern literature should thank the authors, who dedicated hours, days, and even years of their lives to warn us about our mistakes before it is too late. If we read Antigone now and see how King Creon suffered from his pride, we can save ourselves.

Victoria Scott, Grade 10
St Francis Catholic High School, FL

2000 Valentine Storm

On February 14, 2000, was the worst day of my life. I say this because a hurricane hit in Camilla, GA. My mother had just come home from the hospital with my new baby brother. Early that morning, my mother said that she heard something that sounded like a train. She got up, took my brother and me into the other room and told my grandmother to wake up. When she came back in the room, it was almost too late, because the tree was coming through the roof. I heard my mother crying out to God, thanking Him for watching over us. When the storm was over, my grandmother walked around the inside of the house to see if everything was fine. She couldn't go outside because there was still storming going on. I count it as a blessing each and every day of my life because we're still living. Yes, the roof on our house was destroyed and we had to move with my aunt until the roof was repaired. We then finally moved back into our home after about a month and a half and then moved to Pelham. I didn't want to move because I knew that I would not be able to see my friends anymore. I didn't want to make new friends, but I did make new friends. When it's storming now, I stop what I'm doing, and take a moment to pray. The valuable lesson to me is being careful and stay prayed up.

Yashika L. Holton, Grade 12
Pelham High School, GA

Lung Cancer in Progress

According to the American Cancer Society, lung cancer is the number one cause of cancer deaths among men and women in the United States. It is extremely difficult to detect lung cancer early. Symptoms can include a cough that will not go away, chest pain, hoarseness, shortness of breath, bloody or rust-colored sputum, and recurring infections such as bronchitis and pneumonia. Lung cancer can be caused by smoking, secondhand smoke, asbestos, radon gas, and contact with certain chemicals and substances like uranium, chromium, and nickel.

Approximately 85 to 87% of all cases of lung cancer are caused by tobacco use. This makes lung cancer one of the most preventable cancers. My grandmother was just recently diagnosed with lung cancer. She had smoked for about 45 years of her life. Family members encouraged her to stop smoking about 5 years ago. She did with lots of help and support. She says it was one of the most difficult things she has had to do. We all hope it will save her life.

Lung cancer is difficult to treat effectively. There are three standard ways: surgery, radiation therapy, and chemotherapy. Laser therapy can also be used. The doctor recommended that my grandmother have surgery immediately. The surgery went well and the doctor has given her a good prognosis for recovery. Many others are not as fortunate. Prevent lung cancer by stop smoking today!

Stephanie Maddux, Grade 12
Walker Valley High School, TN

Unconditional

Since the day I was born, I've known that I'm lucky. I've never doubted that I was loved, and have always been supported by my family in anything I wanted to do. Though I never doubted that I was loved, I never fully comprehended how much my family cared for me until recently. Four months ago, I found out I was pregnant. Given the fact that I'm seventeen, my parents weren't thrilled, and to be honest, neither was I. However, since I decided to raise my baby, my family has shown me just how loved I really am.

To begin with, my baby's father, my on-off boyfriend of three years said he was going to be there to help me. One month later his whole tune changed.

As soon as my parents realized he was going to walk away, they told me not to worry. As long as I completed high school and still planned on attending college, we had a place to live. They've made it very clear that no matter what, they'll do what it takes to help me succeed and achieve my dreams, even with my baby.

I won't say I'm not nervous or a little scared, because I am, but I truly don't think I could do it without my family behind me. They truly are amazing people, and have made me see that I made the right choice, and that I'm loved unconditionally.

Sage Beasley, Grade 12

9/11/01

September 11th is a time where all Americans came together. We saw the major threat and horror that could come from other nations. At this time our pride of being an American boosted. It made our thoughts sharp. We knew our mission, avenge our fellow fallen Americans. The first thing that happened is we got in our minds that we wanted payback and no one would attack the U.S. like that and get away with it. So our brothers and sisters of the armed forces rallied together for a siege in the Middle East. We made it a quest to find the person behind the Twin Towers and Pentagon disasters. Also we made it part of our quest to free the foreign countries from harsh tyrants.

So today we fight on foreign land to make sure our own freedom is kept, and make sure other peoples of the world have the same opportunity.

Juan Jose Benitez, Grade 10
Slater High School, MO

Peace and Tranquility

What's important to me is my family and friends, my higher pleasures according to Socrates. They make me content, and without them, my life wouldn't be great. And living in constant grief, is no reason to continue living, hence mankind's quest for companionship. Though there are personal pleasures in life that I need as well, like fine art, music and stories. They're vital to me because it makes me question and reflect about life, religion, existence, thought, beauty, love, and serenity.

And last of all, a world worth living for, a world with no hostilities, poverty or any anguish. That makes everyone feel functional, like there's purpose in their being, like they're important. Because what's important and vital for me, are actual peace and tranquility among fellow men and women we jointly exist with.

William Willis, Grade 11
Plant City High School, FL

My Dog Mia

My dog, Mia, is fun, mean, and loving all at the same time. She is a tan and white puppy that loves to play and run around.

She is fun when you want to play or be chased. She loves playing fetch but once she gets what you threw, she brings it to you half way and you have to get it from her. Mia is a spoiled brat. She only eats warm bones and she only drinks ice water.

Mia gets mean if she doesn't know you and you just try to walk to the house. She is very protective when it comes to the family. She even tries to keep my brothers out of the house just because she doesn't like them. She even loves to nibble on you not bite but just put your ankle in her mouth.

My dog is very loving when she wants to be. When she knows you feel bad, she will climb up in your lap and just try to make you feel better.

Daneilya Whitney, Grade 11
Southside High School, NC

My World Today

Probably since the invention of the Internet, my cousin attached herself to the computer and became to believe that she was living in Earth II. Fast access to every information written since the invention of writing, e-mails that somehow teleported one's message to the other end of the Earth, easy one-two-three steps that processed one's order from the internet and spontaneously sent the product in front of one's doorstep, my cousin was "addicted" to the magnetism of Internet and its friend, Speed. She was, as my aunt called it, experiencing an "adolescent" phase, which she said through the "home" phone, which is now a useless piece of device that cannot match the mighty effectiveness of cell phones. She would eventually get out of it, Aunt said back then.

Well, the next time I saw my cousin, she was sitting on her desk with two-inch thick glasses, a bad hairdo, and a strange habit of calling downstairs with her cell phone to tell her mother she wasn't hungry yet. I hope no one would become a zombie like my cousin who still lives in Earth II. But inevitably, many of my friends, cousins and children I used to baby-sit have already grown absorbing America's convenient society and have transformed into indolent potatoes. Inevitably, those around me defend speed over tradition and classical lifestyles. Inevitably, much of my own life is dependent on speed. Speed will go far, but will self-destruct.

Bora Kang, Grade 11
Union Grove High School, GA

Offense of the Century

We have the Tomcats take on the Devils for the world championship. These two football teams are considered to be the fiercest teams in the world. The Tomcats are known for their great ability to move the ball on offense.

As the two teams captains go to the middle of the field for the toss, the coin is flipped, and the Tomcats will receive the ball. As each team lines up, the adrenaline pumps, the crowd's at the top of their lungs screaming. As the kicker runs to kick the ball he boots a nice kick all the way to the one-yard line where the receiver takes a knee thinking he's in the end zone. The hollering fans quiet as their team takes the field on offense. Sweat already dripping down players' arms, adrenaline pumping more than ever. Here is where the Tomcats set the bar. Tomcats line up in I-formation, the fullback to the left two steps. The quarterback barking out the snap calls like a dog protecting its turf. HUT, then the ball is snapped all the receivers shoot off the line like rockets pumping their arms back and forth. As the quarterback drops back, he surveys the field to find his receiver. Swiveling his head left and right he finds his receiver and throws, he's wide open on a fly route. Stretching his hands out like rubber bands he catches the ball for a record, 99-yard pass for a touchdown.

Christopher Stone, Grade 10
Stanton College Preparatory School, FL

Friends and Family

I am most thankful for my friends and family. I do not know where I would be without them. I can't think of life without them.

My friends and family are my life. If I get in a bind, if I got into trouble, if I need a place to stay, I can always count on friends and family. If I didn't have them I wouldn't have anything. They encourage me to stay in school. If I need a ride somewhere, I can always have someone to count on.

I really would not have a life without them. I wouldn't have anyone to help me when I need them. It would be a lonely world without them. I would not have any encouragement to stay in school, to lead me right from wrong, to guide me, or to care for me.

This is why I am most thankful for my family and my friends. I would be nowhere in life without them. I am blessed to have the friends and family that I have in my life.

James Kennedy, Grade 11
Southside High School, NC

Healthy Living

"Hurry, I feel his pulse weakening! He's going! I can't resuscitate him…" Today, teens lie around pushing buttons on the remote while stuffing their face. They refuse to eat healthy or exercise daily. Most kids don't realize the effect that obesity will have on them in the future. Teens should feel obligated to lead a healthy lifestyle.

Other points of view exist. Most people would argue that children work very hard in school, so when they come home, they deserve a good long break. Other people would say, "Oh, they're just children, let them have fun and relax while they still can." Other people, especially parents, would say, let your children do and eat whatever they want, they're just children.

Teens should feel obligated to exercise and lead a healthy lifestyle. It could affect their entire future and the future of their offspring. Leading a healthy lifestyle could extend teens' life spans, and make their life more enjoyable.

Meaghan Ritchie, Grade 10
Greenwood High School, KY

My Family

I have a family that is funny and cool because with my family I go places and we have the most exciting time. We cut up and joke and enjoy each other.

Now me and my family are real close. I have a couple that are like me. My cousins, for instance, have a neighborhood where they live and we hang around and cut up such things as boxing, and playing basketball and it is real fun to us. We are so close that we call ourselves brothers because we are always there for each other and we have each other's backs no matter what. I think anyone that met my family would have a good time with them because they are real cool to get along with and you would have a good time with them. This is what I think of my family.

Antwan McCuller, Grade 11
Southside High School, NC

The Opposite of What I Thought

The thought of my grandma coming to America was something that I dreamed of since the day I left her. The thought of me seeing her made me feel like she was already here. When I left her, I was afraid I wouldn't see her again, because she was too far and too old to travel the distance.

She promised that we would see each other again. After seven long years that promise became a reality. I was so excited to see her, but didn't know what to expect. Would she be grumpy or nice, mean or loving, emotional or happy.

My parents kept calling me from the airport telling met when the plane would arrive. The close the time came, the more I thought about what she would be like.

When she landed and arrived at our home, everything was what I hoped for and wanted. A few days later everything changed completely. My grandma thought I was the nine-year old little boy she last saw. She asked if I could take down the trash, so the laundry, the dishes, or even check the mail by myself.

We finally knew who she really was, her constant drinking only made it harder for us to communicate with her. In the end, it was a good thing she came out, because we could see the bad side of her and what my mom had to go through. She was the exact opposite of what I thought.

Mate Fabian, Grade 10
Countryside High School, FL

A Source of Encouragement

The life of Johnny Gunther definitely presents a source of motivation and strength for those who struggle in life. Johnny was a boy with a deep interest in life and education, but could not fulfill his dreams due to a brain tumor causing his life to end at the age of seventeen. He struggled immensely due to x-ray appointments, surgeries, vision loss, weakness on his left side, and instances of amnesia. These interruptions caused Johnny to become frustrated, but never hindered his perseverance. After an operation in which the tumor seemed to be dead, Johnny does better and regains his eyesight, but the bump on his head mysteriously grows back along with amnesia, sickness, a blood vessel burst, and eventually unconsciousness. Little did Johnny know, he would never awake.

Johnny was an inspiration with his fascination of education, always asking for larger textbooks. He was always anxious to go back to school and someday attend Harvard. He was interested in several occupations such as a physicist, chemist, mathematician, poet, or cook. "I have so much to do! And there's so little time!" Even though his life was short, he accomplished a chemistry experiment, a list of chess precepts, graduated high school, and wrote the "Unbeliever's Prayer." People can be encouraged by his persevering character, always willing to keep going. His experience can show people to keep going no matter what life throws out. If Johnny Gunther could accomplish so much in his short life, so can everybody.

Brittany Wilson, Grade 11
Village Christian Academy, NC

The First Use of a Cell Phone

Cell phones have turned away from being *just* a phone; they are a completely separate life for some people. Cell phones can now do almost as much as a basic computer. Before texting and IM, music and ringtones, bluetooth and GPS, the cell phone was a two pound block costing around $3,500.

On April 3, 1973, Martin Cooper was the first person to introduce this new type of technology. As he walked through the streets of downtown New York, people stared in awe. No one had ever seen a phone without wires. The cordless phone was not released into the public until the 1980s. The first call Martin Cooper ever made with the newly invented cell phone was to his rival at AT&T's Bell Labs.

In 1992, Martin Cooper began the ArrayComm Company. ArrayComm created the core-adapted antenna, which increases the capacity and coverage of a cell phone. ArrayComm also helped bring about the use of broadband technology with cell phones. Without the help of this company, cell phones might not exist.

Jake Wegrzyn, Grade 11
Providence Classical School, AL

Homework Overload

Homework has a purpose to increase the knowledge of the student; however, an excessive amount of homework could end up being counterproductive. Homework takes away from a student's free time and can have a negative effect on learning.

Too much homework reduces leisure time a student has outside of school. A student will spend the whole day in school working, and then will return home to additional work. This can leave a student unable to exercise or pursue extracurricular activities. This will hinder the development of talents outside of school subjects. Excess homework can also interfere with a student's time to spend with friends and family. Homework is time-consuming and is intrusive to a student's free time.

An immoderate amount of homework can have a negative effect on learning. A Pennsylvania State study shows that countries with students who score high have teachers who assign minimal homework, and students who score low are assigned a lot of homework. Students tend to multitask while doing assignments at home which lowers the quality of education received. There is a large amount of research to support that homework is of little educational value, and that it has an adverse effect on learning.

Homework can have a negative effect on learning and takes away from a student's free time. With increasing amounts of homework being assigned each year, this could potentially be harmful to education. It turns out homework may not be serving its purpose.

Darci Shofler, Grade 11
Grove High School, OK

Where to Begin: Musicians' Struggle to Remain Creative

For thousands of years, music has been composed of many different genres and instruments. Even in the past one hundred years, music has adapted to a variety of trends and lifestyles. It's mind-boggling to think of the process so many individuals have gone through to help contribute to the millions and millions of songs in the world today.

Like many writers, musicians also experience their own form of "writer's block." It can be an accomplishment in itself to simply get one minute's worth of music on paper, on tape, or on computer. There are several factors that cause music "block." Some musician's might find it hard to concentrate and be creative if they have been dealing with hardships in their life. Others might not like the music they have created.

With as many determined artists and groups making music in the world, it can be hard to develop a new style of music that no one has heard before. The biggest problem musicians face is finding their own sound that distinguishes themselves from all the rest. Some give up too early in their lives as musicians to really test their ideas and tweak and modify them. Instead, they are left with a generic sound that everyone has heard before.

Even with music "block," music is changing. Little by little, musical experiments are shaping the future of what we will soon be reaching the ears of listeners. The lives of radios are soon to be recharged.

Logan Dedmon, Grade 11
Camden Central High School, TN

Judgment

"The only devils in the world are those running around in our own hearts and that is where all of our battles ought to be fought." – Ghandi. Today we live in a very judgmental world. People are quick to point out the faults in others before taking a look at themselves. Many teenagers are especially quick to decide that they know what is best for everyone.

Just because someone follows a different religion or has a different lifestyle that you don't agree with doesn't mean that you have the right to judge them for it. Growing up in the Bible Belt this can be especially prominent. People like to argue about whether or not different lifestyles, like homosexuality, are sins. However, no matter what you believe, it is not your place to decide if it's right or wrong. The world would be a lot happier place if people worried about ways to improve themselves and less about the wrong doing of others.

Today there are billions of people, all of whom are very different. Part of the beauty of the world we live in is its diversity, with many people's cultures and ways of life. We all have to share this world together and we should try to make the best of it. We should stop judging and condemning not only so that we are not likewise judged but also so we can try to live peacefully with everyone.

Zach Martin, Grade 10
Greenwood High School, KY

The Thrill of the Sound

The stadium lights shining. The crowd roaring. The instruments sparkling from the stadium lights. All of this gives the band an amazing aura. There is nothing more exciting than the thrill of the first show for a marching band. Watching an amazing marching band sends chills down the spine of everyone in the stadium. The way the ensemble moves as one shows the unity of the band and musicians. To achieve greatness, all of the musicians have to work diligently.

When people watch a superior band it seems easy because they perform well. It is not effortless. The band has to memorize challenging music as well as learn how to march on a field of one hundred yards. They have to be in step, which can be difficult with 100 or more people. It takes time and concentration to learn how to march to a precise place on the field so they can form the pictures correctly. In addition to all this, they are expected to play the music perfectly the entire time. Marching band takes skill and dedication from every musician involved.

Though it is difficult, the end product is a breathtaking array of visuals and sound. After a good show, the band takes the final steps off the field feeling like artists. The crowds roaring fills everyone in the band with a sense of accomplishment. They know they made something beautiful. The thrill of the sound leaves everyone's hearts racing.

Heather Lungren, Grade 11
Grove High School, OK

Heritage

Heritage is something that is passed from one generation to another. Do you know your heritage? Do you think it's important to know where you came from? Heritage is a major part of American society. Heritage shows you how you got to where you are.

Heritage is a very interesting thing. Who knows you may be related to George Washington or Davy Crockett. It shows you what your family and others did before you where born. Heritage is something you share with your whole family. It can also be something that is shared with a state, nation, or even a faith. Heritage can also be seen as traditions. Your family might meet at a certain place every year for a holiday. Or it may be changing because someone has passed away. Heritage will always progress, but it never leaves unless you forget. New heritage is made as those we love tell it to us. It is then passed on to the next generation through us. Heritage is continued by talking about what you and others have been through.

"The heritage of the past is the seed that brings forth the harvest of the future." The author of this quote is unknown but it explains the value of heritage perfectly. If you don't know your heritage you should find it out. You may be surprised! Heritage is what makes you who you are.

Ryan Dunkerson, Grade 11
Owasso High School, OK

World Changers

Hundreds of dollars required for participation, fifty students, eight hours driving time, one reason, to serve.

A national corporation called "World Changers," allows youth groups to gather in different locations to fix underprivileged houses of local residents. Having so many people with the same beliefs surrounding me along with transforming a stranger's house in a week, really left me with a mix of emotions.

Surrounded with people who are of the same faith is really supporting and inspires me to stand up for what I believe. It reassures me that I'm not the only one who believes and I'm not alone.

The labor provided to residents is influential on both ends. The organization is split into work groups and sent to a house to work on for the week. My team was composed of people I had never met before from all over America, but we were all bonded by a common religious goal, to serve. Throughout the week, I built a house and relationships. When the week was over, I felt incredibly accomplished. More importantly, residents felt relief and a sense of gratitude.

The trip is the most influential thing I've experienced so far in my life. It has shaped who I am as a person, made me stronger as an individual, and motivated me to make a difference. Knowing strength can happen even though I'm a teenager is really inspiring. I've been to this event three times and every year I return changed for the better.

Tori Short, Grade 11
Countryside High School, FL

Fear in the Life of a Teenager

Teenagers are very plagued by fear. I'm a teen who is very plagued by fear. My fear isn't heights, dogs, or rats. It's reality. Teens have to think about whether or not they will live to see eighteen. In the life of a teen, things happen right in front of you every day. You have to walk down the street hoping that a group of boys doesn't try to pick a fight with you. As a teen, you have to be cautious about what color you wear. If you're seen with too much red or too much blue, someone in a gang is liable to fight you. You have to wake up every day wondering if you are going to make it back in the house. You don't know if someone who doesn't like you will drive by and shoot you. It's sad to see teens dying over shoes, rims and all those other material things.

Criminals these days possess assault rifles and bulletproof vests too. You have to worry if you are going to get caught in crossfire or not because someone shorted someone over drugs. Teens are shooting at each other and the bullets are killing our future doctors and lawyers. To get over that fear, my friends and I united together to stop violence and drug abuse.

Carlos Wilson, Grade 11
City University School of Liberal Arts, TN

The Real Hero

A hero can be many people such as your parents, friends, or even teachers. I believe it doesn't take much to be a hero. A hero can be pointed out by a pure person, an outstanding Christian or even a person that can be looked up to. Heroes are all over the place, to me, my hero is my dad. He has been through some crazy moments in life and is still one of the best mentors I could ask for. He has shown me everything I know in baseball, and baseball is one of my most favorite sports. He taught me to play basketball and he also taught me how to through a football. My dad is awesome; he is patient when it comes to teaching me something and if I'm wrong he doesn't get mad he just says, "Try again son you can do it!" He taught me how to clean my gun and how to use it effectively and safely. My dad really is awesome; he's my hero!

Hunter Bennett, Grade 11
Trinity Christian Academy, AL

Climbing Is Success

Goals are personal. They are intangible and subjective, yet they hold a powerful purpose for everyone. These aspirations that we hold tend to be fluid and dynamic, giving the impression that they are fickle and whimsical dreams more than a creed. The importance of these goals, however, lies more in the significance of the imagination that breeds them than the goals' ends. Every goal contains a piece of who we are as people, similar in our ever-changing nature to our aims, and in developing hopes, dreams, and plans of action we more fully realize who that person is. For many years, I found it difficult to set firm objectives for myself, seeing that choosing to climb the precariously placed ladder of fulfillment brought perils in that each rung presented an opportunity to fall back to the ground. Realizing that these goals were not the object of consequence, but that the true realization of ambition resided in the age old cliché of the journey over the ends prompted me to change my thinking. The ultimate meaning of goals is that they surpass what we can grasp today, but remain a beacon spotlighting the potential we have developed to reach them tomorrow.

Evan Halton, Grade 11
Owasso High School, OK

Mountains or Seashore?

For a vacation, I prefer the mountains to the seashore. When I was younger, my family went to Gatlinburg, Tennessee, in October instead of Myrtle Beach in July. I prefer cold weather to hot weather, so I was in awe at the snowcapped mountains covered in pine trees. The sand on the seashore burns a person's feet, the salty ocean water stings one's eyes, and sometimes there are jellyfish in the water. My dad and I rode the chair lift up the mountain and then took picture at the top of it. At the beach, everything looks the same. In the mountains, a person can ski, snowboard, or just have fun in the snow.

Ashli Sellers, Grade 11
New Covenant Christian School, SC

Pops

When I arrived in my hometown, I thought the common nostalgic thought that people are supposed to feel when they return home, "It's good to be home," but not in this case. I arrived late morning in my birthplace of Milwaukee, Wisconsin for my grandfather's funeral, whom we called Papa or simply "Pops." The weather was cloudy, but it wasn't raining; it was just calm, neither peaceful nor violent; and very purgatory-ish.

Strangely enough, I have grown to be fond of this placid atmosphere. The forgotten Wisconsin breeze felt so soothing to feel. However, this was no time to catch up with my roots, excluding my familial ones. The trip proved to be three days of stifled sadness. I had trouble realizing the fact that someone close to me had died. It wasn't as if I was constantly in sorrow; I just seemed to feel nothing at all. It was cloudy, but lacking the ability to rain. My grandfather was the patriarch of my family, but on the trip I didn't receive any enlightening advice. There was a lack of comic relief that my grandfather had provided ever so much.

Then the funeral day came. I felt dysphoric, melancholy. I tried to cry, but failed again. I realized what was holding my aqueous calamities back, whenever I thought of my grandfather, I would go back to the good times.

Dan Litzow, Grade 10
Germantown High School, TN

Happiness: A Universal Feeling

One of the few things in the world that everyone understands is happiness. Happiness is not just for the young nor is it just for the old. It wraps its greedy fingers around all who dare believe in it.

Those who experience true happiness at least once in their life find themselves addicted to its almost euphoric feeling of satisfaction. People strive to fill their empty hearts with joyful and playful memories, which remind them of the times in which they were truly happy.

The exceptional thing about happiness is that it does not discriminate against black or white or any other color for that matter. It spreads itself to all those who will cherish its ultimate feeling of ecstasy. There are many words for happiness in the world, which is why it's a universal. For even if people don't understand other languages they still recognize its extreme feeling of rapture and what this feeling defines.

When you are honestly happy it does not take a rocket scientist to figure it out. Happiness takes on a certain being in which someone walks a little straighter, stands a little taller, and smiles a little softer. One seems so serene and at peace with the world that others want to share this same feeling. This is why people strive to be truly happy and why they fight to share their happiness with others.

Sarah Rainbolt, Grade 11
Bishop Verot High School, FL

The Real Truth About Life

The default notices come in the mail. The phone never stops ringing. Mortgage lenders are coming to your house. Who are these people or why are these letters coming in the mail? One word says it all, foreclosure. The percent of foreclosure in the United States has soared this past year by an astonishing thirty six percent. This number has doubled from last year. Families with infants and elderly family members are being driven out from their homes and being forced to find another place to live. Some families never find another house to live in or another house they can afford, and those families that once had heat and running water now live on the streets, trying to keep their families alive. Adults try their hardest to keep up with the mortgage payments but if one day your payments on your house increase by a few hundred dollars a month, how can anyone keep up? How are parents supposed to tell their children that their house is being taken away? How can anyone say that to anyone for that fact? I have personally gone through this experience and I know other families who have also. It is one of the hardest events in a teenager's life when you have to pack all of your things and you do not know where you or your family is moving to. With the raising foreclosure rates in the United States, don't you think someone should help?

Cassandra Pawelec, Grade 11
Vero Beach High School, FL

A Notable Hero

Jim Thorpe was the greatest athlete of the 20th century. He is and has been an American hero to many. He showed perseverance, leadership, and commitment.

It was evident that Thorpe was born with perseverance in his blood. Even after the 1912 Olympics where his medals were stripped from him, he still continued to fulfill his passion and love for sports. Baseball was the reason his medals were taken and his name out of the record books. However, he had never quit something before and was not going to start now.

Jim Thorpe has shown excellent skills of leadership. He showed to never give up on your dreams, because one thing went wrong. If everyone gave up when something unexpected happened, our society would not be as advanced as it is today. Even King Gustav V told Thorpe he was the greatest athlete in the world. Thorpe knew this meant something, and was going to continue being an athlete.

Commitment is a quality every hero should have, and Thorpe definitely did. He was not just committed to sports. He was also quite vocal with matters of Indian Affairs, as Thorpe was a Pottawatomie Indian and a descendant of the last Sauk and Fox chief Black Hawk. He also had another love, football. He was instrumental in forming the American Professional Football Association; known today as the NFL.

As you can see, Jim Thorpe's qualities of perseverance, leadership, and commitment make him a hero to me and many Americans today.

Mikka Harman, Grade 10
Mulhall-Orlando High School, OK

Still Alive

I felt scared, nervous, worried. I didn't know what was coming next. I could smell the fear of everyone else. They were just as scared as I was. I heard silence; except for the pounding of beats of my erratic heart. I saw the smoke and dust coming down the street.

It was September 11, 2001, such a beautiful day. Not a cloud in the sky. I remember it as if it just happened. My mom, sister and I sat at home glued to the TV, waiting to see what would happen next, or maybe we could catch a glimpse of my dad or brother. They both worked in the city. We hadn't heard from either of them all day, because the cell phone towers were down.

As I looked outside, I saw the smoke and dust filling my street as if it was some sort of possessed fog coming to engulf the houses of Brand Drive. We ran to the windows and closed them quickly, so the smoke could not come in to get us, too.

We stayed up almost all night waiting for my dad and brother to come home; if they were going to at all. We heard the back door open just past midnight. Somehow, through all the struggle in Manhattan, they found each other and made it home. That night was the first time I ever saw my dad cry. That day was the scariest day of my life, but my family is *still alive*.

Julia Obelenus, Grade 11
Hopewell High School, NC

Homework!

Aww homework! Is this the thought you get when homework is assigned? All people who have gone to school have had this thought process. However, people do not generally think about why homework is important or how it helps us. Homework is one of the most important aspects to school through its ability to teach and more importantly getting a person a better future.

Homework plays a big part in the education of students. Students learn around seventy percent from homework and the rest from teachers and others. From my experiences, teachers give a student an introduction to the material while homework gives the experience and practice for the material. Homework does what a teacher doesn't have time to do in class which leads the student to become independent. Homework indirectly gets a person a greater future. Getting good grades on homework will lead to knowing the material for quizzes and tests. By having good grades and knowing the material, more career opportunities will be open which leads to success. Also by accomplishing each homework assignment, a student gets a good work ethic which is needed in a career. Through doing homework, a student can manipulate his or her life to do whatever he or she wants.

Homework is a daily chore in a teenager's life but helps a student in learning the material and creating a better future for the student. Understanding that homework is helpful in these ways listed will help a student feel further prepared.

Laly Vang, Grade 11
Owasso High School, OK

Teachers

Students usually find school to be excruciating, or even unbearable, but they are able to work through the stress and pain they associate with it and move on to another year of struggles. Sometimes, though, even the best of students simply cannot persevere and find the idea of giving up very tempting. This may be due to an incompatibility with the subject matter or an incompetent teacher.

While it may seem to some parents that subjects are becoming increasingly more difficult, this idea may spring from the large amount of time that has passed since they have received formal training in an academic area. Parents forget the vast amount of time that they themselves spent studying, doing homework, and moaning. However, an adult who cannot recall a particularly disliked teacher is hard to find.

Teachers strike a chord in their pupils, and can shape their world view. But when an instructor misinforms or does not properly teach, the students can forever have a warped view of that topic. Schools frequently overlook the flaws of certain teachers because of their history at the institution or their overqualifications. These drawbacks, though, may overshadow their positive qualities. Teachers like this can neither relate to their students nor relate the information to them in an effective manner.

The school systems should observe such professors, try to learn from them, and discover that the failure of a student not only occurs because of the faults of the student, but it also occurs because of the teacher.

Laurel Bergau, Grade 11
Bishop Verot High School, FL

Friendship Is Forever

In 1978 in the small village called Ghandruk near Mount Everest located in Nepal. Two baby boys were born in two different Sherpa families. One of the baby's name was Tenzing and another's name was Nima. Unfortunately Nima's mom died after he was born and his father raised him. The two boys grew up together and were best friends as their parents were. When Nima was five his father died while climbing mountains. Tenzing's parents adopted Nima because he was their best friend's son and also Nima did not have anyone except his best friend's family. They grew up together. They were the kind of best friends that could not be separated by anyone. They shared the same dream, and the dream was to climb the mountains as their ancestors did it.

Though his best friend was not with him in this world to climb and succeed with him, but he was in his heart forever. Tenzing was in every part of Nima's life whether he was alive or not. The last journey with his best friend was rough but there were happy moments to remember. He never regretted it for going and losing his best friend, but was happy that his best friend would have been proud of him.

Amita Sheroa, Grade 12
Greenwood High School, KY

Born to Be, But Not Wild and Free

The wild mustangs of the west have long been a symbol of the disappearing frontier. Once more than 2 million mustangs roamed miles of land across America. Towards the turn of the 19th century, however, their freedom to wander across the plains was taken, and the number of large herds declined.

As technology began to take over the horses' jobs on ranches, the wild mustangs that were once respected became worthless and a nuisance. The government stepped in and ordered the removal of these pests. Thousands of horses were rounded up and sold to slaughter houses, bringing great profit to those who captured them. Therefore, their numbers shrank faster and faster.

"Wild Horse Annie" was the one who ended this massacre of America's once prized symbol. She campaigned widely against the capture and slaughter of these beautiful creatures. Due to the thousands of letters sent to Congress opposing the slaughter of the wild horses, a new act was passed in 1971 to protect America's "living symbols of the historic and pioneer spirit of the West." Nevertheless, by then the mustangs' numbers had fallen to less than 17,000.

Today their number has increased to around 39,000. Still, their range of travel is shortened every year with the increase of population. The Bureau of Land Management holds a yearly roundup to capture hundreds of horses, which are put in sanctuaries or adopted out to the public. Although protected from slaughter, the wild mustangs are not truly wild and free.

Cori Webb, Grade 11
Rossville Christian Academy, TN

My First Week of School

On August 21, 2007 I began my first day of my junior year in high school. I found out the first period of the first day that we need to wear our school ID's around our neck on lanyards and if we don't, or we forget we automatically get a detention. The days following that completed my first week didn't improve at all. The schedule at our school is horrible and confusing. I haven't met a student yet who has conquered the feat of memorizing it. The main campus now has three resource officers, three security guards, and three student administrators that constantly patrol our campus. The only thing our school is short of is matching orange jumpsuits and handcuffs. Our first three weeks of school brought on the task of changing our schedule three times. Now they're questioning the entire foundation of our schedule and are talking about changing it. We have been reduced to only two short Wednesdays a month and every class is 32 minutes. By the time we have adjusted to the class the bell rings and we are on our way to the next class. To put icing on the cake, because our school is under much construction our entire campus is one big trailer park. No one should worry though because our trailers are anchored for the promising threat of a hurricane.

Max Trage, Grade 11
Vero Beach High School, FL

What Is Life?

Am I alive? Of course. Or am I? I, through "lucky" circumstances, have immigrated to the wonderful United States of America. Every day I wake up, eat breakfast, pack my backpack, go to school, sit in various classes for 3 hours, eat lunch, sit for 3 more hours, go home, watch TV, eat dinner, do my homework, and go to sleep. Weekends are just as monotonous as weekdays. Back in my country of birth, I used to play every day during school. I remember those glorious days I spent in elementary school, swinging on monkey bars, throwing baseballs, or kicking a bottle cap around (it is soccer with a bottle cap) with many fellow students. These seemingly trivial recreations not only kept the spirit of the student body high, but they also kept me lively and animated. I lost most of the opportunities to invigorate myself when I moved to the States. I spent two years at a public school; the recreations in that school differed greatly than that of my elementary school. No longer was I able to run and jump and kick as I did before; no longer did I feel the pure joy of playing with my classmates after a full day of school. I long for the good old days when school meant fun with my friends; oh how I wish students would get together and be active instead of listening to their iPods and iPhones and iWhatnots! I want to active again. I want to be alive.

Youming Lin, Grade 11
Owasso High School, OK

My Hero Dustin Soper

Dustin Soper is my hero and one of my best friends because he's trustworthy, caring, and brave. Dustin has always been there when I need someone. He has never let me down and doesn't let anyone give me any problems. I guess you could say he's like my older brother.

It's hard to find someone who cares about me more than Dustin does. I know he cares by the way he treats me. If I have a bad day he is always the first one to ask what's wrong, and he know how to make me smile. He is good at sticking up for me when I need a little help.

Dustin is one of the bravest people I know. He will stick up for anyone who needs it. He's always comfortable with himself and who he is. He never lets people underestimate him or tell him that he is anything less than himself.

Dustin is one person I know I can trust with anything. I can tell him anything and I know that no one else will find out. I know if I ever need anything he will be right there with me.

Dustin and I are alike in so many ways. We can both trust each other with anything, and we have a lot of fun together. These are just a few of the reasons that Dustin Soper is my hero.

Kayle Golay, Grade 11
Mulhall-Orlando High School, OK

The Bracero Project

This past summer my family went to New Mexico. Just the thought of this trip was thrilling to me, as if I were traversing to a barren, desert wasteland, also known as the Southwest. I had never been anywhere outside of the South.

The most intriguing thing I looked forward to was not just the desert terrain, it was my being exposed to Mexican/Southwestern culture. Here in my hometown many people shun the Mexican community and look down upon the Spanish-speaking people. I was so curious to see how the general attitude was toward the Mexican population in New "Mexico."

One morning, while we ate breakfast in the hotel lobby, a man, who had previously had a conversation with my parents in the pool, began to speak to us again. Somehow we mentioned how there were so many more Mexican people than in Memphis (Las Cruces is about 50 miles from Mexico and has a 68% Mexican population). The man said, "Look around. You see how most of the people doing dirty jobs are Mexican? That's because during World War I, the government created the Bracero Project to bring Mexicans here to work." On the way back home, I contemplated Mexican subculture in America. When I got home, I explained my trip to my friend's father, who said the people who hate Mexicans the most are the ones who have never seen any. I realized then that racism and prejudice only arises out of ignorance of other people.

Rudy Saliba, Grade 11
Germantown High School, TN

Admire

The person I most admire is such a beautiful person, inside and out. At the age of twelve-years-old, she began to face the ups and downs in life. It all started with her horrible relationship with her father. It became apparent it was not a typical daughter-father relationship. He was aggressive and controlling; it eventually led to physical and emotional abuse. She had no one to turn to and so she turned to the streets and men. She became a very angry person with herself and others that triggered her anger. She just didn't love herself like she should have. She had problems with controlling herself emotionally. She ran away from her problems. She slept in places you would never think of. At age 14, she got locked up. The young lady was sent to a division of youth services. There she served her time in a group setting. At age 16, she got pregnant. On May 25, 2006, she had her pride and joy, her daughter. On her child's first birthday, she was battling difficult aspects of her life. She was trying to get her life together, but on her baby's birthday, she was raped. It has made her more aware and sometimes scared. The only way she knows how to cope with her life is through writing. The person whom I admire so much is me.

Porsha Lewis, Grade 11

Dream On

As one falls asleep, the mind takes the sleeper on a journey through dreamland. This mysterious phenomenon launches the mind through dimensions of the imagination, with experiences that may be frightful, pleasing, strange, or otherwise unrealistic. A dream is the subconscious visions in the brain, experienced usually while sleeping. Dreams happen without control of the dreamer, and are most commonly forgotten by the time one awakens. But what causes dreams to take place?

Dreams have been evaluated on scientific, spiritual, and philosophical levels. Neurologists' studies on dreaming discovered that during rapid eye movement sleep state, discovered by Eugene Aserinsky, a dreamer's brain activity imitates qualities of being awake, producing strong dreams that more people remember. Scientists have discovered many factors about dreams, also proposing several new theories explaining dreams; however, there is no definite reason as to why dreams transpire.

Philosophically, dream interpreters Sigmund Freud and Carl Jung suggest dreams are the interaction between the unconscious and conscious, where the unconscious dominates. Freud viewed dreams as brain protection during sleep, which might be invaded with unacceptable wishes; Jung proposed dreams compensate for waking life's attitudes. Dreaming, whether during sleep or in waking consciousness (daydreaming), can solve everyday problems in life, produce inspiration, or clear the mind of useless material.

Spiritually and culturally, some view dreams as messages of the supernatural or godly realm, perhaps even predictions of the future. Whatever you believe about sleep imaginings, you will continue to dream about unexplainable travels through mental fantasyland.

Gabrielle Lyew Kong, Grade 11
Bishop Verot High School, FL

Beauty and Dirt

"On earth there is no heaven, but there are pieces of it." — Jules Renard.

I'm in the Bahamas, on the beach. The light shining down upon me is so bright that it almost blinds me. Perfection is a word I want to use. The soft sand, the light blue water, the bright sun overlooking expensive yachts in the water. As I look to the left I see a beach not belonging to my hotel. It's full of beer bottles, trash and dead fish. I am disgusted and ask myself: what world is this? One in which dreams are broken and perfectionism is an ideal? The world is not like a story, full of lullabies and roses, or blue jays singing in the morning; for that is what a good story needs. The world is cruel like a volcano, striking unexpectedly when least expected by people meaning no harm. This tale is filled with dirt and beauty, but please do not despair for the mixture is what we need. After all is said and proven you must get the point, behind beauty is always hidden dirt.

Pim Van der Sluis, Grade 12
Baylor School, TN

What History Means to Me

The past means a lot to me because so many things went on that have bettered the American way of life. By that I mean without the things that Martin Luther King Jr. had accomplished the world would be a little crazy. Civil rights plays a lot in the past because rules were changed and everyone was treated equally after some bad things went on. I think a life without equal rights would not be good for the people and the economy in that matter. Because of all the diversified people in the world change the looks on peoples views about a lot of things. I also think by knowing history it would not be easy for it to repeat itself since everyone chooses to know that some things are wrong and should never be done again. The Civil Rights Era has a lot to do with the way the world is today because people are not forced to do things that they don't want to and are not judge by certain people because of the color of their skin, or their beliefs on religion. I think that it is wrong to discriminate people just for certain reasons that are not important. By knowing the mistakes that the people in the past made makes me not want to make them either at least when it comes to judging people, and discriminate against them for unimportant reasons. So no one should go back and repeat history like that since nothing good ever came out of it then so it should not be repeated.

Adasha Dennis, Grade 12
Walker Valley High School, TN

Changing the World My Way

If I could change one thing about the world it would be the starvation of our children. This is something that's been on my mind for a while. Poverty is something that's going to be a part of this world forever, which is why this would be what I would change about the world. Everyone is created equal. Everyone has the equal and ample amount of opportunity to be successful. This is something that adults can utilize to the best of their ability, where as children on the other hand are innocent. They are still under the care of their parents. Children don't have any control over their lives and future when starving. They can't contribute their full potential in school or know when, how, or where their next meal will come from.

Programs such as the Feed the Need Foundation inspired me and I try to give as much as I can, especially since children are our future. I can't even imagine being hungry and unable to eat. Sometimes people don't understand how fortunate they are. They will always complain about who has this and who has that, but there's someone in the world that's less fortunate than others and wishes that they at least had something. So if I could change one thing about the world it would be saving our hungry children.

Kevia Pratcher, Grade 11
City University School of Liberal Arts, TN

The Last Time

It has been almost one and a half years since my grandmother's death. She died on April 20, 2006. The last time I saw her was on Easter Sunday 2006. She seemed so happy and energetic. There was just something about her, but I couldn't think of what it was. The sparkle in her eyes and the way her face looked; it just made her look younger. Easter would be the last time I would see the expressions on her face. It would be the last time I would see her eyes and the last time I would be able to feel her silken hands.

Around the time she died, it had been a hard time with our family because her daughter (my mom) was in the hospital diagnosed with Guillain-Barre. The night my grandma Bone died, she did not want to be alone. Bone called my Aunt Julie to come and get my grandma. So Bone stayed the night with Julie. That night Julie and Bone joked around about getting Bone a hearing aid. That night, Bone went to bed with her first great grandson and she never woke up. That was the last time I would get to do anything with her. However, she is still here with me in spirit. I still love her and remember everything that she did, like it was yesterday.

Felicia Christy, Grade 10
Slater High School, MO

My U.S. Hero

We all as a society look up to many people. I guess you can call them your hero. My hero is Steve Owens, he is an awesome football player who was a great leader, and he was committed, and very generous to the kids in the state of Oklahoma.

Steve Owens was a leader as a football player. He started his high school career at Miami Oklahoma High School. At the time he was a halfback who averaged 7.2 yards a carry and gained 4,000 yards at his hometown. Then after his high school career he got a scholarship to the University of Oklahoma, leading the Sooners to the Orange Bowl playing Tennessee, winning 26-24.

He was so committed that he, in 1969, won the greatest award in college football, the Heisman trophy, which is given to the most outstanding college football player of the year. The following year he entered the NFL draft getting the 19th pick to the Detroit Lions. After he accomplished his dreams on being a great football player he retired with 1,035 runs in 246 carries. He was the first Lion to run over 1,000 yards. He was accepted to the Football Hall of Fame.

Not only was he a great football player but also he was generous enough to be the founder of the Norman Public School Foundation and the Miami Public School Foundation. He was also involved with many other foundations such as the Make-a-Wish Foundation.

We all have heroes. Mine is Steve Owens, who is a great leader, committed, and very generous to the boys and girls of Oklahoma.

Aaron Cooper, Grade 10
Mulhall-Orlando High School, OK

Drinking and Driving — It Can Be Stopped!

Every two minutes, a person is injured in an alcohol-related collision. Every thirty-one minutes, someone is killed in an alcohol-related accident. These are stunning facts that should make everyone think twice about drinking and driving. Unfortunately, since many people are not responsible enough to know when not to drive, measures should be taken to prevent drunk driving and the thousands of injuries and deaths that result from it.

Law enforcement officers arrest many people every day for drunk driving. However, police officers are unable to catch every person who is guilty of drinking and driving. Nor are they able to prevent the majority of tragic injuries and deaths due to alcohol-related collisions. Now, in the twenty-first century, we have new technology such as breathalyzers, steering wheels and seats that can measure the blood alcohol level of the driver before the vehicle starts. If the driver has an illegal blood alcohol level for driving, the car will not start.

These new technologies have the potential to greatly reduce the number of alcohol-related collisions. If every car had one of these sensors, drinking and driving would not be so common everywhere. Even people who have not yet been caught drinking and driving should have to have these sensors in their vehicles. In the big picture, saving lives is more than worth the expense of putting these lifesaving sensors in all vehicles.

Kevin Joslyn, Grade 10
Deltona High School, FL

Addiction Without Reality

To me, addiction is something that goes from being a want to becoming a need. The only things that I have needed in my life were food, water, and sleep. In the year of 1997, those three needs slowly decreased until I was left with only one.

It was a subtle change in diet at first. I lied to my parents and said I had already eaten. The loss of energy was a sign of my body telling me that it was starving. I was, but when my body said that, my mind easily replied, "no, just one more." I didn't need much energy for what I was doing anyway.

At night, when my parents came in my room to tuck me in, I would already be asleep in their eyes. They would quietly leave and shut the door to my room. And just as quietly, I would roll out of bed and go to work again. My body was aware of the change in sleeping habits. My body once again asked my mind, "Can he get some rest?" My mind would retort, "No, just one more."

My body understood that this was now a war. My body tried to put itself into hibernation. But my mind was too powerful. My mind seemed to change into a dictator of myself as my body put up an undignified surrender. My mind won the war.

My name is Daniel R. Platt and I am a video game addict.

Daniel R. Platt, Grade 12
Florida State University/Florida High School, FL

Freedom

To me, freedom is a treasured gift. This gift was not bought with money but with lives. Thousands of people have given their lives so that I can be free. I am free to make my own choices, and to worship my own God. I have the freedom of speech and freedom to ask questions. I have the freedom to be whatever I want to be. I have the freedom to vote for whomever I choose. I can be in control of my life.

Hundreds of privileges that we, as Americans take for granted every day, are privileges that millions are not allowed to even contemplate. I have the freedom to go on vacation without asking the government's permission. I can buy and sell a car without asking the government's permission. I do not have to ask permission to see my family in another city. When I grow up and get married, I have the right to have as many children as I want, without asking the government's permission. Millions upon millions have been thrown in jail for not asking the government's permission. Why do millions continue to live like this? Why haven't we, as citizens of the United States of America, done anything about it? We, as Americans have the privilege, the duty, and the freedom to help give other nations freedom, and yet we sigh and turn our backs to the millions who are suffering. I hope that everyone will realize why it is important to give everyone the freedom that they deserve.

Haley Mader, Grade 10
Haynes Academy for Advanced Studies, LA

Exercise

Many medical experts think people need to get more exercise. I believe the same thing. Exercising is the best thing for the human body. It makes you feel good about yourself, you're more energetic, and it makes you want to eat well. Working out stimulates your mind and also relieves stress.

First thing I want to talk about is how it makes you feel good about yourself. What I mean is that you can wear what you always wear. When you're out walking around in your town and where you like to go and hang out, there are people looking at you and saying you look really good. How did you do it? What you should say is that I worked really hard and spent a lot of time in the gym, and it paid off.

Second of all the energy that you will have from exercise is great. The three years of boxing that I have under my belt was the best way I got fit. Well, the days I didn't train, or I had a fight; I was ready to do something at all times.

With all of the nutritious foods that you can eat, you will not gain too much weight. Vegetables are some of the best there is. It depends on the calories in the food because you need a certain amount a day to gain weight and turn it into muscle.

Adam Hanley, Grade 10
Gadsden Job Corps Center, AL

My Getaway

My getaway is the peaceful Fordyce, Arkansas. It is one of the only places where my dad and I can escape the stresses of school and work. When we go there we are surrounded by nature as we walk in the woods. The sky-scraping trees loom over us. An abundance of deer, hogs, and several species of small animals inhabit the area. The nippy breeze numbs my face when I drive a four-wheeler down the dirt road that meanders through and around the land our friends rent.

In our friend's bunkhouse numerous NCAA 2004 football video games are played on the Playstation. However when there is an Arkansas Razorbacks game on TV, the video games are turned off and the volume is turned up. Everyone stops what he or she is doing and either steps inside the bunkhouse to watch the game on television or turns their vehicle's radio on while leaving its doors open so the sound is loud enough for everyone sitting around the campfire to hear. On nights when there isn't a game on we ordinarily go to Leola to eat at Dorey's Catfish Restaurant, known for its savory buffet. After returning to camp my dad and I hang out with friends and family. Once it gets late we go to our family's own little red bunkhouse and go to sleep. We sleep better there than in our own beds. When it is time to depart none of us are ready to go.

Hunter Pettie, Grade 10
Germantown High School, TN

Biggest Problem with Education

The biggest problem with the school system today is the lack of funding. Funding is essential to a school's system. An inadequate source of funding can endanger a child's education.

One of the most important things funding accomplishes is upgrades. Buildings may be in poor shape, which can range from minor problems to whole building issues. Fixing this costs money. If there isn't enough money, then these projects go unfinished. This affects the child's health. An unsafe school is the worst place to receive an education.

Also, lack of funding can really affect a child's education. A lack in funding causes insufficient supplies and books. Without enough books to issue one per child, learning becomes difficult. Also, it is difficult to have a hands-on experience without enough supplies.

Finally, lack of funding can cause lack of extracurricular activities. Some may think that these activities are mere leisure. They are just as important as English and math. Those activities help us with our social skills. They are priceless to a child's education. Also, many of these activities create scholarships. This is highly important to someone who plans to attend college.

To reiterate, without funding, receiving a proper education is impossible. Our children are the key to the future, and our future is looking bleak. Students deserve much better, and it is up to us to change this.

Treshain Norfleet, Grade 11
City University School of Liberal Arts, TN

Transit

Change, it's a scary thing and it seems to be the theme of life. More so now than it has ever been, or it could be that being so close to graduating change just seems to be more apparent. It's in everyone one's eyes when they walk down the hallway at school. You can tell we're all on edge, all the time, just waiting for the next thing to hit us like a brick. It's scary to think that just a few years ago all we were worried about was what we were eating for lunch, now it's about, what am I doing for the rest of my life?

This metamorphosis that is happening is the most real thing that I can think of to write about. The funny thing is, is it's also the one thing I wish I could run from and forget about. When I talk to my friends the conversation is always about the future, sometimes I want to scream and change the subject to Grey's Anatomy. I think that that's what we all want but we know sooner or later we have to face the inevitable.

One day we'll be grateful we went through the transitions to get to wherever it is we are headed. Who knows, maybe we will ask for more changes to come our way. All that is certain is that our greatest wish would be that everything would just slow down.

Shawna Standiford, Grade 11
Owasso High School, OK

Study Session

It is Tuesday night. The time is 8:08 Post Meridian. The sun has set. The night sky outside gleams orange with the sulfur street lights speckling the landscape. Reggae tunes erupt from the speakers. Strange men walk around the café, sweeping the floor. Three girls surround me, estrogen oozing from their pores. A mechanical and inhuman glow radiates from my classmates' laptops and spills over the mauve table. Our binders lay scattered across the counter. Tensions run high as our eyes scan through the pages of our notebooks like the spotlights of a jail yard. Taco Bell tacos and the girls' fruity smoothies pollute the workspace.

My eyes drift onto one of my friend's computers. She has ever so cleverly tattooed the word "Love" replacing the L with a question mark so to represent the intrigue that is the emotion's companion. Presidential and Congressional governments, amendments, Full Faith and Credit, and domiciliary: these words flood my brain and spill out through my eyes. I pull at my hair, as if that was some ancient Chinese method for relieving stress. My friends all look tired; it's as if all the teachers conspired to give us as much homework in one night as humanly possible. I attempt to collect my straying mental threads and place them back in my head. Fed up with it all, I slam my clenched fists onto the desk, thinking, "To hell with it all! I've had enough of this! I'll just wing it…like always!"

Brian Worley, Grade 12
Germantown High School, TN

Breaking Away

Running serves as a form of escape for me, a chance to get away from everything wrong, to distance myself from things bothering me, to distract myself from my feelings. When I run, I don't think; I'm free from anything trying to hold me back. Even though it's hard, even though it hurts, I feel better once I'm done. It is as though I have accomplished something, even though I haven't gone very far. People say that it's weird that I enjoy something as mindless or difficult as running, but to me, it's more than just a sport. It's a way to release all the tension, all the problems in my life, to just let go and break free from all the ties that bind me to my life. When I run, I'm myself. It's raw, it's hard, but I love every step of it. The blood, the sweat, the pain that comes with it is all just a part of the experience. If it were easy, I wouldn't feel as strong, as proud, after a difficult day. If I didn't have to work, I wouldn't enjoy it, I couldn't lose myself in the constant rhythm of my strides, or the mental freedom that comes from focusing on just moving forward, moving faster. Why do I put myself through this day in, day out, regardless of the weather, or my problems, or the agony? Because it feels so good when I stop.

Meredith Gunder, Grade 11
Bishop Verot High School, FL

The Airplane

For centuries, man has watched the birds fly and designed machines so he too could fly like the birds. Inventors have been designing flying machines since the late 1400s. Model gliders flew with success in the 1860s and the first motorized airplane was flown by John Stringfellow in 1848. The Wright brothers flew the first full scale airplane successfully at Kitty Hawk, North Carolina on December 17, 1903. The Wright Flyer flew 120 feet. It was a wood frame, fabric covered airplane powered by a gasoline engine.

Glenn H. Curtis designed the Curtis Jenny. The Jenny was the first plane to use ailerons, flaps on the wings, as control surfaces. After WWI, the airplane industry began. Ford Motor Company built the first all metal airplane; it was called the Ford Trimotor Transport. Great Britain developed the first jet airliner; it was the De Havilland Comet. The first supersonic flight was powered by rocket engines and was flown in 1947, by the Bell X-1. The concord was the first supersonic jet airliner, and was build by the British and French governments; it first flew in 1969.

The Wright brothers built the first successful airplane, and it has evolved throughout history into the supersonic jets of today. Now the United States Government is working on an airplane that will carry passengers to the edge of space. Airplanes have changed the way we live our lives, and they will continue to develop with new designs and materials.

Mark Robinson, Grade 12
Rossville Christian Academy, TN

Bump, Set, Spike!

I love volleyball! In my experience playing this energizing sport, I have discovered some important traits that an aspiring great volleyball player should have.

I think that teamwork is one of the vital function that the players should have. Teamwork is people working together as one for the same goal to become the best and take state. If people on the team have bad attitudes, or do not get along, that team will fall apart and become unsuccessful. Each player has to encourage that other player so that you can become more confident in yourself and others. Another great trait to have is perseverance in always trying to improve. One should never think that he is as good as he can ever be. Communication is a great factor in playing the game. Letting others know that you have the ball (by saying "Got it!") will prevent the players from colliding with each other and prevent the volleyball from getting out of control. Just always try to think logically and make smart plays, and if you mess up, just shake if off and remember that you only lost one point, and you can get that point back. If your coach scolds you for messing up, do not get mad or upset at him, respect him and do as he says.

If you remember these important points, and work hard at them, you can become a great volleyball player and successfully Bump, Set, Spike!

Michelle Plummer, Grade 11
Trinity Christian Academy, AL

Sugar

I have been told that scent is the strongest mortal association with memory, but I have to disagree. Though fragrances remind me of my past, only in the taste of my grandmother's sugar cookies lies my childhood.

Ever since I can remember, my grandma, whom I call Amma, has made crispy cookies in a massive batch at the dawn of each week. As a youngin', I watched her add flour, butter, vanilla, and scoops of sparkly sweet crystals into a bowl, mix it with knowing motion, and flatten the treats into pale patties. Amma never needed to measure her ingredients: "You just know," she had explained.

While her coins baked to yellow treasures, she busied herself in the garden. Taking care of family and flowers are all that has ever mattered to her. When I was younger, I walked with her among the flowers and tinkling wind-chimes; Amma identified the different varieties of blooms and I nodded my head in childish ignorance and love.

By that time, Amma's cookies would have been baked into soft, golden tea cakes. She would take them from the oven, place three for me on an emerald saucer, and stack the rest in her faded tan canister. I was always allowed to dive into the cookie jar when I desired.

Her cookies were delicate, crisp, and very sweet, very much like my grandmother herself. They remind me of blissful days of my kid years.

Ashley Hicks, Grade 11
Germantown High School, TN

Music of the Heart

There are so many different genres of music, ranging from classical to country, hip-hop to jazz. Music means different things to different people. Some music touches people's hearts because the lyrics are so true and heartfelt. Others use it as a method to escape the real world. Music is a way to express ones self when one can't find any other way. It is a time to use words not so often used. It is a chance for one's creative side to come out and no one can criticize it. If we feel the need to scream our feelings then we should. It is an outlet only music can offer. Or if we feel the need to just use instruments rather than vocals, then that is our choice and our choice alone. Some people even prefer music that is a'capella, or just vocals. There are so many ways music can be portrayed and people take advantage of that. They will take into consideration that some people don't just listen to one particular genre. Most people will listen to two or more, and each genre has its own affect on people. Some will make people feel the emotions that the song is trying to convey, such as anger or sadness. For me, country is my choice of music. It affects me more than any other genre. I believe that it, of all other genres of music, shows the most emotion.

Christen Barrett, Grade 12
Lee County Sr High School, NC

Jack Frost's Holiday

When one thinks about winter, do heavy coats and gloves come to mind? Or does the smell of hot chocolate and marshmallows fill one's dreams? I personally think about both of the choices. The season winter can be filled with exciting memories.

A blanket of snow on Christmas day is what I have hoped for every year during winter. I am sad to say that I have only experienced real snow one time on Christmas day. Winter is the time of year when my family seems like it bonds. We have special traditions we do every year. We go to Gatlinburg in Tennessee, and we always celebrate Jesus's birthday on Christmas day. A lot of people don't like winter because everything is basically dead outside. The season in Alabama is totally different compared to Maryland. I like winter in Alabama, because it's not too cold, but it still can be chilly outside. Another thing that I like about winter is that you can build a nice warm fireplace. One can also make sweet and tasty treats, like s'mores. Decorating is a huge hobby to do in winter, because you have a large selection to choose from. Snowmen and angels are the popular decoration from inside and outside.

Food is another wonderful thing in winter. It's soups galore and hot meals. My grandmother can make the best potato soup and vegetable soup. My favorite thing about winter is making cookies with my grandma.

Ashleigh Collins, Grade 12
Trinity Christian Academy, AL

Backpacking Brings Benefits

Backpacking has long been part of the American tradition. Years ago, when the Native Americans traveled through the wilderness carrying limited supplies, they were participating in, possibly initiating, the sport of backpacking. As time has continued to trek forward, so have many others as more and more outdoor enthusiasts learn of this wonderful recreational activity. This rigorous sport requires that a person carry his/her essential belongings in a well-fitted backpack as miles of trail pass beneath their boots. To be successful in completing a backpacking trip, it is imperative that the hiker gather his/her outdoor equipment and slowly eliminate those items that serve little or no purpose. Through this trimming down process, the backpacker can determine what objects are absolutely needed to survive and enjoy their time out-of-doors.

As one participates in this activity, he/she gains a realization of the innumerable benefits of such an event. First of all, this aerobic exercise improves overall health and increases muscle mass. Exercises such as this cause beta-endorphins to be released in the brain, giving a feeling of well-being to the athlete. Secondly, being relatively alone and independent of all others amidst the beauty of the earth, a strong appreciation for nature is developed and a sense of confidence is built. These qualities would help improve the lives of individuals across the globe.

Joshua Gathro, Grade 10
Stanton College Preparatory School, FL

The Greatness of Life

My favorite hobbies or interests that I enjoy doing are playing baseball, spending time with my friends and family and playing music (violin). I am most thankful for being able to spend time with my friends and family every day and being healthy and strong, along with I play the violin during school hours in class and after school.

I am also thankful for believing in God because He is the one who made me who I am today. It's a great opportunity to learn more about the teachings of Christianity and all the religious beliefs and practices. Growing up in a good society with people of the same beliefs learning to help one another in times of need, taking special care to our family and friends. Also I take time to pray to God for our existence and being good model citizens, doing the right things all the time with being kind and forgiving.

Believing has set big goals in my life which I hope to accomplish such as playing for the New York Yankees in the major leagues for baseball or becoming a sports medicine doctor. Along with having a big house, having luxury cars and a yacht, staying close to my friends and family are important to me as well. Also I would love to travel all over the world and staying healthy and enjoy my life to the fullest. These are things that are the most important to me and I cannot picture my life without it.

Stefan Singh, Grade 11
Miami Killian Sr High School, FL

Palestine

"Amro, run and take cover," said my little cousin. As I looked up, I saw five gunmen shooting. They had no souls for shooting at pedestrians. I was scared for my life. I was running through the streets of Ramallah as I saw M-16 bullets passing me shooting people down. I cannot remember if I saw anyone being killed but I do remember that I saw grown adults and little children screaming in pain. Then the gunmen had come to the city to kill the soldiers for not fulfilling their duty. The gunmen shot at the common people for about ten minutes. They did not walk the streets to kill anybody, but stayed in their car shooting. I remember telling my cousin that everything would be all right.

The gunmen left ten minutes after the shooting began. Everybody came from hiding to notice the horrific scenes of what happened. The ambulances came, one after another, picking up the wounded. I recall that one of my friends was shot in the leg and I said, "Doesn't that hurt?" and he said, "As long as God is with me nothing bad will happen." He went off to the hospital and my cousin and I stayed in the city to help clean. We saw cars that had been shot with shapes of triangles and squares. It was a terrifying day, but like most people say, "Things happen but you have to live life to the fullest."

Amro Quran, Grade 10
Germantown High School, TN

Putting My Life on the Line — A Drumline

Have you ever felt the feeling of doing something so extraordinary that you wish you could do it forever? Luckily, I can say yes because I am a member of an elite marching band's drumline. That feeling you get after marching a ten minute show is so unique that there isn't any way to replicate it.

Many people say that band is stupid, but they are totally wrong. They don't understand the commitment it takes to go out on the field and perform. The performers have spent up to two hundred and fifty hours of practice and rehearsals in a season that is only three to four months long. That kind of dedication is so huge that it is just amazing to see the three hundred students committing to it every day.

Not only do these three hundred performers have to dedicate their time, but they also have to memorize ten minutes of music and ninety drill sets. Their music contains insane solos, dramatic volume changes, and problematic rhythms just to name a few. Their sets of drill take up different amounts of time, contain difficult direction changes, and have massive to diminutive step sizes. Talk about tremendous mental concentration.

Every day I'm thankful for my opportunity to be on a drumline, because that feeling I get after performing is not like any other feeling. Band has shaped my skills in leadership, commitment, and trust so much, I don't know who I would be without it.

Andrew Lynch, Grade 11
Owasso High School, OK

September 11: The Tragedy of a Scapegoat

It is easier to blame than to take the blame. On September 11, 2001, two planes crashed into the World Trade Centers. Although it was terrorists that committed the act, Muslims are being condemned; therefore, they are being persecuted, unfairly judged, and mistreated.

Generally, Muslims are persecuted because of 9-11. They have become scapegoats for terrorists. Before that date, Muslims blended into the community. Now, they are unjustly accused; consequently, they are beginning to defy those who think they should hide their faith, and they resent non-Muslims for their lack of knowledge of their faith.

Furthermore, these people are unfairly judged. Not all of them are terrorists; however, the government has domestically grouped them together, and they are being told to condemn the terrorist actions of other Muslims. The largest problem is both they and their culture are misunderstood.

Finally, Muslims are mistreated. They are often more closely watched by airport security, and the use of stop and search is used more frequently. Muslims are both assaulted and insulted by people who fear or dislike them; therefore, they are recoiling and making barriers for themselves.

September 11, 2001, was a dark day, blackened by evil. The terrorists took the lives of thousands and destroyed the lives of millions; consequently, Muslims are being condemned for an act they did not commit. Sadly, it is always convenient to have a scapegoat.

Ashley Pericas, Grade 10
Jessieville High School, AR

Respect in Society

What if, right now, everybody on the Earth lost their sense of respect to others; would the world be the same, or very different? Many would say that society would be more corrupt than it is now. Yet, in my opinion, society has already achieved this level of corruption due to the lack of respect.

Respect is a hard thing to find. Few people actually show respect in their lives constantly. Many might disagree with me, saying that respect *is* shown by a lot of people. They claim that as long as we act in a proper manner face to face then we are showing respect. But respect goes a lot deeper than that. Respect means not talking bad behind someone's back, or poking fun of others. Respect is helping others whenever we don't really like them. We rarely see this level of respect in society.

If respect can be found in our society, the corrupt nature that is prevalent will be stunned. People need to realize what respect really is, instead of just assuming that they know. Respect is not something wanted, but something needed by everyone.

Nathan Lee, Grade 10
Greenwood High School, KY

Father Figure

Although by definition, a father is a man who has begotten a child, a good father is much more. He is responsible; he loves, rewards, punishes, and teaches his child.

A father provides his child with food, clothing, shelter, education, medical visits, and other necessities. He takes good care of his family.

As head of the household, it is the father's responsibility to teach his child about God. The Bible promises, "Train up a child in the way he should go, and when he is old, he will not depart from it."

A father deeply loves his child, wants the best for him, and does not want him to be hurt. He protects his child and makes decisions to benefit him.

Sometimes, a father holds on when he should let go. It is hard for a father to watch his child grow up, but it is inevitable.

Punishment comes with loving. Without consequences for wrongdoing, a child will become spoiled and rude. The father hates the punishment, but it is in the best interests of the child who must know how to obey authority.

However, a child needs to be rewarded for good behavior, good grades, awards, and honors in school. Ignoring a child's accomplishments could cause rebellion.

A father must spend time with his child. Material possessions cannot replace him. A father wants his child to be successful, happy, and able to someday guide his own family.

Natalie Hammonds, Grade 12
New Covenant Christian School, SC

Hurricane Katrina

Have you ever had a hurricane hit where you stay? If not, you are lucky. I have had on hit where I live, and it was a bad one. It destroyed a lot of things also.

When Katrina began to hit, we went to the store to get ham and bread because the electricity went out. My lights, telephone, and water had cut off. It was so dark we had to light candles to see. At first, the phone was still on so we could get in contact with other people.

Then when it started to rain and thunder I just went to sleep, so I couldn't hear it. It was raining so hard that it flooded some yards over by my house. My pole in my yard was leaning and it caught the lines that hook up to the telephone. The phone went off for about three weeks. Our water came back on, and that was good. My TV went out. This was awful because I can't live without my TV or a phone, but I survived.

In conclusion, Hurricane Katrina was a bad storm that hit Philadelphia, Mississippi. It affected so many things in my surrounding environment. After all the damage, everything came back together. They built new houses, picked up the fallen trees, and everything went back to normal.

Mandrius Huddleston, Grade 10
Philadelphia High School, MS

Jesus

Though I may have many things in my life, there is only one person who is above all else — the single most important factor in my life. His name is Jesus. He is the only true thing that has given me an undoubtedly important reason for living. Without him I am nothing. I am nothing but a wondering soul that roams up and down the earth with no purpose, pride, hope, or existence. He is everything to me. Jesus is the sunshine that brightens even that of my darkest days. He is the air I breathe. Without him every lyric that udders itself from the tip of my lips means nothing. I am but a broken vessel without him.

My only purpose in life is to please him, to worship him at every waking moment. Jesus died for me on the cross. Just think about that. He sacrificed his life for a torn sinner like me. With that said and with that in mind, I would be a fool not to live out my life in debt to him. Why did he die for me? He died for me because he loved me so much. He could have commanded the lightning that rolls through the heavens to come and strike the Roman soldiers, but he didn't. He had a passion that was too strong for his flesh to overcome.

Bradley Cannon, Grade 11
Southside High School, NC

We Who Are About to Die Salute You

Imagine you are in an arena, tens of thousands of people staring down at you, watching your every move. The sun is beating down your sweat soaked spine while you stare at your adversary. The metal sword in your hand becomes slippery and hard to hold as you see your enemy run toward you with his spear rising to your vitals. It all sounds pretty scary, doesn't it?

That is exactly what gladiators of ancient Rome had to go through every time they stepped inside the arena. Gladiators that the Romans used in the arena games were slaves, sentenced criminals, and prisoners of war. Some, however, wanted to be gladiators and volunteered for the job, these people were mostly lower class and wanted to be famous and receive awards that went with the job.

Gladiators were classified as "infamous," meaning they were beneath the law, not considered citizens. This did not stop the gladiators from becoming famous among the Romans. Often times graffiti could be seen dedicated to famous gladiators or chanting and gossiping could be heard in public. The not so well known or famous gladiators could sometimes only fight a couple of times a year, while others fought a lot more.

The reward for gladiators that were skilled enough was freedom. They would receive a wooden sword called a rudis and they would be free. From there, most would be trainers to other gladiators or become freelance bodyguards. What would you do if you won your freedom?

Rebecca Tangney, Grade 11

Communication Devices

I think that communication devices have affected our society in a positive way because you can call someone, email, or organize things. It has made life easier to me. I think communication with others would be harder without them.

First, it's good because you can call and talk to someone from your home. You can call from a cell phone while you're gone somewhere. If you had an emergency, you would be able to call for help. You can call family out of state and keep in touch with them.

Second, you can email someone from the computer. It's good because you can keep in touch with family even if you didn't have a phone. It's an easy way of sending a message to someone because they can receive it right then. You wouldn't have to wait to receive something through mail.

Last, it's easier to organize things to keep up with them. It helps you find things easier if they are organized. You can plan things from day to day. There are calendars on computers to help you organize things.

In conclusion, communication devices have made things easier. It's a lot easier to call someone to tell them something than having to go there. You can email something to someone. It's better to organize things than to have to look for them. So it's great that we have communication devices.

Crystal Thompson, Grade 12
Gadsden Job Corps Center, AL

The Essence of Me

The peace, the tranquility, and the significant feelings that give life a deeper meaning. All of these qualities embrace me when I'm in my own utopia of happiness; art. Art, and just being creative, fills my soul with contentment; it's my addiction, my drug that keeps me going. Without it, I don't know what I'd do to get by. Art makes up the colors of my spirit, and my colors are daring and bursting with life.

In making art, I do my own style. That's the wonderful thing about it; I don't have to conform, I can be who I want to be. I love how I can be having the worst day, and with paper, be able to calm myself down and let my emotions out, let the feelings just spill onto the page. Emotions really do the art, we're just there to let them out, to guide them, and to enjoy the ride. We're the audience and the performers, both at the same time.

In my opinion, there's never a "right" or "wrong" in art; all styles can be appreciated. That's the pay off too, knowing that pictures from the heart can truly inspire and give reason to humanity. I'm one of those people, one who tries to stir the soul, and my artistic tranquility has sculpted my being. Creating art has always defined me and brightened my spirit, and I cherish how it makes me "me."

Jaclyn Melcher, Grade 10
Assumption High School, KY

Twelfth of Twelve

It was November 11, 2005. Grand Nationals is the biggest band contest of the year. Sixty bands from all over the country were there to see who was the best of the best. Nationals are made up of a series of rounds; preliminaries, semi finals, and finals. We participated in this event with the hopes of making finals. Twelve bands went on to finals and we hoped to be in that twelve. In the past, the highest round we had made was semifinals. I knew we had not made finals before and if we wanted to, we had to give the performance of a lifetime.

We did. Our semifinals performance was as close to perfect as you could possibly imagine. Everyone was spot on in the music and in the formations. We changed out of uniform and went to eat dinner. Finally, we made our way to the stadium. The entire band held hands while they announced the finalists. They announced nine and our name had not been called. Then the announcer said, "And the Owa- -." He was cut off by our screams because we had made finals. We were all crying for joy. Everyone was hugging each other and screaming. Our finals performance was not as great as our semifinals one. We didn't really care though because we had made finals. We placed twelfth out of twelve. It was okay though. We had worked hard to get that far and it was well deserved.

Audra Waggoner, Grade 11
Owasso High School, OK

Practice Makes Perfect

As a child, one may often hear the saying, "practice makes perfect." The more you practice, the better you will become. But, just how much should one practice? The unexpected answer is that practice doesn't make perfect. If you practice until you are perfect, you will only be perfect in that for a brief time.

The definition of practice in the dictionary is: "To do or engage in regularly; to do repeatedly in order to learn something or become proficient." One can practice, practice, and practice, yet still not be perfected; only the practicing will become perfected. So, the way you practice will be the determining factor in perfection.

An example of this would be in school. A student can study very hard, and very long for a test, yet still fail. The determining factor in this example would be the studying. If the student did not study the correct material, or not enough of the material, it will show when it is time to prove perfection. What you practice will eventually become your permanence.

Another example would be in sports. If you practice lazily, you will play lazily in a game. On the other hand, if you practice to the best of your ability, you will play to the best of your ability.

In conclusion, practice does not make perfect, but, practice makes permanent!

Alexis Heimlich, Grade 11
Bishop Verot High School, FL

Cherish Every Moment

We all lose someone that is close to us at some point in our lives, whether it has already occurred, or is yet to happen. With this loss of a loved one, we realize how much they meant to us and how much we wish we could get them back.

I must have heard the saying, "You never know what you've got 'til it's gone" a hundred times. I never thought much of it though.

Then one day my world turned dark and clouds of sorrow engulfed me. My uncle passed away. My family and I knew he had been sick, but never thought his precious life would be taken.

He was the one, who could brighten my day, even when I was in the foulest mood. He was the one, who could make me laugh without saying a single word, and he was the one, who I trusted to be there in my time of need.

Even when he felt like he didn't have enough strength to get out of bed in the morning, he still made the best of things. When the odds were against him and his fight against this tragic disease, he would say that this was the path God has chosen for him.

His strength taught me to cherish every moment of life, even if the next moment could be my last. Not a day goes by that I don't think about him and remember how much he meant to me.

Stefany Joustra, Grade 11
Countryside High School, FL

Avoiding Stereotypes

Today's world's people base their first impressions on stereotypes. Stereotypes can be accurate, totally offensive, or even completely inaccurate. Basing impressions of people on stereotypes isn't the best thing to do, for all that you know, the blond woman that you automatically assume is stupid, based on a common stereotype, could be one of the world's greatest minds. Sure, using stereotypes helps protect us in certain situations, but most of the time they are very inaccurate. Stereotypes governing the behavior of certain people wearing certain clothing is the most abused. Let's say that you see a person with many piercings, decked out in black, and with tons of chains walking down the sidewalk. What is the first thing that comes to your mind? You probably assume that that person isn't the best person to associate with due to a stereotype. For all you know, that person could be the most responsible, caring person you could ever meet. Of course, that person could be like you first perceived, but that is beside the point. Basically, stereotyping can be good or really, really bad, but it is best to refrain from it and actually get to know people better instead of assuming they are something other than they actually are.

Mitchel Spears, Grade 11
Camden Central High School, TN

Tribute

Six years ago evil fell on America. Freedom was lost as people were trapped beneath the rubble. Six years ago two twin brothers fell. Six years ago families cried as fear and shock was seen in America's eyes as two silver bullets shot through twins. So many people keep on saying forget about what happened, its over. That's just the thing it's not over. As I write this I'm thinking about my uncle whom I'm close with and his friends who are overseas fighting for everything each one of us holds dear. They are fighting for our freedom; our right to stand up for what is right or wrong. Many people seem to forget or not think about what happened six years ago. But there are the ones who lost loved ones on that day, the ones who worry every day if their soldier is still alive. What those people do every day is something so brave and honorable that no one in this world can know unless they are there and that their job every day is to wake up, grab a gun and protect the country they know and love. This is a tribute to the soldiers fighting for our lives, the ones who put their lives on the line everyday to save ours. This is a tribute to those lives lost and their families who got left behind. Support the troops, remember the forgotten.

Alyssa White, Grade 11

John F. Kennedy: A True American Hero

On November 22, 1963, the nation was suddenly overcome by grief and utter shock. The president, John Fitzgerald Kennedy, was struck by an assassin's bullet as he and his motorcade paraded through Dallas, Texas. It is a terrible tragedy that will forever be remembered as one of the darkest days in American history. He will forever be remembered for his courage, leadership, and faith in our country.

John Fitzgerald Kennedy was born on May 29, 1917 in the town of Brookline, Massachusetts. He graduated from Harvard University in the year 1940. Shortly after graduation, he entered the Navy.

After the war, Kennedy began a career in politics. In 1953 he earned a seat in Congress. Also during the year of 1953, John married his wife Jacqueline Bouvier. John remained a congressman for six years. He then entered the presidential election of 1960.

In 1961, Kennedy became the youngest president in history. His efforts, the equal rights movement, opened doors to thousands of Americans that without him wouldn't have the opportunity. 1962 brought on the Cuban missile crisis. There was evidence that the Russians were attempting to install nuclear missiles in Cuba. Fearing the worst, Kennedy ordered that all weapons headed for Cuba must be quarantined. The Russians eventually backed down, avoiding war.

John F. Kennedy was a great leader, father, and husband. He will go down in history as one of the greatest leaders of our country.

Jared Austin, Grade 10
Mulhall-Orlando High School, OK

Pets

Almost since the beginning of man, there have been domesticated animals. Although animals were originally used as protection or maybe to hunt, pets have evolved into something completely different. True, some pets are still used for protection and hunting, but many of these animals are first and foremost companions.

It always seems like there are cat or dog people. Some people cannot stand cats or dogs. I happen to have both. Dogs can be true companions because they love to be with people. They often follow their masters around and aim to please. Dogs have the "pack" instinct that makes them want to have companions. Cats have an entirely different personality — most cats act aloof and regal. In ancient Egypt, cats were revered as gods, and they have never forgotten it.

There have been many studies showing the health benefits of having animals. Logically, if you have a dog you will have better health because of the energy involved in caring for a dog — walking and playing. But mentally, pets can deeply affect someone. They provide companionship, comfort, and often can make you laugh. Sometimes people take this companionship a little too far, having their little dogs spoiled rotten. These dogs serve as their babies, and the dogs certainly do not argue.

My pets are very important to me. Animals have always played an important part in my family, and will continue to do so for the rest of my life.

Maureen McLaughlin, Grade 11
Bishop Verot High School, FL

Teen Life

Do parents really know, or do they just think they do? I believe they think they know what we go through. Times are changing and teens are changing. It is different every day. Some choose to worship God, but most choose other life styles, usually bad ones. Drugs, death, alcohol, and sex play a big role in the life of a teenager. There is a lot of peer pressure, too! To go with the crowd, to do it because everyone else is, and most do. The cell phone is also a big issue, too. They cause many teen deaths because of texting and talking while driving. Teenagers like to party and drink and have a good time, but what most don't realize is that it's ruining their lives and others around them. I choose to not go with the crowd and stay away from drugs, alcohol, and all of those other bad things, but that doesn't mean I do not have my share of peer pressure as well. People can change in an instant because of peer pressure. People are bullied into doing things every day. Bullies play a big role in teen lives too. Some actually commit suicide over bullies because no one will do anything. I think that parents don't understand what we have to go through. Most parents these days are not involved with their children and that's one main reason some are so bad. Thank you for taking the time to read my essay.

Lisa Joyner, Grade 11
Emanuel County Institute, GA

The Athlete's Conduct

When a child or teenager is involved in athletics he is automatically put into an institution which teaches him right from wrong. Whether the practices keep a teenager off the streets, or the game in which the player takes part teaches him valuable life lessons, a participant is always learning. Sports, as well as other organized clubs or teams, can keep a child on the right path, and out of trouble. This is attributed to the time that the sport demands, and the coaches and principles which shape the sport.

While a teenager can be getting into trouble on the streets, football players are working to better themselves. The time that a player puts towards the sport keeps him focused as well as motivated. In addition, sports teach important lessons and principles in every aspect of the game. Fair play, modesty, and respect are all core pieces in the sport of football. This sends the children home every day with a sense of self-worth, and more motivation to come back the next day. This motivation can carry a one time athlete through their life.

Athletes are held to higher standards because of these aspects of the games they play. The game teaches them to cope with that pressure and perform the way they strive to. An athlete sets an example for his peers, and acts with discipline at all times.

Matt Timpanelli, Grade 11
Bishop Verot High School, FL

The Frosty Season

I am very fond of snow and the fall season. Something about it cheers my spirit. It is almost as if my entire look on things changes with each season. I just feel more comfortable in the late seasons of the year. There are many enjoyable things to do in the winter when it snows.

When I was little I would go sledding with my parents, and on the way over to where we would be sledding, they would tell my sister and I stories of when they were children. My mom and I would go see my sister at her school ice-skating practice, and then we would come home and make hot cocoa together. Sometimes we would walk to the lake and see how it froze over the boardwalk. We would always go over to my Aunt Mimi's and eat her Christmas cookies.

My favorite thing to do was to shovel snow! I remember getting up in the morning before school started to see if the front door would open. I remember several times where my parents would have to call family to dig us out because the snow was so high that we could not open our front door! One of the things I loved to do was make snow angels and try not to leave footprints anywhere near the angel. I remember one time it had snowed so much that my sister and I climbed up the mounds of snow and peered down a basketball hoop!

Jenna deStefano, Grade 11
North Forsyth High School, GA

My Mother

My mother, Michelle Moore is the best mother you will ever meet. She has four children, my older sister, younger brother, and I. I bet you are wondering about the fourth child, aren't you? My mother is pregnant, and very excited. The only thing is that she is overweight and thirty six years old. She has four more months to go until she has another one of us to take care of.

Michelle is beautiful and very kind hearted. She would do anything for me. Although she hasn't had the best life, she makes things work. My mom was raised by her mother and her stepfather since she was little. She has been married twice and divorced twice also. She married mine and my sister's father, Vernon Fleetwood first and my brother's father, Mike Moore, second. She is currently engaged to the baby's father, John Reeves. Michelle's first husband was thirty two, and passed away with a heart condition. Her second husband is thirty five and lives in Boonville. No matter what my mom has been through, she is still the best mom ever.

Michelle works at Fitzgibbon Hospital, from 6:30 a.m.-3:30 p.m. As soon as she gets home she cooks, cleans and helps all her children with their homework. My mom also helps my sister with her college decisions. She never stops doing things, and I could never ask for a better mom. She is my role model and is the best one anyone could ever have.

Cecilia Bernice Fleetwood, Grade 10
Slater High School, MO

Keep "God" in the Pledge of Allegiance

Why do people want to take "God" out of the Pledge of Allegiance? I think this is ridiculous. I can think of a number of reasons to support my belief.

The main reason I believe "God" should remain in the pledge is because this is what our nation was founded on. This is the basis for our Constitution. You can't just throw away our values and all that God has created. After all, our nation's motto is "In God We Trust."

The statement "One Nation Under God" does not endorse any religion, and after all, there is only one "God." No one is forced to recite the Pledge of Allegiance. Requiring a person to repeat the Pledge would certainly be unconstitutional. But no one is required to do so. People can refuse to say the Pledge or can just leave out the word "God." This right was given to us in The Freedom of Speech provision of the Constitution.

I think everyone should be allowed to openly express his or her beliefs. The government cannot put God in the schools, nor can it take Him out. That is up to each individual.

We must not allow judges to use the very Constitutional right that guarantees our religious freedom as a tool to take that freedom away. We must speak out and stand our ground. Liberty is a reward of those who obey God and keep his commandments.

Adam Guilbeaux, Grade 12
St Thomas More High School, LA

The Most Important Person in My Life

Every single person in this world has someone important in their life. I however have my mother as the most important person in mine. For some other people it maybe their mother, father, or other relative. Although I chose my mom because she is the one who supports me through everything I do. Whether it be a show I am in, an award I receive, or something as large as following my dreams, my mom is there to support me. My mom is also always there for everything I do. She always attends my band concerts; to me my mom is like a cheerleader. My mom is someone important to me as well because she molded me into who I am. That is a large reason why people would choose a person to be the most important thing in their life. My mom helped me become myself and show me to be kind to others as well as to help out others. When things get tough at school she is there to comfort me and help me get through things. She appreciates what I do for her, even the smallest things; I rarely expect her to. My mom is someone who shows me reality, and is always there for me, as well as my little brother. These are the qualities people cherish when they choose that the most important thing in their life, someone they are close to, in which they complete you.

Rosalind Alifonso, Grade 11
Osceola County School of Arts, FL

Originally Me

I wasted my first fourteen years trying desperately not to be me. In elementary and middle school, I was ditched by my friends as they gradually became "the cool girls," leaving me and my purple glasses in their dust. Nothing would have made me happier than to shop with them at Abercrombie and be allowed to go to movies (without parents!) on the weekends with them. Sadly, I was always one step behind the cool girls; always one rung down on the ladder of life.

Then, as I began to mature into an adult, I realized that I liked me. I realized the basis of the "cool" label — those girls were only cool because they weren't themselves!

Luckily, I caught myself before falling into sameness. Now, I love all of the funky clothes hanging in my closet — from my mom's old 80's-wear to the classic Gap sweaters. My beautiful, size-8 body is my temple — I'd never sacrifice it to conform to the body standards of today's average high-schooler. I'm wildly opinionated on various subjects, and each of my opinions comes from my own mind — no one else's.

It's taken years of tears and downfalls and yearning to be someone else, but I've finally come love who I am. Sure, there are people who can't respect that fact, and who don't like me. Now that I love me, though, I know that it's just their loss.

Sydney Lewis, Grade 10
Druid Hills High School, GA

Are We Doing Our Part?

In the United States of America, we are blessed with many opportunities and responsibilities. As stewards of our land, it is our responsibility to harness the power of our natural resources. Through research and conservation practices, we are continually learning more about using our Oklahoma winds, water, and plants to generate energy.

The powerful winds that sweep across our plains have the potential to remove soil particles, but we have the means to harness the wind and generate electrical power. The new wind turbines that have been placed on farms particularly in western Oklahoma have become very important in the conservation attempts of modern times.

Abundant rainfall has the potential to cause flooding and results in erosion of the soil, but with the proper conservation methods in place, these waters can be stored for later use or used to turn turbines to generate electricity. Hydropower is very similar to wind energy, yet unlike wind, it can be captured and stored.

Plants have become great sources of renewable energy in recent years. Modern technology is now allowing us to produce alternative fuels from common crops. These fuels are gentler on our environment and are helping to reduce our dependence on foreign oil. Some of the most common alternative fuels being used include: ethanol and biodiesel.

If we as Americans will make use of these conservation practices and continue to look for others, then our world will be a better place to live now and for years to come.

Jordan Miller, Grade 10
Mulhall-Orlando High School, OK

My Family in Cuba

One day my grandmother was telling me about when they lived in Cuba. She was telling me about how involved their family was in the government. Then she told me something that I couldn't believe. She told me that her uncle was president for Cuba for a day. There was a presidential election and the new president Batista was a holy man and he wanted to keep the Sabbath so he would not be put into the office until that Monday. Since the country had to have a president they had to have someone as a place holder for one day, so my great uncle was picked to be that place holder. Batista served his four years and he didn't do a very good job, so when his term was over he fled the country only to return to take it over by brute force again. Then there was a revolution and Fidel Castro came to power. That's when my grandfather left the country, leaving family behind to find work. He then raised enough money to get passage for my grandmother and aunt to come to Florida. At this time my grandmother was pregnant with my father. This was the story of rise and fall of my family in Cuba.

Chris Edelmann, Grade 11
Vero Beach High School, FL

Creative Cooking

Ever cooked omelets in Ziploc® baggies? What about baking turkey in a trash can? These are a few methods of cooking that are creative. Creative cooking is excellent for all ages, brings people together to experiment with different forms of cooking, and most importantly, to have fun!

Creative cooking is perfect for anyone. No matter what age or ability, anyone can learn to cook creatively. All ages can wrap food in foil or drop a baggie in boiling water. Dishes can be as difficult as broccoli quiche, as simple as pizza rolls, or as creative as Pepsi chicken. It only takes not being afraid to use imagination while creating.

Many creative cooking events bring together the whole family. Cook-offs are favorites, especially when groups cook the same thing. Each personal recipe is their favorite and it's fun to find whose is best. Stick cooking, vagabond stoves, and box oven baking are methods that several people can work together to prepare a meal.

A fun learning experience can be made of creative cooking. Combining imagination and food has led to many new recipes that are unsurpassed favorites. Ever wonder who combined marshmallow, chocolate, and graham crackers to create the winning S'More? That's the fun of cooking.

Any unusual cooking is coined as creative cooking. Great for children to even the elderly, it makes wonderful bonding occasions, and offers fun times. Give someone a list of ingredients, a different way to cook; and you have creative cooking going on.

Elyssa Kaufman, Grade 11
Owasso High School, OK

Responsibility

It's the time of our lives, high school that is. Every teen wants to enjoy these four short years. There's sports, friends, relationships, weekends, school work, and not to mention JOBS! As a teen, feeling stressed out is anything but out of the ordinary, however not all of us are irresponsible.

Many parents and administrators would say that all teens should be able to balance good grades, a decent social life, and a job. Guess what? We can't! Some parents want us to get jobs to teach us responsibility, what they don't know are the many responsibilities we face each day. It is understandable that we as teens are encouraged to be responsible. The fact remains that we must be responsible to survive. The fault here is the fact that we don't need added pressure to being a teenager. It is already hard enough.

Not every teenager needs a job to teach them responsibility. Each new day, we face pressures to drink, smoke, steal, cheat, lie, and be the best at everything. With every decision we make, we consider the outcomes. We aren't stupid, but we do need help. The help we need is to feel support from our elders, not added pressures. We are aware of the lives ahead of us, the real world, and the importance of responsibility.

Emma Fredrick, Grade 10
Greenwood High School, KY

A Life Changing Event

Hello, my name is Casey Calcagno. I am going to tell you a story about an event in that changed my life. Hurricane Katrina happened in August 2005 and destroyed New Orleans. Of course nobody was happy or excited about all the damage it caused but there was some good things that came out of it. There were plenty of New Orleans schools damaged by this storm. I attend St. Charles Catholic which is located in La Place, Louisiana. My school took in about 200 students from the storm. Everybody at St. Charles was nervous and angry about all these students coming to our school. We thought it would change everything in fact it did. Lots of people made plenty of new friends and some enemies. My friends and I thought this would be a bad thing since all these girls were coming from all girls' schools. We thought they would act bossy and preppy but we were wrong. They ended up being the nicest people we've ever met. I met my best friend because of this experience and I am glad about it. I am not happy about the storm destroying everything but I am thankful that it brought me my best friend.

Casey Calcagno, Grade 10
St Charles Catholic High School, LA

No Words to Say

I remember the giggles and screams of excitement as the boys chased the girls through the halls of the church. The ladies' room was always a great escape, the one place the boys wouldn't dare to follow. I was the ringleader of the girls, fast and mischievous. He led the boys, just as rambunctious as me.

We reigned as king and queen of the mountain. We were the heart of the sexiest rivalry and our little crush just added fuel to the flames. Not overly anxious to sit quietly in the service, we preferred the naughty things children do when parents aren't looking. Ours was a time of naivety.

One day, my parents sat me down on the couch. The king of the mountain was in the hospital.

Day one, nothing sank in. Day two was spent in the private lounge outside the ER praying, surrounded by old men with beards and Bibles. Day three was convincing myself he wouldn't die. Day four found me by his side, staring at his unconscious form in the dim light.

Our mothers stood behind me.

"You can talk to him if you want. The doctors say he might be able to hear you."

His lips were black and his head was bandaged, his bed looking uninviting and the many machines humming softly. I took a step closer, whispering the only thing I could.

"What is there to say?"

Day six, I said a prayer he hadn't heard me before he died.

Heidi Newman, Grade 12
Germantown High School, TN

My Lover

Standing in front of hundreds, the lights illuminating every inch of my skin, hiding nothing; sharing with the world the most raw emotions, releasing words and feelings withheld for so long, I perform. Theatre is the all-consuming lover of my life. It is a greedy lover, yet highly satisfying and rewarding. It takes me to a world far away from the hustle of every day to a world that is new, fresh and ready to be experienced.

Theatre is my therapist. Taking on another character, fully experiencing things anew as someone else, I am able to relinquish my fears, my thoughts and my worries. I am given a second chance as someone else, fully able to live through raw emotions for the first time in someone else's point of view, learning and growing with that person. In doing so, I am able to give my personal emotional being a reprieve, letting it wait until I return refreshed and more learned, ready to confront it with newfound determination.

I am able to receive credit and glory for having taken a piece of myself and releasing it. That is the most glorious feeling anyone could ever imagine. Not the feeling received from the cheers, screaming and clapping, but the feeling of having untied an emotional knot that had been tied and tightened for so long. Theatre is a cliché part of me. It is my passion, my fire, my lifestyle, my best friend, my elixir of life; theatre is my lover.

Corey Thompson, Grade 12
Newnan High School, GA

There Is Entertainment Tonight

"There's Mammy – get her!" I ran after my grandmother with my water gun. It was the annual summer barbecue at Mammy and Grampy's house and this was the yearly water gun fight. My cousins and I wore bathing suits, and Mammy wore a black trash bag over her clothes with a neck hole and arm holes. Mammy soaked us, just like we drenched her. Whenever my sisters and I are with our mammy we have many moments of laughter and excitement. I believe that having a fun relationship with my grandmother helps to build love between us.

I love to spend time with my grandmother. My sisters and I play a variety of games with her. Scrabble is our favorite game to play because we made up our own rules. When we play our version of Scrabble we are up past one o'clock in the morning laughing and talking. Laughing together makes it so that we hardly get angry at each other. If there is a disagreement we simply think about how much we enjoy each others company and do not even argue.

The fun I have at the barbecues are memories that I will always have to remember how much fun my grandmother is. When we play games together we talk and grow even closer than we already are. Laughing and spending time with my grandmother is so important to me. We have fun and demonstrate our love for each other by laughing and doing activities together.

Rachel Ricciardelli, Grade 12
Hopewell High School, NC

Drugs in the Teen World

Drugs and teenage drug use is the increasing problem among teenagers in today's high schools. Most drug use begins in the preteen and teenage years. During these years, adolescents are faced with difficult tasks of discovering their self identity.

One of the most important reasons of teenage drug usage is peer pressure. Peer pressure represents social influences that affect adolescents; it can have a positive or negative effect, depending on a person's social group. We are greatly influenced by the people around us. In today's schools, drugs are very common and peer pressure usually is the reason for their usage. If the people in your social group use drugs, there will be pressure. Teenagers might try drugs just to fit in the social norms; even if a person had no intentions of using drugs, one might do it just to be considered "cool" by his friends. Unfortunately, today drugs are considered to be an acceptable social phenomenon by many teenagers.

Here is a personal example of drug use from a teenager. "When I started using, it was only on weekends, at parties. I used drugs "recreationally" and therefore thought I had no addiction problem. I used drugs like marijuana to fit socially. I had problems in my life, emotionally, that drugs only seemed to solve. Drugs made my problems worse. I almost died!"

In today's society, drugs are around teenagers at all times. They fill our schools, neighborhoods, etc. It is our responsibility to know what's right from wrong!

Khalyn Jones, Grade 10
Grady High School, GA

The Music Man

Music is the key that impacts the souls of those who are lucky enough to osculate it. Yet not many people get to enjoy this impervious force. So I would have to say that the man who brought this to my life in a magnified glass is the one who has impacted my life the most.

Mr. Vincent Raymond Parrulli, is the one person I know that I can trust with anything. He helps me in so many ways that it would seem that his heart is bigger than this Earth. He had made me the music lover I am today. He is the "father-figure" to me as he makes me laugh when I feel I am no good at my instrument or just in general.

The way he will cry in front of his whole class, trying to show us that music can really mean something, and that it isn't just notes on paper. It's a feeling; a meaning, and playing it differently makes it completely a different piece.

He is the man that placed the mallets in my hand and helped me make the sound that pulls your heart out from any rock it may be hiding under. He may just be a teacher, but there is something that makes him different from the others. Just talking to him, you know that he cares. Just by the way he will tell you that everything is going to be okay.

He's one man that I will never forget; *Ever.*

Amy Little, Grade 11
Countryside High School, FL

Scary Saturday Socials

Every weekend is an adventure with my friends. Though, they always start out the same. Friday is usually football games, Saturday is movie day, and Sunday is whatever we want. Personally, my favorite day has to be Saturday. Not only is it the one day of the week you can sleep late and stay up late, but with my friends it's movie day.

Movie day consists of all my friends arriving at my house and picking a movie. Of course, there is usual eating of teenage junk food. There is candy, pizza, chips, and just about everything else that can destroy your arteries. When you get a group of people together, there is bound to be a discrepancy over the topic. The movie always comes down to a comedy or a horror film. Considering that we have more guys than girls in our group, we continually watch horror films. You might think "Why don't the girls just overrule the boys?" It may sound crazy, but us girls actually like scary movies. Maybe it's the adrenaline rush you get, when the main character's in a life threatening situation. Could it be the way your heart pumps so fast you think it could explode? Perhaps it is the thickening plot twists. Or could it be the simple fact that we like being scared? Either way, it's what I look forward to all week at school. My Saturday social is the light at the end of a homework tunnel.

Tara Lewis, Grade 11
Germantown High School, TN

True Friends

What are friends? Better yet, what is a true friend? A true friend is somebody that you know will always be there for you no matter what. They will stick up for you in a heartbeat before they even realize they're doing it. Sometimes even when they know you were wrong. But they will also let you fight your own battles.

Having somebody who you know will always be there for you is a great thing to have. But is also sometimes a hard thing to find. Some friends say they will be there for you when you need them, but then when it comes down to it, they're never there when you need them. But when you find a friend that is always there, then that's when you know you have found a "true friend."

Being a "true friend" is sticking up for your friend when the rest won't. Trust me, those kinds of friends truly are hard to find because a lot of friends don't want to start a conflict. But a "true friend" won't care because they don't like hearing their friend being talked about.

But then again they will let you fight your own battles. Because they know that one day, they might not be there, and you have to know how to stick up for yourself.

So basically if you have a true friend, don't take advantage of them because you might not be blessed with another one.

Carrie Tyrkala, Grade 11
Southside High School, NC

Music: God's Gift to Mankind

The pitter-patter of rain on a window, the bluebird's marvelous song; these are some of the melodic sounds of nature with which God blessed his creatures. He gave us this blessing through which an individual can liberate feelings of affection or ecstasy, anguish or bliss whenever needed. But what is this God-given gift to mankind that aids the human race in many ways? This endowment is music, given to humans at the very establishment of time, and developed in innumerable ways throughout the ages.

Music was given to man as a gift, but some have abused that gift. Music was given for the sole purpose of bringing glory to God, but being an excellent singer or playing an instrument exceptionally well has become a way to gain personal affluence and admiration, instead of the pure form of worship it was intended to be. When an individual sings the words of a song or taps out a rhythm, does he think about what it communicates? Is the message one that focuses on his Creator, or rather is it a message bringing attention to personal grief or contentment?

Most people enjoy listening to music, including myself. I also take pleasure in performing with my voice and the piano and flute. But the next time I hear the melodious song of bluebirds, I will remember the God who formed that bluebird, the same God who shaped me in my mother's womb, and who created the beautiful sounds of music.

Danielle Henderson, Grade 10
Blue Ridge Christian School, MO

Facing Fear

The fear of going through surgery is great, but the fear of losing one's dream is even greater. This is an experience I have to face this week as the operation on my thyroid approaches. I have a dream to sing. It is my calling, the one thing I am passionate about. Unfortunately, my vocal cords are next to my thyroid. I could lose everything in just one slip of the doctor's hand.

Having faith that I will make it through surgery with my vocal cords still intact is extremely difficult. Terror washes over me every time I imagine myself being unable to carry a tune, hold a note, or sing my favorite songs. However, I have hope. Until something ends, there is always hope that things will turn out differently. As Jack Canfield states: "You have to believe it's possible and believe in yourself. Because after you've decided what you want, you have to believe it's possible, and possible for you, not just for other people." Along with faith and hope, I must have courage going into this ordeal. Aristotle says, "You will never do anything in this world without courage. It is the greatest quality of the mind next to honor."

Facing the loss of a dream is a horrible feeling. You always obsess and worry about it until the event occurs. However, the joy of waking up at the end is the best thing I will ever experience.

Leah Moore, Grade 11
Harvester Christian Academy, GA

The History of Pepsi-Cola

The year was 1893 and Caleb D. Bradham, a young pharmacist, had begun experimenting with different soda or "soft" drinks. Bradham had a drug store soda fountain in New Bern, North Carolina. On August 28,1898, "Brad's Drink," on of Bradham's formulas, was renamed "Pepsi-Cola." The drink became so popular in 1902 that Caleb had to devote all of his time and energy to making Pepsi-Cola. The first advertisements for Pepsi-Cola appeared in a local. The growing of the company meant that "Doc" Bradham needed a bigger building to produce his product. The new building, known as the "Bishop Factory," cost the "Doc" $5,000.

In 1934 Pepsi became a big hit by selling a 12 oz. soda for five cents. Other competitors, such as Coca-Cola, were selling their 6 oz. beverages for five cents. Pepsi was one of the few companies able to survive the Great Depression. Pepsi-Cola begins to expand by merging with Frito-Lay in 1965. In the '70's, Purchase, NY becomes the headquarters and Pepsi becomes the single largest sold soft drink in America.

Pepsi is the first to introduce beverage bottles containing recycled plastic into the marketplace in the early '90's. This is the first time recycled plastic is used in direct contact with food packaging. In the mid '90's Pepsi-Cola profits surpasses 1 billion dollars. In 1998 Pepsi celebrates its 100 year anniversary. Pepsi, in 2002, became the official sponsor of the National Football League.

Matthew Gallagher, Grade 11
Vero Beach High School, FL

Careers

I have thought long and hard about what I want to be when I am done with college. Mostly throughout my life I have wanted to be a lawyer. Besides the years that I wanted to be an astronaut, being a lawyer only seemed to fit me. I've always been skillful at debate in my classes. I am fascinated with the court room and trying to convince the jury that my client is innocent. Being a lawyer means a great deal more than just winning my cases. I want to be able to say that I won "fair and square," not because I lied and cheated. I also want to have the clean conscious and know that I put the right person in prison. I know that most people become lawyers and say they are not going to be the lying and shady lawyers, but I know I couldn't live with myself if I was dishonest like that. I hope that when I'm a lawyer people will want me because they can trust me and they know that I will work my hardest to make sure that they are given their rights as a person. Becoming a lawyer will take an immense amount of work, but I'm willing to take the time and energy to be a well trained attorney.

Braelyn Mitchem, Grade 11
Owasso High School, OK

The Big Bang

As I pressed the gas and began my flight backwards, my car slammed to a sudden stop. After smacking into the unforgiving object, all I could feel was shock and disbelief. As I sat there unable to breathe, all I could think of was my parents' reaction. My friend who was accompanying me rushed out of the car to inspect the damage. Upon reaching the back of my car she screamed, "Wow, you may not want to come back here!" My life as I knew it was over.

The fact that this was my first accident was horrific enough, but that I rammed into the concession stand in the school parking lot made it even worse. Just as I gathered enough nerve to look at the damage, the baseball team drove through the parking lot. I couldn't believe my luck; I wanted to get the attention of some of the older players, but definitely not this way. My hopes of getting a date with one of them flew right out the window. This was every girl's nightmare.

When I got home the only solution I could think of was to cry. Instead of being mad, My mom just laughed at how pitiful I was. My dad was able to get my jeep fixed in a body shop owned by a family friend so that I would not have to file a claim. As far as the insurance company knows, I am still a perfect teen driver!

Nicole Crihfield, Grade 12
Germantown High School, TN

Family Time

My essay is about family and how we care for each other. As time goes on it seems each generation is becoming more independent earlier and earlier, families are drifting farther apart, and suddenly quality family time is no longer a priority.

I am one of four children in which the ages range from six to eighteen. My father is a forty-three year old combat disabled military veteran and is unable to work or do much, while my mom is thirty-five, she has a very good career that she is still excelling in. Since my father is disabled and my mother is often working the kids, many times, are left to help each other out. Although we do argue and fight sometimes, we love each other more than anything. We are always there to help out whenever we may need assistance or even if we just need someone to talk to. Even though my mom is often busy she probably gives the best advice I have ever heard. Everything I am going through or have been through she can relate to it and can understand my point of view and where I am coming from on various topics, which helps me through a lot.

In conclusion, many families are not very close anymore and they just don't have time for each other anymore. Even though it is often hard to set time aside just to talk or simply ask how the other persons day has been it can make a difference.

Samantha Howard, Grade 12
Walker Valley High School, TN

How Do You Measure a Year?

As I approach the end of my senior year, one question keeps echoing in my head: "How do you measure a year?" Every year I measure differently. I have measured this final year of adolescence by growth, character, and change.

This year has presented more difficult circumstances than I have ever faced in my life. I am eternally grateful for every tear, every scream, every laugh, and every little pain that got me to where I stand today.

I often ask myself, "What is it that defines me?" I am one who will stand up for what I believe in, and sit down when I need someone to believe in me. I am a realist, seeing things as they are, but also a romantic, searching for the hidden meaning within.

I always feared change. I now know that change is the perfect medicine for a lost soul. It molded my hopes and dreams and altered my actions. It prepared me to embark on this amazing adventure. Now I look at change with excitement.

As this year comes to a close, I realize that it has prepared me for what lies ahead. I had to undergo change and growth to find myself. I am so grateful for the opportunity. I am ready to embark on this new grand adventure called adulthood. Instead of cowering in a corner I stand tall in the open. I have grown. I have found myself. I have changed. This is how I measure my year.

Karrie Kelley, Grade 12
Madison Academy, AL

John Grisham

John Grisham is my favorite writer. He is known for writing many bestsellers. Most of his books are now major motion pictures such as "The Pelican Brief," starring Julia Roberts and Denzel Washington, and "The Client" starring Susan Sarandon and Tommy Lee Jones.

His novels are mainly about law seeing as before he was known as a writer he was practicing law for nearly a decade in a small Southaven Mississippi law practice, in which he specialized in criminal defense and personal injury litigation. Also he has written a book dealing with football because in high school he was a Quarterback for the football team; they also have to do with people on the run from the law. He has written 20 novels, I have only read 18 of them.

I love reading Grisham's novels because of his style in writing; his way of writing draws you in, making you want to read more. The way he writes makes you feel like you are there. Like in the novel "Bleachers" the words he uses makes you feel like you are there watching the football game. Out of all the books I have read my favorite book is "The Runaway Jury" it was the first novel I ever read; this book gave me a passion for reading. Out of all the movies that I have seen, "The Client" is still my all-time favorite. I'm still waiting to read his latest novels "The Innocent Man" and "Playing For Pizza."

Natalie Rodriguez, Grade 10
Deltona High School, FL

Riding in Style

The modern American road is a symphony of different vehicles, whether they be Mini-Coops to the Accord to the Hummer. The roads in this great nation were once ruled by those that wanted to get somewhere, ones who wanted style, ones who wanted speed and others, just good gas mileage.

But today things are radically different. With new tax laws giving SUV owners tax refunds and breaks for their vehicles of choice, the new style is size. This new trend towards larger, pointless SUVs that pose a real danger to those who do not have size on their side.

This era, in which gas is at a premium, gas guzzlers like the Ford Excursion and others like it, which get 15-20 MPG, do not help in our dependence on oil from other nations to survive in this modern world.

Many an SUV owner cites safety as their reason for owning a civilian version of a battle tank, they say that their vehicle of choice has saved their own lives as well as their families'. It does not help when one of these monsters gets mishandled and runs over another car that it shares the road with.

To that, the question that begs to be asked is at what cost? At what cost does the modern American drive around city streets? At what cost do we drive long and lonesome country roads? At what cost is this style, this trend, this murder?

When does it end?

Alex Petersen, Grade 12
Rock Bridge Sr High School, MO

Friendship

Friendship has been a declaration that we, as people, have incorporated into our speech since the word has been first used. According to Webster, friendship is "a relationship with someone you know, trust, and like." An individual who sympathizes with you and supports you is considered a friend. To me, friendship is so much more than that.

True friendship is where both people neither give or take more than they should; there is a mutual balance. Friendship shows through all actions and speech. You go out of your way to make sure your friend is feeling okay when you notice even the slightest change in their demeanor. You know that your friend will always be there for you, even when it isn't convenient for them.

The time spent together isn't a hassle, or a chore one must complete in order to achieve happiness. For both people, there are merits. You enjoy the peace between each other, knowing you can act like yourself. There are no walls between you, no secrets.

Friendship is both a necessity to life but also a luxury. Knowing you have friends that accept you for who you are and still put up with you, is one of the many goals people wish to achieve.

Jessica Cespedes, Grade 11
Bishop Verot High School, FL

Friend

What makes a friend? From person to person this definition differs, but more often than not this is more than just a definition. For the average person a friend is one who they are able to confide in. Truly finding trust in a person is something that many people go through life without finding.

A number of people underestimate the value of a friend because they have never been without them. How does one go about finding appreciation for a friend without losing that friend? Usually this comes from an event of importance that a friend guided or supported a person through. Many people go through life at this point without experiencing anything that testing. When that time comes when the world shows itself for what it is and not what the person believed it to be, then the value of a friend can be found. This usually comes at one time and not gradually due to the person's ignorance of the events around them.

When the farces of personalities fail to support them, they learn who they should surround themselves with and the type of people they would rather associate with. But sometimes through small hardships or through the experiences of others around them, people develop an innate sense of what makes a good person. Sometimes though you may know what makes a good person and can accept the others around you but those cannot see what makes you a good person. A friend waits for that revelation.

Andrew Corbett, Grade 11
Bishop Verot High School, FL

Passion for Dancing

Sixth grade was a major turning point in my life. It was the exact year I decided to try out for the school dance team. I was shocked during the first day of tryouts. This was not the kind of dancing I expected we would be doing. The music was entirely too fast and the choreography was extremely difficult. The veteran dancers picked up on the moves instantly, while the inexperienced dancers stood around looking more lost than ever. I remember standing there silently and wanting, more than anything to run out of the gymnasium and go home to my parents. When the day finally ended, I rushed to grab my bags and bolted out of the gym.

The next day, at tryouts, I had finally caught the gist of what was happening. I guess practicing for six hours the night before helped a great deal. While many of the other girls were lost and confused, I knew exactly what I was doing. I had begun to get a little optimistic about the final day of tryouts. When that day had finally arrived, I almost cheered. As I walked into the judging room, I took a deep breath and exhaled. There was no need to worry myself. What I remember after that is a blur. The one thing I do remember is the list of who made it. Fortunately for me, I had made it! This would be the beginning of a very long, dancing journey for me.

Courtney Miller, Grade 10
Germantown High School, TN

The Tsunami That Ruined Asia

Tsunami is a very long wave of seismic origin that is caused by a submarine or coastal earthquake, landslide or even by a volcanic corruption. These types of waves have hundreds of miles length and a period of the order of a quarter of an hour. In Japanese the word means a harbor wave.

On December 26, 2004 in South East Asia, the earth's crust had been shifted ever so slightly, resulting in an unforgettable devastation to all humankind living there. Relatively in a small movement, the earth's crust accumulated a huge amount of energy and manifested itself as a mega thrust earthquake above the seabed. This was a largest ocean earthquake with huge water wave, which generated a Tsunami.

This is the fourth largest in the world since the year 1990. Tsunami waves are able to travel far — even touching the western coasts of North and South America within minutes, hours and days. Then later the world stood by watching disaster of unforgettable proportions unfold. The media was filled with information on the number of deaths, aid effort and long-term implications of the events that took place shortly before, during, and after the onslaught of the killer waves in order to understand the significance of the Tsunami, as well as a discussion of the science behind the disaster, places and the aftermath.

Thamoda Rodrigo, Grade 11
Little Rock Central High School, AR

Individuality

Individuality is a very important feature in the lives of people around the world. Being yourself around people help to make better friends, a better reputation among your peers and a better feeling about yourself. These features will make you a better person all around.

Being and individual will help to make better friends because they are making friends with "you" not someone you're pretending to be. By you being yourself you find that you have much more in common with your friends.

You will have a better reputation among your peers when you act as yourself and not someone you think people want you to be. When you act like someone your not it is like lying to everyone you're around. Your friends may not be able to trust you because you do not always act or say the same things that you may around other people.

The way you feel about yourself will be more satisfying because you do not have to constantly change how you act around different people. You will also get gratification from knowing that you're not lying to anyone.

By being yourself you will be a happier person and lead a better social life. You will have friends who you will have many things in common with. You will not have to worry about being caught in a lie. This will make your life easier and have you worry about how you're supposed to act easier.

Steven Bippus, Grade 11
Owasso High School, OK

Listen Up Freshmen

Rising freshmen, I'm sure you have heard about how high school will be. I remember hearing about how much better it is than middle school. Television, however, shows that it's scary, but don't worry, it's not.

Sure, there are the popular kids, the mean girls, the nerds, and so on, but that's not the only kind of people here. Most of my friends and I have no idea what clique we'd be in. We're smart, but not nerdy; well-known, but not because of a bad reputation. Get my point?

Television also shows how freshmen get beaten up all the time in high school. Honestly I haven't seen that many fights since I started here over a year ago. Yeah, there are those typical fights when people talk bad about each other, but it's never over little things like bumping into someone in the hall. And whoever started telling people that you'll get thrown into trash cans was just trying to scare you. I don't think anyone at my school has been thrown into a trash can, ever.

As you can see there are a lot of things wrong with TV and how it portrays high school. These are some of the best years of your life, and if you do the right things you won't have to worry about making friends, getting in fights, or failing classes. Keep this in mind and you'll do fine, I promise.

Allison Leonard, Grade 10
Louisburg High School, NC

The Skateboard

The most influential object I have ever picked up would have to be my skateboard. My skateboard has always pushed me to do my best and to not cease until my best is accomplished. A skateboard will punish you when you are not striving for perfection, through falling, and will make you rejoice when you have succeeded your goal.

My skateboard is something that I treasure, not only because of the value that it holds, but the memories it has created. Through my skateboard I have met new people, gone new places, and learned many lessons. Once you become a skateboarder it will open your eyes in a way you have never seen before. A person may see a set of stairs or a curb on a sidewalk simply as they are, but a skateboarder looks beyond its physical aspects and sees what can be created through it. The skateboarder will see himself being thrown down the stair set to accomplish his goal of landing a trick. A skateboarder, once he has overcome the fear of falling, will try anything just to accomplish his own personal goal of achieving greatness.

My skateboard has changed my entire life. It has changed the way I look at the world and skateboarding will always be in my life simply because of the love I have towards it. These are some of the reasons why a skateboard is the most influential object I have ever picked up.

Jonathon Cheek, Grade 11
Trinity Christian Academy, AL

Crew

Crew, a water sport that has been around for centuries, but it is not only a way to keep in shape, it's an art form and it's a lifestyle. Rowing is a sport of perfection. The single is the loneliest boat, with only one person and two oars. Singles are challenging to keep balanced, but once that skill is mastered you can start racing.

Racing is the most exciting part of rowing; sprint season has a race length of 1,500 meters, that's about 200 strokes and around seven minutes of rowing. Sprint races are fast and painful, and over as quickly as they begin.

Poised and ready to start, waiting, "Ready, ROW!" Your muscles clench, you start to drive down the slide, stroke by stroke you power down the course. Looking left, there is a boat waiting, just waiting for you to mess up so they can take your gold. Focus, now only 200 meters left, it's time to sprint. Pulling faster, you have no limits, but all you can think is "Hey legs, move faster!" Now less than 50 meters to go, bubbles rushing under your boat, water splashing, and crowds cheering. That was the last stroke, you stop rowing with only enough energy to acknowledge the signal of a race ended.

Crew is a sport for only the toughest of people. This required inner strength can be gained just as physical strength can, and in crew mental strength is 80% of your power.

Katie Brennan, Grade 10
Stanton College Preparatory School, FL

Image

An image is the general or public perception of a person, company or public figure. It can be perceived by careful calculation aimed at creating widespread goodwill or opinion. Your image can, as some people use the phrase, "it can make you or break you." Since I have the desire to portray myself as an intellectual young man, and would be seeking a career in the criminal justice field, it would be difficult to convince someone I was serious, if I choose to express myself by keeping up the fad or norm of some youth in my age bracket.

I have chosen to venture away from the media influence of stereotyping youth who express their selves in the choice of hairstyles, clothing and body jewelry. My choice to be a positive influence was made from my awareness of my younger cousin trying to mimic my actions. There are several people in my life that have demonstrated the importance of dress, good behavior and self-esteem which will aid in my future development.

I understand the importance of staying focused on my goals and dreams. I can accomplish this by associating with people with similar goals and aspirations. Peers with the same goals can help develop a positive and productive image. A positive image is not necessarily captured in one's dress alone, but also in how one articulates in speech and action.

Terrance Washington, Grade 12
North Miami Sr High School, FL

Shake Hands and Be Friendly

"Shake hands and be friendly," is written on a headstone for a man by the name of Orange Lee Rodgers. I knew him as Brother Orange. He was that elderly, African American in my life.

Orange Rodgers went to church with me and we had a bond. A musical bond is what we had. Orange loved to sing. He sang all the time. I miss hearing him sing. Especially the song titled, "Amazing Grace."

At the beginning of December, on a Thursday, I was told by my mother that Orange had died that morning. I didn't want and, to this day, still don't want to believe that he was dead. I know he is but I refuse to believe it. I never cry at funerals. Recently my great aunt passed away. I didn't shed one tear. I cried at Orange's funeral because I was extremely close to him.

I'm going to tell you a memory of Orange I will forever hold dear to me. I was singing a Christmas carol one Sunday and he said, "Garrett, you're going be like everyone else, swearing in every song."

I responded, "No way brother. That is never going to happen and I promise you that."

As I end my essay I leave with this: to this day I have kept my promise. I miss Orange more than anything. When I'm discouraged I still turn to him. Every day I repeat his words. "Shake hands and be friendly."

Garrett McCorkle, Grade 11
Smith-Cotton High School, MO

Photograph

My mother would always tell me what a harsh man he was, but I could never believe her. I only had one picture of my Grandpa. I look at it for hours just thinking what it would be like if he was still here. The picture was of us. I cherished it, it was my gold, to me precious and priceless I would never let it go. He stood straight with his shoulders back like a good soldier. He would have been retired a few years from the Army in this particular photograph, but still he look as if he was wearing his uniform. His white thick hair was mounted onto his head no wind could blow it. His expressionless face glared into the soul. He wore green plaid shorts and a white shirt. He tucked it in and a belt to hold up his shorts. I rested on his hip one hand over his shoulder, the other around his neck. I couldn't have been older than a year. He would bounce me on his hip repeating "Up and down to and fro," over and over. Most kids have living Grandpa's but I don't. I am one of the few who remember very little about their Grandpa. Sometimes people feel incomplete because they didn't have a chance to know their Grandpa. All I need is that photograph and that one memory in my life where it was just me and him.

Samantha Delzell, Grade 12
Hopewell High School, NC

Embracing Individuality

Throughout everyone's lifetime, people claim distinct personalities. Although many people fail to embrace their individuality, I do. Amazingly, I have been fortunate enough to possess qualities of friendliness, perseverance, and uniqueness.

Naturally, I am an individualistic person with many friendly aspects. This simply implies that my ability to relate to and understand others has made me distinct. My sense of humor has helped me to not only meet people but also make lifetime friends. Lastly, I have been complimented on my million-dollar smile. I live all my days to the fullest, so my motto is why not smile?

With great appreciation, I have been granted the gift of perseverance. At a young age, it was instilled inside of me that I am destined for greatness! Therefore, I have a strong will and belief that I will succeed. Also, along this life's journey, I have the gift of wisdom to help carry me. With this gift, I have only high expectations for myself, friends, and family.

My overall characteristic, which will never be duplicated, is that I am uniquely different. I have an open heart that enables me to love all, understand most, and relate to others. Thus, I am well-rounded and open-minded. Moreover, I have the distinctness to shine from the inside out, enhancing my natural beauty.

In conclusion, my qualities of friendliness help me through the day. My attitude of perseverance helps make things happen. But most of all these qualities have made me uniquely different and irreplaceable.

Kenyatta Henderson, Grade 11
LeFlore Preparatory Academy, AL

I Love

I love everything that is nature, sweet, or anything that makes me feel happy and good on the inside.

I love the way the sun feels when it first touches my skin in the morning. I love to look at an acorn and know that it will one day stand taller than my house. I love how it is so silent outside on a cold winter night. I also love the sound of rain hitting my window as I fall asleep. I love how no one fears the wind, even though they can't see it.

I love the feeling I get when chocolate melts in my mouth. Or how Twizzlers never get old. I love it when I taste something I've never tasted before. I love the smell of fresh peaches being rinsed off. I also love when my mom makes pancakes, and she puts a slice of butter in the middle. I love watching it melt in the center of that pancake.

I love my family and how they will do anything to make me happy. I love it when my brother knows when I am sad and he comes in my room to give me a give hug.

Tasha Talley, Grade 12
Newnan High School, GA

The Ultimate Role Model

What makes a role model? Who is worthy to be looked up to for guidance? A real role model always thinks of those who are watching and learning from them before anything else. They have their audience's best interest at heart. The ultimate role model is a caring teacher.

If one would look around a school, one would find some of the world's best role models; however, to be a teacher, one doesn't have to have a degree in education. Moms and dads and grandparents are teachers. Friends and even strangers can be teachers. To be a teacher, all one needs is an audience to listen, but to be a worthy role model, one has to want to teach for the right reasons. A worthy role model teaches to enlighten and to give joy.

John Steinbeck said, "Teaching might even be the greatest of the arts since the medium is the human mind and spirit." He understood the gratification of teaching. When we look back at our childhoods, we will not remember looking up to the man who created steel or who lowered taxes in the 1970s. We will remember the second grade teacher who sparked our interest in reading the perfect book about dragons. We will remember "Papa" teaching us to fish using string and hot-dog pieces. We will remember the true role models of our lives and hope that we will someday have a chance to equally impact a student.

Paige Bolduc, Grade 11
Logan-Rogersville High School, MO

Deciding Your Future: It's Tough

Have you decided where you're going to school yet? As a junior I believe that I've been asked that more over the past few months than at any other point in my life. I don't know about any other high school students, but now that I must seriously try to answer that question, life seems much more complicated.

Before, college was a thing of the future. Now my world revolves around the words "college applications." Any time I receive a grade or participate in an activity my first thought is, how it will appear to prospective admissions boards. Suddenly I've begun to realize that in approximately a year my life, up to this point, will be being scrutinized, the way a prospective buyer looks at a house. That's a scary thought!

There are many other decisions and changes that go along with graduating high school and beginning college. For most people it will be their first time living on their own. No longer will your parents be there to do the laundry and tell you when to study. You have to start making decisions for yourself and that can be a frightening step.

Another forbidding undertaking for many students is choosing a profession. It's nothing to take lightly and I sometimes wonder if I'm actually mature enough to make that decision. What the future holds is a mystery, but I believe if you work hard it will be something to look forward to.

Allison Hedge, Grade 11
Camden Central High School, TN

My Sunshine

The love of a mother is one that no other love can compare to. It will not break. It only grows stronger within time. Regardless of what happens, there will always be that helping hand and the shoulder to cry on.

My mom is my best friend. And my backbone. The bond we have shared is unlike anything I've ever had. I admire every characteristic about her.

Her personality and smile lights up a room. The strength she has though, is what sticks out the most.

When she was fourteen, her father was found murdered. The pain she felt is unfathomable in my mind. Every day she has to deal with the constant pain and heartache of not having her dad.

Not until recently have I truly understood the anguish she has felt in the past thirty years of her life. The man who was an accessory to the murder of her father, will be getting out of prison in a matter of months.

With everything that's going on in my mother's life, she is still there for me day in and day out. Whenever. Wherever.

She has created a life for me that she didn't have. She has put everything into making my brothers life, and mine, the best it can be.

She is my sunshine. My best friend, and the person I look up to most.

Chelsea Kuhlman, Grade 10
Countryside High School, FL

What I Learned in Life

Life is a lesson that has to be learned, and it is being taught to us daily. It's up to us to decide whether we want to take heed and learn the lesson, or try and make it on our own. I am 17 years of age and there have been some situations in my life that I have learned from, and there have also been situations where I failed to pay attention to the lesson. I have lost a brother and 5 friends as victims to violence but still I fail to learn the lesson. I say this because I'm still conflicted with violence around me; I sometimes tend to act before I think. I am not the only guilty one of this action but realizing creates better understanding. Now I understand that by helping prevent violence, I can help create world peace. I have gained from my mother. She taught me first and foremost to love and respect myself. As a child I used to say "yes ma'am," not knowing what I was agreeing to, but as I grew, I learned that when mama said "respect yourself" she meant positively present myself to the world. And when mama said to "love yourself" she meant I can't learn to love anything or anyone else if I don't love myself. With these lessons I am promised to make it, with my head held high looking over temptations, fears, and set backs in my life.

Keya Rogers, Grade 12
Grandview Alternative School, MO

Band in Everyday Life

As an active band member at our high school, I have discovered many great life lessons are learned. Most often there is only one day in a week that I don't have band practice or a competition. It is a lot of hard work but there are many rewards that come with all the work and effort. The most noticeable reward is doing well at competitions. One of the best moments I have of band was when our high school made Grand National finals for the first time. It was a once-in-a-lifetime moment that made all the hard work worth while. Winning competitions is great, but I think band has most of its influence on us after high school.

Band teaches us skills we need in everyday life. For instance, the fact that we practice all the time, teaches us to learn how to prioritize our time. I definitely procrastinate less during band season because I do a better job of planning ahead in my schoolwork, as to avoid become overwhelmed. Band also teaches us to work with other people. It takes a team effort to accomplish the things we need to do on the field and that makes us understand how important it is for us to work with each other. The lessons we learn from band will stay with us for the rest of our lives, making it a worthwhile contribution of our time and effort.

Morgan McCulley, Grade 11
Owasso High School, OK

American Hypocrisy

It is often said that the more things change, the more they stay the same. There is no vice president running for either party, yet the status quo will not change. Despite promises of the diversity of presidential candidates, choices seem strangely similar to previous elections. Candidates claim conservative and/or liberal views, as well as a political philosophy: if we hold one political view then we must hate the other. The need for a national reconciliation is immense, yet neither the democrats nor the republicans seem interested in providing one.

Our Founding Fathers believed that a free and independent press was vital to the success of any functioning democracy. Yet, our free and democratic press spent three weeks covering the death of Anna Nicole Smith while American soldiers continue to die in a needless war. American's must realize that eventually something has "got to give," as long as our society remains polarized and oblivious to the world, we will be vulnerable to populism. Our representatives use divisive issues like abortion to further widen the fault lines that run amongst American society, it causes us to ignore the real travesty. As Americans, we must realize that freedom is nonnegotiable, and the American government is not responsible for maintaining global hegemony. Rather, government must be committed to its citizens. There is need of genuine national dialogue on what is good for this country rather then listening to the extremist ideologues hijacking our political system.

Mike Robinson, Grade 11
Grady High School, GA

What Is Love?

What is love? According to Merriam-Webster Dictionary love is a strong affection for another arising out of kinship or personal ties. It is also described as an unselfish loyal and benevolent concern for the good of another. Love has been spoken about for centuries all over the world. Where did it come from? Are we as humans capable of loving from birth or is it something that is taught? Is love just a physical response that the body has when you are in close contact with someone for extended period of time or is it a sensation that can take over your thoughts, something so strong that it can have power over everything we do or think. Does a child recognize who or how to love? I have heard it expressed as a reaction the body has that makes you want to reproduce and all animals feel it. Is love the strongest feeling a human can experience? Does it overpower hate, vengeance, or pain? It seems that love can be different depending on who you ask. I think love is different for every person and nobody can really say what love is.

Diane Wilson, Grade 11
White Station High School, TN

Miami

We all have our favorite cities that we love and represent. To me, it's the city of Miami. "Yo amo Miami," which is Spanish for "I love Miami," since Miami is greatly populated by Hispanics. That's one thing I like about Miami, all the different cultures that live amongst it. Miami is filled with Caribbean, Central American, and South American ties, along with its Caucasian inhabitants.

Miami is also the home of many things that I like, like the phenomenal Miami Hurricanes, the blue Miami Dolphins, the blazing Miami Heat, and the grand slamming Florida Marlins. Growing up as a kid in the 1990's wasn't easy, especially where you lived. At first, my family lived in La Pequeña Habana (Little Havana); a neighborhood known for its large number of Cuban refugees. But if you head east from Little Havana, you'd hit one of the most glorious areas in Miami, South Beach.

Today, South Beach section of Miami Beach is a major entertainment destination with hundreds of nightclubs, restaurants, and oceanfront hotels. Downtown Miami is also a nice area to visit, and if you'd like a nicer experience, then walking around in the downtown area is wonderful. Looking up at the sky-high skyscrapers, seeing a lot of different faces, getting a hot dog snack with a soda at the corner. Then afterwards, getting on the metro rail, which is nice because you get a nice view of the downtown area. Later getting off and having a nice walk over to the Bayside Mall. Bayside Mall is a stellar place not only because it's an outside mall, but you can take a boat tour to famous areas around the Miami Islands (Shaq's House, Scarface Mansion, etc.). I'd keep going forever, but I hope you understand me and my point of views.

Ricardo Oliva, Grade 11
Vero Beach High School, FL

Interpreting Dreams

Dreams can be interpreted in various ways, but the exact origin of dream interpretation is a mystery to mankind. Among the first interpretations of dreams that are documented can be found in the Bible.

The further analysis of dreams occurred by the Greeks, most notably a philosopher named Aristotle. Aristotle found that dreams occurred when the body experienced disturbances, which in turn caused the senses to act up. He found that this occurrence allowed for dreams to take place, in what he called sense perception.

In the 19th century, a philosopher named Sigmund Freud had a significant impact on dream analyzing. He found that through dreams one can discover their unconscious desires and thought. Freud adopted the belief of dream symbols, finding that some symbols were universally known. But he abandoned the belief that dreams had a prophetic nature.

There are symbols in dreams that are believed to be universal, although different cultures find that the same dream my have a different interpretation. There are dream symbols which include baptisms, which depicts a rebirth of some kind, or death, which is believed to signify the death of a specific habit or a feeling of hostility towards someone.

Vanessa De La Rosa, Grade 11
Bishop Verot High School, FL

Nature's Splendor

This morning I swam through the salty sea and did not feel welcome. Realizing I have always rushed into her churning embrace with zeal; this morning I tiptoe through the foaming waves. She batters me and I haul my surfboard back to shore a little embarrassed as I cough and sputter. Her punishment is a sting; in my eyes and throat and nose. I do not complain, for I know it is deserved. I have not toiled or sacrificed for nature. I have not and she knows. The temperamental sea will take pity on me, grant me temporary peace, and a natural inexplicable happiness from her waters. I thank her with my silence and choose to leave her shore unmarked and untainted.

I lie on the warm sand and listen to the crash of her waves; I realize it is both a soothing and ominous sound. It is a reprimanding crash and reminder. I hear a thousand lives ending, destruction, explosion, and I am soothed and disturbed by its rhythms. It is the sound of an entity in existence longer and fuller in life than any being of flesh and blood. I feel ashamed and guilty in its presence. I fail to understand how the Earth can be pure and perfect while we sit flawed and speckled. I feel a reverential awe to kiss the Earth, praise the skies, drink in her beauty, and savor it on my tongue; as if it would never appear in this perfection again.

Alexa Oliveras, Grade 11
Douglas Anderson School of the Arts, FL

The Rare Sensation

It's the daydreaming that doesn't let you think about anything. It mesmerizes you with the strong, heartfelt emotion it gives you. Nothing else matters, no one else matters. It's the only thing that makes you feel like a child on Christmas morning, excited enough to try something new and be confident enough to finish.

And that's what it is; it's something new that you've never felt before. Even if there's been times you claim it, it's never been stronger than when it's true and you feel like there hasn't been anything like it. Neither friends, nor family can make the feeling go away. Because your heart knows the only person you need to stay alive, the only person making your life an exhilarating sky dive, is right there with you. Without them, you're a nervous young performer in front of millions of criticizing fans. You get out of breath, almost like asthma. It doesn't stop unless the inhaler cures you. They are the inhaler for the asthma-cursed child.

You start doing crazy things. Like a hip-hop artist who loves gardening, or a shy student playing the main role in a high school play. Those things tell you how much the person affects your life and what goes on in it.

It's love, and it's the most beautiful sensation in the world that, unfortunately, not many people in this world will get to experience.

Francisco Alonso, Grade 11
Miami Killian Sr High School, FL

A Second September 11th?

During the summer of 2007, a steam pipe exploded in Manhattan. Witnesses to the explosion had no idea what had happened. Many feared it was another terrorist attack. The news reported that women took off their shoes and dropped their purses so they could get to safety more quickly. Employees in the buildings that surrounded the explosion said the chaos was the same as the tragedy of the World Trade Centers.

Twenty-five were injured, including several firemen and police officers. One woman died due to cardiac arrest. Two of the twenty-five injured arrived at a hospital in critical condition. While the emergency response teams cleaned up the scene, concerns arose that there could be asbestos in the air. So victims of the explosion may have been exposed to the toxin, therefore causing future health problems. Many of the main subway lines were closed for days because of the concern of asbestos contamination.

The pipe explosion left a huge crater in the middle of Lexington Avenue, and a truck lay in the middle of the crater. City officials closed several city blocks for further investigation of asbestos in the air. They later reported that the air was clear of the toxin and the victims exposed should not have any long-term side effects. It is clear from the reaction of the New Yorkers that the terror of September 11th continues to haunt them today.

Erica Graham, Grade 11
Owasso High School, OK

Hunting

I enjoy hunting. I have been going hunting ever since I was about two months old. Hunting is when most of my father-daughter time is spent.

Hunting season usually opens the second week in October, unless you go bow-hunting or black powder hunting. Bow-hunting and black powder season starts earlier than rifle season.

My dad and I deer hunt. We hunt the deer with dogs. When you hunt with dogs you are running the deer to you with the dogs chasing the deer. We hunt with at least five or more people, but no more than ten. We hunt like this because if you hunt with less than five people it is hard to keep track of the dogs and if you hunt with more than ten people it is crowded.

If you do not hunt with dogs and you sit in a tree stand, tripod, ground blind or in your truck, you are still hunting. After we finish dog hunting, the remainder of my day is spent sitting in a tree stand or a tripod until it gets dark outside.

I enjoy hunting a great deal and during hunting season I am never home. I love hunting. It is something I will continue to do throughout the remainder of my life.

Ashton Hathaway, Grade 11
Southside High School, NC

Living

Abraham Lincoln once said, "In the end, it's not the years in your life that count. It's the life in your years." But what is life? The dictionary might define it as: "a state of existence." But answer me honestly, who would define life as "simply existing?" No one. But I think the real question is, "What does it mean *to live?*"

Everyone seems to have an answer to that question. Some might say that to really live, one needs to skydive, climb mountains, cross oceans, travel the world. Some people think living consists of eating, sleeping, and then repeating the two-step cycle; in other words: don't do anything for anyone else, just exist for your own enjoyment. Others might say that to live, one must live the "American Dream," have a successful career, raise a family, live in a nice house, and go to church on Sundays.

But to me, truly living means more than *what* I do. It has everything to do with my attitude and the passion I put behind whatever I am involved in. It seems to me that so many people go through life, ending up accomplishing their dreams and goals and yet are still unhappy. When one's life is over, what makes up the legacy he or she leaves behind? The tangible accomplishments he or she achieved, or the love, devotion, commitment, and wholehearted passion that person put into everything he or she worked for? I have come to believe it's the latter.

Sarah Gray, Grade 11
Germantown High School, TN

If I Could Change the World

If I could change one thing in the world, I would change the gas prices. I would make them lower because right now they are too high. I would take them down about $1.50 a gallon. People need to get around, and they cannot do that because gas costs too much. Some can't even go to work. Some people can't afford food because they are paying for gas. They can't make any money because they spend it all on gas. Now, as a teenager you can't go to the movies every Friday. Because, your parents say they don't have any gas money. And teenagers can't make enough money to pay for gas either. And we can't get clothes as often as we used to, and we can't go out and eat as often either. Why? All because, we have to pay for gas. Now, you see more people walking or riding bikes. But, that puts them in danger of getting hit by a car. So that's why if I could change anything in the world it would be the gas prices because we want to do more things and go more places, but we have to pay for gas to do those things.

Corbin Carter, Grade 10
City University School of Liberal Arts, TN

What an Inspiration

Oprah Winfrey is almost the most influential person in the 20th century. She has shown the world that she is passionate, generous, and intellectual.

Oprah has a deep love for others, showing that she is passionate. Rather than creating another talk show, she created compassion and intimacy as a way to talk to each other. In 1991, she initiated the National Child Protection Act to establish a national database of convicted child abusers. Oprah's Angel Network is a public charity that supports women, children, and families with educational and empowerment initiatives.

Her generosity shows in everything she does. Oprah was named one of the 100 most influential people of the 20th century by "Time" magazine for two years in a row. She created the "world's largest piggy bank" program, so that people throughout the country could contribute spare change to raise over one million dollars. This amount was matched by Oprah. The program was developed to send disadvantaged kids to college.

Intellectual is the best word to describe Oprah. She started HARPO Productions in 1988. Her company creates feature films, prime-time TV specials, and home videos. Global media leader and philanthropist have made her one of the most respected and admired public figures in society. She believes influence is the union of power and purpose.

Oprah is such a powerful and respected person, and her beliefs are so valuable. She is a role model for many people, young and old, across the world. She has made a difference.

Kass Pfeiffer, Grade 10
Mulhall-Orlando High School, OK

Most Important Thing in My Life

The most important thing in my life is my family and dreams. The reason my family is important is because without them, I probably would not be the person I am today. My family is always there for me during the good and the bad times. My family stand by me. If I am wrong, they will still love and care for me. No matter what happens!

The other thing important to me is my dreams. The reason my dreams are important to me, is because my dreams are what I expect from myself later in life. I also know I am going to work hard to fulfill my dreams. My dreams are to be a good role model for my nephews and nieces within my family. I want to show them hard work pays off and to never give up!

I would like to be rich to get my family members out of bad neighborhoods and out of bad home settings. With that, I shall put them in a better home, so they can have the same opportunity as other children. I want to give them the same chance as anyone else to succeed.

So, thus being said, it's obvious my family along with my dreams is my most important obligations. My family with my dreams is to change my family for the better. That way, the new generation (or mine), can and will enjoy life and "knock the struggle." These are my important values, which I would like to establish in my lifetime.

Durell Dowdell, Grade 12
Grandview Alternative School, MO

Imhotep the World Shaper

Imhotep has been disfigured as the leader of the undead in *The Mummy*. In truth, he is one of the greatest figures in history. He was an architect and a doctor who shaped history even though it has denied him a title he deserves.

Imhotep designed the first Egyptian pyramid, for King Djoser of the third Dynasty; it is dubbed the Step Pyramid and is located at Saqqara. The pyramid started out as a Mastaba, a rectangular crypt; later, new layers were added to it to give it its current shape. This pyramid inspired the creation of one of the Seven Wonders of the World, The Great Pyramid of Khufu. The pyramids are one of Imhotep's many accomplishments and contributions to the world.

Imhotep was also a healer. He lived at least one thousand years before Hippocrates, and there is evidence that he cut portions of skull out to relieve pressure or even to operate on the brain; in addition, the patient also showed evidence that he survived the surgery. It is also believed that Hippocrates studied from Egyptian dictations of medical procedures, possibly even some from Imhotep himself. That might lead one to think that Hippocrates is not the Father of Modern Medicine but Imhotep is.

These are some of his amazing accomplishments. He was revered as a God in Egyptian culture as well as in Greek and Roman culture. Imhotep may not be well known, but he sculpted the life and history that we know.

Breanna Justine Bernard, Grade 12
Lee County Sr High School, NC

Oh Woe Is Me, Oh Woe Is Me

Constant chatter. Stomping through halls. Bored voices repeatedly uttering the same words they did last year. Icons that accompany the words "high school." And for the loner, these images come with as much pain as nails on a chalkboard. Some think of high school as their glory days, the time of their lives in which they are invincible, unhindered by rules, regulations and physical limitations. They appear to own the world, instead of the other way around. They casually stroll into the classrooms, looking through eyes that know everything and need nothing. However, there are others. Those that feel high school is full of headaches, crashes, bangs, shouts, laughing, shrieking, annoyances and the occasional decent day. Then, when they need it most, right when they're going to snap, something amazing happens. Every pessimistic, run-down, slightly-hated, wannabe loner receives a second wind, a renewal of tolerating energy that makes them want to actually socialize with the world. They make an acquaintance, if not a friend. Some last years, while others only exist for a short time, a week, perhaps a month. But, to every one of them, it will be worth it. Because there's no such thing as a loner.

Cheyenne Dela Cruz, Grade 11
Academics Plus Charter School, AR

Why Teens Should Text in Class

Communication is vital for mankind, and if it is not established all will be lost. Most people don't come to think about the forms of communication we have today. Things like the internet, radio and TV. Above all there is a super gadget that makes the world spin, the cell telephone. In America, wireless technology rules the society.

All of the fancy gadgets dominate the market today, especially the cell phones. They are easy to acquire, cheap to maintain. Most of the phones are microscopic and easily fit in a palm of a toddler. Their size makes them efficient to sneak out in class. The advancing technology makes phones that even a fifth grader can use.

Many teens are tempted to text during class. The schools just keep fighting against the cell phones. It's pointless, teenagers will never listen no matter how many referrals are given to them. The schools need to give up, like the iPod, stop hindering teens and let them do it; after all it doesn't disturb the class.

After all, most teachers just gave up on reporting students that repeatedly text in class. It's less of a distraction letting a student text rather then stopping the entire class. Communication is impossible to stop, were there is a will there is a way. Teens constantly find new ways to text in class. So the schools need to stop wasting time resisting the text message epidemic and just go with the flow.

Edouard Pavlyuchek, Grade 10
Deltona High School, FL

My Passion

In my 15 years of living I have never felt so passionate about something like this. It makes my blood rush and my adrenaline go up. When I hear the words and the beat, it takes me to another place. People never seem to guess what I'm talking about. Then when I say the word, music, everybody seems to agree. Music is a whole other thing to me than something you sing along to or dance to. It's very different to me. To me, it's a way to escape from the world. There isn't one day that I don't go home and put my radio up to a point where my mom screams at me to put it down.

I love to listen to what the meaning of the song is. Some people just hear music to have noise around but I hear to see what the artist is saying. I love the beat in the background and how the words flow so freely. It's like hearing poetry but in a more enjoyable way. Music is my savior and without it, I don't think I'd be able to cooperate with the way the world changes so much. Music is so relatable and my passion.

Paulina Hernandez, Grade 10
Deltona High School, FL

The Long Cut

Taking a short cut does not always save time. Sometimes a short cut can actually get you lost. About three summers ago, my family was planning to take a trip up to the mountains for vacation. We were riding down the road, and my dad thought that he knew a short cut. He really didn't. He took a back road then turned onto a couple of other roads, and before he knew it, we were lost. He was saying that he knew where we were, but he really had no earthly idea. It takes only three hours to get to the mountains, and we had already been on the road for over three hours. When my dad finally admitted that we were lost, he asked for help. With the correct directions, we finally reached the mountains after about six hours. In this case, taking a short cut definitely did not save us time.

Stephen Miles, Grade 11
New Covenant Christian School, SC

Friends

Many people say that the people you hang out with are the people that will shape your future and affect you lifestyle. I find that this is not true. I have an extremely wide variety of friends, some bad, and some good. I myself, do not do anything bad, such as drugs, drinking, smoking, or any other type of delinquency. My mom does not tell me who I can and cannot be friends with and she does not limit what I do with them. She has trust in me and knows that if I'm faced with certain situations I will pick the better choice.

People that have strict parents that are always paranoid of them making a bunch of bad choices, normally will, because they see it as a way to rebel and a way of experiencing things on their own. I think that parenting has more of an influence on your actions than the way your friends act do.

Keith Owens, Grade 12
Walker Valley High School, TN

Personal Attacks

Millions of people have no clue what it's like to have a sibling, let alone to be the youngest. Growing up the youngest child of course has its advantages, but with two older siblings it can get complicated. My brother is five years older than me, while my sister is only two.

Being the only male child, my brother played rough. He hated me and loved my sister. To him, I was the ultimate pest. I always wanted to be around my brother because he was "cool." He was older and I looked up to him. I took every opportunity I could to be with him, but he just found it annoying. When he'd get aggravated with me, I'd run to my parents.

It seemed the harder I tried, the more annoyed he got. I took this as a personal attack. I couldn't understand how I was so different from my sister and why he liked her more. My sister always took his side, while my parents usually took mine. My parents would tell them that they were older and I just didn't understand.

As I grew older, I began to realize I needed my own space. I realized that this was all my brother had wanted too. It was not a personal attack. If I had learned anything from being the youngest of three, it was not to take everything personally. It took only time to figure this out.

Kayla Brewer, Grade 11
Camden Central High School, TN

Music Appreciation

Music appreciation is something that seems to be absent among young music listeners today. Sure, enjoying Fall Out Boy and Soulja Boy is perfectly fine, but if you don't know where it all came from, you're considered ignorant in the world of music. You have to know where it all started because as we all (should) know there is nothing original in music — ever. Every new thing just feeds off of something old.

It seems like the adolescents of today are brainwashed by these new music fads like emo, screamo and others. While I will admit I have been know to listen to some of the bands that fall under these categories, I am also knowledgeable enough to realize these dazed genres won't be around in another five years.

No one appreciates quality music anymore; they demand carbon copy bands with no talent and who are lacking creativity. This makes it easy for bands not to have to work hard because they realize they can receive a record contract for having the tightest pants. What really matters are the bands who have made musical history, changed the world, and are still talked about and listened to 20, 30, 40, 50 years later. Great music is either never heard or makes history. A person who claims to be a music fan can't tell you the story behind Robert Johnson and The Crossroads is a very sad thing. In my opinion, we are currently going through a musical epidemic.

Lauren Pintar, Grade 12
Germantown High School, TN

I Will Not Lose

To others, there may be plenty of differences between a dream and a goal, but to me, they are mutual. I feel that they are mutual because my goals in life are my dreams. I feel that I can achieve anything I please. In retrospect, I do have dreams. I dream that I will someday be an NBA basketball player, I want to play college ball while studying to be an architect. That is my back-up plan; I should say it is my second primary dream.

My third primary dream is to become a hip-hop icon. With that being carefully thought out, I am motivated by an inspirational phrase, recited by a famous hip-hop artist/icon, who is also an entrepreneur, Jay-Z, "I will not lose." My goals are simply to fulfill my dreams. All I must do is finish high school, which I am handling right now, go to college to pursue my architecture career, continue staying focused and making my music, and keep playing basketball while doing all of the above. While completing my dreams/goals, I would like to be an entrepreneur. I want to give back to communities and help out those less fortunate. That is simply my dreams, goals, and plans summed up. By remaining focused, "I will not lose!"

Gerard Knighten, Grade 12
Grandview Alternative School, MO

The Teacher Salary Problem

Most people with jobs have to deal with irritating people all the time. Rude customers, senile elderly, children with sticky fingers stealing from the penny jar. But these workers only deal with these irritants two or three times a day. Teachers deal with these people, multiplied by thirty, and must control them for eight to nine hours every day.

People would assume that teachers are paid handsomely for their troubles. However, they are very much mistaken. Teachers are incredibly underpaid. People who have jobs like computer technician sit at a computer every-day for hours on end, experiencing very little social activity, and are paid over forty thousand dollars, while teachers walk around, saying the same thing over and over to blank faces, and are paid only around thirty thousand dollars. When you take into account the price of their housing, groceries, gasoline, and taxes, teachers are paid even less for a job that, in the end, is much more difficult than being a computer technician.

In other parts of the world, education takes on a much larger role in shaping lives, unlike in the United States, where education is taken for granted. In these parts of the world, teachers are paid more than in America, just for this reason of importance. Teachers are still looked at as scholars, people of a higher echelon of genius, even the bringers of peace to some war-torn lands. In America, they are treated like any other person, and are not given credit for their work.

Tyler Watson, Grade 11
Bishop Verot High School, FL

No Longer a Victim

Every nine seconds, a woman in America reports being abused by their partner. Of those women 81% reported being pushed, shoved, or grabbed. 61% were threatened to be hit. 44% reported having something thrown at them. 38% were beaten or choked. 36% were slapped. 27% were kicked, hit, or bit. 16% were sexually assaulted.

I fall in these statistics. It started slowly, with mental abuse. He would call me fat and worthless. I have always had low self-esteem, so I believed him. He said if I left I would be alone forever. He said no one would ever love me. Then the pushing started. It was followed by kicking and hitting. I went through things no woman should ever have to experience.

Women who familiarize themselves with the tactics of these predators may recognize it soon enough to get out safely. Some of the tactics include isolating a woman from her friends and family, criticizing a woman constantly, or control all of the woman's income. You may be being abused of you stay with him because he threatens suicide if you leave, you have stopped expressing opinions when he doesn't agree with them, or are genuinely afraid of your partner.

Every month, six American women are murdered by their abusers. Silence will not stop these attacks. I no longer think of myself as a victim, but a crusader. Abuse is still happening. By exposing it, we can stop it.

Taylor Beth Ellis, Grade 11

Do Video Games Cause Violence?

Video games have had a bad reputation for violence ever since the shooting at Columbine High School. This is because the two shooters loved to play a game called Doom. This first-person shooting game was known for its violence and goriness. The question we have to ask ourselves is; are video games really the problem?

I will have to admit that some video games are extremely violent. They may play a factor in violence. Even if they do it would be one small factor among many larger ones. To completely blame violence on one thing is unreasonable. Some people just look for a scapegoat that seems logical, that can't fight back.

Another mistake that many people make is to think that correlation means cause. While this is sometimes true it doesn't have to be. Just because a game is played before someone shoots another person doesn't mean that the game caused him or her to do it. There are many factors that cause violence such as poverty, abuse, and peer pressure.

Some people like to blame anything but themselves. Parents who let their kids play violent games and watch gory movies seem to never take responsibility for their child's action. People need to learn that they can't always blame bad things on someone or something else. I was raised to take responsibility for my actions not to blame it on inanimate objects.

Corey McCubbin, Grade 10
Seneca High School, SC

A Week in D.C.

Students all over America taking an AP course in any U.S. or World history course should take a field trip to Washington D.C. within the year that they are in that class. The field trip should be strictly school related but at the same time fun and interesting. Reasons for this are: the students would get a more in depth view of what happens in a nation's capital, and they would get to see some famous memorials as well.

If the students take a day to get to Washington D.C. on a bus, the next two or three days could be spent visiting the capital, and maybe even attending a house or Senate meeting to see how this country really works. They would also learn more of the people making big decisions for this country. If the students get a visual view of how things are run in this country, they are more likely to pass the end of the year AP Exam with a higher grade than they would without going to Washington D.C.

The next following days could be spent touring famous memorials such as: the Lincoln Memorial, the World War II Memorial, etc. This stage of the trip would get students more interested in those time eras and would reassure them to study more about those subjects.

If all AP history students were to spend a week in Washington D.C., there would be many positive effects in the future of those students.

Matt Sullivan, Grade 11
Owasso High School, OK

I Am Not One Bubble

We have all had to fill out forms where we are asked to bubble in our ethnicity. The directions state you can only fill in one bubble. What do you do if you are someone like me, when more than one bubble applies?

I have been rebellious in the past. I would fill in all bubbles that applied to my ethnicity. It was my attempt to change the rules in a passive aggressive way. However, one day my teacher called me up to her desk. I knew it was about the whole bubble thing. She told me I was only allowed to fill in one of the bubbles, so much for my attempted coup. I now just choose one. This leaves me feeling like I have to leave off a part of who I am.

People want to fit me into one bubble. I get asked all the time, "What are you?" because I do not fit in one bubble. A girl in my class once asked me if I was mixed. I told her I was. I then watched her walk back to her friends and tell them, "I told you." Mexican, Arab and Hawaiian are some of the other ethnicities people have guessed. I wonder why they need to know. If you do not look like one particular race, people become curious. I understand that. I am not one bubble.

Rachel Goar, Grade 10
Germantown High School, TN

What My Mom Means to Me

Anyone can be a mother but it takes a very special person to be a mom. My mom means the world to me. I don't know what I would do without her. She is always there for me when I need something and she is there when I need someone to talk to. When my parents got a divorce, I lived with my mom, but eventually I moved in with my dad. Yeah, my dad had a girlfriend and I called her mom but it's not the same as my real mom. I felt like I couldn't talk to my dad's girlfriend, and it was hard not being able to talk to my mom. I really didn't like living with my dad because I didn't have my mom. When I lived with my dad, it was the time when I needed my mom the most. My mom has taught me so much. My mom is the world's greatest-loving mom ever. She helps me through all of my problems, and she taught me how to lead a good life. My mom and I have had our problems, but we still have our mother-daughter relationship. We are very close. I feel like I can talk to my mom whenever I need to and she will listen. She doesn't go and run her mouth to everyone about everything we talk about. I wouldn't trade my mom for anything in the world. I love my mom with all of my heart.

Kimberly Dawn Carr, Grade 11
Lakeland High School, MO

The American Influence

"According to the A.C. Nielsen Co., the average American watches more than 4 hours of TV each day. In a 65-year life, that person will have spent 9 years glued to the tube." Nearly every home has a television set, some with one in every room. We as Americans should be aware of the affects that TV has on our minds, bodies.

Each day everything our eyes observe and our brain takes in affects us in some way. What we see can impacts us in big ways that we may sometimes not notice. Television provides easy access to violence and bad language; anyone can turn on a TV and be exposed to it. Though not all TV is bad, we need to be careful not to misuse it.

It is not new to anyone that Americans are physically out of shape. If only we could inspire a nation to do away with the television and become interested in becoming a healthy nation. The only problem is that TV has become this nations norm. We need a solution before the consequences get worse.

Whether it's the news, a game show, or cartoons, Americans love to be entertained by the television. We need to consider what we are letting influence our thoughts and activities. As Mr. Newton Minow said, "The power of instantaneous sight and sound is without precedent in mankind's history. This is an awesome power. It has limitless capabilities for good, and for evil."

Katherine Swearingen, Grade 11
Owasso High School, OK

Being Green

Have you ever wondered why living "green" is a big deal? By living "green," one can help the environment in more ways than imaginable. Helping the environment is a large part of being "green," but it also makes one feel good about oneself by living that way. By recycling, reusing, and saving energy our world is being helped in various ways.

Recycling, instead of throwing away, is a great way of giving back to the environment. At my house, there are different recycle bins for numerous items. I recycle aluminum cans, plastics, glass, paper, used oil, and even batteries. Recycling does take a little extra work, but not too much, and it is extremely beneficial. Reusing items, such as water bottles is a good way to be "green" also. When finished with a water bottle, refill it and use it again. Do not throw it away.

Saving energy is an enormously, significant part of living "green." For example, replace normal light bulbs with compact fluorescent light bulbs. The switch saves energy and money. Compact fluorescent bulbs don't burn out as fast as normal bulbs do. Even though at the store the fluorescent bulbs are a bit more expensive, over time one will notice the savings in energy and money. Next time you find yourself throwing something away or changing light bulbs, think of what you can do to help the environment.

Sam Peyton, Grade 11
Owasso High School, OK

The Untarnished Buds

Have you ever looked into a child's eyes? When you do, you'll see a beauty that lies within them that you could no longer see within your own eyes. Children are the positive thinkers, the never ending explorers, and the greatest gift known to man. Their imagination and creativity excels past even the most influential scientist and scholars of history. Unlike children, adults have transformed into corrupt robots. Their ways are not open minded. Adults are stuck in a bottomless pit of repetitive lifestyles. There is no longer room to uncover the hidden or dive into the unexplained. However, in the eyes of an innocent minded child, anything is possible and open to discovery.

Children have not yet reached that decaying moment in life. They are still mischievous, little hunters determined to capture the innocence of life, but delicate little buds, which have not been kissed by the rays of regret or blown away by the conformities of society. Oblivious to the dark, stricken misfortunes of the world, they have not yet been rooted into ways that are indecent or compressed into foolish debauchery. No, that is the mindset of an adult who has found pleasure in the exposure to the adulterate world. The shine, that they once cast, has faded over the years where as a child's has simply illuminated and filled the world with its light. Children will continue to blossom as long as the world's immorality does not reach them.

Katie Bain, Grade 11
Owasso High School, OK

Justice for All?

Remember the old days in kindergarten when we were so excited to recite the Pledge of Allegiance? Of course we were excited to memorize much of anything. I can remember running around my house, hand over heart, serious as can be, reciting the Pledge. So naive the mind of a child is. As I grew older and became, in my eyes, more knowledgeable I started to think more about the Pledge and what it really said: Liberty and Justice for all. Nowadays I think we've lost sight of what our government is really about.

Our representative officials have become more preoccupied with image and are flirting more and more with the line of discrimination. Isn't the job of our government and its officials to keep us safe in our homes and our voices heard where and when it matters? Since when is gay marriage, or the banning there of, relevant to homeland security? Is that "Liberty and Justice for all?" I think not. Our country prides itself on the separation of church and state, but does it really? Can any one government or country honestly say that the two are complete and separate entities? Our country was founded on the basis of religious freedom so why wouldn't we have religion in our government to an extent? Lately our country has lost touch with its roots and needs to reunite itself with the reasons it was originally founded: Liberty and Justice for all.

Victoria Bridewell, Grade 11
Camden Central High School, TN

Athletic Training

Do you like helping people? I do, and becoming an athletic trainer was one of the greatest things in my life. Being an athletic trainer can be very helpful throughout your life. It can help you in an emergency situation, it educates you, and it helps you with people skills. An athletic trainer is very interesting and exciting job.

Having the skills of an athletic trainer can help you out in an emergency situation. You could help someone if they were choking, unconscious, bleeding, and much more. These skills are very good to have handy when something goes terribly wrong. This job also educates you in many different ways. It helps you learn the human anatomy, how to assess an injury, and how to make people get better. But most importantly you learn people skills. You work with all unique people when being a trainer. You have to deal with their attitudes and how to make them calm down or quit crying or even make them happy. This job is very essential to life. It helps in many ways and can be useful. Athletic training is a lot of fun too. You learn about different sports, and how they are played effectively. In conclusion, becoming an athletic trainer can help you throughout life in any way. It's a good experience.

Candace Spencer, Grade 11
Owasso High School, OK

9:24 A.M.

My sister and I were trying to find some decent clothes in the dark. It was 4:30, maybe 5 o'clock A.M. on July 26th, 2004. My mom was starting to feel contractions and our phone was disconnected. My sister and I had to walk to our neighbor's house to call my dad.

Since my baby sister's been in my life, every day is brighter, even when the sun doesn't shine. There's not a day that goes by that she doesn't put a smile on my face, or make me cry from laughter.

I've come to realize how hard it is to be a parent, although she's only my baby sister. She's taught me so much in her 3 short years. Like how to live my life as if today were my last day, but explore it as if it were my first; and just as she teaches me, I try and teach her anything she's willing to take in.

I know she looks up to me, so I try to do everything right. Even when she's not around, I'm careful and thoughtful of my actions, while still doing what's best for me.

At 9:24 A.M. that day my life was changed forever. Kimberly Elizabeth Castillo was born. She means the world to me and she knows it. She has the passion for life that inspires me, makes me look up to her, and has impacted my life forever.

Jennifer Castillo, Grade 11
Countryside High School, FL

Trials for a Wii

It was cold and unusually arid that night, but a young man would brave the weather for the love of video games.

Arriving outside Circuit City late in the afternoon, he would have hours to wait until midnight for the release of the Nintendo Wii. His determination was unfaltering; neither hunger nor dropping temperatures could drive him away empty handed.

Time marched slowly on and his pains for food increased. Much to his surprise, the cavalry arrived with steamy hot hamburgers from Wendy's. Despite his aching stomach, he first stole the warmth from his meal by stuffing it under his shirt to absorb the burger's heat.

The minutes crept by slowly, but inevitably the clock did sound and it was midnight. His reward was to be the first in line for the new console, but to no avail. The clerk would not accept his mother's credit card. With a heavy heart, the brave young man sat and waited and waited outside the store that once offered so much hope, but now only despair and 'what could have beens' remained.

Suddenly, like a mounted knight triumphantly riding downhill, they approached; the family that would lead him to his Wii. With borrowed cash and a warm ride home, a sudden flush of emotion overcame him. He did it!

He had stood the cold, the aches of hunger, the agonizing pain of near defeat. Now he was home in his warm bed, with his new Wii safely by.

Alexandra Harris, Grade 11
Vero Beach High School, FL

Roller Coaster

Life is like a roller coaster, exciting, yet scary. We can't wait until we're old enough to ride, but when we hit the first hill we're terrified. I was thirteen when I rode my first roller coaster; now I'm sixteen and I'm just learning how life works. When we're young, things seem so much more fun, then we realize life isn't always fun. It's scary, and then we get used to it and then BAM, something new happens out of nowhere. But you can't get off and sometimes you get stuck, or so it seems, then things go full speed ahead and you barely have time to think; all you can do is scream. You may have to choose which roller coaster to ride and if you think it's too scary, you pass it up and go for another. Like any other choice, you never seem to think that could be easier than it looks.

Catelyn Nicole Young, Grade 10
Slater High School, MO

Preserving Our Environment

Preserving our environment is important to me for several reasons. The Earth is very big and there are many trees to give us air, shade and food. The massive sun gives our planet energy for heat and energy for the plants to grow. The Earth contains many animals and their homes. Animals and plants provide life to exist on our planet.

If there is pollution on our planet, life as we know it will end. We should not throw waste into the water or on the ground. This could harm the animals and plants. Toxic waste from chemicals that farmers use on their crops also pollutes our plants and drinking water. The Earth will die with all the toxic waste killing it. The emissions from cars are bad for the air we breathe because they produce too much carbon dioxide in the air. We will not be able to breathe if there is too much carbon dioxide in the air. If we take good care of our planet, we should live for a very long time.

Jacob Anderson, Grade 11
Easter Seals of South Florida School, FL

Hurdles

Trying new things brings diversity and creativity into life. I never played any sports, attended dance classes, or took music lessons when I was young, but I decided to step outside of my boundaries when I entered high school. I tend to be an extroverted person, but adding something new to my life ignited a spark of fear inside of me. I joined the volleyball team because the game intrigued me! Many obstacles frustrated me in the beginning, but I found that succeeding involves dedication. I realized that I had to practice with enthusiasm and had to have a positive attitude. New challenges allow a person to experience how unique the world is and how people can express themselves through all avenues of life. Now that I am more adventurous and flexible, I have a more exciting life.

Angela Hendrix, Grade 12
New Covenant Christian School, SC

One Lane Highway

The pressure mounts with every shot, every roll. One missed pin could cost one the game of his or her life. I have practiced for years using a number of techniques, bowling balls, and mindsets, but have never been able to crack what seems to be the unreachable score: three hundred, twelve strikes in a row. Every throw is different down this one lane highway; the bowling ball could break too much, not enough, or right into what we call "the pocket," the sweetest spot in the game.

I have only once come within reach of three hundred. I struck on the first three shots of the game; no big deal in most games, but today was different. Today I had a certain niche for the sport, one that I have never been able to find again since that day. The fourth through seventh shots were much like the first three: strikes. I began to realize what was happening; unfortunately, so were my teammates. There I was with seven strikes in a row, only five away from sheer glory and the coveted three hundred ring. However, one of my teammates uttered the six vilest words in the history of bowling; "He's got a three hundred going." Right at the moment I knew I was jinxed; no one can surmount the six unspeakable words. My next shot left one pin standing; my final score was a measly two hundred and fifty-seven.

Brian Vinson, Grade 11
Germantown High School, TN

Technology's Tomorrow

From the invention of the light bulb in 1879 to the handheld, touch screen mp3 players of the new generation, technology is a spreading trend of the world. Grandparent's of the new generation cannot believe or comprehend some of the new technological inventions. Technology is growing at such a fast exponential rate, that as of right now, tomorrow is a new invention waiting.

In 1936, during World War II, the first programmable computer named Z1 was invented with a sixty four word memory. Microsoft, a graphical user interface operating system, helped place a computer in virtually every household in 1983. Recently, the boundless possibilities of developing the newest technologies are hard to imagine. For instance, the internet has changed the lives of the young generation. Students no longer go to the library to sift through encyclopedias to do research papers; they simply type their subject into the search bar on Google.

What is in store for the future is limitless. Scientists and inventors are combining to advance technology to an inexplicable level. Computers, cell phones, and games are on such an innovative level, they are hard to imagine as being real. This century is the most technological the earth has seen, but what happens tomorrow will amaze the world.

Hayley Archer, Grade 11
Owasso High School, OK

An Angel at Sixteen

The pain shot through me, in more than just a physical form as I walked out of my best friend's intensive care room. I fell to the cold tile floor as soon as I reached the hallway. I lost all my composure in the tears streaming down my face.

How could this really be happening? No one had the answer. All we knew was she'd been hit by a truck while crossing six lanes of traffic after she stepped off her bus, just as she did every day.

There seemed to be a cloud of haze hanging above the ICU waiting room that Sunday. Groups of people sat together and prayed; others brought food, and some, like me, held each other, pretending to be strong.

In the back of the my mind, I suppose I knew nothing would be the same. I dreaded the revealing of her test results. They hit harder than any freight train. It concluded she was "brain dead," at least that's what the strange lady in the coat had said. The room seemed to split with the cries of heart break.

Her heart ceased beating at exactly five o'clock after she was removed from life support. As I stood by her bed, I thought of all the joy she'd brought to my life. Rebecca Marie McKinney showed me the value of family, love, and forgiveness.

It can't be measured, how much of an impact she's had on my life, but I do know, God gained an angel at sixteen.

Jordan Gentry, Grade 11
Countryside High School, FL

Teardrops Forever Falling

How does an individual persevere after having their world crumble to pieces? Only one who has experienced these circumstances can give a proper answer to such a question. Who knew that the human heart could handle such anguish as mine did the day of March 25, 2007?

I had just returned home from volleyball practice and was running inside to avoid the rain, not realizing the dismay I was about to endure. Both my parents had tears streaming down their face, an emotion I rarely saw. My sister and I sat before them, startled and apprehensive. My dad began to speak words that seemed foreign to me. He was leaving us; my parents were separating.

At that moment, I became deaf to everything around me. My dad spoke but no words came out, my sister ran hoping to somehow escape this turmoil, and I sat there paralyzed, speechless for words. I ran to my room with all the life left in me and opened my window as I heard his car engine start up. I screamed at my dad to come back; however, he never looked up as I so wished he would. As he drove away, the rain intermixing with the tears upon my face, I knew my life would never be the same.

A person must rebuild their inner selves when torn apart by such high measures, as I have had to do. There you have it, a five minute story that has forever changed my life.

Mandy Brady, Grade 11
Owasso High School, OK

My Father

One of the first things people tell me when they meet me is that I remind them of my dad. We have a little saying around my house, and it goes, "Everybody loves Geoff, but Mama's always right." I've never met someone who dislikes my father, a quality I have inherited well. The difference is that my dad is a good listener, which comes from working in education for 15 years. It takes a special kind of person to teach special ed. students for 11 years, and my dad is just that kind of person. There aren't many specific words to describe my father. He's kind of a parental anomaly in that he is 100% committed to his job but he manages not to sacrifice things in his personal life.

When he was 14, he had a diving accident that left him in a coma. He would never be able to play any contact sport like he had wanted to, not even basketball. This is my worst fear, to be immobile or unable to play football. But somehow he pushed through, continuing his other passion — playing the drums. He became a successful drummer and I'm told he left people speechless when in his prime. I will never know everything there is to know about my dad, or even fully understand him, but what I do know is that he's a great role model and he loves our family with all his heart.

Evan Woodson, Grade 11
Owasso High School, OK

1980 Days Straight and Counting

One thousand nine hundred and eighty days straight, regardless of my health, rain or shine, I'm in school each and every day. My classmates may think I'm strange, but it's a personal goal of mine. Now that I'm only several months away from graduating from high school, I hope I'll remain healthy so that I can fulfill this mission.

There were days when I wanted to stay home to nurse a cold, a fever, or even a slight headache, but I'm well aware that even a single day missed in class can be detrimental to a student and their ability to learn and understand an assignment. For example, one situation stands out in my mind — it was during my sophomore year, I woke up with a fever. I not only got up and went to school, but I managed to stay the entire day so that I would not miss an important chemistry exam.

Developing good habits during a person's formative years will benefit you later on in life. I feel that this habit that I've established from a young child will benefit me during my college life and in my future career. Having a flawless attendance record will prove to my teachers, instructors and future employers that I'm someone who is responsible, dependable and reliable regardless of my physical or mental condition. In addition, the fact that I possess these qualities proves that I am a dedicated student.

Channa Chuck, Grade 12
Miami Palmetto Sr High School, FL

Light

"You are the way, the truth and the light. We're living all for you." Six months ago I figured I was living for my parents, even my boyfriend. Now I realize how stupid I was to think that. Today I have someone who is strong and trustworthy to live for, and his name is Jesus Christ. Not once has He let me down or broke my heart. He's been there for me when I didn't know who else would be. He's always here and I wouldn't have it any other way.

Almost half a year ago, I broke up with my boyfriend. I couldn't handle the pressure or risk being hurt more than I already had, so I ended it. For months I cried and I listened to him tell me one thing, but mean another. After so much, I gave up. I turned to friends who I thought would be the light of my world. They, too, let me down. One night my friend Briana called me and asked me to go to her youth group 'Liv It.' I ended up giving myself to God that night and ever since then my whole life has changed. I found the true light and it's Him. Today people look and see the real me, a girl who can't keep her mouth closed and never wants to stop smiling. God has given me His strength to pick up my life again and keep moving.

Michelle Coffman, Grade 10
Deltona High School, FL

Hard Hitting Life Lessons

Muscles tired, body aching, scorching heat, hands shaking, half of practice is still to come. Football isn't for everyone; only the strong minded and dedicated will even stand a chance. Whether it is the daily practice, or the constant pressure to be great, much heart is needed to keep up. When I'm out on that field, I represent more than just myself; I represent my family, friends, and entire school.

I have played football for over 7 years now, and have learned many things important in life. Such as hard work, determination, never quit fighting, and to play my very hardest every down.

Soon I noticed that what I learned on the field, I was using in my everyday life. I stopped complaining about little things and just "got it done." School became easier and was no longer a chore. This soon became true for most other annoyances in my life.

Being on any kind of team brings people together. Many of my closest friends I met on football teams. Team isn't a good word to use though; it's more like *family*. We got through all the hard and good times…together.

Whenever my team loses, we all take the hat. Likewise, when we win, we all share the glory. Teams where every player cares about one another usually do the best. I love this sport, football has taught me lessons I will remember for the rest of my life.

Justin Brooks, Grade 11
Countryside High School, FL

Run Free

Legend says that settlers tamed the Wild West. The west was never to be tamed or won for that matter. The horses were the true pioneers of the west. They were born, lived, and died on that land. Why would you take that away? How could you expect them to understand marked boundaries and where not to graze? So how do we as people have the right to send them into shacks where they will never see the light of day?

In the early 1900s, horses roamed the west, freely going wherever and whenever they wanted. It was their home! To the settlers it seemed to be too much. The wild horses could strip a whole field in a night; they became useless to humans. Today there are only thirty thousand or so left. Compare that to millions roaming the land, back where we called the *free west*, but there is no such place anymore.

All United States slaughterhouses have been shut down. There are foreign slaughterhouses still today that take our beloved animals' lives. Do not believe that they are only taking the old horses not good for anything. How could someone be so cruel to buy a horse with so much potential and put him in a house with other scared horses who are bullied into what is called the kill-box, where they are tortured until they are almost dead. Finally they dismember their bodies. Some of the horses are still half alive. They never had a chance!

Ariah Wolfe, Grade 10
Grady High School, GA

Home School Does Equal Real School

Home schools are real schools with real kids and should be treated as such. Kids in home schools are often treated differently from kids in "regular" schools. An example of this treatment is the day I attempted to get my learner's permit.

On the day I turned fifteen, my father took me to the DMV to acquire my learner's permit. I stood in line just like the people in front of me with my report card issued by my home school association in my hand. When I got to the front of the line the lady at the desk informed me that since I was home schooled, I had to have special papers to get my permit.

The driver's manual said nothing about requiring home schooled students to have anything different from anyone else. According to the manual, I needed my report card, which I had. She said that wasn't good enough, I needed a letter from my home school association, which was closed that day.

I returned home and searched our family files until I found my acceptance letter from SCAIHS.

Although I work very hard in school and get good grades, I received many dirty looks from my tester that day. They treated me like I was scum, because I wanted to have the same privileges every kid in school gets. I think that home schooled students should be treated no differently from the kids in school.

Marie Williams, Grade 10
Stoneridge Academy, SC

Scapegoat

Packages clung tightly to its benefactor as a sea of fur grazed under it; small hoofs struck against earth in a harmonious chorus; with each step, the fall and rise of those clunks stimulated brusque breathing, for the load was a weighty burden. The odor of these creatures would pain the nose of unattached beings that walked on two legs, recklessly. The heaviest penalty was that of the sun's. Sunlight, the miraculous patron that provided and rewarded, continued to offer its gift upon the backs of these animals, these scapegoats.

No person holds perfection in his hand. Consequently, to obtain this admiration of the first, they disarray the hands of another. "Scapegoats" are those held responsible for faults of others. A child breaks a vase; to avoid punishment, he points his chubby fingers at the nearest figure. Royals are not so different; they hold power over a group. Once the group turns their heads to another, monarchs must sever the disturbance. Soon, events ensue chaotic; no one likes to admit to their errors, so they find a substitute. Continuous burdens shift, creating a cage.

Individuals run pass fields of green; small fingers finding their way into tiny pockets of trees, droplets fleeing on sleet leaves, and insignificant balls of green peas. They cannot see those little goats; they're blind to dots upon this globe. When images of black and white are spattered with red, only then will they remember trapdoors that lead to another's canvas.

Anna Huynh, Grade 10
Jessieville High School, AR

Parents, Teens, and Schoolwork

"Aw Mom, how come I have to study?" "Amber you'll thank me someday." You never believed our parents when they said that you would thank them one day. I mean come on you would rather go to the movies then study English right? You might think your parents don't know what you're going through, but they do 'cause they went to school too. You may use the excuse, "They are ruining my life," they're not. Your parents are just trying to form your future. Teens should listen to their parents when it comes to schoolwork.

But others hold different point of view apart form mine. One part of the parents say "Kids are kids let them have fun while they can." The other part of the parents want their kids to be great in school and take school seriously. Either way kids need a little of both.

Teens should take their parents advice when it comes to schoolwork. The teenagers should also have some freedom. Schoolwork is important even though you might not think of it that way. Your parents are hard on you and push you to succeed in many ways. But all they are doing is helping your future.

Amber Powell, Grade 10
Greenwood High School, KY

Audition

I sit, palms sweaty, breathing shallow, against the wall as the others take their turn. Some do well, some very well indeed. Some should have practiced more. What will the reaction to mine be? Stop thinking and focus. No. Keep thinking. And wait to hear your name. Someone else goes. She stands up and recites the lines she's prepared with all the poise and emotion she can muster through her obviously shaken nerves. She sits and can breathe again.

"Michael Horton."

So much for thinking. I stand, mind and body seemingly numb from the vicious battles of butterflies within me. At a nod from the judges, I state my name and the title of my piece with as much confidence as can be expressed with a frightened, quivering voice. Then, I turn to my right, steady myself, and become Jean for the dozen seconds it takes to present the lines. At the final syllable of the last word of his final line, Jean dies, to be replaced once again by Michael, who straightens, nods, and says "End scene."

"Thank you."

I sit, palms sweaty, breathing deeper now, against the wall as the rest take their turn. All I can do now is wait to see my name on the list tomorrow. Or not. The moments that should have been different occur to me in a flood, but I won't think about that now. I erect a temporary dam against those damaging streams of thought and watch the others audition, hoping.

Michael Horton, Grade 11
Germantown High School, TN

The Influencing Men

Mr. Kevin Daughtry, my eleventh grade AP English teacher, would always have a smile on his face or a kind word to say to anyone. He would always greet kids with kind words and be the first to lend the helping hand. He inspired me to become a high school English teacher because he portrayed a love for teaching. He showed me that touching a young person's life is a gift, and that some are simply meant to teach. He opened my eyes to the interesting and challenging side of the English language, yet let me figure out the perplex world of literature on my own. Without Mr. Daughtry, I would never made the decision to be a high school English teacher. Sitting as a senior at North Johnston High School, I believe teaching is my calling in life.

Another teacher who has influenced my life and my career choice greatly is Mr. Jesse Woodard. Not only is he one of my best friends, he was my high school Physical Science teacher and my Sports Medicine instructor. Now, four years from the time I started working with him as an assistant athletic trainer, he has shown me that after teaching English all day, I want to leave the classroom and do Athletic Training for high school sports teams. He has shown me that Sports Medicine is a rewarding career. Without Mr. Woodard, I would not have been introduced to the field of athletic training.

Chad Holloman, Grade 12
North Johnston High School, NC

Violent Video Games

The ever popular world of video games continues to grow even more.

Through new technology advancements and the increasingly realistic and exciting nature of electronic games, they have became enormously more popular with children and youth. 79% of American children now play computer or video games on a regular basis. Children between the ages of seven and seventeen play for an average of eight hours a week. Is this safe for children? How do violent video games affect a child's emotions? What about their thoughts and aggressiveness towards everyday obstacles?

Games are a great way of teaching a child basic strategy and problem solving. Many of them cause a child to use logic and reason to come to conclusions. Yet there are games that are very controversial. These include games that have mature content with much gory violence and antisocial behavior. They are considered to be inappropriate for all children and harmful to some.

Studies measuring 7th and 8th grade children rated that the ones who spent more time playing violent video games have more aggressive behaviors, and it is just the opposite for the children who do not play these violent video games. The ones who do play a fair amount of violent video games are more apt to engage in fights at school and have negative attitudes.

Video games will continue to be an exciting and growing part of children's media diet. As long as children have access to them, then policy debates will continue.

Joshua San Mateo, Grade 10
Stanton College Preparatory School, FL

The Most Significant Event That Happened in My Life

The one thing which has impacted my life was when I almost lost my older sister, Cierra. It was the same night of my great grandmother's funeral when she was hanging out with her boyfriend, Fletcher.

When Cierra got through hanging out with her boyfriend, she got a phone call; it was my uncle. He asked her if she wanted to come over and stay all night, because he and my aunt wanted her to. While she was watching TV, she saw two men running around in the kitchen. One man ran in the room where she was and asked her, "Where is the money?"

She said she tried to get up, but he had a gun to her head; the next thing she knew, he pistol whipped her. She woke up with a lot of blood running down the side of her face. I got a phone call right before midnight when somebody told me that my sister was in the hospital, fighting for her life.

Two weeks later, she got out. She left the hospital with head injuries. The robbers never took anything; they just ran out of the house when my uncle got up, and we still don't know who did it. To this day, I really thank God for being on my sister's side that night; it wasn't time for her to go. She is still here with me until this day…

Miesha Chrisman, Grade 10
Grandview Alternative School, MO

Last Name Guggi

My family are the most important people in my life. Each person has uniquely influence me. My mom, dad, and three older sisters have affected me in more ways than I can count.

My dad has taught me all I know about sports. In baseball, he taught me how to bunt a runner to next base and how to swing for the fences. In golf, he showed when to lay up before the lake and when to hit the driver off the deck. He has always been there to show me the way.

My mom has taught me right from wrong, morals, and how to stay away from trouble. She has influenced my crowd of friends while showing me, who to stay away from. Also, she taught me to do good deeds and to help others.

Finally, my sisters have influenced me with my decision making. They teach me from their mistakes so that I don't make the same ones. They also show me when to play it safe and when not to be afraid to take risks. The best advice my sisters gave me was, "Go big or Go home." They told me never give up on my dreams and always strive for what I want, not matter the cost.

My family means a great deal to me. The vacations, dinners, and even the occasional fights have brought us closer together over the years. My mom, dad, and sisters have each influenced my life in their own ways.

David Guggi, Grade 11
Countryside High School, FL

A Little League Memory

When I was eleven, I played in the Little League state tournament. In our first game, we played Tulsa. They had a pitcher who threw the ball about 70 mph. In the first two innings he didn't give up a hit. I was up to bat in the third inning with a man on first, and we really needed to get a big inning started. The first pitch came and hit me right in the face. I collapsed immediately and whimpered. Our catcher's dad was a doctor, and he came out and cleaned up the blood. I wouldn't leave the field until the game was over, and I needed to go to the emergency room. We went after the game, and the doctors took some X-rays. They couldn't see through the swelling, so they didn't think anything was broken. My mom asked if I was all right and the only positive thing I could think of was, "At least I didn't strike out."

We played the next day, but the doctors said I couldn't play for the rest of the tournament. We won that game and then had a day off. Two days after I got hit in the face I played anyway, against doctor's orders. I got to bat in the fourth inning and faced the same kid who hit me in the face two days before. I was terrified, but luckily I walked. I played baseball for two more years and never got hit by a pitch again.

Walker Botts, Grade 10
Grove High School, OK

Troubled Past

I'm choosing to write about the way my father's death has changed me. He died when I was ten-years-old, on November 14, 1999 at 8:25 PM. I was the one to hug him last. Before anything bad happened, he was just going in for surgery in Taos and then that's when something bad happened with his oxygen and he ended up becoming brain dead. He was a vegetable then and that's when they ended up hooking him up to a ventilator which was used to control his breathing functions. Then that's when he was transferred to St. Vincent's Hospital in Santa Fe, New Mexico. There I was taken to a meeting held by my family and the doctors. Where they all gave me, a 10-year-old boy, the decision of whether or not to cut off his ventilator and kill him or keep him on it alive and like a vegetable. Well, I ask you now, what would your decision be? Mine was to let him go. If my own dad can't say my name, something's wrong. To be honest, it was for the best. After that, I started slangin' and bangin'. I spent periods of times in and out of jails and then started going in and out of counseling. Then I started living on the streets and the corner. It was a struggle moving from friends' to friends' houses, to apartments and to dark allies. Finally my mom let me stay at her house, and finally I'm here in Grandview and will be until I graduate.

Will Schuster, Grade 10
Grandview Alternative School, MO

Driving

Today in America, it has been proven time and time again that driving is a dangerous act. Hardly ever does a day go by without a devastating accident just within the town of Jacksonville; just imagine the whole United States. Various causes account for the high rates of automobile accidents including driving under the influence (DUI), young, inexperienced drivers, and the nature of driving alone. A DUI is often thought of as subordinate and not a threat, but statistics prove otherwise. Not only is DUI involved with alcohol, but drugs as well, including prescription medicine. In order to prevent accidents caused from substance use, harsher laws need to be made to enforce it. When substances mix with young, inexperienced drivers, the outcome is worse. Driving is already dangerous enough with the reckless driving such as running stop signs or red lights. The inability of people to use sense and reason is accounted for many deaths and preventable injuries. However, of all the driving concerns, young people are the worst. Statistics show the majority of accidents result from drivers under the age of 18, despite being a small portion of drivers on the road. In order to lower such statistics, obtaining a license should be made more difficult or the driving age should be raised. The driving age is already amongst a much debated subject. No matter the cause, it is proven that driving is dangerous and needs adjustments to improve the safety of our youth, and other citizens, too.

Andrew Lepore, Grade 10
Stanton College Preparatory School, FL

Nature

Nature is as beautiful as the heavens above. You never know what you're going to see, but you know it will be beautiful and different. This is why I love my secret place.

My favorite place to go is just this little stream. I go here to think. It is nothing big but it means a lot to me. It is beautiful! Just imagine walking on old train tracks and off to the side you see a stream. The tracks make this magnificent, old bridge that goes over this stream.

As I reach the bridge I walk down the side to get under the bridge. I sit here on a rock thinking of life. I close my eyes envisioning my choices. The wrong. The right.

I hear crickets chirping, fish jumping, cars in the distance, and nothing. I feel wind as it blows through my hair as if it was a brush. To love or not. What if I died today? Would I be happy with my choices? Would God be happy with me? These are some ideas that go through my head. Always wondering if I made the right choice.

Nature is wonderful in many ways. It allows you to be free. Not holding you back or judging you by who you are. Be as if a bird flying free in God's wonderful nature.

Glenda Moses, Grade 11
McMinn County High School, TN

Why One Should Play Guitar Hero 2

Not many people, if any, strongly encourage the playing of video games because of the strong influence they have upon the sedentary lifestyle; either making one who does many physical activities into a sedentary person, or one who further sinks into the routine. But in fact many benefits are to be had if one decided to start playing the popular game *Guitar Hero 2*.

One such reason is an exposure to classic rock. As one plays the game, the opening songs are classics from the 70s and 80s. Not all people have had the pleasure to listen to the fine workings of classic rock, except for *Guitar Hero 2*.

Another benefit is increased hand-eye coordination, specifically the fingers rather than the thumbs. Because of the unique controller used to play *Guitar Hero*, it is not just the thumbs that get trained in hand-eye coordination, but the 2nd through 5th fingers as they push the coordinating fret button as they strum the guitar.

Another benefit is that aspiring musicians can learn rhythm and beat as well as gain stamina for the real instruments. *Guitar Hero* forces songs to be played at the speeds in which they were originally written, forcing the player to learn the beat. Also the constant strumming down with the respective arm (right or left) would make the player able to play longer and faster.

The greatest reason to play *Guitar Hero 2* is that it is the best game ever, period.

Phil Palmon, Grade 11
Bishop Verot High School, FL

A Brother's Gift

I was seven when Tim was born and that is when everything changed. I was no longer the princess. The worst part I was bumped up to the middle child, which meant that I was the one who got in trouble the most and somehow I received more chores. On the other hand if Tim hadn't been born who would I watch a movie with every Saturday night? Who would be able to quote lines from SpongeBob, and who would be there to make me feel joy after both my grandfathers died.

My brother likes movies the most. He can repeat a whole scene from many movies like *Finding Nemo* to *Pearl Harbor*. He says a line and quizzes me about what movie it's from. Most of the time I can tell what movie it is and then other times I have no clue. I guess the real significance of this, is that it is our way of sharing.

Tim is one of the smartest kids in his class. He watches the History and Discovery channels religiously, but as a normal 10-year old he watches SpongeBob, and he relates to each member of my family as a character they resemble.

The best thing about Tim is that when I come home from a trip, he is always the one who is so excited to see me that I'm on the ground because of his bear hugs.

Without Tim, I would never be the person I am today.

Anne Harrington, Grade 11
Countryside High School, FL

Life to Its Fullest

Most people wake up in the morning, shower, brush their teeth, get dressed, and get on with their days. They miss the beauty and wonders of life and let small miracles pass them by. They don't take full advantage of the potential greatness life offers, but if they lived every day as if it were their last, their lives would be more full, rich, and meaningful.

When we rush through life, we miss so much that is significant to our spirit, like a sunrise, one so beautiful, it leaves you in awe with your mind unable to think of words gorgeous enough to explain it. Living a sequence of days as if they were our "last days" however, might slow us down enough to let us enjoy things like a simple smile that can turn your mindset around or the clean, fresh scent of the Earth after a heavy downpour. This would also help us put the events of our lives into perspective so we don't blow through, leaving the really important things unsaid and undone.

If you were told that you only had one day to live, you probably wouldn't saunter to the office or go skipping off to school. As Tim McGraw sings in his song "Live Like You Were Dying," you'd probably "go skydiving, rocky mountain climbing, you'd love deeper, and speak sweeter." If everyone could pretend for one day that it was their last, it would change their lives forever, and make it all worthwhile.

Danielle Macaro, Grade 12
Hale High School, MO

My Grandpa, My Dad

I was four when my mother packed our things and moved my sister and myself into a tiny one bedroom home with my grandpa. From the moment we walked through the door, my grandpa became more than my grandpa, he became a surrogate father. He was present in all the ways a father can be; physically, financially, and emotionally.

One can imagine my devastation when he was diagnosed with a terminal illness. Now not only would I have to watch him die, but I would have to watch him deteriorate and suffer. ALS started its course in his arms, crippling them, and will eventually take his whole body. His inability to swallow without choking has made a feeding tube necessary, and we anticipate wheelchair confinement is in his very near future. For a man in his seventies who has worked nonstop as a farmer since adolescence, a more cruel fate does not exist. Yet somehow, despite his viscous prognosis, he remains with bitterness.

In his final time, my grandpa has yet again managed to teach me some of life's most valuable lessons. He has managed to teach me to appreciate each and every moment and to consider each one a blessing. He has taught me that bitterness is a vice, and acceptance is a virtue. Most important he has taught me to live candidly, while there is still time.

Lillian Sanders, Grade 12
Slater High School, MO

The Journey

Growing up in Hungary, every little boy has dreamed of visiting America. Fortunately for me, that came true when I was ten years old. My parents announced that we needed a better life and we would soon move to America. What we didn't realize was how hard things would be. Learning the language, finding a job for my parents, and adjusting to traditions was incredibly hard.

Excited and nervous we hopped on a schedule plane. After sixteen hours of flying and a day stay at New York, we found ourselves in the beautiful sunshine state. We soon arrived in a two-room apartment. We liked the small place, but the struggles that came after, were in immense proportions, and hit us with shock.

My mom couldn't get a job, the language was incredibly hard and we were drowning in financial debt. I remember my family's life in great depression. My mom would cry almost ever night, and my dad would work himself to death. Life seemed to be unfair.

Within time things were better. We found some great friends and my mom and dad are now holding stable jobs. I have the best parents in the world. They left a world of friends and family, so my brothers and I could be happier. Though we are still struggling here and there, we have fought incredibly hard and are now standing on our own two feet. I thank God for every happy day I get to share with my family.

Milan Fabian, Grade 11
Countryside High School, FL

The Game of the Stick

As not only the fastest growing sport, but also the fastest sport played on two feet, lacrosse has experienced drastic changes since its origins among fifteenth century Native American tribes. Sometimes lasting for several days, lacrosse was originally played by hundreds of men on fields stretching several miles long, as a way of settling disputes or preparing young men for combat. Players were often seriously injured or killed, and early balls were sometimes made out of the heads of a rival tribe. Since the 1600's, lacrosse has evolved into a more civilized and safe game. The objective, to use sticks to pass and catch a ball for the purpose of scoring goals, has remained the same, but modern lacrosse games are played on a regulation field by a set number of players for an established period of time. Men's lacrosse has retained a certain degree of the violence or physical contact common in the original game, but women's lacrosse, a non-contact sport, has developed into a game of intense skill and finesse rather than brute force. Rules, protective padding and helmets, referees, and a lengthy list of personal fouls, ranging from minor to major, help to prevent modern lacrosse from reaching the intensity and extremity which was achieved by the original, more deadly version of the "game of the stick."

Hillary Gunder, Grade 11
Bishop Verot High School, FL

What I Would Be

There are many important people in my life. For instance my family, friends, and people at school.

The most important people in my family would be my mother, and my boyfriend, Floyd. My mother taught me how to love, be considerate, and also how to be determined by motivating me. The reason Floyd is so important, is because he was the first person to show me compassion, and how to love. He also showed me how to be kind and caring. Without those two people in my life, I would be a bitter person.

As for my friends, Aleshia and Kelly, they help guide me down the right path, to make the right decisions. They both also have always been there to comfort me when I have been in a crisis, to give me good advice. So without my two friends, Aleshia and Kelly, I would be an emotional wreck.

In school my teachers are important to me, because they are great examples on my schooling. My teachers are examples of success mentally, as well as in life. When I acknowledge their success it urges me to become better academically. Without the good influences of my teachers, I wouldn't have made it this far in my schooling.

Although there are many important people in my life, they all serve as great influences in helping make the person I am growing into.

Nichole Edwards, Grade 11
Southside High School, NC

Reading

When asked the question, "What do you like to do in your spare time?" most kids respond with a sport or maybe even hanging with friends. When someone asks me that question, I respond by saying reading. Yes, I hang out with my friends often, but you can't do that twenty-four seven (even if you wanted to). So when I'm not with friends, I'm usually in my room or on the couch with a book in my hands and my head deeply indulged within it.

Reading is great for many reasons. It improves one's vocabulary skills and reading comprehension. Due to that fact that I read often, now when I'm asked to read something and then tell someone about it, I can usually remember everything that happened or was in the passage, which helps a lot in English when your teacher surprises you with a reading comprehension test (though it only helps if you actually read the chapters).

It also, in my opinion, is a great pastime that could, if more kids would do it, keep a lot of teenagers out of trouble (drugs, crime, etc.). It would give them something to do that helps them instead of having them on the streets doing stuff that just hurts them in the long run.

Reading is important for many reasons. Maybe you have different reasons on why reading is important to you. Whatever they are, they are important because they keep you reading.

Andrea Weatherford, Grade 10
Germantown High School, TN

The Nonexistent "Real World"

What is the "Real World?" If asked, almost every person would have a different opinion. Well, I believe that there is no such thing as the "real world."

We, my senior class and I, have, on occasion, been informed from some of our authorities that we are not in the "real world." Their reasoning for this is that we do not know the stresses according to their adult lives. But I believe that we have burdens that can be as difficult as if not more so, than their own. We have to worry about making good grades and choices so that we can be accepted to a preferred college. This is an anxiety because we are preparing for our future. Adults do have worries, such as pay bills and have a job, but we have jobs after we have endured a seven hour school day. I see their point of view; although, I do not believe that we are not in the "real world."

Elderly, retired people would probably say that those younger than they are too distraught about minuscule things that do not matter in the end. They also could say that the younger generation is not in the "real world" does not know what life is about.

These views of what the "real world" proves that there is no distinct definition. It is only a point of view or opinion. This is what gives me reason to believe that their "real world" does not exist.

Madison McLean, Grade 12
Trinity Christian Academy, AL

Hope for My Home

Whenever a person hears the word "home," he envisions a house with a beautiful green lawn, tall blooming trees, and the mouthwatering scents of homemade cookies; the place he grew up in. Whenever I think of my house, I still see this image; a beautiful lawn which demanded countless hours of strenuous work; the blooming trees, and my mom making delicious foods. But when I think of the word "home," I see broken streets, beggars littering the streets, smog forming a layer under the sky, and a green and white flag, with a star and crescent right in the middle. When I think of home, I see my homeland, my birthplace, Karachi, Pakistan.

I was born on January 22, 1991 in Karachi, a city in the destitute country of Pakistan. In Karachi, there are so many shootings daily that no one ever cares unless it is a politician, celebrity, or a religious leader. Electricity is so scarce that for hours, even days, families live without it, and lie outside to catch a breeze, to cool down from the searing heat.

But now, see something else when I see home. Where I see dying beggars on the streets, I also see the Aga Khan Hospital, the biggest hospital in all of Asia. Where I see people living without electricity, I also see hydroelectric dam that will soon solve this crisis. Now, I see hope for this country, for the people to have a life without these troubles.

Asad Ali Sajwani, Grade 11
Germantown High School, TN

Sticks and Stones

The old saying says that words can't hurt you, but the truth is words can completely tear you down and make you feel like nothing. Words when put into sentences can affect someone's whole outlook on life or their emotional being. If you tell someone they're fat or ugly it could cause someone to develop a psychological problem like an eating disorder.

Words spoken in a derogative manner can cut like knife, lacerating one's self-esteem. Even if it's something like a racial joke, you may think it's funny, but if someone is affected by what has just been said, then they could end up feeling completely degraded.

Even the strongest person in the world probably couldn't withstand a massive verbal beating. When you say something mean to someone that really affects them, it can remain in the back of their mind for days, weeks, months. Saying something harsh to someone is bad enough, but spreading something humiliating about them to a large group of people is atrocious. Having your mind manifested with ideas that everyone is saying something hateful about you is the worst emotional pain you can go through. Someone disliking you is hard enough, but when they're saying vicious things to and about you that is 100 times worse. Everyone should think before they speak because as fast as words can compliment, they can offend someone even faster. Although they say sticks and stones can break your bones, honestly words can completely annihilate you on the inside.

LeeAnne Sine, Grade 11
Vero Beach High School, FL

Addiction

"Coffee keeps me awake!" Many people exclaim this when asked for the reasons why they drink coffee. That cup of joe stimulates them to stay awake throughout the day, thus achieving their daily tasks successfully.

Coffee comes in a variety of flavors and it can either be hot or cold. Coffee companies such as Starbucks, Barney's, and Dunkin' Donuts have been recognized for the types of coffee they sell. With their artificial flavorings, taste buds are taken for a ride.

Although many may say that it's rather ridiculous to pay $3.00 for a cup of coffee, people still buy them. Why? Coffee is an addiction nationwide. Chocolate, energy drinks, and even energy gum have become the nation's latest sensation and there seems to be no slowing down. Americans love their coffee; they like the taste and do not mind paying for it.

And recently, many coffee company chains provide a trendier and more modern atmosphere with music which ranges from Ella Fitzgerald to Paolo Nutini. All Americans are addicted, like it or not, and that's perfectly fine.

Milagros Aliaga, Grade 11
Bishop Verot High School, FL

In Need of a Change

If I could change one thing in the world, I would change the negative expectations that are set for black teenagers. Most black teens are set for failure before given a chance to succeed. I believe that if this problem was removed from our world it would build more confidence in our generation. Although the majority of teens are proving society right as far as responsibility and respect, I would like for change to happen.

Since young black females and males are seen as sinful and uneducated, I guess we feel like we should go along with that stereotype. I've accepted the fact that we all are human and humans make mistakes. But these days teens know the consequences that come with their actions, and yet they still do it.

Additionally, I would change the decisions that teens make, especially in black communities. Our young minds can't process that society is recording our moves and sadly our mistakes are overruling our accomplishments. It is time that our generation stands up as one and proves the world wrong, and show them that we are here to present them with more than the ideas that have been previously established for us.

As a young teen in this day and age, I will make an attempt to break the chain of ignorance and no education that is supposedly possessed by me and my peers. I know that this cannot be achieved over night but a change from one individual is a start.

Destini Johnson, Grade 11
City University School of Liberal Arts, TN

Moving Forward

I enjoy running. Not the slow fifteen mile runs but the fast 5k races. The 5k is my specialty. I was not an experienced runner until last summer. I started because I found out I could run a mile in six minutes and twelve seconds. I had run few 5ks before that point, but I had run cross-country in my middle school. The team was not that good, and I did not enjoy it. I would actually think of excuses to get out of running. I have grown taller since middle school, and I think that was the key to my improvement. I developed a longer stride, but that was not everything. I naturally developed a breathing rhythm that worked. I found out just last week that my style was one of the most common. I ran about ten 5ks in 2006 and 2007. I ran each one at an average of twenty minutes. Twenty minutes is not a fast time, but for someone who did not train, it was blazing. These races were run for different charities.

When school started, I had been running for the Germantown High School cross-country team for two weeks. I was steadily improving until I was injured. Running maybe ten miles a month to forty miles a week took a toll. I was out three weeks. All of my running has taught me perseverance; the only way to finish, or get something done is to just keep moving forward.

James Tatum, Grade 10
Germantown High School, TN

My Team

I have been going to Rossville since fifth grade. I have always been in love with our basketball program. We have won three championships in the last ten years. I had always dreamed of wearing a Rossville jersey and playing on our floor.

I started practicing with our high school team in seventh grade. I feel that we had the best team that year. Coach Vincent Askew really taught me a lot of new techniques. That year we easily won our second state championship. I was not able to play in the game, but I was proud to have practiced with them.

My eighth grade year we hired a new coach, Tavis Rutherford. He is probably the best coach I have ever had, he taught me and the team so much. With our talent and his coaching we won our second straight state championship. Due to the fact that I was only in the eighth grade, I was not able to receive a state ring. After seeing those rings I worked out even harder so I might get one some day.

My ninth grade year I was finally able to officially join the team. Coach Tavis Rutherford left right before the season started. Our whole team was very disappointed but continued to work hard. That year we made it to the state tournament, but lost to I.C. 95 to 100. It was a good game but we just could not pull it off.

This year we are working very hard to bring the state title back to Rossville Christian Academy.

Daniel Banks, Grade 11
Rossville Christian Academy, TN

The "Write" Stuff

Is it important for adults to be able to write well in today's world? In today's world it is important for adults to be able to write because writing is 80% of the world's fundamentals which means we need critical thinkers, problem solvers, and political environmentalists who can communicate well. Writing is important in all areas of society.

First, the best way to explain how important to other environmental strategies writing is would be to state what would happen if we were to neglect this issue. Environmentalists don't depend on election trends to be neglected since they devoted significant resources to supporting pro-environmental candidates, which encodes writing with literature.

Next, critical thinkers have a lot to do with writing. Critical thinkers are honest with themselves according to what they do not know. They watch their limitations in public speaking as well as mistakes on paper.

In addition, the world is a map that must be read and written. You would have to understand the literature to understand directions. Also, being an adult mean taking care of what's important in the society, the economy and the livelihood of everyday people which can only be expressed with good communication skills.

In conclusion, a long healthy life is no accident. It begins with good sense; it also depends on good habits. The world is set up to have exceptions of all humans. The chemical of writing is the combination of thoughts on paper.

Donnell Hubbard, Grade 10
Gadsden Job Corps Center, AL

Dancing Feathers

Have you ever seen something or thought of something that reminded you of someone? I have seen things that remind me of my grandfather who passed away six years ago. I see feathers that just float around in the air and it's like time has stopped and all I see is this feather dancing around like it's a sign that my grandfather is still here watching over me. I believe that my grandfather is in heaven and he is watching me and making sure that my life is headed in the right direction like he used to when he was alive. Even though he is not alive I know he loves and still cares for me because he shows me signs like the feathers, which lets me know that it is true. I love my grandfather and every time I see one of those feathers it makes me think that he's there watching from above and he's just letting me know he still cares. I only wish that he were still alive for I would give anything just to hug him once more. I loved him and I always will. He will always have a place in my heart and I hope he keeps sending me signs that he's still here because when it comes time that we will be reunited in heaven it will be far greater.

Laura Bordwine, Grade 11
Owasso High School, OK

Go Bogo for Shoes

What is some thing you never leave the house without, and they always match? Shoes of course, the key point of an outfit. Shoes are one of my favorite things to have. I have so many pairs and not enough feet to wear them.

There are several types of shoes that I want to talk about. Dress shoes are a key thing to have. Everyone should have at least two pairs of dress shoes, a black pair and a brown pair. Brown and black go with everything. A pair of tennis shoes would be a good thing to have. I buy tennis shoes for looks not for athletic use. If a pair of tennis shoes goes with my outfit then I'll wear them. Another type of shoes is casual shoes. A casual shoe would be a boat shoe. I have many pairs of casual shoes. They should be comfortable shoes and go with almost everything. Mary Janes are another casual shoe. They come in many colors and styles. Summer shoes are another one of my favorites. Flip flops are a style of summer shoes. They come in many colors, some with a back and others with heels. An open toe shoe would also be considered a summer shoe. Colorful shoes are a good thing to have! It adds flavor to your outfit and it completes it.

The first thing I look at when I approach someone is their shoes. So a good thing is to have nice shoes on wherever you go!

Katlyn Dabbs, Grade 12
Trinity Christian Academy, AL

The Sport of Rodeo

In the sport of rodeo, there are numerous timed events that can be participated in.

First, barrel racing is an event normally participated by only cowgirls. In this event there are three barrels in which there is a clover-leaf pattern to follow. The challenge of this event is mainly to get the quickest time and leave all three barrels standing.

Next, the cowboys compete in an event called team roping. There are two riders and two horses and their goal is to work together as a team to rope a steer. One of the cowboys will rope the head and after the head of the steer is caught, the other cowboy tries to rope the steer's two back feet. Finally, if they are successful, the clock will stop, and the team with the fastest time will walk away with the victory.

Last, but definitely not least, the most dangerous, the most favored, and the most nerve-racking event in which the cowboys participate is bull riding. The stock owners bring in their unsurpassed bucking bulls and the cowboys try to stay on their back for at least eight seconds.

In conclusion, these are only a few of the events in the sport of rodeo. At the end of the rodeo, the rider may walk away with a gold buckle, a cash prize, or an objective to work harder to achieve the rider's dream.

Lauren Wilson, Grade 11
Escambia Academy, AL

Hurricane Season 2004

In 2004 Florida had a very active hurricane season. My hometown of Vero Beach was hit by Hurricane Frances and Hurricane Jeanne.

Like other Floridians, my family and I were preparing for Hurricane Frances, but also enduring the loss of my Uncle Carter. Right after the funeral the men boarded up the windows on our homes and the women got necessary supplies. We finished just in time.

Though we were stuck in a house without power we remained strong. When Frances was over we ran outside to see the damage. Our homes suffered minor damage compared to others.

A few weeks later we heard about Hurricane Jeanne and her expected strength. Once more we waited in huge lines to get our surplus of supplies, because we didn't know how bad it would be so we prepared for the worst. Luckily we didn't have to board up our windows, because we left the old wood on.

Once again we waited it out, but when it was over my family was in shock. Our oak tree almost fell on our house and needed to be cut down immediately. The roof on our house had patches of missing shingles. Our yard was littered with debris and holding water.

All of the damage has been repaired since Hurricane Jeanne. Fortunately, all of my family members lived through both hurricanes. My experience with Hurricane Frances and Jeanne was frightening. Hopefully we won't have another hurricane for a long time.

Sabrina Curry, Grade 11
Vero Beach High School, FL

Trust

Trust in the Lord your God. Most people worry too much about the little details of their lives. When people worry about things it stresses people out and they can't live their life to the fullest. People should pray to God and not worry about the little things, they should trust Him.

Other points of view exist. There are people who say they pray to God but they say He doesn't answer. There are people who say God doesn't care so people shouldn't pray. There are people who say even if they pray to God, they still worry. These statements are false in most cases. God will always answer prayers, although it may not be the answer people want and people may have to wait for His answer. God always cares. If God didn't care He wouldn't have taken the time to make the human body so complex. He wouldn't have made each flower so detailed and provide water and sunlight for it to grow if He did not care. If you pray and you truly trust in God then you will not worry.

People should pray to God, and trust that He will take care of their worries. Don't worry. Do pray. God will answer because He loves you, He cares about you, He always answers prayers, and you trust Him.

Chelsea Cooper, Grade 10
Greenwood High School, KY

My Revolutionary March

I slowly boarded a large charter bus where I would be spending the majority of the next two days exploring myself. At that moment in my life, as an independent, biracial teen, I had been contemplating which part of my heritage I wanted to embrace, mainly because of the recent events of the Jena 6. "Am I black or white?" I pondered to myself as I climbed what seemed to be an endless flight of steps onto the bus.

For a lengthy seven hours, I rode in the back of the bus sharing and discussing common interests in life with my black friends. At that time, I thought that I knew for sure with whom I wanted to identify with.

We finally reached our destination: Jena, Louisiana. To my surprise, I stepped off the bus into a crowd of 25,000 people who all shared a common goal of peacefully overcoming the injustices of the Jena 6. I figured that the crowd would only contain African Americans, but it also included members of the second part of my heritage. Together as one unit, we marched up the streets of Jena to the revolutionary courthouse and the infamous Jena High School.

Looking into the mixed crowd, I realized that I could embrace both sides of me. If two different groups of people could unite to reach a common goal, why could I not let my heritages work together within me to achieve my individuality?

Michael McGee, Grade 11
Germantown High School, TN

My Best Friend, My Father

It was eight in the evening. The sky was a deep purple and I could see the leaves of the palm tree outside my window swaying gently.

My phone rang. I stood up from where I was sitting to answer; it was my father. He calls me every day to check up on me and see how I am feeling. "Fine," I usually say. But tonight there was a different answer.

"I am having trouble with this essay," I spoke nonchalantly; "I have no idea how to start it." I told him the subject matter. He suggested to think about what makes me happy, what gets me through tough situations when I feel I cannot cope. I thanked him for the inspiration and we shortly ended our conversation.

"I love you," he said.

"Love you too." I hung up the phone.

My father is a huge inspiration and teacher. Every time we are together, he is like a friend, telling me about his past and how he achieved even in tough situations. He inspires me to do well in school and to stay away from trouble.

Our relationship is open and is one I do not have with any other person in my life.

Shelley Rush, Grade 11
Countryside High School, FL

Where I'm From

Some people think they really know who you are, when really you're just a mere blur in front of their face. Like the dust blowing in the wind, or the breeze of a stream blowing through your hair. You know they can't feel the way you do. They do not know how it feels to be in your shoes. They don't know where you've been, or what your intentions on life really are. Where you're from can affect things like who likes you, who looks up to you, or who gives you their respect in the short term. Although in long term talk, the respect is earned by who you are, and what you're about. I see this myself from my past experiences. When I was young, the family moved around a lot because of many different reasons. Of course, that meant I had to go to a new school and meet new friends. This was very hard for me at this time because I was young and didn't know what to expect going to a new school. The longer I went there, the more I got to know people, and was more respected for who I was and what I was about. After living in one place for a while I would end up moving again very soon and have to start all over. Now living in Slater for seven years, I've begun to be proud of where I'm from.

Jermie Pittman, Grade 10
Slater High School, MO

The Red Scapegoat

A scapegoat, also known as a group or individual who is blamed for others' actions, is a way of slipping through the cracks, so only one gets burned. It is often an object of irrational hostility. Throughout history, America has produced many scapegoats for its obscene actions, such as the communist Red Scare in the 1920s.

To begin, a new threat had risen to the Americans who greatly feared communism. Emotions were rising, which led them into a xenophobic repression. They now had a scapegoat, provided by the red scare, because they were no longer fighting the Germans. Many also feared the decline of cheap immigrant labor and wanted to eliminate confining government controls upon themselves.

Tragically, the American "Reds" were persecuted for the communism in Europe. They were branded for most of their lives, even if merely accused. Senator McCarthy went after communist sympathizers, not just the communists. They were arrested in their own homes, thrown into jail without an attorney and interrogated. The Department of Justice held total disregard for their American rights. These Americans were treated somewhat like the women of the widely known Salem Witch Trials.

Eventually, the Red Scare died down, but didn't fade away completely. There are still many communist organizations running countries we Americans interact with every day. Scapegoats have been a common occurrence throughout history and prove only one thing: it is easier to point your finger at the whole rather than at one individual.

Olive Davis, Grade 12
Jessieville High School, AR

I Always Wanted to Be a Princess

My hero is known to me for her brave sense of courage. She lived a great life, and died an unjust death. She learned from her mistakes, loved to help others; had fun, but could be serious.

Seeing her parents divorce, Diana swore to marry once, only for love, and never for money. Diana fell in love with Prince Charles and the world fell in love with Diana. In love together they had two boys, Harry and William. Both had extramarital affairs, and divorced in August of 1996. She was hurt, but stayed true to her children. She always remembered her duties as a mother.

In her spare time, Diana hugged AIDS patients and land-mine victims. She liked to help and succeeded at it. Her biggest achievement was raising awareness of several issues including AIDS and homelessness. She enjoyed being the most famous woman in the world and used it to help others.

Diana knew what she wanted to portray by what she wore and never failed to make a statement. Even if she wanted to "dress down" she wore jackets with special designs, made to never crease. She was well-dressed and the designers knew what to make for her.

Princess Diana was too famous, if at all possible. She died in a car accident, being pursued by photographers. Some people believe it was murder, others believe it was an accident. People gather to mourn her death to this day. What we don't realize is that she's still here in spirit! Honorable Diana Frances Spencer will always be my hero.

Kayleigh Hope, Grade 11
Mulhall-Orlando High School, OK

Who's Handicap?

Who has the right to park in a handicap parking spot? A lot of people park in handicap spots when they don't have a sticker. Excuses that I have heard are, I was running late today or my ankle was really hurting today. What about those people who don't have an arm or leg, what do they do? I think leaving those spaces open is respectful. It is along the same line as respecting your elders.

I know a man who is a paraplegic, who is a person who is paralyzed from the waist down or the lower limbs could be caused by a spinal cord injury. Which has two daughters that both play two sports. At the school, they have handicap spots but are in small supply, just like any other school. When all the people are running late to a game or match and they park in the handicap places, what does he do? He would not be able to go to their games because he couldn't get the wheelchair around to the side of his truck between the other cars to get himself out.

What if it was your dad, brother, friend and he could not get out of his car to come see you. I think they should raise the ticket costs and maybe people will stop parking in those spots. Police and security guards should pay more attention to all these things!!

Karli Booher, Grade 12
Walker Valley High School, TN

Education Today

Today when kids think about an important event in America's history, what are they thinking? Do they think about the Founding Fathers: "Wow, those men were so smart!"? Do they think about the American Revolution: "Those men really thought about the direction they were headed and wanted to change it"? It would show promise for today's kids if that was what they believed. However it is more common for today's kids to think, "When am I ever going to need to know who fought a battle with Native Americans in Tennessee?" or "I know what the American Revolution was about so why am I still learning minute details?" Kids today want to learn more about the history of a video game than the history of our country.

This attitude shows that teachers are facing something entirely new. More students are focusing on what happened rather than why or how it happened. Children are becoming impatient and want summaries of the material rather than a textbook. Students want extra credit, test reviews, and study guides so they can know exactly what is on the test and only study that. There is no interest in actual learning anymore. Students only care about getting good grades so they can go to college, get a good job, and become rich. Soon students who really want to learn and know anything other than how to text during school without getting caught will have to study at a foreign school.

Katie Bridson, Grade 11
Germantown High School, TN

Friends vs Family

The single most positive force in a teenager's life is family. Other people might say their friends are their most positive force. Friends are good but they come and go and aren't guaranteed to always be there when you need them, unlike most families. My family is always there when I need them. I feel a lot more comfortable at home than any other place. When I am at home, I can totally relax. I don't have to worry about my hair, whether my breath smells or anything else that deals with me having to look a certain way. When I'm with my family, I can be myself.

The main reason my family is the most positive force in my life is because I know they will be there for me if I need them. If I need advice about school, friends, or just life, they will always be there to give it, and I know that they will not judge me. I can trust what they are telling me because they have my best interest in mind and they won't tell me anything that might harm me or get me into any trouble. They always support me. Friends are easier to tell things to sometimes but if it's something you want to be kept secret, they are not always going to do that, unlike family who are very supportive, honest, and encouraging.

Alexis Tuggle, Grade 11
City University School of Liberal Arts, TN

American Families

When looking into today's families you see a massive pull apart from the way it used to be. Families used to value that time they spent together helping and enjoying each other and the presence they bring. Playing games, eating dinner, and taking family vacations is becoming a thing of the past. Bringing our families back together again and uniting the bonds they used to have could strengthen and improve the moral values of American society greatly! Look back to Roman society and you see a decrease in morality and values as the empire began to decline. Rape, thievery, and abuse all increased. Family togetherness was little to nothing, most likely being the cause of all these acts. The same thing is beginning to happen here in America. Families drift, the values and morals parents are to project on their children lessen; children grow up with these pathetic ideas, and things continue to worsen. If there is to be any hope for a better America things need to be changed in the home, because that is the start of every person's well-being. Children who grow up with their mom, dad, brothers, and sisters, who spend time together, and proven to become more accomplished and successful people. All due to the fact that they have the support they need at all times! Families are the roots of everything within a country; do you want to see a better America tomorrow? How about starting at home.

Jon Grossman, Grade 11
Vero Beach High School, FL

Alvin Weidman

My grandfather, Alvin Weidman, whom I call Pap, is the most courageous and strong person I know.

When Pap turned eighteen, he decided to join the Navy. However, because his family was extremely poor, he was severely malnourished. The day that he went to enlist, he stood four feet and eleven inches tall, and weighed only ninety-nine pounds. He was turned down and told to come back when he grew. Pap refused to go home.

He was sent to the office of an officer of higher position, who again told him that he was too small and had to go home. Pap again refused to go home and began to cry. The officer reluctantly agreed to let him join. He warned him that his time in the Navy was going to be extremely tough. He told him the others would be very cruel to him about his size and he explained how grueling the training would be. He gave Pap his card and told him to call him if things got too difficult and he would give him an honorable discharge. Still, Pap wanted to go.

The officer was right about everything, but Pap never gave in. The other guys did torture him daily and the training was extremely difficult. At the beginning of his training, a buddy would help him carry his equipment, because Pap was too weak.

Pap's great inner strength and courage touches me so deeply and makes me so proud that he is my grandfather.

Jillian Palmer, Grade 11
Bishop Verot High School, FL

In My Spare Time

From my point of view, the hobbies of my choice I like to do in my spare time are reading, singing, and dancing.

First, in my spare time, I like to read. The reason that I like reading is because you can learn a lot of things from reading such as: how to write poetry, and activities in the everyday life that interest you. Reading also keeps me occupied when I am bored, and when I have nothing else to do. That's why I like reading.

Secondly, in my spare time, I like to sing. The reason I like singing is I like to sing my favorite songs that come on the television and the radio. I also like to sing when that annoying someone gets on my nerves, and aggravates me, so I sing to drown them out. I also sing in church and in the shower to get my tone up. But most nights when I feel down, depressed, or stressed I sing my favorite song until I fall asleep. That's why I like singing.

Lastly, in my spare time, I like to dance. I like to dance because I'm good at it, and because I have been dancing since I can remember. That's what I have been doing many years with my friends and that's what we love to do. So that's why I love dancing.

So those are the hobbies that I like to do in my spare time: reading, singing, and dancing.

Ta'Keyna Carter, Grade 11
Southside High School, NC

No Regrets

Police cars at the apartment I called home — I could see them from my bus stop. I assumed that my brother had done something stupid again and they were going to give him "a slap on the wrist" — like usual. I was wrong. They were there for an arrest, two to be exact.

My sister's school had seen the burn mark my brother left on her arm. My mother hadn't taken her to see a doctor. She knew the way to treat it was to keep it covered, and she instructed my sister as such. Obviously, my sister chose not to obey.

I saw my mother being read her rights and put into handcuffs. My brother was taken to the Juvenile Detention Center. My three younger siblings and I were tossed into the Foster Care System, being placed with our aunt and uncle.

This occurred two years ago, and yet, these few hours are as vivid in my memory as if it was just this afternoon. During the past two years, I've moved five times. Flaws in our Dependency Court have been revealed to me. I'm determined to some day fix these problems. This experience has made me the person that I am.

The most important lesson I've learned is to live my life without regret. EVERYTHING happens for a reason. What happens must happen. I wouldn't have it any other way.

Bryanna Dunne, Grade 11
Countryside High School, FL

The Truth About Respect

Respect. It is a word that is heard often from parents, teachers, and on occasion, people not even known. Being respectful has nothing to do with the way people are raised, beliefs, ethnicity, or age. It is simply the way a civilized person should behave, in public or at home.

People today have forgot what respect is about. It is a word that many people live by, and others have never heard of. Respect is simply an action that should require no thought; it should be a voluntary movement of the body. There are several other names for the word respect, like polite, kind, formal, and modest.

People know little of what the word really means. In the dictionary, respect means 1) relation to a particular thing or situation, 2) act of giving particular attention, or 3) high or special regard. Respect in my mind, means what you give or get according to actions. Examples of polite or respectful words include please, thank you, and excuse me.

So the next time you are headed out of the grocery store, hold the door for the person behind you. Or if someone holds the door for you, say thank you as you walk by. You will truly feel better knowing that you know manners.

Danae Elizabeth Eddy, Grade 10
Slater High School, MO

Why We Believe

Everyone who watches sports does do for one reason, and that is the feeling they get when they have witnessed something incredible. Whether it is a game-winning goal in a backyard soccer game, or a buzzer-beating heave from mid-court in the finals of the NCAA Tournament, nothing tastes sweeter than seeing your squad triumph over what seemed insurmountable odds. Although we as sports fans love to champion our team, often praying to God that if He will let us prevail this one time we'll go to church every Sunday, we must also suffer stomach-wrenching failures.

Many times after heart-rending losses we spectators do not know how to react. We are stunned. I remember sitting in a stadium until there was no one left but the janitorial staff and me, staring in disbelief at an empty field because we had squandered another opportunity at greatness, or at least another week's worth of bragging rights. It is our commission as fans not only to storm the field and rejoice with our team when they seize the elusive victory, but also to weep with them when they suffer an agonizing defeat. It is experiences like these that show our true character as devotees and make us return each season to cheer and jeer our beloved lineup in hopes of sharing in their glory and reveling in a few, brief moments of jubilation. That is what we live for, and that is why we are fans.

Sam Evans, Grade 10
Germantown High School, TN

Lucas Aaron

It was June 15th, 2007, 8:10 in the morning. My life changed. I was seventeen years old when my mother decided to have a baby at the age of forty-two. I remember walking into the hospital with her. It all felt surreal. The doctors came in and wheeled my mom away. I was left to change into a pair of mismatched scrubs. Minutes felt like hours as I waited for them to come back for me. Walking into the delivery room I heard the doctor say, "We've already started. Would you like to look over the curtain as the baby is born?"

I replied, "Um, no thank you," as I pictured myself passed out on the delivery room floor. Minutes passed, and I heard crying. Lucas Aaron was born, 10 lbs. and 21 inches long. Tears came to my eyes when I saw my little brother for the first time.

I cut the cord, and was the first to hold him. I already knew that there was going to be a special connection between me and my brother. It is a day I will always remember, and one day I will be able to share that moment with him.

Sammi Smalley, Grade 12
Slater High School, MO

Like an Eagle

You don't have to be free. You don't have to fly through thunderstorms. You only have to let the animal in you out. Tell me about your depression and I'll tell you about my joy. Meanwhile, his world turns; the eagle flies through the air with his wonderful, wide wings.

The sky is a light blue shallow creek in which the salmon gather in the deeper parts when they see the eagle's shadow circling around the creek. The world like an eagle is superior and terrifying. However scared you are to be yourself continue to be free like that eagle hovering.

Stephan Jaeger, Grade 12
Baylor School, TN

My Family

I would like to tell you about my family. I have three brothers and one sister; I also have two nieces and one nephew. My dad is a pastor at Edward Christian Church, my mom, she works at National Spinning. My brother's name is D.C., which that stands for David Clayton he is 25 years old. He is in a band called Ghost Riders. DC has a little girl, Cierra, who is five years. My brother Daniel, he has a little girl named Emery. She is almost nine months. Daniel is a sheriff for Beaufort County. It is so cool. My brother Nick, he does not have any children right now. He is only 20 years old. He lives with us. He is trying to get a job.

My sister Tamela she is the one with the big boy Dillion. What I mean is he was born at ten pounds and five ounces. When he came out my dad said that the doctors had to chase Dillion off the playground. I have a great family. They are the best thing that has ever happened to me. God has given me the most precious gift.

Bethany Linton, Grade 11
Southside High School, NC

Parents

Why can't we just please our parents sometimes? Parents' standards are a lot higher these days, while young adults continue to work hard. Parents may not realize this, but their children do try to meet their regulations. Most of the time, teens find it very difficult to live up to their parents' standards.

Other points of view do exist, or not everyone would agree that teens find it difficult to live up to their parents' standards. If parents are lenient on their children they will be good friends, but if a parent does not say, "no," the child will do anything that he or she wants to. A lot of parents would say, "Well, they just need to listen to me," but teens have a lot going on at that age, and it's not that easy.

Teenagers have a hard time trying to meet their parents' regulations. Every teen will be rebellious, because it is just the age. To a young adult, it is very frustrating when you cannot please your parents.

Lauren Ackerman, Grade 10
Greenwood High School, KY

Unblinded

America, a land of "amber waves of grain," is one of the most affluent countries in the world. Those who have a "plentiful supply of goods," are often blinded to the needs of others less fortunate. It is hard to empathize with the poor and downtrodden engaged in death or life struggles yet compassion demands a response.

A privilege I will never forget was going on a mission trip to the inner streets of Chicago. Due to the dangers, my parents almost prevented me from participating. Unlike home, Chicago offered a unique atmosphere that made me uncomfortable. The trip occurred the week of July 4, 2007. As a native told us of the many times he experienced shootings, we were startled by a firework explosion that resembled a gunshot.

The purpose of the mission was to offer kids a safe environment by providing a free basketball clinic that proved to be moving and successful. In church, several attendees offered their testimonies including a boy named Juan who loved basketball, but couldn't play in school because of his grades. His parents confided that the wrong crowd was influencing Juan. At camp, Juan requested a safe haven where people would help him with his schoolwork while he avoided trouble.

Stepping outside my comfort zone allowed me an opportunity to see the benefits of compassion firsthand. Being involved in a mission trip to an area of less affluence, challenged me to recognize the needs of those around me. I became unblinded.

Ashley Prentice, Grade 11
Owasso High School, OK

No Better Word

It was May 20, 2006 when the words erupted right out of his mouth and straight to my heart. With pride he said, "Kiarra I want you to be mine, will you go with me?" The tears fell and I said "yes." I know what you are thinking, she act like he proposed and to answer that question it's called love, and there's no better word.

Everyone thought it was the cutest thing. He is a football player and I am a cheerleader. Darius simply means everything to me and he is my best friend. People need to understand everyone is different and not all hearts are made the same. There is someone out there for everybody, therefore be patient and it will arrive.

Love is that four letter word that society as a whole tends to abuse. Some accept it as a major in their life and for some it's minor. There's always that special person in your life you don't ever want to lose, but at the same time you can't live with them and you can't live with out. So when it comes down to it you're in love, and there's no better feeling in this world being happy and proudly loved.

I appreciate everything in my life. I can proudly say "I don't ever want to lose him," and I respect that word called love. Sometimes if you love someone set them free, and if they come back it was meant to be!

Kiarra Roberson, Grade 12
Hopewell High School, NC

Poverty Exists Everywhere

Most people travel in their lives. I've been graced into a family that recognizes the importance in my seeing what the world outside the United States is like. Every year my parents take my brother and I to the Dominican Republic.

While there we get to try activities that are scarce in the United States. My dad and I enjoy an extreme sport: kite boarding. I'm proud of my father and his resolve not to let age get in his way. We also enjoy the other natural beauties of the Dominican Republic such as the Caribbean waters.

I'm also exposed to third world conditions. Poverty exists everywhere and it has made me realize that when people tell most Americans "You don't know how good you have it," that they really don't. The hovels that some Dominicans live in would fit in some American's homes. Children that have high levels of intelligence are reduced to scrapping for food.

The vendors in the street try and do business while being undercut by their cheating neighbors which the government leaves unchecked. Most Dominicans in touristy locations have taught themselves English by listening to the language from passersby. Most are in jobs that they are unsuited for, but cannot leave for fear of bankruptcy and inconsistency of businesses.

This experience has shown me much of what most Americans take for granted. I can only thank my parents for exposing me to the world that America has turned a blind eye.

Paul S. Polgar, Grade 11
Countryside High School, FL

A True Friend

Among life's most valuable treasures are true friends. A true friend is rare. However, the relationship is permanent and fulfilling.

A true friend is willing to accept one's flaws, and she will love her friend regardless of her mistakes. Others look for the flaws in people, judge them, and look forward to their failures.

A true friend encourages one to make right decisions and never purposefully leads her in the wrong way. She is always thinking in the best interests of her loved ones.

Friends will be optimistic while others are pessimistic. They will help a person to have a wise and calm reaction. Friends will be honest, even if it means saying that a person is wrong.

A true friend will be protective and will not let others talk in an insulting way about her friend. She will be indignant when someone hurts her friend.

In adversity, a friend will listen intently and focus on what one's problem, rather than making her friend listen while she talks. She will learn details and show great concern about the predicament.

Finally, a true friend will eschew jealousy; she will be selfless. She will not resent her friend's accomplishments, but she will be happy in her friend's achievements.

Being a true friend is hard and time-consuming. Friendship cannot happen instantly, but it must grow and mature through the experiences friends will face together. Always remember: to have a true friend, one must be a true friend.

Melly Helm, Grade 12
New Covenant Christian School, SC

Skateboarding

Flying down a smoothed, paved road! The thrill of launching off a ramp, and getting big air! The frightening attempt of ollieing the biggest set of stairs you've ever seen! And being able to land it! These are things that goes through a skater's mind. They are the reasons we do them too. This is what goes through all the skaters, young and old.

Skating, to me, is my everyday way of life. In everything I do I think about skating. The way I visualize objects, places, and everything else is based on skateboarding. I can look at a square and think of a way to skate it. Going to places like the mall or a park I look at the details of what the surface of the ground is. I ask myself, "Is it too rough? What tricks could I do? Is it too hard for me?" Sometimes I get advice or help from my friends. Skating with a group of your closest friends is the best way to skate. They can push you. They give confidence. Helping and going to organizations like Unity Skate Church is a great way to make and meet friends.

Skating is not just a sport. It's a way of life for me, and for many others. They may be young or old, but we all have the passion for skateboarding.

Carson Waldrop, Grade 10
Shades Mountain Christian School, AL

Death in the Neighborhood

As the sun shines on my face I awoke to the sound of sirens ringing in my ear, I turned over thinking that it was just a dream as I hear the front door slam shut. Then there was the sound of my mom's bare feet on the pavement outside my bedroom window. As I jumped out of bed I heard my dad trying to rock my baby sister, Kayleigh, back to sleep. I was afraid to open the bedroom door to ask what happened, so I didn't. I went back to my room to look out my window to find my other two siblings, Megan and Jon looking out the window already.

Megan was on the verge of tears and when I opened my mouth to ask why, she pointed out the window down the street to our neighbor's house. As I looked out the window I saw the ambulance taking a small figure out of the house on a stretcher covered in a sheet. I burst into tears. When my mom came home I found out for sure that my four year old neighbor, Faith Marie Whittle, had died.

The funeral and wake were scheduled for five days later. The wake was marked by many tears. Then the funeral was marked by even more. We all miss her very much. Anyone who knew her knew how pure and innocent this child was, and she will be in our hearts forever and always.

Jessica Newton, Grade 11
Vero Beach High School, FL

That Green Stuff

It was that look, the same one every time. It was characterized by the squinting, disapproving doubt in the stare. I could probably have recognized it from a distance since I was so acquainted with it. I also got it when a proud peer student in Spanish 2 asked me what foreign language I was taking. Their only reply to my answer was, "Latin! Why? It's a dead language." That look typically, more often than not, originated from the contents of my cerulean lunch box. For some oblivious reason to me, people continuously had to point out "that green stuff," as they called it.

I guess people just didn't comprehend that eating healthy food was a part of who I am, a part of how I grew up, and a part of what I enjoyed. Since sports are a significant part of my life, drinking soda has never been worth all of the health problems. The best advice I received was from a person who always seemed to be on a pure-sugar only diet. He said, "Why you try so hard? You gonna die anyway."

When I was much younger, I let it get to me. I would stand up for myself, but there was always this minute part of me deep down inching to cry out from the stabbing, throbbing pain. I began to accept who I was, no longer humiliated by my most preferred foods: from broccoli, lettuce, and grapes to even the avocado and kiwi.

DR Itayem, Grade 10
Germantown High School, TN

What You May Not Know About Diabetes

You might know someone who has diabetes, but do you really understand what it's all about? Diabetes has to do with the pancreas' beta cells that produce insulin. Insulin is what enables your body to absorb sugar (fuel). It attaches to insulin receptors on a cell's outer membrane (wall). The insulin then lures sugar and directs it to the cells inside.

In diabetics, not enough insulin is made or not used in the right way. So cells cannot take in sugar, giving them no fuel. Unused sugar is left in the blood. So the kidneys work harder to filter out the excess glucose, the urine then become sugary. Overworked kidneys soon lose their ability to take in water as needed, causing many bathroom trips.

Type one diabetes is where a person produces no insulin. Type two is when a person is unable to use what they produce. So why doesn't insulin do its job? The theory is that for type one diabetes, the person's own immune system destroys the insulin producing cells. For type two, an over mass-produced protein call poly peptide might be at fault.

Type one diabetic symptoms include rapid weight loss, constant hunger and diabetic coma. For type two, symptoms include fatigue, extreme thirst and blurred vision. Still, certain tests must be taken to confirm that someone is diabetic. For example, a blood test might be taken. Still, a diabetic can have a normal life.

Tabitha Gill, Grade 11
Vero Beach High School, FL

Falling

The darkness of the looming opening curled around me as my hands tightly gripped the metal sides. I mentally prepared my four-year-old mind for the oncoming whirling confusion of metal and plastic. As I glanced down the ground stretched away from my lone tower as it began to sprout towards the clouds. I gulped; this edge of the world would soon free-fall into a blur of color. There was no going back for the line of other kids awaiting the same fate had grown to epic proportion and their restlessness had been slowly eating away at my persona as they chattered, birds twittering nervously and raising their feathers to the sky.

"Come on, hurry up," the raven nearest me chirped impatiently. The time had come for me to delve into the madness of the rabbit hole. Scooting towards the gaping chute, I quickly attempted to calculate my approach. Suddenly, a kick from behind sent me spinning down the slippery slope to the awaiting wood chip strewn ground. I frantically jammed my foot at the wall beside while simultaneously pushing myself sideways. The momentum stopped me and I hung there, helplessly feeling the friction of my shoe against metal slowly begin to slip. "Hey kid, you're clogging the slide!" I dropped to the bottom, a stone succumbing to gravity, and flew, sprawling onto the ground. Spitting wood chips out of my mouth, I lay there until the next kid went sailing down the slide and landed on top of me.

A.J. Tirrell, Grade 12
Germantown High School, TN

On Your Mark, Get Set, Go!

Cross country is a team sport that takes determination and commitment to succeed. Determination is having what it takes to not quit and reach your goal. Cross country races are run on roads or in woods. A normal race is 3.1 miles or 5k. Boys and girls will normally run separate unless it is a small cross country meet.

The state cross country meet is in October. In the last few weeks before the state meet, I try to fit in many speed workouts to condition myself. In the state race the team must have at least five runners or the team will not be scored. The team with the lowest score is the champion.

Marathons fall in about the same group as cross country. A marathon is about 26.6 miles. My cross country coach, Joel Lambert, has run in the Boston Marathon. To run a marathon takes running many miles a day and determination to reach a goal. Cross country, marathons, and any sport teaches athletes to not quit and to stick with it. The lesson that being active in sports teaches me will help me the rest of my life.

Running and being in shape are healthy for my body. Even walking or jogging will be enough to get someone in shape. My Paw Paw is 89, and he still walks two miles a day. He has a garden that he works in every day. So many young people today are out of shape; it is not healthy for America.

Wade Matthews, Grade 10
Escambia Academy, AL

What Do You Get Out of It

With friends, there comes peer pressure. With family, there comes responsibility. Everyone has their own opinion about what's good for them and what isn't. In my opinion, I feel that family is a more positive force than friends.

With family, you receive confidence, motivation, and the thought of loved ones supporting you. Your family gives you the courage to do what's right. They have been in your shoes before so they know how you feel and the kinds of things you go through. Your family supports you in whatever it is that you want to succeed in. They will try as hard as you to accomplish your biggest goals. The reason for this is called love and you can get a lot of it from them.

Friends, on the other hand, cause too much drama. Sometimes you may think a person is your friend and they're not. Friends cause you to do things that you know aren't right. Fake, jealously, and hatred are some of the words that come to mind when I think about friends and my future. You may think they have your back but they could quickly turn on you.

Essentially, your family is the best thing for you now and you should be blessed.

Brittany Foster, Grade 11
City University School of Liberal Arts, TN

Being Drug Free and Be Healthy

People are dying because they are eating junk food instead of eating nutritious foods from the recommended food pyramid. People do not exercise daily. Do you know that there are seven spoonfuls of sugar in coke and about fifty-one percent of the U.S. only eat nutritious family meals once a day? People should not want to be underweight or overweight, just in between. Americans should not take diet pills because they don't know if they are allergic to them or if they are damaging organs.

Kids are doing drugs and selling them to make money and they don't really care if they are living a healthy life. Some families let their kids do that stuff and they don't realize their kids could be taken to juvenile services. Many times, their parents could be sued or be called child abusers.

On television, the ads on cigarette commercials say that people can stay younger and can also win prizes. Tobacco can cause different kinds of cancer, and that's the way the governors are trying to state "No Tobacco" at school. That is why I am glad I am drug-free and healthy.

Cord Carter, Grade 10
Haworth High School, OK

Do Children Fight Against Cancer?

Do you realize that the leading reason for death in children of fifteen years of age and younger is cancer? The estimated number of deaths in 2007 for cancer is about 1,545. The approximate number of children diagnosed with cancer this year is about 10,400 just in the United States. The good news is that the advances in cancer therapy will allow about 79 percent of these children to survive five years or more. That still doesn't sound great, but compared to the survival rates in 1970, this is astounding. In 1970 the five year survival rate was less than 50 percent.

So, do the same types of cancer that affect adults affect children? The answer is no. The types of cancer that most adults fight are skin, prostate, breast, lung, and colorectal cancers. However children mostly fight leukemia, brain and nervous system tumors, lymphomas, bone cancers, soft tissue sarcomas, kidney cancers, eye cancers, and adrenal gland cancers. Another difference between adults and children cancer is that the organs of children are not fully mature and react to treatment differently.

The most dominant types of cancer are leukemia, brain and other nervous system cancers. These two types of cancer alone make up over 50 percent of the childhood cancers. In fact, leukemia is the most common childhood cancer. The second most common cancer in kids is brain and other nervous system cancers which makes up about 22 percent of cancer in children.

Kelsey Lucas, Grade 10
Stanton College Preparatory School, FL

True Love

I can finally say I've made the right decision. I've accepted who my father is, and have moved forward with my life. I've stopped waiting for a change I know I'll never see.

"Daddy, daddy, look at my picture!" I wobbled over to him at the age of four, carrying what I felt was a masterpiece. "Oh," he grumbled, while on the phone. He began jotting numbers down over the drawing, like I was invisible.

Emotionally, I could never count on him. He believed gifts and money in the mail could equal emotional support. I saw him maybe five times out of the year.

It is probably morally wrong to hate your father, but I did. This hate engulfed me and controlled my life. I hated that my mom was overwhelmed having to raise us alone, and I loathed the effect it was having on my younger brother.

I remember when I let him go. He called some random night, drunkenly talking about the past. I cried the whole night, hurt again by his words. I had never felt so unloved.

My anger slowly fizzled. I had no more tears left to shed, my smile returned. I realized what I have, and what I've had all along. My mom is my rock. My friends are my shield. When I need someone, they are there; no questions asked. I don't need him; I have so much more.

I was searching for love, and I had it. I was born with it.

Rachel Lindo, Grade 11
Countryside High School, FL

Mt. Magazine

Thick brush cracked and splintered under my muddied hiking boots as I made my way through an intertwining net of gnarled branches and vines. Staring contentedly at my feet, I treaded carefully across a cliff cut by decades of erosion. The thick autumn air choked the warmth out of my breath, creating a swirl of vapors which quickly dissipated before my wind-whipped eyes. The clouds hung low, trapped in the slithering valleys of the Ozark Mountains. Like a sea of pearl vapors, the fog splashed jovially against the cliff face upon which I stood. A twig snapped behind me and I whirled around; the beast was mere feet from where I stood.

A patch of brown in the deep green canvas moved slightly, flowing with the branches in the wind. Its pink nose blew steam in a gentle plume and its velvet eyes shone in the first rays of sunlight. The nimble creature was statuesque and noble; a king among peasants. With a swift prance the doe disappeared from sight, yet the memory of its beauty remained vivid in my memory.

With the November sun winking on the horizon, light was fading as swift as the closing curtain at the end of a performance. With a fleeting glance towards the gross expenditure of mountains that protruded from the earth like goose bumps of a shivering child's arm, I turned around and proceeded back towards the campsite. The itinerant creature would forever remind me of the time I spent on Mt. Magazine.

Paolo Vignali, Grade 11
Germantown High School, TN

Racism Today

White's only, no colors allowed. The world used to be like that, but now it just comes in different forms. Many people say racial jokes every day, but many say they're just playing. Some people actually believe they're playing and they may be joking. People today still use slurs to offend people in negative ways. Believe it or not, racism still occurs today. This is horrible, upsetting and just plain wrong.

Everyone experiences racism every day no matter where they are. It goes on at schools, in the work place, and even at super markets. Racism hurts people in many ways. Some are physical like destroying people's property or setting things on fire in their front yard. Many people use racism verbally like saying things such as "go back where you came from" or "you're in America, speak the language" or "I'm not getting on a plane with these people who bombed us!" People who aren't a different color don't realize how much this hurts people's feelings.

So what is a person to do? Just sit back and watch. I know we can't change the way people are raised or the way they think. We need this to change; in all actuality this will always be a problem in the world. We as people, a society, a community, as ONE world need to get together and end this epidemic.

Ayla Espinosa, Grade 10
Greenwood High School, KY

Good Friends

I love having good friends because they help you stay on the right track. They can help you determine right from wrong when you are in a stressful situation. Some of the best friends that I have are on color guard together. I can talk to them about anything and they can tell me anything. We have some good laughs about silly things like boys, pop culture, and TV programs. We hang out all the time because color guard and band are our life and we really do not have time for anything else. It is fine though because at the end of the day we like to hang out together. We practice almost every day perfecting our routine and drill. Most of them are very levelheaded too so they do not think that they are the best. We also work well together and that helps to get things accomplished. Most of them are going off to college next year but hopefully we will stay in touch for many years. It is great that I found a sport that is enjoyable and I can be myself. It is great that I do not have to have a fake personality to get along with my guard members. Being in such a great group of girls has taught me to have a calmer personality and listen better to what my peers have to tell me knowing that they are there to help me and have my best interest in mind.

Katie Hazelton, Grade 11
Bob Jones High School, AL

Modern Day Civil Rights Movement

It has been almost fifty years since Dr. Martin Luther King, Jr. changed the idea of equality for all. It's disturbing to know that even though blacks are welcomed into society they are still discriminated against because of their threat to corporate America. African Americans are almost always used as scapegoats because they're apparently easy to be framed as criminals. Theory is that African Americans aren't expected to reach the average success that Caucasians do, causing blacks to be discriminated against in the twenty-first century.

Since Dr. King changed the face of the civil rights movement in the mid 1900's there has since been a new travesty. Trouble started at Jena High School in Louisiana when six black students asked and were given permission to sit under "the white tree." Following a series of fights, three of the Jena Six were in a local convenience store and a white adversary entered the store with a rifle. In an attempt to self-defend, the black boys assaulted the white boy and confiscated his rifle. The white boy suffered minor injuries and was released from the hospital within an hour. The three blacks were arrested and charged with attempted murder and robbery.

Since then, protests have taken place in Louisiana in an attempt to free Mychal Bell. All attempts have proven to be worthwhile; Mychal has since been released on a $45,000 bond. In support of Mychal, I wore all black, made posters for my teacher to use in the protest and wrote him a letter. I will always remember his triumphant story in this modern day rights movement.

Sara Grace Wallace, Grade 10
Kennedy Charter School, NC

Porcelain Dolls

Porcelain dolls remind me of Christmas. Every Christmas my Grandma Bone would buy all of her granddaughters a Porcelain Doll. As Christmases went on I collected many Porcelain Dolls. Then one day came that no one expected, and Bone passed away. When she passed away no one thought about the Porcelain Dolls, but when Christmas came it felt as if something other than just her was missing. As my aunts passed out the presents I knew what was missing, the Porcelain Dolls. Then we began to open the presents and just as I had suspected, no doll. As I got to the last present I wasn't expecting what I got. I opened it up and there it was the Porcelain Doll, and from none other than Bone. How could this be? It turned out that she had bought extra dolls last Christmas and already had them wrapped and signed. As I looked at the doll my face brightened up, and I realized that Bone was there the whole time. Even though I couldn't see her she was there. I now have the dolls sitting on my dresser next to my bed, and every morning when I wake up and see the dolls I think of Bone. My Porcelain Dolls bring back great memories and mean a lot to me.

Niki Kruger, Grade 10
Slater High School, MO

A Contest on Edge

It was the fall of 2006 when that joyful feeling of accomplishment overwhelmed my band mates and me. The Germantown High School Varsity Band was struggling to perfect the marching show for the upcoming contest. We competed in two major contests and proved ourselves to be a fairly descent band. However, the upcoming contest, the Arkansas Band Contest, was the most important. This was the last contest the marching band would participate in for the year and the last contest for the seniors.

A week before the contest, I felt that all the practice was paying off. Our band director, Mr. Byrd, began to yell at us less frequently, because he was either tired of it or could not find as many errors as before.

We were ready for the contest. As soon as we arrived, we headed to the warm-up area for a sound check. Within minutes, we were on the field. The show seemed much slower than usual because of the pressure and silence of the audience. After seven agonizing minutes, our show was over. We waited in the stand for the nerve-racking results. "Third place goes to Humolt High School!" said the announcer. "Second place goes to Shierwood High School! First place for the Arkansas Band Contest goes to..." At this point, a thunder of screams and shouts erupted from the Germantown fans. I looked down the field to see the Germantown High School Varsity Band swarming around an enormous trophy. We won.

Christopher Range, Grade 10
Germantown High School, TN

Show Day

It's worth it, the three short months that we give up for each other. All hundred and fifty people in the competition marching band would have to agree that for the short ten minutes of pure heart and mind, it's worth it. We complain a lot, after all we do have other priorities such as school to deal with, but we love marching. There is no way that we would put ourselves through the August heat, and October cold wind every year, if we all did not love marching. It begins in August, outside just standing on the black top for hours. Next we go inside and work for hours getting our music the very best we can. It's this time that we all begin losing our minds and just want to start working on what we have been waiting for since last November, the show. Finally we get the drill and we work and work and work but it still won't be perfect. We practice almost every day no matter what, sun or rain. Our feet are sore, calves are cramped, mouth is dry, lips are chapped, backs are breaking and we can't breath, must have been a good practice. But soon the practices will stop and we all know that, so we make every practice, a performance. When we step on the field, the energy runs through each of us and we are all thinking one thing — show day.

Rita Jones, Grade 11
Owasso High School, OK

From the Heart

I am a member of The Pride of Owasso High School Marching Band. We spend hours upon countless hours practicing. For the first half of the school year our schedule is school, band practice, home to do homework, and if we are lucky, we get some sleep. When people think of band students they think, "Band nerd," and yes, I am. I'm proud to say that I enjoy doing what I do. We are frequently asked why we are in marching band. Well, here is why: When you're standing on the field and you can feel the energy from the people around you, you look up at your drum major and wait for him to start. You're waiting to show all those people what you've worked for. It's halfway through the show and you look at your drum majors and they can't help but smile because they know we've put our heart into that show. There is no greater feeling than standing in the last set and we play the last note and everyone in the stands gives you a standing ovation. When you march off that field and you look at the freshman and you can see that they finally understand why we work as hard as we do. It's all for that moment, when it doesn't matter what place we get because we did our best, put our hearts into it, and left it all on the field!

Caitlin Kelly, Grade 11
Owasso High School, OK

Why Teens Do Drugs

Have you ever wondered why teenagers do drugs? Why it is so easy for them to smoke and pop pills, but they gripe and complain about having to open a book and read a few pages out of it?

Teenagers do drugs because of peer pressure, thinking it looks cool, and just the pleasure of "fitting in." They say whatever to what their parents have to say, and listen to everything that their friends tell them. Teenagers who do drugs say they do it because it takes their stress away, calms them down, and it's just fun to get high. My opinion on teen drug use is that I don't approve of it. I think it is just an excuse to run and hide from their problems instead of facing them like they should. Some side affects of drug use is depression, suicide, and just frying your brain. I know people who have or are doing rugs and they have told me they chose to start drugs either because they thought it was cool or they just plain like experiencing the pleasure of it. What I don't think they realize is that it is messing their brains up and it's just hurting their future.

Even though you may be pushed to try drugs, think of the outcome and what it may do to you when you're older and how it could affect your future. Don't let your friends try to pressure you into something you don't want to do. It's your life and your choices.

Megan Brashear, Grade 10
Greenwood High School, KY

Illusions

Illusion is defined in the dictionary as "something that deceives by producing a false or misleading impression of real life." This definition, although literally correct, does not give the word justice. When a person thinks of an illusion, the thought of a magician or a trivial optical illusion that gains attention only through the blindness of a whim are common situations performed in their mind. Quaint little images that compose an unexpected figure, viewed only for amusement.

Sadly, illusions cannot be restrained to such a simple limitation. Illusions in reality are everywhere, in every face of every person you will ever come in contact with. In most situations, the illusion is almost never pleasing. In a common optical illusion, to discover the answer it is as simple as taking a different perspective.

Unfortunately, this process becomes much more difficult when applied to our lives and our relationships with others. We dislike seeing things differently than we would normally, because they are often upsetting or painful. So we block the option, either consciously or subconsciously, and continue on with our lives, never questioning our composed reality; succumbing to an illusion concocted through our own means.

By following this world we choose to view, we only lead ourselves to our own undoing. We choose not to realize the faults of others, to not conceive their true intentions. We picture things as they should be, and disregard any harsh truth we encounter. We wander into a pit in full view.

Jake Sharma, Grade 11
Bishop Verot High School, FL

Life's Challenges

Life has a funny way of testing us. Just when you seem to be making the best of things or when you start taking things for granted, life has a way of complicating and showing you how you're messing up. Unfortunately, my realization came a week after my birthday when my mom was diagnosed with cancer.

See, my mom and I have always been really close until I started working, spending more time with my friends, and dating. Before that March I can honestly say I didn't talk to my mom much about anything and it was like I was always too busy to make time. Then I get this huge blow to my chest, and I realize I've been taking my mom, my family for granted and I felt horrible. I mean just the pure shock of the situation floored me. So I started making changes, I prioritized my life and put everything in perspective. I go with my mom to treatments, I sit and talk to her, I miss my mom to tell you the truth. I just know that since I have seen the error of my ways, something is going to change and she will be better. Life has tested me rather harshly, and I hope I passed.

Chris Southerland, Grade 12
Walker Valley High School, TN

What Really Matters?

What really matters? I've asked myself this several times, and I always come up with the same answer: family. Without my family I wouldn't be who I am today; they support me, guide me, and are always there for me when I need them the most.

My family are the people who shaped me into the person I am today. Ever since I was born my parents were there, teaching me and watching out for me, and my brothers were there driving me crazy but always watching out for me. I've learned so many important life lessons from them and they continue to teach me, even now in high school. I can always talk to my parents about my problems. They listen to me, and offer their advice. I don't always listen to them, though later I wish I had.

My brothers are always there to cheer me up by constant teasing. They're also great for help with homework, or just for having fun. Having three brothers has really helped me learn to stand up for myself.

When I make mistakes, I know that my family will be there for me. Let's face it, we all make mistakes and stumble in life. Families are the people who are there to catch us when we fall and help put us back on our feet. So, what really matters? My answer will always be the same: my family, always and forever.

Katherine Gale, Grade 10
Rock Bridge Sr High School, MO

Hiking Blind

It is amazing how things that you once hated can grow on you. When I was little, my parents would take me hiking, and I hated it. I complained that my feet hurt, that it was too long, and boring. Then one day we went hiking on a trail in Rocky Mountain National Park. Going up, I was complaining about my feet but gradually I started to notice how clear and pure the streams were as we walked over them. I noticed how green all the pines were and how clean the air was. As we got higher up, my family stopped to eat some lunch and relax. From that point you could look over the cliff and see for miles. After resting, we walked a short ways and came to a beautiful waterfall. I felt the mist and loved the thunderous sound it made as it landed in a small pond that branched out into all the tiny streams we had passed earlier. When my family made it back down to the car, my dad took off my shoes to see why my feet hurt and it turned out I did have a blister. I was so entranced by the beauty of the mountains on the way down that I had not noticed for a while that my feet even hurt.

I learned that day that if all you do is complain, you'll miss out on the beauty of life.

Ciera Fegel, Grade 11
Owasso High School, OK

Empty Heart

Can you imagine losing your father at a young age? I had to experience that at the tender age of 5. It was the summer of 1995, and my mother and I were sitting at home watching television. The news was on, and breaking news flashed across the television set. It said, "We have just caught the suspect that serial murderer at the gas station trying to rob the gas station." My mom hurried and turned the television off and ran to get the phone. She called my grandpa and started crying to him.

It turns out that my dad killed 5 people in Kansas City, Kansas. I never thought that my dad was the kind of man to take other peoples' lives, but that goes to show you that you don't know people as well as you think. My father was the kind of man who always put his family first in life.

A few months after my father was arrested I remember I woke up and I wanted my dad and forgot that he was in jail. I don't know how many times I looked up and my father wasn't there for me. I felt that my dad ran out on me when I needed him the most. My heart is empty because I haven't had a father figure in my life. Looking back on it now, I always wished that I had my dad.

Chavierre R. Walker, Grade 10
Grandview Alternative School, MO

Why Louisville?

The Fleur-de-lis: the new heartagram of the youth culture? Maybe, in Louisville anyway. But that would be too shallow a statement to make. That would be because any Louisvile-born child could tell you that pride is only part of the ticket; to be in the city is something else altogether. It's kind of like Kentucky's best kept little secret, if not the stereotyped shame of the U.S. The inbreeding history of our state can be overpowering, but in essence: tourists that flock here know nothing.

The point: people who think they've seen every place worth visiting can only pen Kentucky as being good for pumping out horses and whiskey. And if they have graced Louisville with their presence for the once-a-year Derby, they haven't *really* seen Louisville. What other city has a fan following for itself? And that's not the same as people who say they love New York or LA...to be part of the "cult following" of Louisville is to really know the territory, to know and envision every aspect of it, to know its spirit and people, and to appreciate that it goes beyond the novelties of "charming" places to shop and eat. The city has personality, and that's that. It's got quirk, trash, oddities, and beauty. It's what chic places want to pretend to have; the wreckage they want to glamorize. You can neither leave, no matter how far you get or how hard you try, or truly want to leave.

Brooke Hernando, Grade 12
Assumption High School, KY

Multiple Personality Disorder

An experiment practiced during the early days of Shakespearean drama — a practice that still persists to this day — was that of having different actors portray, say, Hamlet at different points in the play, depending on whether it was the character's compassionate self, or bored self, and so on. In such situations, it's essentially true that we are seeing different "characters" playing the same "role" in one play — or even scene. This can be confusing or fruitless, depending on how it is used. But it is not, in itself, bad theater — it shows how differently a certain character can react during a certain situation.

There is certainly nothing wrong with this multiple-actor idea. But the usual result of such experimentation is, like I noted, a sort of lack of identification with the character. I think animation is particularly suffering from this nowadays — when the audience becomes, unwittingly, alienated from the characters — which arises from a lack of vitality and life in the animation itself.

There are excellent instances of "life" in the Disney animated features *Snow White and the Seven Dwarfs* and *Pinocchio;* in Warner animated shorts like *Coal Black and de Sebben Dwarfs, Book Revue,* and *Duck Amuck;* and in MGM cartoons like *King-Size Canary* and *Bad Luck Blackie.* But it's because these films have been demoted to kiddie ghettos that current "adult" animators have discarded them — but in doing that, they will never be able to recapture the emotional depth that those films possessed.

Jessie Smith, Grade 10
Plainview High School, OK

A Serious Problem

Global warming is a major issue in the world today. It is caused from the pollution that humans put in the air, which causes the green house effect, which causes global warming. It has made a big impact on animal life, as well as people. It's been causing animals to migrate to other places so they can survive. The more animals migrate, the more environments are going to be destroyed. Global warming is causing a whole cycle of problems that the humans have caused. But it's not too late; we can still help these cute animals from becoming endangered, or at least slow it down. Humans can help them in many ways. For example, we can donate money to foundations or zoos. Instead of driving alone, you can car pool, use public transport, walk or ride a bike, use clothesline instead of dryers and plant trees when we cut them down for our use. If everybody does a little bit every day to help the planet, like not putting so much pollution in the air, we can slow down global warming. Global warming is also causing ice caps to melt, which is causing the sea level to rise. That is a problem because if the sea levels rise it will mean loss of land mass, which will probably cause more violence over land.

Erica Cook, Grade 11
Grandview Alternative School, MO

My Life Support

When I say life support, I don't mean a machine that breathed for me after a horrific accident. I mean my parents. My parents have been there for me and my two brothers through everything. They support us in everything we do, even when we don't succeed. My parents and I don't have the perfect relationship. We do disagree occasionally, but I know what they do and say is for my own good. I feel my parents have raised me well. I know right from wrong, and I know that what the crowd is doing is not always right. I have to be my own person and have my own thoughts. I hope the morals they have taught me show in my personality. I think I am a good role model, but I also think it is because of my mom and dad. When you're younger you don't really pay a whole lot of attention to what your parents say. Now that I'm older I try to pay more attention to them, and try to appreciate them though it doesn't always work. I just hope that one day when I have kids I am as good of a parent to my children as my parents are to me and my brothers. So all you kids out there, next time your parents do something for you appreciate their love.

Alexsis Nicole Griffith, Grade 10
Slater High School, MO

To Win

My heart was racing one hundred miles per hour. My adrenaline was pumping. My throat felt sore as butterflies churned in my stomach. Lights nearly blinded my eyes with ESPN cameras fifteen feet away from my face. We stood stiff with the fake grins from ear to ear. We waited for the music to start during the ten seconds that felt like a year. This was it. Our one shot. If one wrong step, movement, or motion went wrong in the next two minutes and thirty seconds, we would be done. Everything we had worked for an entire year came up to the next two and a half minutes. All the sweat, teas, and pain for a year could mean everything, or it could be meaningless.

At that moment, winning was everything. Why should we do something if we do not give it our all and strive to be the best? The music boomed. We yelled, stunted, and tumbled in synchronization the best we could. Suddenly, the music stopped. We exploded in excitement and screams because we knew we had just won by only doing our very best. Still breathless ad now with a bona fide smile plastered to our faces, we walked off the mat with our heads held high. Results were later announced. The Universal Cheerleading Association National Finalist Results: 20th, 15th, 10th, 5th, 3rd, 2nd. Tears flooded our eyes as the announcer shouted: "From Germantown, Tennessee, 2006 National Champions…Germantown High School!"

Caitlin Hanisco, Grade 11
Germantown High School, TN

The Impossibility of a Christian God

God, cannot exist. It is said, that you cannot prove the NON existence of anything. But this is not true, using logical reasoning and common sense you can deduce that a round square cannot exist. The same can be said of God. Look at the evidence.

A God, as presented by the Christian church, is an omnipotent, omniscient, benevolent being. Now, this causes strife because omnipotence and benevolence is impossible. Science has already proven that you cannot know the position, and the momentum of an atom at any given time. Also, to know everything, means God knows everything that IS, everything that WAS, and everything that will be. It is impossible. This means, from the beginning of time, God knows everything that will happen. This means that he has already predetermined his own path, free will which makes him not all powerful because he is stuck to a specific path and if he is not all powerful, he is not a God. If he changes his path, he is not all knowing, and therefore, not a God.

God cannot be all powerful and all good at the same time. If he is all good, there would be no evil in the world, and if he was all powerful, he would get rid of this evil. And if he made the claim that Satan or the Devil created evil then that means that God is NOT the only being who can create. And if that is true, who is to say Satan and not God created the universe?

Diego Villasenor, Grade 10
Deltona High School, FL

My Sister and Me

I, Ashley Nichole Manning, was born November 16th, 1990. I have an older sister named Amanda Renee Manning, born September 8th, 1986. As kids, we were never really that close because she had her older friends and I was so young that I was more of a nag than my sister could handle. As we grew older, so did our love for each other, we still had our sister moments where we almost hated each other. In the year 2005 she signed up for four years of duty in the U.S. Army. It was then that I realized just how much I loved her and how much she did for me every day. After she left I tried to talk to her as much as possible by sending letters and having conversations with her on the phone. There was too much time between our communications so we started to e-mail each other on a regular basis.

When Amanda first went into the Army we became so close that we were more than sisters, we were friends. Every year since then, I felt our relationship has spread further apart. I still love my sister very much and I know that she loves me too. One day I hope that we will be just as close as when both of our eyes were opened to how much we needed each other. Until that time I plan to do all that I can to keep the lines of communication open and to make sure that my sister knows how important she is to me.

Ashley Nichole Manning, Grade 11
Southside High School, NC

Don't Give Up

I was a normal four-year-old with a normal loving family. My mom told me my dad was given a purple heart in the Vietnam war. I knew he was a brave, honorable soldier and I wanted to be just like him. That's why I played army man with the kids at my mom's daycare.

I remember he loved me. So much so that even though he was in a wheelchair, he would take me out to play.

There was a hill in front of the apartment we lived in, and it taunted me. One day he took me outside to play and I tried to climb it, but failed. He kept telling me, "Don't give up and keep trying." Twenty attempts later I did it. I was so proud and so was he.

A few months passed and my dad became sick. Mom moved his bed in the living room.

She filled the room with chairs and I knew something was wrong. She protected me from seeing in the room, but I stormed in. My dad was lying down, his head in my mom's lap.

The chairs were filled with men in suits. I didn't care, my dad was sick. I wanted to be by him, he was always there for me.

I remember my mom crying and I laid beside him with her.

Now I know he contracted cancer from "Agent Orange" in Vietnam.

Shortly after he died, I learned one thing from him: "Don't give up."

Anthony Long, Grade 12
Countryside High School, FL

High School

High school. The place where you see bullies stuffing nerds in trash cans, where it is so expansive that you lose your way, the place I learned none of this was true. The first day, my very *first* day, I knew that all the hype, all the buzz, all the exaggeration was nothing but a farce. During what I thought was my last summer alive, I kept hearing how high school was going to be the death of me and how, if I survived, that I would want it to be the death of me. Such things included the infamous Freshman Friday and the belief that there was a pool on V building (there is not by the way). I decided that I was going to do what I normally do if I were at school, survive.

My first class was upon me as I looked around nervously in anticipation for what might happen. Class started and my teacher and my peers made acquaintances and the teacher motioned for us to sit, then started to speak. What she said sent a shot of relief through my body, like when you get the goose bumps on a cold day. My teacher quickly dispelled every known story that I and everyone else heard. That was when I came to a very comforting realization. I was going to enjoy high school.

Tyler Woodling, Grade 11
Germantown High School, TN

Black, White, Tan

Even at a young age, one wants to fit in. No one wants to be left out of made fun of because he is in some way different from others. Everyone is different in his or her own way, and no one was made exactly the same. It is called being unique, and there is nothing wrong with being proud of oneself for the way he was made. People can be different in a number of ways. They could have different color hair; they could have different likes and dislikes; or they could have different talents. But the problem seems to come when people differ in religion, sex, race, or nationality.

There is no reason to discriminate against others because of the way they look, what they believe in, or where they came from. America was founded so that the people who lived here could be free and live as they wanted. Equality is important because everyone is all the same, even though they may seem different. Everyone was made in the image of God and deserves to be treated equally and with respect. Maybe if everyone could learn to discriminate less, they world would be a more peaceful place.

Jessie Braud, Grade 12
St Charles Catholic High School, LA

Conversions

China, France, Algeria, Brazil, and Australia: all these countries and more use the metric system as their official system for measurements. Who is not on the list? The United States is the only country using a different system, the English System. In this, Americans need to conform. Due to several incidents caused by having different systems of measurement, it seems prudent to change the United States' measurement system to that of the rest of the world.

For starters, the metric system is easier to work with mathematically than the abnormal numbers of the English System. There are, for example, exactly a thousand meters in a kilometer, whereas in the English System, one mile equals 5,280 feet. Does it take rocket scientists to do conversions? Maybe it does. A NASA spacecraft going into orbit around Mars crashed and was destroyed because of a conversion mistake, wasting enormous amounts of effort and money. In another incident, eight people died on an airplane that was accidentally told crucial numbers from two different systems.

Not only will it be easier if Americans change to the metric system it will also be safer in dealing with international affairs. The US government has indeed made metrication efforts, but it is the common people who do not seem to be interested in using such things as Celsius instead of Fahrenheit. Nonetheless, it does not, in fact, take a rocket scientist to see that such equations as $F = 9/5C + 32$ should not be necessary.

Magdalena Sudibjo, Grade 10
Mount St Mary Academy, AR

Doors Within the Pages

Reading is an education experience that can broaden your horizon. It opens up your mind to new words that expand your vocabulary. Every time you read, it speeds up your reading ability. Reading can also spark an imagination that can change the world.

New worlds open not only imaginary worlds but also new cultures. The customs of different countries are explained in the pages of history books. Politics are discussed and written down in many volumes. Wars are discussed and written down so we may read about them and not repeat the mistakes of the past.

Reading can also help open doors in your own life. There are many self-help books, and many religions have their religious books. Books can influence your thinking and your way of life. Different books influence people in different ways. In my opinion, the Bible is the best book to set your life upon.

Some books are just for laughs. They open up and expand children's and adult's imagination to new worlds. Others give people hide-a-way worlds that they can escape from their hectic lifestyles.

Reading books is both educational and humorous. Each time a book is opened and read a new door is opened. These doors may lead to learning about the world around you or to expanding the inner worlds of your imagination. So no matter what you read, the door that is opened will lead to a new path of learning in your life and will broaden your horizon.

Dawna L. Kay, Grade 11
Trinity Christian Academy, AL

Mom My Hero

What is it that makes a hero? To me a hero is someone who is always there and who has experienced and also accomplished so much in their lifetime. It's also someone who has been through a lot, but has never given up even if things got really hard and they thought they couldn't get through. A hero is the one in the end who held up strong even when they didn't think they could. To me that's truly a hero.

My mom is my hero. She is so strong and she has accomplished so much in her life. She is truly the strongest person I know. She has had a lot of struggles in her life and at times, almost gave up, but she always thought of us kids and that kept her going. She had her own kids taken from her by our dad. One day she was at work and he took us out of daycare and went to her work to mess up her car. After that she didn't knew where we were for a year, but she kept her head up high and never gave up. To me that takes a lot. I believe if my mom can keep going through all that, then I know I can. My mom has inspired me in so many ways. She is truly my hero.

Wendi Daugherty, Grade 12
Lee County Sr High School, NC

The Ultimate Evil

A day that not only impacted my life, but millions of others was September 11, 2001. The details of that day are still very vivid in my mind. I was in fifth grade at Liberty Elementary sitting in my classroom and I knew something had happened, but I was not sure what it was. The teachers were scurrying about and talking to each other, but I was still confused. Finally, the school day ended. I usually walked home because I lived only a block away, but suddenly I saw my mom. My mom was wearing a purple shirt and told me she was going to walk me home this day. As we walked she explained to me the details of what happened on this tragic day.

When we arrived home the television was on replaying the crashes over and over. Also, my dad's best friend lived in New York at the time and I remember how worried my father was, until he found out his friend was okay. I felt terrible for the victims, but I was only in fifth grade and it seemed as if there was nothing I could do. I was very sad with mixed feelings and the next couple of days I was very upset. This was a day that affected me personally, but also millions of others across this country.

Athena Padgett, Grade 11
Owasso High School, OK

My Favorite Season

Everyone has a favorite season for some particular reason. My favorite season is summer. Summer is great because you can do basically anything. It's a great time for camping, horseback riding, and tubing. There are endless possibilities.

My family goes to Green Acres because we have a permanent campsite there. I love going down there and just hanging out with all my friends. When we're all hanging out, it's fun and relaxing. We go swimming, play sports, and have dances. Those are just some of the many activities we do when we're all there.

Summertime is a great time for horseback riding. There is a lot of sunshine and the wind on the back of a horse cools you right down. There is nothing like going down a nature trail on an amazing animal on a sunny day and enjoying the scenery.

Now if it's really hot and you just can't take anymore heat, going out on a boat and tubing will cool you down fast. If you've ever been then you know what I'm talking about. When you're in a tube being pulled by a boat at 35 mph all you get is water and wind hitting you. That is a great way of cooling down and having fun at the same time.

These are the reasons for why summer is my favorite season. I can't participate in any of these activities in the winter because it's too cold.

Codie Whealton, Grade 11

Do I Follow God's Word?

"Do I follow God's word or not?" That's a question a lot of teens ask themselves every day. They don't always know that they are asking this question, most times they look at the surface question. If I am asked to do something for someone, I simply ask myself, "Do I want to do this or not?", but if I make myself look deeper into it, I end up asking myself "Is this something God wants me to do?" Every day teens are faced with one single question — "Do I please God in all I do?"

To be sure that you please God in everything you do, ask yourself. Whenever you are asked to do or say something, ask "What would Jesus do?" or "Will God be pleased with my actions?" Some people will say that this doesn't make your decision any faster and that it doesn't help them at all. Well, with me, it does and to be honest with you, it has saved me a lot of trouble by asking these simple questions.

So, you do please God in all you do, right? I hope you do. If you're not sure, just ask yourselves those simple questions, be sure to answer them truthfully, because God is watching you all the time, even when you don't want Him to or don't think He is!

Courtney Peterson, Grade 10
Greenwood High School, KY

First Cry

In Vancouver, BC Women's Hospital had delivered a 7.4 pound baby girl, she had ten little toes, ten wiggling fingers, and two beautiful blue eyes. I've waited my whole life for Maya. After thirteen years, three miscarriages, twenty-seven hours of labor, and a cesarean, my baby cousin was born.

Flushed of color and air, she had finally arrived, although she put up quite a fight. Maya was all but vivacious, purple in the cheeks with blue and green fingertips.

She instantly became the most important person in my life; I spend every summer with her. Knowing I belonged to her, she woke me up every morning. Once she realized I liked to sleep in she'd lie in her bed waiting for my eyes to open. A wide smile would creep across her face, revealing barely six teeth. She was devastated when I left, having no one to sing "Little People" songs with.

She's talked about me since her first words. We bond quickly every year, despite her fear of me trying to take her grandparents away. My behavior and actions reflect on her; equally, she makes me a better person.

She's my other half and represents so much of me. I believe I'll look up to her more than she'll look up to me.

I love her immensely; I can't believe she almost didn't make it. The happiest moment of my life was at 4:42 on the morning of June 6th, 2004, when I heard her first cry.

Tea Zubic, Grade 11
Countryside High School, FL

Please Don't Smoke

I think that it's bad to smoke and it isn't good for your health. But for some reason I don't understand, people still do it and they know the consequences.

Smoking is one of the worst things you can do for your health. Many things can go wrong and many diseases can come from smoking. There are all types of cancers and other life threatening things that you can get by just simply taking a puff of the cigarette. I know first hand what it is like to almost lose someone because of it. My grandma had a heart attack because she had smoked on a daily basis since she was fifteen years old. So is your life or one of your loved ones important to you?

What people don't realize are the addictive qualities that cigarettes have. It's the nicotine in the cigarettes that make you have to have one every five minutes. People think that it's cool if they smoke and it makes you fit in, but you don't have to smoke for people to like you. They will like you just as much if you don't. Most people start when they are young and they just say they will have one and from that point on they are hooked for life or until their early death.

Smoking is a horrible habit that no one should do. Cigarettes should be banned because they do no good, they only hurt many people's lives and I'm sure everyone will feel the effects of it at least once in their life.

Holden Kerns, Grade 11
Southside High School, NC

Telephone Technology

Technology in communications has evolved greatly in the past thirty years. Thirty years ago, here in rural Fayette County, most people were still using a party line. A party line consists of several neighbors sharing a single telephone line. Many times, if you needed to use the telephone, you would have to wait until your neighbor got off the phone. There was always a chance that someone was listening to your conversation. I think it's amazing that most everyone has a cell phone now. Cell phones are now more than just a phone. They are used for taking pictures, video, sending written text, and are even internet connected. All of this is a long way from Alexander Graham Bell's idea of the telephone.

With all the new telephone advancement in mind, I wonder where telephone technology will be in the next thirty years. Nano technology is a new concept. Nano technology refers to the creation of material, devices and systems on a scale of one to one-hundred nanometers. Nanometers are billionths of a meter. This means we will be using devices as small as a single molecule. I feel this is hard to believe even though technology has developed the way it is currently. People thought that man would never walk on the moon. We know that anything is possible. We already know that today's communication technology will be outdated tomorrow. It is hard to keep up with the constant changes in this field.

A.J. Beshires, Grade 11
Rossville Christian Academy, TN

Abortion…Life and Death

In clinics across the nation, women from different walks of life enter looking to remove babies from their lives. Should this practice of a "one and done" with humans be allowed to continue? Certainly children can be sent to an adoption agency instead of killed from an early stage of life.

Research has shown that babies move at a very early stage after conception, clutching of the fist, wiggling the toes, and kicking are all pre-birth movements. For a child to move, their brain must be active and alert, meaning that they must have thoughts no matter how small or trivial, babies are thinking.

Adoption agencies can be found anywhere in the United States. So why should we destroy an innocent life instead of finding it a home with a family that will love that baby? Everyone deserves a chance at life to see what life gives them. It's written in the constitution "life, liberty, and the pursuit of happiness." How can we then, if we are following our written laws, kill a baby before it has a chance to experience all the world has to offer?

Who has the right to decide matters as great as this? Who has the wisdom to decide who lives and who dies? Who has a chance at life and who does not? Who can grow to be married, a doctor, a preacher, or maybe even president? No one has that wisdom. No one can decide the fate of an innocent human life.

AJ Mondin, Grade 10
Deltona High School, FL

Criminal Investigator

My dream is to be a criminal investigator. I was first inspired by my aunt. She works in the courtroom and participates in the same aspirations I have. She makes sure criminals go to jail. I feel that her career and my dream go hand and hand because we have to put those terrible people behind bars. I am able to go to her for advice and more information about my dream.

Some may think that this job is too dangerous. I would like to be an investigator because I want to put criminals behind bars for killing innocent people. I really feel that I should pursue this job for all those people who lost a family member to crime. I want to help girls in the world who were raped and killed. I want to find criminals and let them pay for consequences of their behavior.

We live in a world full of crazy people who have sick minds that want to hurt anyone. I want to be a helping hand, a friend, a hero. I want to bring justice even if it means risking my life. I will do it. I do not like seeing people hurt emotionally and physically. I feel like people need to make a difference in the world no matter what age you are.

Gabrielle Alexis, Grade 12
Tropical Christian School, FL

Suicide

Have you ever experienced a loss due to suicide? This silent killer has killed many young teens. Many people ask why do teens go through this? And what can we do to prevent it?

First, many people have thought of suicide and attempted it. I have known many people who have thought of suicide but have overcome their struggles. Most teens that attempt suicide do it either because they don't feel loved, feel that there is no use in their life, or young relationship problems. It is a fact that suicide is the third leading cause of death from people between the ages of 15 and 24. On an average day, six youths die from suicide related causes.

Finally, many people have tried to prevent suicide. There are many organizations which try to show teens that there are people out there who care for them and they're not the only ones who feel this way. One organization that I like is To Write Love On Her Arms. The founder of the organization's friend said that there was no suicide prevention. This is his attempt to prove him wrong.

In conclusion, many young teens have been killed by suicide. I believe that it is very important that we become more aware of suicide and how to prevent it. My personal answer for suicide is to show your friend God and tell them that He cares for them unconditionally even if no one else does.

Andrew Hall, Grade 10
Haynes Academy for Advanced Studies, LA

Freedom at Last

I turn the key into the ignition and feel the car rumble beneath me. Like a monster just waking up, the machine "vrooms" loudly as it regains its strength. As I check my mirrors and adjust the seat, I start to realize how exhilarating this is. Finally, I am on my own. I used to think riding my bike past these quaint homes was fun; now I zoom past them in pure bliss. The cars beside me make amused and confused faces when they see a tiny redheaded girl driving a huge soccer-mom van. I do not care though; I am free!

The process of getting here was long and hard. Hours and hours of practice. Chaotic times when my mother was screaming, jamming her foot on an invisible brake in the passenger seat. The full week of Driver's Ed, ten to five, was excruciatingly painful. There there were the driving exams, possibly some of the most nerve wracking times of my life. The thought never crossed my mind that it took this amount of practice and patience into getting one's license.

Although the journey has been difficult, I would not have had it any other way. The feeling I received after grasping my license for the first time, still warm from the machine, could not have been better. Excitement, relief, jubilation, and shock all overwhelmed me at one time. I would not trade this moment for the world.

Ramey Arnold, Grade 10
Germantown High School, TN

My Last 1st Week of School in 11th Grade

There was no reason to be nervous and I especially had no reason to be. I woke up at 4 in the morning knowing it was my 1st day of 11th grade. I couldn't seem to get back to sleep for hours, but before I knew it, my dad was waking me up to face the wretched day. It was so easy to get up seeing as my nerves were on the tip of their toes. I got out of bed and proceeded to cut tags off my new outfit.

I got dressed and after a quick once over in my full length mirror, I proceeded to the bathroom. I had gotten a full blowout the day before at the salon, but after a long night of restless sleep, it could use some touching up.

I felt a combination of quickening nerves and a growling sensation in my stomach. After a quick look in the mirror to notice my acne medication waging war with the newly sprouted pimples, I ran downstairs to grab a healthy Nature Valley Bar.

When I came back upstairs, my straightener was hot; I attempted to iron out the menacing crimp that was taking over the mid section of my hair. As I was just beginning the fine art of my makeup, the power went out.

Fabulous.

I have the worst luck EVER!

Since it was already time to go, I trotted to the car. Thank goodness the sun decided that yes indeed, it was early enough to come up that morning because I got to do my makeup on the way to school.

After a stressful morning of the power outage, I was ready to begin my 1st day of school.

Mia Vanatta, Grade 11
Vero Beach High School, FL

A Little Goes a Long Way

"40,000 dollars!" His father exclaimed in disbelief, the college tuition letter wavering in his trembling hand. There was silence for a moment as the family sat around the dinner table digesting the news. It was certainly hard to swallow and left a bitter aftertaste. They, like many other American families, are finding out first hand just how expensive it can be. Teens should do everything they can in getting college scholarships.

Not everyone believes that you should go out of your way for "trivial amounts of money." They will say that you should be accepted on grades alone. This is true for the small percent that get accepted based solely on grades, but they look at more than just G.P.A's. The majority must go out of their way for "trivial amounts of money."

College can get you ahead, but all that knowledge isn't cheap. Students should try to get extra scholarships via school involvement or grants to get the extra push. Having good grades doesn't do it anymore. Colleges look for involved students. So get involved. A little community service can go a long way.

Jacob Hughes, Grade 10
Greenwood High School, KY

My Individuality

My individuality, or the characteristics that distinguish me from everyone else, are what make me who I am. My loyalty, ambition, and personal style make up my individuality.

My loyalty sets me apart from others because I am loyal to all of my friends, family, and myself. If two of my friends are arguing over something, I don't choose sides. I simply observe both arguments, choose two positive and negative aspects of each argument, and present a compromising solution both of my friends can live with. In doing this I stay true to my friends and my personal values.

My ambition sets me apart from the pack because it lets me fight for what I want and gives me the drive to get where I want to be in life. My ambition has helped shape who I am because I have had to change certain aspects of my life to get where I am today.

My personal style helps me stand apart from the rest because I can express myself, show my moods, and how I feel inside. My personal style makes me unique because I mix up different styles on different days to match my mood so I can show my individuality inside and out.

My individuality comes from my ambition to complete my goals, my loyalty that keeps me true to my friends and myself, and my personal style that lets me express myself.

Alyssa Hamman, Grade 11
Southside High School, NC

The Cheapest Spa Treatment

Over the past summer, I have been to two continents, entered different worlds, and met over one hundred people. How, might one ask, could you accomplish this? The answer is simple: reading. After a stressful day, just opening a book can put me at ease. I can lose myself and become the characters. I am able to leave the realistic world and enter another just by the turn of a page.

Many of my fellow students miss out on this relaxation technique called reading a book. They will say it is "boring" and "uninteresting." Or, some will complain, "I don't have the time." My belief is that if you find a book on a topic that interests you, you WILL find it interesting and exciting. It can seem difficult to multitask between schoolwork and reading. There simply aren't enough hours in the day. But, by just reading a few pages, it can gradually become something you enjoy.

Reading has opened many doors in my life. By reading various genres of books, I have been inspired, saddened, overjoyed, angered, and relieved. I have gained knowledge through books I wouldn't have gained elsewhere. But most important of all, reading can relax me like no other, being the cheapest spa treatment!

Alex Hastings, Grade 11
Camden Central High School, TN

Heroes

Music. Everyone listens to it. No matter the genre, there's a sound for everyone. My sound fits in many genres; call them what you will, but to me, they're heroes. Fall Out Boy took a path into the industry of music that was all their own.

When you start a band, you may have thoughts such as: "What happens if this goes somewhere?" "Let's do this for fame and fortune…" Not in this case. This band was made up of guys who were sick of the scene. Bands like Green Day, Lifetime, and others inspired them to go a different direction.

They stayed true to their original plan; not wanting to be another "one hit wonder," like bands before, they took it slow. Fall Out Boy is smart; they know how to manage themselves. Many bands and artists get caught up in fame; they forget to make the decisions that are in their best interest. Fall Out Boy wasn't ready to jump in.

When bands become established, they tend to lose their friends and fans they've made along the way; not these guys. Their fans change as their music does. That is why when compared to other bands, Fall Out Boy has one of the biggest fan bases of all.

Fall Out Boy changed my life. Through their lyrics, they have helped me through some of the hardest times in my life. No matter how big they become, they will always be my heroes.

Rachel Xanders, Grade 11
Mulhall-Orlando High School, OK

Religious Contentment

Life without fundamental beliefs, is like a ship tossed about on a stormy sea. There are few things in life that are dependable. Fortunately for me, I have enough to make my life blissful and complete. There is my family, whom I know will always be there when I need them, and there is my religion. I come from a family of mixed faiths, where everyone worships God, in his or her own beliefs and his or her own ways. Therefore, I would never consider myself ultra-religious. In fact it is only within the past four or so years that I have even become interested in my religion.

No, that's wrong. I have always been interested, but as a young child, I found the intricacies of Judaism difficult and complicated to understand. Over the past few years, I have become more intimate with the subject: studying it, asking questions of my family, friends, and rabbis, and becoming involved in the Jewish community, which is more extensive than I ever dreamed it could be. I have learned many essential life lessons, including the fact that I will never understand everything there is to know about Judaism. However, the most significant lesson I have learned is finding and loving God, your family and friends, and most importantly yourself and your own beliefs is what truly matters in life. With these vital lessons in mind and heart, I am like a ship floating safely in the harbor of Judaism's arms.

Katelyn Zeno, Grade 11
Germantown High School, TN

My First Week as a Junior

An early morning wake-up followed by a quick, choked down breakfast told me that the first day of school had come. Knowing that the school is run by the dimmer colors of the rainbow, I was expecting a very memorable first couple of weeks. What I got was more than I bargained for. Built for maximum capacity of 600 students the new cafeteria really is a sight to see. Too bad our administrators hoped to squeeze 1350 students into it! It's ironic how much our administrators stress math's importance, yet they fail at even simple division. Four weeks later this was fixed. Although this fix received much applause, it only made me giggle. We should be able to look up to them, but if we, as students, follow their example of ignorance then nothing would ever get done.

Furthermore, another problem is transportation. Our school is located on two separate campuses, one down the street form the other. Busses transport students between them. This year the bus loading area could better be considered a war zone. Hundreds of students were pushing to find a seat. How can we be expected to learn if we cannot even get to our classes?

If things ever go bad for me in life then at least I can look back on my school administrators and think, "well, at least I've not fallen that low." And that, to me, is a very encouraging thought.

Chip Dougherty, Grade 11
Vero Beach High School, FL

My Hero

My hero would be my Grandpa Hopkins in Nevada. He is the grandparent that I can talk to without him judging me. He is very intelligent, generous, and is strong.

He is intelligent because he can figure out things easily. He likes to figure out how to use the new technology that comes out. It only take him a short time, too. Even though he didn't get past an eighth grade education he is very quick at everything.

He is generous because he helps a lot of people overcome their frustrations. He also lends out a hand to anyone in need that he can see.

He is strong because he is not easily discouraged by anything. When he was eight years old, he was removed from his home and raised by the state. Despite this, he still grew up to be a kind and caring person. Also, a couple of years ago he had emphysema and didn't give up hope.

My grandfather has played a good role in my life. He has taught me when it's the right time to do something and when I should take a minute to think to myself if I will regret it later. That's why I look up to him as a hero.

Danielle Pangburn, Grade 12
Mulhall-Orlando High School, OK

4x4 What For?

My first experience with a four wheel drive truck was in grade school. My uncle and I went to his hunting lease to work on some things. The road to get there was muddy and you needed a four wheel drive truck to get through it. He put the truck in four wheel drive, and I couldn't believe the difference it made in the traction.

Four wheel drive trucks come in handy frequently. If you need to get somewhere, but in order to get there, you have to go through mud, then it will obviously come in handy. If you need to pull a tree out of the ground, a two wheel drive might not be able to do it because it doesn't have the option to use four wheel drive low. Four wheel drive low is when power goes to all four wheels, but uses lower gears so you can use more of the engine's power because of the higher rpm's it's producing.

So to conclude, I strongly believe four wheel drive definitely out performs two wheel drive vehicles. I know this for a fact because I drive a truck that is four wheel drive and I've noticed the definite increase in traction in four wheel drive than in two wheel drive. I would never buy a two wheel drive truck over a four wheel drive truck.

Cody Lane, Grade 12
St Thomas More High School, LA

Left Behind But Valuable

I never thought that my life would change completely by the time I was ten years old, but it did. For Christmas in 2000, I received four horseback riding lessons. I met the horse I would be riding as soon as I got there. He was a Quarter Horse named Skip. My first lesson went very well and I was all smiles when I jumped off his back.

When I went to put Skip in the pasture, I noticed a black horse that looked like no one had paid attention to it in years. When I questioned the owner of the barn, he told me that her owner had left her there and moved off to Texas, promising to return for her. He said that after five years of waiting he assumed she was never coming back.

The next lesson, my instructor informed me that I would be riding that black horse whose name was Shadow. The lesson went extremely well and Shadow and I "clicked". The owner of the barn gave Shadow to me for my eleventh birthday.

Shadow taught me many "life lessons". She taught me about trust, responsibility, sharing, and caring. Shadow is now 25, which is quite old in horse years. This past summer, at the Mississippi Northeast District 4H Horse Show, Shadow and I walked away with the Grand Champion award. It is hard to believe that someone left her, but I guess it was fate that we found each other.

Samantha King, Grade 11
Rossville Christian Academy, TN

My September 11th

Do you remember where you were on September 11, 2001? I sure do. I was in 5th grade, in the classroom of the biggest history buff, news junky, Mr. Jones, surrounded by tons of historical newspapers and memorabilia dating back to the 1800's. We were all doing our class work when about 8:50 AM Mr. Jones got a phone call from the P.E. teacher telling him to turn on the television. So Mr. Jones immediately put down the phone and grabbed the television remote to turn on the news. The sound of the television being turned on got all of our attention, but after watching the news for a few minutes all of us were terrified of what we were seeing. Mr. Jones turned off the television to calm us down and told us to get back to work.

Later that day as I was walking home from the bus stop, I noticed my mom was standing outside waiting for me. As we were walking up to the front door she was telling all about what had happened with the planes and the towers. We went into the house and my sister told me that as they were watching television, a news report broke through showing the live footage of the north tower burning and few minutes later they saw the second plane fly into the south tower.

Jessica Harrell, Grade 11
Vero Beach High School, FL

Live, Love, Laugh

"Live, love, laugh," this saying pretty much sums up my grandmother. She was a huge inspiration to me throughout my life.

My grandmother, also known as Mama Jack by her grandchildren, was diagnosed with Lou Gehrig's disease or ALS in 2002. This disease attacks a person's muscles and causes them to deteriorate. The disease made everyday tasks seems impossible. Through all of this she kept up with her fourteen grandchildren as much as possible. She was determined to not let her ALS stop her from living her life to the fullest.

Mama Jack loved having a big family. Even though she had many grandkids, she never forgot a birthday gift, or to send a card no matter what holiday it was. Mama Jack loved to see the family together, so every summer she would plan for all of us to meet at a beach house in North Carolina. She tried as hard as she could to get the family together at least once a year.

When there are fourteen children running around, some pretty funny situations occur. Mama Jack loved laughing at the things we would do. Every summer we would have giant squirt gun fights. She would help us in any way she could, especially in filling up the squirt guns.

My grandmother was a huge inspiration to me. She loved life even through the toughest times; she loved being around family, and she always found a reason to laugh. Someday I wish to be like her.

Caitlin O'Connor, Grade 11
Countryside High School, FL

Fighting

Fighting can be considered one of the most human acts ever done. Though animals occasionally fight they do it for reasons which could ultimately determine their life or death, such as a food source, or a habitat. However humans have a lust for fighting, hockey has become a popular sport for many because one can suspect that there will be at least one fight in the course of the game. Nothing grabs the sports world's attention like the news that two baseball teams cleared the dugouts to have at each other, or to hear that two football teams got over excited in a game. Our children grow up playing games in which the goal is to kill as many "bad guys" as possible. Young teenagers take pride in the fact that they have never lost a fight, or that no one is man enough to fight them. How does this human lust for fighting help us in our lives? Most of us aren't going to be prize heavyweight fighters, or hot headed athletes; most of us are going to end up working a job in which cooperation is the key to success. So are we helping ourselves by our fascination with fighting, or are we crippling ourselves for the future?

Josh Doragh, Grade 11
Bishop Verot High School, FL

Common

"What's your middle name?" asks one of my friends. I reply with a hint of hesitation, dreading the imminent jaw drop, "I don't have one."

Not having a middle name has become quite a predicament for me ever since preschool. Some of my friends had four and some, considered to be royalty in their clan in Nigeria, even had names long enough to circle the Earth once and back. I had none. Null. Zip. Zero. Looking at the glass half full, I have come to embrace the middle-namelessness in the most comical way possible, knowing my mother almost gave me the middle name "Common" because it sounded like my Chinese name.

The "uniqueness" I have amongst my peers doesn't stop there. Usually when my friends are picked up from school, the music on their stereo is from the radio and at a reasonable volume. However, when I am picked up, the moment I crack open the door to the car, shrieking of seismic proportions is emitted from within. That would be the traditional Chinese opera my parents enjoy so much. I can't quite grasp why they like it so much because all it sounds like is high-pitched screaming set to a nonexistent melody.

Looking back on my grade school years, I chuckle, remembering how conscientious I was about my Chinese heritage. Today, I love every aspect of being who I am. No middle name and all.

Allison Yu, Grade 11
Germantown High School, TN

Running

I clenched my hands until I thought my fingernails were going to pierce my palm. I tried to manage a smile but couldn't. I was still thinking about my nerves when the race began; I yelped when I heard the shot of the race official's gun.

The other runners took off, some laughing and others serious. As I worked to keep up with the leaders, I heard spectators cheering. I heard my name and resisted the urge to smile.

Girls passed me on the downhill, but I kept my pace steady, knowing what I would do on the uphill. At the end of the downhill, I sped up in preparation for the steep incline ahead. When I reached the top, I passed three runners.

I saw leaders starting up the second hill just ahead. I knew I'd make it to the top first; I'd been practicing for weeks.

My muscles shook with exhaustion, but I pushed harder. I was with the front runners, the four of us jockeying for the top spot. I tried to get away from them, but it was no good. Finally, we came to the straightway.

Time slowed down; I saw the clock counting the long seconds it took me to get to the finish line. I realized that I was going to make it and sprinted the last 20 meters faster than I ever had. "22:22!" shouted the race official. He handed me my place card, and I collapsed after those hard, long 3.2 miles.

Mariah Burch, Grade 10
Grady High School, GA

The Biggest Problem in Schools/Education

The biggest problem with schools and education today is the administration. The administration includes most principals. Nowadays most students aren't getting the education they need. There are several reasons that this is the case, such as principals who are not caring for the students, teachers who are not teaching the students what they need to know, or students who just don't want their education. But I think the main reason is the administration. They are not working to help the students get what they need to become successful in life. Principals, to me, play a big part in their students' education. They should determine all of the students who really want to learn and try to help them towards being successful in life. They should also do more to help the students that don't want to learn find motivation. They should continue helping the students that want to learn achieve better.

I feel that if more principals were really involved and in tune with their students, the educational system and environment would be better than it is now. If administration actually took the time out to sit down and to get to really know their students, the student body would be more respectful and willing to learn and succeed in life.

Amber Jones, Grade 11
City University School of Liberal Arts, TN

Crossroads of the Worm

I stand on the sidewalk, the sun beaming down my neck, staring down at the wilting purple-black body. It slowly curls and uncurls, suggesting the pain it would voice if physically capable to cry out its anguish. Here on the crossroads of Beaverwood Street and Oakleigh Lane, I stand at a crossroad. I can pick up this simplest of creatures, the earthworm, the *Caenorhabditis elegans*, and deliver to safety that is the soft, damp heave that is Mother Nature. Or I can leave it out to die by allowing this plain creature shrivel up to die in the harsh heat of the flaming sun.

I am, and always have been, a lover of all animals. I already know that I *will* set this worm back into the dirt, back into its home. Is it the worms fault that innate instinct orders it to lay out, soaking the cool rain? Is it the worm's fault that it cannot, and usually, *will not*, reach the end of the sidewalk that separates hot concrete from cool grass?

We all need help in this life. Whether it is a consoling hug from a friend or smile from a complete stranger, everyone needs someone. Why not help our fellowman, even the common earthworm, when in its time of need? Next time when you are walking outside on a hot day and see the scattered bodies withering on the ground, help a buddy out: pick him up and deliver him to the lands of safety.

Hillary Robson, Grade 12
Germantown High School, TN

Me, Myself and I

It's hard to understand the simple things when you are from another country. Some things that seem obvious to everyone else don't make sense to me at all. I struggle with vocabulary words, history of the country, and many other things. Since Spanish is my first language, I usually get confused with spelling and pronunciation. It's not easy to move around, especially during teenage years.

I moved to the United States from Argentina about two years ago. All my relatives live in Argentina, except for my parents and my younger sister. We get to go visit my family twice a year, but not for a long time. It's hard to make our schedules work, and we never have enough time to see everyone.

When we first moved, I was afraid I wouldn't like living in the United States. The school system and the people were different. The town was different, and so was the lifestyle. Knowing there was nothing I could do about it, I walked in to school with a smile on my face. I made great friends almost immediately, and I truly appreciate them being there for me at all times.

I got involved in many school activities which helped me learn new things, and meet new people. When you move, you learn how to adapt to different styles of life, religion and races. It helps you change in a good way, and keep your eyes open for new adventures.

Samanta Pesek, Grade 11
Owasso High School, OK

What People Don't Know About Me

Some people look at me and say, "she thinks she's the stuff, she thinks she's got it all." People judge me before they get to know me. What people don't know about me is that I am a strong black woman. I can care less what others think. What people also don't know is that I use the negativity, and the slander and the doubt to get where I am today. I use all the pain in me to go on. I am proud of who I am. I've learned from my mistakes; I strive for the best in life. I don't give up when people put me down. I use that to keep on going. There was a point in time where I almost gave up on everything. At that time I had lost my first child, my only son. And I used to question God. I used to ask why? For the longest time, I questioned his will. That's until I came across a story in the Bible about Job. Job was a man who strongly believed in God. No matter what happened in Jobs life, he kept going on. Because of that story, I feel I can do anything. So, to the people who say mean things about me, I laugh, because they don't know me. They don't know my loving heart. I am a wonderful person to get to know.

Ry'shawn Mitchell, Grade 12
Grandview Alternative School, MO

Effect

Ever wonder why that girl never talks? Ever wonder why she slumps down in her chair when someone looks her way? Probably because someone has twisted up every word she has ever spoken and has had something to say about every aspect of her life. Maybe what she had to say could have changed the way you think about things, opened your mind a bit. She might actually be a human just like you and have ideas and feelings she has the desire to express. She shouldn't be afraid of what they might say, but she is. Does that even phase you?

Teens these days don't think, don't care, and they most definitely don't see the effect they have on the people that are around them. Even when you are whispering behind someone's back, the other person usually knows. When you give someone looks in the hallway like "I'm so much better than you" they will remember that. Cliques and stereotypes affect high school students on a daily basis. If you don't get invited to the most popular guy-in-schools party, then you're obviously not worthy of living, duh. Since your ideas are different than the person beside you, yours aren't worth sharing.

So in order to make themselves feel better, most teens find things they don't like about the person sitting next to them. Why does it matter if you make the weird feel bad? The person beside you is probably thinking the same thing about you.

Ashli Alford, Grade 10
Greenwood High School, KY

My Purse, My Life

Every time one of my friends mentions a need for some obscure item, I reach into the depths of my purse, and we share a laugh. I'm notorious for my obsession with purses, and the need to be prepared for anything. Ever since I started carrying a bag the summer before high school, that bag, and each subsequent one, has been dubbed my "life" by my pals.

My collection of purses has continued to grow in the four years since that summer. I have at least thirty now. But not only is the number of purses I have a topic of humor. The fact that only a few of them are small purses amuses my friends, too. Most of them are large enough to double as my book bag.

I believe the fact that my friends find most amusing, though, is the selection of items to be found within my bag. I've been known to carry anything from spare pencils to fabric pens, Benadryl to Rolaids, nail files to Swiss Army knives, and any number of other odd items. My friends call my purses my life because I always have what we need and none of us could live without it. It's something that all of us bond over.

Now, every Christmas and birthday I can expect at least one purse, accompanied by some teasing and laughs. I love being able to share something with my friends that makes me happy and leaves a quirky memory for me to cherish.

Amelia Grace Fizer, Grade 12
Slater High School, MO

My Family

If there is one thing in this world that means more to me than anything else, it's my family. If it were not for my family I'd be nowhere. Family is the only thing that keeps me going when there is nothing else to go for.

My family and I spend most of our time watching TV together. On the weekends we all do our own thing unless there is something that needs to be done together. As long as you get what needs to be done, done, mom and dad will let me do just about anything.

I really enjoy doing things with my family. I really like going out to eat on special occasions. Mostly I like just being able to get along with my family, because when one person's mad, everyone's mad.

I am most thankful for having the best family anyone could ask for. Even though my family has problems and trouble (like most families do) they're still the best anyone could ever ask for. When you have no one else to help, to turn to, family is always there.

If I did not have my family I do not know what I would do. Family is the only thing I have to turn to sometimes, if they were not there when I turned, who knows were I'd be. Like daddy always says, "When there's no one else, there's family!"

Jessica Smith, Grade 11
Southside High School, NC

An Everyday Struggle

Something happened a year ago that changed my life forever. The night of Oct. 18th 2006 I was trying out for a competitive volleyball team, when I took a wrong fall and hurt my knee. At this time I knew something bad had happened but I never thought the outcome would be this. After seeing a few doctors I soon found out that I had torn about everything I could tear in my knee. It would require a big surgery, and the outcome was unknown until the surgery was over. We thought it went well. Until months later I was still unable to bend my knee past ninety degrees. I kept working hard with a therapist for a few more months until the doctor required another surgery to try and progress the bending. This helped tremendously, but still ten months from the original accident I was still struggling with everyday activities. The doctor told me it was one of the worst cases he has seen in a young teenager, but the rest was up to therapy and I. To this day I wake up stiff and unable to bend my knee until I start moving around. This will affect me the rest of my life but I am certain that I will heal. I will not let this burden get in my way, soon enough I will be able to crisscross applesauce once again.

Kelsey Sailor, Grade 11
Owasso High School, OK

Capital Punishment

Capital punishment is a hotly debated topic in today's society. Capital punishment is important to the morality of the nation. When someone is murdered, the family of the one who was murdered wants restitution. They want that person to be punished.

This form of punishment was instated to protect the citizens and to promote morality. If a stiff punishment is in place for a certain crime, then that crime is less likely to be committed. If a killer is aware of the punishment before he commits the deed, he is more likely to think about it twice.

Our nation has quickly drifted away from capital punishment. We do not have strict rules in place to justly punish murderers. They have nothing to fear. They can go out, commit their crimes, and come home without having to worry about retaliation. Even if they are sent to prison, they live a life of ease. If teens see older people committing murder with no retaliation, then there is no reason why they would not go and kill someone too.

So does this nation encourage lawlessness? If it refuses to punish the evildoers, then it is refusing to create a moral society. If these criminals continue being pardoned, this nation is soon to become a scary place. A lack of enforcement of capital punishment promotes an immoral society.

Leigh Steward, Grade 11
Providence Classical School, AL

Love, Respect and Encouragement

As years passed I began to realize that my life is very important to me. Without God and nana I don't know where I would be. My parents mean a lot to me but when I don't want to converse with my parents I always have grandma. My mom and I don't have a close relationship like my dad and I, but there come times when we are mad with one another and I don't want to converse with them. I have grandma to turn to.

I'm very thankful for grandma because I can go to her 24 hours a day and 7 days a week and she's there. Grandma shows me the love and respect that I don't get when I feel I deserve it. When I want to just throw my hands up and say "I give up," grandma is the one that encourages me, "It's all right." Days I walk around with my head hung down I can hear grandma saying, "It's going to be all right" or "Look up to the hills from which cometh your health cause all your health cometh from the Lord," or "You're too blessed to be stressed." When I didn't always understand things in life I'd go to grandma and she'd say "fall on your knees and go to God in prayer." If I was to lose grandma I don't know what I'd do. No one can ever replace grandma because she'll always be the one I turn to.

Aleisha Hardy, Grade 11
Southside High School, NC

Our Heroes of 9-11

Even though I was only nine years old on Sept. 11, 2001, it is a day that will live with me forever. I did not find out about the terrorist attacks until a few days later because my parents and school were trying to protect us, and thought it would be best if we did not know right away about the devastation at the World Trade Center and all the people who died on the planes. They were trying to find a way to tell us, even when they could not understand it completely. The images that I have seen since that day are etched into my memory.

There are many heroes because of their actions before, during and after the terrorist attacks of 9-11. It took a lot of courage to know that you would die by taking control of a flight or by not, or could die by going into a burning, collapsing building or could get sick by looking for survivors in the rubble. It takes a hero to sign up for military duty knowing there is a chance you will fight in Iraq. There are many heroes of 9-11, including my cousins who are in the 101st Airborne, the Navy and my cousin's boyfriend who is now serving in Iraq. Civilians working in Iraq helping our soldiers are heroes. Heroes from past, present and future have put all of our lives in front of their own, and I thank them!

Jason Sellers, Grade 10
Florida Virtual Middle-High School, FL

Motivation

Motivation is key when you're a high school student. Most people don't just go home and do homework to get good grades unless they are motivated to do so. Motivation may come in many different forms. For some it comes in the form of sports, some might have parents that motivate them by giving them a car to drive as long as they keep their grades up, and others may use college as a motivation.

Motivation in the form of sports just means that you have to stay eligible to play sports in high school so you must pass all your classes. Some coaches require more than a "passing" grade which is even more motivation to do well. The reason that sports motivate some of us is simply the fact that we love competition. A little friendly competition never hurt anyone and it can only make you a better athlete.

My parents, as well as those of a few of my friends use a car as motivation. When you make good grades your insurance costs much less. My parents constantly remind me that if I let my grades slip then I won't have the luxury of a car anymore and that definitely keeps me motivated to do my best.

The same goes with college; for some the only way they'll make it to college is on scholarship, academic or athletic, and staying motivated to make good grades may help them reach their dreams.

Hannah Boss, Grade 11

Tupac Shakur

Tupac Shakur a rapper, an actor, a good to be around guy. He was brave, heroic, and thoughtful. Tupac was born on June 16, 1971 in the great city of New York City, New York. He was killed in Las Vegas, Nevada by a drive-by. He then went to the hospital where he died seven days later.

Tupac's bravery shows through all of his life until his death. His family was involved in drugs, rebelling, and even murder. Tupac had been shot prior to the shooting of his death in 1996. Although it didn't kill him it made him stronger and braver. This is what defined him.

Tupac's heroism shows because he fought for what he knew it would make him stronger. He worked and refused to give up until he finally got to do his dream of acting, singing and living the American dream. That is why he is a hero to me and a hero to many other people.

Thoughtful, he tried to stop the hate between whites and blacks violence racism and the hatred of police toward people. To quote Tupac "They got the wars and the drugs so the police can bother me." He also tried to keep his friends and family away from enemies.

Tupac lived his life in hate, love, peace, war, and any other possible scenario. Someone can think of he loved his family and friend and career. Tupac loved poetry and it helped tell his story when he died. So this is why Tupac Shakur was great.

Ben Zimmer, Grade 11
Mulhall-Orlando High School, OK

Grand Nationals

During my freshman year, I participated in the marching band. After a lot of practice, sweat, hard work, and determination our band was finally ready to compete in one of the biggest marching contests in the world, Grand Nationals in Indianapolis, IN. After a solid preliminary performance, our band traveled to the University of Indiana to rehearse in their domed practice field. After the practice our entire band sat in a circle and held hands as we listened to some soft music. This gathering was extremely powerful in showing us all that we were a family and gave us a great energy boost.

The next day, we competed in the semifinals and were able to absolutely knock out one of the best shows that we ever done. That afternoon, we went to announcement ceremony and were forced to sit at the very top row. As they announced the names of the finalists, we sat there with great anticipation. The public announcer had soon read off the names of 11 out the 12 spots available and our name had still not been called. As we sat there with our eyes closed in anticipation all we could hear was "and finally, the Owasso High School Marching Band." Because of this, our area went nuts. Although, we didn't win the competition I still get chills down my back when I watch a copy of our performance. This was a great experience in which I will always remember.

Andy Simmons, Grade 11
Owasso High School, OK

Do Things Really Happen for a Reason?

Ever since I was a little girl and I'd get into some sort of trouble, my mom would say it must have happened for a reason. "Do things really happen for a reason?" is a question that most people ask themselves. As I got older, I started to question myself. Did the mistakes I made happen so I could learn from them, or did I just do it because of me? I was adopted and as I got older and started to notice that I realized that my family started to treat me differently than the others. Then at night I'd go in my room and cry, and repeatedly say to myself, there has to be a reason. But I couldn't find a reason why adults would treat a child so differently. Deep down inside it hurts so bad that words can't describe it. So, this year, little did I know this question would be a part of my life. Just when I thought everything was going along just great and I thought I met the right man, I wound up pregnant. Now, my baby's father won't talk to me like he used to. I feel rage because he won't even try to make an attempt to help me. Besides being pregnant and the sickness, I feel horrible, because I know I could have done much better than that. I sit and ask myself, do things really happen for a reason?

Isabela King, Grade 10
Grandview Alternative School, MO

World Changers

In July of 2006 I decided to go on a mission trip called "World Changers" with my church in Sedalia. The "World Changers" mission trip lasted a week and during this time we drove up to Trenton, Missouri. While in Trenton, we did volunteer work on other people's houses because they couldn't afford to pay professionals to do all the labor. Some of the work we did included putting shingles on roofs and painting people's houses. There were many different churches from many different states, and we were all separated into different crews of about eight people each. Normally in each crew there was a devotional leader (who read a daily devotional to the crew each day), a medic (who was in charge of all the cuts and scrapes that might have been made), and a crew leader (who was in charge of the crew itself and gave instructions on what we were to do for that day).

I liked everybody that was in my crew, mainly because we all got along and never got into an argument. Because of this, my crew finished our job (roofing a small house) after the first two days of working and went to help other crews who had a much harder roofing job. We spent the remainder of our week in Trenton picking up shingles from the ground and putting them in a dumpster and putting even more shingles on a house that hadn't been reroofed in many years. Our work was much appreciated.

Matthew Warren Fisher, Grade 10
Slater High School, MO

From Life in the Big City to Small Town Life

Let's say that your life is going great, you got your friends and schools going good. Then your parents come and tell you, "We're moving." I know you feel like your world is crashing down around you, or someone just slapped you right across the face it's a complete shock. And the worst part about it, you have to move to a really small town out in the middle of nowhere.

Believe me, I know just how you feel because the same thing happened to me. Leaving your friends, and possibly family, having to move away from everything and everybody you know and love. Yes, it's bad at first, but you will learn how to get over it, I did. But you never know, you could like living in a smaller town than a big city. Some advantages are there aren't as many people, and not having to deal with all the hassle of the big city like traffic jams and trying to find a place to park when you go to work. Even though you have to leave all your friends eventually you will make new ones, it may take some time, but it will happen, you just have to be patient.

You will make new friends, get used to a new school, and you will adjust to a small town. The whole moral of this is basically, "Don't judge a book by its cover," or just simply put, don't say you don't like something until you've tried it.

Laura Dennis, Grade 10
Trinity Christian Academy, AL

My Lost Love

I walk among the shifting crowds viewing life as still shots in time, trying to find something I've held with me since I was 6 years old, something that has grown and matured through the years just as I have, so it has become a part of me. I can still feel bits and pieces of it such as the way my hands felt against its surface as I spun it around on my fingers, playing with the intricate pathways along its circular structure losing myself in its beauty as I dream of the game. I can still hear the sounds, of how it contacted the floor and vibrated and sang with the speed of my body as it moved through my legs into the hands of other people, but most of all, the deathly quiet swish the net made as it sunk, without brushing rim or backboard. I remember the sweat that flooded out as my mind pushed my body to continue on. I can still taste the tears that leaked my frustration and all the pain: the price of winning.

Oh how I remember the passion, the love I possessed for that bloated sphere of leather. A lost love is like a lost self, like losing something apart of you. You're now missing something. You're lighter, misshapen; as I am, lost, wandering around in a world that has turned foggy because of a now blurred vision caused by my lost love.

Darah Patterson, Grade 11
Germantown High School, TN

Becoming a Jew

Butterflies squirm around in my stomach. It's August 7, 2004. Two years prior I selected this date for my Bat Mitzvah. I never thought the day would arrive so fast. I woke up to find my house filled with relatives: a very warm, hectic setting. I commenced my morning routine as if it were a normal day: took a shower, styled my hair, and slipped on my newly bought outfit.

Then it was off to the Temple. Being the Bat Mitzvah, "daughter of commandment," I arrived early to have photos taken of this acclaimed occasion. The service started at 10:30 a.m. My nerves wanted 10:30 a.m. to never come; it did.

Before the Rabbis and I walked onto the bima, or alter, I proudly put on my talliet, prayer shawl, for the first time. Then it was show time. Most of the actual service is a blur in my memory now, but I do remember the most important part of the service: the Torah reading.

As I read the Hebrew words, I thought of how the exact Torah I was reading from originated in Czechoslovakia, where my great-great grandpa resided, and how I was reading some of the most holy words in the world. The experience was exhilarating.

After the service, parties came to pass, but that didn't matter. What mattered to me was that I committed myself to be a Jew. I was to be recognized as an adult Jew in the world.

Amy Fenton, Grade 11
Germantown High School, TN

Fishing

Fishing is a sport, a relaxing hobby, and a way of forgetting one's woes and living a life away from the harsh realities and consequences. There are several different purposes for, and styles of fishing; however, the end of a great fishing trip always results in a great amount of pleasure and happiness, as well as a good amount of knowledge gained from the experience. Fishing serves as a sport for the serious fisherman who base their lives upon the necessity of such a pleasurable and carefree occupation. As a relaxing hobby, fishing soothes the mind and allows a break or recess from the continual stresses of work or school. This hobby also gives a person the capabilities to begin to understand and assimilate into a part of nature. Fishing also takes the place of a reason for taking a vacation or some time to reflect on past or present experiences, as well as helping to relax the mind and serve as a beneficial way of becoming one with one's own self as well as nature. The results of fishing are beneficial for the most part, and the best part is knowing that you provided dinner for the rest of the family through the skills and knowledge of any experienced angler.

Patrick Rickert, Grade 11
Bishop Verot High School, FL

Who He Once Was

"Daddy's Girl" my shirt read on the first day of kindergarten. I can remember clenching my father's hand tightly as he walked me to my class.

I was nervous, but my dad just kept telling me everything was going to be okay. When it was time for him to leave, he said, "Remember, I love you Peanut."

As the years went by, my father changed; he became distant and unreliable. Then one Saturday morning, my mom woke me up in tears, for she had learned of the ongoing affair between my father and his boss.

Shortly after, my father moved out. At first, we all tried to forgive him and maintain a relationship, but he couldn't bare his guilt alone. He began to blame my mom and his children for all of his choices.

Slowly, he started to alienate my brother and I and enjoy his new life. Eventually, my father made no time, nor room for his children at all.

It's been months now since I've seen or heard from my father and in spite of the pain I've felt, I look back on this event in my life as something positive. It has made me more aware of what I do have in my life, rather than don't.

Each day I am grateful for my faith, friends, and family; all of which helped me through this tough time.

Today, my father is blind to who he has become, but I'll always see him for who he once was.

Sarah Shehorn, Grade 11
Countryside High School, FL

A Good Friend

Everyone has friends but not everyone has good friends that you can trust and count on. My name is Shantia and I will be writing on having good friends and my opinion of what a good friend is. My opinion of what a good friend is, is a trustworthy person, someone who you can depend on, and a friend that will always be by your side.

I think being trustworthy is what makes a good friend because if you don't have trust then you don't have anything. Nobody wants a friend that you can't trust and cannot keep anything with. You should be able to tell your friend anything and don't have to worry about them telling anyone else.

I also think having a good friend should be someone you can depend on. Your friend should be someone that you can go to for advice and they help you in every way. You should be able to count on your friend to be there whenever you are going through or are in need.

And finally, I think your friend should always be by your side. Your friend should be by your side through thick and through thin. You should never be afraid of your friend not being by your side. If you have to, then you don't have a good friend.

Shantia Satterthwaite, Grade 11
Southside High School, NC

Mahatma Gandhi

Mahatma Gandhi was a humanist who inspired people worldwide with his theory of nonviolence, stating: "The weak can never forgive. Forgiveness is the attribute of the strong." Gandhi has led Mother India through the steps in governing and protecting herself from foreign interference, and in uniting the many castes, religions, etc. that caused much negligence for the people. Taking into consideration the size and population of India, the fact that Gandhi was successful in setting aside the differences, and allying the people to work as a whole, proves to be an essential factor, for it helped the process of unification tremendously.

The principles of Gandhi have unequivocally left their distinct mark on the world. Despite the numerous clashes between India and Pakistan, both countries have shown extraordinary restraint in preventing the situation from escalating into a nuclear war. Nothing can prove the relevance of Gandhi in today's society better than the liberation of South Africa and the fight for civil rights in the USA, both happening in the age of the "weapons of mass destruction" and both proving to the world how powerful nonviolence can be.

Mahatma Gandhi had stated, "An eye for an eye only ends up making the whole world blind." If we pay no attention to nonviolence and think of it as irrelevant, there is no doubt that the world we leave behind will be on the verge of destruction made none other than by mankind which is blinded by hatred and prejudice.

Alisha Rathi, Grade 10
Stanton College Preparatory School, FL

Blink

"7:22 AM" my clock yells at me in angry red blinking script. That's wrong of course, I've neglected my clock so much that it's never been fixed to the correct time after the numerously many accounts of power surges that set it back to 12:00 AM. This, of course, is why it blinks. It almost demands attention, it's crying for help. If I actually were to look at this clock every day and keep its time maintained it wouldn't HAVE TO blink. But it blinks, once about every second. This clock is by no means alone, for I sleep and spend time beside it every day, but it is lonely. I am sorry for the clock, because I know I can do something about it; I simply choose not to. Maybe today is a day for change, however. Perhaps today the clock will stop waiting for me or anyone else who's been in my room to pay it attention and make it happy. It is certainly possible that today or any other day this clock will stop crying out for attention and love and do something crazy, perhaps insane, and just move itself over to the correct time and stop blinking. It's a shame that this is impossible. Everyone knows the nature of a clock is that it is built in such a way that only someone else can satisfy its need. Perhaps this is the nature of all human beings.

Alfred Kilzi, Grade 11
Miami Killian Sr High School, FL

Always Forgive, Never Forget

My grandfather was a horrible man. He was even convicted of murder. Because of that, my parents only let me meet him once.

He died a few weeks ago and I know, this sounds terrible, but it didn't really bother me. I was actually glad the world was rid of such a bad person.

I felt that way until my mom told me about the last time she saw him. She said that he was in a coma and brain dead at that point, but she wanted to talk to him anyway. She hadn't spoken to him since she was 8, when her mother died.

She had been put up for adoption because he would always beat her. So she decided to see him one last time to tell him how much he hurt her.

But when she saw him with a machine breathing for him, she realized that he was completely helpless, just like when she was a little girl. She then decided that she shouldn't be mean.

Instead she walked over to him, held his hand, told him that she forgave him and loved him, and then left.

About an hour later the doctors took him off life support, and he passed away peacefully.

When my mom told me about how she was able to forgive him after all the terrible things he did to her, it changed my life. It taught me to always forgive and never forget.

Heather Marker, Grade 12
Countryside High School, FL

My Childhood

It starts when I was born. I was born into a dysfunctional family. My dad drank and my mom, well didn't do anything. My dad had three jobs, no sleep and still took more care of me than "Mickey" did. I started to live with my grandma when I was nine months old.

After that, things still weren't normal for a young child. My mother and her brother Bill kidnapped me three times! The first I don't really remember but the second time I could still, to this day, be able to press charges for attempted murder. My uncle and Mickey tried to drown me and my uncle tried to run me over with his car when I was three. I haven't seen them since I was six. I have an older brother I've never met, a little brother that I haven't seen since he was born, and a sister that I haven't seen since she was three years old!

I'm a whole lot better than what I was back then. I still have dreams to be in the military, more likely the Marines. I have really good grades. I miss my brothers and sister. She has made me a stronger person unknowingly. Hate is a harsh word, but to think of it, I hate her. But I can thank her for making me all that I am.

Wilkie Calhoun, Grade 10
Deltona High School, FL

Relax and Throw

It was the summer before my junior year in high school when I decided to get serious about pitching. I no longer wanted to be the "bad" pitcher or the "easy" pitcher. I wanted to actually be a threat to our competition. Now it was time to get serious; working on strategies and change-ups.

That's when my training plan began. Sacrificing my summer mornings and nights, I was on the field, ball in hand, working on my pitches. There were good days and bad, and always frustration. Concentrating on gaining speed and improving accuracy, I was determined to get better and escape from the mediocre category.

There were days when I loved pitching, when I felt like I was going to make something of myself, and the days when frustration got the best of me, and all I wanted to do was quit. On the other hand I was always reassured by my parents that I was doing my part and working hard. "It will come, you just have to relax and throw," said my mother, who is also my coach.

Now I'm pitching in my junior year in high school and all my hard work is beginning to pay off. Don't get me wrong, there are still so many things I have left to improve, but overall it's like night and day from my previous pitching years. The practices haven't let up nor has my determination. All that's left to do is keep working hard, relax, and throw.

Rachel Rebecca Gonzalez, Grade 11
Slater High School, MO

Prince of Darkness or Just Simply Misunderstood?

December 3, 1948 in Birmingham, England, John Michael (Ozzy) Osbourne was born. Born fourth of six children, his family was middle class. He is not a great war general or never made a tremendous social move in society. What makes him a hero is he has faced adversity, controversy, and severe addictions and overcome them all.

What does Ozzy have in common with Albert Einstein, Henry Ford, and Walt Disney? He suffers from dyslexia. Yet he has written three books. He experienced tremors and found out that he has the genetic condition Parkins Syndrome; symptoms are similar to Parkinson's disease.

Ozzy is controversy. Osbourne has always been portrayed as a "devil worshipper," but states that it is done in good fun. His song "Suicide Solution" is believed to have convinced two teenagers to commit suicide, however it is about the dangers of alcohol abuse.

Ozzy Osbourne has a well-documented career of abuse. His most famous encounter would be biting the heads off of a bat and two doves. Under the influence of alcohol, he urinated on the Alamo at a photo shoot and attempted to kill his wife/manager Sharon.

As you see, as a young man, Ozzy was not a model citizen. Now he realized the bad he has done and has completely changed his ways. Osbourne has overcome poverty, alcohol and drug addiction, and not cared about what others think of him. That is why Ozzy Osbourne is my hero.

Justun Kukuk, Grade 10
Mulhall-Orlando High School, OK

Surf's Up

Everyone has their own opinion on what sport they think is the best. Well, although basketball, baseball, and football are pretty entertaining and fun to play, none of them compare to surfing. To me, surfing is the best sport out there. Surfing is not only really entertaining and exciting to watch, but it's even more fun to do. Getting up before the sun, putting on your bathing suit, board shorts, and rash guard, and waxing your board are all preparations before you hit the water. Then you paddle out to where the waves are smooth, and wait for a nice wave. Once you see one, you have to paddle in hard, so you can catch up to speed with the wave, let it take you, and then pop up. Once you're standing, you drop down the face, and then turn right or left, depending on how you ride. After those basic steps, it's all up to you. If you're a long boarder you can just chill and ride it out, or for the fancy riders you can do some cross stepping, hang five or even ten. And if you ride a short board, you can do cutbacks, or other aerial tricks.

All of this might sound easy, but it's actually hard. Even some pro surfers like Kelly Slater and Keala Kennelly bail off or don't make the drop. Also, you can die easily, especially if you're doing big wave surfing, or around reefs.

Maria Kosar, Grade 10
Deltona High School, FL

Life Without

As I live day by day, I think about all of the things that make me feel important. Oh how life will be without them.

I sit and think. I picture my greatest joys — my family, my life, and my friends.

If I did not have my life, I wouldn't be here to shine my light or my warm love to all the ones I love and grow to love. Without life I wouldn't have a chance to find my way. I'll just be living a hollow life with no hope.

Family and friends are also very important to me. My family and friends keep me going. They put the burning light in my heart, which makes me fight for my life and my future with hope in plain sight. If I didn't have them I would be nobody, lost, without hope, fighting for an empty future, a shallow tomorrow. If they weren't here the flames that are burning in my heart would turn to an icy cold river flowing with anger.

Without the things that are important to me, I would be broken (like a kid that can't find his favorite toy). But with the things that are important to me, I am whole.

Angel Brown, Grade 11
Southside High School, NC

Our Mission

Through school, I was taught to dream of an equal and harmonious society. I was reassured that my country would one day have basic values of human rights and freedom. But when witnessing widespread of poverty to the point of human trafficking, I wonder how can my fantasy become a reality…Little did I know that the Vietnamese government has been brainwashing students and the general public through their education system and the media. This wake-up call arrived when I stepped foot on the American soil — a transition to what I was taught of an ideal society, but didn't see until now.

Now in America, I'm blessed with values of freedom and human rights. It's such a privilege that I live in a society where human rights are respected; when in countries like Vietnam and Burma, these basic values don't even exist due to the cruel regime of communism. Here, people are being muted from speaking their mind. People are being stopped from expressing their religion.

Now I'm asking you, World, let's unite and bring down communism! Friends of all colors and different tongues, let's unite and bring freedom and human rights to Vietnam, Burma, and many other nations where they're deprived of such basic human values. Dear World, it's just you and I to make this difference and save innocent lives from perishing. We have got to start today for the success of tomorrow!

Down with communism! Freedom for the people!

Thu Tran, Grade 12
Paul L Dunbar High School, KY

All About Life

When school started this year, it almost became innate for me to not get any sleep because I was taking AP Biology. At first I felt highly annoyed and irritated by the fact that a class was indirectly taking away my freedom to live a normal life or even function properly as a human due to my lack of sleep. I thought that AP Biology was going to continuously hinder my happiness through its difficult techniques and far out, but at the same time real, concepts. It wasn't until my class reached the chapter on macromolecules that I began to understand the biological concept of life. By that time, I had slowly gotten back into a normal routine of getting more than three hours of sleep at night. I also had begun to understand how to study for and complete my homework from that class with enough time left over to complete my other work.

Now, AP Biology comes easier to me, and as time progresses I am becoming more attached to this study or way of understanding life. It is the one subject that brings a smile to my face. I find myself relating everyday simple occurrences to concepts I learned about in AP Biology. In fact, whenever I am overcome with happiness of my final realization of something, my friend automatically knows it deals with AP Biology. I appreciate this class very much; AP Biology is my life and I love living it.

Ezinwanne Rosemary Emelue, Grade 11
Germantown High School, TN

The Characteristics of an Ideal American

The characteristics of an ideal American are what you believe that everyone in American should live up to. Everyone has different characteristics that they believe make the ideal America. There are not right or wrong characteristics, just different ones. I will share with you the characteristics I believe make the ideal American.

The first characteristic I chose was honesty. The ideal American must be honest. Honesty is the main characteristic I want to see in people, because I like to trust people and the ideal American would be one of my best of friends. My ideal American would be able to tell a story without saying "no lie" every five seconds. The second characteristic I chose is hardworking. My dad used to tell me, "If you work hard the people around you will respect you." I chose that characteristic because I've worked hard all of my life and I have the respect of my parents and I believe the ideal American would be the same way. The third and final characteristic I chose was patriotism. I don't believe, I know, the ideal American would be patriotic. I know the ideal American would be behind our troops; he would believe in freedom and liberty for all, and would never back down from terrorism.

Those are three characteristics I chose to describe my ideal American — the honest, hardworking, patriotic American. In my eyes that would be the Ideal American.

EJ Winfrey, Grade 11
Trinity Christian Academy, AL

Friends with a Stranger

People know my favorite color. You could look at me and notice my taste in clothing or hair styling. A stranger can hear my proper speaking skills or a friend may enjoy my constant laughter. Friends like to believe that they know a lot about me and what I like. They feel informed and in reality, they are in the dark. People I meet prejudge or rely on stereotypes until they take time and observe. They would not ever believe the things they don't know.

People see me as a cool and fashionable person. I'm considered a popular person that is well liked and fun. Actually, I would consider myself as a nerd, or maybe a geek. I don't mean this in an offensive way. I'm proud of my excessive interests in certain activities. I understand that I become enthused with computers and electronics. I construct and design websites for large companies or individuals. I also specialize in fixing computers whether the job is small or large. I am a classically trained pianist that works every day for two hours. I perform at recitals every week and play incredibly difficult pieces. These things of course, are what pay for my expensive shoes that maintain my popularity. I also read for fun, write poetry, write songs, and even cook often. I may be ashamed of these skills or hobbies. My friends are completely unaware of these hobbies and skills and this leads me to say, they are friends with a stranger.

Sheldon Neal, Grade 12
Grandview Alternative School, MO

Faith

Faith, it's what separates me from the crowd. It's my own motivation. Because of my faith, I can stand strong, no matter what life may throw upon my shoulders. Some say that believing in a God is a waste of time or that there is no such thing as a God, but I feel in my heart, that there is a higher force out there in this vast universe that we have yet to understand. To have faith means that you believe strongly in something. Whether it be having extreme confidence in yourself or with others. As a Christian, I have faith in many things in life, such as me getting good grades, excelling in life, and hopefully becoming youth pastor in my church.

Faith can have many different meanings for a lot of people. Some feel that to have faith, means that you are optimistic about life, and that you have a positive outlook on difficult situations. To me, faith is a strong belief in my God and myself. When a situation's rough, I am able to pull through and strive on. Plus, in the end, I am a stronger individual. Life to me is a giant test. We are faced with many obstacles, but it's how we handle these obstacles that will determine the outcome of it. Since I have faith, I approach things with a positive mindset, while others might take a more negative approach. All in all, having faith means believing in myself.

David Garcia, Grade 10
Deltona High School, FL

Audrey Hepburn, a Star Worthy of Praise

Audrey Hepburn was an Academy Award and Tony Award winning Anglo-Dutch actress of film and theater, a fashion model, ballerina, Broadway stage performer, and humanitarian. She was raised under Nazi rule during WWII and trained to become a ballerina before pursuing an acting career.

She was one of Hollywood's leading actresses during the 1950s and 1960s, and won four more Academy Award nominations. She was one of Hollywood's biggest stars and was a major fashion icon of her time. People admired and imitated her chic fashion ideas. She starred in many famous movies such as *Breakfast at Tiffany's* and *My Fair Lady*.

Until her death in 1993, she served as a Goodwill ambassador for UNICEF, was honored with the Presidential Medal of Freedom for her work, and by 1999 was awarded the third greatest star of all time by the American Film Institute. Hepburn's fame still endures today and she has been one of Hollywood's few admirable actresses; always retaining humility, and then giving back to the world through UNICEF.

Jackie McCaw, Grade 11
Bishop Verot High School, FL

Lesley Gore: The History of a Teenage Classic

Lesley Gore was born in New York; on May 2nd 1946, as Lesley Goldstein, although her family was in the process of changing their name back to their original Russian name, Gore. Her parents agreed in her early teens, that she would need professional training for her talent of singing.

When her cousin Allen needed a back-up singer for his band since the lead singer was sick, he gave Lesley the job. It just so happened, that was the night that Mercury Record's President Irving Green heard her.

Soon after that night, she and her vocal coach, Myron Earnheart, recorded some demos and sent them to the booking agent, Joe Glaser. Joe listened to them and Irvine Green went and introduced her to Quincy Jones.

"It's My Party" became so popular, that, as quite common in the 60s, the follow up to it was an "answer song" a kind of continuation of the original story.

Leslie Gore had become the teenage bearer for angst, her next release "She's A Fool" and "You Don't Own Me," united teenage girls around the world as someone who seemed to be going through the same thing they were. She provided a declaration of independence with a feminist theme that was advanced for the early 1964s.

Leslie Gore recorded eleven top 40 hits in total, all before her 21st birthday. She continued to entertain her audiences all over the world!

Alyssa Strickland, Grade 10
Glenpool High School, OK

Child Abuse

Child abuse, though often overlooked, continues to be a rising problem in the United States. The Justice Department verifies about 2.7 million cases a year and over 2,000 deaths due to abuse or neglect. The government's inability to control the money devoted to child abuse and prevention directly leads to the escalating number of child abuse cases and deaths.

The immediate and long-term effects of child abuse costs the U.S. about $100 billion each year. The federal government spends $9.9 billion; the state governments, $7.9 billion; and organizations and charities, $2.2 billion. The American people pay the other $80 billion through taxes.

The government fails to focus on prevention; therefore, more money is spent than necessary. Prevention solutions have been proven to work and save millions of dollars. For example, the Chicago Child Parent Center preschool programs in low income neighborhoods cut the abuse and neglect rates in half. These programs served as a kindergarten for the children and a training session for the parents, in which they learned life skills and parenting skills. For the children saved by these programs in Chicago alone, it was estimated to be a total of $2.6 billion in savings.

Child abuse cannot be eliminated, but it can be limited. The government must redirect their funds and use different programs to combat the increasing problem of child abuse. Focusing on prevention will eventually lead to a decrease in abuse rates, and to a decline in expenses placed on the government and the American people.

Christine Dearden, Grade 11
Bishop Verot High School, FL

The Ride of a Lifetime

I had the thrill of my life when I got to experience a rollercoaster at Cedar Point Amusement Park in Sandusky, Ohio. The Top Thrill Dragster was built in 2003 and broke two existing records. The ride stood at 420 feet tall and reached speeds of 120 mph. The moment I stepped into the line, my head was rushing with adrenaline. The line was packed, due to its popularity in the rollercoaster world. Standing in line and watching passengers board the dragster made me anxious for my turn. I was with my dad, and we experienced this together. As the line moved on, it was our turn to buckle ourselves in. Pulling out we waited for the stoplight to turn green. Once it turned to green we hit 120 mph and we were shot in the sky before I could blink. Reaching the top of the hill, the whole park became visible for a split second and then we plummeted at a 180 degree angle downwards. We screeched to a stop and then both looked at each other and just laughed. The coaster was the biggest rush of my life and I wish I was standing in line to ride it again. I have the right to say that I've rode the tallest and fastest rollercoaster in the world, and you haven't.

Harrison Haugland, Grade 12
Bixby High School, OK

Unexplainable Reasons

Perfect definition of a role model. A straight A student who never missed school. His life was nearly perfect. Well, that's what everyone thought. I always looked up to him. He was always there for me and he told me to not do what other people did. I wonder why he didn't listen to his own advice.

He met a couple of friends in college that were used to dealing with negative things life offered, such as drugs. In his eyes, they were the best friends anyone could ask for, but he was wrong. At first it was just weed, then came the needles. He wasn't the person I used to admire. He wasn't the big brother I looked up to.

We tried seeking help, but by the time we tried to help, it was too late. He was infected with HIV because of the injections. We didn't know the reason he started doing those things but he was too ashamed to give us an explanation. My family quickly blamed his friends. I realized that, even though his friends got him involved in that, you have the right to make your own decisions in life and that was his. I don't judge him for what happened to him, but I know that now I have to be there for him.

Gineyda Cornelio, Grade 11
Vero Beach High School, FL

Dream, Work Hard, and Never Give Up

"Don't be pushed by your problems," it has been said. But instead, "be led by your dreams." If given the chance to say one thing to the whole world, I would share with people how they should follow their dreams.

First, "Before your dreams can come true, you have to have those dreams," states Joyce Brothers. Without taking time to develop a dream, one cannot possibly achieve anything. For example, let's look at the Supremes, a group of friends who enjoyed singing together. They dreamed of singing professionally, overcame obstacles, and became one of the most popular singing groups of the 60s.

Secondly, one must work hard to make those dreams happen. You must pursue the education you need to reach the goals you have made, whether it is learning a trade so you can make money for your family, or learning about healthcare so you can better your AIDS-stricken community.

But the most important part of following your dreams is never giving up. What if Thomas Edison had never developed his dream of the light bulb? Did you know it took over two-hundred tries for him to perfect the light bulb? This is a true example of following your dreams and persevering.

"Destiny is not a matter of chance; it is a matter of choice. It is not a thing to be waited for; it is a thing to be achieved," William Jennings Bryan noted. Making our dreams come true is up to us.

Bethany Pate, Grade 11
Eastern Hills Academy, AL

I'm Different

From the time I was 5 years old, I have been a little different from most girls I know. I've been a little plumper, and a lot more muscular. I've been more athletics, and a lot less girlie. I've been a real "tomboy."

My mom has always said that I am not different, I'm special. She says that I'm unique. She did not seem to think that when she made me do ballet or no softball. She also did not seem to think that when she would force me into the frilly, pink dress I despised. I've always been the boy that my dad and granddad never had. They put me in more sports than any person could imagine, and they took me golfing and fishing "with the boys." They understood me, and they did not try to change me. My mom and grandma, on the other hand, didn't know what planet I came from.

Today, I'm still different. I'm still not stick thin, and I still have some muscle tone. I still play more sports than most people know about. I know I'm not like every other girl; I'm not the cheerleader my mom wants to be. I have come to realize that being different is okay. I'm proud just being me.

Aislyn Taylor, Grade 10
Germantown High School, TN

Standing in the Limelight with Companions

The sound of music rings even to this day in my ear resonating from a time not so long ago in a place not so far away on a crowded stage where I once sat barricaded by walls of benevolence and amiability. As the music began its initial ritual of vibrations, I felt the cooling sensation of dried tears sweltering down my rigid cheeks as I fought the malevolent depression of a soon-to-be separation from companions. These emotions were those that I felt shortly before walking off the stage in the T. Earl Hinton Music Hall in the Wright Music Building at Middle Tennessee State University for the last time as one amongst a crowd of name-tag-wearing, dorm-food-surviving, cafeteria-food-risk-taking Tennessee Governor's School for the Arts students in the summer of 2007.

No denial can be made of the changes felt by everyone during the span of the five weeks in Corlew Hall. We survived the dorm flood from the top to the bottom floor; we survived the nightly game of surreal "Blitzball" on the sixth floor; we survived the Chinese-food-Nazi. We had grown together as brothers and sisters with a deep love for one another.

On the last day, emotions ran high as tears flooded the eyes of everyone, even those who rarely cry. Compassion so strong cannot be merely sewn from the wombs of companionship or from the wounds of bigotry and apathy. We will forever stand proud of our unique companionship and will long for another.

Philip Shapiro, Grade 11
Germantown High School, TN

Go Organic

In recent years, organically grown foods and other products have become more and more visible in the everyday market in America. This is doubtlessly a result of a nationwide movement towards improved health consciousness. People have read news reports about young children experiencing maturity issues due to the ingestion of certain chemicals in milk, and are similarly wary of these chemicals causing illnesses such as cancer.

Organic products seem to provide a solution to those who want to protect their families from unnecessary chemical consumption. Organically grown foods and animal products are those produced without the use of preservatives, pesticides, artificial growth hormones, human waste, antibiotics, genetic modification, or cruelty, many of which have been thought at some time to perhaps cause serious health issues in humans. Organic produce has a positive effect on consumers as they will not take in unnecessary chemicals as they ingest organic food.

Despite this, there are negative aspects to organic products for human consumption as well. Some preservatives and pesticides not used in organic farming help keep growing foods healthy and safe from harm caused by insects or disease. Organic farmers do take precautions, natural or otherwise, to protect their products from these things, however.

Foods are not the only consumer products now labeled as organic. Organically grown cotton is now widely used to create more natural clothing.

Many people support the organic movement for health, labor, and ethical reasons, all of which can be justified by the very foundations of organic farming.

Kaitlin Sovich, Grade 11
Bishop Verot High School, FL

The Power of Words

They enthrall me. They force me to spend hours poring over them. Have you ever wondered how stories can hold such power over you, so much that you forget about everything else? What makes fictional tales so fascinating?

They make me dream of faraway places and put me in other people's shoes. Stories teach me how to fly and how to be myself. Through stories I learn how to persevere, though the world is unfair. Dreams are even born and hopes are rekindled through messages of courage, love, family, and friendship. Lessons are learned thanks to the experiences of the characters. Everything divulged in stories may be lies but they tell me the truth.

Ultimately, for me, stories are ways to escape the real world. As A.C. Benson, a British poet and author, once said, "All the best stories in the world are but one story in reality, the story of escape. It is the only thing which interests us all and at all times, how to escape."

Merissa Johnson, Grade 12
Academics Plus Charter School, AR

Is Education on Your Mind?

With education in mind, many questions are raised concerning whether or not a person of my stature would succumb to the stress of not being able to learn about life. It is troublesome to be reminded of those days when young women were denied the privilege of going to school and learning essential factors about the world and the people who inhabit it. Young women were subjected to the expectations of the society, which clearly expressed the stereotypical idea that a woman's only duties were to listen to her husband, care for the children, and take care of all the responsibilities in the home. For this reason, imagining myself without a good education proves to be an arduous task.

In the same way, I cannot fathom complying with the rules and regulations and having my voice stifled. For me this presents obstacles that would be hard to handle. In fact, it is important for me to understand that I have been blessed to be able to receive an education. Therefore, in order to pay homage to the freedom that I have, I wake up in the morning with a smile on my face and the anticipation of what's going to happen in school on my mind. In order to make sure that I do not stray from the right path, praying to God for faith and determination to excel in the endeavors of my heart are most important.

Malinda Estrada, Grade 12
LeFlore Preparatory Academy, AL

Country Living

Living on a farm has its benefits. I have never felt any need to live in town, nor have I been present to think that anywhere else would suffice what I have here. The green of grass in my jeans is only the paint of the wild. Ever since I was able to acknowledge where I was, I knew I lived in a kingdom. The fairies, the goblins, dinosaurs and Siberian tigers all had their place on these twenty acres. I remember roaming about and trying to find a way to unleash myself from the grip of the evil inferno, my brother. Among the trees I could hide from his penetrating gaze, and perhaps with my ice and water powers I could in fact put out his rage. So many times my brother and I would find ourselves lost in time and space as simply two entities among the stars. We also had dogs and cats and other animals to keep us busy. My Ginger would become a gazelle as I threw a sharpened spear in the air. Novice play, but my dog did not like it so much. Setting up sticks was also fun as I would try to get Ginger and my other dog Diogi to jump them like the Olympics. So many laughs and games of enchantment hold my heart even today.

Shaping me and giving birth to so many of my dreams was this piece of land. I will treasure it forever as my home.

Jessie Bushyhead, Grade 11
Owasso High School, OK

It's My Life

What started out as a night of fun, ended in a night of death and sorrow. Three teenagers thought it was okay to drink and drive. Before they knew it, their speed increased to over seventy-five mph. They ran a stop sign, clipped one car, and crashed into another, killing themselves and the driver in the other car. The one survivor in the other car is my friend's cousin; the driver was her husband.

Thousands of young teens die each year from drinking and driving, risking lives for a few hours of fun. They are making bad choices by putting other lives in jeopardy and their own. Breaking the law, and for what? Just to have fun?

Peers and relatives may pressure or influence young teens to think drinking and driving is not bad, it's cool, and it's another way to have fun. Wrong! There are many different ways to have fun which don't involve drinking and driving. Some different ways to have fun include going to the park, swimming, fishing, hanging out with friends, and watching movies.

The law of Missouri states that the legal age to drink is twenty-one. Anyone, even a minor, who is caught drinking and driving is charged with a DWI (Driving While Intoxicated). Their license could get revoked, and in some cases, the driver who was intoxicated could be charged with attempted manslaughter.

Don't make bad choices; do what's right. Just think to yourself *It's My Life*.

Jana Knowles, Grade 12
Lakeland High School, MO

Dare Devil

The human mind is a very strange thing. There's something in it that makes us want to do the craziest, stupidest things, and like it. Some people jump off of buildings; some fling themselves into the air thousands of feet up and some people try to go as fast as they can. I'm one of the guys in the last category. Just one problem, when you go fast, you tend to crash.

It was a day like any other, the sun was shining, a breeze was blowing, and I was as happy as a 12 year old could be. Unbeknownst to me at that time, I was about to beat the crud out of myself. I walked outside, the sun glaring down at me, and went over to the garage to grab my bike and helmet. The first few times I went up and down the steep road by my house were nothing out of the ordinary, but then that something stupid part of my brain kicked in. I went zooming down the hill, fast as I could, and tried to turn into my driveway to get to the sidewalk. My house is built on a hill, so there's a brick wall built next to the sidewalk. Unfortunately, I forgot to pull on the emergency breaks. Let's just say that a red brick wall doesn't make the most effective airbag. The doctor said I'd probably have cracked my skull open if it wasn't for the helmet. Guess I'm just lucky.

Johnathan Drury, Grade 10
Germantown High School, TN

Change

Change. It's never a simple thing to do, and not many people are generally able to adapt to something that they do not see eye to eye to. Change. Very few people see the positive aspects of it. Change. It's secretly a vital part of life; one we could, by no means, live without. It helps us to experience numerous things, develop as individuals, and move on with our lives.

Change. Experience comes from change. Throughout life you experience everything; from suffering, to bliss, from sorrow to joy. Eventually, you learn from these experiences, which help you make decisions to steer the wheel of life into whichever direction you may choose.

Change. Our individual characteristics come from change. Events that you pass in the course of life mold your personality. This is all change. This is why we are all different. Without change, your lives would be basic and straightforward.

Change. Moving on with our lives comes from change. However, the most important thing to do is acknowledge change as it comes. Not many people are capable of this; however, those that are, seem to be the happiest in life.

Change. It's never a simple thing to do, and not many people are generally able to adapt to something they do not see eye to eye with. Change. Very few people see the positive aspects of it. Change. It's secretly an important part of life, one we could never live without. It helps us to experience many things, grow as individuals, and move on with our lives. Change.

Amanda Bloomer, Grade 11
Vero Beach High School, FL

Learning to Fly

It was the year 1997, a year that transformed the rest of my life. Before that bleak period of my childhood fell upon me, I was an ordinary little girl. Raised in a sheltered Christian home with loving parents, I had the best any seven-year-old could ask for. However, that life I had known would forever be stripped from my innocent mind. A shadow, I thought I deeply knew and trusted, came in the night and stole what I could never replace. I was broken inside and out. My family nearly fell to pieces like a shattered glass. Although the path was narrow and rough, my family and I survived. As years passed by, I rebuilt myself. I grew stronger, braver, and more confident in my own skin. I realized that no matter the situation, inspirational or horrendous, you will come out on the other side, holding your head high knowing who you are and rising above and beyond your dreams. Though it might not have been my choice to learn in such a way, or time, I accepted my circumstance and I'm proud of the unique individual I am. I hope to one day alleviate the pain and confusion of a lost child that I once was.

Sheridan Smith, Grade 11
Owasso High School, OK

What I Love…

I love the feeling that overwhelms me when I close my eyes and escape the dark auditorium room that I'm sitting in listening to the Atlanta Symphony. I love picturing myself sitting on that stage one day, giving people the same chill bumps that are swarming my body. I love the far away places I am taken by those accelerandos, decrescendos, and every musical effect that I know they are working so hard to relay to me. I love being a part of music.

I have been playing the piano and clarinet for six years. It is not only my passion, but it is also my escape. It is my vent and my inspiration to work harder. It has become more than a hobby through the years. Music will always be a part of my life. I love the countless hours that I have spent practicing, and I love the sweaty palms and shaky knees that I still get every time I walk on stage to perform. I love the resonance of sound left lingering after the last note is played, and I love the music of the audience clapping with an obvious tone of awe. But most of all, I love giving people music.

Mary Leflet, Grade 12
Newnan High School, GA

Motivation

My inspiration originates with a factory worker of six children whose strength is as admirable as her life. My mother is the person I can proudly declare as my hero without feeling any shame whatsoever.

When poverty is enforced by society every day is full of suffering. Her childhood was spent working on a farm with the heat that surpassed one hundred degrees Fahrenheit. School was expensive and walking twenty miles every day was the punishment for desiring an education. Imperfect chores resulted in being flogged with a rope that left an inflammation and sometimes caused the skin to split and bleed. Reality was cruel.

Trying to escape poverty, she left to work in The United States. She knew the American dream was a complete lie, but for us she was willing to sacrifice her life. For ten years she worked in a chicken factory standing every day for eight hours on the hard concrete and slippery floor. These are the only jobs available to the undocumented criminals.

The future, the present, and the past are identical to my mother. Even now at almost fifty years of age, she must work in a disgusting place being humiliated by those who criticize people like her without seeing that we are all humans, not animals.

I admire that she doesn't hide any part of her life. Her loving actions have taught me the meaning of humanity. Like my mother I will "jump for the skies" even though "many have died but [I] can still try."

Janeth Valente, Grade 12
Lee County Sr High School, NC

A Life Changing Adventure

International mission trips are a once in a lifetime experience. Mine encompassed, leaving my home town of Clearwater, Florida, and traveling to a small island called Ariri off the coast of Brazil, even traveling to another part of the world, Juarez, Mexico.

Lifelong memories are made while discovering new places most people don't visit. Knowing that I have affected someone's life who is entrenched in poverty has brought me long lasting memories that I will never forget.

Knowing what I did, such as building two houses in four days, to starting the foundation for a community center, made a big impact on someone's life. This is very comforting. Passing the keys off to a husband and wife, who are about to have a child, and knowing that they can now have a safe house with a locked door, just makes the experience even more worthwhile.

Long lasting memories, whether it be through pictures or through remembrance, will never be forgotten. Doing these mission trips have really made me appreciate everything I have, even the simplest things like flushing a toilet. I grew so much closer to my fellow youth group friends and the organizations we traveled with.

It's hard to say goodbye once the week is over. Friendships were built and communities were brought together. By taking this step forward to ending poverty in this community, it may even have created a new lease on life for the families we helped.

Shelby Hanna, Grade 11
Countryside High School, FL

The Beauty of Music

No matter where you go on the planet you'll hear this. No, I'm not talking about conversations, I'm talking about music. It doesn't matter who you are or where you come from, the odds are you listen to music. One of the best parts about music is you have the choice to pick what you listen to. The best part is there are so many different kinds of music to choose from. There is everything from country to rap, from heavy metal rock to even classical. Whatever you can think of, I'm sure there's a type of music for it.

Music is also a great thing because many jobs come from it whether you play in an orchestra or in a rock band. Music is all about expressing yourself. Sometimes you can figure a person out by the type of music they listen to, but be careful not to stereotype. There is also such a wide variety of music that there are plenty of songs out there for you to relate to and make a connection to. Songs always have more meaning to you when you can make a connection. For a lot of people music is personal because music can bring out your emotions, like when you're heartbroken, excited, or even when you're sad. There is a song for everything which is the beauty about music.

Emily Dike, Grade 10
Deltona High School, FL

Faith Is Hope

Faith is the most important part of my life and the reason I get up every single morning. Faith is defined as, "Confidence or trust in another person or thing." The most important part of my faith is my belief in Jesus Christ as my savior. Not only my faith in Him but the faith that my parents will be there for me, my friends will pick me up when I am down, and even having faith that when I sit down, the chair will hold me up.

Whether people believe that there is a God or not is up to them but saying that someone does not have faith is absurd. This person doesn't need my belief system to have faith. Believing in God or not, one has faith every day whether it's getting into a car and having faith that it will get him where he needs to go, or as complex as having faith that his life means something to get him through the day. The reason faith is so important to me is because I know how important it is to the world. For faith is hope and without hope, we are nothing.

Martin Beamer, Grade 11
Platte County R-III High School, MO

Life in Marching

My name is Cameron Taylor and I'm seventeen years old. I am a junior at Owasso High School in Owasso, Oklahoma. I am a member of the Pride of Owasso Marching Band. Life in the marching band is an amazing experience. The marching band activity teaches you many things that you will always take with you wherever you go. It has taught me leadership and responsibility.

The Pride of Owasso has taught me a lot about leadership. With this, I have learned how to lead people, set good examples, and act the right way when it comes to being around younger people. My leadership has grown over the years with my confidence. Without leadership, the band program would fall apart and cease to exist. Leadership makes up a big part of the Owasso Marching Band and has improved my ways of leadership personally.

Responsibility is another thing that I've learned with being in the band. Our responsibility varies from always keeping up with our music, learning our show drills, having everything we need for competition, or just showing up on time for rehearsal. School work is also important. I always have to keep up with my work and grades regardless of the time I have. My responsibility has improved much with my studies and grades.

Being in the Pride Of Owasso has made me a different person ever since I joined. I've learned so many great things that will help me in my future including leadership and responsibility.

Cameron Taylor, Grade 11
Owasso High School, OK

Timely Travel

Whether it's a stretch of highway or a hiking trail, traveling connects with the soul and needs of a person. Once man's mental, financial, spiritual and physical state achieves acme, that man searches for adventure and new settings. Man questions himself asking, "What is just beyond the ridge?" The human mind gains experience and exposure while traveling between two points. Between point A and B memories form and man feels a sense of understanding.

Man must obtain certain needs before travel can be enjoyed. Maslow's hierarchical pyramid suggests that travel lies in the self-actualization stage which is at the apex of the pyramid.

National and international travel has its roots in the Industrial Revolution when trains and boats started to span land and ocean. As technology expands into man's life, tasks and goals can become achieved easier. Bullet trains, cheap airfare, cruises, travel websites, embassies, and space tourism all illustrate how travel flourishes in modern society.

International travel mixes cultures and opens people's minds and hearts to the lives of others. People want to see all they can and be everywhere; and they should, since nothing can last forever. Today's world wonders may not stand in the next millennium.

People love the feel for adventure and still get to stay in their comfort zone. Travel offers a natural high that hits on all senses of the body.

John Gavin, Grade 11
Bishop Verot High School, FL

Vero Beach High School

My first week at Vero Beach High School as a junior has been pretty chaotic. It consisted of loafing around massive books and binders, writing seemingly pointless essays, and smoldering in the heat of the current trailer park of a school I attend. The bathrooms are gnarly and humid. I have to run to lunch to get a seat and if I'm lucky, maybe something to eat. I don't notice very many people in the sea of nameless faces coming and going, with the threat of being trampled ever present. My lanyard is also good at getting in the way of things, yet another burden of the new school year. Getting written up because I honestly forgot about my lanyard is bogus.

I used to enjoy my attendance at Vero Beach High School, back when I had time and space to comfortably eat food and not have to rush just to be on time. It used to be that my locker held my several books and binders all day instead of my awkwardly positioned arms. This year has been so hectic and the pizza I probably won't have time to eat does not make up for it.

Anthony Cooper, Grade 11
Vero Beach High School, FL

Step 1: A Way to Succeed!

Do people REALLY know the way to succeed? Some people would say yes, some would say no. If everyone clearly understood the meaning of success, I think that more people would understand HOW to succeed. The definition of succeed is to accomplish what is attempted or intended. Sometimes, something that is attempted or intended, might seem impossible or awfully hard to accomplish.

How would you accomplish something that seems impossible? Simply by doing these three things: Having positive friends, having the right attitude about life and different situations, and just by frankly being determined. Statistics show that 73 percent of people who surround themselves by positive people, and positive things, have a positive outlook or outcome on life. This also goes to follow that having the right attitude about life and different situations, keeps your mind free from negativity. Being free from negativity, keeps you determined and eager to stay in that positive atmosphere. People who succeed in life, are not only happy, but make the people in their life who are supporting them feel like they've accomplished something great.

So, when wanting to know how to succeed, it's very simple. Just surround yourself with positive friends, have the right attitude about life and different situations, and stay determined. Never give up, it's one step away!

Shashana Hill, Grade 11
Trinity Christian Academy, AL

The Value of Money

Parents should teach their children the value of money. Children will be helped so much more in the affairs of life if they learn the value of money earlier in life. The most important reason to learn the value of money is God's Word says that we are to be frugal with our money (which means to know the "value" of money). God also wants us to be faithful givers to him. In 2 Corinthians 9: 6-7, it says that "Whomever sows sparingly will reap sparingly, but whoever sows generously will reap generously." It also says that God loves a cheerful giver. Being taught the value of money early in life — people will know that they do not waste money and can be trusted — can also help your child's reputation. Teaching your child to spend money wisely will also help them avoid marital conflict. They will need to know how to set aside money for food, clothing, hygienic, on bills and much more, and learn how to set aside money for extra things they would like to possess. They, along with their spouse, will be able to plan out how much money is spent on things without disagreement if both know the value of money. About eighty percent of divorces are caused by conflicts over money. Knowing the value of money, children can pay for college stress-free by saving at an early age. Knowing the value of money will greatly help your child's life in the future.

Charis Athon, Grade 11
Trinity Christian Academy, AL

School Uniforms

There is an old saying, "If you dress for success, you will be successful." This is one of the reasons why all schools should require school uniforms. School uniforms can be beneficial in three ways. First, uniforms can be helpful in the classroom setting. Second, uniforms promote a positive image to the community. Finally, the uniforms can ease relationships between students.

In the classroom, school uniforms can create a better atmosphere for learning. When everyone is dressed alike, there are fewer distractions among students. Uniforms are also helpful for the teachers. Less time is spent monitoring and enforcing dress code violations.

Uniforms promote a positive image of the school to the community. When visitors come to campus, the uniforms show unity and a sense of pride in the school. Monogrammed uniforms are also good publicity for the school throughout the community.

Among friends, uniforms take away the peer pressure of how to dress. Not all students can afford to wear the clothes that are popular. Uniforms help break down these economic barriers. This leads to better fellowship among students.

It is a good idea for all schools to require school uniforms. They provide a better environment for learning in the classroom as well as showing school pride to the community. Perhaps the most important benefit of school uniforms is creating equality within the student body. Our school recently adopted a uniform policy, and the benefits listed above are already obvious.

Will Krech, Grade 11
Rossville Christian Academy, TN

Everyone Is Equal

Equality is something that is very important to me. I feel that America should be a place that people can come and live and have a good life.

America is a free country. We have people from all different countries. People come to America to be free and live the best possible life. You can have a good job, and be wealthy here in America. Equality is another thing that is very important in America. There are all different cultures living in America.

America used to be segregated. People even went to different schools based on what color you were, or what your race is. People were not able to walk outside into their front yards, without getting attacked by someone else. Those were hard times.

Now, equality is something very important in America. People are no longer segregated, and now everyone is together. Equality is important.

Andrea Henries, Grade 11
Southside High School, NC

Identity

When you look in the mirror who looks back? Do you like who you see or do you want to change? How well do you know this person? I know what I see in the mirror. I see lies.

Staring back at me is a girl who has everything going for her. She's surrounded by people who love her and is always wearing a smile, laughing or making jokes. She's a straight-A student and the teacher's favorite. She's even an all-star athlete, playing every sport she can and a top-performer on every team.

But this isn't the girl I truly am. It's the facade I put up for everyone — my shield against the pain and cruelness of my world. In reality all I am under this heavy veil is a stressed-out adolescent trying to attain a balance between the sports teams, school and a job. I feel desperately alone because though I'm surrounded by people, none truly know me. They don't know my fears and insecurities or hopes and dreams. None of them are brave or determined enough to see my shield, break it down and pick up the pieces of the shattered girl waiting to be saved.

So until that person comes, I'll continue to look into my mirror and put on my armor to protect myself. They'll only see what I want them to. Lies.

Caitlin Dellar, Grade 11
Academics Plus Charter School, AR

Solo Eyes

A gentle bead of water slides sluggishly across the rigidly contoured surface of a bright crimson sugar maple leaf. The plump droplet moves slowly, casting crystal explosions of light into the hazy atmosphere, small and unseen but not insignificant. The tree emits an aura of light, red and glowing with a misty magnificence only captured in the earliest moments of dawn's exposure. This spectacle is viewed in all its beauty by the most accepting eye, the solo viewer, in the company of only the dawn. He takes in all details, every intricacy is noticed, and appreciated. This moment is as brief as the single flutter of the dragonfly's narrow wing and seemingly as insignificant, insignificant unless observed, and observed in a state of complete self isolation, the only way to drench one's perception in the vast pool of natural beauty.

Happiness comes as a product of knowing oneself, and knowing oneself in full. It's in the stereotypical confines of the wilderness that we all embark on our own personal epic. How are we expected to enter into a world plump with human populous, and attempt to meet people, when most are unable to cypher themselves from the herd. A journey is necessary in one's life, an exploration of one's personal limits outside of social confines. Otherwise the world's beauty is left only to the few courageous solo eyes who are living life for the drones who know themselves only as deep as others can see.

Luke Cottam, Grade 12
Germantown High School, TN

Growth

People grow accustomed to what they have always known. Life can become simple, warm and familiar. Only when the simple things that we used for support for so long crumble, can we find out just how tall and sturdy we can stand on our own.

Cicadas' familiar buzzes merged with the warm Arkansas summer air. The old gravel road, unpaved with memories of first time driving, red-staining popsicles, and hot chocolate with small marshmallows as pure as clouds, still curved in the same direction. With each step the young boy knew that the previous could very well be his last on that sacred road. Sixteen years of junk resigned in two bags on his shoulders. The old Edie Bower bags were falling apart at the seams, but still hung by threads. As the boy loaded the bags into the black Expedition at the road's end, he gave a final look back. Never had the mundane looked so refreshing.

The young boy never imagined how hard living could be. Waking up, getting dressed, living, even going to sleep all seemed so new, but it was all so ancient. He began to live a life not supported by familiar columns or old branches. He tested himself by how far he could go, and surprised himself at how far he went. He grew again from the rubble of a shattered life, while always remembering the past (because it was a beautiful past), and treasuring every moment of the potentially beautiful present.

Rob Moore, Grade 11
Germantown High School, TN

Family

What are you most thankful for? I am most thankful for my family. My mom loves and supports me no matter what. Uncle Rusty and his family love me for me.

My mom supports all my decisions. Once I was supposed to go to West Virginia. I had paid all the money to go, but decided I didn't want to go and she wasn't mad at me one bit. My mom helps me keep my dreams alive and encourages me every day to be the best I can be. My mom knows that I love photography and she's always trying to get me to take classes at the local community college.

Uncle Rusty and his family are the people I go to when I'm home. They always invite me to their house. When I'm there I know I'm loved. Last Christmas I stayed with them for three days and helped shop for Christmas presents. My aunt Donna also knows I love photography and has offered to let me borrow her camera.

Family is the most important thing to me. Without family, I would feel lonely and would probably give up a lot of my dreams, but they support and love me every day. My mom encourages my hopes and dreams. While Uncle Rusty and his family take care of me when I'm at my home and away from home. No matter what, I know that I'll always have someone there to love and support me all throughout life.

Ashley Withers, Grade 11
Southside High School, NC

Music of My Life

Joining marching band has helped me make many friends. Friends who are funny, helpful, encouraging, and talented. They have always been there for me. Whenever I am upset, they are there to make me laugh and support me. They are the kind of friends who you could spend hours with, or talk to or just be with. Who knows what life would have been like if I had never known them?

Not only have my friends made a difference in my life, but also music. Music that can soothe, excite, and comfort the soul. Music has brought my friends and I together. Our talent is to play notes into beautiful songs that can raise the spirit of one. Without music in my world, life would be impossible.

Playing and marching in front of thousands of people has built more courage and endurance in me than ever before, too. (To clear my mind of all the strangers staring at me and noises surrounding the environment.) To forget about the rising temperature inside my uniform, sores covering my every muscle. To just focus on the music and steps to take. Clearing my mind, body, and spirit.

I have now realized that heroes can be anything you want them to be…people or memories. Marching band has been that hero to me. It was the music of my life.

Brandan Tillman, Grade 11
Countryside High School, FL

A Difficult Time

Although I was only a young child, I remember it like it was only yesterday. My mother came home one day and told me that I was going to have a baby sister. The further along her pregnancy went, the less work she was able to do. One day something happened and I knew it was not good because my dad had to call an ambulance. When the paramedics arrived they loaded my mom into the ambulance. When my dad and I arrived at the hospital, my mom told us that the doctor said that everything was okay, but I thought otherwise. On May 9, 1998, I returned later to the hospital and saw my mom lying in the bed looking depressed. After hours of talking, my dad told me that my sister's name was Ashley Faith Scott, and that she did not survive. After constant crying, I decided that I wanted to see my sister and the doctor brought her into the room. She was so small and cold, but we took pictures and held her as if she were not dead but only sleeping. Hours later, the rest of my family and my pastor arrived, he gave words of encouragement and prayed for my family. That was a very difficult situation for me to deal with at such a young age. Many times I wonder how different our family we would be with her in our lives. This year she would have been nine years old.

LaTroya Scott, Grade 10
Baton Rouge Magnet High School, LA

Do I Have To?

As a society, we've thrived on the complex nature of opposites. Counting down the thousands on the list, there has always been one opposite, though, that the emotional thrall is profound knowledge. Basking in the cliché world of a teenage heart and the world around us, we find love and hate. While these are very powerful and seductive emotions, how much of what human creatures do is only because we think we should? The world can splash around the words, but are they truly real or are we just giving them manifestation because we need an excuse for our actions? Our mind is just a series of conscious and subconscious thoughts, but honestly, do we rule the thought, or does the thought rule us?

Countless times, the argument to love with the heart has been heard. But in all honesty, the heart is just an organ. It is the brain and its minions of the body that cause us to react in such a way that we wish, desperately, to fling ourselves into precarious situations. But when are we going to just stop and ask ourselves, "Am I really embarrassed or, because I am human, do I feel like I should be embarrassed?" With the ruling thought of how we should act, no one realizes that they aren't acting at their own body's will at all. People react on the immediate, self-gratifying thought, and in the end, the thought always wins.

Allison Batt, Grade 12
Rock Bridge Sr High School, MO

Sports

One way to release stress during the hectic school year is to play sports; two sports that I enjoy participating in are tennis and cross country. I have participated in these sports for a majority of my high school experience. I have been playing tennis since I was about nine years old. I practiced tennis every day for about three consecutive years. My freshman year I made the varsity tennis team and I had a lot of fun on it. Another demanding but fun sport I participated in was cross-country. The conditioning began in April and lasted through the summer until November. Even during the summer we practiced for five days a week for two hours. We were able to take a three week break in June, but that was the only break that we got. It was a very challenging and demanding sport, but I enjoyed doing it. In August the season started and we had our first meet towards the end of August. I ran on the varsity team and finished about 5th out of seven in all the races. Our season lasted until early November. Our team almost made it to the state final, but one of our runners suffered an injury during the race. I continued both of these sports and I am still running cross country right now. I am glad that high schools across the country offer sports programs because they help to enrich the students at those schools.

Gregory Lambros, Grade 11
Bishop Verot High School, FL

The Real Football

Nervous and excited at the same time, I slip on my red jersey along with the rest of my teammates. It's game day. The opponent is Houston, our rivals since anyone can remember, and our ultimate conquerors in the previous games. Thirteen girls make up the entire Varsity squad, a fraction of all the other schools in our district. Our coach briefly sums up what we need to do. The whistle sounds two times piercing the silence, and eleven girls including me step onto the playing field. One more sound of the whistle starts the game. The ball is knocked into the defensive side. The ball rolls swiftly to me in the far corner. People begin to swarm around me in the few seconds that I hold the ball. I quickly direct it away from the mob and successfully pass to a teammate. We make several attempts to put one in the net throughout the game. Houston rifles two that make it in.

The final moments seal our fate. We lose two to nothing. Our coach talks with us after the game. He is not upset. We were supposed to be massacred by this team. No one feels ashamed, but proud. We held our own with a team ranked state wide, and we knew how well our team had played. No subs for eighty minutes of constant running. Houston subbed every ten or so. We lost, but for us, it felt just like a win.

Madelon Crosson, Grade 11
Germantown High School, TN

Audie Murphy

Audie Leon Murphy was a legend in his own time. Audie was an orphan at age sixteen. He lived for only 46 years. Audie always seemed to have courage beyond his years. He made a huge influence on America and her people. He was both emotionally and physically strong and had the heart of a hero.

Audie made a huge impact on American history, and he influenced many in the process. He made a good soldier and a great role model. He touched people's lives in many ways. He protected his fellow soldiers and in many cases saved their lives.

In the army you must be both physically and mentally strong and being strong happened to be one of Audie's good qualities. He entered the army at the age of sixteen and became a world known hero.

Do you think you could hold off an attack by Germans single handed? Would you continue trying to protect your brothers in battle if you became wounded? Audie was always willing to help people. He cared more for others than for himself.

He may have been one of few that actually fought for his country because he had faith in it. Most would probably say he was a very unique hero that loved his freedom.

Sarah Johnson, Grade 11
Mulhall-Orlando High School, OK

Let's Give Back to Our Mother

What can I do? What can I do?!? This pops into my head every time I see a garbage truck hit the gas pedal making dark charcoal smoke appear out of the pipe or when the topic of global warming comes on the five o'clock news every other day. These issues affect how we live in the future. Preserving our environment will only reinforce our future in this place we call Earth.

Most people could care less about the environment, but I'm not one of them. We may think that we have all the time in the world to fix our problems such as rising temperatures, and emission of green house gases (making the hole in the ozone bigger if you didn't know) there are simple things one can do to try and make a difference in the world. It may not make a difference, but standing around and seeing the environment crumble shows that you have no heart. I for one cleaned up garbage around my neighborhood all summer, recycle, unplug items that aren't in use and I'm now the president of my school's environmental club.

The environment doesn't need fundraising events, what it needs more than anything is your help. Rachel Carson once said "It is a curious situation that the sea, from which life first arose, should now be threatened by the activities of one form of that life." I know what I can do to help. What can you do?

Brittany Wojnar, Grade 11
Miami Killian Sr High School, FL

What People Don't Know About Me

There are a plethora of things that people don't know about me. Starting with my life, my past, the journey I have been through. You can't walk a mile in my shoes. When I was born premature, (actually coming out 5 months too early), I had heart defects, and many of my main organs were not developed. Coming up in life, there were many struggles. Until I was older, I was parentless, so my attitude changed dramatically over time. My father got murdered when I was in the sixth grade, and I almost lost my mother to breast cancer. Somehow I encouraged myself to move on. I know my father would want to see me succeed. I have learned that friends are not everything, so I am not interested in friends. I am dispassionate about what people think about me. On a normal day, I am very secluded and devious. I observe people daily. Nonetheless, in my 8th grade year, I was molested by my cousins, and in early 2007 I was raped. There are many things people don't know about me. It has changed me as a person, because it has made me realize life will never be perfect. It also has made me stronger, because if I wouldn't have been through my trials in life, I wouldn't be the person I am today; a warrior, survivor, and resilient, independent, strong woman!

Donna Irons, Grade 11
Grandview Alternative School, MO

November Morning

She was born on November 16, 1998 in a little hospital room in Mobile, Alabama to two young, energetic parents. Her hair was thin, like her mother's, and brown, like her father's. She was my niece. I didn't hold her in the hospital; a six-year-old's arms are unreliable. I did hold her eventually, but I can't say I remember when. The memories have faded together as the other seven precious little monsters have entered into my world.

My sister, not my mother, awoke me that November morning. Instantly, I knew something was happening. She told me that Dottie, my sister-in-law was in the hospital. I was going to be an uncle. I didn't go to school that day. How could I with the excitement? It was perfect Southern bliss. A young man from a big, Catholic family and a young woman from a town none other than Tillman's Corner were having a baby.

I don't remember sitting in a waiting room for hours. I don't remember anyone worrying. However, I do remember walking into the hospital room. I saw my brother, as proud and as worried as can be. I saw Dottie, who still amazes me with her strength and love as a mother, holding the baby. I think I cried. If I did, it wasn't for attention. I used to cry for attention. No, if I cried, it was because I was realizing that I could love something without even knowing it.

A.J. Heinz, Grade 10
Germantown High School, TN

Injustice

Injustice. It tangles my veins with anger. It makes my blood flow with rage. It spikes my heart with sadness. It takes people down, it creates an indomitable fire, and it flaws our society. Injustice is around every corner. People don't exactly embrace the contrast that each person possesses. Equality exists only on paper for some, and is used at a catalyst for our nation. But, the equality doesn't always exist naturally in every person. Will we ever live in a world where injustice doesn't have an antonym and equality is felt as commonly as being happy? No. Not for a long time. White people are going to continue to feel superior to everyone else. Homophobics are going to continue to hate. Dorks and nerds are still going to be taken advantage of, or teased for being "different." Even in our judicial system, people are still going to be sent to prison for crimes they never committed. Teenage girls are going to continue to gossip about each other as if it's war. Poverty will continue to have roots planted on the world's society. The world is still growing up. One day, the world may have global peace, but the concept is hard to conceive, like the idea of infinity. But, it won't be anytime soon. As much as injustice and inequality may upset and corrupt our world, it will never disappear, which is a truly depressing thought.

Christine Lindquist, Grade 11
Vero Beach High School, FL

Soil Conservation

Soil is one of the world's most valuable natural resources, yet it is not fully recognized for its significant importance. Without soil, we would be unable to maintain the basic needs of our daily lives. Healthy soil is required for plant and food production for humans and animals. Healthy soil is also required to help maintain many of our other basic needs, such as medications and clothing; it is the foundation for our homes, businesses, and roads, and it helps keep our economy productive and stable. Besides all of this, healthy soil produces plants that help filter pollution for the ground, air, and waterways.

Now that we know the great importance of soil, we should take great care to conserve it, because once it's destroyed; it is gone forever, and we would be unable to sustain life on Earth. Soil takes millions of years to form; it forms at a rate of about 1 cm every 100 to 400 years and would take 3,000 to 12,000 years to form productive land.

Healthy soil is destroyed by erosion, which is the wearing away of the land caused by wind, water, and weather conditions. Once erosion removes the topsoil, the rich nutrients needed for plant growth are destroyed. Without soil and plants, the land becomes unable to support life.

Stacy Keith, Grade 12
McCreary Central High School, KY

Big Girls Don't Cry

We leisurely lined up by twos awaiting the signal that we could come into the church. The only thing I could think of was not to cry. I felt as if I was over mourning for the piece of my heart that was so savagely ripped out by fate. As I walked through the lofty doorway, a disheartening ambiance came over me, causing my naturally jovial spirit to die. The stench coming from the elaborate box propped in front of the pulpit was bewitching me as I came closer to it. This was the most frightening time of my young life. I looked to my right only to see the same feelings written on my cousin's face. We never went to funerals because we considered ourselves as too young to go. We both were wondering the same thing; are we ready for this?

As we neared the end of the isle, I saw my pastor at the podium. The words he uttered were inaudible to my ears. Before I knew it, I was standing in front of the casket. What I saw befuddled me. I did no see the lovable person I would previously see every day. It was merely an empty shell. The man who raised me was no longer there. Like a barren Dogwood, the life in him was gone.

Fighting back tears, I wandered to my seat in the pew. I could no longer hold back the tears. Though I was a big girl, I cried.

Amber Bryson, Grade 10
Germantown High School, TN

Close Encounters of the Wild Kind

Mountain vacations can be very memorable. The dizzying heights, the fields of wildflowers, and the occasional wild animal sighting can make for some of life's most notable trips.

My family went on a vacation to Montana's Glacier National Park. While we were there, we hiked up to the top of a mountain where there was a beautiful lake. As we reached the top, the lake came in view, and it was a gorgeous deep blue-green, perfectly framed by bright wildflowers. It was even more beautiful than I had imagined.

Still on the trail, I raised my camera to take some photos. I heard a noise nearby, but thought nothing of it as it was probably other hikers. A moment later, I heard my mother call my name, but I was concentrating on taking my photo and didn't answer. She called to me again, saying "Get out of the way! NOW!!" I turned to see what the problem was. Three steps away from me was a huge mountain goat with her baby. She was in a hurry and not about to give up the trail! I didn't want to butt heads with her, so I leapt off the trail.

With my heart still pounding, we hiked back down to the road. In a meadow nearby stood the mountain goat and her baby, calmly munching on grass. I may have just been an obstacle in her path, but she is a striking memory in mine.

Jocelyn Pipkin, Grade 11
Owasso High School, OK

Thespian at Heart

Imagine a theatre. The kind with numerous seats, and a shiny stage with wooden floors, perfected with a set of velvet red curtains. Then, a spotlight is waiting center stage for its act. This spotlight is mine, because the stage surrounding it is my life. The audience is made up of friends, family, and onlookers who have helped me grow into a better character I never thought I'd become.

The thought of theatre, when I first entered my high school building, was completely foreign to me. I never thought I'd adapt to the stage life so easily, but I have with pride. I enjoy the exciting new challenges it brings.

This adaptation has drastically affected my life when it came to being social and coming "out of my box." Because of Musical Theatre and the Drama Club, I have made best friends and memories with a wide variety of people, with the result of just being myself.

My own family even notices how committed I become, when I am involved with a show. It puts a smile on my face to know that they are proud of me. They support me with anything I do and I honor that.

Theatre is very precious to me. Although after high school I may not continue with the performing aspect of it, I will always be a thespian at heart. My role in this world is just as important to me, as the cast and crew in my life.

Kristina Pabon, Grade 11
Countryside High School, FL

Impact of Music in My Life

Music has impacted my life in many ways. From my beginnings on the piano, to the saxophone and now the guitar, I have gained a greater self-confidence in myself and in my performance ability.

Confidence plays a big part in performing and practicing music. Throughout performances and tryouts, it is essential to be able to recover quickly from a mistake or to accept new information and process it rapidly. Sight reading, taking a piece of music and reading it for the first time, is a perfect example of having confidence while you play.

In my opinion, performance is the most important part of music. To me, a performance is not just entertainment, but it is creating a connection with my audience and demonstrating to them the reasons I love music. Performing also overflows into how I live my life. Whether I am performing music on a stage or performing my life as a soundtrack, I want to make it worth remembering, because a real performance is unforgettable.

Music is something that I have a passion for. The experiences I have gained through music have been life-changing. Confidence in myself, growing in my knowledge and skill and performing for an audience of one are all values that will influence my life greatly.

Jeffrey Payne, Grade 11
Owasso High School, OK

One Thing I Would Change in My Life…

The one thing I would change in my life is disrespecting my parents. I have been a disrespectful child in the past. I had kicked my mother and called her all types of names. I know I was wrong, and I wish I could take it back. I love my mother even though we have been through a lot. When disrespecting the people that brought you into this world, days are taken from your life. God said, "Honor thy mother and father."

That means whatever my parents do to me no matter how bad it is I must forgive them. I should also love and respect them. That's what God said, and that's what I must do. My mother makes me mad all the time, but I still love her and care for her.

I haven't really disrespected my father because I used to be scared of him. Well not anymore. My parents have taught me a lot because they have already been through what I am going through. Sometimes when I see young people disrespecting their parents, I get mad. I get mad because they don't know when their parents' time is up on this Earth. When someone dies, that means they are gone, and there is no coming back.

Keyonna Thomas, Grade 11
Gadsden Job Corps Center, AL

Prideless Passion

"Generosity is giving more than you can, and pride is taking less than you need." This statement made by Kahlil Gibran is my outlook on my passion to volunteer. Servanthood is done in willingness and not pride. Being able to learn something about myself, being in an environment around my career possibilities, and making somebody's day just makes volunteering even more interesting. Working with children at a hospital every Wednesday and Sunday doesn't take away from my life, but adds. Working with sick children exposes me to new ideas about life. I have a calmness in me when I see they are happy. I like to see them comfortable and not focusing on the environment around them. Playing games with them, watching TV, or coloring just for the little time we have I bring joy to their life that is filled with pain. I listen to them and ask them questions so we could have a bond. All I need is one moment to let them know someone cares.

I also choose to volunteer with children because I want to be a nurse, and nurses often become close to patients just like volunteers. To form a trust and a bond, nurses see their patients almost every day. Nursing will be a great opportunity for me to serve people. Having a passion to serve others in your life will grant you respect and help you gain leadership that will guarantee you success in anything you pursue.

Stacey Pugh, Grade 12
North County Christian High School, MO

Hero

We all have heroes. For some of us, it may be a famous athlete or celebrity. For others, it may be a teacher or coach. But for me, my hero is my father. He is extremely hardworking, and he's a loyal friend. He is also a good family man.

My father is a very hardworking man. As a child he learned the meaning of hard-work by working in his father's grocery store. Because of that, he has been able to be successful. Also, he has worked to instill that hardworking mentality in myself as well as my siblings.

My father is also a loyal friend. He has stood by his friends through the good times and bad times. In fact, there have been times where I've asked him why he stands by them and puts so much faith in them. He always tells me that if you're good to people and you help them, when you need a hand, they'll help you. I now truly believe that.

Finally, my father is a good family man. He has an extremely stressful job, yet he never lets it get the best of him at home. Also, he emphasizes family above everything else, because if you don't have your family, then what do you have?

Because of my father I know the importance of being loyal and hardworking, as well as the importance of family. I hope that one day I will be able to be half the man my father is.

Alex Busken, Grade 12
Bob Jones High School, AL

The Power of Music

For as long as humans have walked the earth, music has shaped the culture of our world. Music is not only a form of enjoyment and pleasure; it portrays every emotion imaginable, and acts as words that cannot be described by simply speaking. From the very beginning of time, music has been used in a variety of ways for different reasons. Because the sound or lyrics of a song is filled with emotion, one can jump into the shoes of the musician and catch a glimpse of what he was feeling as he wrote it.

The great power of music is everywhere. From the majestic sound of a string orchestra, to the rock and roll of the 1980s, music has been used in many aspects of the world's ever changing culture. Whether a musical work is sung with meaningful lyrics, constructed with melodies of many different instruments, or the communication of a flock of song birds, music surrounds everyone and everything.

It is difficult to imagine a world without the beauty of music. Much of history is based upon the musical influences and sounds of each era. It is an importance that brings color, beauty, and vibrancy to everyday life. Music is the musician's opinion, poem, and diary. Hans Christian Anderson, a nineteenth century writer, said, "Where words fail, music speaks." Sometimes, when it is difficult to say what one feels, music can better describe feelings, and can often speak much louder than words.

Maren Engel, Grade 11
Owasso High School, OK

Beneath the Surface: A True Glimpse of Self

When you wander through a library it is like entering into a new kingdom, all the books cry out to you from their shelves, small subjects or counselors begging your eyes to fall upon each of them, to take note of them. You are drawn to the brown, thick one with gold lettering and take it but another book with a splash of red on the spine and large, curvy letters jumps out to you and you slip it off the shelf also. The books begin to leap into your arms; you cannot stop them.

Upon arriving home you eagerly find the brown one and immerse yourself into it, hearing naught but the turning of the pages and the world of the story — soon you devour them all. You read classics and discover that fictional characters embody you, despite being from different eras; that you are in all the books. Upon reading *Pride and Prejudice* you can whole heatedly agree with Mr. Darcy that, "[A young lady] must yet add something more substantial, in the improvement of her mind by extensive reading," because you know a book is more than words and pages. A book is about meaning. You have discovered that books reach past your outward self you present to others, to the very true core of who you are and thus what it means to be human.

Ashley Jones, Grade 11
Rock Bridge Sr High School, MO

Death

Death is unfortunately something everyone must experience in his or her life, whether it is one's self of the ones they love. It is a topic left unspoken, but I see it as an understanding crucial for the continuation of life. Understanding death, especially at a young age, should be mandatory. The death of someone close to you can be overly-devastating and, at an early ate, life-threatening.

I experienced the death of a very close friend of mine when I was twelve. I began to question life and what is to come of it. Thoughts of death, religion, and afterlife flew through my mind. I have never thought of these things, until this moment in my life. Sleepless nights, filled with nightmares then consumed my life. I lost my grip on reality, and slowly but surely — I was slipping into hell. Submitting to what has recently overpowered me, I lost a mental fight with death.

Guidance and parental help has since then rescued me from the hole I was trapped in. I suffered a devastating blow, and allowing others to help has sewn the gash left from his death. There will forever be a scar in my mind, but I now how to keep it that way. Giving help and understanding of death at an early age is nothing but beneficial. Everyone experiences death, so why not be prepared?

Tyler Berretta, Grade 12
Germantown High School, TN

Daddy's Little Girl

It was during the summer before third grade and I remember my mom pulling up to the house and getting out of the car surrounded by my family members, something was wrong I knew right away. I ran next door looking for an escape from the dreaded news I knew was awaiting me at my house, as I walked back over I thought of all the things that could be wrong but nothing prepared me for what she was about to tell me. As I sat on my bed holding my mom's hands I held my breath, her eyes filled with tears as she tried to think of the words to tell me that my Dad had passed away today in the hospital. My life froze, I didn't believe her, I couldn't hold the tears back any longer I had to get out of there. All of the memories of me and my Dad flashed before me, I didn't know what to think as I sat in my house thinking about how we would live our lives without him there. Death seemed like such a permanent thing, I had never experienced anything like this before, everything was so perfect and for something as life changing as this to happen seemed like a dream. Why would God do this to us is the question I asked myself for years, now I see how this experience has helped me to become a stronger person and to really hold onto the things in life that matter most.

Gabrielle Muller, Grade 10
Stanton College Preparatory School, FL

A Summer with Koreans

Summer is always a time for new experiences to happen. Everyone usually has a busy summer filled with camps, vacationing, or seeing family. For my summer, I helped at a Korea Heritage Camp. It's a great camp, and it has taught me a lot. I, a Korean adoptee, am very involved in this camp, and I'm up for anything that it offers.

Every summer, Dillon International offers heritage camps to help adoptees come together and learn about their culture. I'm too old to go as a camper, but I help as a counselor at the Korea Camp. I've been a counselor for 2 years, and I still love it. I always learn something new. This camp helps me understand about my culture and ties me into things that are happening in South Korea now. Also, being a counselor, I help the younger kids learn about their heritage and seeing them having a fun time is great. The camp teaches different classes like: cooking, language, dancing, tae-kwan do, and Korean culture. It also brings adopted children together. I've met so many people through this camp and have made several long-lasting friendships. If anyone had the opportunity to go to it, I would definitely recommend it! It offers so many eye-opening things for kids, and that's why I enjoy it. I don't know what it would be like without this camp, but I'm so thankful that I can go to it!

Tori Thomas, Grade 11
Owasso High School, OK

Good-bye for Now

"We did it!" he shouted when he first saw me. "We did it" is all he could say. As I sit here watching him on stage, taking the diploma with his left hand then shaking the hands of principals and other board members with his right, I'm mesmerized. Years of memories flash within nanoseconds — birthday parties starting at age five, weekends in the house due to punishments, holiday mornings around the stove, and haunted houses on warm October nights.

Here they come; I can feel them. Hot tears gush down my face. Seeing him end the first chapter of the beginning is too overwhelming. The expression of pride is glued to the faces of my grandmother and aunt. We've all waited so long for this day. Believe it or not, there was a time where we didn't think he would make it through. All the stomach-aching laughter, long hours, stress, jokes, and work…it all leads up to this day. At this moment I realize watching him leave is not going to be easy. I can't imagine life with my cousin so far away. Who's going to stay up late and watch old movies with me? He's leaving and I'm sitting here with tears rolling down my cheeks.

Here it is: "I now present to you the graduating class of 2007." They throw their hats in the air. "We did it!" he screams as he looks at me with utter excitement. "No, you did it," I scream back. "You did it!"

Bria Brown, Grade 12
Germantown High School, TN

The Purpose of Life

The purpose of life is one of the most asked (and most important) questions in one's lifetime and is regrettably the hardest to answer. Are we just random occurrences, or is there a specific purpose, a guideline or path that we were meant to tread? If we are here for a reason, why should we follow it, yet if there is no purpose to life, then why live? These are several of the branches of thought that stem from the question that we seek to answer.

The purpose of something is defined as such by its creator, for a pot does not know it's purpose; only the creator does. This leads to the question "Is there a creator?" to which there are 3 logical possibilities. The first possibility is that there is no creator and thus, there is no purpose to life. Keep in mind that either everything must have existed or the creator(s) who created everything existed forever. Time cannot have a beginning or an end. The second, however, is that there is a creator(s) whom has a purpose (or purposes) for us, thus delving into the science we call religion. The third is that there is a creator(s) but it has no purpose for us. This would be no different from the first option.

All in all, the purpose of life, as so many things do, come down to the religions. Which religion is true for you?

George Hagler, Grade 10
Starrs Mill High School, GA

Krumping

In krumping, dancers are in a lashing-out-breakneck-rhythm-and-pace-pushing-each-other-scrambling-and-releasing-aggression state of mind. Through krumping, dancers use anger and frustration to change negative energy into positive. Krumping is an interesting example of the way dance styles change from one to another at different times.

Krumping is graded by different levels of difficulty. For example, "Beasty," it's aggressive beast-like and powerful. It's similar to "Bully" but more creative. "Technical" is a mix of flashy and smooth moves that has more of a crowd-pleasing style. "Goofy" was pioneered by the krumping legend, named Goofy. It's the least aggressive of the krumping styles, but usually funny and energetic.

The chain between religion and dance is also part of krumping. Another legend named Tommy the Clown, turned to dancing after finding Christ in prison and his group of krumpers are all committed Christians who talk of finding a spirit in krumping or in other words, getting krump for Christ. Traditional African dance came together with spirit and dance after western Christianity tried to separate dance and worship. Dividing the weak flesh of the body and mind, the young people today now have rediscovered this connection.

Terrence Windley, Grade 11
Southside High School, NC

Dr. King

He came to this surface to serve a purpose, which he did profoundly. Martin Luther King Jr. was dedicated to serving his brothers and sisters and all of America to get the justice and equality that every citizen in this world deserves — respect, honor, and a feeling of a sense of purpose in life. In 1963, he spoke one of the greatest speeches, that I know of; that was "I Have A Dream." This speech inspired many people of different ethnicities and gave them the motivation to survive through such a time with racism and other barriers that tried to hold people back. Martin Luther King's dreams promoted more dreams, which was his overall goal. His march on Washington was another big event in his life. This march's purpose was to end the segregation in public schools, increase minimum wage, and have justice. As we know, these events helped pave the way to end segregation, which is why he was such a profound leader. His strength to make the world a better place to live, unfortunately also led to his assassination. King left behind many people that loved him and were moved by his messages in the 1960's. In the end, set out to do something profoundly because you'll never know how much of an impact it will make on your life and the lives of others in the future. We all should have a dream and we should set out to fulfill that dream without any setbacks.

Jocelyn Sanders, Grade 11
Little Rock Central High School, AR

Growing Up

After a grueling day of nonstop academic stimulation, I speedily drove home, hoping to throw on some clothes and make it to work at my appointed time, 3 p.m. I rushed through the front door, and was greeted by my mother, with the routine, "How was your day at school?" and of course a hug. As I embraced her, I instinctively tried to rest my head against her shoulder, but as my head went forward, my chin collided with the top of her forehead, a slightly painful experience. We both went to accomplish our intended activities and chores for the day, but it amazed me how much I learned about myself from that seemingly irrelevant experience. In that moment the realization that life was going by way too quickly hit me. Underlying the physical pain, I could see a deep symbolism within the incident. It is as if some heavenly entity were trying to tell me that I was about to turn 18, and that it was time to grow up and free myself from the limits of teenage life and make a transition into the realm of adulthood. Although the occurrence seemed trivial at first, it turned out to teach me something of great significance. It taught me that although I have lived 17 years on Earth, I still had plenty of life ahead of me.

Joel Lewis, Grade 12
Germantown High School, TN

Controlled Chaos

Within the hustle and hustle of what we call New York City, there is life. New York City is what I like to call controlled chaos. Form a bird's eye view; it looks like a bunch of people just running around with no destination, right? I must say you are quite wrong.

New York City is so much more. Everyone has a place in this "Big Apple" whether it be watching the stock market, taking a stroll in Central Park or running a million dollar company. It is without a doubt the city that never sleeps. You may think that there are way too many people and it is just a crowded mess but those people are what keep that place in business. New York for me is like a diverse jungle where you can be who you want and work your way to the top. So I am proud to say I was a New Yorker. If you can make it in that city, you can handle whatever life will throw at you.

Nicole Quattrock, Grade 10

BMR

It was by far the busiest weekend of my life. Recruit training would commence on Monday, and final preparations were still in progress. During these last days before departure, I busied myself packing my sea bag, studying Basic Military Requirements, and running — running as I had been for weeks of uncertain anticipation. Push-ups, sit-ups, and stretches were part of my daily routine, and adequate sleep was a necessity. Carefully, I inspected my uniforms, not overlooking the slightest flaw. There was no turning back. Upon arrival at the base, I would begin ten days of torture, or so I had been told. Finally, orientation day came, and I knew that I was ready.

Jonathan Atkinson, Grade 11
New Covenant Christian School, SC

What Is True Love

What is true love? Love can be a challenge, a word, sex, sorrow, change and other expressions. Love is best seen in loyalty and actions, not as emotion. Love is not in how we feel; emotions are certainly involved, but they shouldn't be our only standard or principle of love. Love requires a structure of integrity, truthfulness, and unity. There is no fear in love, but having a perfect love can be feared, and one who fears in love is not perfect. True love is very patient and so kind; it's not disrespectful or jealous. Love isn't about wrong, but always about right. Love is not because of his/her beauty, but because you have a condition in which your happiness for one another is unrefutable. To be loved is happiness, but to love and not be loved in return, equals sadness and darkness on someone's soul. True love means loving someone without change; trusting someone without doubting; being with someone without listening to what others have to say, and having a path that starts at "forever" and ending at "never."

Amber Horn, Grade 12
Grandview Alternative School, MO

The Life of a Teenager

Many teens, since the dawn of time have been going through a thing I would like to call peer pressure. Peer pressure plays a big role in a teen's life; this can cause dangerous decisions we as teens make. Teens sometimes feel as if they must wear what it is in style in order to fit in, just so we can be cool. We as teens should be able to dress however we want to dress; who says what is in style and what's out? That's when we as teens are at our best when we don't have to be self-conscious about what we have on. Many teens today have fears of going places at all because they don't want to be laughed at or ridiculed about what they have on. School is a big place where peer pressure gets all of its attention, all because they feel uncomfortable with what they have on. These days wherever you go you must be on point with what you have on; everything just has to be new and clean.

A while back Memphis City Schools enforced a uniform policy where all Memphis City School students must wear a uniform to school. It doesn't help; teens go through the same things every day, teens are still being judged, checked, and criticized every day. We as teens should help each other and not put each other down. We should be there for one another, instead of looking for a reason to talk badly of someone.

Nicholas Mackey, Grade 12
City University School of Liberal Arts, TN

Cheerleading

Usually when most people hear the word "cheerleader" they think of really preppy girls. But, the truth is most of them are not. I know that I'm definitely not. Some people don't really consider cheerleading a sport, but what else would you call it, a past time? We have practices a lot and compete. So I'd say it's definitely a sport. It's my favorite sport and I like it a lot!

A lot of people think cheerleading isn't hard work. They are wrong! I have to lift up people and throw them in the air, tumble, condition, and learn a cheerleading routine. I think tumbling is the hardest, like learning all the flips and everything. It's also very dangerous. I have never gotten seriously injured doing it, but I have fallen a lot. My favorite part of cheerleading is definitely the tumbling. Even though it is hard, it always pays off when I learn a new flip. Conditioning is also really hard. We run so much and do suicides, which are the worst. After a long practice I just want to go home, but we have to condition. But I think the reason I have for liking cheerleading so much is it's just so fun. Just being with all my friends and learning to flip and just going to the competitions, it's all so much fun. All the cheerleaders are like my family. Even though it can be hard, it's still a good experience.

Jenna Kline, Grade 10
Deltona High School, FL

A True American Hero

Former NFL player, husband, and role model, Patrick D. Tillman possessed all of these qualities and more. Pat Tillman was a very popular player for the Arizona Cardinals. After 9/11 he gave up a thirty-five million dollar contract to join the military to protect his country. Through sacrifice, bravery, and honor did he live by to be a true hero for many people.

His sacrifice was incredible. He gave up his job, life, money, home, and everything he owned to protect all of us in the fight against terror.

Bravery was another quality of life this young man possessed. When he saw his own men under fire by local terrorists he sprang quickly into action to help fend off the attackers. But to no avail, his effort was useless when a bullet took his life.

Honor is one choice word I would use to describe Patrick D. Tillman. To protect his country was his one main worry. With people like him, I too am honored to live in the same country.

If a man who had it all, millions of dollars living the American dream, can just give it all up to serve his country, then respectively, I too think we all can do one thing or another to help serve our country and the others around us to help make this country a better place for our children and generations to come.

Jacob Beck, Grade 12
Mulhall-Orlando High School, OK

The First Drop

The first drop is terrifying, exciting, and amazing. Your first free falling dive is all of these things, and more. The excitement found in scuba diving is unparalleled by anything in the world. The blood starts to pound in your ears, the pressure is all around you, it seems like it will never end, but it does. Although the fall only lasts for a few seconds, during that time you are free, and nothing will ever compare to that feeling.

While the fall is amazing, your first time is the scariest thing you will ever attempt. The darkness is all around you, there's no sound but the blood in your veins, and the air in your regulator. It seems like you are alone in the world, and that is very frightening. However, no matter how scared you are, the minute it is over you're ready to do it again.

Scuba diving is an experience that appeals to the primitive aspects of the soul. Your thirst for adventure, the need to be free, and the urge to experience something greater than yourself, anything your soul craves, scuba diving will supply it. After your first time you will agree, it is an experience beyond words. The sheer amazement of it will astound you.

Taylor Pate, Grade 11
Owasso High School, OK

The Human Hand

The human hand is different from any other hand in the world. It is a feature that has helped to separate our race from that of the animal kingdom. One of the main differences between our hand and those of the animals is an opposable thumb and the flexibility of our hands.

Now imagine that we did not have these features to our anatomy. Our thumbs would be just like another one of our fingers that sticks straight out. Our hands wouldn't be flexible and every motion that we made would be stiff. Try to imagine having sticks as fingers and a flat square piece of wood as your hand. What would have happened to our race over time? Would we have been able to build the pyramids or the Great Wall of China? Would we have been able to do the normal everyday activities that we take for granted?

Earlier in the football season I had broken a bone in my hand. The bone that I had broken runs from the knuckle on my ring finger to my wrist. It split lengthwise like a piece of wood being split by an axe. I waited until the following Monday before I went to the doctor. He told me the news and said that I shouldn't have waited to get treatment.

In conclusion, try to go an entire day without using one of your hands. If for some reason you find that it is not very hard, then you must not have a very challenging life to begin with. Lastly, protect your hand; you only get two.

John Robert Lovelace, Grade 12
Rossville Christian Academy, TN

Toads

Toads are the naughty, handsome princes transformed by magical means into a bumpy amphibian whose only hope of ever being vaguely attractive again is to sucker some lovely maiden into kissing them. Task difficulty aside, being a toad is considered quite repulsive and an unacceptable state. I would imagine the *real* toad is very offended.

So I, defender of all toads, am setting the record straight. I, a reasonably attractive maiden whom would surely meet the requirements to be a toad-kisser, would choose not to kiss the toad, not because it is a toad, but instead so it would remain a toad. Toads are enormously more entertaining than what I would imagine princes to be; I can poke a toad and it hops, I can poke it again if the first time was insufficient, I can have races — mine versus my friend's, it eats what I dislike, and when I'm done I can set it free with no emotional baggage. I have never heard of a prince doing any of the former; if I were to poke a prince he is more likely to stab me with a sword than hop, if I were to poke him a second time he *would* if he hadn't already, a prince would probably be very upset if I were to ask him to race my friend's prince to see whose is better, and princes tend to be very clingy. Thus I'll keep my toads and keep my toad-kissing friends away from them.

Ali Edge, Grade 11
Germantown High School, TN

Childhood Story

When I was about six-years-old, I had to take care of my brother and myself. My mom was on drugs so consistently; I think sometimes she forgot she had four children. I remember how my mom looked; she was ugly. She looked as if she weighted 90 lbs. and hadn't slept in days, if not weeks.

I ended up with my grandma at the age of two. It sounds all good, but my grandma drank constantly from when I was six until I was sixteen-years-old.

My brother is a year older than me, but if you ask other people, they would say he is my little brother because he acts like a kid. When he was about 10-years-old, he cried because he did not have money for a field trip. Trying to act older, I gave him some money I had been saving for a bike, because I knew my grandma did not have money for him or a bike for me. I always saved the money I earned.

I'm 18-years-old and living my life like I want. My brother is in jail, looking at 7 years. My mom is in jail. My grandma is still getting drunk at the age of 62. As for me, I am doing well. Many things have happened over the years; I cannot forget it at all, but I can forgive the people that hurt me, like my dad, mom, and grandma.

Jessica Maness, Grade 12
Grandview Alternative School, MO

Expelling the Beast

As I line up to fight, I remind myself of the positions of my feet, hands, the tip of the blade and the fact that I was lining up to fence my father. The adrenaline I gain from a few minutes of ducking, attacking, guarding, gaining the points and pokes inherent in the sport carries me through the night until I fall, exhausted, onto my bed. A week later I repeat. Although my opponent changes, I usually play the part of a life sized pin cushion.

Fencing, a long forgotten sport of nobility and fair fight, brings forth the aggressive, competitive beast that has saved man from everything since the saber toothed tiger to the bus that isn't slowing quite fast enough. It allows an aggressive, physical outlet for anger and rage while reminding the beast of the humanity through conscious actions. In fencing, there are lines that are not crossed, lines never approached and lines that have been scuffed away by familiarity. Revenge is taken lightly; and the beast is banished by all of the shiny swords and the expert wielding of them.

Fencing, founded from dueling and swordplay, has evolved into a peaceful sport that simply shows the expertise, speed, and good humor of the fighters. The human mind is played in a physical competition with an atmosphere of very little aggression. No one wants to be angry while others have thin blades of metal, even if they are blunt.

Abby Durnett, Grade 11
Germantown High School, TN

Why Is It Important to Have a Good Education and Follow Your Dreams?

I believe it's important to have a good education and follow your dreams because it helps you in life. A good education can help you get a good paying job and open you up to many things in life. When you follow your dreams, you have fun doing what you do best, instead of doing something you don't like. For example say John is good in mechanics but he likes to teach and it was his dream to teach. Just because he is good at it doesn't mean he likes it. By having a good education and following your dreams, you can live life to its fullest with no regrets. The people who have a bad education or no education at all can't get through life very well like others who do. Having a bad education isn't something good on a resume when applying for a job. The people who don't follow their dreams are sometimes unhappy with their life and sometimes things don't go as they want. This is why I believe it's important to have a good education and follow your dreams.

Carlton Littlejohn, Grade 11
Southside High School, NC

Me

Today is the biggest day of my life, October 4, which is my birthday. I love this time of the year because I get to go shopping, eat cake, and hang out with my friends.

Well today I'm going to tell you what I spend most of my time doing.

I spend most of my time eating, talking to friends, playing video games, and on the computer. Now don't get me wrong, I spend time studying but just not as much as I should.

What do I enjoy doing? I enjoy singing, reading poetry, and just chilling with my friends. I started singing as a young child in the Y.P.C.L choir of Jones Chapel located in Aurora, NC. I like reading poetry, but I especially love poems. I love to read love poems, because I can really relate to them. Well, some of them.

I am also a caring person. I care about everybody. It doesn't matter if I had a problem with someone and if something would happen to that person I would care about him or her. I'm not a mean person; I have a spot in my heart where I care about a lot of people. Even if they have done something to hurt me I will still care for them and love them, 'cause I believe in God and I know that I'm going to leave from here one day and when I do I want to go to Heaven. So I have no problem showing love.

Do I believe in myself? I believe in myself, I have faith in my abilities. I know that I can do all things if I set my mind to it. I try not to ever say the word can't. Because I feel that I can do all things.

Bryanna Morning, Grade 11
Southside High School, NC

A Stroll Unremembered

It was just after midnight on New Year's Day as I opened the door to leave the grand ballroom. As the enormous snowy white doors shut behind me, and the music faded from my ears, I headed for the elevators on the other side of the eerie rocking deck. The swells pounded the sides of the ship and the clouds thundered. I quickly stepped inside the elevator and descended to the first floor. I shuffled down the narrow hall and slid my card through the lock device. Stumbling inside, I hastily climbed in my top bunk, and with the television on, slipped away from reality into the dreams of a 12-year-old.

After what seemed to be only minutes later, I awoke to find myself staring through several glass doors at the downpour nearly flooding the deck before the water ran off the edge. A tingling numbness engulfed my body, and I looked down to discover goose bumps covering my whole figure. Sluggishly, I retreated towards the elevator behind me and as I emerged from the sleepy daze I shivered due to the whistling breeze, which seemed to entangle my entire being. Reminiscing, I realized that I was on the eleventh floor of the ship, no one was around, no clothes covered me but boxers and I had no key to a room that I had unknowingly escaped. This was the first and only time I have ever sleepwalked. An experience I don't remember, but will never forget.

Elliot Bertasi, Grade 11
Germantown High School, TN

A Common Enemy

This world needs unity. Just as the new America needed unity to survive, the world needs it now. Looking at the past, we can learn how to unify people. What has unified people, regardless of race, religion, or country? A common enemy. World War II is a terrific example of this.

When the world was threatened by a common enemy, they joined together — and won. Once the common enemy is gone, the people are back at each others' throats. How do you solve that problem? The common enemy cannot lose. It must be a constant threat, not necessarily in the form of a war, but a threat that endangers everyone, no matter who or where they are. If everyone is threatened, they all must bond together to fight that enemy, but that enemy cannot lose. Ah, but the people must not realize the invincibility of that enemy! If they give up, what use is the enemy? What does the enemy do if the people give up? They willingly give up, disappear, and leave the people to reestablish their world. After the world is rebuilt, there will come a time of prosperity, of greatness — and the enemy must strike again. It's a cycle that is necessary for the world to survive against itself. At the rate things are currently happening, the world will destroy itself from the inside out soon. The world doesn't need a hero, it needs an enemy.

Wesley Clawson, Grade 11
Owasso High School, OK

H₂O No

One arid summer afternoon in 1995, a battle was amidst. Jeanie, the baby-sitter, called my siblings and me to arms. We formed lines at the various sinks with buckets at our sides. The cool water from the faucet encompassed the rubber bombs for ammo. Finally, the ammo filled the containers to capacity.

My eldest brother, Bradley, broke away from the company. The rest of us, unaware of what was to come, followed suit to the outdoors. The sun beat down upon our heads in the stillness of the day. We were bewildered as to where our new target, Bradley, had disappeared to. That was until an object above us blocked out the sun leaving us in a prolonged darkness. The bomb came careening to the earth with a resulting splash effect upon impact.

We then realized that the enemy had retreated to a higher ground where none of us dared to go…the roof. Our group of four scattered across the yard forming harder to hit individual targets. The missiles dries up as fast as they rained down upon us. Everyone was being pelted with orbs of refreshingly cool water. Two hours passed without a victor.

The last of the ammo was consumed by the now damp ground. The battlefield was covered by countless remnants of thin rubber pieces. Soaked from head to toe, we trudged back to base. A verbal agreement was made to end the childish activity of war. The battle was over at last.

Kevin Hudspeth, Grade 11
Germantown High School, TN

Pep-Rally

The scene had been set. It was so quiet you could hear a pin drop, until "FRESHMEN!" The crowd went crazy. For the first time in years the freshmen class had just won a pep-rally. Standing in the front row, she jumped up and down; everything seemed to happen in slow motion. They stormed the court, all sharing the joy of their recent win. Jealously, the upper classmen couldn't resist, they had to start trouble. From that point on, it was a blur. Knocked down to the ground, she couldn't breathe, didn't know what to do. More and more people were crashing down on top of her. Using her only defense, she dug her nails deeper into whoever and whatever was on top of her. She saw it all stop, her life, thought it to be gone, felt it might be the end. Finally the crowd parted and there she was, crying hysterically, not knowing what else to do. Rescue came and swept her away to the home of the injured. Friends and family members came to check on her. Hours, that seemed like days later, she left, went to the comfort of her home. It was over; she was safe, left only with a neck brace for a few days. One memory she would like to forget, but will always remember.

Amy Richardson, Grade 10
Stanton College Preparatory School, FL

Spirit Lifters

There are three things in my life that I could not live without: music, art, and writing. I enjoy all of these things in their turn and they all lift my spirits above my everyday troubles. I often spend most of my free time drawing and writing, and I listen to music whenever I am doing either activity or at any appropriate opportunity.

The ability to draw and paint is my God-given talent, so I take no credit for anything that I am able to produce. I spend much of my free time drawing whatever I feel like. I also have taken three art courses at my high school and plan to take the fourth soon. I feel as though my art has improved immensely under the direction of my art teacher, Heather Lattimore, and I am thankful for her and her guidance.

Writing is also something at which I naturally excel. I enjoy it immensely and hope to be an author someday. I write in my spare time about whatever I am moved to write. I have a bad habit of over explaining things, however, and I'm finding this two-hundred and fifty word limit rather hard to follow.

Music is something that I truly believe that I would die without. If I were to suddenly become deaf, I would probably go crazy from the lack of music in my life. It inspires me in both my art and writing and generally leaves me feeling good inside.

Samantha Garrett, Grade 12
Walker Valley High School, TN

Little Sister

"I'll be parked under the trees!" Mom calls as I sprint towards the door. I start signing the Big Brother Big Sister sign-in book. I hear a high-pitched squeal and the sound of someone running towards me. I grab the counter and wait for the impact. I'm jerked sideways as 5-year-old April, my Little Sister, slams into me with a hug that I gladly return. "So what are we doing today?" I ask as she slips her hand into mine and leads me over to a table where there are books strewn about. "Reading," she says, making a face. We collapse onto a hard bench and look at the books. "Okay, how about we read Dora?" I ask, glancing over in time to see a look of dread pass over April's face. "You don't like reading, do you April." I state. Mutely, she nods. "And why, pray tell, don't you like to read?" I question, using an accent that makes her giggle. She suddenly becomes somber and mutters, "'Cause I can't read the big words and then Jeremy calls me stupid."

"Well let me impart all of my one year of high school wisdom," I intone, "All boys are goofy and don't need to be listened to. Anyway you can read better than I could when I was your age!" April's eyes become huge. "Really?" she asked in an awed voice. "Yup" I replied. From that day on, any day that we met, we would read.

Margaret Durnett, Grade 10
Germantown High School, TN

Child Abuse

When you hear these words what comes to mind — cruelty, inhumanity? Touchy subject?

Most people don't truly know the reasons why parents abuse their children. Often abuse is the result of stress overload. Stress progresses from many situations. For example, if a parent has had a difficult week at work and is in over their head in paperwork and deadlines, often when they come home they take their frustration out on their innocent children. Poverty is another stressful situation that leads to child abuse. When parents are barely able to make ends meet and are on the verge of losing their job, they begin to blame their children. They start to resent them and sooner or later the stress builds up. They release this stress by abusing their children. Also, another motive for child abuse is the fact that the parent themselves were raised in an abusive household. They only know how to handle situations as their parents did.

Abuse is bad enough, but it is awful that people take their fury and frustration out on their naive children that have no control in what happens in their parents' lives.

Heather Cathcart, Grade 11
Vero Beach High School, FL

Jena Six

The year is 2007 and we are still dealing with racism in our lives. This is very evident in the South, and one town in particular, Jena, Louisiana. The term Jena Six refers to six black teenagers. Many people believe the arrests and charges against them were racially discriminatory and excessive.

The teenagers were charged with attempted murder in the second degree and conspiracy to commit murder. They beat up a white student after a racial incident. The incident went as follows: there is a "white tree" for shade, under which only white people sit. A black student asked to sit there and the principal said he could sit wherever he wanted. However, the following morning there were nooses hanging from the tree. The white students who were responsible for the nooses were only given three days of in-school suspension. The superintendent was quoted saying, "Adolescents play pranks. I don't think it was a threat against anybody." This statement fueled racial tensions and led to the six teens beating the white student.

The white student had apparently made racial and degrading comments to one of the Jena Six. Mychal Bell, sixteen at the time of the attack, was charged as an adult. He was charged with aggravated battery in the second degree and conspiracy to commit aggravated battery. He was found guilty by an all white jury.

All of these incidents have brought to light how racist our country still is. Hopefully these teens will be rightfully punished.

Stacia Sarwinski, Grade 11
Grove High School, OK

Mind Over Body

Pole-vaulting is a very unique sport. There are many challenges to it. The main challenge is getting over what your brain is telling you not to do. It is a major mind over body task to clear a bar high in the air. Your mind goes through many processes to tell you to not do something, to keep you safe. In pole-vaulting, you are running fast, turning yourself upside down, and springing yourself in the air. All just to clear a bar and fall onto a mat. Your brain is constantly being an inhibitor and tells you not to do it. While running down the track with a pole that is about to spring you up in the air, your mind's first instinct is to slow down, to get past this you have to constantly think of your speed instead of how scary it can be. The next task is to turn upside down and don't flag your legs, but your mind is telling you no, you have to conquer many fears to get a good technique. So to be a good pole-vaulter, you have to overcome that and keep your pace up and jump when your mind says no. To be as good as Sergei Bubka, the World Record holder for pole-vaulting, you have to have more than just physical strength, but mind strength also. This sport doesn't only get you into shape and challenge you, it makes you mentally stronger.

Sarah Ramsay, Grade 11
Owasso High School, OK

Carpe Diem

Carpe diem is Latin for "seize the day." I believe that living by this saying is essential to enjoying life's benefits and taking advantage of all of the "golden moments" in life. I'm sure everyone's had the opportunity to do something very special but didn't take advantage of the opportunity. Soon it becomes vital to seize these moments because there isn't a guarantee that there will be another time to shine. Carpe diem can apply to any aspect of life, including school. I'm sure every student has or had a problem with procrastinating in school, especially while trying to juggle a social life or extra curricular activity. However, we must discipline ourselves to take advantage of today because there isn't always a tomorrow. Living by this idiom also gives great motivation.

After realizing that life is short and you must do everything you can during this lifetime, you'll set your goals higher and want to achieve more. As you grow older, you'll find that the things you most regret are the things that you didn't do. Seizing the day will also produce a more amusing lifestyle by allowing you to live more freely. When you're aware that life doesn't last forever, you'll try to have fun while you can and you won't stay "down in the dumps" for long. So go for it now! Don't wait until tomorrow because the future isn't promised to anyone.

Deysia Collier, Grade 10
Stanton College Preparatory School, FL

Fighting Irish

A sea of glittering gold and emerald green fills the slate gray stadium as people file into their red oak benches. The clash of symbols and roaring of trumpets fill the stadium as I walk to take my numbered seat. My gently aged grandfather sits next to me feeling like an emperor presiding over his golden kingdom. As the great game begins, my grandfather, also known as "Poppy," watches as the little, entertaining leprechaun with a little jig in his step bounds around the field. Poppy glances to the right and asks his youngest son to get him a soda, a pretzel, and maybe some popcorn. My grandfather stands up to reach for his wallet, but seems to have "lost" it. He guards his wallet as though it was Fort Knox.

The six-foot-two Irish Guardsmen march across the field to amuse their emperor. The citizens of the empire scream until they are blue in the face and the golden helmets of the team storm back onto the killing ground. They throw the straggling teams into the cobbled prison to rot for eternity. The band of the emperor takes the field and plays his favorite song, then sprints over to the opposing, hubris team and plays the fight song, proving to them that they have lost the battle, and the war. My grandfather, the emperor, stand up and walks silently out of the stadium.

Robert Sheehan, Grade 10
Germantown High School, TN

The Job That Changed Me

During the summer between freshman and sophomore year, I didn't realize how much I was going to change. I had got my first job at a restaurant about two miles from where I lived. I was a hard worker. I wanted to be at work anytime the restaurant was open so that I could earn more money. I had many dreams and goals for myself, but a couple months into the summer, those goals and dreams had changed.

I started wanting to fit in with the cooks at the restaurant. I thought they were cool because they were older than me and they liked to party. It astonished me that they were actually starting to notice who I was. I started to change who I was to please them. My life started turning upside down. My parents and I would argue all the time because they wouldn't let me go hang out with the guys from work. They would tell me that they weren't good people and I would defend them with everything I had.

I didn't realize that my parents were right, until it was almost too late. I was at my lowest point, when I started to become wiser about the decisions I was making. I quit my job at the restaurant and today I think it was the best decision I have ever made. The lesson that I learned changed my life. Don't change who you are to please someone else.

Katherine Barr, Grade 11
Owasso High School, OK

My Inspiration

"To teach is to touch a life forever." Sometimes, when I wish I could escape the harsh world outside, I think of school. Two teachers there are my inspiration.

The first was my AP Language teacher. When she very first walked into class, electricity flew and we knew this was not someone to cross. Her stern face and tall stature made her appear menacing and cold. After a few weeks and several long, after-school conversations, her carefully constructed mask fell and I was finally given the privilege of "seeing" her. She is a very beautiful woman and appears much younger than her sixty-one years. We eat together every day and no matter how terrible I feel she can always make me laugh. She is a grandmother of sorts and can outwit me in every discussion.

The second was my chemistry teacher. She is also very beautiful in every way. One thing keeps her from being absolutely perfect, she suffers from Lupus. Despite her illness she comes to school every day with a smile, eager to teach us everything she can. I sometimes can't help but stare at her and marvel at how amazing she really is. She goes out of her way to help me, sacrificing herself and her time to make sure I succeed.

I like to think that knowing these two extraordinary women has made me a better person; they impact my life every day. I hope one day I too will be an inspiring teacher.

Lesli Lewis, Grade 12
Owasso High School, OK

Being Me

Before my sophomore year I never thought about what kind of person I was. I've always known I live a great life, my family supports me, and my friends were here to back me up. Not long ago, I evaluated my life and realized how truly blessed I am, and what an individual I am. I have my friends I can vent to and celebrate with. I look up to my brothers at everything, and call to them for advice. I remember being in preschool and going with my mom to take my brothers to Larkin Bailey Elementary, and I couldn't wait to be in 'real' school.

Well, I made it to elementary school and I vividly can recall going to their sixth grade enrollment, which then I was eager to start the sixth grade and elementary school all of a sudden wasn't so fun. Every year seemed like this, and they were one step ahead of me leading me in the right path. Now they are at college, and last year I wanted to be out of high school and in college too. I realized I am finally in high school, and I don't want to wish the most enjoyable years of my life away. My brothers shaped me into the person I am and I no longer want to live my life exactly like theirs. They influence me in positive ways but I have my own goals and achievements I am to accomplish.

Paige Colpitt, Grade 11
Owasso High School, OK

If Only to Believe

It is easy to do. Really, anyone can do it; football players, English professors, and even doctors around the world do this: believe. Everyone does not necessarily believe all the time, no, but that is not the point. The point is that people have the choice of whether to believe it or not, the choice of whether to give up or keep going. Nobody can get very far in life if no one believes in them, or if they do not believe in themselves. Belief boosts people's self-esteem, helping them get through whatever it is that is opposing them. It helps them get through the hard times, the average times, and the best times.

For example: football players need to believe they will win a game in order to do well, English professors need to believe they will get through all the term papers they must grade, and doctors must believe they will go through an important procedure safely. It may sound cheesy and cliché, but by believing in oneself, it is likely that the football player's team has a better chance of winning, the professor will get his homework done, and the doctor will have a successful surgery. Therein if one only believes, everything may not be solved, but the chances of success are higher and the chances of finding personal happiness, with friends or family, skyrockets. Overall, to believe is to make it through life and through anything that comes your way…Believe it!

Tegan Thomas, Grade 10
Germantown High School, TN

Honesty's Role

Honesty in life is an important quality, which many struggle to embrace. As stated by William Shakespeare, "No legacy is so rich as honesty." Honesty is important in many aspects of life, such as school, work, and in our government. However, to me, honesty has a greater weight and meaning in schools.

For a student to be able to take a test without cheating, even if they didn't study, is an achievement worthy of honesty. By being honest, students will have a positive characteristic and will succeed in life far easier than those who lack honesty. Honesty in schools also means not copying homework. The strength taken to admit that you haven't done your homework is far better than the guilt which sticks on any cheater. Honesty defines true education and character and prevents its opposite from disrupting a true learning environment. Fraud, deceit, lying, cheating, all contradict the true meaning of honesty and destroy the integrity of many students. As stated by Sophocles "better to fail with honor, than succeed by fraud." It's always far more valuable to uphold honesty and treasure it over the temptations of cheating.

Joshua Diaz, Grade 11
Miami Killian Sr High School, FL

Time

It had been over seven years, but I still wasn't ready to overlook my past. No, I couldn't possibly. I would be disowning a member of my own family, and that would only add guilt to my already condemned conscience. I didn't think that I would be able to deal with anymore worry than was already on my mind, but it was eminent. The time had come to face it. I had come to terms with my past.

After over five years of dating, my mother had finally announced to my brother and me that she was now ready to wed another man. After a few days of thinking over this idea of a new man in our lives, my brother and I still had yet to come around to the shocking subject. After being married to our father and having two children with him, it seemed strange to see her moving on in what seemed like such a short span of time. All of a sudden this colossal change in the form of my step-father-to-be was creeping its way into my life, and I had no idea how to act or how to feel. However, I didn't have long to make up my mind and figure out my feelings. The next day it seemed, the wedding was here and I found myself slowly walking down the long aisle towards the altar. At that moment, I knew things would never be the same.

Brittni Brewer, Grade 11
Germantown High School, TN

Crack Cocaine

Crack cocaine use is a growing problem in the United States. 7.9 million people are currently addicted to the drug. Not only are the addicts affected, but also all of society feels the effects. Crack is known as a gateway drug. Crack users usually start out only taking crack, but they will eventually move on to other substances in order to prolong the high.

Crack is a freebase form of cocaine. Cocaine hydrochloride is concentrated by heating it in a solution of baking soda until the water evaporates. When this solution is heated, it makes a cracking sound, which is why the drug was named crack. Crack interferes with the process of reabsorbing dopamine in the brain. Dopamine is associated with the pleasure centers of the brain, so when it builds up in the wrong places, the user feels an intense sensation of euphoria. This sensation only lasts about ten to fifteen minutes; the high is gone even before the body starts breaking down the drug. After the first high, the user will never be able to reach that same level of pleasure, but instead will continue looking for it; thus, an addict is created.

Crack cocaine is a life-damaging drug. There are many available options for treatment of addiction to crack, but none of them can accomplish anything without the participation and acceptance of the addict. The first step to recovering has to be taken by the addict, and that can be a difficult step to take.

Samantha Easley, Grade 11
West Limestone High School, AL

Swimming

Swimming is an interesting activity. It appeals to a wide range of people of all ages, physical abilities and skills. Swimming, a skill acquired by many people when they are young, becomes a lifelong recreational and physical activity.

Swimming is also a very competitive sport with high numbers of participants. Competition in swimming takes place at the high school, college, masters and club levels. Participants race in various distances and strokes. Also, at most of the levels of swimming there are relays for teams to participate in.

Finally, a revolutionary new type of swimming that has become popular in the last few decades is called open water swimming. Open water swimming consists of a swimming race that does not take place in a pool but in a lake or an ocean. Many people that are great at swimming in a pool are not good at open water swimming because open water swimming is a completely different type of sport. The participant must perfect the art of swimming against the current and navigating through a sometimes treacherous course. Many people do not like to swim in open water because they are afraid of sea life.

Jordan Williams, Grade 11
Bishop Verot High School, FL

Being a Senior

Twelfth grade. The defining year of my life as it is now. The choices I make now decide what I'll do for the rest of my life. Five AP classes plus innumerable college applications merely adds up to a ball of stress, ready to burst at any give moment. Unlike many of my peers I chose the path less chosen, senior year is supposed to be fun, I hear. But I try not to let the idea of working less entice me and realize that although my work's hard it will be rewarding.

The uncertainty of this time is what frightens me the most: there's the immediate uncertainty of high school and the ever pending abyss known as college. With that growing uncertainty comes a great sense of self doubt, questioning whether or not I am qualified enough for certain schools, leaving me distraught over the whole process. I try to find wisdom in some of the absurdity surrounding me. I truly know what it means to seize the day, leaving nothing to be pondered; I'd hate to look back years from now and regret not doing something because of fear.

At least one thing is certain: I'm not the same girl who entered the ninth grade. I've grown in myself, despite the fear created by this year, I'm more confident than I've ever been. I'm also proud of my friendships created but more importantly of those that have lasted throughout high school, which has been know to kill friendships.

LaRonda Mitchell, Grade 12
Germantown High School, TN

School Uniformity?

Should all schools require their students to wear uniforms? What are the benefits and the drawbacks? Students should be able to wear whatever they choose, within reason, and should learn to deal with the diversity caused by clothing.

Uniforms cut down on the pressures of wearing the "right clothes" to school. While this can be beneficial to the students during high school, it can hinder them after they graduate and enter the working world. High school is supposed to prepare you for the real world in which people do not wear uniforms. In forcing students to wear uniforms, they fail to learn how to deal with people who may dress better than them.

Students should also be able to dress however they feel like dressing. There should be a school dress code to reduce the amount of distractions in the classroom, but the students should be able to express themselves somewhat in their clothing. If a student feels like relaxing, they should be able to wear sweat pants and a hoodie; if a student feels like dressing up one day, they should be able to don a skirt and a dress shirt.

In allowing free dress, students will learn that not everything in the real world is fair. Some people will dress better than you and some will dress worse. People have to learn to deal with that diversity in high school so that they can cope with it later in life.

Laura Sadler, Grade 11
Owasso High School, OK

Cooking Together

Every year my family and I, along with our church, cook apple butter at the Arrow Rock Craft Festival. Thinking about it now brings back so many memories. The day starts out early in misty morning; a light fog hangs over the small town and the hot fire begins to bring out the sweet aroma of the apples cooking mixing with the fresh morning air. The women dress up in traditional attire of our early settlers to bring something to the picture of us working like early settlers would. As I stand there stirring apples so they don't burn, the heat from the fire starts making me get very hot and someone comes to relieve me. Pretty soon after the apple butter gets cooking, I can hear people coming to see what it is we are doing. After long and torturous hours of stirring and getting smoke in my eyes, it is finally time to put apple butter in the jars. As the assembly line is formed, I join the end of the line and prepare to put labels on the jars. Finally we completed making apple butter and enjoy the scene of customers hurrying to buy some before it is all gone. Satisfied workers are ready to call it a day and head home for some needed rest.

Andrea Borgman, Grade 12
Slater High School, MO

Page 143

Pets Are My Passion

Growing up, I always lived with a pet. I cherish Nija, my Eskimo-spitz Catahoula mixed breed dog. Nija helps me grow physically and mentally, knowing my deepest thoughts and darkest secrets. Fortunately, our bond today is stronger that ever. Having animals around me the majority of my life always has me wondering what can I do if my bird refuses to eat or if Nija's nose is dry. What type of education could help me learn these things? I have decided that I am happier saving the lives of animals, giving them back the joy they always share with me.

Animal Planet is a fantastic source of education in the veterinarian field. This channel enlightens me on many different qualities and characteristics one must have to endure this type of work: courage, kind spirit, sympathy and a honest and soft side. All of the previous qualities and characteristics are of great success. Starting with courage, one must be confident about the situation, thinking positively no matter the outcome. A kind spirit takes a key position in this situation because one must be kind, showing that hope is still alive. Lastly, just being able to feel where a little kid is coming from gives a warm feeling in all hearts.

Everyone's passion is not the same, knowing that everyone is different. My passion has always been my love for animals and I will prove this by becoming an emergency veterinarian.

Kiara Wallace, Grade 12
Baton Rouge Magnet High School, LA

Grades 7-8-9

Top Essay Grades 7-8-9

What I Will Never Become

Most kids have a parent for a role model. I do not. I was six years old when my biological mother dropped in. It was a short visit; she just left my little brother and was gone.

Last October, the phone rang. Dad said, "Honey that was your mother. We are going to pick her up." Now my questions could be answered. Why did you not visit or call? Did you not love us? Look what you missed: no first steps or first teeth, no first hug, nor Band-Aids or tears, kisses, tucked in bed, or held when we were sick. These are questions that I was sure you held the answers to.

When we arrived at Lamar, my first impression was she looks so old. My hopes quickly faded. I was meeting a stranger. I wanted to break down and cry, and then ask her, "Do you love me?" Instead she said, "Hi, you are getting big." I answered hi and then just listened, I had my questions answered. I learned her first love was alcohol, drugs, and living for the party. I learned that I will never become what I saw that day. She looked at me with drugged-hazed eyes and still never said, "I love you."

I do not want your pity for I learned another thing that day. I have a role model. My adoptive mom is a very strong woman. She is a nurse, and I will be too. Thanks, Mom. I love you.

Darby Bartlett, Grade 8
Greenfield Jr/Sr High School, MO

Top Essay Grades 7-8-9

Part of the World

Harmony, in musical terms, is defined as a variety of pitches sung together to create a colorful sound throughout a piece of music. What would life be like if every person's song was sung in unison? If each individual behaved and thought exactly alike, the world could never succeed. The universe, like a giant puzzle, needs this diversity known as individualism, to create harmony.

There is a certain essence of humanity that unites each person of the world. Whether someone is living in a poverty-stricken, third-world country or thriving as the daughter of a wealthy business owner, both look into the same sky each night and understand that someone else is seeing that sky too. This unity is precious.

Harmony can assist the creation process of this unity. If the insignificant dissidence of feuding ethnicities and accusing discriminations were pushed away, humanity would find, buried beneath all the hate and injustice are the stories of each being, connected, like a chorus, singing different pieces of the song of life.

Every soul has the same basic needs: love, nourishment, happiness, and acceptance. The future of our world relies solely on our capability to welcome new ideas. With diversity, the human race can achieve wonders past its fullest potential. Harmony is when the sopranos, altos, tenors, and basses weave together an enriching song, created through the spirit of diversity. Every soul is a crucial part of the earth's beauteous song.

Allie Fry, Grade 9
Nerinx Hall High School, MO

Top Essay Grades 7-8-9

My Life, Your Life, Our Life

Sometimes, in this life, we spend too much time thinking about ourselves. We hardly ever stop and really appreciate everything around us; the trees, the leaves, and the shadows. Just everything.

Have you ever gone outside when it was raining and just walked around, enjoying the feel of the rain on your skin? I have, and it might sound weird, but even the smallest things are important and wonderful.

And yet, this fabulous world of ours is breaking down. Littering, pollution, and the poisoning of our resources are only a few of the many things that we are doing to ruin our planet. And most of these things can be easily prevented.

It is said that roughly ninety-eight percent of all the organisms that have lived on Earth are extinct. That's thousands of species completely wiped out. Some people who read this will say that most of those species died of natural causes. But, think, humans haven't exactly helped.

The mammoth, mastodon, and saber-toothed tiger, all killed by humans. The bengal tiger, panda, and spotted owl, there are only a few hundred left because we are destroying their homes.

In fifty years, maybe longer, maybe shorter, you might not be able to go outside when it rains, because it would be poisoned. You wouldn't be able to breathe the air outside either, because of the pollution. Think, your grandchildren may never see a blue sky, or smell a rose, or feel the rain streaming down their face.

Whitley Grindle, Grade 8
Lumpkin County Middle School, GA

Top Essay Grades 7-8-9

The Music Flowing Through Me

The music comes naturally. I hear the beats, notes, and tones flowing through my fingers as I play the oboe. I play what I feel and what I think. My emotion comes through my voice as I sing out loud. I play oboe in our town orchestra, my school singing group, and in my oboe lessons. I sing in my church choir, and my school singing group. I can't get enough of the music. I express myself through the melodious song.

I cannot live without music. It is the food which my soul feeds on. The songs are addictive. There is not a minute that passes by when I do not have a song stuck in my head. I love music.

I would say music has deeply affected my life. I have been playing oboe for four and a half years. I have been singing since I could talk. Music has taught me discipline. Music has taught me that without practice I can never achieve greatness. I chose which high school I'm going to from their music program. I have met the most fantastic people from my years of music education. I hope to be in music for the rest of my life and learn new techniques, instruments, and theories every day.

Megan Hathcock, Grade 8
Holy Spirit Regional School, AL

Top Essay Grades 7-8-9

Keep Holding On

On April, 12, 2003, my life was forever changed. While attending my grandmother's wedding in Baltimore, I began suffering from a terrible headache. When the pain would not go away, my parents rushed me to the hospital where I was diagnosed with a blood clot in my brain. Within an hour, I was undergoing neurosurgery to remove the clot. I now know how precious life is and how the people who helped me recover are true heroes.

After the surgery, I suffered a stroke and remained in a coma for seven days. The doctors feared I suffered permanent damage. For seven weeks I remained in the hospital recovering. The doctors, nurses, and therapists all helped me physically and emotionally. My family and friends all prayed for me and sent me cheerful cards to keep my spirits up.

Once stable, I was air transported to Children's Hospital in St. Louis. I spent eight intensive weeks going through occupational, speech, and physical therapy. I had to relearn how to walk and to regain use of my right hand. Whenever I was lonely, tired, or depressed, the medical staff and my friends would come to my rescue. They motivated me and encouraged me to keep making progress even when I didn't think I could. My classmates even shaved their heads, mirroring my own shaved head.

Today I am back in school and back to normal. I will never forget those heroes who helped me get my life back and never let me give up.

Matt Kammer, Grade 8
St Gerard Majella School, MO

Top Essay Grades 7-8-9

Dare to Be Different

Originality. In the dictionary, it's defined as the freshness of aspect, design, or style. To me, this definition adds up to one thing — being yourself, no matter what any of your peers say. If you want to wear your hair short and wear clothes that aren't from any popular store, then go for it, no matter what any of your "friends" think! If they insult you for being different, then they really weren't your friends to begin with, anyway!

A company called Life Is Good® has a motto that states: "Do what you like, like what you do." If everyone lived their lives by that saying, then a lot of peer pressure would be eliminated, and everyone would like who they are, instead of pretending to be happy and realizing just how unhappy they are with themselves in the quiet moments of the day.

Our world would be completely boring and devoid of any creativity if everyone looked the same, talked the same, did the same things, and were just plain identical to each other. God made us all different and unique for a reason, so don't let what anyone says keep you from showing the world who *you* are, and not someone's opinion on who you should be. Be original and don't change yourself for anyone! It's not always easy to be original, but you'll find that if you are true to yourself, you'll be much happier during those precious quiet moments of the day, and you'll live life in the best possible way.

Erin Tracy, Grade 8
Bak Middle School of the Arts, FL

Top Essay Grades 7-8-9

Urban Clear-Cutting

What happened to the tall oak behind your house? What became of the mighty pines that once stood where rows of houses now stand? Chances are, if you live in a relatively new area in almost any city, there are no trees, and if there are trees, they only date back to the time when the neighborhood was created. Even if you live in an older subdivision, where there were once trees behind your house, now there is an ugly field of dirt, with the occasional bulldozer.

Yes, America is growing. Yes, we need more space. Yes, we could use more houses. But are these reasons to cut down all trees in an area? Trees provide food and homes for many animals, and humans enjoy trees as well. Most people have sat beneath a tree to enjoy a good book, or climbed up into its sturdy branches. I want future generations to enjoy this pastime and not live in a treeless barren land.

Developing houses in any city is a necessity. Nevertheless, is *development* a viable reason to clear cut every tree in sight? While building houses, leave some trees for the sake of animals, the environment, and children of future generations. It is a shame for a 200 year old tree to get cut down for the sake of dollars and cents. So I ask developers that before they cut down that old tree that has been there since our country's conception, to think about who they are affecting.

Allison Underwood, Grade 8
Providence Classical School, AL

Top Essay Grades 7-8-9

My Heroes

Standing on the front line, bullets flaring past without even flinching, American soldiers risk their lives for the sake of their homeland. A United States army medal is more than ribbon and gold. It is a sign that the recipient has risked his or her life in an effort to protect their proud country. Each day many soldiers do their daily war tasks without being recognized enough for the great effort they put forth to keep our country's freedom and equality. Great honor and respect should be given to our U.S. warriors. Helping our soldiers by sending them food, encouraging messages, and other things they may miss while overseas is a great way to display thankfulness and honor towards them.

U.S. military men put up with harsh conditions, such as overheating barren terrain, insufficient food supply, and vigorous physical training and work for the sake of their country's people. Thousands of soldiers have died fighting for "the land of the free and the home of the brave," or as many know it, America. Soldiers are very brave to risk their lives but are also very proud to be serving their country. Without the present and past U.S. soldiers, our country would not have the freedom and independence for which it is known. I am proud to say I do not have one hero but a full army of them that fight to protect my family and me every day.

Taylor Wagner, Grade 8
St Gerard Majella School, MO

Top Essay Grades 7-8-9

Wallpaper Students

If you were to stop in your school and look around, how many wallpaper kids would you see? Wallpaper kids are the ones who don't get noticed, who go through school getting picked on by a variety of students. These kids go to school knowing their fellow students don't care about them — and the message's hammered in every time they're bullied. They learn to hate school, grow miserable, and eventually snap.

It's always in schools where students commit lethal crimes, and it's always wallpaper kids — the lonely ones with unnoticed problems — who do it. Did you know that most male students say they can get a gun in just one day or less? What's going to stop them from using it if they've got issues? Most people can't understand this. But being ignored every day at the place where students spend most of their time can give people problems. Always being given wordless messages saying how worthless they are can drive someone to a breaking point.

There's little teachers can do to spot — or stop — these messages. And students don't realize how much damage they're doing, because they only see their own small scale actions instead of the actions of the entire school. Wallpaper students shouldn't be told that bullying is part of school or of growing up. Students need to work together to be more conscious of the consequences of their actions. After all, it's never just one person who turns somebody else into a wallpaper kid.

Allison Wigger, Grade 8
West Jr High School, MO

Top Essay Grades 7-8-9

Time

No one ever realizes how fast time flies. Some people are too busy to relax. Time flies, fast. Time is precious. Sometimes time is is too hard to find.

Sometimes people just work too much. Life is a beautiful thing. Time is what lets you enjoy life. Most people just need to stop and enjoy life the way it is. Some people can't see the beauty of life because they are too busy to stop and acknowledge it.

However, time flies by fast enough that we don't get to enjoy it. When people do get time to spend with family or friends, it goes by too quickly. The saying, "time flies when you're having fun," is a true statement. I think that we could all use a little extra time.

Time is a precious thing. Time is not something that we can choose to have, it is something we are given. Time is like a loose button, if it is misplaced, it could be lost forever. You can't get back the time you've lost, so live in the moment, and have fun while you can. You will never know what you can do, if you don't take the time to try.

Finally, time is important, but sometimes it's just hard to find. If you don't pay attention, time can just slip by. Time is precious and can be missed when not used. Time is the president of all life, it is what makes the world go 'round.

Sarah Wilson, Grade 8
Pigeon Forge Middle School, TN

Nothing Lasts Forever

Being in 6th grade was a walk in the park. I thought the only reason I survived was my older brother, Andrew. He tutored me through studying methods for the test I was cramming for and informed me what sets a teacher in kill mode. However everything eventually comes to an end. Once my brother graduated from 8th grade to the never ending halls of upper school, my life went plunging downhill. He was never there to support me at my tennis matches because of late classes. I would never get the chance to spend time with him. When it seemed like he made the long journey home just to hang out with me, he would retire to his Philadelphia Eagle painted room to spend the rest of the time studying for an exam in biology or finish his geometry which looked like cavemen drawings. I felt like Mrs. Bonitz, his evil math teacher, was loading him up with homework just so I would be miserable. I was foolish for thinking this.

Andrew still guided me through school and goofed off in his spare time. On the weekends, he would procrastinate to do his homework just to play a mindless video game with me, or he'd offer to answer any of my questions about math or Spanish (never English). Even when it seems like Andrew has gone with the wind, I know he will always be my guardian, my best friend, and most importantly my big brother.

Jeffrey Shibata, Grade 7
Baylor School, TN

A Famous Oklahoma Writer...Who Is She?

Even though Oklahoma will soon be 100 years old one of the most poplar and best known writers of young adult fiction will only be 59. S. E. Hinton is not only famous in Oklahoma, but world wide. Her books have been taught in some schools and banned from others. Her novels have changed the way people look at young adult literature.

Susan Eloise Hinton was born in Tulsa, OK. She has always enjoyed reading, but wasn't satisfied with the literature that was being written for young adults. This influenced her to write the novel, *The Outsiders*. *The Outsiders* was Susan's first novel, published when she was 16 by Viking Publishing.

During a recent book signing event in Tulsa where she was promoting her new book, *Tim's Story*, she discussed what it was like to have her book come to life, having a part in a movie, and how proud she is to be from Oklahoma.

I am amazed at how much I have enjoyed reading S. E. Hinton's books. Her books are enjoyable to read, the time passes so quickly while I am reading one of her books. My friends and I have had some great conversations about S. E. Hinton's books.

I agree with S. E. Hinton when she wrote, "Anything you read can influence your work, so I try to read good stuff."

Tiffany Harper, Grade 9
Chelsea Jr High School, OK

Wildlife Conservation Keeping Life on Earth

Conservation is a very important thing in our world. We need animals to help us survive. Animals keep the ecosystem running smoothly. For example, the scientists think that because of the ice melting from global warning polar bears are disappearing a little at a time. Animals also have amazing abilities such as echolocation, night vision, and super sensitive hearing. Humans sometimes overlook the animals around them and therefore they do not respect animals and their importance. Humans are the cause of what is happening. We are polluting the ocean, rivers, and ponds. We are using chemicals that destroy and kill animals and our environment. Every time we cut down a tree we are killing a place where an animal might live and nurture their young. Every time we decide to build something new we are destroying homes and habitats. If we do not protect these animals how will they keep our planet intact? Animals are just as important as we are. Another example of an animal being threatened by pollution is the Bald Eagle, our national bird. These animals are eating and drinking out of contaminated food sources. We share the world with many magnificent creatures and we need to protect them not destroy them or we destroy ourselves. We all need to make it a priority to make and keep people aware of the need for conservation in our world or we will pay the price.

Atarah Fish, Grade 7
Home School, GA

Broken Heart

She was independent and attractive. Everyone wanted to be her. She walked with courage and bravery, maintaining her flawless individuality. Her attitude screamed she had it all together.

Her gold hair slinked down her back and her crystal eyes glistened on her genuine skin. She seemed to have everyone wrapped around her fingers.

No one knew what hid behind her perfect smile.

She returned to her empty home. Dad was at work. Mother had left her. All she wanted was a family. Dad was never home. She had no mother to laugh with, tell her problems to, or cry in the arms of. Only when no one was watching could she truly fall apart. She concealed herself in her room, alone as usual, and cried herself to sleep, her broken heart slithering out of grasp.

She wondered if anyone else had failed, or had fallen. When she took a glance around, everyone seemed so strong. She determined they'd soon discover that she didn't belong anywhere. Would it unbind her if she revealed the truth behind the person they expected her to be? Would their arms be sincere, or would they be thoughtless? She hid it all away, as if everything was all right. Maybe if she believed it, they'd all believe it too. Her routine was convincing, and she recited every line by heart. So with her painted smile, she played the part, again.

Why do we use our smiles to hide our pain?

Haiden Redmond, Grade 7
Aletheia Christian Academy, FL

Mexican Immigrants

These days people take one look at a Mexican and automatically assume that they are an immigrant. That's what is wrong with America. We don't realize that there are Caucasian and African Americans that are immigrants too. Why do we automatically think that Mexicans are the only ones that have to go back to their country? We are all humans, and we should all be treated like humans. If it weren't for Mexicans we would do without a whole lot. They build our houses. They pick the oranges in Florida, and peaches in Georgia. They have families they need to take care of and provide for. How are they different from us? We are all the same inside and out. Like our fellow American Dr. Martin Luther King Jr. said, "I have a dream." Well, I too have a dream. I dream that all Caucasians, African Americans, and Mexicans can come together as one. If Mexican immigrants have to be deported then so should all the other immigrants. No one should be treated like he or she is nothing. No one should feel lower than low. So I stand before you, saying that if many years ago one man could make Caucasians and African Americans come together and put aside all their differences, then why can't we do the same with Mexicans? We should all put aside our difference with them. The way we did many years ago. We all need a change every once in a while.

Brittney Stanley, Grade 9
Triton High School, NC

When It All Passes!

There she is again. Playing ol' sol. Every time you turn that corner after you waltz through the door you will see a ninety-year old lady playing solitaire. That old lady would be my great-grandma Ada. She is one of the sweetest ladies you will ever meet.

My favorite thing to do with my Grandma Ada is listen to her tell me old, old stories. It is so interesting listening to what she has been through in her life! She is always here for me.

There are a few things I hate to see my grandma do, and that is cry or see her in pain. But she makes me feel better by saying "When it all passes, it will all be the same." I get worried about her sometimes when she refuses to take her medicine.

She loves to watch fireworks on the Fourth of July. She also loves some good ol' Indian cooking. Did I mention she is a full-blood Indian? She is the best grandma in the whole world! I love her with all my heart. I have no clue what I would do without her.

She knows more things about Indians than I know about softball, and that's a lot! My grandma has a very outgoing personality. She has nine kids and only seven are still alive.

My grandma is very traditional. She goes to stomp dances, feasts, and other Indian events. This wonderful lady was very ecstatic that she got to celebrate Oklahoma's centennial this year.

Dani Hutt, Grade 8
Chelsea Jr High School, OK

Literature's Importance

Literature is important in many ways, but several reasons stand out. One of these reasons is how literature entertains us. Another reason is how literature teaches us and connects us about our past.

Literature evokes extreme emotions of the human psyche. For hundreds of years Shakespeare used politics, love, death, religion, and humor to amuse people by writing plays. Edgar Allen Poe wrote poems and short stories that still keep people horrified and turning pages. Also, J.K. Rowling manipulated fans of her books by making her books suspenseful and interesting. With these forms of literature, these authors have enthralled readers and play attendees.

Without literature, connecting with our past would not be possible. One way literature educates us is how conflict plays out. Conflict is the problems of the past, present and future. *The Bible* is a perfect illustration of educating literature. It teaches us about Christianity, and it tells us about what times were like in the past. Conflict is the base of learning; so, transitively, if learning is knowledge then literature is the base of knowledge.

Without literature, entertainment would not be possible. Without literature, teaching and connecting with our past would not be possible. Without literature, cultures would die out. Without literature there would be no life. I suppose that we all could be hunter-gatherers, but we would still use literature in the form of stories by painting on cave walls, but I don't think that that would go over too well.

Sean Davison, Grade 8
Heritage Hall School, OK

The Worst Day Ever

The worst day on Earth was September 11, 2001 also known as 9/11. It was a horrible day. A firefighter was on his way to golf when he heard people blaring over his scanner inside his truck; he turned his truck around and headed to the firehouse. He got his gear and put it into his truck and headed toward the World Trade Center. He ran 2 miles with 75 pounds of gear on him. It immortalized him at the same time.

It is pretty sad that we have to live in fear of people bombing us or flying planes into buildings. I wake up every morning wondering if I'm still going to be alive at the end of the day. A lot of times I don't want to go to public areas, because I'm scared of what's going to happen. No one in my family died in 9/11, but I feel the same pain as everyone else. On September 11, people just go their way and don't even bother to take a moment of silence on September 11 here in Stroud, OK. We don't know where the next terrorist will be at, but as long as we live in this world, we will always have to fear people.

Tommy Mason, Grade 7
Stroud Middle School, OK

The Heroes of September 11, 2001

September 11, 2001, dawned a normal day until the hearts and lives of millions were shattered. On that bright, crisp morning, children and parents were walking out the door while some stayed to enjoy a quick cup of coffee. Turning on the news, you sat frozen as your eyes witnessed a horrific sight. America was under attack.

Two hijacked planes crashed into the World Trade Center in New York. You watched intently, tears streaming from your eyes, as the two buildings burst into flames. Innocent, everyday people plummeted to their death rather than being trapped inside the building. You saw the panic-stricken faces of people frantically searching for a way of escape, but finding none. Firefighters, police officers, off-duty men and women, and everyday people charged in, risking their lives to evacuate as many as possible. It was as if you were watching a horror movie, but without the screen.

Two more planes were headed toward the Pentagon and Washington D.C. After the Twin Towers collapsed, the Pentagon was hit. The brave men and women of Flight 93, heading towards Washington D.C., received phone calls from loved ones and realized they were aboard a hijacked plane. They overtook the hijackers and crashed into a field rather than flying on as intended. They died that day as heroes.

Ordinary men and women gave their lives for others. Nearly 3000 died that day. Although a tragedy, September 11, 2001, is not only about horror, but also about heroes.

Kelsey De Jong, Grade 7
Blue Ridge Christian School, MO

No Friends! What?

"Friends are useless. They are back-stabbing and ignorant, and you cannot trust them with anything, especially secrets." What? I was shocked to hear what one of my classmates thought of friends. I gaped in disbelief. How could anyone say this about friends, to whom I always go for encouragement and assurance?

Friends are supposed to be companions and chums, people who hold a lofty place in your mind and heart. My friends are always there for me, helping me through tough situations. We argue sometimes, but because we have been through so much together, this seems like nothing more than a bump on a lengthy road.

Many people believe friendships are similar to climbing a long rope with many knots; you need to use the lower ones to get to the top. Anybody who exercises this theory (whether they benefit from their displeasing way of thinking or not) is utterly incorrect. Other people actually feel they are above the concept of friendship. Those select few in between are the ones who flourish and prosper in life.

I cherish friendships now and always will. Keep in mind that friends, especially best friends, are special. Once you've found that true companion, hang on tight. It'll be a rough ride, but there will be lots of fun and laughter, and of course, secrets, along the way. Just wait! You'll see.

Claire Mullaney, Grade 7
St Joseph Elementary School, MO

My Little Slice of Paradise

One of my favorite things to do in my free time is to play games. Games! Games! Games! I like almost every type of game. I enjoy playing games at amusement parks, playing a variety of games with my friends and family, and playing games on all different kinds of systems.

Several times this past month I walked past a new store in the mall called "The Edge," which is a new style of game playing. This past weekend, I went to the mall with my aunt and it was the perfect timing because there were only a few people inside. As I entered the store I was amazed by what I saw. The room was at a nice cool temperature, kids and adults of all ages were playing and enjoying the games, and I saw many big screen TVs setup in their own unique area with a comfy sofa for you to sit on and a large variety of games to play. Even the newest games that just came out were on display. Everyone that worked there treated me like I was the king of the world!!! You can play by the hour or join on a monthly basis. There are also tournaments to enter and if you get hungry by the smell of the food there is even a cafe.

For someone like me who really likes games this is my little slice of paradise.

Kodi Bell, Grade 8
Eagles Landing Middle School, FL

Opinions

Opinions. Everyone has them, and everyone's is different. But they help make our country diverse and interesting. This society would be extremely boring if everyone thought the same way.

Here in the United States, we have the right to have an opinion, and the right to talk about it freely. People *really* take advantage of that. It's wonderful for all the people who understand that everyone believes differently, but bad for those who don't. The people who aren't willing to tolerate others' opinions create problems. They think people who don't agree with them are unintelligent. They start hating others. They create untrue stereotypes. They refuse to see the other side of arguments. This happens much too often in the world around us. Ignorance is surrounding everything now. People will simply refuse to accept others' opinions. And then they will try to force theirs' on others! Yes, ignorance is swallowing everything. Does no one realize that we are *lucky* to be able to even talk about what we think? That doesn't mean we should put people down for it! So many people are abusing this right. Respect is all I'm asking for people. And a little kindness would help too.

Opinions are awesome. Our country rocks because we are allowed to talk about them! Opinions help make every person an individual. So please, be a civil human being when talking about your opinions. And try to keep an open mind.

Sarah Zimmerman, Grade 8
Southwest Jr High School, AR

The Day America Cried

It was January 28, 1982 when the Challenger was taking its tenth and final trip into space. A teacher named Christa McAuliffe was going to be on the space shuttle, and she was going to be the first civilian in space, beating 11,000 candidates. At Kennedy Space Center around 11:40 A.M., the shuttle took flight, and about 73 seconds later, the disaster was over, and seven lives were lost. Billions mourned the lives of Francis Scobee, Ellison Onizuka, Judith Resnick, Ronald McNair, Christa McAuliffe, pilot Michael Smith, and Gregory Jarvis.

The six day and 34 minute mission was never completed because of a default in a rocket booster that ignited the main liquid fuel tank. The Challenger was enveloped into flames before exploding into the ocean. The Challenger was successful from 1982 to 1986. It took NASA 10 years to launch another shuttle into space.

I can imagine the memories it brought back for the families and how many people cried for the seven lives that were lost that day. I believe they died doing what they believed in, and they died for their love of space and adventure.

Ashley Parnell, Grade 7
Stroud Middle School, OK

My Nana

One of the most influential people that is in my life is Nana. My Nana is so giving towards others. She loves just spending time with me and showing her love towards me. Last, she teaches me how to treat other people and is someone I look up to. Therefore, my Nana is very important to me.

My Nana shows love towards others by helping them out. She will stop what she's doing to go and pick me up. You can just ask and she is there. When people are in trouble she is there to lend them a helping hand. She encourages me every day to go and help other people. In addition, she shows love in many ways.

Next, my Nana enjoys just spending time with me and showing love. She calls almost every day wondering if I'm ok, or if I need to stay at her house. She always keeps her house open for guests. She is always the one to hold events. As a result, she doesn't like her house to be empty.

Last, my Nana has qualities that I hope to have. All the things she does for other people encourages me. As I have grown up, I have noticed that even though she calls me constantly, and worries about me I know that it's all out of love. Eventually, I'll get over it and want to spend time with her a lot more.

In conclusion, my Nana has been more to me than just some old woman. She has been so giving to other people. She loves spending time with me and showing her love to me. Last, she has taught me how to treat others. Furthermore, my Nana is someone that I love very much and enjoy spending my time with.

Kendyl Chambers, Grade 8
Pigeon Forge Middle School, TN

My Private Grounds

My backyard leads to an unknown world, one where I can think alone except for the sounds of cheerful bird songs and the rushing of air past leaves. It contains a soft and moist cushion of green grass for my bare feet. Also, it is a calming place to collect my thoughts, after having a long day. I can release all of my emotions with one simple breath.

Some people use their lawns as a way to express their personalities by decorating them for certain holidays, whereas others use them as leisurely activities by gardening. I, however, use this area to practice soccer, but it also serves as a home for my dog. As versatile as this area of my house is, for me it is mainly used for one purpose: a place where I can relax. Just stepping outside is soothing, especially with all of the sweet aromas of roses and strawberry plants. Sometimes I even do my homework outside because it is a great location where I can really concentrate. Above all, I can also pray there. I just don't understand how some people dislike the outdoors, because for me it is one of my favorite places in the world.

Selma Padilla, Grade 7
White Station Middle School, TN

Gary Powers and the U-2 Crisis of 1960

Gary Powers was an American pilot who flew his Air Force-issued U-2 plane over the Soviet Union during the Cold War. The principle of his flights was to spy on the Soviets. No one would've thought that this trained pilot and his sophisticated spy plane would cause the U-2 Crisis of 1960.

There was one key reason that everyone expected U-2 planes to be safe over Soviet ground — the plane could fly to heights of eighty thousand feet, much higher than any Soviet weapon could reach.

Suddenly, on May 1, 1960, Gary and his plane were shot down over the Soviet Union by a missile. Gary made a parachute landing, survived, and was captured by the Soviets. Gary was sentenced to Soviet prison for ten years.

After Powers had been missing, the American government was questioned about the plane. The U.S. government replied that the U-2 was a weather research craft and the plane had crashed because the pilot had experienced oxygen problems. The U.S. lied, and it worked until the Soviet Union displayed the alive and well Gary Powers in front of the world twenty-one months after his capture.

Not only was Gary still alive, but the plane itself was still mostly intact. The Soviets were able to recover important photographs from the plane, the surveillance camera, and other things. Later, Gary was exchanged for a Soviet spy the *Americans* had captured.

This story became known as the U-2 Crisis and was an important event in the Cold War.

Savannah Silver, Grade 8
Providence Classical School, AL

Nature's Greatest Artwork

I had a quiver in both my soul and body as I exited the door of my school. Something in my brain told me that an incredible event was approaching at a rapid pace.

I began to ponder and puzzle over this bizarre feeling, no — bizarre instinct. Great happenings and events flashed through my mind. Things like the Second Coming, reaching Mars, and discovering aliens wove in and out of my reverie. As my visions became more and more maniacal, my strange quivering continuously grew stronger.

When I pulled into the driveway of my country home, I began to hear the bangs of shotguns and blasts of rifles. Soon the ear-piercing honking of geese and clamorous quacking of ducks filled the air. Everything melted into one big symphony, with the guns as percussion and the birds as the brass and woodwinds. The wind became a light, gentle flute.

As my comrade, also known as my dog, came to my side, the sun began to sink, and the great natural symphony came to the big finale. We settled on our favorite hill and began to watch the show. The sun slid behind the trees, and the sky turned a deep, royal purple, and the clouds a valiant scarlet. The autumn wind had its last dance of the evening. The song ended, the light drifted to sleep, and the sun said, "Farewell."

As night's blanket tucked me in, I had a culminating thought. "This is what is important to me."

Thomas Miller, Grade 7
White Station Middle School, TN

Space Exploration

Have you ever wondered about space exploration? I have and would like to discuss some facts and opinions. These are my opinions on exploring space. For one we should not stop exploring space. Also NASA should not stop making new things to help explore. The universe could hold many planets that are inhabited by other life forms. The Earth will not get over populated by colonizing other planets. Finally in the future we could have the technology to leave the Solar System.

These are some facts on space exploration. Space travel has always been thought of. Then in 1969 it became reality. Last year the British scientists found another planet that could be habitable, and its sun is called the Red Dwarf Star. Also last week a Japanese space craft found a sun spot on the sun that could be a giant Trilobite (a Trilobite is a bug that lived millions of years ago). Next month NASA will show a new map of space. Finally NASA plans to setup a camp on the moon.

To summarize, these are my opinions and facts on exploring space. I hope that space is more fascinating to you now.

Joseph Warnix, Grade 7
Henry L Sneed Middle School, SC

My Life

My life revolves around my friends and my family. Oh and of course a 13-year-old girl has to have guy problems. Well I have them almost every day dealing with the same guys.

I love all my friends. They are my life. My number one best friend is also my cousin, Britany. She understands me unlike most people. I can talk to her about almost anything. If it's guy problems or personal problems, it doesn't matter. That's the only one of many reasons I love Britany Tedder.

My family has a lot of difficulties. Sometimes we argue and sometimes we fight. I still love them and they all still love me. My daddy helps me with a lot of things. When my boyfriend that I really liked broke up with me my daddy was there for me to comfort me. He is there for me unlike my momma. I live with her, but she neglects me all the time. But I have to love her.

Kayla Tedder, Grade 8
Seminole County Middle/High School, GA

Having Good Friends

Having good friends is very important to me. There are several reasons why. I need someone to talk to that will keep a secret and is a real friend. I need support from my friends when I am sad or hurt or lonely. My friends help me when I am sick, and when I need money to pay bills. My friends make me happy when we are together.

If we did not have friends, we would be very lonely because we wouldn't have anyone to talk to when we need help or to keep our secrets. We would be sad because we would be all by ourselves. We would feel helpless because there is no one to help us. We would feel alone with no one to play or to go to places with us like the movies or the park.

Samantha Aviles, Grade 8
Easter Seals of South Florida School, FL

My Private Escape

Have you ever been in a situation where you feel like all of the stress of the world has joined together and unleashed its wrath on you? Well, I have, and believe me, it doesn't go away on its own.

If I have a nerve-wracking day and feel like my head's about to pop, the only thing that can ease my nerves and soothe my soul is to hear the overwhelmingly sweet melody from the most majestic instrument ever known to man, the piano.

The reason why the piano is important to me is because it is like my gateway of relief. From an elegant piece down to just simply playing scales on the piano is extremely relaxing, and it's also something that I can call my own. In my house, I have to share everything. including my room, with my little sister, Natasha. Playing piano is almost like a sanctuary to me.

The next time I'm caught in a jam or I just need something to help clear my mind, I will be playing my piano to break off into my private, musical escape.

Ana Beatriz Maclin, Grade 7
White Station Middle School, TN

The War Unleashed

I think President Bush is going in the right direction with the war in Iraq. I think he is stopping 9/11 from repeating. Also, the president has the right ideas about how to handle the war and we are making progress. I think we should continue the war until our goal is met.

I believe that if we leave Iraq, being the only super power there, terrorists will regain power and attack other countries while America ignores them until they gain enough power to attack the United States. We're in Iraq because they killed thousands of innocent people on 9/11 like flies to be swatted away. We cannot let that happen again.

I also believe that President Bush is making the right decisions on the war. What we spend on the war is nothing compared to American's 17 billion dollar yearly budget. The soldiers in Iraq voluntarily went to fight. We did not force them to go. We should send as many as possible.

I believe we are making great progress in Iraq. In the news they only show death and money because that is what sells the story. There are a lot of good things going on in the war; we've crushed a terrorist empire and we are doing great stuff in Iraq every day. A great democracy has been formed.

In conclusion I support the war in Iraq. We cannot let 9/11 happen again. I believe in what President Bush is doing. I believe we should stay in Iraq.

Ethan Thomas, Grade 8
Pigeon Forge Middle School, TN

Why I Am an American Patriot

What does it mean to be a patriot? It means you would be willing to give your life for your country. It means you are loyal, passionate, and bonded to your country. It means you would do anything to help your country and the people in it.

I know that the patriots in our country do many things; firefighters save people's lives, policemen protect the people in our community. So what could I do to show my patriotism? I know I cannot rescue people from burning buildings, or pull over a speeding car, but I can do little things.

In every community there are many small problems, like broken memorials, overgrown graveyards, or a tunnel with graffiti on it. As a kid, I can help clean up places that have been here for many years. By donating my time as a volunteer, I show my love for our community.

One more way I can show that I am an American Patriot is by praying for soldiers. This gives everyone courage that our friends will come home. We do not just worry about ourselves; we worry about the other people in need. I may be suffering a small bit for helping others, but it is all worth the turnout. This turnout is peace.

That is why I think I am an American Patriot.

Kendra Efker, Grade 8
Father McCartan Memorial School, MO

Shooting Clays

I get up at eight o'clock every Saturday morning to shoot clays at my uncle's field. Clays are very tricky because they can turn slightly throwing you off course. They can also shatter in mid air if they go too fast. I love waking up to shoot at clays.

Clays train you for hunting doves, and ducks, which are tricky, like the clays. For instance if you were to practice shooting clays two weeks before dove season you would greatly increase your chances. Believe it or not shooting clays is actually a sport. Because it is not as famous as football, baseball, basketball, or even golf it is rarely on television. Clays will blow up after you shoot them, as in the they break into tiny pieces. In conclusion clays help you train for hunting birds.

Waking up to shoot clays is a great way to wake up in my opinion. Getting up at eight o'clock is not so bad when you know you will smell gun smoke in minutes. Clays are fun to shoot at on a cool Saturday morning. They are also very tricky when they turn. They are especially fun when you have some friendly competition from your dad. Waking up in the morning is fun most of the time.

Trevor Spain, Grade 7
Greenfield Jr/Sr High School, MO

Jimmy Carter an Inspiration to Everyone

Jimmy Carter is a wonderful human being. He has done great things for this country. For example he got us through the Iran hostage situation as well as the energy crisis of 1979. He always did the right thing even though half the time the country disagreed with him. Although the public was not fond of him I believe he was the greatest president in the history of our country.

When I was a child my mom and dad were always talking about politics and how our government had gotten much worse. I remember asking my mom who she thought the greatest president was, and she said Jimmy Carter. Of course at the time I had no idea who Jimmy Carter was.

Two years ago I got into politics because of 9/11, but mainly because George Bush was screwing up the country and I believed I could do something. Unfortunately I was wrong. I read up on our government and the history about it. I learned a ton of information and a lot of it came from Jimmy Carter. The first thing he taught me was politics was like gambling, if you put too much hope on one candidate you are bound to lose. Also he taught me that when there is a crisis do not panic, stay calm and everything will work out.

In the past few years, Jimmy Carter is not president but he is still helping third world countries with peace and war related problems. As well as this he visited Israel and Palestine and watched as hundreds of people were slaughtered. After this experience he wrote a book about how horribly the Israelis treated the Palestinians. So knowing this and all of the other great achievements of Jimmy Carter how do you feel about him?

Jules Crespy, Grade 9
West Jr High School, MO

The Best Internet Game Ever

Super Crazy Guitar Maniac Deluxe 2 is the best internet game ever! It is very much like *Dance Dance Revolution*, it has lots of different songs to choose from, and you can unlock a lot of things. These are my favorite reasons for liking *Super Crazy Guitar Maniac Deluxe 2*.

If you like *Dance Dance Revolution*, you will love this game. The only thing different is you use the arrow keys and the letters a, s, and d. It doesn't burn off calories like *DDR* but it's just as fun and exciting.

My next reason why I like *Super Crazy Guitar Maniac Deluxe 2* is because it has a lot of different songs to choose from. They are not songs that you hear too much but they are good. There are 14 or 16 songs; depending on which version you load. My favorite song is "Broked It."

Last are the things that you can unlock in this game. You can unlock different guitars by getting perfects on songs and by getting a certain number of awards. You can also unlock new songs on the game.

This is why I like *Super Crazy Guitar Maniac Deluxe 2*. It is like *Dance Dance Revolution*, it has a lot of different songs to choose from, and you can unlock a lot of things. *Super Crazy Guitar Maniac Deluxe 2* is the best internet game ever and I really think you should try it out now!

Eric Bauer, Grade 7
Sebastian River Middle School, FL

Midtown Is Memphis

"One generation plants the trees, the other gets the shade," states the old Chinese proverb about community. This is especially true in Midtown, where we continue to sit under trees planted by our ancestors centuries before. These forefathers also planted seeds of culture that would grow into our current community.

Even though I've lived in East Memphis my whole life, I feel as though my heart is in Midtown. When I travel there, nothing excites me more than knowing that I am driving through the historic architecture of our hometown. Something about the artistic feel of the locale fills me with joy and inspiration. For example, the Brooks Museum of Art shines with creative glory in the noonday sun.

Midtown has numerous festivals and entertaining activities, where Memphians gather as a community. These include the Scottish Festival, the Cooper Young Festival, and the Mid-South Fair. At the Scottish Fest you can relish the taste of meat pie while some get in touch with their heritage. The Cooper Young Festival is the art festival featuring the creative side of Memphis. Finally, at the Mid-South Fair, the smell of pronto pups and cotton candy fills the air. Originally a celebration of our agricultural roots, it is now a place where people of all backgrounds come together.

Midtown is a palette on which various cultures mix and form a uniquely Memphis personality. Just as in the past, this persona will continue to attract and delight for generations to come.

Ethan Williford, Grade 7
White Station Middle School, TN

History of Video Games

The history of video games is so interesting I would like to share it with you. A man named Ralph Baer in 1949 was assigned to build a television set. But he wanted to make it the best television set ever. He wanted to make a game in the set. He didn't know what game to make. But his manager said he couldn't any ways. It actually took him 18 years for his ideas to be put into reality. Soon other people would share his idea like Willy Higinbotham, Steve Russell, and Nolan Bushnell. Willy designed a tennis game played on an oscilloscope, Steve made a space game on the DEC PDP-1 mainframe computer, and Nolan played this space game and dreamed of creating more games.

Some of the games that were created from Willy, Steve, and Nolan's ideas were Space Invaders, Centipede, Frogger, and Pong. Some of these games are still played today. Atari, Sega, Phillips, and Sony made the games that are created today and in the past as well.

Video games are seen as the jump-start for teenage violence. In 1975 the company Exidy Games came out with the Death Race 2000. The game was taken off the market because of the violence in the game. The reason was because you earned points for running over stick figures which resembled humans.

Now, the video games systems are Playstation 1, 2, and 3, Xbox, Xbox 360, Gamecube, Wii, and handheld systems are Gameboy Advance, SP and Ds, and Playstation Portable.

Derek Lewis, Grade 7

The Best Book Ever Written

I think that the Bible is the best book ever written. It applies to a variety of aspects in all of our lives. It tell us how to live, how to treat others, and most of all how to be saved.

The Bible tells us how the world came to exist. It also informs us of our purpose while on the earth. I would hate not knowing my purpose while I am here. God created humans so that He could have fellowship with them. It tells us how sin came into the picture and hindered us in our relationship with God.

Luckily, God had a plan. The Bible says and prophesies that God's one and only Son, Jesus Christ, came to the world to die for all. That is one of the best reasons I like the Bible.

The Bible tells us how to live and treat others. Jesus told this best in the book of Matthew in the fifth and sixth chapter. They tell how God blesses those who keep His word.

Though you can keep these commandments they won't get you into Heaven. Heaven is the place of perfection. It won't be any size, shape, or form of sin. The way to get into Heaven is to accept Jesus as Lord and Savior of your life.

In conclusion, those are some reasons why I think that the Bible is the best book ever written.

Alex Crittendon, Grade 8
Dyer Elementary & Jr High School, TN

Marquitta's Life

The best day ever was on June 8, 1993, in Bainbridge, GA. It was a baby girl named Marquitta. She was very adorable and she was something special. Her cute red cheeks were just as cute as a red bow. Her eyes glistened from the light above and made her smile shine. Marquitta was the perfect and chosen one. She grew up in Donalsonville GA.

She was one year old when she started walking really well. Everyone was expecting her to, but it wasn't so good when she was tearing down everything. She started talking well when she was 2 and grew into a fine young lady.

Finally, at this time she was 13 years old and she had just become a young cute teen. She settled her life for the best and she is something really amazing. Marquitta is a good person when you get to know her.

Marquitta Taylor, Grade 8
Seminole County Middle/High School, GA

Foster Care

Have you ever been in foster care? Well if you have then you know what it's like, and if you haven't then you probably don't know what it's like. To be honest with you I've never been in foster care. I know a lot about it though. The main reason I know a lot about it is, because I have a friend that has two sisters, and they are in foster care. I know that it can be hard for some people. Especially those that are little and they grow up and need to be told that their parents did not want them. Some of the foster parents are mean, but there can be nice ones too. Like my friend and her two sisters, they have great foster parents that teach them respect, they give them a good education, and they love these girls with all their heart. I know this, because I can just look at them and I can tell that if these girls were to leave their hearts would be broken. But, if you're a foster parent I'm proud of you. So let me tell you something if you have kids or are going to have kids don't put them in foster care, because you'll regret it one of these days.

Sierra Wagner, Grade 8
Pine View Elementary School, TN

Our Heroes

I strongly feel the war in Iraq is really important to me because my friends' fathers are there. Even though I don't have a mother or father there, I am still worried for them. I pray every night that the war will stop and all the troops come home. to me the war is pointless and we shouldn't be there but at the same time, I understand that we can't come home. This war has taught me stand up for people and be a better person. I think we should all support our troops because they are fighting for us. Do you think if they risk their lives for our rights we should take the time out to support them and pray? All the soldiers there are my heroes and this is important to me. I think this war should be important to everyone whether you're for or against the war you need to support our troops!

Kayley McRae, Grade 8
Heritage Hall School, OK

The Tale of Braille

Louis Braille invented Braille, a system of writing for the blind. He was also blind. He became blind because of an accident when he was three years old. His family found him rather annoying (in his three-years-old way). He was bored and went to his father's workshop and decided to make a harness like his father. He was using an awl, and it slipped and fell into his eye. Soon after, it got infected. Then it spread to the other eye.

At first, he was oblivious being blind. After that, he stayed at home, and then after a while, he was sent to a school for the blind in Paris. He loved to read even though he couldn't see the letters. At the school for the blind, there was only about eight books all in raised print, a very expensive way of making books. Only a few words, even only sometimes one, could fit on a page. Otherwise, they couldn't feel it.

Braille really wanted to read. When he was twelve and he heard about this code that the French military had thought of, but it was hard to learn and very complicated. He had to find a better way. He decided to use a code based on the night writer code, a series of bumps that were felt with the fingers. It took him about a year, as it was still complicated but easier to learn. Still, making it was hard. He used paper on a board and a stylus to make the letters; he based it on the night writer code.

Ken Beck, Grade 7
Stroud Middle School, OK

My Hospital Nightmare

It was already dark outside, the day had flown by, me and my family didn't even eat dinner. We were so exhausted that we had no desire to cook. My mom and dad ordered sushi for us to eat. We gathered around the television eating our dinner almost half asleep. As soon as we finished we all jumped into our beds and fell right asleep. A couple hours later I woke up to nausea and pain in my stomach. It was as if I was on a boat rocking back and forth. I tried to use the bathroom, drink some water and eat some bread. Nothing was working.

I woke my parents and told them about how I was feeling. They tried just about everything: the last thing they could have done was to take me to the emergency room, which they did. As we arrived, the hospital nurse admitted me to a room right away. The doctor did his testing and found food poisoning from either the rice or fish I had eaten. They had to do numerous painful tests to make sure nothing was infected. My mom and aunt Jill held my hand through every procedure, and felt my pain. I was in the hospital for a week but then got better. Through this experience I know my family will be there for me no matter what I go through in life.

Eric Getz, Grade 8
Eagles Landing Middle School, FL

Things We Take for Granted

Have you ever sat down and wondered, what if we didn't have the everyday things that are common in our lives, and that we take for granted? We also take life for granted. Life is the most precious thing we have.

There are lots of common everyday things we take for granted. Such as: automobiles, cell phones, house phones, computers, lawn mowers, and televisions. For instance, what if we never had cars? Can you imagine how hard it would be to get back and forth to work and to the grocery store. If you had to walk everywhere you went you would probably quit work and stay home every day. What if there were no cell phones or house phones? You would not be able to call your friends or your boss to let him know you were sick and could not come to work. What if you had a medical emergency and could not call an ambulance to take you to the hospital. What if computers had not been invented, you would not be able to get on the internet and search for things on Ebay or even research information for your homework. Without television it would be hard to get weather and news information. The thing that is the most important that we take for granted is life. Life seems even more important when you have Christ as your Savior.

These are just a few of the everyday things we take for granted. I hope this has boggled your mind and caused you to think about all of the things in your life that are precious and are gifts from God that we take for granted every day.

Taylor Walker, Grade 8
Trinity Christian Academy, AL

My Father

My dad can do anything. His name is Harold Dempsey Woosley. He is not my biological father, but my foster dad. He is 65 years old, we live in Chelsea Oklahoma. It has been a pretty good town in the five years that I've lived here. My dad grew up in West Virginia; he lived there for a long tome, and learned how to swim in Lake Michigan.

He teaches me things like how to work on cars. He fixes, and does body work on cars, trucks, and anything else you can imagine. He is really good at math, and can read almost four chapter books each evening. He usually works from 6:00 or 7:00 a.m. to 1:00 or 2:00 p.m. every day. He puts up with a lot of things from everyone without getting mad. He lets me slide with a lot of things, but he lets me know when I do wrong. He has always been there for me since I have been with him. I think he is one of the best people in Oklahoma. He has been almost everywhere in the United States. He is strong as an ox, and as sly and a fox. He loves to joke around a lot. I know that he is not famous, but he has a really good point in a lot of lives. He always makes people laugh, and feel good about themselves.

Ely Woosley, Grade 7
Chelsea Jr High School, OK

I Meet the Tree

I was four years old and I had a miniature dirt bike. I was used to my dad traveling with me, but he decided I needed to take a spin on it by myself. I wanted to be just like him, but I was frightened. I didn't know how to ride it except for the part where you twist down the throttle and that made you go. I got all geared up and put my helmet on. My dad got the mini bike started, I got on, and I was ready to go. I put the bike in full speed and took the seemingly long journey, even though it was only about twenty feet. I didn't know how to stop it and I wasn't sure how to turn. Right there was a humongous pine tree right in front of me and I smacked right into it! I tumbled over the handle bars and my parents were in shock of amazement. Luckily, I only had a bruise on my leg, but after that, I didn't ride the dirt bike for a couple years after that.

Jasmine Kemman, Grade 7
Osceola Creek Middle School, FL

The Best Gift

Who do you talk to when you're upset? Who is the first person you talk to after something exciting happens? Often this person is your best friend. It would be hard going through the long, hard journey of life without someone walking beside you. Without friends you wouldn't have anyone to tell your deepest secrets or desires to, no one to spend time with, and nobody that can always make you smile.

Friends are important to me because if I'm having a bad day, they can always cheer me up. If I have a problem, my friends are always there for me, finding ways to help. When I'm writing stories, I know that I can bounce ideas off of them and always get truthful answers. Friends are an emotional support system holding you up through the good, the bad, and the worse. They are people that know everything about you and that you can trust with anything. Although being a good friend is sometimes hard, it is well worth it because friendship is the best gift you can receive.

Kristen Bilgere, Grade 8
St Gerard Majella School, MO

The Sims

Do you like video games? I personally think that *The Sims* is one of the coolest there is. You can do some pretty cool things on this game. You create a sim and basically rule their world. You tell them what to do and they do it. Recently The Sim's games creators made The *Sim's 2 Pets*, which is an awesome game. You can create either a cat or a dog, as well as your sim. It's just like real life: you have to make sure to feed, clean, and give your pet lots of attention. If not, it might run away.

Other things you can do is get a job. There are at least ten different job options. Every day if you have the right amount of friends and if you're happy enough you get a promotion. If you get enough promotions you get to go to work in a limo. I think *The Sims* is an awesome game.

Amber Fields, Grade 8
Dyer Elementary & Jr High School, TN

Heroes Are Dads

My dad deserves to be a hero. He is a Jack-of-all-trades who can build anything. He is incredibly smart and can figure out any problem thrown at him. He always has an answer for even my hardest questions. My dad is extremely fun to be around. He will wrestle with me and build all sorts of crazy contraptions and diabolical devices with me. We build potato cannons and rocket-propelled potato launchers. He still wrestles with me even though I am taller than he is.

My dad taught me everything I know. He taught me what I know from our endless hours tinkering with old radios and computers. We put in a computer network in church. We built and installed a radio network for a summer camp. We go on trips together to the dump and mess around with the crushers or go to Radio Shack to pick up parts.

Our favorite hobby is HAM Radio. We both have our HAM Radio licenses. Our favorite activity with HAM Radio is to volunteer at public service events together. Some of the events we volunteer at are the MS 150 Bike Tour, the Tour de Cure Bike Tour, The American Diabetes Association Walk, and The MS Society Walk.

My dad sacrifices his time and money for me. He works really hard to give me a great life and make me happy. He is always there for me when I need him. My dad is my hero.

Samuel Freeze, Grade 8
Leesville Road Middle School, NC

Hamzah's Artistic Skill

Art is an important part of my life. It started in kindergarten when I started to illustrate a lot of animals. I kept on making these creations and continued even today. Then a little bit later, I took the art test and scored a ninety-six on it. I am now in the art program and Jefferson Parish School System said that I should continue the art program up until high school.

The theme of my drawings, sculptures, or anything I do, changes almost every year. When I was 4, or somewhere around that age, I started to draw animals and dinosaurs and I loved to make clay creations of them. The teachers said that my sculptures were so good, that she had put them on display for everyone to see. Then when I moved from Pakistan to Austin, I had made a friend over there that was totally obsessed with cars. Every day when I went to his house, we always talked about cars and we had always played his favorite game: *Grand Turismo 2*. Then, I had started to get obsessed with cars too! I started to make drawings and some clay sculptures of cars and did it until 3rd grade. When I was in 3rd grade I had lost a little interest in cars and then learned about dragons and mythical creatures. Now, I have moved back to cars and other things in life. This is the history of my artistic skill.

Hamzah Khan, Grade 7
Haynes Academy for Advanced Studies, LA

Mothers

My topic is about why mothers are mothers, and why children and teens love and hate them.

The reason our mothers exist is so we can live. Even if we don't understand them, you still love them. Sometimes you might think they hate you, but you've got to understand they still love you. If you follow the Ten Commandments, you will make sure they know you love them.

Tell your mother you love her a lot. Try not to get in so much trouble. They don't want to hurt you, they would rather buy you stuff. Mothers love and care for you, but you have to love them, too.

We must always love our mothers no matter what. They love you more than anything in the world. So, love your mother because they do so much.

Adrianne Curry, Grade 7
Trinity Christian Academy, AL

The Deadly Night of 1912

Titanic was the sister of Britannica. She was on her very first voyage when on April 15, 1912 she sank to her watery grave.

Titanic was sailing from England to the New York harbor. Titanic was cruising along in the frigid Atlantic Ocean. It was around 11:40 p.m. April 14, 1912, when suddenly CRASH! Titanic skidded into an iceberg. This left the Titanic with a nasty scar. Rapidly, the furnace room was filling with water. The ship had six cavities and the crew knew that the ship would still stay above water with two cavities filled. Quickly they tried to get the men to safety, but they were taking on water too fast for them to react. While the crew was trying to escape, Captain Edward John Smith was trying to calm the people from panicking.

Slowly, they were first evacuating the women and children, then the men and the poverty people. Around 2:20 a.m. April 15, 1912 the Titanic broke into two sections, and sank quickly to the bottom of the Atlantic Ocean, never to be risen from its watery grave.

Erica Beck, Grade 8

Talent + Hard Work

If I could write about anything, it would be about my sports career. In my life, I have played in over 400-career basketball and football games combined and ran at over 40 track meets. I am a sports fanatic, but these three are by far my favorite.

Now, of the three, football stands out as my all time favorite sport, and without it I don't think I could live. I am the leading tackler on my football team. Someday I hope to take my talent and dedication to the college level and then to the pros. My dream is to play for the LSU Tigers. If I add hard work to my talent, I can fulfill my dreams. My dad always says, "Talent doesn't beat hard work if talent doesn't work hard." I'm going to keep that in mind and turn these dreams into reality.

Markus Wakefield, Grade 8
Heritage Hall School, OK

My Best Friend

My best friend was my grandpa. A person who I could talk to when I needed to talk to someone. I told him stuff I never told anybody in my life. I told it to him because I knew he wouldn't tell anybody. My grandpa was an awesome cook; he could cook a home meal dinner in like 30 minutes. That's not the only thing cool about him. Grandpa was a daredevil. One time he wrestled his pig that weighed 230 pounds. I mean this was a huge pig and its teeth were like the size of my index finger. He also jumped off this cliff at Lake Tenkiller. It was a huge cliff. Yet my grandpa was one awesome person who would do anything you wanted to do. He was a cool person, and he made as much out of his life as I could. He also loved dogs. Everywhere we went we had to bring his dogs with us. There was this one dog he loved the most, and he was name was Poncho. It was a wiener dog, and it was mean to people it didn't know. It was most definitely not the sharpest tool in the shed. My grandpa and I were walking to the truck. Poncho was chasing his tail, and he fell in a hole. It was funny! Grandpa died two years ago from cancer.

Blake Gordon, Grade 7
Stroud Middle School, OK

Solitude in School

Ever since I was enrolled in the Sevier County school system, I haven't pondered the thought of overcoming my antisociality. It started in about 2nd grade. I became so obsessed in my schoolwork, that I thought of nothing more. When we would go outside and people would asunder into their own little coteries, I always strayed askew to them. Another thing that made me alienate myself from them was the cacophony of vulgarness and the way they beleaguered anyone who was different. Finally, I was always a little more intelligent and mature than my fellow pupils and it was this gift that made me an outcast among them.

I have always been an A-B student. In previous grades I was mocked and teased for being a learning freak. Now I'm everybody's favorite partner in projects.

Recess; my least favorite time of the day. The rebellious ways and vulgarness of my pupils was almost too much to bear. Every day hearing them gloat of acts such as drugs made me giddy.

Dork, geek, loser. Common names of those choosing an education over rebellion. If you're different, enjoy school, or aren't part of a certain stuck-up coterie of *popular* people then, if they even take the effort to notice that you're there, you're just another one of their targets to take out their problems on.

In conclusion, enjoying learning and keeping to yourself is not being a loser, dork, or geek. As a matter of fact you're probably doing yourself a very good fait accompli for the future and no matter what people say they can't take that away from you. So if it makes you happy it doesn't matter what anyone else thinks!

Cherisse Wilkins, Grade 8
Pigeon Forge Middle School, TN

The Sweet Sound of Music

Imagining a world without music is very difficult. Think about how much it influences our lives. Where would themes for TV, background music for movies, and that annoying song that gets stuck in my head be without it? Like an android, talking would be an endless drone.

At my piano, I feel as if a river of angelic, pure melodies flows out of my fingers. Because I'm tiny and petite in size, it is tricky for me to have control over so many things, but when I play music, I have control over everything. I alone control whether the tune sounds like a tame, purring kitten or a vicious, roaring lion. Making music is a wonderful way to express emotions.

Musicians aren't the only ones influenced by beautiful tunes. If I look around, I'm sure to find someone humming their favorite song. When I watch movies, I don't think about the background music. But without it, the movie isn't half as good.

Like everything else, music isn't flawless. Life is a little bit like a concert when I think about it. The concert will be sounding perfect when I play an obviously wrong note. I feel horrible, but I have no choice but to move on. Eventually, everything turns out to be all right.

Each person has a favorite type of music, but I can't make up my mind. People say something pretty is eye candy, right? Well, all music is ear candy for me.

Elizabeth Ji, Grade 7
White Station Middle School, TN

Oklahoma's Great Kicker

Young National Football League "NFL" kicker Josh brown lines up to knock down the 61 yard field goal after practice. He gets his steps, gives the que to snap the ball, kicks it, and it flies through the goal post. This is just one of the many kicks he made during his college career.

Josh Brown began his life in Tulsa, OK when in the 8th grade he moved to Foyil, OK and that's when he started playing football. While attending Foyil Public Schools Josh played many positions in football including running back, safety, punter, place kicker, kickoff returner, and punt returner. He also won state in high-jump jumping a whopping 6 foot 8 inches. He later went on to play college football, for the NCAA, at the University of Nebraska.

After entering the NFL draft in 2003 and being picked in the 8th round 7th pick, 222nd overall pick, Brown continued his football career with the Seattle Seahawks as a place kicker even though we know he is capable of much more. While with the Seahawks his career long field goal is 48 yards. Brown is now ranked one of the best kickers in the NFL right now and has many more games to be played for the Seahawks and possibly many more teams.

Justin Platner, Grade 8
Chelsea Jr High School, OK

What R&B Means to Me

To me R&B means more than rhythm and blues, it is the art of sound. It relaxes the soul and soothes the mind. R&B is soft and isn't difficult to understand. That's my kind of music!

I listen to all types of R&B. Some are romantic, some sad, and some tell life stories or experiences.

There are many different composers of R&B music. For example; J. Holiday, Fantasia, Musiq Soulchild, and Mariah Carey, who are also my favorites. When I listen to R&B I think of all the good things that have and can happen to me.

Listening to R&B music is one of my favorite hobbies. It calms me down when I'm angry or sad. I listen to it when I'm cleaning, doing homework, or sleeping. From this you should know what R&B means to me.

Jasmine Stone, Grade 8
Turner Middle School, GA

Volleyball

Volleyball is a fun sport. I absolutely love the sport of volleyball. It is played by six people on each team.

In volleyball, you have six people on each side of the court. You have a setter, a spiker, a server and three people to back them up. One side serves the ball and the other side plays defense to retrieve the ball and score a point. If the ball is served out of bounds the opposite team gets the ball. If you want to be a good player you must practice every day with the team and without the team. You must also show team work in order to win the game and everyone needs to work together and encourage one another in order to accomplish the task. You must move your feet to get to the ball. I love volleyball because I like playing on a team. I like showing team work and good sportsmanship.

God gave us volleyball to enjoy and as a talent for us to be able to play the sport with good attitudes and Godly manners for the audience to witness; also for us to show good sportsmanship when we don't win.

Alicia Franklin, Grade 8
Trinity Christian Academy, AL

America at Its Worst

What I chose to write about is the U.S. Civil War. This was a war fought between North and the South. Or the Union and Confederate states. This war was about slavery. How the North thought it was wrong and the South wanted it. A lot of the South just wanted slavery for the money. See this way they didn't have to pay for manual labor. They wanted people to pick their things that they grew without having to pay them. But the North thought that owning people was wrong. This was a very upsetting time for the United States. There was brother fighting brother, families getting ripped apart, and houses getting destroyed. Thousands of people died in this war. But in the end the North won. Slavery was made illegal and the North was happy. But that still remains one of the biggest tragedies ever in the U.S. history.

Anna Madden, Grade 7
Excelsior Springs Middle School, MO

When Mae Went to Heaven

Sometimes, when something seems bad, good things can come from it. When I found out that Mae Moss had cancer, I couldn't believe it. Mae was my best friends' grandma, but I felt as though she was my grandma too. Mae was taken to a hospital then later transferred to a nursing home. She wasn't herself and she was in pain. When Mae Moss died it was sad; however good came out of her death.

At first, Mae's death seemed horrible, but good came from it. She gave a lot of encouragement to people and she was an example towards everyone. When she died, a lot of people felt like they lost a family member, even if they were not a relative. Good came out of her death though. Somebody unexpectedly came to ask her for forgiveness. Mae's family, that hadn't come together for a long time, were all at the nursing home to see her. Also, Mae told us that since a lot of people were coming to visit her, it was like having her visitation before her funeral. The best thing that came out of her death, was showing us the hope she had in spending eternity with God in heaven.

I realized after Mae died that her purpose on earth had been fulfilled. God was ready for her to be with Him, and Mae was ready to go to heaven. When Mae Moss died it was sad, but in the end good things came from it.

Shelby Creson, Grade 8
College Heights Christian School, MO

Building an Acoustic Guitar

The making of guitars, also known as luthiery, is a long and difficult process. For some people, like my dad, it's how they make a living. There are many steps to making a guitar: shaping the body, neck and putting on the finish.

To bend the guitar's sides, the wood is soaked in water, then bent over a heat blanket that is on top of a mold. The guitar's back is then cut out from a hardwood, then braced for stiffness. Next the guitar's top plate is cut from a softwood. The top is then thinned and braced.

The guitar's neck is made from mahogany. It is cut out, then rough shaped, then sanded. The peghead is the area where the turning pegs are placed. The fingerboard is usually made of ebony and it must be fretted with metal frets.

The finish on the guitar is important because it is what people see and feel. First you prepare the wood by sanding it with fine sandpaper, then blow all the wood dust out of the pores in the wood. Next you wipe on a coat of shellac. Next you spray as many as twelve coats of lacquer, spraying only four coats a day. Then you rub out and polish the finish with super fine sandpaper and rubbing compounds.

Making of guitars is a long and difficult process with many steps, like shaping the body, the neck, and putting on the finish. For some people it's how they make a living.

Nathan Mermer, Grade 7
Sebastian River Middle School, FL

Global Warming

Global warming is the climate change and warming of the globe. No one is sure when global warming started, but they now know when consequences could conclude, in between 10 and 35 years, if actions aren't taken. Global warming by what scientists have said, is caused by the pollution of the air and burning of CO_2 emissions. CO_2 emissions are fossil fuels and other air polluting gases, like gasoline, and coal. Other things that pollute the air and harm the planet are things like not recycling the making of plastic bottles and appliances, and not conserving energy. All of this pollution has led to melting of the polar ice caps in both Antarctica and Greenland. The melting of these glaciers scientists believe can cause catastrophic consequences. They say it could cause the gulf stream in the Atlantic Ocean to stop, stopping the flow of warm water which warms the surface of the ground. That would cause an ice age in parts of North America, South America, Africa, and Europe. Others believe that the warming of the planet would overwhelm any cooling. That would cause more hurricanes and cyclones in the oceans of the Pacific and Atlantic. Also there could be more droughts world wide, making food scarce. Which could lead to wars over remaining food, water, and fuel. Ways to fight global warming are by conserving energy, and using cleaner fuels. To conserve energy, turn off lights when not in use, and use the compact fluorescent bulb. But most importantly, find cleaner fuels like solar wind electricity and hydrogen, to stop this crisis.

Nicholas Faldetta, Grade 7
Harvard Academy, FL

Construction Zone*

When you think of construction you think of sweaty workers on a hot summer day. I would have never thought of my house as a construction zone, until the day the fathers on 116th Terrace helped knock down a wall in my house. During that time all the children of 116th Terrace gathered into my bedroom. While all the tools were banging all the kids were playing. All the children were going crazy jumping on my bed, running around, throwing clothes everywhere and playing hide and go seek. There was yelling and screaming, pushing and shoving, it was a room of wild animals. We were all having fun while being crazy, but yet I was a little upset my room was a total disaster. We all really had and awesome time though. Telling secrets, playing games, listening to music, and being with each other. The children of 116th Terrace all were like a part of my family. We did everything together, from teaching each other to tie our shoes to playing football at the park across the street. I'll never forget that day with the friends that will always be with me.

AnnaLina Felicella, Grade 7
Osceola Creek Middle School, FL
*Dedicated to the children of 116th Terrace.

Beauty from Pain

In some people's lives God will make beauty come from pain. I, in my short years, have experienced this already.

I was a premature baby born to an unmarried girl of fifteen. I was abandoned at a hotel along with my one year old brother. We were placed in an emergency foster home for a week. They sent us to another foster home when I was only two months old. We had been there for only an hour when Bonnie called a nurse and asked her to come look at me on her lunch hour because I was sick and she was nervous. When she walked in the door my one year old brother ran up to her, held up his arms and said "Momma" and she saw me sick with thin grey skin and enormous blue eyes. God moved in her heart and she knew at that moment we were supposed to be hers. She and her husband had lost four babies and hadn't considered adoption. This started to the journey to where I am now. With much effort and patience our adoption became complete on June 23, 1997.

I went from being homeless to being part of a large, loving family. I have three brothers and a mom and dad. I believe God has put me here for a special purpose. He has truly brought beauty from pain.

Natalie Gariss, Grade 8
College Heights Christian School, MO

Preserving Our Environment

Preserving our environment is a concern of many people today. We are discovering new ways to help our environment. We are using prescribed burns, wildlife refuges, and pollution control to help.

Prescribed burns are a good way to help the environment and people. They reduce the risk of wildfire by making the grass green so it will not catch fire. They also control Eastern Red Cedar, which helps the wildlife. Burning the land reduces human asthma and allergy problems.

Wildlife refuges help the native habitat in that area. They manage the native wildlife species. Wildlife refuges also protect the land from development in that area.

Pollution control is another concern. Air pollution causes harm to the atmosphere and plants. Chemicals being dumped into the water can cause great damage. The animals and fish that need the water could get injured from the contaminated water. If these things were stopped then we would not have these problems.

Harm done to the environment can cause even more harm to the animals and people. We depend on our environment to meet our needs. Prescribed burns are a great way to preserve the environment since they reduce many risks. Wildlife refuges help maintain the habitats and prevent development from occurring. A wildlife injury from pollution harms our food sources if the water is polluted. Controlling pollution will help our wildlife problems. Preserving the environment should not be an issue that we take lightly. If we want our environment to stay then we need to control pollution and use these practices to help out the environment.

Ashley Weir, Grade 9

Try Again

Cheering and applause recedes from the atmosphere and everyone holds their breath again. Adrenaline pumps through me once more. I am ready. I have practiced this over and over again. Time grips at my heart and pumps it harder with every second passing. My arms float calmly at my sides. I swallow and breathe heavily. A whistle screams and everyone is alert. The crisp sound that shot through the air has awakened them. They are all staring at one target…the volleyball. "Serve receive!" a faint voice shouts from afar. "Boom!!!" Time stands still as the volleyball floats toward our side of the court. I find myself at the net, ready to set. "Mi-ne!" someone screams. They are unsure of themselves. I become ready for anything. The ball hovers over the net and suddenly time bolts out a shock wave of energy and movement. A fist barely reaches the ball and smashes into it. A player is on the floor and other teammates stand and let their shoulder sink. They have given up. A surge of aggression throws me spiraling toward the ball, hands clasped above my head. I keep track of gravity and push my hands upward. The ball rockets up speeding parallel to the net, but it is too late. Others were not ready for a save. Arms flail and it crashes out of bounds. A whistle sounds. It is time to get back up and try again.

Natalie Braden, Grade 8
Heritage Hall School, OK

When I Got My Braces

Getting braces is a very difficult process to experience. When I went to get my braces on, I was very nervous, and I had to miss two hours of school.

I left school and went straight to my orthodontist appointment. When I got to the orthodontist's office and was called back, I went to the treatment room. The orthodontic assistant laid me back in a large reclining chair, put clear plastic holders in my mouth to hold it open, and then cleaned my teeth. A suction tube was placed in my mouth to make the gums around my teeth as dry as possible. She then put a special type of glue on my teeth. The orthodontist laid the little metal square parts of the braces on my teeth before the glue dried. While the glue was hardening, she removed all the excess. To help the glue harden she used a special light. After that, she put the metal wires in place.

After my appointment, I returned to school. I was able to eat pain free right after I got my braces, but later, during my other classes, my teeth gradually began to start hurting. I was so sore that night, I could hardly eat and my gums hurt for a few days. I had to get used to the feel of braces, because they are very uncomfortable. Braces make you feel like you have a bunch of metal behind your lips. Braces may hurt, but they help straighten your teeth.

Lydia Todd, Grade 7
Providence Classical School, AL

What My Family Means to Me

My family is so hard on me. They want me to make the right choices. My mother is the working lady! She makes sure I come to school each and every day. She makes sure I don't play in school. My daddy is the money man he gives me money every day, that's why I love him so much. I love my sister so much that when she leaves the house I am like where you going, she is like nowhere that is why I love my sister so much. Now my brother means a lot to me. When I am in trouble he is there to help with my problems. He keeps me out of trouble. My brother and sister are so helpful. In my family they help around the house and help my grandmother with her bills. My mother and daddy make sure I have clothes on my back and shoes on my feet. When you see my family you will see a big happy family.

Le'Nard Brown, Grade 8
Turner Middle School, GA

What My Family Means to Me

My family means a lot to me. Most of the time we have fun together. They make sure I come to school each and every day. Also, my family makes sure that I make the right choices in life. One example is that I have a roof over my head. Another reason is that I have food at the table, clothes on my back, and someone whom I can talk to.

Although my dad doesn't live with me, he still shows love. My family sends me to school to learn, and not to play. They want me to show a good example for my sisters. My family's goal for me is to go to college, and be successful in life. Another thing they want me to do is to have a great job.

Finally my family means a lot to me to be supportive of me. My family will sacrifice their last dime for me and every Sunday they always are cooking big dinners. For example, when we are having company, my family loves to cook. The most important thing that my family means to me is that they love me a lot and I cherish all of them as well.

Quivadas Hutchison, Grade 8
Turner Middle School, GA

Stand Up

A time I stood up for myself was when I was twelve years old. My friend, Blaine, and I were walking by an abandoned house. Blaine took a lighter and a piece of paper out of his pocket. He wanted to burn down the house, and I took the lighter out of his hand. He asked why I had done that, and I said, "We can't burn down a house."

He said I was no fun, and he tried to take the lighter out of my hand. I took my hand out of his reach and threw the lighter into a field. He started toward the field, and I grabbed him and started dragging him home to tell his mom.

When we got there, his mom was on the porch. I told her what Blaine had wanted to do. He was punished for a couple of weeks. When his punishment ended, Blaine came to my house, and he thanked me for what I had done. We played at the house, and we are friends forever.

Brett Simmons, Grade 8
Delcambre High School, LA

The Great Declaration of Independence

There are many great things about the Declaration of Independence; the 1300 words that made this country free. Who do we to thank for this? Well, the 56 great human beings who made it possible.

One such man is Thomas Stone; a lawyer who died following his wife at the age of 44. Some even came from simple merchants like one of the greatest, John Hancock, who died at age of 83. One of the smartest men ever, Ben Franklin, died at age of 84. Even a future president, Thomas Jefferson who died at 62.

July 4, 1776 is one of the most important days ever in America. Today we call it Independence Day or the 4th of July. When we say this, all kids think BBQ or fireworks or even camping, but what they should think is freedom, liberty, and the red, white, and blue.

They should be saying God Bless America, or at least, God Bless our troops in Iraq. Say to yourself, what does it mean to you? When you look at 56 names on that parchment you think things were so bad back then, and we have it so good thanks to them. So the next time you see July 4th on your calendar, instead of thinking fireworks, say a little thanks to those 56 people — the great signers of the Declaration of Independence.

Sean Huff, Grade 7
Stroud Middle School, OK

The First Shot Heard Around the World: The Events on March 5, 1770

People today know what the Boston Massacre was. However, many don't know how the Boston Massacre was the first bold trigger of revolutionary spirits in the colonies. It impacted everyone in America, and many in Great Britain, during that time and provoked a sense of patriotism. Three events played a role in the start of the revolution: the Townshend Acts, the Massacre, and Captain Thomas Preston's trial.

The Townshend Acts were taxes on widely used products, though tea was the only tax that lasted. This tax brought about a disapproval of the government. Colonists protested the act, and this led to an increase in Regulars in cities.

Now known as the Boston Massacre, March 5, 1770 was a dispute between a wigmaker and an officer over a debt that escalated into a shooting. As tempers rose, Redcoats shot into a crowd killing 5 men. This murder fueled the Patriot cause and made people choose sides: freedom or loyalty.

Captain Thomas Preston was the leader of the Regulars on the day of the Massacre and six months later was tried for murder. The topic of the hearing was whether or not Preston ordered the men to fire. He was cleared of all charges, and 2 of the 8 officers were convicted of manslaughter.

Though the Boston Massacre wasn't a mass killing, it was the day that first shot of the coming revolution happened. It was the first time Regulars had shot colonists, and this day led to independence.

Rana Aliani, Grade 8
The Barstow School, MO

My Own World: Books

I'm flying like the wind over the grasslands. The real world stays behind me, waiting for me to return from those wonderful books. Creative books pull me into themselves, away from everything else. They make me feel like I'm a soaring star running wild through the universe. Nobody can catch me, for I am too evasive for them. I race back into my books, who help me escape, blocking out all my troubles.

I'm a navy ship in the thrashing seas. I set my course and battle vicious, plundering pirates. After many weeks of carefree treasure hunting, I finally catch a glimpse of the harbor and the lighthouse. I fight on through the harshness of the world, back into my haven: my books. I'm safe now, dry and cozy, in my books.

With sudden violence, Reality drags me from my sanctuary, and I must give up the struggle to face the brutal world. Miserable, I bid goodbye to my books, who forlornly say farewell. Already I feel a dark shadow creeping upon me and a chill crawling up my spine. I must face Reality now and be ready to shine and show the world what I can do.

Patrick Harrison, Grade 7
White Station Middle School, TN

Mexico

Let me tell you a little about Mexico. A holiday that we celebrate in Mexico is Day of the Dead Ones on November 2nd. A Quinceañera is a big party with everybody. This is an important date in Mexico; the Independence Day of Mexico. This is a reason why you should visit Mexico.

On Day of the Dead Ones people go to the cemetery and bring food to the dead ones. An enchilada is a tortilla filled with chicken inside (good). Pozole is like a hot, spicy soup that tastes very good. We also celebrate Our Lady of Guadalupe (religion). I just gave you another reason to visit Mexico.

A Quinceañera is very important for a teenage girl. There is always plenty of food like mole, meat, and more. You go to church, then to the party room, and eat and much more. When the Quinceañera comes out, behind her comes the Mariachis. You get to share really important moments with everybody.

The Independence Day of Mexico is important. People decorate their cars with Mexico's flag. At night the president yells "Viva Mexico!" A parade is done; some people go walking and others go driving. They sell food and snacks.

You should visit Mexico. There is a lot of culture and interesting things. You should go to a Quinceañera. You should go and see the Independence of Mexico. Mexicans believe a lot of Our Lady of Guadalupe. I gave you a lot of reasons to visit Mexico, so hurry. Mexico is a very tourist place.

Maria Vazquez, Grade 7
Sebastian River Middle School, FL

A Score

Pure satisfaction is the only thing I feel when I score a goal. I am usually battling in the back trying to keep people from scoring. However, on this occasion our center midfielder arrived late so I got the chance to play up. I tried to take advantage of this chance right away, pushing forward every chance I got. Despite my attempts to score, I could not penetrate their defense. With endless drops of sweat pouring off of me, I knew a sub would come soon. Making up my mind, I received the ball and began a give and go along the left sideline; I had to score. My attempt once again failed. By this time, I was breathing heavily, but there were no excuses, getting on the board first was imperative if we wanted to win the game. Finally, a chance arose: I got the pass from our defense, turned, and saw nothing but beautiful green grass. In an instant, I shot off. This was the daylight I needed, nothing but one defender and the goalie. Sprinting as fast as I could, my mind was racing: should I be a good teammate and pass it to my streaking companion or go for the gold myself? I faked left and cut right. I had a perfect shot. Swinging back with all my might, I launched the ball into its curving flight pattern. It wailed in right over the goalie's outstretched arms. I was screaming at the top of my lungs, feeling only one thing: pure satisfaction.

Rob Jaffe, Grade 7
White Station Middle School, TN

Queen Elizabeth

Queen Elizabeth was one of the greatest rulers in England. She loved England very much and did whatever it took to protect it. Elizabeth was Henry VIII and Anne Boleyn's daughter. She had a half-sister named Mary and a half-brother named Edward VI. Elizabeth was greatly loved by England.

Religion was very important in the sixteenth and seventeenth centuries. Three hundred people were martyred by Elizabeth's Catholic half-sister, Queen Bloody Mary, during her reign. Mary wanted to kill Elizabeth too, since she was Protestant. During Elizabeth's 45 year reign, Englishmen encouraged Good Queen Bess to murder her cousin, Mary Stuart, for religious reasons.

Elizabeth, who was a strategic military leader, won against the Spanish Armada. King Philip II was the Spanish leader, and in his defeat he said, "I sent my ships to fight against men and not against the winds and waves of God."

Elizabeth was such a dedicated and focused queen that she never got married. The fact that she never got married earned her the name of "The Virgin Queen." Her people returned that dedication and loved her greatly.

In summary, Queen Elizabeth loved her people a lot. Although Mary wanted to kill her, Good Queen Bess turned out to be one of the greatest rulers in England. Elizabeth was a great military leader. The Virgin Queen was also a strong Protestant and ready to stand up for her faith. Elizabeth was a dedicated queen and was loved by her people a lot.

Faith Buckley, Grade 7
Providence Classical School, AL

Danger Behind the Wheel

You see them, barely peering over the steering wheel, stopping at imaginary stop signs, not stopping at real stop signs, driving slow in the fast lane, and drifting into other lanes. They drive with their blinkers on even over a bridge. It's hazardous for them to drive during the day, but at night they pose an even bigger threat. They are the elderly drivers.

As people grow older, their senses become duller; thus, their driving skills decreases. But, like all of us, they don't want their independence taken away from them. However, sooner or later, it has to be. Recently, an elderly woman made headlines when she drove through a school cafeteria, killing a student and injuring a few others.

It is common knowledge that some people age differently than others. My eighty-five-year-old great uncle is in excellent heath. He is as nimble as a cat, takes no medication, and wakes up at 5:30 every morning to take care of his farm. Others can lose their senses even at an early age. Should the family be responsible for taking their keys, or should the government pass a law? Whatever the verdict, is independence worth the risk of human life?

Jack Witthaus, Grade 8
St Gerard Majella School, MO

Role Models

Great role models are people we look up to, but what does it take to be a great role model? It takes hard work, discipline, and determination; those three things are the foundation to a great role model. They don't do anything illegal and have a positive message to send to other people.

In life role models work hard to reach their goals and they succeed at them. That's why we look up to them in such a high fashion and admire them. Great role models like Dwyane Wade exemplify hard work by practicing every day becoming better at what they do. Some great role models started from being bad and someone who didn't care about life. Then they turned around and became good little by little.

Great role models have always had good discipline everywhere either in public or private places they have good discipline. They know when it's play time and when it's time to work, they don't fool around. They set a good example for other people to follow. If a role model doesn't have discipline he would be sending a bad example to kids and others.

Determination to role models is probably the most important thing about them. If someone doesn't have determination they won't make it anywhere. When a role model is determined to something, they do it no matter what. Great role models are made of hard work, discipline and determination. That's what it takes.

Federico Molina, Grade 8
Ponce De Leon Middle School, FL

The Military Protects Us as They Serve in Iraq
(The Brave Will Rise, the Weak Will Fall)

The war in Iraq has ended people's lives. The war is a good thing though; it has given us a sense of protection and safeness. The war in Iraq would have come no matter what we did. The war would have started one way or another because of the disagreements of the United States government and the Iraqi government. The dispute between them is how to run their country, and how to just do things your way and not try it their way just once. But, we are going to fight back with all the firepower we have and give them a kick right in the rear to show them how the Americans do this thing. We are not just going to sit around and let them take over our country. The war will soon end, and our troops will come home with the sense of pride and a good feeling, because they served our country, and they deserve the respect that you would give to the president of the United States.

The feeling of having a soldier there gives you mixed emotions, and it makes you worry a lot. When the war comes to an end, the soldiers will stand at attention, and yell at the top of their lungs, "Hooah! we are victorious." The men and women there that have fallen in battle should be honored equally, because they fought and lost their lives for their country, and they protected us.

Keith Woolverton, Grade 7
Stroud Middle School, OK

My Bat Mitzvah

September twenty-ninth at six fifty in the morning, and my alarm clock goes buzzing off to the newest songs on the radio. I rolled out of bed extremely excited. I ate a bagel, brushed my teeth, and did my hair. It was the big day I have been waiting for my Bat-Mitzvah. My family and I hurried to Temple Israel to meet my friend and her family. I was having my Bat-Mitzvah with Rachel, my best friend. Rachel and I took some pictures and told our families, who had come from near and far, what they needed to do during the Bat-Mitzvah service.

Rachel and everyone else who would be seated up on the bimah, which is like a pulpit, went back behind it to a little meeting room where she and I shared a prayer and calmed down. Rachel and I were not nervous though until we got out on the bimah. We went through the whole service, reading out of the Torah, saying what it means to us, leading the service, and thanking special people for coming.

Afterwards, Rachel and I were so happy and everybody was saying Mazel Tov, which means congratulations, about how good we had been. All I could say was "thank you" to every person who came to compliment me. This was an experience I will never forget, and I will always remember how important my Bat-Mitzvah is to me.

Cara Levi, Grade 7
White Station Middle School, TN

Moving

When writing about something true in my life, the first thing that comes to mind is moving. Moving is not fun. You lose your friends. You also have to transfer schools and start all over again. But you do get to go through everything and find new things. Here's an explanation.

To begin, when you move the hardest part is saying good-bye to your friends. When you get to school you just wanna bury yourself under a rock and never come out. When your friends ask you "What's wrong?" you have to tell them. Now you have to leave and make new friends. Sometimes you can't stop yourself from thinking, "Who am I going to talk to? Who am I going to share secrets with?" But somehow, you can always make new friends and everything seems all right again.

Next, when you move you have to start all over again when working hard for grades. It makes you feel like you've worked so hard for it just to be yanked away like snatching candy from a baby. You have to work extra hard when moving because at your new school, you don't have as many grades as everyone else. But usually you work so hard you can bring up your grade without even knowing it!

Also, there's one thing that kinda benefits. When you move, you get to go through everything you own. Most of the time you always find something you forgot you had or something you have lost.

So to conclude, writing about something true in my life is about moving. You lose your friends, but you make new ones. You have to start over when moving, but that's ok. You also get to go through all your stuff so that's good. Moving can be good and bad!

Amber Kinton, Grade 8
Pigeon Forge Middle School, TN

Important Challenges

I have had many challenges in my life, two of them have occurred during this past year. One will affect me for the rest of my life and the other is a tough personal goal. Two stress fractures and a displaced vertebra in my back will affect me for the rest of my life and pose a difficult challenge because I have to work hard to achieve my personal goals. I have to do back exercises everyday to strengthen my muscles to keep my backbones in place. Months ago Dr. Herndon, my doctor, questioned whether or not I would be able to participate in the activities and sports I enjoy most. Because of my diligence and hard work, I can take part in my sports, such as wakeboarding, dance, swimming, being a cheerleader, and many other activities. One of the sports I am able to enjoy is wakeboarding; this is the subject of my personal goal mentioned above. I have decided I am going to clear the wake, so every weekend we go to the lake I work hard to achieve this goal. I have cleared 4/5th of the wake; this is still short of my goal. I want to clear the wake because I have not seen a girl my age do this. I will clear the wake because I am very persistent, and I am determined to be successful.

Hayley Bock, Grade 8
Heritage Hall School, OK

Stranded

A few years ago my uncle invited my family to come to Florida to stay for the Fourth of July. He was going to have fireworks and he wanted my brother and me to be able to see them. So, we decided to go and stay for a week and we would come home that night after we watched the fireworks. It took us around 8 hours to get there, it was about 2 a.m. when we got there. So, we went to bed and every day we would either go swimming or we would go on the boat. It was the Fourth of July and this was our last day there. It was about time for the fireworks to start. We put down the anchor and we watched the fireworks. When it was over we looked at the water and it was not even a foot deep. We were STUCK!!! So, we called the coast guard and my dad had to walk from our boat to the coast guard's boat. He had to bring a rope and have it tied up to the other boat. The whole time my dad was walking across there was mullet jumping everywhere. The coast guard could not get us out. We had to spend the night on the boat and it was HORRIBLE!!! It had dirt in the bottom of the boat and it was cold. I will always remember that Fourth of July!!!

Christin Cox, Grade 8
Rhea Central Elementary School, TN

Caring for Goats

Goats are fun animals to raise. They also serve many useful purposes. They produce milk and meat, as well as, fiber for spinning into yarn. Goats also make excellent weed eaters. Caring for goats is not difficult. They require simple housing, will eat just about anything, and come in many different breeds.

The housing for goats does not have to be fancy. You can easily use an old shed for a goat house. Goats need a shelter that is well ventilated and provides protection from the elements. Since goats like company and you will probably have at least two, you will need plenty of space. You will also need strong fences, because they love to escape.

Goats graze pasture and browse woodland. When they do this, it costs less to maintain in hay or other goat supplements. If you are letting your goats graze or browse, you have to be careful that they don't eat poisonous plants such as milkweed, horse nettle, and Mountain Laurel.

There are many different breeds of goats. These include dairy, meat, and fiber goats. Dairy goats are ones that produce more milk than is needed to feed their babies. All over the world, many people eat goat meat. The three main goats in the U.S. are Boer, Spanish, and San Clemente. The goats which have long hair that can be spun into yarn are fiber goats such as Angora and Cashmere.

Goats are fun to raise, as long as you keep them away from your mom's flowers!

Clark Hunter, Grade 7
Stroud Middle School, OK

Who's Next?

"Home run!" We can hear the announcer's loud, excited voice. Then the thunderous roar from the excited crowd as we are getting our tickets for the Oklahoma State Softball Tournament in Oklahoma City, Oklahoma.

As I am walking through the front gates, I smell the popcorn. The sounds of the crowd cheering for their team and people talking to each other are ringing in my ears. I see the tan bricks on the outside wall of the stadium. Then I see it, the ASA softball field.

The softball field is beautiful! The fresh mowed, green grass is shining in the blinding sunlight. The dirt is muddy brown and is raked to perfection. The bases are as white as the clouds on a summer day. The fence is baby blue with a yellow railing at the top. The dugouts underneath the ground are filled with the softball players.

As the game before Chelsea's finished, Chelsea went on the field to warm up. The game was very tense. Everybody was nervous and on the edge of their seats. What was special about the game was that the Chelsea Lady Dragons softball team won the state championship in Oklahoma's centennial year, 2007.

I like going to the ASA softball fields not only because I love softball, but also because of the history of it and all of the people who have played on the fields. So when I go back next year, I will ask myself, who's next?

Darian Marone, Grade 7
Chelsea Jr High School, OK

Swimming

Swimming is my topic. Why did I choose swimming? Because I love it. First of all, it is really fun. Secondly, it builds up your strength. Lastly, it is relaxing.

Swimming is really fun. You go to swim meets and hang out with your friends. You also get to go to the concession stand and eat lots of candy and power bars. Plus, you really feel proud when you win your races. That is the first reason why I like swimming.

The second reason why I like swimming is because you build up your strength, technique, and speed. Each day you attend practice you get stronger. As you are swimming you try to go as fast as you can so you can improve in meets. Also, as you are swimming your coach shows you the proper technique. When you learn the proper technique there is an increased chance of you getting faster. That is the second reason why I like swimming.

Not only does swimming help you become a stronger swimmer and allow you to have fun, it's also relaxing. When you are swimming you can forget about everything. Your mind is set free. That is the third reason why I like swimming.

Those are some pretty good reasons as to why I like swimming, right? I know what everyone is thinking about right now. Going to swim and to see if those reasons are really true. Go ahead try it. I'm sure you'll agree.

Erin Trumbach, Grade 7
Boyet Jr High School, LA

Ancient Inventor

Do you know who invented the Cherokee Alphabet? It was invented by a guy named Sequoyah. Sequoyah was a tall Indian who wore a red turban on his head with feathers sticking out of it.

Sequoyah accomplished a lot in his long life. He was a skilled silversmith, a talented painter, and a skilled soldier.

Sequoyah was born in the 1770's at a village called Tuskegee located in the Rocky Mountains in present day Tennessee. In 1829 Sequoyah settled in a place called Skin Bayou near present day Sallisaw Oklahoma. Sequoyah never learned how to speak English even though he understood when he heard it. In many ways Sequoyah was among one of the greatest Cherokee people.

Sequoyah's one room log cabin (which he built himself in 1829) is protected by a stone covering. The cabin is now a national historic landmark and is open to the public.

Jeffery Cordrey, Grade 8
Chelsea Jr High School, OK

My Grandma

My grandma died on September 6, 2006. It has been a year since she has been dead and now that she's gone my family doesn't do anything anymore. We don't go on family vacations. We don't even have family reunions or anything and if we do go on family vacations or have family reunions there is either going to be some arguing or fighting.

I think the reason this is happening is because my grandma is gone. Everybody has stress on them. I know all of us miss the old times with my grandma on special holidays. We would record the whole family just having fun and laughing. Now my grandma is gone in a better place none of that even happens anymore.

If my grand ma was to be living right now I could go up to her and ask for anything I wanted and she would give it to me. Sometimes I wish my grandma was here. That is just how much I miss her. My grandma will always be in my heart form this day on until the day that I die. I love you Grandma.

Shanikiqa Groomes, Grade 8
Seminole County Middle/High School, GA

My Heroes

My heroes have to be my family. They are great! They always support me. All of my family helps me in some way. My grandparents always encourage me and tell me how good I do. My greatest hero is my mom, I can talk to her about anything. I love her so much, I love talking to her. She is like my best friend. My dad helps me do my homework and explains to me everything that I don't understand. My brother helps me in sports and other things. They all love me so much. My other hero is Jesus. I mean He died for my sins. He was perfect and He loved all people even His enemies. I love all of my heroes and I hope I will be able to be encouraging to my friends and family like they are to me.

Olivia King, Grade 7
Rhea Central Elementary School, TN

Pictures of the Past

Fall is coming, and I remember that this is how the weather was before I went to Kenya. The air is getting cool, and the leaves are changing. I grab the photo album containing pictures of my trips to Kenya and India, and I burrow into the warmth of my bed, ready to remember.

I went to Kenya, the most beautiful country in Africa, when I was seven years old. Benina, my doll, went with me. In every picture from that trip, her fuzzy head is poking out of my arms. Her cloth skin looks black as licorice against my white skin. Her red, embroidered mouth is in a little "o," as if she is crying to me. She is in every picture because I needed her with me.

I flip to the pictures of my trip to India, which I took earlier this year. While there, I rode elephants, saw comical lime-green parrots, became a teenager, and tread upon the marble floors of the Taj Mahal. I notice something that is different from the Kenya pictures. Benina is not in any of them. A feeling of joy bubbles up inside of me as I realize I no longer need a favorite toy to comfort me. I am growing up.

Suddenly I hear a strange noise outside. Without thinking, I grab Benina, who is on the bed beside me. I hold her tight and whisper into her ear, "I might be thirteen, but I'm not completely grown up yet."

Molly Marietta, Grade 8
Moseley Elementary School, OK

Cabin Time Is Chilling Time

Enid, Mississippi is where my lake house is located. There my family and I like to fish in our private pond where we have bass and brim. Enid Lake is where the world's biggest crappie was caught. Hunting deer is something my dad and I enjoy together. We go down there around once a month. We have a four-wheeler, a John Deer Gator, and a three-wheeler. We will occasionally bring friends and family along with us. It is twice the fun with someone extra to tag along. In the day Enid is clear with bright skies, but at night is where its beauty is really held.

When we have a fire I will just look up in the sky and see billions of stars that appear to be right where I can grab them. A pesky beaver will come out at night and slap its black tail and cut down all our trees. In our pond we have five mini type islands. I really enjoy taking the boat out and casting a couple of times. In the winter you can't do as much really, but you don't have to worry about mosquitoes and mowing the grass. Slipping on a jacket and walking up the gravel road and not having to worry about the scorching heat is marvelous.

My cabin is a thirty-seven acre piece of paradise where my family can come to lounge around and spend quality time.

Evan Ross, Grade 7
White Station Middle School, TN

Stop Motion Animation

Stop motion animation makes a physically manipulated object appear to move. The object is moved by very small amounts of space between individual pictures creating the illusion of movement when the pictures are played as a continuous sequence. Clay figures have been used in stop motion animations. Known as clay mation, for their ease of repositioning.

Stop motion is a great way to have fun, but it takes a long time to do. It is very hard to make stop motion films. When you make stop motion films you have to use a certain amount of pictures per second. The amount of pictures per second for movies is 30 pictures. So if you make a movie that is 30 seconds long it will take 900 pictures. Therefore it would take a very large amount of your time to make a stop motion film. Many movies and television shows like Wallace and Gromet have been made by stop motion. These movies have been more than 90 minutes long. The directors and producers had a have a lot of time on their hands to make these movies. Stop motions films have been a great success.

Stop motion films have been a great success even though they take a very long time to make. Stop motions films are very fun to make. My dad and I have made stop motion films, and we had a blast making them. But we also saw how much effort you have to put into them.

Kristen Athon, Grade 8
Trinity Christian Academy, AL

A Journey to My Birthland

A person always has a special attachment to his or her birthplace. So do I. My birthplace is India, which is very rich in different cultures and religions. Although I have been here in America for a long time, I still miss my birthland. Some of my best friends are still there. Finally, September 27th, 2006 was the day when I reached India with my family.

Indian culture is very interesting. There are all different kinds of people, different lifestyles, food, and clothing. Whoever goes to India really enjoys the Indian culture. I also enjoy different kinds of food. My brother and my little sister also enjoy it.

India is a country that has many different religions. Hindus, Muslims, Sikhs, Christians, Jains, Bhudhists; all live in India and celebrate each other's festivals together. I belong to the Sikh religion and visited many Sikh Gurudwaras. We offered prayers and got mental peace. We also visited Hindu temples.

My best friends were also waiting for me. I enjoyed my time a lot with my old friends. We played our favorite game, cricket. My great-grandparents, grandparents, aunts, and uncles also live in India. They were so happy to see us.

A person always has a special attachment to his or her birthland. I am also attached to the place where I spent beautiful times in my early life. As we still have family and friends in India, I plan to visit every 2 years. I really enjoyed my trip.

Tegpreet Singh, Grade 7
Sebastian River Middle School, FL

My Best Friend, Kerry

Friend. Your sister or brother mysteriously separated from you at birth. The other half of you. On the first day of fourth grade, I met all that and more when Kerry Cleys came to St. Mary's.

A girl with lots of freckles, monkey ears, and a purple giraffe print book bag was sitting Indian-style in line, waiting for Mrs. Campbell to take her new fourth grade class upstairs. Throughout fourth and fifth grade, Kerry and I were hardly ever apart. However, our friendship would soon be put to the test.

Things didn't turn out how I had hoped. On the last day of school in 2005, it was the last day I was going to be with Kerry at St. Mary's, because she was now going to attend St. Joseph's.

However, I think that our separation has strengthened our friendship. Carowinds, comparing yearbooks, and sharing hilarious stories about our schools are just some of the great times Kerry and I have had in the summer. Even though a different school usually means new friends, Kerry and I are still as close as ever. Kerry's personality is the same one I knew in fourth grade: loyal and entertaining.

The thing I remember most about Kerry is her famous quote, "Laugh as much as possible, because it adds one extra minute to your life." Wherever I end up in life, I will always be able to call Kerry my best friend.

Colleen Campbell, Grade 8
St Mary's School, SC

Statement to Folks

In middle school I received good grades. I was so determined to get straight A's; I did my homework, sat in front of the classroom, and took the time out to study. By doing all of that I got six A's and 2 B's. But ever since 8th grade when I transferred schools, I have become lazy and procrastinating.

My report cards always had a D or an F. My highest GPA was a 2.9, pitiful, I know. Every time report cards were sent home, I would look at mine and say, "Next time I'll be on the honor roll," and it never happened, but since I had grades okay enough to stay in the magnet program, I got accepted to Baton Rouge High School.

I told all my friends that I was going to Baton Rouge High, and they'd laugh and tell me I'm going to fail the eighth grade. One day, a friend said, "You're going to be gone before the semester is over." Even my mom thought I would fail, but I passed the eighth grade.

Now I go to Baton Rouge High, and I'm doing okay, but I plan to prove a point to everyone around me. I'm going to accomplish my goals so I can get out of high school, and graduate as one of the top in my class.

Janetta Ross, Grade 9
Baton Rouge Magnet High School, LA

Car Crash

My brother and I will never forget the day I was "hit" by a car. We used to always ride home from school along 162nd. One blistering day we were very animated and trying to get home as soon as possible. My brother yelled out, "Race you!" We started to accelerate. Then all of a sudden I heard a myriad amount of noise behind us. It was just a golf cart going in the opposite direction. I looked at my brother deftly and he grinned. All of sudden his face went sour as a lemon and he shrilled at the top of his lungs, "Stop!" I didn't stop but made a face that queried him. Then I quickly turned my head and everything went black.

It felt like an eternity, but it only took a couple seconds for me to get up. I felt like I was hit by a car. I looked up and realized that I was hit by a car. My knee became cramped and thrived in pain. After a while when I collected my bearings, I figured out that I ran into a parked pickup truck. The people that owned the truck came rushing out saying they heard a heap of clamor. They made sure I was fine and offered to take me home in their truck of doom. I got up and told them I would make it. I then slowly walked home and rested for days.

We'll never forget that day.

Tim Sumell, Grade 7
Osceola Creek Middle School, FL

Touring Treasures

In the summer of 2005, my family and I embarked on a two-week journey to Alaska. The first week was a land tour, and the second week we were to take a cruise. During the first week we toured Mt. McKinley National Park, and the most amazing thing happened.

As we neared the middle of the tour, our park guide spotted a female grizzly bear and her two cubs. The family stopped about thirty feet away from our bus, and the mother began to nurse her cubs right in front of us. We were particularly intrigued by this unusual happening and couldn't believe that a protective mother grizzly would feel so safe around people. Nonetheless, we didn't question and just took as many pictures as we could. We did, however, question our guide on how rare this sighting was, and she said in her seventeen years or so of working in the park, this had only happened twice before. After about eight or ten minutes, the grizzly family got up and disappeared around a nearby giant rock. All of the astonished people on the tour where chattering about our incredible experience. I was a little surprised myself. Once our throng of people had settled down, we drove on to view the rest of the park.

Looking back toward one of the mountains in the park, I noticed the three brown grizzlies climbing steadily up the side of it. My intimate experience of wildlife was truly incredible.

Amelia Ramsey, Grade 7
White Station Middle School, TN

The Life of Others

My name is Batiste Stewart and this is my story. I was born on September 20, 1993, in Bainbridge, Georgia. I live in Donalsonville, Georgia.

I have 3 sisters and 4 brothers. I was raised up around a lot of grown folks. My mom and me have always struggled. We try so hard to get everything right. When we needed help we didn't depend on other people. We tried our best, to work everything out. People try their best to help us, but we didn't need it. My mom depended on herself. So, we found out how to get on the right track. What would I do if we didn't have what we have now in the world? Some people would not have anywhere to stay. I was in the place people are in today. What if you lived in Africa where the disease is real? Who do you thing they are over there? The life of others is all about thinking of others, not yourself. Let's help people in other countries.

Batiste Stewart, Grade 8
Seminole County Middle/High School, GA

Stop Horse Slaughtering

Have you ever been to a Horse Slaughter House, probably not. Well then I'll be the first to tell you about how cruel they are. Horse Slaughter Houses are cruel and mean.

You may not know this but horses are badly abused and mistreated in Slaughter Houses. They are put on trailer for long periods of time with out food or water.

Workers there hit the horses on the head with scissors, hammers, and even axes to kill horses. Some horses are even shot! Foals are taken from their mothers and some foals die due to this. Horses starve and go thirsty for weeks on end. Some horses get so weak they cannot even stand up.

This is just some things that I hate about Horses Slaughter Houses. I love horses and cannot stand to see them suffer like that. You may not care, but now you at least know about this problem. Horse Slaughter Houses are cruel and just down right mean to horses.

Texanna Edwards, Grade 8
Dyer Elementary & Jr High School, TN

Imaginize Me!

I think it is good to have a big imagination. If you don't have a very good imagination, it can be hard to picture something out of a book. I think that people with good imagination can have more fun than people without good ones.

If you want to be someone like a cartoon creator, video game designer, comic book writer, or even an artist, you need to have a good imagination. Sometimes, a person with a big imagination can go to some fun careers.

Sometimes, it can be useful to have a balance between imagination and intelligence. The two skills can cooperate with each other to think of neat, easy, and fun ways to remember notes. Big imaginers can be big thinkers with a balance!

Dakota Warren, Grade 8
Dyer Elementary & Jr High School, TN

Comforts of a Clean America
from an Immigrant's Point of View

Most of the people in America agree that America is a great country. For me, America's splendor is made up of small things such as good sanitation.

Three years ago I moved to America from Latvia. Even though Europe is considered advanced some of its parts are not. For example; when going out, be prepared to see a considerable amount of stray dogs and cats roaming the streets due to the lack of shelters and animal control. However, in America if a stray animal is seen it is immediately captured and transported to a shelter. This process results in less fleas to catch, less "bombs" to step into, which pleases people, and improves the sanitary conditions.

Furthermore, because of the good sanitary conditions the streets are kept clean and neat. Arriving here I was surprised to see barely any graffiti on the walls, or cigarette butts and garbage on the streets. Being used to filthy streets the positive change had a good effect on me.

In summation, the good sanitary conditions provide much comfort to me because I don't have to be afraid of stray animal chasing me all over the street or getting my shoes dirty because of many cigarette butts attached to them. I believe that if more countries learn to keep themselves orderly, together we all might make a positive impact on the world by saving our planet and leading healthier and cleaner lifestyles.

Zlata Gogoleva, Grade 9
West Orange High School, FL

Prayer for Peace

The booms of exploding bombs and the crashes of breaking windows are the sounds that can be heard on the news when they are talking about Israel. It must be horrifying living in constant fear of suicide bombers. Most places in Israel are peaceful and there are no signs of war. In others there are nervous pedestrians, army tanks and men with guns all around. In some places, the bomb threat is so high that people who go there are thought of as crazy. One of these places is Hebron. This is the city where the Patriarchs and Matriarchs are said to be buried. In this type of city, there are metal detectors everywhere to find bombs and guns. There are also soldiers every eight or nine steps. It is very scary. These people wish for peace so their families can live without fear of a bomb going off every moment.

In the Jewish prayer, "A Prayer for Peace," we recite, "Nation shall not lift sword against nation, and let them learn war no more." This is one of the most touching prayers in my eyes. Israel is such a holy place to so many nations. Spilling blood and fighting is not resolving anything and it is spoiling the Holy Land. "Let them study war no more."

Karen Schaeffer, Grade 7
White Station Middle School, TN

Stuck!!!

I will never forget the time when my sister Amy, my brother Eric, Arrielle, and I went out to my pond to go out on our little boat. We had planned to row out to the middle, tie up to the fountain, and eat a little lunch. We had packed an amazing lunch filled with our favorite meals, drinks, and desserts!

I used the little paddle to push us off the shoreline and then threw it back.

We soon waded out to the middle. When we arrived I simply asked Arrielle for the rope. I saw her eyes open wide with fear and look back on the shoreline where I saw our rope, our lunches, and our paddle! Amy and Eric burst out laughing. Arrielle's eyes widened in fear. She looked ready to cry!

Amy said, still laughing, "Swim!!! Grab the boat and swim!!!"

Arrielle said, "Heck no!! I might be wearing a bathing suit but this is from Holister!"

"It's our only way, Ari," I said back.

"But…fine but you're buying me a new one!" Arrielle said.

We hopped out and grabbed the end of the boat and started swimming, making sure no pond water got in our mouths. We got to the shore very quickly but to Arrielle and me it felt like an eternity. When we got to the shore, we ran into the house dripping with water. When my mom saw us she laughed so hard.

Samantha Chung, Grade 7
Osceola Creek Middle School, FL

Baseball

Baseball is a very popular sport. There are many rules in the game of baseball to learn. Before you play, you need to learn the object of the game. Last, you need to learn how to play.

Here are the basic rules of baseball. First, every time a person on your team goes around all the bases without getting out, your team gets a point. If you hit the ball and the person with the ball tags you, you are out. These are the basic rules of baseball.

You also need to learn the object of the game before you can play. The object of the game is to score as many points as you can. Whichever team has the most points at the end of the game wins.

Next, you need to learn how to play. When it is your turn at bat, you swing your bat at good pitches. If you hit the ball, run as fast as you can to first base; if you can, run to the next base. Try to avoid getting tagged by the person with the ball. If you are fielding, try to catch the ball. If the ball hits the ground, throw it to the pitcher or any base. Try to practice every day to improve.

Baseball is a fun sport. To play, you should learn the rules, object of the game, and how to play. You should also practice.

Joey LeBourdais, Grade 7
Sebastian River Middle School, FL

The Porch

"Crash!" I was sitting on my large gray, soft sofa in the living room watching "Saving Shiloh" when I heard another "crash!" The sound came from behind me. I walked over to the cold, gray door, unlocked it, and went outside. I saw that the plant stand and the blue food dish were turned over on their sides. I was looking for what could have done that, when I saw my gray hyperactive kitten Gracie hanging off the porch by her two front paws. Then, I saw my other kitten named Midnight below her staring up at me. I got Gracie and Midnight, stood the plant stand upright and the blue food dish back up and played with my kittens.

The next day I came outside to feed the cats. They looked like they all wanted to do was play. So I stayed outside and played with Gracie and Midnight. Like always the little hyperactive kittens like to play rough. At other times they were sweet and loved to lay on my lap and get some attention. The reason I love the porch so much is because it is a place where I can do my homework. Like right now I'm writing this paper on my porch, and I can get away from my brothers and sisters. I love to just sit outside and play with the kittens.

Lily Sanders, Grade 7
Chelsea Jr High School, OK

Poetry

In the beginning there was pen, paper, and a creative drive. As the pen moved about the page, a poem took form. These words, verses, lines, and rhymes expressed the thoughts and images trapped inside a cluttered mind. Countless hours of devotion, creatively spilling your guts out, into the hopes that the thing that was created would connect to others, a gateway to your mind laid out for all to see. Living on through what you wrote, like a silent voice that reaches out, grabs, and pulls them in. Just so that they can feel as you feel, and experience a new part of their mind and make a connection with you and what you had to say.

Amanda Steiner, Grade 8
Louis C Saeger Middle School, MO

The Bible Zone

As I walk in the doors of Bible Zone, I see the kids running around, next I see the main office, then you will see the kitchen, and finally the sanctuary. Bible Zone is a place for the first through fifth grades to learn about Jesus or a Bible study every Wednesday.

As a worker I make sure the kids are safe at home and while with me. I also help them learn about Jesus. We play games to help learn the Bible verses. We have class outside on the real big playground.

The kids like me because I buy them stuff for participating. I got the job because I am good with kids, and I attended Bible Zone for five years. Bible Zone is located in Oolagah, Oklahoma. This town has been around since 1907. Hey! That's right it is Oklahoma's birthday! I love this state and Bible Zone.

Sabrina Prescott, Grade 7
Chelsea Jr High School, OK

One of the Greatest Passions of Our Time

Baseball is one of the most renowned sports of our time and is also my favorite sport to play, watch, and learn from, but baseball is more than a sport if you honestly love the game. For instance, my love for the sport reaches out to a Major League Baseball team called the Boston Red Sox, and I watch almost every single one of their games, keep up with their stats, and make sure they are doing well, thus I have become very attached to this team. In fact, Jason Varitek is my favorite catcher of all time for Boston because we both share the same position and even have some of the same attributes when it comes down to throwing someone out at second base as they make an attempt to steal the bag.

Also, being a Red Sox fan means that you despise that one team…if you are a MLB fan, you know of the rivalry between the New York Yankees and the Red Sox, but in recent years this rivalry has become more of a hatred towards each other because of Red Sox players going to NYY for trades and fights breaking out between the two teams while playing. All in all baseball is not a game to the people who honestly know and love it but it's more of a passion to individuals who cheer when they win, cry when they lose, and make sure that this game is passed on to generations after us.

Katie Wilson, Grade 8
Heritage Hall School, OK

Jim Thorpe an American Athlete

Did you know that Jim Thorpe went to the Olympics? Who is Jim Thorpe? He was one of the best athletes I have ever heard of. He played football, baseball, basketball, and participated in field. In football he could drop-kick a ball for a record distance and place-kick it 40 yards, and punt 80 yards. Jim played college football where he scored 29 touchdowns, made 38 extra points, and kicked four field goals in 1912. His positions were running back and defensive back. Jim played for six professional teams. He played six years of major league baseball too. In track and field, he could jump five feet nine inches. He could run the 100-yard dash in 10 seconds flat, and the 120-yard high hurdles in 15 seconds. He could also broad jump 23 feet six inches and high jump six feet five inches.

Jim Thorpe was a full blood Indian. His fox name was "Meskwak." After he stopped playing sports he settled down and got married to Iva Miller. They had four children, Jim Jr. who died at the age of two, Gale, Charlotte, and Grace. In 1925 the got divorced and in 1926 he got married again to Freeda KirkPatrick who was the manager for his baseball team at that time. They had four sons Carol, William, Richard, and John. By the 1950s John had no money and left shortly after he was hospitalized for lip cancer. By March 28, 1953 Jim Thorpe died.

Hayden Delozier, Grade 9
Chelsea Jr High School, OK

Over in the Blink of an Eye

The swish of metal blades cut through the silence as we salute in. Just minutes ago, we were getting warmed up and doing stretches. Preparing us well, our coach has drilled us hard, getting us ready to spar against each other. It's hard, but at the same time, it's relaxing. Fencing gives me a sense of accomplishment, without anyone yelling at me from the sidelines, telling me how to throw the ball, or catch it.

Taking a deep breath, I advance toward my friend, enemy, and target. Near his shoulder is where I attack first. He blocks it and we return to our original stances. It only takes a second, and a blink of an eye can end the game. My enemy lunges, attacking fiercely. I block him and attack him near his belt. For several seconds we do a dance: attacking, blocking, sidestepping, deceiving, and lunging. In the end, he lands a touch on me and time is called. We salute out, and I walk toward my friend and shake his hand, commenting on a good game. I approach another friend and request a bout. He accepts the challenge, and we line up again at the familiar strips. We salute each other in and come *un garde*. Sweat from the last bout still clings to my forehead, and my bones ache. I don't care though; I'm ready for anything. I once again approach my foe, this time with a plan. He lashes out, but I block him. Beneath his mask, I see a grin. I smile back and attack. And so the dance begins again…

Navin Gallimore, Grade 7
White Station Middle School, TN

9-11

About six years ago something terrible happened, something that caused us to go into war: 9-11. This was a very big disaster, many people died from it.

What actually happened on 9-11 was that Osama bin Laden, the leader of a terrorist group called the al-Qaeda, ordered nineteen men from his group, to attack. A plane crashed into the Pentagon, the Twin Towers, and they were planning to crash a plane into the White House. Thankfully, the passengers took control of the plane causing it to crash somewhere in Pennsylvania. The Twin Towers went down first, one plane in each tower. The Pentagon went down second.

No one really knew what was happening, until after it happened. It brought devastation across America. So many family members passed away, which is why all Americans have a moment of silence in remembrance of those who died in this tragedy.

The song, "I'm Proud to Be an American" by Lee Greenwood, was written long before this. A video was made using this song, to help Americans remember this tragedy. Whenever I hear about attacks, I remember this song. We are all proud American. We had to fight to get to where we are today. I think every single American would "Proudly stand up and defend her still today 'cause there ain't no doubt I love this land God bless the U.S.A."

Megan Hinson, Grade 7
Tropical Christian School, FL

The Treasure

"Soma, Soma, Soma," my mom tells me in Kiswahili. It means read, read, read. When I went to Zanzibar in Africa to visit my family, education meant everything. I wasn't surprised, but I got angry because some people here, not all people, don't take school seriously. Education is priceless just like the magnificent smile on my face, just kidding. I went to Africa last summer and boy was it torture. The schools were horrible and sometimes the teachers wouldn't even show up for a week so during that hour we would just stay there waiting for our next class. Not only that but when I was there I was in sixth grade and I had just turned eleven, and everyone in my class was thirteen or fourteen and in some cases fifteen, which is freaky because they don't know as much as we do. If you lived in Africa your parents would tell you, "Soma," because they want you to grow up and be wealthy enough to send them money. I consider myself lucky because I'm here in America going to school trying to get outstanding grades. I wouldn't trade my life for anything. Every day my mom and dad get e-mails and phone calls from Africa saying please send money, from a lot of people in our family. They always e-mail because they don't have enough money to talk to us on the phone. This is what gives me a passion to learn and work hard. Don't turn down opportunities.

Ilham Mohamed Adam, Grade 7
White Station Middle School, TN

The Old Tree House

I remember the old tree house in the property that my neighbors owned. It was just dense forest with plenty of trees and a little trail cut through it. It was really fun to explore with a neat sandy field in the back of it that I'm sure no one knew about until we discovered it. We would play hide-and-go-seek in the empty lot. One day we decided that it would be fun to build a tree house. The neighbor certainly never used it and we could use a home away from home; when we were tired from playing, but just not ready to go home yet, we thought. With that image in our head, we got to work.

We would grab anything that would help us build our tree house. Nails and wood that wasn't being used went right to the tree house. With pegs of wood that was nailed to a tree as the ladder and sheets of wood as the floor and roof, it wasn't the best tree house, but it was ours.

It was great to hang out and eat lunch in, but we barely had enough room to move. It was missing pieces and we often had to make repairs, yet it was sturdy and withheld the most ferocious hurricanes and heavy rains. It was our fabulous abode where we would hang out until it and our memories were destroyed. I will never forget that remarkable place where I spent my young childhood at.

Rachel Warren, Grade 7
Osceola Creek Middle School, FL

Jim and I

Did you know one of the greatest athletes ever lived was from my state? His name was Jim Thorpe. He was a true Native American. He was born in Indian territory near Prague, Oklahoma. When he was a teenager, he was sent to an Indian training school in Kansas. I can't imagine being him back in that time. He was a football star, track star, field star, and baseball star. He was excellent in all sports. He and I are kind of alike. We're both good at football, track, and baseball. In football he could play any position. He could pass, kick, play excellent defense and especially run with the ball. In 1911 he was named to the All American team. This was only for the best players. The next year he went back to play football and he scored an amazing 24 touchdowns and 38 extra points and kicked four field goals in 1912. He rolled up 224 points of Carlisle and helping them to a record 12 wings. I chose to write a story over Jim Thorpe because he was a star in the sports he played. He was in the Olympics and got a lot of gold medals and broke a lot of world records. He played his sports at Carlisle Institute, an Indian trade school in Pennsylvania where he was supposed to learn how to be a tailor. Man it would be nice to be him, because we both like sports and lived in Oklahoma.

Taurus Yorkman, Grade 8
Chelsea Jr High School, OK

Switzerland

Have you ever gone to Switzerland? I have; it's so much fun. You can never be bored. When I first went to Switzerland I felt amazed! Now I will explain more about Switzerland.

It looks astonishing! There are mountains everywhere. You will definitely see lots of cows. While we were going to the rental house, the road only fit one car. So if a car came down we would have to move to the edge. If we moved one more inch we would fall down the steep valley. After that I saw clear glistening lakes.

Now the activities; the fun never stops in Switzerland. The parks have awesome slides, and much more. You can go hiking on the mountains and see the goats, cows, and sheep. If you get the chance you can go visit a glacier. When you go in it, it's very cold. You can go to a very tall mountain to go see snow and the ice castle. First you drive up by car, get on the train, and it takes you in the mountain. When I was on the train I was facing the sky; it was so steep. When you get to the top, you will find yourself on the peak of the mountain in snow. You will see a valley of cold glaciers.

The people that live in Switzerland work on farms, in stores, and in banks.

By now with all the things I told you, I guess you want to go visit Switzerland now.

Tiphaine Olivier, Grade 7
Sebastian River Middle School, FL

Plymouth Plantation

The Plymouth Plantation is an exciting adventure for all who go there. The 1627 English village is a recreation of the small farming town built by the English colonists in the middle of the Wampanoag homeland. The town takes place just seven years after they landed at the New World. In the village there are timber framed houses, raised bed gardens, tended livestock and townspeople of the Plymouth Colony.

The people there are dressed up role players who take on the names, viewpoints, and life history of the people who actually lived in the colony in 1627. Each one of the people has a unique story to tell. Discover the colony's difficult beginnings or listen to the gossip of the day. Just go up to them and ask about the religious beliefs, where they keep extra clothes or the relationships with the Wampanoag peoples.

The tour around the village is self-guided. Do not be afraid to walk in on colonist as they eat, question them as they work, or join a lively conversation in the street. Most of the objects in and around their houses are modern reproductions designed for everyday use and can be handled gently.

The people at the Wampanoag Home site talk from the past, but tell their story as a current story. These people have lived in the southeastern New England for over 12,000 years. Step into a traditions wetu (house). In each wetu you can touch soft furs watch a fire or watch food be cooked.

Bridget L. Cotter, Grade 8
The Barstow School, MO

The Message Left by Rachel Scott

Rachel Joy Scott is an amazing girl. Rachel Scott was the first person to get shot at the Columbine High School shooting on April 20, 1999. She always was nice to everybody.

After the Columbine shooting Rachel's parents got a phone call from a man about 1,000 miles away from where Rachel's parents live. And he was saying, "He saw a girl's eyes crying on a flower that was growing out of the ground." Her parents didn't believe him at the time. Her parents got another phone call two or three days after that and it was from the police station saying, "Rachel's backpack is at the station." So Rachel's dad went and got the backpack and looked inside it to see if her journal was in there. The last thing that she wrote before she got shot was a girl's eyes crying onto a growing flower. Then Rachel's parents believed the man after what they had seen.

Two years after Rachel's death her parents moved an old dresser in her room. On the back of the dresser was a set of hand prints from when Rachel was thirteen years old. In the hands she had wrote, "My name is Rachel Joy Scott and one day these hands will touch millions of people's hearts." After the Columbine High School shooting Rachel Joy Scott has touched millions of people's hearts and will continue to touch several people's hearts from all around the world.

Meggan Decker, Grade 8
Greenfield Jr/Sr High School, MO

The Rivalry

Lockwood Tigers girl's basketball is Greenfield Lady Wildcats biggest rivalry. In 2006 Greenfield girls had the worst game. Greenfield has won every game. Our last game was against Lockwood.

The first half of the game, the scores were back and forth. We were up by two with one half to go. We made all of our shots that quarter and we were up by eight. In the fourth quarter we started to lose control of the ball. With two minutes to go we were only up by two. We had possession of the ball. Audrey threw the ball to Paige and Paige threw the ball to Samantha. Samantha went up for the lay-up and made it. Lockwood had the ball. They made a three pointer and got fouled. She made both free throws. They were up by one. It's the fourth quarter and there was six seconds left in the game. I throw the ball to Audrey. She was at half court. I yell, "Shoot the ball!" Within seconds the ball was in the air, rolling around the rim. The ball flew out of the net. Lockwood had won. We shook the other team's hands and said good game. Our coach said we had a good season and we would beat them next year.

A couple days later we got over it and our lives moved on, but we will never forget that day. This year is our time to shine. We will beat our biggest rivalry this year.

Taylor Shepard, Grade 7
Greenfield Jr/Sr High School, MO

Soccer

Have you ever had a sport you just loved? You watched it all the time and also played it all the time? That's me, and that sport is soccer. My favorite things about soccer is the feeling and smell of the fields, the determination to win and get better, and training knowing that I'm getting better each time I train.

The feeling of the breeze in your face is great in the hot air. If you're playing in the morning then you can smell the newly cut grass. Also when you know you're doing good then it makes you feel good and then you know you have gotten better.

I always have the determination to win. I have the determination to keep going even when I'm tired. Also I have the determination to get better.

I train about three days a week, have two games, and I have 3 school practices a week. I train as hard as I can and I get better. Then after training, it feels good to know I did well.

The feeling, the determination, and the training are all reasons why soccer is my favorite sport. It's also why I'm at the soccer fields about half my week. If you don't already play then maybe you should give it a try and like soccer or any other sport as much as me.

Kadin Campbell, Grade 7
Sebastian River Middle School, FL

A Famous Cherokee Indian

Did you know that Sequoyah invented the Cherokee Alphabet and the syllabus? He was born is the 1770's in a Cherokee village called Tuskegee in the Smokey Mountains. His name Sequoyah means "sparrow."

Sequoyah was an artist and he gave the gift of reading and writing to his people so they could communicate with each other. He got a silver medal for all the hard work that he did.

He had gray hair. He is a Cherokee Indian. He carried a knife and smoked a pipe. He wore a blue and red robe and turban with a feather in it.

In 1829, Sequoyah moved to a town named Sallisaw, Oklahoma where he built a one room log cabin and his house is now a national historic landmark open to the public.

Sequoyah was a very famous person. He had a town and school named after him. He died in 1843. Happy 100th birthday Oklahoma.

Jacob Miers, Grade 8
Chelsea Jr High School, OK

Friends and Friendship

Friendship is the greatest gift one can have in their life. Friendship is not something to take for granted by using it to rule over others, but friendship is to honor and admire one for who they truly are. Friendship is not what you take from a relationship but is what you give to a relationship.

A good and true friend is someone I can entrust with all my secrets. If I were to confide in my friend, I would know that it would be safe. If they did tell others, I would not consider them a true friend. A friend I would appreciate and treasure would be someone I could always feel comfortable around. I wish I had many friends as this. I have only one or two friends that have these wonderful traits. I could never ask for a better friend than those I already have.

Friendship is a wonderful treasure never to be thrown away.

Courtney Marie Gibby, Grade 7
Bowens Mill Christian Center, GA

The Virtue of Friendship

Friendship is to seek out the best for others, even if you have to make a sacrifice in a good way. Friends are faithful and loyal to each other in the good and the bad times. Benevolence is true friendship, also known as the virtue in the middle, but what leads us away from the bulls eye? The friendship of utility is a way to use someone else's gifts for your own good.

How to practice friendship is first to appreciate everything and everyone around you. Second, you need to include everyone. Third, you need to treat everyone with the utmost respect and care.

We need friendship because it is within our nature to have true joy and friendship. God's desire is to bring us into a relationship with him. Friendship helps strengthen our connection to everything around us.

Hannah Lorenzen, Grade 7
St Mary's School, SC

Uncle Kevin

My uncle Kevin is my hero. He is the deputy commander of Homeland Security for the state of Tennessee. He also won a Bronze Star for something he did in Afghanistan. He's met the vice-president, been on Air Force One, and he works for the president! Those are only a few reasons Uncle Kevin is my hero.

Uncle Kevin is the deputy commander of Homeland Security which basically means he's the second-in-command. I think his job is awesome, although it stinks that he doesn't get to see his family much because of it. I don't think there is anyone better for his job than Uncle Kevin. You have to agree, his job sounds as exciting as an action movie.

When Uncle Kevin was in Afghanistan he was awarded a Bronze Star. He planned an attack and not one of his troops were harmed in anyway! It's difficult to plan an attack and have it go so successfully. Mr. Pitts, my teacher, said that if he got a Bronze Star he must have done something really good. That is why I think Uncle Kevin is awesome.

Uncle Kevin's job is hard and requires him to be out of town most of the time. He goes through a lot of training that requires hard work. Uncle Kevin is in charge of the troops that clear the airport and check for assassins if the president comes to Tennessee. He also checks Air Force One before he leaves.

Uncle Kevin is awesome! He has a cool job. He's basically a war hero. He's met some of the most powerful people in America! He rocks and I hope that one day I might be as successful as him.

Patrick Taylor, Grade 8
Pigeon Forge Middle School, TN

Little Monster

My life has changed dramatically since my nephew Kaden moved in with my family. Before he moved in I would come home to a clean quiet house. Now when I open the front door it's like walking into the eye of a hurricane. There's toys all over the living room floor, and you can't imagine what his room looks like. My mom is usually telling him "No no Kaden put it back." Or she is chasing him around the house while trying to cook dinner.

I used to just have to clean up after myself, but now I have to help clean up after me and Kaden. He loves to read his books, but the only problem is he pulls all of them out and doesn't put them back. He just leaves them there for me to pick up. My mom used to have to ask me, but now I automatically do it because I know she has a lot of other things she needs to do.

Having a baby in the house can sometimes be a drag. Like when he screams because something isn't going his way or when he doesn't get his nap out, but there are also some good things about him. It is so much fun to take him outside and watch him play with the dogs, and I like to jump on the trampoline with him. I get mad at him sometimes, but I don't think I could live without him in my life.

Sarah Moore, Grade 7
Baylor School, TN

Behind the Mask

Everyone always thinks that other peoples' lives are so… perfect. They're so beautiful, so smart, so perfect. But deep down everyone knows — there is no such thing as perfection. We are all shadowed every single day by the mask we put on to hide what really goes on inside. Inside our minds, inside our hearts, inside dark rooms with the door locked and the blinds shut. Do we really know each other? Do we really know ourselves? Or do we somehow also get mixed in with the ones we hide from? Do we forget ourselves in the never ending journey of perfection? Perfection — a funny thing — is it real or is it just a figment of an unrealistic being? Something that we will never reach, saying we will never be good enough, that we may never touch it. Just a thought we search for, but never seem to find. And for some reason, we keep it all behind a mask.

Heather Paugh, Grade 8
Dunbar Magnet School, AL

Small Preserving Methods

When you start to preserve your environment, you must find the easiest way for you to do it. You can choose from many different ways, such as planting a garden, choosing a more friendly environment car, and one of the easiest ways to preserve, recycling. Any of these ways could make a difference in the way your environment looks and the way you feel.

When you preserve your environment the small things are what matter the most. Like throwing that piece of metal in the recycling bin instead of the trash. The small things add up to be big after you do them for awhile. Wouldn't you feel better seeing more animals being able to survive in your environment, after you have picked up trash or planted plants that the animals could feed off?

Another thing about preservation is that the more you preserve, the cleaner your air will be. Everyone can benefit when the air is clean. You will feel better because you're not sucking in toxic gases. The better you feel the more you can enjoy the environment. It's a win-win situation.

Everything in your environment is connected. If someone were to dump toxic waste in the river next to your house, then the plants, birds, and animals would consume the water. They would become ill, then humans would consume them as food and become ill as well, causing a chain reaction that could end badly.

If you don't preserve your environment, things like this could happen even by accident. Preserving your environment is very important. It could be fatal if you don't. Instead of buying that Hummer, buy that hybrid, or pick up that piece of trash and throw it in the trash. It may take time, but you will see a difference in your environment.

Katlin Trejo Martinez, Grade 9
Mulhall-Orlando High School, OK

How We Get Through Each Day

As the bell rings at Stroud Middle School, the hall gets as crowded as ever. I always wondered why the halls get this way, but I never got the right idea.

When the tardy bell rings at 8:15 a.m., most of the kids are in their classrooms. For the first four hours of the day, it is pretty calm, but at lunch, it gets pretty wild. Almost everybody runs to lunch, including me. I am one of the first ones to get to the cafeteria every day.

After lunch, most of the seventh grade boys have athletics and so do the seventh grade girls. After athletics, most of us go to the old elementary where the city is making it into an alternative school. After sixth hour, most of us go to the high school for art, band, or choir.

After school, almost all of the 6th, 7th, and 8th grade boys have football practice from 3:00 p.m. to 5:30 p.m. That is what goes on at the Stroud Middle School.

James Catron, Grade 7
Stroud Middle School, OK

Barrel Racing

Barrel racing is a very high speed sport. It takes balance and strength to stay on the horse while going around three barrels. It also takes courage to stay on a galloping horse that turns on a dime.

In running barrels you need a fast, flexible horse. The course is set in a clover leaf pattern. You can have a running start through the gate to the first barrel. The person with the lowest time is the winner. A good run is considered to be between seventeen to eighteen seconds. People that race want a horse from fourteen to fourteen point three hands tall. The reason they don't want a very tall horse is because if it was too tall then the horse wouldn't be able to make the turns easily. Though racing is exciting, it is also very dangerous. It is easy for a horse to stumble on a clod of dirt, slide while turning around the barrels, or lose its footing.

Barrel racing can be for anyone as long as you are dedicated to practicing. Although, you also need to have faith in your horse to do its job properly and accurately. If you do both of these things you can become very successful.

Heather Clay, Grade 8
Trinity Christian Academy, AL

How Trees Affect Our Lives

Trees can affect our lives in many different ways. If it weren't for trees, we would not be here. Also, if it weren't for trees we wouldn't have desks, paper, houses, etc…

Trees can save lives in many different ways. If you were lost in the woods, you could eat the pecans from a pecan tree. If it's cold, you could get some wood and build a fire. If you were stranded on an island, you could drink the juice and eat the fruit of coconuts.

God has given us trees to improve our lives. He gave us trees for shelter, oxygen, paper, and food. It would be hard for us to survive without trees.

Dustin McCullars, Grade 7
Trinity Christian Academy, AL

Turmoils of the Briny Blue

The weather report for the day was really not a good one for the activities that were on the itinerary. The clouds were thick and the sky was gray. As I glanced at the horizon, the ocean seemed to go forever into nowhere. The water looked serene, but I found out it is not calm at the Gulf of Mexico. On one particular day, I had to muster my intrepid nature.

The current tore over the ocean floor. Staggering because of the power of the water, I jumped up as each wave crashed incessantly. The brown, salty water stung and burned my eyes. With each wave, I was pushed further away from the grainy, light sand. Like a mountain climb, waves became more forceful and higher.

Yet, I had determination and won. Initially, I made a choice to enter the body of water knowing the danger. Innocently, my family wanted to have some fun and laugh at my aunt for snapping pictures of our feet in the water. Soon, the mood changed and danger lurked. The gulf was filled with seaweed gravitating to our ankles. My mother kept yelling when the distasteful, salty water flew in her mouth. Clearly, the sea can represent life's turmoil. When you see challenges, do not let it stop you from persevering. This can hold you back from making your greatest accomplishments. In retrospect, this wasn't a day of battle against nature, but instead, it was a day to spend time with my loving family.

Ramona Durham, Grade 7
White Station Middle School, TN

Lovin' My Dog

There are many things that are important in my life but the one thing that I love and cherish is…my dog. Why? Well he's amazing! My dog's name is Tucker, obedient, and a soccer player.

First, his name is Tucker. The main reasons why he's silly is well…because he's a dog. I mean they aren't so bright, or smart or whatever you want to say. Maybe mentally challenged, but…I LOVE HIM. He snores, barks at nothing, and is a soccer dog!

Secondly, he is very obedient. He sits when he is told, or whatever he is told, he will do it. Even in his sleep. He's so gentlemanlike he crosses his paws! But he runs away almost every other day. Even though he does this, we don't care, he comes back in 5 minutes.

Thirdly, he's a soccer player. Tucker is so small he just bumps the soccer ball around with his head. Although, he can get it anywhere. Tucker used to be better than my sister. Then she went to soccer practice.

In conclusion, I love my dog for more than 3 reasons but I really don't want to write down probably 10 long, annoying paragraphs. So I just gave 3 reasons why he is an ordinary, silly dog, very obedient, and a soccer dog. Tucker is truly an amazing but strange dog who I love.

Claire Johnson, Grade 8

Everlasting Affects of the Media

Ever since the late nineteenth century the media has had a strong affect on the American population. The media can make something look incredible or denounce something else. The media includes newspapers, television, the radio, and web pages. Almost every American adult either watches the evening news or in the morning reads the newspaper over a cup of coffee. The views expressed in each of these tabloids or news shows can alter your opinion of different issues.

For example, an election is coming up and you decide to watch *Fox News* one night about the election. Depending on what their views on the issues are, you will walk away with their perspective. If they love the republican candidate and completely hate the democratic candidate it will be biased. But it will still change your opinion.

Also the media has an everlasting affect on celebrities. Yes, the news of Michael Vick has absolutely no affect on us. But it is what sells stories. The media decides to talk about Paris Hilton going to jail for twenty-two days instead of North Korean nuclear tests. That is what sells stories and is what America wants to see. The media's influence has Americans more interested in Lindsey Lohan rather than the genocide in Darfur. The media has negative and positive affects on things. Although one thing is for sure: it is a very powerful and dominating. The media frenzy is very influential and lingers over the opinion of people everywhere.

Ben Taylor, Grade 8
Brandon Academy, FL

The Music in Our Ears

There will always be one thing that's bigger in my life than schoolwork or sports. It's music. Singing for me is what I like to do most that has to do with music. But I wouldn't find that being a career for me in the future. Being a pop star is too much work and you have no privacy. I mean, do you see what happens to celebrities today when they are exposed to a camera? Anyway, all I'm trying to say is that music plays a huge part in our society. There are so many things it does; like writing words to a song to vent your feelings or just for fun. You can play an instrument or be the lead singer in a rock band. Last of all, you can listen to it.

Of course, music has its downsides, too. People are changing it and changing the meaning of it. They're making it inappropriate for kids of young ages and sending the wrong message. Ten years ago, music was nothing like it is now. Now it's all about women and sex, and it's offensive. It's the twenty-first century, but songs can be about girls and love without being inappropriate.

The music going into our ears is important. Also, remember some of it is trash. It doesn't mean stop listening to it. Make music a part of your life and have fun with it!

Maya Rose, Grade 7
Bak Middle School of the Arts, FL

Real Family Values

I eagerly cross another day off the calendar. My mind, consumed with thoughts of happiness, is unable to focus on my chores. I am anxious about an upcoming family vacation. With aunts and uncles scattered around the country, I am easily engulfed in a wave of excitement whenever relatives are able to visit. In addition to diverse locations, differences in schedules make it hard to gather together. However, once everything is coordinated, the enjoyment brought about by the presence of my extended family offsets all the stress that we endured while planning the trip. When I am with my relatives, all of my troubles seem to melt away. This is the reason why I find such joy when I am with my family. My life is greatly enhanced by seeing my aunts and uncles, and cousins. My family provides support and encouragement to me. They challenge me to live my best life. Large family gatherings allow me to interact and share with a group of people who love and cherish me. No matter the trials and tribulations that are encountered getting together, I believe the ending result makes it all worthwhile.

Ted Schmitt, Grade 8
St Gerard Majella School, MO

The Day the World Changed

9-11, what do these numbers mean to you? To some they're just numbers, but to Americans this is a date that our country changed forever. Security tightened, the economy plummeted and Americans became more unified.

Security tightened immensely. People were profiled because of their color, religion and national origin. A color-coded threat alert system was introduced, but instead of warning Americans of danger it just added to the confusion. Airport security was one example.

America's economy paid greatly as a result of the terror attacks. The whole travel industry was shut down for days. Tourism, which is an immense part of the American economy, was also shut down. Gas prices rose quickly putting a squeeze on the wallets of many American families.

With all the bad things 9-11 brought it also brought something very good. The unification of America. Americans finally realized if they didn't band together and help one another this great country would fall, because America is like a mighty oak tree and its roots are the people. Without its roots a tree dies and without its people America will fall. Many realized that tomorrow may never come as it never came for 3,000 people who were killed that dreadful day. So people started to live life to the fullest, never knowing the answer to one of the greatest questions ever asked "will I die today?"

9-11 changed the world in so many ways three topics could never define it all. But I chose the ones that meant the most to me. Security status, world economy, and the unification of this great country we call America. When you think of the digits 9-11 do you still think of just numbers or do you think of the day that shook America to the core?

Rachel Henson, Grade 8
Eclectic Middle School, AL

Teachers

All teachers have one main purpose and that is to teach their students. I can tell you four things that all teachers do to try to help students. One, by breaking it down step by step, making sure you understand the lesson they are teaching you. Two, they can tutor you during lunch, before school, and after school. Three, calling your parents to discuss how you can get help. Four, putting you into a special group with other students who have trouble understanding the lesson.

Breaking down the lesson is really helpful to kids. It helps them understand what each part means and how to use it in a sentence or a problem.

Tutoring can help kids get better grades. Teaching them the lessons over and over or in different ways until they learn the lesson that they had trouble with.

Sometimes, teachers calling your parents is a good thing other times its a bad thing. But this is going to be a good thing. Having your teacher call your parents to discuss how to help you in class will really get your grades up in class.

Getting put into a group with kids at the same level will help you feel like you are not the only one at that pace. Trust me, I know how it feels to be at a slow pace.

So trust your teachers when they say they're going to help you improve your grades. Good Luck In SCHOOL!

Khadijah Khan, Grade 7
Tarpon Springs Middle School, FL

What Would Life Be Without Friends?

We all know that everyone needs a friend, but do you know how much they can change your life? Ask yourself this, when I am mad at my family, who do I always go to? Usually, we all say my friends. So we all need a "back-up person" to listen and understand what problems we have. Imagine life without them. Where would you be?

When you are mad, who is there to make you laugh? Of course, the answer is your very close friends. Friends are caring, loving, and understanding. They always cheer you up, and you get along great. That's what a good friend is. Good friends can never be found right away. You have to look very carefully and be very social.

Even in my life, I have had friends since kindergarten that I have had some good and bad times with. We all know that friends fight, but at the end of the day they will be there for you. In my lifetime, I have learned that my best friends are the most important people in my life. Good friends will let you know if something is good, bad, pretty, or ugly, but they will not lie. You can always trust them. Friends will go to the ends of the earth until they find what you need. That's what makes a good friend. That's someone that can change your life.

Danielle Rohling, Grade 8
St Gerard Majella School, MO

Bryan

On May 21, 1998, my little brother Bryan was born. Bryan is nine years old and is my wonderful and awesome little brother. When I was younger, I remember going to places with my family and him. Bryan always makes things more fun, and he entertains me without him knowing it. Bryan is one of my four siblings. I have an older brother, younger brother, Bryan, and two younger sisters. My older brother and I make unusual nicknames for him like "ocra," "little gardener," and many more. Although he gets mad at me a lot, when we do get along, we have a fun and good time. Bryan is a cute and loving kid unless he gets mad at you. Bryan always puts a smile on my face and cheers me up. Sometimes I will play sports with him and try to help him out, but usually he doesn't want my help. Anytime I am with Bryan things are better than they normally would be. Bryan has impacted my life dramatically and has made my life more exciting. My life without Bryan wouldn't be nearly as fun.

Sean Badock, Grade 8
St Gerard Majella School, MO

My Family

My family is from Atlanta, Georgia. Everybody in the house where I live consists of my family. In the house where I live there are 3 of us which includes: my mom, my little brother and myself.

My mom is the head of the house and whatever she says goes. If she is angry, she wants to be left alone. My mom is also the kind of person that if you need something, if she has it she will give it to you. She is great.

My little brother is the security guard of the house. He is also known as the goofy one. My little brother likes to play a lot and sometimes I might have to put him in his place. He is a good person to hang around only if his attitude is right.

These two people mean the most to me. If they weren't a part of my life I would perish. I love them with all my heart. So all I'm trying to say is that those two people are the best.

Xavier Lawson, Grade 8
Turner Middle School, GA

Monster Trucks

A time I did something fun was when my dad took me to see a Monster Truck show for the first time in my life. My favorite Monster Truck was Bigfoot. He won a lot. He was fast on the races and high on the jumps. Captain America was the only truck that beat Bigfoot. My favorite dune buggy was the Tiger. He had high jumps and sharp turns. Tiger won the dune buggy competition. The grand finale was a junkyard tractor painted green with fake wings, as a dragon. The tractor picked up a car and crunched it, then dropped it, and hit it. Then the tractor opened its mouth and fireworks came out like fire! Then the tractor repeated the actions over and over again until the car was demolished. Monster trucks, dune buggies, and a dragon car made for one of the best days in my young life.

Harland James Barker, Grade 7
Benton County School of the Arts, AR

Family Values

Family is a very important factor in a child's life. Enjoy playing in your backyard, with your parents, siblings, and pets. Just simple things like that can help kids. Sometimes when kids don't have the family members impacting there life, they get into bad situations. Life is very inconsistent, one day you will not have a dad, a mom, a brother or sister, or even have a place to sleep. You have to take life by the reigns and make the most of it. Whenever you are a parent you have a mission from God, to give he or she a home, be good to them and lead them in a thriving direction. Family values teach a kid a lot. If your dad or mom is a drunk or druggy, you will be depressed or end up like them if they don't have that extra push and that is family values.

Ross Clifton, Grade 8

The Person I Admire Most

The person I admire most is my mother. Why? Because she teaches me things in life that I really need to know. I also admire her because of the way she is herself all the time. My mother keeps it real at all times. My mother is my joy, we have our ups and downs but I love her to death. My mother is the person who I can be around at any time.

Rosie Mapp is like my best friend; my mother will try and get us whatever the family needs. She will do anything for her children. That's my hero! She made me who I am today. She is my good luck charm, my world, my joy and my inspiration.

I do not know what I would do without her. And she is the most special and precious person to me and she is Miss Rosie Marie Mapp.

Mary Mapp, Grade 8
Turner Middle School, GA

Becoming a Kiowa Princess

Every summer since I was nine years old I have been going to Kanakuk, a Christian summer camp in Missouri. If you go to Kanakuk for a two week session you will be put into a tribe; either Kiowas or Kickapoos for the girls and Choctaws or Cherokees for the boys. Once you are put into one of these tribes you will always stay in that tribe no matter what term or Kanakuk camp you attend. During the day you might have a tribal competition like water polo, whiffle ball, knock out, or a dress up game. At the end of the term each tribe elects a princess or a chief to serve for the next year. Being a princess or a chief is a real honor; your tribe nominates about ten girls and boys then they vote. I was elected to be the Kiowa princess. Throughout the year I will have fun, but time consuming tasks. For example making a spirit stick, designing T-shirts, memorizing Bible verses, and coming up with new tribe cheers are just a few of the tasks I need to complete. This position has grown me closer to Christ and I hope that I can help others know how much He loves them too. When the summer comes around I know I will be ready to lead the Kiowa's to victory!

Katelyn King, Grade 8
Heritage Hall School, OK

Lunar and Solar Calendars

Lunar calendars are the first type of calendars ever to come into existence and use in life. Our ancient ancestors used these calendars, but many cultures and religions still use them today. The first man-made lunar calendar dates back 32,000 years ago!

Lunar calendars work based on the phases of the moon. Each month is corresponding to a phase of the moon. In addition, a lunar year consists of 12 lunations, or 355.37 days. Mot new months are determined by the sighting of the lunar crescent.

The most used lunar calendar is the Islamic calendar. Most Muslim countries use the Islamic calendar. Even though lunar calendars are an old way of determining the days, months, and years it is still used profoundly all over the world.

Unlike the lunar calendar, the solar calendar can be determined years in advance, because it is measured by the position of the Earth on its revolution around the sun. The calendar that most people are familiar with and used most in the world today is the Gregorian calendar. The Gregorian calendar has 29, 30, or 31 days in a month, and 365 or 366 days in a year. The Gregorian calendar repeats itself every 46,097 days. This calendar was made because the lunar calendar had flaws in calculating Easter. The Gregorian calendar deals with problems that are in the lunar calendar by dropping days.

Shahzad Aslam, Grade 8
The Barstow School, MO

Polo

Polo was my neighbor's dog. He was sooo sweet (and stupid). Francheska and Veleska were our friends, so we made 2 different club houses around our houses in the wooded lots. When they got him, we changed the location of the clubhouse. We chose one that was diagonal to their house on the other side of the street, so we'd play around with the boys and Hogan. He was a sweet German Shepherd. He loved to play with us and Polo.

Then, when our 2nd lot was cleared, he (Polo) chased the BOBCAT around, nearly getting run over. When that was finished, we went back to playing in the woods. My two older sisters, Francheska, and her younger sister had found an old hunting stand, and propped it against a pine tree. They'd look out for boys while we (me and Veleska) played along the trail with Hogan and Polo.

When Polo died, (of course) we were sad. Polo was buried near his home on the lot where our original clubhouse lay. I keep going into that patch of woods to find the pipe that was part of our space, and it's a lot smaller than I remember.

Rachel Kelly, Grade 7
Osceola Creek Middle School, FL

Spending Time with My Family

Time is not to be wasted because it is a very valuable thing. It should be used wisely and carefully. I try to use most of my time with my family. They are so special to me just because they are loving, caring, and helpful to me. When I need help or when I'm hurt they are always there for me. Sometimes we get in fights, but that's all right because we still love each other. Spending time with my family is what is important to me and it always will be.

William Rohrkaste, Grade 8
St Gerard Majella School, MO

Will Rogers — 28 Years Older Than Our State!

"I never met a man I didn't like!" What a beautiful quote that people still say to this day. This quote was said by Will Rogers. A man on a horse with a hat on his head and a lovely smile that said, "Howdy Friend." A humble and proud man who was all about his country.

William Penn Adair Rogers was born in 1879, on the family ranch, in the Cherokee Nation, near what would later become Oologah, Oklahoma. He died in 1935, when he was 56 years old. He was over six feet tall, about 200 pounds, grey and white hair, and the most sharp and intense eyes that say I am who I am.

You see, William was a man of the land. Always on a horse, and always had a greeting smile on his face when he rode past you. I bet it was cool for him back then. He got to see our beloved state grow into what it is today. Our state is turning 100 years old and he was one man that was there on Oklahoma's first birthday. He is just 28 years older than Oklahoma, and he gave this land something to remember. He loved everyone and hated no one, and also taught people to just be who they are. Like what he did. A man on a horse riding free.

Amber Schwarz, Grade 8
Chelsea Jr High School, OK

Grandpa

Over the past fourteen years of my life, I have grown close to my grandfather. Since I was a baby, he has played an important role in my life. Even today as a teenager, I cherish the time spent with him.

When I was a little girl, I looked upon my grandpa as a man with great knowledge. I remember asking him questions about outer space or electricity and his lengthy complicated answers. Although I didn't understand most of his explanations, he amazed me with his wisdom.

I was lucky to grow up around my grandfather. We would swim in his pool together, watch trains pass while eating ice cream side by side, and chat with each other. He was supportive, caring, and trustworthy.

Today my bond with my grandpa continues to strengthen. I started interviewing him two years ago. He shares stories, opinions, and facts about his life. I love my grandpa very much and I know in the future we'll be closer than ever.

Krista Gmelich, Grade 8
St Gerard Majella School, MO

Turn Up the Volume!

Among a screaming audience, you spot a dimly lit stage. Upon it, a dark figure moves himself into a familiar position. Then, when you least expect it, the spotlight is set on the guitarist and you hear the brilliant sound of a small plastic pick striking a metal string. Your heart throbs with excitement in your chest as you listen to the guitarists' synchronized notes come together to play your favorite song.

The guitar is the emblem of rock music itself with its many mesmerizing notes and chords. To play it with expertise puts the crowd in awe while the strings are plucked at the perfect time to form the intended melody.

Guitarists are completely essential to rock bands all over the world. In some cases, the guitar player may make or break the aura and popularity of the band. Through skillful playing, a guitarist can become a legend, forever etched in the list of the greatest musicians ever to live.

The guitar is important to me because I love music, and music isn't always as powerful as it could be with instrumental accompaniment. For that very reason, the guitar is a cornerstone of music, as is any other instrument. But because of the various tunes, shapes, and methods of playing the guitar, to me it is the most diverse and unique instrument you can find.

Tom Blood, Grade 8
St Gerard Majella School, MO

Opinions Are Just That

There was a point in my life where everything hurt my feelings. Everything that was said about me hit me in the heart. What people thought of me mattered so much.

Entering the middle school life is what I was doing. School and grades where heavy on my chest, but what bothered me the most was if people liked or disliked me. I wanted to get along with everyone.

I found out that my so called friends were talking behind my back. I know. People are always going to talk no matter who a person is. So, I was crazy for thinking I wouldn't be targeted. I found out really quick that I wasn't the only one but at the time I felt like it was all on me and felt so bad about myself. I was trying to make everyone happy and forgot about myself.

My mother always told me from that point on that everyone has their turn. I didn't understand it at first but I see that she was saying that it was someone being talked about before me and my time was now and that someone will be after me. I soon grew tired of worrying myself about what people said and thought. I learned to love myself for who I am. Today I don't let things like that get to me as it once did, I love myself and opinions are opinions not the end of the world.

Briya Hood, Grade 9
Baton Rouge Magnet High School, LA

Knowing of Death May Be a Call Away

"Steven answer the phone" my mom called out. "All right mom" I answered back. So I picked up the telephone and screaming noises were coming through the phone. My reaction was that my little cousin was joking on the phone, wanting to talk with my sister. "Stop screaming so loud" I laughed. Suddenly my aunt's voice said "Dude, Dude!" Dude is my nickname. At that point I knew something was wrong. She said "Put your daddy on the phone" screaming. So I ran to my parents' bedroom. My dad said "Hello!" My aunt dropped her phone.

One minute later my dad was gone. Now this was my mom's sister, so she wasn't sitting and waiting for a phone call. My mom wanted answers right then. We called everybody in our family, to ask them. No one knew. We later received a phone call. All of a sudden I hear a "No he did not!" My uncle has been shot.

I had to go outside to catch air. "God, please let Uncle Mike be okay." I prayed. There was this white light; it was dark outside so it must have been a sign that everything would be okay. The phone rang again. "Put your mom on the phone." So I did. My mom started bursting out in tears. She said my uncle has been killed. I started thinking about his visit four hours ago. How I finished talking with him. How someone you love can be gone that quick?

Steven Jackson Jr., Grade 9
Baton Rouge Magnet High School, LA

Divorce

Divorce has a negative impact on the children, and adults in the family. Some of the children whose parents divorce will have a disrupted life and routine. In the adult stress becomes a problem. Making tension between everyone in the family. Divorce negatively affects the entire family.

If the parents divorce it might disturb the child's life and routine. The child will become ill-mannered. To think the child has to deal with living with only one parent. If the child has to worry about who they are going to spend time with it might confuse them. They will have to think about living at two different houses.

Divorces can also be stressful for adults. The divorce can lead to fighting over who gets to keep the child. It could also break into arguments over who is dating another person. The parents might so stress out that blaming the child for their divorce. On rare occasions some of the divorces could cause suicide.

So before you even think about getting divorced go over the consequences. That your child life and routine will be disrupted, and it can be stress for adults. If you think about it divorce is good and bad for everyone. Do you want your family to suffer from divorce?

Chardonay Gant, Grade 7
Mineral Springs Middle School, NC

My Guitar

Boump boummmp naa naa na na na na nough. Oh excuse me I'm just practicing my favorite song by Lynyrd Skynyrd called "Free Bird." Oh! While we're on the subject let me tell you about my guitar and the basics.

To begin with, the first thing you need to play guitar is a guitar. One thing that is good to have is a pick. Picks are little triangular objects that are used to strum with. If you need picks I suggest you get non-see-through. See-through picks are too flimsy to strum with. Non-see-through picks are more firm and easier to use.

In addition, the next thing you need to know about is frets. Frets are the spaces in between the two rods on the longest part called the neck. Play higher sounds you move towards the base or body of the guitar. To get lower you strum the top note on the first fret.

In conclusion, you learned the basics so it's up to you. Are you ready to rock? If you say yes then get out there and make it happen.

Rory Grandison, Grade 7
Sebastian River Middle School, FL

Small Things

The small things count for more than you think. Whether it's a peach or a tree or a window, it counts. When my younger sister was two, she was bitten by our three year old golden retriever, Comet. He completely mauled her. She was in reconstructive surgery for about three hours. The whole time she was awake. The reason was, because she ate a peach. That peach made it so she couldn't get the medicine and would make her vomit, which would suffocate her.

So, my little sister was in surgery, getting 120 stitches in her face and six in her arm, she was awake. It was three hours of nothing but my parents singing, "Who lives in a pineapple under the sea…" *SpongeBob*, another small thing. So, next time you hear "Don't sweat the small stuff," make sure to think about them and see how they might affect you. Is there a reason my sister ate the peach? Was it to make her stronger? Or was she just hungry?

Sarah Bowen, Grade 8
Heritage Hall School, OK

Crab Trap

One day, when I was about 4 years old, I was walking on a dock, in a place we have in the Everglades. My mom wasn't paying attention to me. I walked off the dock and I landed in a crab trap. Splash, my mom heard the noise. She looked over the side and I was laying there in the trap. My mom jumped over the side and saved me.

Later on that day we were at the hospital, nothing bad really happened. My mom had more cuts and bruises than I did.

I am so happy to have a mom like mine that will risk her life for me. That is a memory that I have from when I was little.

Cody Ehrlund, Grade 7
Osceola Creek Middle School, FL

Soldier

Several times throughout the last few months, he has encountered death from inches away. He gets shot at, and his past injuries are sore, but he keeps moving forward. He depends on his weapons for survival; his ammunition keeps him alive through the restless, tension-filled days and nights. Every day, he sees the broken bodies lying in the streets and gutters. Men, women, and children alike lay, lifeless, now finally without any fears. Some of these bodies belonged to his friends. The cries of the wounded echo through the barren city. Orphaned children roam the roads, whimpering and not knowing what to do. What food he may get through the day is barely enough to keep him away from starvation. He hasn't bathed in weeks. He waits for the mail to see if there is anything from home. He finally receives a letter, and holds it close to catch a whiff of his love's perfume. A single tear escapes his eye, but upon reencountering mangled bodies of the innocent, he remembers why he is fighting and he brushes away his momentary hesitance. He clutches the cross hanging on his chain and pleads for guidance from God. He knows that he may never see his family or friends back at home ever again. He knows that there is a possibility that he will never have the chance to meet his newborn son. He knows. And yet he fights. He fights for your rights, your freedom, your protection. He fights for you.

Kalyani Hawaldar, Grade 8
James Weldon Johnson Middle School, FL

Music

Everywhere we go we hear music; it is the art of arranging sounds in combinations of rhythm, harmony, and melody. All three of these, if combined, can create a sound to please and interest the listener. Music plays a very important role in the world.

There are many different types of music including Blues, Rhythm and Blues, Pop, Jazz, and Hip-hop. Blues is an older form of music that developed from southern black American songs. It has a slow tempo. Unlike the Blues, Hip-hop is a more modern-day form of music. It has a more upbeat tempo.

Many people enjoy various types of music. Personally, I like the smooth sounds of Rhythm and Blues. Hearing those great artists mix cadence with a little bit of flavor, is what I enjoy most. Jazz is another one of my favorites. There are many forms of Jazz. From Ella Fitzgerald's scatting, to Scott Joplin's Ragtime. All of these things and much more come together to make Jazz.

Music is a lot more than just something people listen to. For some people, music is a passion. They eat, sleep, live, and die by music. Therefore, music is more than just entertainment; music is a way of life.

Kinsey Blackamore, Grade 8
Turner Middle School, GA

Old Antwan

I love playing football in my yard, but there was this one day that I remember the most. Antwan and Rayfield came over to my house to play football. We started to throw some passes but Antwan kept on smacking the balls down.

We took a break and decided a game plan with my team. We went back out there and passed the ball again, but unfortunately, Antwan blocked the pass again.

A few days later I had a shade tree buried into my yard where we played football. Nick, Matt, and I went outside to play football. The shade tree kept on getting in the way so we ended up calling the tree Old Antwan.

Michael Pacillo, Grade 7
Osceola Creek Middle School, FL

Jonas Salk

Jonas Salk is an American hero who invented a cure for polio. In April 1955 people in America rejoiced when they heard that Salk and other scientists invented the cure. Polio was a disease that struck without warning and usually left your arms or legs paralyzed.

When Salk graduated from the University of Michigan, he invented a vaccine for the flu that helped millions of soldiers in W.W.II. In 1947, Salk set up a lab at the University of Pittsburgh where he and others worked on the cure for polio. By the mid 1970's America was polio free, and before Salk died he started looking for a cure for AIDS.

When Jonas Salk died he had helped millions by inventing cures for diseases. Jonas Salk was an extraordinary person by taking his time and effort to help other people. I think Jonas Salk still inspires people till this day, and he inspires me by how he cared for other people.

Adam Johnson, Grade 7
St Mary's School, SC

What You Need During a Hurricane

Here in Florida we can get some bad hurricanes. During hurricanes you need to make sure that you are prepared. If you don't have the right type of food, flashlights, candles it can be pretty hard to do anything including eating.

When the power goes out you can't eat half the things that you eat on a daily basis because your stove and your fridge does not work. And even if you do keep food in your fridge it won't stay fresh for long. You mostly eat canned foods, hamburgers, hotdogs, steaks or anything else you can cook on the barbeque. Another thing that you need to make sure you have is enough candles and or lighters, and flashlights with extra backup batteries. At night you will have a lot of trouble getting around because there is little or no light around you so you tend to bump into a lot of things around you. Also you want to make sure that you have plenty of gas in your car because after the storm you will want to be able to travel and it is very hard to get gas right before and after a hurricane because everyone wants gas at the same time and there is only so much gas that there is, so you need to get some before it is all gone.

Alexis Cohen, Grade 8

The Great Gift of Faith

Being a virtue of extreme importance in our lives, faith is a gift from God that should not be taken for granted. To further this virtue, we must know that faith is a supernatural gift from God that enables us to believe in all that God has revealed to us because He, who can neither deceive nor be deceived, has revealed it. Faith perfects the human intellect by enlightening our minds to God's revelation. A virtue related to faith is prudence because, like faith, it helps in perfecting the intellect. Faith is a virtue that can help us to reach heaven, but we must remember that it is purely a gift and cannot be merited by our actions.

Although this great virtue is freely given to us by God and cannot be earned by human acts, we can show gratitude for it in many ways, especially during the season of Lent. One way for us to show gratitude for faith is for us to read the Bible, for this is God's revelation to us, which we must believe. We can also show gratitude for faith by using it to assist us in believing God's word in our daily lives. My Lenten practices have helped me to be appreciative of faith because I have read more of Sacred Scripture, which has helped me to be ever grateful for my gift of faith. We should always show gratitude for this awesome gift, which helps us to believe in what God reveals.

Mark Schott, Grade 8
St Mary's School, SC

The Man Will Rogers

"Shucks, I was just an old cowhand that had a little luck. Why all this here fuss about me?" That was just one of the quotes that William Penn Adair Rogers said. He was born on a farm in the Cherokee Nation around Oologah, Oklahoma in 1879.

When Rogers was a boy he was taught to rope by a freed slave, so he could know how to use a lasso to work the Texas Longhorn cattle on the old family ranch. When Rogers grew older he was listed in the Guinness Book of Records by throwing three different lassos at once. The way he did it was: one rope caught the horse's neck, one of them looped around the rider, and the other looped all four of the horse's legs. His hard-earned roping skills won him trick-roping jobs in wild west shows. He also started telling small jokes.

After Rogers dropped out of school at the end of 10th grade, he set out to be a cowboy in a cattle drive. They said he always told everybody that he regretted dropping out but he still kept on learning by reading, thinking, and talking to all kinds of people. He ended up doing pretty good in life. He was a star of Broadway shows and 71 movies. Around the time of the 1920s and the 1930s, he also was a popular radio broadcaster and a newspaper columnist.

He died in a plane crash with a friend who was named Wiley Post, they were on their way to Alaska. You can still go visit the ranch that he was born on, in Oologah, Oklahoma. You can also go visit the Will Rogers Memorial Museum in Claremore Oklahoma.

Dalton Nelson, Grade 8
Chelsea Jr High School, OK

Brooklyn Memories

One hot summer day, my entire family and I went to Prospect Park in Brooklyn, New York which was around twelve blocks from my house near New Utrecht and Fort Hamilton.

That day, there was around forty of us, each one of us brought our mountain bikes and all of our gear to ride around the nine mile track. On the way you see many of Brooklyn's beautiful landmarks and a side of nature to the enormous borough. Many of which include elegant ponds, lakes, animals, and trees. We would also find statues of famous Dutch, English, and Italian explorers like Giovanni De Verrazano who first came to explore the area.

People were running around, playing football, having a picnic or just laying down watching the beauty of the park. After a couple times around we laid on the grass, my dad and some of my uncles would go and buy some Kentucky Fried Chicken for everyone. This wasn't the last time we would do this, it was more of a monthly tradition.

Going to Prospect Park is a great way to collaborate with my family. I will never forget these wonderful memories, and I hope I can be a part of this activity the next time I return to Brooklyn.

Matthew Baquero, Grade 7
Osceola Creek Middle School, FL

The American Citizen's Freedom

All American citizens are guaranteed certain freedoms. Among these are three major ones: freedom of religion, freedom of speech, and freedom of the press. These freedoms are a great privilege as well as a huge responsibility.

American citizens have the freedom of religion. No one can legally harass another person because of his or her religious beliefs. One may choose to worship whomever or whatever they please. Separation of church and state is also a part of this freedom. While many people responsibly use this freedom, others abuse it and use it as an excuse to completely remove God from the leadership and authorities of the country.

Freedoms of speech and of the press are other benefits of being an American citizen. Unlike some countries, in America no one can be arrested or persecuted for their words. All citizens are entitled the right to openly declare their thought either through words from the mouth or on paper. Americans need to be responsible and use their words to encourage others instead of putting them down.

Many people have considered it their duty to give their lives in order to maintain these freedoms. It is the American people's duty to use them in the proper way so that generations to come may continue to enjoy these much appreciated freedoms.

Joanna Stalcup, Grade 7
Blue Ridge Christian School, MO

The Forever Engraved Experience

After a great beginning for my eighth grade volleyball season, my coach told my team about Club Volleyball. Volleyball had been going on for about a month, and I loved it a whole bunch. In fact, as my final class ended every day, I would race over to the gym and get changed for practice. Anyway, when my mother picked me up from school that day, I nailed her with questions including if I could try out because I loved volleyball to commenting about the tons of classmates I know who loved it last year and ending with my conclusion that it would be a good experience for me. Eventually my mother answered the begging and pleading with my favorite answer, yes. When the time finally came to try out, they were completely different than anything I had ever seen. First, they took height, wingspan, speed, and vertical height. Then after all seventy-three kids got that taken care of, we broke off into groups, where we did digging, hitting, setting, and serving drills. After three to four hours of tryouts, it was time to go home, hopefully with the feeling that you gave it your all. Just a few weeks later I, Sydney Miles, was called to be a part of one of the club teams. Later I realized the experience that just started, would become engraved in my memory forever.

Sydney Miles, Grade 8

Air Pollution in Cities

Many cities find themselves caught up in the life of pollution. Vehicles, industries, and waste are the main causes of pollution. They can be very harmful to your health.

Vehicles produce several pollutants, such as nitrogen oxides, carbon monoxide, and quantities of particulates of chiefly lead. When in sunlight nitrogen oxides combine with hydrocarbons to form a secondary class of pollutants. In urban areas like L.A., transportation is the main cause of air pollution.

All industries exhibit their own pattern of air pollution. Petroleum refineries take responsibility for hydrocarbon and particulate pollution. Uninsulated high-voltage power lines affect the atmosphere, forming ozone and other hazardous pollutants. Other sources of airborne pollutants caused by factories are radioactive fallout, insecticides, and herbicides.

Waste pollution such as garbage dump sites can also affect our cities. Garbage can produce chemical waste, which deteriorates the ozone. But putting out pollutants acid rain can form. Acid rain can contaminate the water you drink, damage aquatic life and erode buildings.

Air pollution can seriously affect your life and health. It can cause you to have breathing problems such as asthma and serious lung damage. An example of how pollution can affect your life would be, in December 1952, London had 4,000 deaths that were caused by smog in their city. The federal and state governments have passed a number of laws and regulations to reduce air pollution, but they need your help. You can help your community and yourself by recycling or carpools.

Heather McNeil, Grade 9
Mulhall-Orlando High School, OK

The Days to Remember

As a child I had many fun and exciting experiences. I remember things like birthday parties, happy holidays, and other things like vacations and even getting to pick out my first pet. These are all wonderful memories but the best thing that I remember is going boating out on the lake.

It was like all problems went away when the family was all together and having fun. All bad memories and issues seemed to fade away while new memories were created. Just sitting by as you soar over glistening waves with wind blowing your hair is all it takes to create the perfect day. I honestly could never imagine anything as relaxing and fun.

Night time can be the best time on the lake. Whether it's watching stars, fireworks, or the sun setting, on the lake is the best place to be at night. Laying down just listening to gentle waves rock the boat slowly while looking into the beautiful sky can definitely be the best night ever. This is an experience I think everyone should have the privilege to do.

As you can see, the lake is my favorite place to be. I see a trip to the lake as a way to get away from all the stress. Wouldn't it be wonderful if you could make all your stress and worries disappear? I couldn't ask for anything better.

Ginger Medina, Grade 9
Overton High School, TN

Two Different Heroes

Webster's definition of a hero is "a figure in mythology and legend renowned for exceptional courage and fortitude." Even though the definition implies heroes only exist in mythology and legend, I believe heroes exist in real life too. In William Bell's novel, Forbidden City, Alex Jackson and Xin-Hua are both heroes, but in different ways.

Alex Jackson and Xin-Hua both believed China's government was wrong in their decisions to massacre the students and the citizens. Alex and Xin-Hua both fought to stop China's government from covering up the fact that they massacred those people, and they succeeded. Alex and Xin-Hua were adventurous, brave, and heroic.

Alex Jackson and Xin-Hua had very different results that came from their heroic acts. Xin-Hua lost her life because she was helping Alex escape from China. However Alex survived and smuggled a tape to Canada. That tape made Alex's and Xin-Hua's struggles worthwhile, because China was not able to hide the fact that they massacred those students and citizens. Even though Alex and Xin-Hua ended up with different fates, they were both heroic until the end.

Alex Jackson and Xin-Hua are both heroes. Even though Alex's heroism was sparked by his love for his father, and Xin-Hua's heroism was sparked by love for her country, Alex and Xin-Hua both used that spark to help others. Helping others is what makes a true hero.

Kasey Hancock, Grade 7
La Salle Springs Middle School, MO

The Saddest Day in Oklahoma

The day started when people were dropping their kids off at the daycare that was called the Murrah Building, and people were going to work there. About 9:02 A.M. on a Wednesday morning April 19th, 1995, a bomb went off on one side of the building blowing up the whole side of the building. The ninth floor of the building ended up on the first floor and ripped open. The impact of the building was felt far away. Some people thought it was a sonic boom or a natural gas explosion.

Little did they know that the lives of many people would be changed forever. Three minutes after the bombing local workers and police officers started helping people injured in the bombing. Nine stories on the north side of the Alfred P. Murrah Federal Building flattened creating a crater thirty feet deep.

Paramedics, firefighters, rescue and emergency workers started looking for survivors. People were crying out for help. They found parts of a Ryder moving truck that was believed to have carried the bomb. They found out that 168 people had died that day in the Murrah Building, and 19 children had died in there. People from all different states went there to stick things on the fence for all the children and people that died there. Timothy McVeigh got executed June 11th at 7:14 A.M.

Darion Forrest, Grade 7
Stroud Middle School, OK

Hurricane Katrina

On August 29, 2005, Hurricane Katrina made landfall on the Gulf Coast destroying lives, leveling homes, and leaving thousand of survivors with the same story: We lost everything. One year later, many still coped with Katrina's devastation. Some had moved forward, but for others, recovery was at a standstill.

At least 1,836 people lost their lives in Hurricane Katrina and in the subsequent floods, making it the deadliest U.S. hurricane since the 1928 Okeechobee Hurricane. There is no exact account, because many bodies were never recovered and records were destroyed during the hurricane. Thousands more were injured.

Due to this hurricane, many people lost their homes. About 340,000 homes were destroyed by Hurricane Katrina, the largest number of homes ever destroyed by a hurricane in the United States. Many people had nowhere to go; many were in hospitals or large rooms like basements. Some people left New Orleans to avoid being hit by Hurricane Katrina. They didn't have much food to survive off of, so many people lost their lives. This was a sad time in life. One of the United States worst hurricanes did its job and ruined people's lives and homes.

Asheleigh Wheeler, Grade 7
Stroud Middle School, OK

Someone to Remember

Someone to remember in the history of Oklahoma is someone that you can say that has been there for you so you always have a shoulder to cry on. Someone you could tell your treasured secrets to and know that they won't ever tell anyone! Someone you can rely on! That one person is my great grandmother. Her personality is spectacular! She is thoughtful, trustworthy, and incredibly smart. She's seventy-three years old and she also lives is Tulsa, Oklahoma. When I go over to her house she tells me about stories when she was growing up and how much Oklahoma has changed over the years. Just to imagine not having a car to take you places, not to mention not have a neighborhood grocery store, or not having a school where they separated the grades, they all have to be put in the same room. I bet that would be really hard. I think it's amazing how much Oklahoma has changed in the past one hundred years. My grandmother is very nice and is about five-foot-three and is a Native American and has short curly grey and white hair. The years pass by and she keeps on watching the population grow and watches the town change every day she gets out to leave or waters her flowers. The things that she may or may not see will bring back many of her childhood memories. It is very hard to believe that a hundred years have been here and passed. But many will be surprised what will happen in the future because every day there is a new discovery in Oklahoma.

Brittany Cunningham, Grade 8
Chelsea Jr High School, OK

The Shot That Changed Columbus

A shot was fired that would change a community forever. One man was dead and another's life was altered forever. The damage though, wouldn't stop at just those two people. A lasting effect would hang over a city for many years.

One fateful night, my father accidentally shot and killed a man. What seemed most important in the community's eyes was that he was black. Suddenly, the situation went from a tragic loss to a racial storm the likes of the old days in the south. News of the incident covered news stations and approximately six black coalitions came to town claiming that my father shot intentionally because the man was black and that he should be hung. Both sides threw rallies and marches and sent out petitions.

The racial incident skyrocketed and my dad became a household name in our city. Criminal charges were brought against my father that were later dismissed but that didn't mean the controversy ended there. The civil part is ongoing in the court system. My father's health has gone down considerably and another family lost a loved one.

Slowly and surely this event will begin to fade but the effect it left will still be clear. Racial tension is not just something for the history books. Whether or not we choose to admit it we still judge people by the color of their skin every day. This shooting only brought this point into the light for the entire community to face.

Hayley Glisson, Grade 9
Smiths Station High School, AL

Stay Strong

"Stay strong!" This is what my brother Jeremy Tharp told me before he left to go to Iraq. My brother decided to join the military to help pay for college. My brother left January 4, 2007 to go to boot camp in Fort Knox, Kentucky. He spent four months in Kentucky training. Then he went to Fort Hood where he is stationed at for a month. He left to go to Iraq on June 23, 2007 three days after my birthday.

He graduated from Chelsea in 2001. I am kind of like him when it comes to sports. He played football, baseball, and basketball. He was good in football and baseball. When it comes to basketball he is not very good but he never gave up.

He is about six foot one and he is buff. He plans to go to college to be a member of a S.W.A.T. team. He plans on getting married in February after he gets back from Iraq. The girl he is getting married to is from Claremore, Oklahoma. Her name is Amanda Moseley.

Lonnie Tharp, Grade 8
Chelsea Jr High School, OK

Soccer

I see the grassy, white chalk lined field. As I approach the field, the biggest game in the WSMS soccer season is about to start. Out onto the concrete I step, hearing my cleats clang. Joining my other teammates, the Cordova Wolves arrive with smirks on their faces, jittering about the upcoming game. We warm up. Rushed, we join Mr. Pickering to huddle up and quickly discuss plays. He sends the starters onto the field as the referee blows the whistle to start. Running onto the field I see our rivals. The game starts. Having the ball we dribble it down field. I get the ball, passing it to Rachel, my teammate. I watch her strongly kick the ball, past the goalie. Realizing we scored, I cheer my team on. Seeing their faces, I smile with excitement. Cordova kicks off; they pass it back to their defenders, booting it towards our goal. Wolves run down and immediately score, we saw this optimistically. Half time comes. Mr. Pickering, sitting down holding a dry-erase board with the example field on it, congratulates us for an excellent first-half. Very interested in his comments, I listen. The second-half of the exhilarating game starts. They kick off, with a slight advantage. Maya, #22 steals and dribbles the ball toward the Cordova goal. Passing it to Rachel, she shoots at the goal; the fierce goalie caught it, making a strong kick. The ball luckily lands outside the boundary line. Out of the blue, pleased with our lead. Coach calls me, asking me to stay back toward defense, to assure a victory. Without a doubt, I prognosticate that we'll win. The ball stays near the opposite end, giving Cordova no chance to score. The whistle blew, game's over. We all are so overjoyed with the victory.

Mary Beth Perry, Grade 7
White Station Middle School, TN

Rodeo Champion

Larry Mahan once told *The Star-Telegram* of Fort Worth about a man who helped take rodeo to the next level. And then more people started to accept it as a sport, this man was Jim Shoulders.

James Arther Shoulders was born and raised in Tulsa, Oklahoma. When he was 14, he caught a break from working on a wheat harvest for a neighbor; he was earning 25 cents an hour. Jim had been watching a minor league rodeo on the Fourth of July in Oilton, Oklahoma. His older brother had been riding bulls, and he gave it a try and won, or in his words, "I won it and received $18, and said that sure beats the heck out of 25 cents an hour," he told the *Tulsa World* last year.

Jim started competing on a professional circuit while in his teens. He specialized in bareback riding and bull riding, touring in rodeos nearly all year long in his prime. The last time he competed professionally was in 1970, at a rodeo in Houston, Texas.

All together Jim Shoulders won more championships than any other Professional Rodeo Cowboys' Association Cowboy. Sixteen championship titles, five All Around, seven Bull Riding, and four Bareback Riding. He was the only man to win Cheyenne All Around four times and seven time winner of the Calgary Stampede and all in a ten year span.

After retiring shoulders became a stock contractor and started a rodeo riding school at his home in Henryetta, Oklahoma.

Jarrett Phillips, Grade 9
Chelsea Jr High School, OK

What It Takes to Be a Great Role Model

Role models, we've all had them whether it be the neighbors dog or someone revolutionary like Martin Luther King Jr. They are the ones that inspire us to do something worth while with our lives. They are also the ones we look to for help when we have problems.

Most of us choose the people that made a huge difference, not necessarily a dog as mentioned above. Many of these "role models" have existed over time like Joan of Arc, Albert Einstein, and many more. The best part of having a role model is that there is no right or wrong, it's totally up to you.

To become a role model you don't need to have money or be a certain race. The only thing you do have to be is yourself and have your mind set on go. Almost all role models have been diverse in race, beliefs, and even the way they dress, because it's the way they are unique that makes them the pioneers they are.

We should all start making a difference and follow in the steps of these great people. Of course nobody likes anything to be repeated so why don't you do something of your own? Go ahead impress the other people sitting on their couches everywhere. Who knows maybe you will become the next generations amazing role model.

Andrea Pomares, Grade 8
Ponce De Leon Middle School, FL

The Truth About Love

When one says "love" they get this weird fuzzy weightless feeling inside them. But to others they feel a dark pain come back from the past. If you think about it love is like a flower. You have to admire its beauty and thank God He created something so wonderful.

The weird thing is people say "You're only a kid, you have no idea what love is." But that is the thing, we don't know. Kids want to feel something, and the only way we know how to, is to find the empty space in their heart, which is love. The only reason I know so much about love is I have been through real love and fake love. And I love real love.

Some people take love for granted because they have problems and drama in their relationships. But love is complicated: you have to make sacrifices. Love is blind so I say that "Liking someone can come and go, but when you can't breathe around him or her, love is there. Cherish it."

Brooke Hundley, Grade 7
Central Middle School, NC

The Hidden Baseball Field!

One summer day my friends and I were extremely bored. We were always hanging out at each others houses and so it was a normal day. What we didn't know was that the day was about to get very exciting.

We went out exploring and we went into my woods. We were not really looking for anything but we found a lot of stuff. I found a watch and my friends found money, a ring, and a basketball. We were so happy we kept looking all day.

I saw an opening in the trees and I saw my friends were getting tired so I said "Let's see where that leads," we headed to the opening and saw a huge baseball field. We all loved baseball very much so we were so happy that we found our very own baseball field. We played on the field every day until summer was over.

Stephen Harris, Grade 7
Osceola Creek Middle School, FL

The Xbox 360

The Xbox 350 is a unique game console. There are four types of Xbox 360, the Xbox 360, Core Xbox 360, Elite Xbox 360, and the Halo 3 Special Edition Xbox 360.

They make so many different games for the Xbox 360. If you really want the game you can pre-order it so you can get it before they run out of copies. The Xbox 360 has a wireless controller so you can play from far away. You can turn the Xbox 360 off and on with the controller. The games have ratings on them just like movies. The ratings are E, T, and M. E stands for everyone, T stands for teen, and M stands for mature. You can buy all kinds of things for the Xbox 360. You can buy stands, fans, etc.

The Xbox 360 is a good console. You can have a great time playing the Xbox 360. You can play online with other people. You also make new friends from other states and other countries.

Josh McDaniel, Grade 9
Trinity Christian Academy, AL

Living Life to the Fullest

Many times someone will say, "Follow your dreams, don't let anything get you down, and always stay true to your heart!" All these categories fit under the idea of living your life to the fullest. You might be wondering what exactly that means. This can mean many things. For example, when you live your life to the fullest you don't let anything hold you back. You also will live in the moment, and acknowledge your surroundings.

For multiple people holding back is a huge issue in their life. I know from experiences that it's sometimes hard to be yourself or to express your true personality. But if people would, they would see how much more people would accept them. If you let go and see the more important things in life you could realize how great it truly is.

Living in the moment is also a very important step to living life to the fullest. When you live in the moment you don't think, how will this affect what will happen to me tomorrow, or what will she or he think if I do this? You could just forget about your fears or flaws and take the ride of life.

Life is short. Sometimes when you lose a loved one you realize how dear that person was to you. It is crucial to be thankful for every thing you have.

These steps will make an easier way of living your life to the fullest.

Claire Donald, Grade 8
Southwest Jr High School, AR

New York

New York is one of my favorite places to visit. I was born in Long Island, New York and I lived there until I was seven years old. My favorite thing about New York is definitely the winter. Also, the city is a must if you're ever in the state. Another great thing is that the people are so friendly. There is so much to love about New York, but the winter, the city and the people are my favorite.

New York has the greatest winters. It snows like crazy so there is a lot to do. You can build snow people, go sleigh riding or have a snowball fight. It can snow as much as three feet!! Also, the city is awesome. You can literally go outside at any time of night and people will be out. There's always something happening.

People in New York are the friendliest you'll ever meet. They can make friends with almost anyone! Also, they have interesting accents. Some aren't as noticeable as others, but others you can easily recognize. People from New York absolutely love to talk. They basically never stop.

Like I've said, New York is fabulous in my eyes. There are endless things to do. Did you know that in New York City they put up a huge Christmas tree in the winter? It's true, and there's an ice skating rink. New York is amazing.

Erin Fischer, Grade 7
Sebastian River Middle School, FL

Poems and the World Today

The people of the 21st century do not care for literature, especially the poetic arts. Poems help us think and dig for the truth in words. They don't appreciate the skill of words it takes to form these "paintings of words."

It takes exceptional writing skills and a creative mind to form the "slang" or hidden meanings in these writings. Many prefer the new world poems of butterflies and colorful, wonderful worlds, but they don't think of the old world poems. The poems that state truth and morals. These poems tell stories and could help the people today in their lives.

So we see that acceptance of these writings though rare can be vital and can be helpful. If only more read and understood poems they could help themselves and possibly others. Poems are not just words on a page they're ideas and concerns on your heart and minds.

Jonathan Simko, Grade 9
Trinity Christian Academy, AL

New Message

Cell phones are a very controversial subject in our world today. They are very convenient in our very quickly advancing technological world. Though helpful, cell phones also become a bother after surplus attention to them. If more responsibility were used the phones would not be an issue. Unfortunately though, they play a large role in distractions. Not only do you not associate with people normally, your schoolwork and friends, among other things, are impacted. Phones can also permanently remove friends and family from your lives due to impairment while driving or being distracted while doing other things. So be smart and know there is a time and place for everything, and use common sense.

Taylor Hayes, Grade 9
Smiths Station High School, AL

My Life

This story about my life's goals, and the stuff I have already done in my lifetime. I was born on October 9, 1993, at Flowers Hospital. I have played baseball starting with t-ball and worked my way up to fast pitch. I have a lot of baseball trophies that I have won over the years. I have also become a 1st degree black belt, my parents have it framed so I can look at it whenever I want to. I used to play football for my old school GMS. I also have 5 trophies that I have won in world tournaments. I came in 1st in sparring and 3rd in weapons that I have won in my first tournament. My second tournament I won 2nd in form and 3rd in weapons.

In my future I pan to be a CEO of a large company and try to make riches and fame. Then I want to get married and have 2 children. I would try to make a cure of all the diseases. I want to cure the world. It is not fair to die if you get a blood or organ transplant. I want to become someone who can make a difference in this world. If I do not succeed I will try to get my children to help my dream. This is what I have done and what I plan on doing in my future.

C.J. Petersen, Grade 8
Seminole County Middle/High School, GA

Space

I am very interested in astronomy and space. There are very interesting things about space. There are things we have barely discovered about space. There are a lot of planets in the galaxy. There might be life on other planets. There are things to learn about: asteroids, shooting stars, and planets.

There is one very amazing thing in space, asteroids. Asteroids come in a lot of sizes. Some might be the size of a pebble, and others can be the size of a house. When asteroids do hit Earth they might make huge craters in the ground. It is very rare for an asteroid to hit somewhere on Earth.

Another fascinating thing is shooting stars. Shooting stars are very quick. They can be there one minute and gone the next. You can see a lot of shooting stars during a meteor shower. A meteor shower shows many shooting stars flying in the sky. They are very cool to see, and some meteor showers are a once in a lifetime event to see.

The third fascinating thing about space is the planets. They are big and small, but there may be life on some of the planets. There are also so many planets we have never seen or heard of before so it will be very exciting to find a new planet. We might even find a planet where we can breathe, and live on it.

There are so many things in space, things we have never seen or heard before. So we got to find new things about space. It is always fun to find new things about something. There is just so much to learn about space so it will be exciting to find new things.

Branden Manning, Grade 8
Pigeon Forge Middle School, TN

Responsibility Is a Choice

Responsibility is something that everyone needs to learn. You can't go through life without it. If you are not responsible, people tend to think you are unreliable and can't be trusted.

In order to gain someone's trust you have to prove to them that you can handle the consequences of your actions and be accountable. Being accountable includes choosing for yourself between right and wrong and answering for one's conduct.

Those are some steps that help you become responsible. Taking out the trash, cleaning your room, and loading/unloading the dishwasher without being told to do so is being responsible.

You will go farther in life if you are responsible and people can trust you. If people trust you then it is more likely that you will have a job that you love. Life is a lot easier if you take control and do what you are supposed to do.

Kristen Matthews, Grade 9
Escambia Academy, AL

Barry Sanders

One of the people I most admire is Barry Sanders because he is the best running back, in my opinion, in football history. Barry was born in Wichita in 1968. He was seventh of eleven children in his family. He began playing football in sixth grade. He then played football for Oklahoma State University. As running back, he broke 21 NCAA records. Barry also won the Heisman Trophy as a junior at OSU in 1988.

Barry was drafted by the Detroit Lions out of Oklahoma State in the first round in 1989 and won the Rookie of the Year Award in the NFL that season. Barry Sanders, 29, became the third player in National Football League history to rush for over 2,000 yards in a season when he rushed 2,053 yards during the 1997 season. Barry a 5-foot 8-inch, 200 pound running back, was honored as the co-Most Valuable Player of the NFL. He is the first player in league history to break the 1,000-yard rushing mark in nine consecutive seasons.

Kevin Hinton, Grade 8
Heritage Hall School, OK

American Traditions:
Baseball, Apple Pie, and Flying an Airplane?

American citizens are loyal to their country. Some join the military while others enjoy participating in American pastimes. Some enjoy baseball games while others fly the American flag on their front porch while celebrating the 4th of July or Memorial Day. However, there is one American pastime that is now being considered a sport or hobby. I believe aviation is an American pastime that is slowly fading away.

In early 1900, Americans could travel via trains and automobiles but airplanes were not yet practical. This dream traced back to the 15th century when Leonardo da Vinci made sketches of futuristic flying machines. Since then, many aviators have tried and failed to conquer the skies. In 1889 the Wright brothers made cycling another method of transportation famous and they were experimenting with gliding. Their efforts led to the first man powered flight on December 17, 1903. During WW1 top ranking generals thought aviation would not give them an advantage but it contributed to the Allied victory in 1918. After WW1, American aviators Charles Lindbergh, Amelia Earhart, and Chuck Yeager broke many speed and distance records. Aviation advancements helped the Soviets launch Sputnik 1. U.S. President JFK answered by launching Apollo 11 on July 16, 1969. Aviation innovation and military research have produced jets for transportation and military use. They entertain fans with impressive maneuvers and speed during air shows. For these reasons, I strongly believe that aviation has always been and continues to be an American tradition.

Christian Lemus, Grade 8
Safety Harbor Middle School, FL

Lucy

"Rachel, stop daydreaming!" exclaimed my mom from downstairs. "Please take the dog out!"

Startled, and now awake, I walked into the kitchen and put the leash on my black Labrador dog, Lucy. Lucy, unusually small, considering she is a black Lab, is a sweet dog, always excited to see people, and of course, always ready to play "Frisbee" or "ball."

Although I love to daydream when I am restless, playing with Lucy is my favorite activity when I have no other commitments. Hours spent outside with Lucy involve throwing the tennis ball or Frisbee. I can throw it yards away, and Lucy will dash to retrieve it and bring it directly back to me. She can do this forever!

As soon as we return from playing hard outside, I always pour Lucy water. She is usually panting so hard that the water drips everywhere from her mouth and soaks the kitchen floor. After about an hour, Lucy is back in action and ready to go out again to play. However, I am never quite ready to go back outside to resume play so quickly, so I just sit and talk to her. It really seems as though she is listening because she tilts her head and stares right at me as though she understands our conversation.

I hope that Lucy will always be there to listen to me and be there to remain my best friend.

Rachel Glazer, Grade 7
White Station Middle School, TN

The Other Side of the Magnolia

Have you ever had a serene sanctuary in a chaotic world? Let me explain how I found mine.

I was outraged when my parents told me that we were moving. We would be going out of the city and into the suburbs away from my friends. I was inconsolable. That was, until I saw my new yard. Right in the middle was an enormous magnolia tree.

A few years ago, after we'd lived at our new house for a while, I was sitting in my tree thinking private thoughts. Quickly, I swung down off the tree. As I did, I noticed something odd about the overgrown grass. Underneath them, was a pile of old, mossy bricks. They were rust red and slightly crumbling. They smelled of the earth and gave me a serene feeling.

The pile was tucked under a little overhang of branches with oversized leaves, though I could still see my house. It was, as I later found out, the only place that we could reach blossoms to pick. The rest were far up in the tree. The ground was slightly worn in places so that I had little nooks to store things and a place to put my soccer ball so that it wouldn't roll away.

I no longer dress up like a princess or make "salads" out of leaves and grass, but I still go to my special place just to calm down, drink some warm apple cider, and watch the leaves fall.

Andrea Vancil, Grade 7
White Station Middle School, TN

Religion

There are many things different about religions. Many times we look at the differences between religions, and don't notice how much they have in common. Religions have MANY similarities, just like they have their differences too.

The Catholics and Baptists are just two religions, but have many similarities and differences too. For starters, both are Christian, and believe in Christ. Some big similarities are that they equally celebrate the Eucharist, both believe they are and will be saved, each go to mass every Sunday; also following Christ's word is important to both religions, each rely on, and follow the Bible. They are similar in MANY ways.

Secondly, Catholics believe that their work on Earth will affect whether or not they go to heaven, and they believe in a 'Judgment Day' — a day when whether or not they will go to Heaven is decided. They believe that if they act as Christ showed on His days on Earth, followed things given in the Bible, listened and followed God, that they would be saved and earn a place in Heaven by doing good deeds. Catholics believe that they should learn from their sins to become better disciples of God so they can earn their way to Heaven. Baptists believe in 'spontaneous salvation' or being saved without having to do anything — just happening. They believe they are saved BECAUSE they are sinners, and it is a gift of God by His grace. They believe that being good alone won't get you into Heaven. Catholics and Baptists are just two religions, but there still are many religions that are similar to these two in MANY ways.

Alicia McCabe, Grade 7
Incarnate Word School, MO

Jasmine's Escape

I will never forget the time Jasmine escaped. Jasmine is a miniature horse. My neighbor, Morgan cares for her. I have always loved Jasmine, but I was quite disappointed in her on the day she escaped.

Morgan, my friend Madison, and my sister and I were at Morgan's house playing outside when Morgan's mother told her to do her daily chore. Morgan's chore is to clean out the horse's stall. Morgan propped the stall door open with the wheelbarrow. Jasmine is a smart horse, and she knocked over the wheelbarrow and ran straight for the road. All of us ran for Jasmine, but I ran inside to tell our parents what had happened. Jasmine ran and ran. My mother and Morgan's mother were running after the horse in their pajamas. The horse ran down a busy highway, but luckily our mothers got her home safely.

To this day, Morgan doesn't leave the stall door open. On the bright side, Morgan has a fence around her whole yard so this will never happen again. This is one memory I will never forget.

Margaux Keating, Grade 7
Osceola Creek Middle School, FL

Will Rogers

Born November 4, 1879, Will Rogers is known as Oklahoma's' favorite son. He was known to many as a comedian, writer, actor, social commentator, and an America cowboy. He blended his vaudeville acts with a mix of politics and American cowboy. He died before his time, in a plane crash with another favorite Oklahoman, Wiley Post.

Will was raised on the Dog Iron Ranch in Indian Territory near Oolagah, Oklahoma. There he honed his skills as a cowboy. His father was a politician, his mother died when he was 11. Will left school after the 10th grade, he was much more interested in learning how to be a cowboy than getting a formal education.

At an early age he left for Argentina to become a rancher and ended up in South Africa, breaking horses for the British Army. He was in New York when he was discovered, during a rodeo a steer broke out of the arena, of which Will roped before any damage could be done.

He became famous using one-liners, in front of millions of people all over the world, while he was dressed as a cowboy doing rope tricks. "I never met a man I didn't like," was arguably his most famous line. His humor and wit was compared to none.

His death was mourned all over the world. He has museums and statues built in his honor all over the world. He was a modern day Jay Leno in chaps.

Molly Manning, Grade 8
Chelsea Jr High School, OK

When the Lake Came to Lakeview

I am a Katrina victim. Katrina has changed my life forever. I lost everything: my house, friends, neighbors, school, and my city — the city of New Orleans.

It was Saturday. There was a category five hurricane in the Gulf of Mexico. It was drawing near to the city. My step-mom was in a panic. We packed up and got all of our beloved possessions. Dad was still at work shutting down and preparing the oil refinery for the hurricane. The roads were all backed up. We were in the car a long time before we got out of the city. We were praying to Our Lady of Prompt Succer to help keep us safe from the storm. We were going to stay at my grandpa and grandma's house.

When we got there, we watched the news and Katrina was about to hit the city. We watched it all night then it hit. The next day, Dad shows up with the generator then the flooding began.

We watched the flooding of Lakeview on the news. I watched my life being washed away. There was twelve feet of water in the area where my house was located. My house was gone; washed away with the storm.

The move to my new home was sad. I did not fit in. I missed New Orleans. My life literally started anew. Everything was different: the people, the school, my house. Just new everything, and I didn't like it.

Greg Cooper, Grade 7
Holy Ghost Catholic School, LA

Summer Fun

One of the best things I did during my summer was hanging out with my cousins. I think my summer was one of the best because I got to see all my cousins that I hadn't seen for five years. It was very exciting. We had a big party with music, and we danced a lot. We had a lot of nice decorations.

Another very exciting thing that I did during my summer was visiting different places. I had a lot of fun with my family and cousins. We went to a lot of different places in Mexico that are very interesting. We bought a lot of nice things to decorate our house. I hope someday you can go and visit the interesting places I went to.

One of the last fun things that I did before we came back was mudding with my cousins. It was very fun feeling the cool wind blowing on me. One of the things that I liked was getting kinda dirty but after a while it was kinda uncomfortable. It was also very dangerous because the four-wheelers would go sideways.

Well the only part I didn't like was when everyone started to come back. The only thing that made me happy was that I knew that I was going to see my cousins from Fort Pierce when I came back. I have very fun memories from Mexico. I hope I can go for my next vacation.

Jacky Hernandez, Grade 7
Sebastian River Middle School, FL

My Inspiration, Dorothy Parker

Although her education ended when she was thirteen, Dorothy Parker became a famous author, critic, poet, and screenwriter. In addition to those accomplishments, Parker co-founded the Algonquin Round Table. She is world renowned for her witty, sarcastic, yet sometimes offensive writing style. She teaches that even with horrible tragedies in your life, you can overcome them and grow in drastic ways.

Extreme misfortune in Dorothy's childhood affected her writing style. Dorothy's mother died when parker was just one month shy of turning five. Soon after, her father remarried. Her brother Henry died during the sinking of the Titanic in 1912. Only one year later, her father passed away.

The first writing job Dorothy had was when she was hired at *Vanity Fair*. Her comments were offensive to some readers, so despite being an excellent writer, she was fired from her job. The tragedies in her young life taught her to keep going even when things are rough. Soon, because of her persistence, she got a job as an editorial assistant at *Vogue*.

Soon after, Dorothy co-founded the Algonquin Table. The Algonquin Table was a quasi "literary club" where the best writers of the time would lunch at the Algonquin Hotel.

Dorothy Parker's extreme wit and harsh criticism, which was somewhat unheard of in 1920s made her stand out from the hundreds of authors of the time. To be a twelfth as good of a writer as she would be such a blessing.

Mary Frances Zeager, Grade 8
St Mary's School, SC

Why I Hate to Write Essays

I really despise writing essays. The first reason I don't like to write essays is because I can never think of what to write about. Secondly, I am a terrible speller. Thirdly, there has to be three supporting details and I don't like to write that much. As you can see, I hate to write essays.

The first reason I don't like to write essays is because I can never think of what to write about. There are normally a lot of topics, but never one that really captures my attention. There are as many topics as trees in a forest, however it is difficult to choose the right one. In summary, the challenge of choosing a topic overwhelms me.

The second reason I don't like to write essays is because I am a horrible speller. I absolutely hate spelling! Nothing seems to be spelled the way it sounds. Obviously, I am a bad speller.

The third reason I don't like to write essays is because I have to think of three supporting details for the essay. Why do I have to have three elements? I can never think of three! Therefore, yet another reason I don't like to write essays.

As you can tell I don't like to write essays. I can never think of what to write about, I am a bad speller and I have to think of three supporting details for the essay. In conclusion, I hate to write essays!

Michael Newsom, Grade 8
Pigeon Forge Middle School, TN

Legacies

When you pass, do you want to leave a mark? If you could make a statement, what would it be? You can create prevention from what had happened in the past to make a better future. I know, it sounds ridiculous.

Several people tried to make a difference with peace and freedom over the years. Some failed to get their point as public as they wanted. John Lennon created a beautiful song with the lyrics, "All we are saying is give peace a chance." Anne Frank, a Holocaust victim that died at the ripe age of fifteen in a concentration camp, once said, "Whoever is happy will make others happy, too." With that quote, she changed millions. She would not even know it! Rachel Scott was one in many that were shot in the Columbine High School shooting. She said, "Compassion is the greatest form of love humans have to offer." And today, Rachel's family tours throughout the nation to spread her thoughts from her diaries. Those that I just mentioned are only three in billions of people who wish for their theory to be thought of.

Believe it or not, I have a theory as well. I wish for everyone to do whatever he or she wants in order to make him or her content. The definition of "happiness" is a state of well-being and contentment. It is the core of the successful way of living. So, go on and enjoy it.

Hannah Hodge, Grade 8
Greenfield Jr/Sr High School, MO

What My Family Means to Me

My family means everything to me. They spend time with me, celebrate holidays with me and most of all love me. I have a lot of family that is spread out all over the United States in California, North Carolina, Virginia, Florida, Indiana, Illinois, Nevada, Alabama, and Oklahoma.

My favorite time to get together with my relatives is on the holidays. During the holidays my family usually goes back to their home town for a big family reunion. Spending time with my relatives is a great experience, especially in South Bend, IN, home of the Fighting Irish.

When I'm around my family I can be myself because I know they will always love me. While I'm with my relatives I can get to know them better and they can get to know me better. Getting to know your family is a very important thing.

My family is great. I've told you what my family means to me, what does your family mean to you?

Carter Wroblewski, Grade 7
St Mary's School, SC

Going Through Divorce

In my life, I have had many challenges. However, the divorce of my parents stands out as one of the most difficult challenges because, as a child, it was hard to go through not seeing my mom and dad equally. Also, when I would see my friend's parents and both of them together at the same time, it was challenging to not regret what had happened.

Later on in life, when I started to forgive my parents of the divorce, I realized this shouldn't bring me down. In order to reach this, I looked at the bright side and realized God makes everything happen for a reason. Going through a divorce as a young child was difficult, but it all ended up working out for the good.

Katie York, Grade 8
Heritage Hall School, OK

My Football Team

This is my first year playing football. It is a new experience for me. We have practices and games every week. I'm going to tell you about those and my teammates.

Before we practice we stretch our muscles. We do this so we don't injure ourselves. We usually do drills like running the plays. At games if we get penalties we have to do downups. They really hurt. At the end of practice we do suicides. It's basically long and all-out running.

The players on my team are nice. They support each other and give tips. Lots of them are really fast. The one thing is that they complain a lot.

At the games it's really loud. I'm on the kick return team and have to go out on the first play. We've lost every game so far but that's ok.

So as you can see my football team is great. The games are fun and the people are nice. I'm glad to be playing football.

Adam Lukomski, Grade 7
Sebastian River Middle School, FL

Feed the Children

Feed the Children is very serious in Africa. Many children are dying from sickness and hunger. Most children live without their parents and live on their own in the cold and dirty streets or in houses where they live on the hard dirt ground. When the children are starving, they look for food in piles and piles of trash and they can't do anything about it but try to survive the harsh conditions. When they take a bath, they use the muddy river water or they don't take a bath at all. Some children at a young age are abandoned or left in fields and half-eaten by animals or burned in the hot sun. Some children have a disorder and can't move around like some of the kids.

These children need help. Feed the Children is a sponsor to help the children of Africa who need love, food, and a family. If you watch the show you will see how hurtful and serious the situations are these kids go through in a matter of time. Some of these children are dying and they need your help. So be a sponsor; make a better life for the children of Africa. We need to support the needs of these children; you can put a smile on their faces.

Jacolbi Ivory, Grade 7
Bak Middle School of the Arts, FL

Wherever Your Feet May Take You

People all have dreams. Some may want to be a flight attendant flying all around the world, or some may just want to taste food for a living. Whatever it is, just remember to never give up. People may tell you that you won't make it, or you're not capable of doing it. But no matter what anyone says, always follow your dreams.

When a child walks up to their parent, and says, for example, "Mommy, I've decided I want to be a famous singer when I grow up," the parent usually just thinks to themselves "such a wild imagination that child has." Well, it sounds like that parent doesn't really believe in their child.

Kids will give up that dream if someone ever says that to them. It's not fair to anyone, big or small, to have their hopes and dreams crushed by someone not believing in them. No matter what your size, don't let anyone judge you.

Having a dream comes with obstacles. Maybe someone's not smart enough, or not skinny enough. If somebody really wants something bad enough, they'll work for it. But remember not to lose yourself in the process. Maybe someone has a dream, but doesn't "fit the part." It's okay. Everyone's made for something. Everyone will find it eventually.

Dreams are dreams. They may be big; they may be small. People may tell you wrong. It's sometimes hard to reach them. But follow your dreams, and follow wherever your feet may take you.

Savannah Ownby, Grade 8
Pigeon Forge Middle School, TN

The Good, the Bad, and the Ugly

School is filled with opportunities for our futures using education. School can be fun at times but we cannot forget the bad times as well. We just have to push ourselves through and keep going.

School has many astounding things to offer. We have a chance to make many friends and have much fun with one another. If we study hard enough, we may make good grades and instantly feel proud of ourselves.

Along with the good in school is the bad. To succeed in school, teachers require us to study and accomplish homework. Many do not care enough about their grades to perform these activities. If we do not carry out these requests, we might make bad grades and end up getting into trouble.

It is very important to work hard and try your best during school. Having an astonishing education will help us with college and careers in our futures. Education is very important, so do that homework and everything will be just grand.

School can offer us so many things for our futures. If we try hard enough, we can do anything we dream of. If we fall, we'll get right back up anxious to keep going.

Monique Irizarry, Grade 8

Life Is a Roller Coaster

The metaphor, life is a roller coaster, is shockingly true. The examples are all around us. Almost everything we do can be qualified as part of an amusement ride. The roller coaster is a perfect portrayal of the things in life.

With shaking hands, I opened the big, tall door in front of me. The anticipation and nervousness I felt when I walked into my kindergarten class is similar to the slow approach of the peak of a roller coaster. When I saw the faces of my new classmates staring at me, my roller coaster had an abrupt fall. What if they didn't like me? What if they made fun of me because I couldn't even speak the language they spoke? Freezing all my haunting thoughts, a small girl stood up and put her hand out in front of her. Even though I couldn't understand a word she was saying, I understood the meaning. This was unanticipated, but I felt much better. I knew, then, that adjusting in America wasn't going to be too tough. Then came the loopty-loops. I had the challenge of learning English.

In the beginning, I was terrified that I would never learn it. But all the tension had been pointless because I was a fluent English-speaker in no time. Suddenly going to school wasn't frightening; it was fun! Just like a roller coaster, I wasn't afraid; I was actually enjoying it! With its rises and falls, twists and turns, and loopty-loops is life perfectly descried as a roller coaster.

Apoorva Dixit, Grade 7
White Station Middle School, TN

Jealous

I am one of few blondes in my family. Everyone has brown or black hair except my dad, who doesn't have any hair. I have never been happy with my hair. It used to be light blonde, but as I got older my hair turned darker. In seventh grade, I decided to bleach it. My hair turned orange. Finally, my hair started to grow back out, but it was thinner. Now it sticks to my head like someone super glued it down. My mom and sister have thick, curly blonde hair. I would kill for my sister's hair. She can braid it, curl it, wear it down or straighten it. I wish I could braid mine, but it is too short. Allie has hair that smells like the beach, mine hardly even smells like the baby shampoo I use. Babies smell good, but the smell of the beach is something you can't beat. Allie isn't happy with her hair either. She slicks back the curls that run down her cheeks, and she always wears it up. Mom tells her that if she keeps pulling her hair back that tight, it will fall out. I hope not. If it does though, I wouldn't mind having it.

Kate Harper, Grade 8
Baylor School, TN

War Can't Fix Anything

Belligerent nations gain nothing from their many wars. We have seen this statement proven all through time. People fighting for freedom, fighting for land, and some people don't know what they're fighting about. Some people think that Iraq, Iran, and other countries are the only countries that should be classified as belligerent, but we have no room to judge. Over the years Americans have been just as responsible as everyone else for not ending the wars. So are we wrong to have our own opinions? Is it wrong for us to have our own religions? Is it wrong to believe in something that others don't? The answers to all of these questions is no. What's wrong is when a society or certain people try to force you to change, then it becomes wrong, then we become a society that cannot think for ourselves. So the next time you have a debate over wars, we just have to remember we are a belligerent nation.

Katelyn Mayberry, Grade 7
North Iredell Middle School, NC

Baseball

Baseball is fun and exciting sport. Most people don't believe it. I think baseball is much harder than it looks. I believe that catcher is one of the more important positions in the game. The catcher tells the pitcher what kind of pitch to throw and where to throw it. This position can get very stressful at times; if you miss a ball then the other team scores and everyone blames you. If the pitcher throws a strike and you miss it, then the hitter can run to first base and after that he could possibly steal for second and keep going. Even though there are some down points of the game, I would still say baseball is one of the more exciting and challenging sports around.

Kyle Wegrzyn, Grade 9
Providence Classical School, AL

Super Bowl History

The Super Bowl is one of the most important sport events in history. It is that important that someone sold six suite tickets for about $12,500. The first Super Bowl was on January 15, 1967 at Memorial Coliseum in Los Angles, California with the Green Bay Packers defeating the Kansas City Chiefs by the score of 35 to 10.

Before having the name Super Bowl it was just called The NFL-AFL World Championship Game. The Kansas City Chiefs owner Lamar Hunt surprisingly named it after his daughter playing with the toy Super Bowl. Whoever wins the Super Bowl receives the Vince Lombardi Trophy, after Vince Lombardi who was the coach of the Green Bay Packers who led them to win each of the first two Super Bowls. I think it would be very cool to have a trophy named after yourself!

In Super Bowl XXXIV the ads cost about $73,333 per second! The highest attendance in Super Bowl history was 103,985 with the Pittsburgh Steelers against the Los Angles Rams in Super Bowl fourteen.

In 2004, Super Bowl Sunday was the busiest day ever in Domino's history selling about 1.2 million pizzas. The San Francisco 49rs and the Dallas Cowboys both are tied and hold five Super Bowl victories. Winning the Super Bowl is the most important goal in football!

Aldo Gabriele, Grade 7
Incarnate Word Catholic Elementary School, MO

Soccer: The Only Sport

There are lots of things that are important: God, my family, friends, future, and health, but they can all meet on the soccer field. Soccer is my favorite sport, even though I like football, baseball, and basketball. My favorite sport is only soccer.

When I get on the field there's no more school work or worries. My only goal is to enjoy the game that I love. Soccer is also a reward all on its own. After a long day, with work and stress, you can go play and have a good time. Even doing well in soccer is a reward. When the ball hits the net, you now you did a good job in what you love.

What makes soccer even better is having your friends and family with you. You are all having fun, playing, working together, and joking around the whole time. It's just like hanging out but doing something you all like.

Soccer is not just a sport; it's a way to enjoy life. Whenever you walk out on the field with the ball at your feet, the sun shining on your face, your family cheering and having a good time on the sideline, and your friends on the field with you, it's a feeling like no other. Some people think that all sports are alike, but in soccer, it takes more skill, strength, and love for the game. That's why soccer itself, is the world's game.

Juan Carrasquilla, Grade 7
Boyet Jr High School, LA

The Car of My Dreams

The 1968 Camaro is the best car on the planet. The '68 Camaro has a 4-speed engine. There are different types of Camaros, manual and automatic. This car has a top speed of 160 mph on straight-aways, but on turns, it has a top speed of 90 mph.

This car has a V-8 engine. But you hardly find cars with a V-8 engine anymore; you always find cars with V-6 and V-4 engine now a days. I have only seen two cars with a V-8 engine; they are the Dodge Charger and the Mustang GT. I left one car out, so there should be three cars that I've seen with a V-8 engine — the Old Mustang. The '68 Camaro also has 300 horsepower. That's what makes the car go its speed.

The '68 Camaro has brown leather interior. The inside of this car is completely leather, except the dash, the console in the center, and the back window is like carpet. The '68 Camaro has one exhaust pipe. The pipe is 6 inches wide and 2 inches tall. The body frame on this car can be any color you want it to be; here are some examples: red, blue, pink, white, and pearl black. You can also put pin stripes on this car. But, if you wreck this car, it will barely do anything to this car because that's how tough this car is. This is a very expensive and fast car. This car can beat almost any car.

Blake Harris, Grade 7
Stroud Middle School, OK

September 11th, 2001 Attack

It all started on September 11th, 2001 when the hijackers: Al Suqami, Waleed M. Alshehri, Wail M. Alshehri, Alomari, Atta, Moqed, Nawaf Alhazmi, Almihdar, Salem Alhazmi, Hanjour, Alghamdi, Jarrah, Alnami, Al-hazawi, Al-shehhi, Alghamdi, Al Qadi Banihammad, Alshehri, and Hamza Alghamdi destroyed the lives of many people. This was the deadliest attack in the world.

Before the attack, Alsuqami and Waleed M. stabbed two flight attendants and a passenger. One of the attackers learned how to fly planes while living in the United States. They took over the controls turning the plane south and heading toward New York City. They told all the passengers to stay calm; they were heading back to the airport.

On September 11th, it was a sunny day in New York City. At 8:47 A.M., some people looked up and saw a large 767 flying very low over the city. They wondered why the plane flew straight into the ninety-second floor of the north tower.

There was an enormous explosion, and when the smoke cleared, there was a giant hole ten stories high in the side of the building. A large fire began to burn in the top twenty floors. Black smoke billowed out of the hole, and jet fuel and plane parts began spilling out falling to the ground below. The people who witnessed the crash said it looked horrible. Firefighters and ambulance drivers hurried downtown to where the towers were burning. The other hijackers crashed a plane in the Pentagon, and the other plane crashed in a field in Pennsylvania.

Sierra DeGolier, Grade 7
Stroud Middle School, OK

Dumb

After my class had gotten back our homework, I saw I didn't do as well as I thought. I had gotten a fifty-seven. After I read my grade it was like my brain was a bowl of Jell-O. One of my friends, Junamacaby, who sat next to me, got a ninety-six, as usual. Her brain is like a computer. After I went over my homework to see what I missed, Junamacaby asks me what I got, I respond,

"Fifty-seven."

"How could you get that bad of a grade?" she replied.

"I didn't really get it."

"You have to be dumb not to get this. We did this in sixth grade!"

After those words I felt like bricks had landed on my shoulders. I thought I was going to scream! I had never thought of myself as dumb. I had known it had always taken me a little longer, but I never thought people thought of me as dumb. From that day I have worked twice as hard and have improved my grades. Now I'm getting in the nineties on all my homework. I'm not dumb. I just made some careless mistakes and got mixed up. Even Junamacaby made a bad quiz grade. Which is worse than a bad homework grade. Now Junamacaby and I know that not everyone is going to make perfect grades. Now after all that I have realized I'm not dumb, I need to go more slowly on my homework.

Elizabeth Sosna, Grade 7
Baylor School, TN

My Favorite Hobbies

What's your favorite hobby? Well, I have one. Hobbies are important to me because it gives me something to do, so I don't go home and watch TV or lay on the couch all day. Three of my favorite hobbies are playing basketball, going shopping, and cheering at the football and basketball games.

Basketball is valuable to me because it gives me something to do when I am bored. It also gives my body high-quality exercise. When I play basketball I get to be with all my friends. My friends and I work awesome together. That is why basketball is one of my favorite hobbies.

Shopping is a girl thing! My friend and I went to Destin on a family and friend vacation. While we were in Destin, we went to the Destin Commons to go shopping. We had a magnificent meal at Johnny Rockets and bought a lot of clothes at our favorite stores. We had a fun time and enjoyed every moment of it.

My favorite and last hobby is cheerleading. I enjoy cheerleading because I like to support my team. We cheer at all the basketball and football games. They are usually a blast! I love to be with all my friends. That is why cheerleading is my favorite hobby.

Now you know my favorite hobbies, and I hope I interest you in finding yours.

Remember basketball, shopping, and cheerleading are not that bad so, try them out. They're a lot of fun.

Meg Gambel, Grade 7
Holy Ghost Catholic School, LA

Surmounting the Odds

There isn't anything that is comparable to the sensation of endorphins pumping through your body. Energy is given that was never thought possible. Contributing to your team can make you feel so proud. The exhilaration that is experienced when one sprints down the field is like no other. Where might these highs be found? For me, it's on the soccer field.

Where I come from, soccer's a way of life. Kids start playing around kindergarten. Many later go on to exclusive "premier" teams with British coaches, expensive fees, and excruciating practices. I didn't play soccer as a young child, but my sister started soccer when she was little. She somewhat inspired me to begin a quest in 5th grade.

I joined a team. All of my teammates went to a different school. Fortunately, befriending them was easy. We developed a bond over the pleasurable game we loved. Although wins were rare, we never quit playing. Our passion for the game remained constant.

After many losing seasons, something magical happened. Some new players with some serious talent joined the team. The way they performed motivated me and my teammates to strive. Last year we began to win. It was simply remarkable.

No matter what happens, I will always enjoy soccer. Now I'm starting forward for my team. I continue to improve with each passing season. This imperative branch of my life has taught me teamwork, perseverance, and athleticism. But, most importantly soccer has taught me the love for the game.

Melissa Martin, Grade 8
The Barstow School, MO

My Hero

My hero in my life is my dad. He has taught me almost everything I know, and is the nicest person ever created and put into this world. He always understands everything I say, and he helps me when I need it. Everyone's hero should always be joyful and goodhearted. They should also be intelligent and wise in every way.

My hero influenced the music I listen to and the musical instruments I play. He even supports me in almost everything I do in life. He has always been there since the beginning. If I'm sad, he cheers me up. If I'm happy, my dad makes me happier. When I feel sick, my dad is always there for me.

My dad always knows what cool things to say to my friends. He also knows the right time to be funny. It always puts a smile on my face when I see him help people in the grocery store because they don't know their math.

Though my dad is a terrible golfer, and he cannot score a soccer goal for his life, I still love him. He has a great sense of humor for all his misfortunes and difficulties. It's great to go to sleep knowing you have a father like this. One that will never give up and that will never give you up.

Trevor Simpson, Grade 8
Leesville Road Middle School, NC

The Game of Basketball

In this essay, I will tell you all of the set ups of the game, who invented it, and why I love the game of basketball. Also, I will tell you about why or why not people like the sport of basketball.

James Naismith invented the sport of basketball in 1891. In the game of basketball, there are two people that are guards and two people that are in the front. There are usually two referees that make the call. The main important call is traveling or physical contact of each other. Traveling is when you pick up the ball with two hands and walk or when you double dribble the ball. The people in the front, on defense, guard the person with the ball. On offense, the object is to get the ball to the basket. The measurement of the court is 94 feet for the college level. In basketball each side must have at least six players on each team. Each side of the team can have more than six players.

I think that many people should play basketball because it is a good endurance exercise.

Bobby Ruberg, Grade 7
Trinity Christian Academy, AL

Football

Football is a very demanding sport, which requires sacrifice, discipline, and confidence. You have to sacrifice time to be able to play. Discipline is something that is a must to play because you need to listen to the coaches and do what they say. In football confidence is another thing you'll need to succeed. For these reasons football is very demanding.

Sacrificing your time is an important part in football. It is probably one of the most important components of playing football. The sacrificing of your body is something that can hurt at times but you're rewarded with fun. Your time is needed to practice and make yourself better. Furthermore sacrifice is a major component of playing football.

Disciplining yourself is a necessity. It is part of being a coachable player. You need to be coachable so that when you need something done or the coach tells you to do something there aren't questions asked. Discipline yourself to practice without being told. As a result discipline is a major factor in football.

Everything in football comes down to confidence. You need to be confident so you're able to sacrifice and discipline yourself. Self-confidence is a big part in succeeding and believing in yourself to get the job done. Confidence in the team is another thing you must have, so you'll do what needs to be done and not worry about the team. In other words, confidence is the most important factor of football.

Sacrifice, discipline, and confidence is what makes football a demanding sport. Sacrificing your time is essential for playing football. You must discipline yourself to be able to be coached. It all comes down to being confident not only in yourself, but in the team. Finally, all of these things make football a demanding sport.

Mariano Aaron Seth Matthews Muñasque, Grade 8
Pigeon Forge Middle School, TN

Say Cheesy!

Have you ever been told to smile for a picture? We have all been photographed, and we have been forced to smile at one point or another. If you are like me, you don't think you have the best smile. According to my estimation, four out of five of us have a rather awkward smile in photos because it is not a real smile. Smiles caused by laughter or having a good time are real smiles, but in pictures, it is just a forced movement of muscles near the mouth. Don't get me wrong. A lot of people have a really nice smile and enjoy having their pictures taken, and there's nothing wrong with that. For our school pictures this year, some people's smiles looked really nice. But most people talked about how they disliked their own picture and would not let anyone else see it. Most likely, this is because of their fake smiles that do not portray the individual's true appearance. When I look back at yearbooks, I see a clump of photos of kids who look weird and really, really unnatural. Not that there is anything we can do about it. If we all just stared blankly at the camera, it would look even weirder and quite depressing. There truly is no other option. The fact of the matter is, those of us with bad smiles have to look cheesy in photographs, that's how society works. So don't worry about it. We have all taken unwanted pictures.

Michael McLaughlin, Grade 8
St Gerard Majella School, MO

Why

Everyone is entitled to their own opinion. Some people though go over board on their opinion. Politics, religion, and life are brought up to many places including school. Now everyone thinks differently, and yea everyone has the right to talk to their children. What I'm trying to say is that these things can affect your child at school.

Politics are something that is mainly talked about in school. If it's not global warming then it's a presidential election, so on and so on. Yes you can talk about these things at home as much as you want, but that opinion is carried into your daughter or son because as a child I know I want to be just like mom or dad when I grow up. That view though is carried around and when the subject is brought up, and it will be brought up, the different points of views will collide. I'm not saying it will split the school, but what might happen is a fight between friends even good friends.

Religion is a biggy. Since people believe in different things they try to influence that on their child. Some people that think other religions are wrong and that his/hers is right. These people try to teach their children to stay away, harm, or even discriminate someone from that religion. Kids obviously agree to that since that is what they are taught. Some kids even talk about their beliefs in school.

Natalia Castillo, Grade 7
Sagemont Upper School, FL

Grammar Guru

As many of the people in my school know, I am considered a grammar guru. In sixth grade, I became fascinated in grammar and mechanics. Although it's a rather odd interest, I love it. Mrs. Perry, our 6th grade teacher, was and is still a grammar guru and inspired me to love the subject. Her passion for grammar has been so unlike any teacher I have ever had and she explained it in a way that can make sense in anyone's mind. Since English happens to be the language we speak in the United States, I believe everyone should be educated in the topic and become associated with its rules. When we have a paragraph or essay due in English, or any other subject, all of my friends ask me to revise it for them, and I don't mind at all. Mechanics is my favorite part of English because it is connected with punctuation; my favorite part of the language. Punctuation, commas in particular, intrigue me because they are what really make the ordinary sentence different. Last year I was elected to be the editor-in-chief of our school newspaper. This opportunity gave me a chance to look into other various types of writing styles. Grammar guru was a name given to me since I liked English so much, I was like Mrs. Perry. Two years since Mrs. Perry, I still have not received the enthusiasm, from any other teacher, that she had for the subject.

Meg Jarman, Grade 8
Heritage Hall School, OK

A Day at the Lake

It was a hot, summer day in Arizona; a day where swimming just felt right! We did not want to go swimming in the pool, though; so we loaded up the car, picked up the boat, and went to the lake. Lake Saguaro to be exact. We got to the lake, and it was amazing! Seeing the desert and mountains in the background, watching people water-ski and wakeboard, and seeing the stillness of the water all made this experience magnificent.

When we arrived, we got the boat into the water and parked the car. Shortly after we got situated in the boat, we were off. The wind was blowing and the sun was shining. Once we found a nice spot to stay, we all jumped into the cool water. It was so refreshing that I did not want to get out. However, I had to because, for the first time in my life, I was going to go wakeboarding.

I was both excited and scared at the same time, but I knew that I was going to have a blast. My main priority was just to have fun, and hopefully get to my feet, as well. After only a few tries on the wakeboard, my arms were tired. I succeeded in having fun, but not so much in getting to my feet. It was an awesome day, but it was almost over, and we had to head for home. I was disappointed, but knew I would never forget it.

Talia Barraco, Grade 9
Southwest Florida Christian Academy, FL

Life in Turks and Caicos

Turks and Caicos is an amazing group of islands 500 miles south of the Bahamas. In this paradise, I was raised from age five to eleven. "Beautiful by Nature" is the island's slogan which attracts tourists, and it symbolizes the island's economy. Beauty is rampant and can be spotted throughout the many resorts, hotels, and restaurants. Nature is at its finest on the beautiful white beaches that are surrounded by the massive clear blue Atlantic.

There, in the crashing waves, my dad taught me all of my favorite water sports: wakeboarding, skiing, and wakeskating. After water activities, we usually enjoy a meal at my dad's restaurant, Tiki Hut. Sometimes my dad stays on the island for work, weeks at a time, where he remains in our old house there. Sadly, we miss him since the rest of us are here in Oklahoma City.

For a few weeks this past summer, I actually worked at Tiki Hut where I learned the chores of a restaurant employee: clearing and resetting tables, greeting and seating guests, and even delivering meals! Renewing old friendships and building new ones were both a part of the vacation. Although I used to live their full time, I now see that going there on vacation is almost as fulfilling as living there. Now I experience life here and life there.

Kent Camozzi, Grade 8
Heritage Hall School, OK

America

Are the citizens of America really "free?" America was established for religious freedom. If one looks at America now, he sees Christians, Muslims, atheists, evolutionists, and Catholics. Most of these "religions" are tolerated by the nation except for Christianity. Our founding fathers originally based America on Christianity, but now if someone mentions the name of God or Jesus, Americans are offended. People can have license plates and bumper stickers that are not appropriate for children to be reading or looking at, but when a man tries to put a verse from the Bible on a license plate (that he is paying for) the government does not allow it. That is not religious freedom. What would our founding fathers say about this problem?

Our founding fathers or the men who signed the Declaration of Independence, were brave, knowledgeable men who went through problematical hindrances in order to write and sign the Declaration of Independence to help set a superior foundation for our country. Look at America now; do you really think our founding fathers would be proud of what we have become?

Freedom — liberty, independence, and free will are generally what one thinks of when freedom is mentioned. Muslims like having freedom of their beliefs. If Muslims and other religions can talk about what they believe in, but Christians cannot, then where is the religious freedom America is supposed to have?

Abby Runyans, Grade 8
Providence Classical School, AL

My Cousins

My cousins are now 5, 7, and 9 their names are Austin Luke Anderson, Stephen Scott Anderson, and Hunter Mark Anderson. They live with their mom, dad, and grandma, and grandpa. Austin is nine, Stephen is seven, and Hunter if 5, they are all 2 years apart. I do not get to see them very much because they live so far away. They really like to go fishing with their dad they even have their own boat. Their dad owns a lake thy go fishing a lot. They like to catch and fry catfish to eat also they eat blue carp too. By themselves they like to catch rabbits and snakes in their spare time. Also they like to make and made traps to catch rabbits.

On their twenty inch plasma television they like to watch Batman, Superman, and the Teenage Mutant Ninja Turtles. Austin is going into third grade, Stephen is going into first grade, and Hunter is starting preschool. The pets they have are a big fish tank with about ten fish in there. Also they take very good care of their fish by feeding them and changing the water. Their favorite sports are football, basketball, and baseball just like me.

All of them go to a Christian school so they do not get to play sports yet. Their family that goes to Topeka, Kansas goes to The First Baptist Church of Topeka, Kansas.

My cousins are the greatest things in my life.

Jake Anderson, Grade 7
Greenfield Jr/Sr High School, MO

A Hero to Me

By far, my Mom is the hero in my life. The most important thing she does for me is just being there. My daily schedule is extremely hectic! After school, I go straight to school soccer practice for two hours and then I go right to another soccer practice for another two hours. I get home at about eight every night. Plus, before bed, I have to eat, take a shower, and do about two-three hours worth of homework. Why is my daily schedule significant to my Mom being my hero? It is because, throughout all of that chaos, my Mom is there. She picks me up from school soccer and takes me to my other soccer practice. She comes home for a little time for herself, then gets me dinner, and runs back to pick me up. After that, she helps me get organized for the next day of school and helps me get through my homework. Also, she stays up as late as I do, which is often midnight. This is only during the school week. During the weekend, she comes to my soccer games and cheers me on. Whenever I need any new clothes or school supplies, she always helps me out to get them. She will even treat me to nice things like pedicures.

Anyway you word it, she is always there for me! I am always put first, over herself, and that means a whole lot to me. She is my hero!

Abra Floyd, Grade 8
Leesville Road Middle School, NC

The Vietnam War

"Ambush!" This is one of the most feared words in Vietnam. The Vietnam War lasted from 1959-April 30, 1975. The Vietnam War started because the North Vietnamese believed that communism was a better and more profitable way of government. But the Republic of Vietnam (also known as the South Vietnamese), thought that democracy was better. This led to war.

So in 1966, President John F. Kennedy sent five thousand troops over to Vietnam to help the South Vietnamese to defeat the North Vietnamese. But the fighting got worse, and John F. Kennedy sent eleven thousand more troops.

One of the most famous battles of Vietnam was on November 8th, 1969. The 74th Airborne Division was walking in the forest in the Pagasi Delta when they were ambushed. Out of the sixty men left in the division, twelve were wounded and forty eight were killed. That means that everyone in the division was either killed or wounded.

My grandfather was in the 101st Airborne Division during Vietnam, and he told me countless things about the war. He told me about him always thinking he would die any second, how he could hear the shells hissing over his head, and he also told me how many times he and his buddies got lucky. My grandfather was in Vietnam eighteen months and was a corporal in his division. I hope you have learned a lot in reading this essay.

Kaden Birdsong, Grade 7
Stroud Middle School, OK

Chasing My Dreams

People tell me all the time that I can't do something because I'm not talented enough or I am not smart enough. Well, I want to prove those people wrong by fulfilling my dreams.

My biggest dream is to go into the mission field in Africa and help the poor children gain salvation and help them have a better life. I would love to see all of those kids happy and know that they know God and that they are going to heaven. I want to help them be able to eat more food every day and I want them to have better clothes.

Another dream I have is graduating college with awesome grades and owning my own veterinarian business. I want to do this because of my love for animals. There are lots of human doctors in the world, but sometimes it seems like people forget about animals. Sometimes animals are the most important part of our lives. So, my dream is to save animals so they can help us humans.

The last dream that I have is to become the first female professional motocross racer, but this will by far be the hardest dream to fulfill. I want to do this because I love to ride dirt bikes.

No matter if I fulfill my dreams or not I will know in my heart that I tried my best to do so. I will never give up on my dreams no matter what anyone says.

Hannah Fulmer, Grade 8
Mayflower Middle School, AR

Outlining Life

Whenever I'm alone, frightened or sad, there is one thing, one friend that is always there for me. This is someone who has been with me since the beginning — crying with me at birth, and even now, watching over my shoulder. At my saddest moment, happiest moment, and moments of pure emptiness, my shadow stays with me.

When I was a young child, I would sit in my front yard babbling to myself and wonder what the dark spot on the ground was. It looked like me and acted like me, yet when I tried to touch it, it moved. Still today, I often wonder about my shadow: whether I'm playing in my front yard, my shadow trailing behind me like a lost puppy as I swing into the sky; or reading on a moonlit night, my outline fluttering on the wall, grasping the book I'm desperately trying to finish.

My shady silhouette, slightly altered by the lighting, is often a distraction to get away from life, though at other times it reminds me of life. On occasion my shadow varies my profile, and, as life often does, reveals how things aren't. From my shadow, I have learned to be fearless, but cautious, when I am alone; to be independent but not distrustful of others; and to just accept things the way they are, whether I like them or not.

No matter how alone, frightened or sad I may be, my shadow — my friend — will always be with me.

Molly Mulroy, Grade 7
White Station Middle School, TN

A Hidden World

Imagine a placid beach; with sand such a brilliant white that it hurt to look at it. Imagine crystal blue waters so clear you could see the bottom clearly. This is the beach in Hawaii that is best known for its excellent snorkeling.

The most spectacular time of summer vacation was going snorkeling at the beach whose name is impossible to pronounce. Once you put on your snorkel and fins, you have to make your way out to deeper water. After it gets to the point you can almost stand on the coral, put your head under, and prepare to witness another, entirely different, world.

Under the surface, the water is crystal clear, so you can see for several yards ahead. A black fish darts in front of your nose. You turn to see it join a huge school of other identical fish. A little yellow fish swims frantically away when a puffer fish chases it, and it disappears into the labyrinth of coral. A humuhumunukunukuapua'a (or humu), the Hawaiian state fish, is hampered by the coral in his attempt to swim away from you. You are amazed at the world that exists just yards from your own.

You notice that you've been out for an hour! Making your way back, you see many more awesome fish. You make it to the beach, then head for the car. You glance back over your shoulder, just as a wave is crashing on the shore, and wonder if it was imagination or reality.

Kristen Farrenkopf, Grade 7
St Mary's School, SC

My Life as a Sixth Grader

Out of all the good and bad times in my young life, I have to say that sixth grade came out on top. The major things that happened were an accident, senior activities, and graduation.

After my usual morning routine, I stepped into my school, got my pass, and headed to the library (my classroom was being done over so we were in the library). I was glad to be there. Everything in the hallway seemed dark and gloomy. It looked like I was the only happy one in the class. I had absolutely NO idea what was going on. It turned out that a close friend was hit by a car. She had a really serious leg injury. Rosella was the kindest person anyone could ever know, and she was hit.

We sixth graders were seniors which meant senior activities! We had senior breakfast, senior awards, senior movie day, senior barbecue, and senior trip. The senior breakfast was the normal cafeteria breakfast, senior awards was a normal awards assembly, and senior movie day was horrible. We sat on the FLOOR to watch a movie! The senior barbecue and trip were awesome. Too bad Rosella couldn't go to any event.

Graduation was the best. We all had fun. Rosella appeared on the overhead and we all were extremely surprised. All of us thought that she wouldn't make it, including Rosella herself.

As you can see, sixth grade was really unforgettable.

Andria Evans, Grade 7
Sebastian River Middle School, FL

The Only Person in the World I Admire

The only person in the world I really admire is my mother, Cheryl. My mother is the most important person in my life; I would never put anyone else ahead of her. She has been there for me no matter what, through thick and thin. If my mom wasn't here on the earth before me, I wouldn't even be here to say how much she means to me. She's the only woman in my life that I adore. When I was just an infant, I was the only person she would make sure nothing happened to. She is my beautiful, black queen; she is my everything. She is the only one in my life that would make sure I had everything I needed to survive growing up into the young African American man I am today. If I ever wanted to get something for my pleasure, my mom needed to pay a bill or get things we need, my mom would jump in like a superwoman and put me ahead of everything else. My mother is like the apple of my eye; she has done so much for me growing up, I just don't know how to thank her for everything she has done. In conclusion, if my mom wasn't there for me growing up, I have no idea in the world where I would be today. Thank you, Mom.

Jarrett Long, Grade 9
Grandview Alternative School, MO

My Grandpa on the Hill

"My Grandpa on the Hill" is really my grandpa Bob. He has been a farm-boy all of his life. Even when he was 80 he was outside wrestling steers trying to give them shots. When my dad was old enough he went out and worked with him every day.

When Bob was 16 he met my grandma Hazel. Later they moved to Chelsea and he bought over 160 acres of land. He later built a house on the property and it's still standing today. My grandma still lives in the house and she likes it. Even though it is falling apart around her she refuses to move out. My grandpa Bob's favorite thing to do was ride down the hill and go eat a burger at the old Route 66 Café. He used to take my dad, Aunt Connie, and Uncle Johnny out to Grand Lake for the day and maybe even sleep in the back of the truck and stay for another day. When they got back it was right back to work though.

When my grandpa got deathly ill near the end of his time, we had to buy him a motorized wheelchair for him to be able to get around in. I remember playing around in it. Until the day he died he stayed at his front door waiting for us to come by and see him.

Dylan McMahan, Grade 8
Chelsea Jr High School, OK

The Secret Vacation Spot

New Jersey is not viewed as an attractive spot in the tour books; however, each summer my family takes a vacation to a covet town on the Jersey shore called Sea Girt. Sea Girt is only one square mile and it seems as though it stopped progression in the 1930's.

My grandmother spent her summers in Sea Girt with her eight siblings, and they lived in a large house with a wrap around screened in porch. As a child, my mother would return to that house each summer, and our family has continued that tradition. Kindling relationships with cousins, playing games and eating large family meals have been some of my favorite memories in Sea Girt.

New Jersey is sometimes looked at as an undesirable state because of its pollution. Sea Girt is just the opposite of the polluted city. On the contrary, Sea Girt is renowned for its luscious gardens. Its boardwalks have not been commercialized with multiple shops. In contrast, Sea Girt's boardwalks are peaceful, and often we'll ride our bikes on the boardwalk in the early morning and take walks to the pavilion for ice cream after dinner.

Often times, the day starts off with ominous clouds threatening to shower; however, the day evolves into a beautiful one. As breakfast is over, my family and I relax at the beach. We later walk to the pavilion for lunch, but we always swim afterwards.

Sea Girt, New Jersey, is what you would call a diamond in the rough. While the state is known for developing industry and pollution, the shore is helping create memories.

Katie Anderson, Grade 8
St Mary's School, SC

Don't Dis Me

Have you ever heard the expression, "Don't dis me?" "Dis" means to not respect a person. According to Webster's Dictionary, respect is to consider worthy of high regard. It is important to show respect when talking to someone. To show courtesy, one should listen when a person is talking, have appropriate body language and give eye contact.

Interrupting someone when they are talking is not very polite. In other words, listen to what the person is saying instead of worrying about what you are going to say next.

In addition to listening, body language is also important. Body language is paramount; because when a person is talking to someone, the other person should show respect by not rolling their eyes or looking in another direction. Keeping still is also significant. When a person fidgets during a conversation, it is a distraction to the speaker.

Eye contact is essential. For example, if a person was giving a speech and people were laughing or talking with their friends, the speaker might feel like they were wasting their valuable time.

If you show respect, well, one good turn deserves another, you'll earn respect. All anybody wants is for people to regard them. The best reason to show respect is that people will think you are a good-natured person and respect that. To show courtesy, one should listen when a person is talking, have appropriate body language and give eye contact. So remember, don't "dis" anyone.

Tanya Kramer, Grade 8
Holy Ghost Catholic School, LA

Whine

"Tyler Blackmon. M-O-N. Not Blackman (or however else you were planning to spell it). M-O-N." I find myself repeating this throughout the day. Tyler actually comes from Old English meaning "a layer of tile." Great, my life's dream. I cannot wait to hear repeatedly the "Scrape! Smooth! Slap!" of tile laying. Get this, since I was born in the middle of May, I am supposed to be Taurus, a bull. That's like labeling Mother Teresa a terrorist. I am also supposed to be born in the year of the dog. A dog? How boring. Why couldn't the Chinese have a year of the ostrich or a year of the polar bear? Because of my middle name, Steven, I am often Aerosmith's Steven Tyler. I giggle and chuckle when I see myself holding a gleaming red guitar with orange fire roaring up on the stage. I often try to picture myself as a Bob, Brad, Bill, or another one of those one-syllable names that seem to hand you a one-way ticket to fame. I try on Bill. Bill Gates. I sit at the computer I made myself and breathe deeply in the soothing air and the drifting intelligence. But alas, despite all my complaints, I am Tyler. I will have to work myself up that social ladder.

Tyler Blackmon, Grade 8
Baylor School, TN

Be Yourself

One thing that really gets me is hearing how people change themselves. They think they need to be thinner, or other things. People change because they don't like themselves, are under pressure, or to impress someone.

First of all, I think that you should be happy with the way you are. God made you that way for a reason. Some things I don't like about myself, but they're part of me. I don't like to wear makeup because it covers my real face. Everything about everyone makes them unique.

Being in 8th grade, I know about pressures. There are pressures to do wrong things and change yourself. Tons of pressures are found in schools and not many people are strong enough. Some of my friends fall into pressures like cussing. It's crazy. It also helps me realize that I need to stand up to pressures to show others that it's okay.

People change to impress others. I know if you like someone, but they want you to change, they're not worth it. Don't change to be someone's friend, because they will probably leave you anyway. If someone doesn't like me for me, I know that they're not important. I like who I am and I don't want to change.

I'll end with this, "Stand up for what's right, even if you're standing alone." "I know that I can do everything through Christ because he gives me strength." Philippians 4:13. Everyone is unique, so no one should change themselves. NEVER!

Mary Tetrick, Grade 8
Southwest Jr High School, AR

My Parent's Divorce

Ten years ago, when I was about four years old, my parents got a divorce. When I was ten years old, my mom told me that I would be living with my dad. At the time I had no idea what was about to happen; I thought nothing of the matter. When I found out that she was serious, I broke into tears. I was so sad; I really did not know what to think.

I would be staying with my dad all of the time, except weekends and some holidays. I was so accustomed to living with my mom that the thought of living with another parent was out of the question. Once I left my mom's house, I was always crying because I missed her a lot. This would go on for weeks and months. It took about a year and a half before I was completely used to the situation.

Now, it is not so hard, but I still miss my mom. I always look forward to seeing her and my little sister, Destini. My mom, my sister, and I always have a good time. I have had a few good times with my dad, but not as good as with my mom. I am more comfortable at my mom's house; I just feel more at peace and cozy there. I know deep down that everything will work out and that it will be okay.

Brandon Johnson, Grade 9
Baton Rouge Magnet High School, LA

The Many Possible Things

Stuart Allen Roosa was born on August 16, 1933 in Durango, Colorado. When he was young he attended Justus School and Claremore High School in Claremore, Oklahoma. He also studied at Oklahoma State University and the University of Arizona. He graduated with honors and a bachelor's degree of science in Aeronautical Engineering from the University of Colorado. He completed the Advanced Management Course at Harvard Business School in 1973.

When he was older he spent many of his years in the sky with a log of 5,500 hours of flying time. During this time he was a smoke jumper, which is a firefighter that fights fires by dropping water from an airplane.

After that, he joined NASA. He became an astronaut that flew in some of the Apollo flights. In one of the flights he flew around 32 times taking photos while the rest of the crew rook rock samples.

On another one of his flights Alan Shepard and Edgar Mitchell went with him into space. When they got to the moon Roosa had to attach the two rockets together to keep from crashing. The rockets were called Kitty Hawk. They came back with over 100 pounds of lunar samples.

He died several years later on December 12, 1994. If he was still alive today during Oklahoma's centennial I bet he would be be celebrating by flying airplanes all over the place. If Alan Shepard and Edgar Mitchell were still alive they would celebrate with him too.

Geoffrey Bickford, Grade 8
Chelsea Jr High School, OK

My Life

My life began in Berlin, Germany. I was born in a major hospital in Berlin. My mom tells me that life was hard in Berlin, especially for her because she was born in America. We finally moved to America when we had the chance. We moved in with my grandma in Crawford County, Georgia. My mom started taking college classes and she became a lawyer by the time I was ten. Our life was at a turning point.

I didn't see much of my dad in my childhood that I can remember because he and my mom were divorced, but when I did get to see him we went to the movies a lot and played lots of sports such as: baseball, football, and basketball. I knew that baseball and football were my calling. I played as much as I could, and soon I joined the Peach County, Georgia tee-ball team. I loved the sport and soon forgot about footfall and became all about baseball.

Most of my preteen years I played baseball and video games. My life was getting better, because my mom had hit the "jackpot." She got married and her husband (my step-dad) works for Barge Air-Conditioning. I wasn't spoiled, but I got what I needed, and some things I didn't need. All in all, I've been a good student. I plan to change the world by coming up with the next best idea to stop the pollution problem!

Walker L. Hagler, Grade 8
Seminole County Middle/High School, GA

Running

My favorite thing to do is run. Running is fun because it's something I get to do with my mom. It's also very good for you. I think that running is only fun if you're outside. As you can see, I think everybody should run.

I enjoy running because it lets me spend time with my mom. I don't get to do that a lot because she works till about six o'clock; I have karate at seven. Running is a great way to spend time with somebody. Obviously, running with my mom is much better than running alone.

Running is good for you. My mom and I are always on a diet and are trying to lose weight. We run two laps around the park as many days as we can, that's two and a half miles. I haven't lost much weight, but it's still good for me. Therefore, I'm going to keep running anyway.

Running is much easier outside. Running inside doesn't give you anything to look at. It seems like it takes longer too. I would much rather run under the sun than in the air conditioner. In conclusion, I think running inside is as boring as school.

Running is my favorite activity to do. It's a way to spend time with my mom. It is also good for you and keeps you in shape. Running inside is hard compared to running outside. All together, running is my favorite activity to do.

Alex Large, Grade 8
Pigeon Forge Middle School, TN

My Soldier, My Hero, My Dad

I have numerous historical and present-day heroes, but my first and foremost hero is my beloved dad. He is an incredibly hard worker and does not relinquish a job until it is complete. My father is in the army and has been for twenty years. He has faithfully served America in a multitude of places including a full thirteen months in Iraq. Since the news of his deployment arrived on April Fools Day, my family thought it was a practical joke. Unfortunately, it was no joke. My heart was ripped in two when my mother informed me that the terrifying news was true. He would leave the day after Christmas. Every night it was harder and harder to believe that one of my dearest friends would fly across the vast ocean into a dangerous place. The disastrous thought of him never coming back caused my eyes to swell up with salty tears. Christmas night was the hardest night of all. One thought buzzed in my head — he is not coming back for thirteen miserable months and maybe not at all! The horror of my dad gone forever was overwhelming. The morning sun peeked over the hills, and the day my dad had to leave arrived. To my pure delight, he came home one year later safe and sound. The worst of my fears was over. Pride crept into my heart when I realized what he did. He helped secure America's safety. He is my soldier, my hero, my dad.

Hannah Bristol, Grade 8
Providence Classical School, AL

The American Athlete

WA-Too-Hutch, meaning "Bright Path," was a name given to Jim Thorpe who was born in Prague, Oklahoma near Indian Territory. Thorpe later played six years of professional baseball. He also played professional football and set the record for longest drop kick at forty yards and the longest punt at eighty yards. In 1911 he was voted as an All-American and then a couple years later he competed in the Olympics in track and field. During the Olympics he won gold medals and set new records. A little later in life the United States Congress designated Thorpe "The American Athlete" of the country. After Jim Thorpe returned, he left us a very famous saying, "You never learn anything while you're talking." This is the best way I looked at life and during my sports career. Jim Thorpe was one of the best athletes in America; he came from our great state Oklahoma, which is why I decided to write about him for our state centennial. He was born in 1888 and past away the year of 1953. Afterward is when everybody found out his real name which is Jacob Franascus Thorpe.

Blake Russell, Grade 8
Chelsea Jr High School, OK

How September 11, 2001 Changed America

On September 11, 2001, nineteen terrorists hijacked and crashed two airplanes into the Twin Towers. Shortly thereafter, one airplane was crashed into the Pentagon. As a result, security has been intensified. Gas prices increased and the War on Terrorism began.

In the attacks of September 11, the hijackers were able to board planes, even though they carried weapons. They even lacked proper identification. Since then, security at airports and military bases has been intensified to ensure that nothing like the September 11 attacks would ever happen again.

One of the major necessities in our lives are petroleum based products. Of those products, gasoline is the most widely used in the United States. Though gas prices have fallen since the 9/11 attacks, gas prices have climbed to nearly four dollars per gallon in some states.

After the 9/11 attacks, President George Bush declared the War on Terrorism with Osama bin Laden being his prime target. In addition to Osama bin Laden becoming his prime target, all U.S. citizens came under scrutiny. Since the 9/11 attacks, the United States has been engaged in the War on Terrorism on Iraqi soil.

You ask the question, "How has 9/11 changed America?" I would say that it has heightened security concerns. 9/11 has caused government and higher officials to look at alternative fuel resources. It has brought out some Americans' patriotism and support for our troops. It has caused an outcry of opposition from others to end this war. We all suffer the effects of 9/11 daily, whether it be at the airport check-in desk, the gas pumps, or our friends and family defending the feeling of freedom overseas.

Hayley Carden, Grade 8
Eclectic Middle School, AL

A Special Kind of Friendship

It is the best of both worlds to have cousins as some of your closest friends. I have been lucky to enjoy this world with my cousins in Cincinnati. We're close like sisters, but there is no tension of living under the same roof. By using modern conveniences, we are able to keep in contact with each other daily through emails and phone calls.

There is a natural family connection that brings us together at holidays, celebrations, and family gatherings. Being with my cousins make these special occasions even more fun. In my daily life, they are some of the first people I go to when I need to talk. The fact that they live far away sometimes makes us even closer. We have to make an effort to keep in contact, and we get to learn about each other's cities. By talking to my cousins, I am also kept up to date with my other relatives in Cincinnati.

Because we have stayed so close throughout our childhood, despite the fact that we have lived so far away, I am confident that we will stay friends throughout college and adulthood. I'm lucky to have my cousins because they will be my friends for life.

Meg Buckley, Grade 8
St Gerard Majella School, MO

The Nintendo Wii

Nintendo's newest console, the Wii (pronounced "we") is amazing and like no other video game system ever before. The Wii has legendary sales numbers and is outselling both of its competitors, Microsoft and Sony. The system has a revolutionary controller, games that are fun to play, and additional features.

The Wii remote allows the player to be part of the game with its motion-sensor technology. For instance, in a game of bowling, on the game "Wii Sports," the player swings the remote back and forth to make the ball roll and hit the pins. The remote gives me a good workout and provides fun at the same time.

The Wii has fun games both from the past and the present. On the Wii Shop Channel, people can purchase classic games from previous game consoles. These games are just like the original versions. New games that are specially designed for the Wii offer a chance to put the motion sensor to work by making the player move the remote.

The Wii Channels add extra fun to the system with their additional features. The channels allow players to surf the web, create miniature characters, and check the weather and news. Players can also vote on opinion questions, send messages to friends with a Wii or computer, and view and send pictures.

The Wii remote, channels, and games make the console a truly great system. The Nintendo Wii provides fun for everyone and opens up new possibilities for the future of video games.

Chris Kotson, Grade 8
Albemarle School, NC

The Day I Got Stitches

One day on a Saturday afternoon my sister and I were trying to build a brick playhouse. I walked out the back door to go help get bricks. As I was walking toward the bricks already ready to be used, I heard my sister Whitney call my name. When I turned to see what she wanted, everything froze. I was in shock. I touched my head and saw on my hand blood. Then I started crying as blood fell down my face, and I ran inside to tell my mom what had happened. She got a towel and put it where the brick had hit me to stop the bleeding. Then she called my uncle and told him what happened and asked if he would take us to the hospital.

When we made it to the hospital, my mom set me down with my sisters and signed me in to get fixed up. The lady called my name and everyone became angry because I had just arrived and was called before them. The doctor laid me on the table and put drops in the hole to clean it. My mom and two other doctors held me down because it hurt. They didn't numb me or anything so I was constantly trying to get up and run. The doctor put nine stitches in my head. When I came out with a patch over my eye, my sisters were waiting and my uncle drove us home.

Terence Alexander, Grade 9
Baton Rouge Magnet High School, LA

Dinosaurs

In the forest of the cretaceous period, it was very quiet and placid. Quietly a velociraptor woke up from sleeping that night and was covertly hidden under sonic bushes in the labyrinth-like forest. Slowly, a hungry Tyrannosaurus Rex walked up; slowly the velociraptor hung his head out from under the bushes to enhance his sight of the huge Tyrannosaurus Rex.

The Tyrannosaurus Rex was looking around for prey to eat because he was starving. Suddenly the Tyrannosaurus Rex made a loud roar and the velociraptor knew the renowned roar and got scared so he ran away. Unfortunately the Tyrannosaurus Rex caught sight and heard the velociraptor and took off after him.

The velociraptor went deeper and deeper into the forest and the Tyrannosaurus Rex followed close behind. The velociraptor was abrasively tripping over things and the Tyrannosaurus Rex was catching up quickly. Then the velociraptor got cornered in a spot replete with trees so he could not get out and would stay in there until the T-rex could get him to eat.

The velociraptor backed into the tight corner to get away for the noxious and hungry Tyrannosaurus Rex. The Tyrannosaurus Rex could not get his big mouth into the small corner and eventually the velociraptor's strategy nullified the T-rex attempts. Then he went to look for food elsewhere.

Patrick David, Grade 7
St Mary's School, SC

Painful Summer

Next to my family, baseball has been the most important thing to me for years. It is a physical sport, and I have seen many people get injured. I have played for years and have had no injuries. That all changed 8 months ago.

Eight years ago, I began playing baseball for Champion League. As my skills improved, it seemed to me the league was not improving every year. Therefore, I decided to find another league. After many months, I finally found a travel ball team from Piedmont, SC, called the "Carolina Thunder." I went to the practice so I could try out. I made the team! The only bad thing was, we had to run 1.5-2.0 miles every practice, which was about 2 times a week. After four practices, I started developing a mysterious pain in my ankle. I went to physical therapy, wore a cast, and had surgery. After surgery, I noticed that my ankle was not doing any better. As a result, we went up to Duke University Medical Center. After we talked to the doctor at Duke, I had a MRI, and the film was taken to an Orthopedic and Radiological Conference. They determined that I had a rare condition called "Bone Marrow Edema Syndrome." The doctors said, "the only treatment was rest."

Being a 13 year old active boy, it has been hard to rest. I've not enjoyed the rest, but have learned patience.

Robert Wilson, Grade 8
Wilson Home School, SC

My Name: A Family Legacy

My name was the first thing given to me at birth, and will be the last thing thought about at my death. A name is given to all people, no matter your race, culture, ethnicity, or religion.

Among the reasons why I hold my name so dear, is that I possess more than a name, I possess a legacy. A legacy of honor, honesty, and good heartedness came before me and are expected to follow after me. Brought from Romania by my great-grandfather, the name Kaufman emerged when he reached Ellis Island, and had to be able to spell his name. He had apprenticed for a shoemaker in Germany. The word *Kaufman* is German for shoemaker, and he could spell that for he had the business card in his pocket. Originating as Monsky, the name Monroe is the legacy of my father, which his father chose to change it to after World War Two. Lastly, the name Zachary was considered strong and noble by my parents.

Furthermore, the respect I hold for my name is something that nothing and no one can tarnish no matter how hard they try.

Living on in me forever is my name, and hopefully to live on in my children. A name is a magnificent exposé of parental love and devotion to a child, and a name is an elegant reminder of a persons' ancestry.

Finally, my name is a way for me to express my inner being through three simple words, Zachary Kaufman Monroe.

Zachary K. Monroe, Grade 7
White Station Middle School, TN

Pasta Day

Thursday is a terrible day for everyone, because Thursday is pasta day. Everyone dreads Thursdays because they know that pasta will be served at lunch. Fifth hour comes and no one wants it to end. Usually everyone rushes to the cafeteria, like on chicken nugget day, but not on Thursday. The hallways are full, as everyone takes as long as possible at their lockers and walks as slow as molasses to the cafeteria. The smell is dreadful and the taste awful. Some kids think it is so bad that they don't even eat lunch, while others puke the pasta up in their mouths.

Unlike the delicious Italian pasta, school pasta is like eating slimy worms that crawl around in your mouth. A deadly haunting aroma fills the nostrils of students with the smell of eggs that have rotted for over a year, while regular pasta leaves people wanting to smell more. School pasta leaves my hands feeling like a rubber baby toy. When I look at this appalling dish, I see a snake that has been curled up with a curling iron. This kind of pasta is usually not appealing to the average person. This kind of repulsive meal should not be served at school.

Alexis Bumby, Grade 8
West Jr High School, MO

Positions of Football

Football is an exciting sport. Football is a sport of execution and having talented players at key positions. Most people know how football is played, but they don't know the positions. The following are some of the more significant positions and their role in football.

The quarterback is positioned behind the center, and takes the snap from the center. When the quarterback takes the snap, he either hands the ball to the running back, throws the ball down the field, or runs the ball.

The position which is my favorite, is the wide receiver. The wide receiver is responsible for getting open to catch the ball. The wide receiver has to run specific routes and if these routes are not executed properly, the quarterback may be forced to throw an interception.

The running back carries the ball as he runs down the field. They are frequently used as short-yardage receivers. On the offense, the wide receivers and the running backs are generally the fastest.

The place kicker is one position that goes unnoticed many times. Many games are won or lost by the place kicker. One example of this was on the 2005 Alabama team. Three games that year were won by the field goal kicker. The place kicker handles field goal attempts and kickoffs.

I hope that by reading this you have learned some of the positions of football and their functions. I also hope that you have found that football is an exciting sport.

Chelsea Morgan, Grade 8
Trinity Christian Academy, AL

The Greatest Big Sister Ever

Everyone has someone they admire, and the person I admire the most is my older sister, Megan. She is great at basketball, makes great grades, and is the best big sister you could ever have.

Megan has been playing basketball for four years. Watching her play is one way I have become good at this sport. She has taught me so much about the sport, that I've learned more than a coach could ever teach me.

Megan is the smartest ninth grader I've ever known. She is taking tenth grade math and is making an A in the class. She has made straight A's since she started using letter grades in the third grade.

She is the best big sister because she helps me when I ask for it. When I need help in learning how to do something she will explain it to me. Sometimes she might even show me how to do it.

Well, that's why I admire my older sister. She is amazing at basketball, very smart, and is the best big sister ever! If you got to know the real Megan, you would know why I admire her so much. I am very thankful for being her younger sister. We may fight sometimes, but that's what sisters do and I will always admire her no matter what happens.

Amy Aaron, Grade 7
Morris Middle School, OK

Treadmill Mishap

Have you ever seen the commercial for depression where the lady goes and sits on a moving treadmill and rides off? That is one of my favorite commercials.

One day I was bored out of my mind and wanted something exciting to do. I decided to go upstairs to the so called "fitness room." I set the treadmill to 5 mph. I wanted to reenact the commercial.

Once I had checked that everything was in order I sat on the body builder machine. As soon as I sat down, I realized that I was going too fast. I flew off the machine and hit the wall behind the treadmill. My foot got stuck underneath the treadmill but the treadmill kept rolling over it. I finally was able to pull the plug and proceeded to the standing position.

I had a huge burn on my foot. I thought I was going to get in trouble so I decided not to tell my mom. However, the next day was football tryouts. When I went to get ready I couldn't fit my foot in the cleat because of the swelling.

Once we managed to get my cleat on we went to the tryouts. I couldn't run as fast as I normally do but even with my dilemma I was still ranked as an "A" player.

Now that I have a scar to represent the action of a true blonde, I don't think I will try to reenact any commercials again!

Madison Harding, Grade 7
Osceola Creek Middle School, FL

Key West

Today I am going to be telling you a little bit about Key West. In these next three paragraphs I will explain the atmosphere, the things to do while you're in Key West and what the weather is like while you're in Key West.

The atmosphere in Key West is a very laid-back one. The people in Key West are very nice and very outgoing. Whether you are a local, working on Duval Street, or a vacationer from out of town, the mood is the same; carefree and trouble free.

One of the things to do in Key West is ride the conch train. It takes you around the island, giving you some pretty interesting facts about Key West. One more thing you can do while you are in Key West is visit the Key West lighthouse. Climbing all the way up, you can see the view of the island. You also can walk the Duval strip which has a lot of bars and shops you can go into.

One of the events in Key West is the Hemingway look-alike contest. The sunset celebration in Malory Square has some really good acts. The weather in Key West is very beautiful. It never gets hotter than 95 degrees and the humidity always feels low because you are surrounded by water.

I hope you learned a little more about Key West. I hope what I told you makes you want to visit real soon.

James Briggs, Grade 7
Sebastian River Middle School, FL

The Threats and Advantages of MySpace

The MySpace website is a great thing but can be dangerous. MySpace is a good way to contact friends, family, or to meet new people. People on MySpace can be threatening and can hack into your MySpace profile and your personal files.

MySpace threats can be lethal, but there is a way to prevent them through the use of private settings. The private settings have choices to make your profile information private. This makes all your information private so that the person trying to send a message, send friend requests, and all other postings have to know your last name, email address or type random letters and numbers jumbled up for a verification process. These settings can help in the event of someone trying to send a virus.

You can tell many things about a person by what their MySpace looks like. Everyone can customize their layouts, music and pictures. PimpMyProfile.com is one of many websites where you can get a layout for your MySpace. Music can be searched on MySpace from music celebrities' profiles and then placed into yours. It is not the best thing to add a celebrity as a friend because some people join for the wrong reason.

Without being responsible you can endanger your family, your friends, and yourself. Before you get a MySpace, think hard about the dangers and threats that can come to you. If used correctly, it can be fun.

Zachary Clevenger, Grade 7
Trinity Christian Academy, AL

What I Like About My Best Friend…

What's not to like about my best friend! It is someone to lean on when things get tough.

She is someone to talk to when you need to talk. Someone you want to have a good time with each day. My best friend is not only one of the nicest people you will meet but also very generous. If I ever need something, she is the first person to want to help. My best friend is kind and loving and is always there when I need a shoulder to lean on. Have you ever had a friend that just makes you laugh when you look at her? Well, that's how my best friend is. She is a true blonde. Half the time when you talk to her she just looks at you and pretends that she knows exactly what you are talking about. I love her so much. When it comes to school, she is very focused and asks lots of questions, but as soon as she is out the door, it's all talk and all play. These are great qualities to have because it is great to have a serious side along with a fun and enthusiastic side. Every day I learn something new about her and I've known her for a very long time. She is special. If I had to choose my favorite thing about her it would definitely be her personality. Bubbly, hyper, and sarcastic are the best words to describe her. Natalie is my best friend and there are so many things I love about her and I would never change anything about her.

Taylor Ogle, Grade 8
Heritage Hall School, OK

Trials

I once knew a girl named Amina whose Muslim family lived in Africa. One day Amina was bitten by a snake. My family discovered what happened and offered to help. We gave them money for food and told them we would take them to the hospital. When we returned, we found a witch doctor there. The family had taken our money and paid for a witch doctor. When the witch doctor didn't heal her, we offered to help again, but they hired a witch doctor again. By the time we finally got her to the hospital they had to amputate her leg. Afterwards, the same process was carried out on her sister. Eventually, through our outreach, we taught the family about Christ and they were all baptized. Through any trials we have we should always look for the positive in the circumstance.

In our lives we all have trials. Trials come in many different ways. We need to decide to accept them and redirect their meaning. We need to take trials as they come and use them in a productive way. Like in Amina's story, God always has a plan. For Amina, her whole family was saved.

We need to be ready for the trials God gives us. He decides whether we prosper or perish. He guides our path and determines what will be. If we depend on Him, our lives will forever be glorious. Life is a trial in itself and we should all be ready and waiting.

Jadeth Lieb, Grade 8
College Heights Christian School, MO

The Best Birthday Party Ever

A birthday is a fun, enjoying, memorable time. I was determined my twelfth birthday would be extra-special. I was going to have a slumber party. I invited five friends, Destinee, Mima, Jessica, Lautwanese, and Ashleigh, to my house after the spring dance.

We were going to the dance together and then staying up until 3:00 in the morning. This was significant because at my house we must go to bed by midnight on Fridays. On Saturday, the party would conclude with a trip to the movies and lunch.

We had so much fun at my party. We danced and talked at the dance. This was the best girl time we had ever had. This was the best part of my party. I only wish it had been longer.

My friends, mom, and dad are what made this party significant to me. They helped me realize that a party isn't special because of what you do at it. It is special because you celebrate with people that love and care for you. Though you think, even if you already know this, that a party is determined if it is good or not by what you do at your party, it is not. A birthday celebrates when you were born and what you do on it doesn't matter. Who you celebrate with is more important. This may have been the best thing I learned in my life.

Myleka Jefferson, Grade 7
Alexandria Middle Magnet School, LA

Away Traveling

During my lifetime I have been all around the world. I have seen India and Spain. I could probably say I have visited countries in most of the continents. I have also been to places like Ayortha and Auburn, places not located on a map. Transporting myself, I didn't go by any normal means of transportation, such as cars and planes, I went on the wings of a book. Exploring these exotic places, I was still enjoying the comforts of my own home.

Sometimes, I would even travel at night. I got my cell phone and used the light to read by. Every time I heard my mother, I would stop and feign sleep and put the book and light away. After hearing her retreating footsteps, I would take out he book and start again.

Some of the best books to travel in are those in which the author has made up their own world. One of my favorite is the series of *Harry Potter* by J.K. Rowling. The way she describes Hogwarts can always send me off flying on a broomstick. She makes me feel as if I were right there playing quidditch or going into one of the battles.

Every time I pick up a book and sit on my favorite chair, I leave the ordinary world behind and live in the world of the character. I experience their lives for that time while I am traveling. I sit there, in the world of the book, until someone brings me out of my reverie, back to my world, the real world.

Chiyerre Echie, Grade 7
White Station Middle School, TN

Pros and Cons of School Uniforms

Schools that require students to wear uniforms are breaking parental rights. I think that uniforms could cause students to be rebellious; simply because children feel that they are told what to do all of the time, so they do not want to be told what clothes to wear.

A school generally proposes the idea of school uniforms to reduce bullying, but on average, only about 7% of bullying is caused by this issue. Schools should be more worried about bullying because of racial discrimination or bullying due to athletic ability. I agree that there should just be guidelines and dress codes not a strict requirement of something such as khaki pants, polo, and a neck tie.

If a school proposes the idea of school uniforms to stop children from wearing provocative clothing, then uniforms probably should be required, but let the students pick the uniforms; let it be something that they want to wear. If the uniforms are something that the students as a majority do not like, then that is breaking the students' right to freedom of expression. I think that it is easier to get up in the morning and know what you are going to wear, and you can do that with school uniforms.

In conclusion, I believe that schools need to let the children and parents choose their attire. I completely support the idea of school uniforms, not that a board of education decides, but that we as a student body make the decision.

Caleb Ball, Grade 7
Stroud Middle School, OK

Before You Crochet

Have you ever seen a blanket or sweater made of yarn? If yes, then you have probably seen a crocheted item. Crochet is a way to make yarn into cloth and other items using a hook and pattern. Using crochet you can make ruffles, tight-knit cloth and loose-knit cloth; it all depends on your hook and your pattern.

There are lots of hook sizes all used with different yarn for different things. Everyone who crochets has their preference and they all have used different kinds of sizes. Take me, for example, my favorite hook size is a 5.00mm hook but I've made doilies with a 2.5mm hook and a sweater with a 6.00mm hook. All three of them use different yarn types.

My favorite kind of yarn is the regular yarn you get at Wal-Mart, which can be used for almost anything. Other kinds of yarn are best for different things. Thread-like yarn works well for doilies, soft yarn is used for blankets and fuzzy yarn is used for winter items like scarves.

Working with the yarn is fun and easy for anyone who likes to make things with their hands. It is a great way to get new clothes and a great activity for anyone who makes presents. If you're good you almost always make something productive. Now find a pattern and begin!

Alicia Oliphant, Grade 7
Excelsior Springs Middle School, MO

Winning Isn't Everything

Winning is what everyone wants, but winning does not always help you.

Everyone hates to lose, but it can help you. Even I want to win every time I play the sports I love, but you can't always win. Winning makes you more self confident, but does it teach you anything? If you always won would you learn that you can't beat everyone? I know that some people can beat almost anyone at whatever they do, but there is probably someone else that will come along and beat them sometime.

Losing is sometimes good when it teaches you how to accept defeat and how to learn from your mistakes and your opponent's strengths. You can also learn why the opponent beat you and what you need to work on to succeed the next time. I also think that losing helps you and what you need to work on to succeed the next time. I also think that losing helps you to work harder and improve, so that you will not lose the next time you play the same opponent. There are some teams that you can beat convincingly. Now think how they feel? But don't go and lose to them just because you feel bad or don't change your game plan so that they will win. Just take it in to consideration that they feel the same as you do when you lose to an opponent.

Just think about winning and losing. Just think!

Sam Emerson, Grade 8
Heritage Hall School, OK

Female Firefighter

I come from a family of firefighters. I'm the first and only girl. When I started firefighting, the chief was my daddy. My reason for wanting to become a firefighter is because we lost 343 firefighters on September 11, 2001.

Being the only girl and the chief's daughter, you have to work ten times harder. On my first night, nobody liked me because I was a girl. After a year, the boys gave up on trying to run me off from the fire department.

My first year at North Lenoir I got Jr. Firefighter of the Year. This award goes to the person who works really hard. The boys on the department did not like that at all. On October 14, 2007 we all pulled together and brought home the first place trophy at our annual firemen's day. The whole department won first place in every event except one. And we won the overall award.

Now I have been on the department for two and a half years, they have been the best years of my life, so far. I'm also a Jr. Firemen captain and secretary. All the firefighters are like one big family. I may get picked on or talked about at school, but I just think of someone's life I might save one day. Who knows, it could be theirs. The feeling of saving some ones life is PRICELESS, that is why I love being a VOLUNTEER FIREFIGHTER!

Morgan Everett, Grade 8
E B Frink Middle School, NC

Emily Butler, My Best Friend

I could write over one million pages of why I love Emily Butler but, unfortunately I can only write 5 paragraphs. Ever since the fourth grade, Emily has been my best friend. We have been through it all. She is my other half. She has been there for me when I needed her and it is how she handles the hard times and treats others that makes her my hero.

Emily has been through so much. When she was little, she moved from California to Texas. Afterwards, Emily lost her dog, Romeo in October of 2000. This changed her whole life. Following this, I met Emily in the 3rd grade. Unfortunately, three years later I moved far away, leaving her devastated. Although I moved, we still keep in touch every day and are as close as ever.

She has many different qualities that make people love her. Her sense of humor is incredible and it cheers people up. When you're sad, she knows the right thing to say. One of the best qualities she owns is standing up for you even though you're one thousand miles away.

Emily and I are literally the definition of best friends. Our conversations are certainly amazing. She is my sunshine. Obviously she means a lot to me. For example, Emily has helped me to become who I am today: myself and no one else. I honestly don't know what I would do without her.

Despite our locations, our friendship has reminded me that there is always someone there for you at your time of need. Emily is that certain person for me. I'm so glad she moved to Texas, even though I moved to South Carolina. Basically, Emily is my best friend, she completes me, and I wouldn't want it any other way.

Ashlen Conerly, Grade 8
St Mary's School, SC

Imagination of Millions

Walt Disney was a famous Missourian. He opened kid's imagination as he created cartoon characters such as Mickey Mouse, Donald Duck, Goofy and many more adventurous characters. As a kid he would draw on toilet paper with coal because his family didn't have much paper for "doodling" but that didn't make a difference to him just as long as he got his ideas down on something. As he got older and had more practice drawing, he sold as many animations as he could. Turns out that when he grew up he became a very famous cartoonist and a motion picture producer. He won 32 Academy Awards for motion pictures throughout his career. He was also very well known in 1927 for adding sound to his animations. Two of his animations with sound that he was famous for were *Steamboat Willey* and *Snow White*. Still until this day he's remembered as one of the most famous cartoonist and motion picture producers. One of the ways we honor him is by resorts all over America such as Walt Disney World and Walt Disneyland. Still until this day he is remembered through all his achievements as a cartoonist and motion picture producer.

Tania Palacios, Grade 8
West Jr High School, MO

The Greatest Game Ever Played

Football has been played ever since the early 1900's. The sport has evolved into a lifestyle for many Americans. It has become known as the greatest game ever played.

Football players started out wearing nothing but leather helmets for protection. Now they wear cleats, shoulder pads, knee pads, thigh pads, and even gloves. There are two main sides of the ball, offense and defense. The offense's job is to simply move the ball down the field and score a touchdown. The defense is on the other side of the ball. It is the defense's job to stop the other team's offense from scoring. There can be only eleven players on the field at a time for both teams, eleven on offense and eleven on defense. The quarterback may be the most important player on the offense. The quarterback gets all of the credit when the team wins and all of the blame when the team loses. The offensive and defensive line is the two most physically exhausting positions. The linemen may be the biggest players on the team, but they are also the most athletic.

These are all reason why I think that football is the greatest game ever played. It is my favorite sport and I will always love to play it.

Nathan Jackson, Grade 8
Trinity Christian Academy, AL

My Hero

Out of all the people I know and love, my hero would have to be my grandpa, Tom Trentham. The reasons he is my hero are we like the same things, he takes me hunting and fishing, and he cares about me. Because of all these he is my favorite person in the world.

One reason my grandpa is my hero is because we like the same things. We both like to watch football. Both of us like to hunt and fish. We both like to shoot guns. These are only some of the things we do together.

Two of the most fun things in the world to do are to fish and hunt. We fish for trout at the Clinch River below Norris Dam. Every single time we go we always have a blast and catch a lot of fish. We hunt for coon in Newport or in Greene County, Georgia. When we go to Georgia and stay in the cabin we have so much fun. We sleep all day and hunt all night.

The main reason he is my hero is that he cares for me. When I stay at my grandparents' house, if even just a little sound happens, he comes running down the stairs to check on me. He shows how much he cares about me by coming to all of my sport events.

After reading all of this I guess you can tell I really love my grandpa. We both like fishing and hunting, and he supports me. I really love my grandpa and he is my favorite person in the world.

Dalton Bohanan, Grade 8
Pigeon Forge Middle School, TN

Moving

I just moved to Florida and I love it, but I'll tell you about that later on. I will tell you about how it was when I was packing, how it was on the way down to Florida, and how it is now.

Wow! I know now how hard it is to move. We had to pack every day right when we got home from school until dinner. My friends came over to hang out and that led to tears. We had to say goodbye because I had to pack up our moving truck.

Are we there yet? The trip felt like years. We stopped so many times. Bathroom breaks and just to get out and stretch. I got so bored that I slept for hours. We stopped to stay at a hotel then we headed out early that morning. We got closer and closer until we pulled in a driveway to a beautiful house. So me and my sisters ran in to look inside.

It's my house not my vacation house. Now that I realize that the schools are so fun and you have nice teachers. I have a lot more friends than I thought. My house is great and I love my room.

My thought was wrong because I thought I would hate it. Now I could say a kid's most hated words to my parents you were right I was wrong. I love Florida now and I love everything about it!

Shyann Gilbert, Grade 7
Sebastian River Middle School, FL

The Undefeated Dragons

October 6, 2007, the Chelsea Dragons softball team won the state championship in Oklahoma City. They won against Henreyetta, Oklahoma, only winning by one point and being undefeated 42-0. This is really an accomplishment to the girls on this team and that is a huge pride for this small town.

Only if I could be there to watch the greatest coaches, Darryl Ping, Gary Reed, and the funniest one ever Jim Patterson, I really enjoy listening to them during the summer. But, watching them win during the tournaments that were held here just makes me think about all the good times.

Well, we know that this is the first year they actually were sent to state and won undefeated, which I can't believe that they went that far in the whole season. For a small town like this it is awesome for this small town to have girls like this.

October 7, 2007, the Sunday after the tournament coach Gary Reed came to First Assembly of God here in Chelsea and he said in his own words about the team saying. "This game wasn't like others we have played and many like this has given us the strength to carry on and the only thing that was different, there was a good feeling we were being watched over by God himself." That got me really thinking about what wonders that God has done for this little community that have changed through the 100 years of this nice state Oklahoma.

Josh Boggs, Grade 8
Chelsea Jr High School, OK

My Family

Whenever I think of my family, I feel so lucky to have such wonderful people who support me and help me through the hard times. I have many family members but the ones who have influenced me the most are my mom and dad, and my little brother, Jack.

My parents have encouraged me to always go for my goals and dreams. Also, they have always done whatever it takes to let me do whatever activities and other events that I would like to do. They both have worked very hard to allow me to participate in a competitive soccer team, a traveling dance team, and now they are working hard to let me be on the cheerleading team at our school, which is very time consuming and isn't cheap. Although my brother is only three years old, he is another person who influences me a lot. He is just so innocent and he knows right from wrong which reminds me if he can do the right thing so can I. He looks up to me so I always need to be a good leader for him. He is a good example for me and he teaches me new things every day.

In conclusion, I hope you can see why these people are so important to me, how they have changed my life, and made me who I am today. I really wish everyone could be as blessed as I am to have such great people guiding them through their life.

Kenlee Collins, Grade 8
Southwest Jr High School, AR

Mr. Rocky

Mr. Rocky came into my life like a whirlwind. By watching him mature and grow in body and heart I have seen that he exemplifies many wonderful character traits.

If you want love from an animal, then Rocky is the animal you would go to. He comes up to you and he snuggles you. When you are sad he comes and gives you kisses. When he gets tired he comes and snuggles down in your shirt or in your lap. Mr. Rocky is a brilliant squirrel. He was potty trained in about a week. He learned where to eat his food in a few days. When he was a little older he learned some simple commands. He learned what no, come, and his name meant. Mr. Rocky is very funny. When he was very little he thought his bathroom was my grandpa. But he quickly found out it wasn't. A couple months later he figured out that he liked peaches, so when my grandfather was sitting in his chair and was just about to sink his teeth into a peach Rocky ran up and snatched his peach away from him. He then had to run with the peach in his mouth. Poppy chased him all the way across the house. Rocky has a lot of determination and perseverance. When he wants something he does not stop until he has it no matter what the cost. When he was out in his cage one day he wanted to take his blanket to the top of a tree and he didn't stop until he got it up there.

Mr. Rocky is and will always be the best pet ever. These are just a few examples of Mr. Rocky's personality.

Sara Nicole Tice, Grade 8
Southwest Jr High School, AR

Fatal Tragedy in New York

A few years ago there was an unbelievable tragedy in the United States. It was the fall of the World Trade Center in New York City on September 11. That day more than 2,900 people died, not counting the terrorist. I remember being glued to the television, wondering the horrors the people in the buildings went through.

Although it was terrible there were still people in those buildings who were calm. Some of the people called their families telling them that they wouldn't be coming home. They sounded calm because they knew that death was soon to become their present, and they were able to accept that.

Their families, however, weren't so calm. Families were worried. They were just realizing that they were never going to see the member of their family again. The whole United States nation was crushed.

At 10:05, September 11, the south tower of the World Trade Center collapsed. Ten minutes later Flight 93, of American Airlines, crashed. At 10:29 the north tower collapsed. There were no survivors ever found in the rubble.

Even though it was a very dreadful time it has just made the United States stronger. Our country has become more prepared for these situations. We will always be the United States and we will always be one.

Megan Harris, Grade 7
Rhea Central Elementary School, TN

The Deep Blue Sea and Me

Look out yonder and see the blue waves tumble over each other like crisp leaves. Then the waves start to calm down, and I can see for miles. It appears as if the sea is going farther and farther away from me.

I look down near my feet and ponder about the water. I wonder why it is so dark and mysterious, yet bright and full of knowing. Suddenly, I see a gray dolphin peering up from behind a wave. It is by far the most exquisite mammal that lives in the sea. However, there are also seahorses, starfish and many other beautiful sea creatures. Although there are many spectacular living things in the ocean, the dolphin is my favorite.

Yet another thing I adore about the magnificent sea is the way it seems to be calm and gentle. Nothing else can distract me when I am floating with the current and gazing at the clouds. While the majestic water hugs my body, I fade into a blue. Finally, I sit up and come back from my imagination, then come in to shore.

I can see for a hundred miles when I look out into the deep blue sea. The tides are coming in soft and gentle while the dolphins are playing in the waves. I sit and admire the views for as long as I can. I hope that you now know why I adore that deep blue sea along the soothing shore.

Kelsie Henry, Grade 7
Greenfield Jr/Sr High School, MO

It's Only a Dream

The beat of the drums or maybe it was my heart was all I could remember. I had been walking along the beach when suddenly everything went black. I now realize that my vacation paradise had turned into a nightmare. I had been taken captive by the natives. I soon learned that this was a hostile tribe that had lived on this island for many years. They were a tribe of hungry headhunters.

I woke to find myself prisoner in a primitive hut. Although, I was allowed to wander about their village, I knew that there was no chance for me to escape. The natives watched my every move. I wasn't deprived completely. Every day, I drank sweet clean water. I ate delicious tangy fruit and crunchy meat. The thought occurred to me that they were fattening me up for their next big meal. As I explored my new home, filled with strange sounds and smells, I wondered what would be my fate. The shrunken heads decor didn't help my anxiety.

The natives were getting restless. I knew that something was going to happen. As I lay in my hut trying to sleep, I knew that morning would bring answers. Awakened by the smell of bacon cooking or maybe me, I fell out of my bed, I could hear a faint voice calling my name. Wake up Haley, it's only a dream.

Haley Jones, Grade 8
North Iredell Middle School, NC

Small Town Boy

My dad, Bill Huston grew up in small town America, with rusty, red brick roads, markets, and dime stores. This town is called Chelsea, Oklahoma. Bill enjoyed being a child in Chelsea, he liked playing with his buddies, tormenting his younger sister, Shelly along with his teachers, and keeping his parents on his tail.

Bill remembers riding his bicycle while carrying his bb gun with his dog, Bobby K. tagging along beside him. He also remembers when he was four or five. He was looking for grasshoppers to use as fish bait when a red wasp stung him near his eye and he yelled out that a grasshopper had bit him. "There are many other memories but there's not enough paper," says Bill Huston.

Some of his hobbies growing up included camping, fishing, and basically just being outdoors. The sports that he played were football, basketball, baseball, and playing the trumpet in the band. Some of his current hobbies still include hunting and fishing but he also enjoys spending time with his family.

Bill has a full time job as an electrician working for Duvall Electric, but his most important job is being a wonderful loving husband and dad. A good trait about Bill is he brought his daughters up in a good, Christian home and has always provided his family with food and a roof over their heads. The next time you see Bill Huston you will look and know that he is a wonderful Oklahoman.

Hannah Huston, Grade 8
Chelsea Jr High School, OK

Coach Paul "Bear" Bryant

The University of Alabama was founded in 1831. One of the most important things on the campus of Alabama is its football program. This, I believe, is one of the best college football programs in the Southeastern Conference. The most exciting thing in the months of September to November is to wake up to the sounds of thousands of fans crowding the streets trying to be the first ones there on the Promenade.

One of the most important things you will ever learn, coming to the University of Alabama at any time of the year, is that there is a man named Paul "Bear" Bryant. Bryant was one of the best football coaches Alabama ever had. Coach Bryant led Alabama to win over a hundred fifty games in just a twenty-eight year coaching period. Then he died on January 26, 1984. He will always be remembered for both his honors and accomplishments. One of his greatest accomplishments was being a four-time National Coach of the Year.

Although a lot of fans wish that we still had Coach Bryant, we will always be satisfied with what he did for Alabama. Over all, Paul "Bear" Bryant was the University of Alabama's greatest football coach of all times. I believe no one will ever be able to beat Bryant's legendary record and impression he left, not just with Alabama fans, but a lot of other fans too.

Savannah Taylor, Grade 8
Trinity Christian Academy, AL

Chicken Balooza

Chickens are very unique birds for many reasons. Different chickens lay different colored eggs. Chickens' feathers come in many different colors. Chickens can look very different from one another.

Some chickens, like Ameraucanas can lay blue, green, and pink eggs. There are others that lay white eggs, like the Golden Campines. Others such as the Barred Plymouth Rocks lay brown eggs.

Chickens can come in many different colors. The Golden Campine is a personal favorite because its neck is covered with golden feathers. Buff Orfingtons are a sunny shade of yellow. A Rhode Island Red is a rusty red color all over with a bluish green tail. Chickens come in practically every color imaginable.

While most chickens tend to look similar to one another, a chicken called the Frizzle is very unusual. The Frizzle's nickname is the mutant chicken because its feathers go the wrong way. While many chickens have feathers going away from their heads, the Frizzle has feathers going in every direction on its body. The Frizzle is considered to be one of the ugliest birds raised on a farm.

So, it is apparent that chickens can come in many different shapes, sizes, and colors. They can be ugly, pretty and just plain odd. They are very interesting and unique birds. Hopefully, as people learn more about chickens, they will grow to love and appreciate them.

Chris Williams, Grade 8
Stoneridge Academy, SC

How to Have a Healthy Lifestyle

Let me ask you a question? Have you ever wondered what the Bible means when it says, "That your body is a temple of God?" I believe it means that we should keep our bodies healthy. I believe that we should maintain a healthy lifestyle. We can do this by exercising, eating right, drinking the right amount of water, and getting plenty of rest.

One way of keeping our bodies healthy is by choosing the right kinds of food to eat, and not always eating junk food, and other foods that are processed. We also need to drink the right amount of water to flush out all the impurities.

We should exercise every day. Whether it be walking on the treadmill or walking outside, swimming or jogging. It does not matter what you do as long as you are doing something. In addition to this, we should get plenty of rest. This will help us live longer lives as well. It is hard to go through your day or exercise when you are tired.

As I stated earlier, I believe what the Bible says, "That our bodies are a temple of God," and because of this reason we should live a clean healthy lifestyle. I also believe that we should keep our bodies fit, and in good shape. The Bible also says, "That God made us in His image." Therefore by exercising, eating healthy, drinking the right amount of water, and getting plenty of rest, we honor God.

Ryan Reaves, Grade 9
Trinity Christian Academy, AL

Cross Canadian Ragweed

Cross Canadian Ragweed is an alternative country band. They are from Yukon, Oklahoma. Their name is made out of Grady Cross', Cody Canada's, and Randy Ragsdale's last names. The band members include drummer Randy Ragsdale who is the founder of the band, their front man/guitarist is Cody Canada, rhythm guitarist is Grady Cross, and their bassist is Jeremy Plato.

The band's albums consist of *Carney* made in 1998, *Live and Loud at the Wormy Dog Saloon* made in 1999, *Highway 377* which was made in 2001, *Live and Loud at Billy Bob Texas* made in 2002, their album *Purple* was made in 2002, *Soul Gravy* was made in 2004, *Garage* was made in 2005, *Back in Tulsa — Live and Loud at the Cain's Ballroom* was made in 2006, and their latest album is *Mission California*. The album *Purple* is a tribute to the band's "little sister," Mandi Ragsdale who died in an automobile accident. The band has three albums that are Top Country albums. Those albums are *Purple, Soul Gravy*, and *Garage*. Their singles are *17, Constantly, Sick and Tired, Alabama, Fightin For, This Time Around*, and *I believe you*.

Cross Canadian Ragweed is known for touring show after show. They tour mainly in Texas and Oklahoma a lot. But also travel other places.

Seth Walker, Grade 8
Chelsea Jr High School, OK

My School Life

School life for me is different every day because I never know what crazy thing I will do next. Yesterday, I fell on the steps on the way to lunch. It was really funny to my friends because I tried to act like it didn't even happen. It's so weird how one little accident can amuse so many people (except for me). When I went to dance last night, a girl asked me if I fell. She wasn't even in my class and informed me that my clumsiness had spread over the whole eighth grade! That was not the only time I have fell at school and you don't even want to know what else I have done. Anyway as you can tell, my friends (and people in other classes) get MANY laughs out of me. As I was informed, ask anybody in the eighth grade!

Kimberly Ervin, Grade 8
E B Frink Middle School, NC

A Key Virtue

Friendship is the relationship between two people. It means to will the good of another. Friendship is right in the middle of bullies and pushovers, the two things you don't want to be. The friendship of benevolence is the good and true friendship, but friendship of utility is the false and bad friendship.

To be a true friend you must know how to practice friendship. You must learn to love and be true to all of your friends. Without friends life would be lonesome and very boring. Never use friends just because they are smart or have something you like.

Without friends we would be completely lonely. It helps us relate to God and love God. We were made for friendship. I think friendship is a great gift from God and is often taken for granted. True friends will hang on through the toughest times.

Robert Collins, Grade 7
St Mary's School, SC

Wars (My Opinion)

Some people think wars help us. I strongly disagree with them. Wars hurt us in many different ways. I'm sure we all remember 9-11. Do we remember the panic, the pain, and the confusion? Well I do. 9-11 changed our lives forever. What does 9-11 have to do with wars? We all know the answer to that. It's simple. We are at war because of that unforgettable day. We are the ones causing pain and sorrow. Sure it's to keep us safe, but can't we solve our problems without guns and violence? I say we can. Belligerent nations gain nothing from their many wars. We've all heard people say the world would be a better place without wars. Although the majority of people agree at some limit, we do nothing about it! My question to you is will we make it a reality. We don't have the power to change the past, but we do have the power to influence our future. For good or bad, it's up to us. So what will we choose?

Evelyn Espinoza, Grade 8
North Iredell Middle School, NC

Imagination

Webster's Dictionary defines "imagination" as "ability to confront and deal with a problem," and "a creation of the mind." I have chosen this author, because he shows imagination can change your life.

It began in Ireland. His mother and father were A.J. and Flora, and his older brother was Warnie. Warnie and he played in the garden making up animals and people from different worlds. Heroes and bad guys! Animals that could talk!

His life changed at age 9, because his mother died. Warnie and he were sent to school in London, because their mother's death was hard on their father. It was like his father gave up. A teacher named "Knock" helped him to enjoy learning. He went on to Oxford University. But before he could finish school, he was called into the army. He was wounded and sent back to Oxford.

He was a tutor for 26 years. Later, he taught at Oxford and Cambridge. While at Oxford, another war came; England was fighting Germany. He and his brother took in children from the city. Four of those children he later used in one of his stories. Their names were Peter, Susan, Lucy, and Edmund.

He married when he was older, but sadly, she died too.

This man wrote many books. His name is C.S. Lewis, and he wrote "The Chronicles of Narnia."

C.S. Lewis had lots of problems to deal with, and he used his mind and imagination to create answers to his problems. I think imagination has a lot to do with how you handle problems in your life. Are you using your imagination?

Rebekah Baker, Grade 7
Stroud Middle School, OK

The Dirt Bike Crash

The day started like a normal day. We had just got the welder running and started welding. About 5:00 my dad got on my dirt bike. He had got it into third gear, rode by me and started a wheelie. He held it for three seconds and it came straight over on him. The brake by the peg went to his lower calf. Somehow he got up and managed to go to the garage. I drove the wrecked bike back up to the garage and we called 911. They came here very quickly.

When they showed up they tested his heart rate, put a neck brace on him, and wrapped his hurt leg. They tried to take him to the hospital but, he refused to go. So we took him five minutes later after they left. We got him to the emergency room and he was in there for an excruciating three hours. Then the doctor came in and cleaned his cut, then he got three stitches inside and seven outside. After that was over we left and went back home. Now that was something I never want to relive!!!

Nick Hart, Grade 7
Osceola Creek Middle School, FL

A True Friend

What is true friendship? True friendship is called benevolence, when you will the good of another. Friendship is a relationship between two people based on mutual interests. Virtues help us practice good habits of friendship, and lead our lives in the right direction. Friends will help each other out and try to do what makes the other happy. Once you put your friends first and yourself last, you have found true happiness. Another kind of friendship is utility. Utility is when you use people for the benefit of yourself, and is showing selfishness and disrespect.

There are many ways you can practice friendship. You can practice by never allowing teasing or criticism between siblings and friends, by trying to make new friends, and by helping teach good habits of friendship. You should always include everyone; there is no joy in exclusion. Some ways that I will practice to be a good friend and develop good habits are by being kind to my family and showing respect. I will try to include everyone, make others happy, and not gossip. This is something everyone should practice to live a good, happy life. Friendship is very important because we experience true joy and human flourishing in living in communion with others. Friends help you through times of need and are always there for you. Virtues of friendship make us more like God; therefore we need grace to practice them. We should thank God every day for this beautiful gift!

Stephanie Orr, Grade 7
St Mary's School, SC

Don't Worry, You Really Are Beautiful

Something that I feel strongly about is self-esteem issues in children, teenagers, and adults. Some problems that they have are things such as anorexia, bulimia or suicide. Anorexia is to starve oneself due to feeling fat or not liking one's body. Bulimia is defined as frequent episodes of grossly excessive food intake followed by self-induced vomiting to avert weight gain. To be suicidal is defined as dangerous to yourself or your interests. According to http://www.coolnurse.com/suicide_faq.htm, more than 32,000 people in the United States die by suicide, and it is the United State's eighth leading cause of death.

The truth of the matter is that everyone is perfect exactly the way they are, and I don't believe that anybody should feel otherwise. You are who you've made yourself, and you shouldn't let others, or yourself, bring you down. Everybody in this world is so caught up in the picture of "perfect" that society has painted for us. But don't sweat it if you're not skinny enough for anyone else, or too skinny, or if you're not pretty enough, because you don't need to be anything for anyone. Love yourself exactly how you are. In all, don't worry, you really are beautiful — exactly the way you are.

Rachael Becker, Grade 8
Bak Middle School of the Arts, FL

Dare to Be Different

If somebody asked you, "Who is your hero?" what would you say? I would respond with Gerard Way. All throughout middle school, he had very few friends because he was different and didn't fit in. Most of the time he went his own way and did what he wanted to. People picked on him because he was not thought of as "cool," but Gerard didn't care what other people thought of him. He realized that being cool is one of the worst things you could be. High school was a little harder on him, but he kept telling himself, "Don't take anything from anybody." Those words helped him get through high school and college.

While working at a comic book store in New York in 2001, he witnessed the plane crashes into the Twin Towers. Right then and there Gerard decided he wanted to get out and do something with his life, something that will make people remember his existence. He started a band with his brother, Mikey Way, and three of their good friends. They created many songs reflecting their points of view on life and what they have gone through.

In one of their recent songs, Gerard sings, "I am not afraid to keep on living, I am not afraid to walk this world alone." That is telling people that it's okay if you're different or don't have many friends. God put you on this Earth for a reason, so you should do something with your life.

Madeline Menius, Grade 8
St Gerard Majella School, MO

Stay on the Path!

Thousands of people visit Yellowstone National Park every year. Many visitors are antagonized by signs, rules and rangers around every corner. As irritating as these rules may be, they are the result of many deaths in the park years ago.

"Do not approach bears and bison." As simple as this rule may seem, there was a time when people would approach the animals for a picture. This caused many deaths in the park. One woman was killed while feeding a bear by a crowd of people, just after a park ranger told her to stop. Another man was posing for a picture by a bison when it turned and gored him, killing him instantly.

"Stay off the ground in thermal areas!" This is another imperative rule to follow. Many people have died in the park while visiting thermal areas. The ground in these areas is very unstable and can collapse at any time, sending you down into a hot pool or burning geyser, where you will probably painfully burn to death. People have made the fatal mistake of not following this guideline.

And one final rule "Stay on the path at great heights!" Once again, it's important to follow. If you venture to the edge of a cliff, then you could easily slip and fall and die. But some people didn't think of this, and people have fallen to their death in Yellowstone.

So when you visit a national park, follow the rules. Your life just might depend on it!

Jack Schoelz, Grade 8
West Jr High School, MO

My Family

Hi, my name is Irene Reianna Guzman. I'm twelve years old. I was born in Harlingen, Texas. In my family we are seven, mom, dad, three brothers, one sister and I. In my family we are respectful to one another and always use good manners.

My sister Calista Kate is six years old, she loves animals. She also loves playing with our three puppies. My sister is special to me because she is caring and cool to be around. She always keeps me smiling.

I have three brothers, the oldest after me is Nathan Lee. He is two years younger than me and he likes to play football. Then comes Dominic Javier. He said he wants to be a soldier when he grows up. Then is the youngest, Maximus Aurelious; he is thirteen months old, he is a little Tasmanian devil.

Now let me tell you about my mother and father. My mom is the weird one in my family. She is twenty-seven and was born in Harlingen, Texas. She works as a medical assistant. My dad is the strict, clean parent. My dad is thirty-nine and was born in Ft. Myers, Florida. He works as an electrician.

My family means everything to me and I would not change them for anything in the world. I love being the oldest from my brothers and sister and I'm proud to have loving and caring parents. I think I have the best family in the world!

Irene Guzman, Grade 7
Sebastian River Middle School, FL

Falls Creek

Falls Creek, Oklahoma. Fun, games, friends, contest and spiritual growth are just some of the best camp experiences I have had. Falls Creek is located close to Davis, Oklahoma.

As we approached the entrance a man in uniform stopped our vehicle. He was checking our identification. My I.D. bracelet was bright orange. I should have been wearing shades. The new tabernacle was being built. So, we had our church services in the old tabernacle which was just a roof and open sides. I was looking forward to some cool breezes but, we had only hot air. I felt like I needed a long shower. The new tabernacle will have AC.

The Devil's Bathtub was fascinating. It's actually a wading area surrounded by huge rocks with water flowing through. There were thousands of people, well, just seemed like thousands, trying to get a cool spot.

In Baptist Lake there were giant blow up water toys I tried to climb. They were slippery as a slide coated with olive oil. I cannot tell you how many times I splashed into the brown fishy lake water. I was lucky to leave with all my toes.

Our last day at Falls Creek was sad and happy at the same time. I was sad that my first time at Falls Creek was over. Even though we had to clean and spit polish our cabin. I was happy to be going home to my family and bed.

Savannah Sager, Grade 7
Chelsea Jr High School, OK

Having Good Friends

Having good friends is an important part of a person's life. Friends are there to help you when you fall and are there when you need them the most. Friends can put you down too, but they can also bring you back up. When you and your friends have a fight, it's only going to make you and them stronger. My friends are similar to this, but I only have one who is there for me through everything I go through. She helps me make good decisions, and I help her make good decisions as well. She has a good attitude and is a very positive person. She is somebody you would want your children to hang around. She is in church, and she makes good grades. She helps me when I don't understand things. My friend is a good example of excellence in many areas. She loves to play basketball and softball. We both support each other in everything we do, and help each other through the good and the bad. We give each other advice about things that we are experiencing or things that we're going through. I love her more each and every day.

Friends are important. You need someone you can talk to and tell anything to, without them telling the whole school or world. So if you don't have a good friend, it is important that you find someone. Someone you can tell all your secrets to. Someone you can trust, someone you can love forever.

Andreanna Carson, Grade 8
Appling County Middle School, GA

Life

Sometimes in life we all wonder what makes people do the things they do. I know we all think that at some point in our lives we wonder about tragic things like divorce, a death, and what causes them. We think about happy things like romance, children, all of what makes us happy. But again what causes them? These questions make us all ponder about what is good and bad in life. Sometimes we forget what is good in life and it can get better.

Sidney delaRua, Grade 7

Dogs

Dogs are the best four-legged animals to play with. They are cuddly and like to be treated with respect and love. There are multiple types of dogs.

You will need a lot of help to train a dog. If you don't train your dog, they will make a mess everywhere. You will need to buy lots of dog food because they love to eat. You should wash dogs up every two weeks.

When you take dogs outside, you have to be very careful. Dogs like to eat other animals. They also like to chase cats. Dogs are very playful. They like to chew things like shoes. Dogs should be walked every day. Dogs should be taken to the veterinarian. If dogs don't go to their doctor, they will get sick. Dogs have to get plenty of shots.

In conclusion, I love dogs very much. I had plenty of them. They are excellent dogs to care for.

Janecia Thomas, Grade 8
Turner Middle School, GA

The Queen of People's Hearts

Diana, Princess of Wales, was an inspiring person because she was always putting others before herself. Even though she was young, she held great power. Before being married to Charles, Prince of Wales, she was known as Diana Frances Spencer. She and Charles were good friends, and they went on to get married on July 29, 1981. Their wedding was watched by millions on television. They had two sons, Prince William and Prince Henry, also known as Harry.

Diana had many talents and gifts. She was very generous and would often help with charity events. She also supported several music organizations and helped with the Armed Forces. Diana loved music; she was a talented piano player.

After eleven years of marriage to Charles, they divorced on February 28, 1996. A year and a half after their divorce on August 31, 1997, Princess Diana was killed in a traffic accident along with two of her friends. The accident was so devastating because Princess Diana was so young and loved by so many people. Since her death, Diana's sons have continued to support many of Diana's charities and causes. As her famous quote says, "Being a princess isn't all it's cracked up to be." There were a lot of ups and downs to being a princess. Overall, Princess Diana was a great person and is a role model to many people.

Lindsay Fuchs, Grade 8
St Gerard Majella School, MO

The Art of the Gods

Music is the art of the gods. That is what my band teacher has always told me, but I think it is so much more than that. It is more like the life of the Earth or even the entire universe. Even in a thick silence, there still may be an extravagant song flowing through your heart.

All over the world music can be found, even in nature. In nature, tiny raindrops falling from the vast blue sky, birds chirping, and the ocean waves crashing against the shore are all music. Some people just call all of this noise. Obviously they don't commune with nature too well.

When I make music, it soothes my soul. In my head, the war of thoughts call a truce, and I enter a peaceful state of mind. All distractions that were present begin to fade so that I can concentrate on making the most beautiful sounds possible and touching the hearts of everyone who is around me.

Like going to different lands around the world, music is like traveling. Whenever I listen to the different sounds and rhythms of music, I am transported to the heart of the place of its origin. Listening helps me clearly imagine what different people and diverse cultures inhabit these places.

Making music is more than making noise. It can provide solace for the heaviest of hearts and lull a ferocious beast into a deep, sound sleep. However, even the softest of melodies can bring a man to his knees. Furthermore, music should be respected and not considered a trifle commodity.

Jasmine Jefferson, Grade 7
White Station Middle School, TN

Living with a Sister

I have a little sister named Ashley, and as most of you know younger siblings can be very annoying. Like every other teenage girl, I spend most of my mornings in the bathroom getting ready for school. Since I have to share a bedroom and bathroom with her, this makes it impossible to get ready for school. Ashley likes to take her shower in the morning. An example of the way this aggravates me is sometimes after eating breakfast, she leaves a wet, dirty towel on the floor along with her pajamas. When I have to pick up after her, then that takes time out of my schedule.

Another example happened just the other day; I came home to a room covered with clothes that belonged to me, and I asked her, "Why are my clothes all over the place?"

"Because I was looking for clothes to wear tomorrow," she said. I was completely disappointed in her because she didn't have the decency to pick up a mess that she made.

How can I forget about the time I saw the make-up lying open on the counter and feeling angry that I wasn't the last one to use it? My last example would be that I usually have to walk onto the sticky bathroom floor because "someone" insists on using nothing less then half a can of hairspray in one use.

As you can see, living with a younger sister isn't easy, but even though she is hard to deal with sometimes, I can't live without her.

Allie Stiglets, Grade 8
Heritage Hall School, OK

My Mom, an Oklahoma Native

My mom, Janell (Jones) Allen, was born in Vinita, Oklahoma on October 29, 1975. She was the fourth daughter born to Darrel Jones and Carolyn Jones. She came home to live in Chelsea the next day. My mom lived in Chelsea until she was four and then she moved to Adair, Oklahoma. She moved to Tulsa in 1986.

My grandparents moved my mom back to Chelsea the next year. My mom's best friend in school was Rachel Smith. My mom says, "She was a typical teenager. She was always testing the limits of what she could get away with." She says that "she was and is proud to be from Oklahoma."

She met my dad in 1991 when she was 15. They met at the Chelsea Jamboree so they try to go back every year. They dated for one year and got married March 6, 1992. I was born on July 8, 1993.

Mom remembers when the Oklahoma City bombing happened. My mom said that "she was very proud of how everyone came together and stood united."

My mom got her GED in 2003. She said that "it felt good to finally have her diploma." Now she owns a flower shop in Tulsa and she works for a cancer support group in Chelsea. I am proud of my mom. And of my state.

Jonathan Allen, Grade 8

The Deadliest Terrorist Attack in America

The fatal accident that happened on September 11, 2001 was the deadliest terrorist attack on American soil. Why did this occur? The men that arranged this plan did not like what America stood for: freedom, liberty, and the rights of men and women of all races, backgrounds, and beliefs. The attack brought down the Twin Towers in New York City and part of the Pentagon in Washington D.C.

The story has been told that terrorist hijacked four planes. Two of the planes crashed into the Twin Towers. American Airlines Flight 77 was flown into the Pentagon, the headquarters of the military operations, at 9:37 A.M. The other plane was planned to hit the White House, but the passengers found out and took control of the plane. They crashed it into a field in Shanksville, Pennsylvania.

On this fatal day, camera men and photographers captured flames, billowing smoke, and sadly, bodies of people who plunged to their deaths rather than remaining trapped in the buildings. All the while, everyday people continued filming, snapping shots, and watching the terrible scene. People running and screaming, sirens blaring, and crying could be heard through Lower Manhattan.

Hundreds of people died on those planes that horrific day. Thousands died in the buildings. The men that planned this attack wanted Americans to feel afraid and unorganized. They wanted citizens in this country to do what they say by threatening us.

My opinion on this story is, I think it is just wrong what those terrorists did.

Jill Shipman, Grade 7
Stroud Middle School, OK

Life in the 50's

Have you ever wondered what life in the 50's was like? Well I have, I mean who would not be interested in 5 cent sodas or $40.00 cars, maybe I am exaggerating a little about how much money it cost to live in the 50's. The cost of living was a lot less than now! Back in the 50's, there was not a lot of crime, the cost of living was not that high, and people mostly obeyed the laws! Granted, times in the 50's were better than modern times, but it was not a perfect world in the 50's.

People in the 50's did not always follow the rules. Have you ever seen the movie *Grease*? Have you ever read the book *The Outsiders*? The T-birds in *Grease* and the gang in *The Outsiders* did not usually follows the rules.

Also in the 50's, the prices were lower but also the businesses did not pay the employees as much as they pay the employees now. So technically, the prices that we look back on and say were not a lot of money at all in the 50's were a lot of money back then. The employees probably did more work to earn that money because they did not have modern equipment to help them do their jobs. I personally believe that life in the 50's was harder than modern life.

Jenna Powell, Grade 7
Tropical Christian School, FL

My Superhero

My dad is my superhero. First, superheroes are not just super powers in tights. Next, my dad has a lot of jobs to do. Lastly, my dad is the best superhero in my mind.

First of all, some superheroes do not have super powers or tights. My dad does not have super powers, but he has dad powers. Dad powers are like when you come home from a bad day at school. And your dad smiles at you and your bad day turns into a good day. Now that is dad powers.

Next, my dad is not like regular people. He has to be the principal, a stay home dad, and also a taxi driver. he is the head of the high school, except for his boss the superintendent. Who runs the whole school district, the grade school, the junior high, and the high school. He watches us at home so we do not do anything bad. he also drives us to football practice, school, church, and around town.

In conclusion, my superhero is my dad. Super powers do not make the hero. Jobs are what my dad does most of the time. My dad is the best superhero that has ever lived.

Jonathan Anderson, Grade 7
Greenfield Jr/Sr High School, MO

Fascinating Porcupines

Porcupines are fascinating animals. This is how I think they are fascinating. Here is some interesting information about them.

Porcupines range from a bunch of different sizes. Adults can weigh fifteen to twenty pounds. Their quills are two to three inches long. With a six inch long tail, it is about three feet long.

Some of the predators of the porcupine are the puma, coyote, and the bobcat. Porcupines are an easy meal, because they aren't very smart. They live five to seven years in the wild.

The babies are born with their quills at birth. The adults have 30,000 quills when they are full grown. The babies weigh 16 ounces at birth.

All porcupines are herbivores. They eat bark, leaves, ferns, and twigs. They tear the bark off of trees and eat it. That is why they have such sharp claws. They are very good climbers also, and this makes it easier for them to get away from predators. The only problem is that they destroy trees badly because of their sharp claws.

Some people keep porcupines as pets. They make really good pets if you treat them right. You have to feed them so they have the right kind of diet. As long as they don't feel threatened, they are good pets. All you need is to watch out for their quills.

That is how I think porcupines are fascinating. If you want to know more, read a book.

Nicholas Martinez, Grade 7
Stroud Middle School, OK

The Most Important Person in My Life

The most important person in my life is my mom, Annesha Mungo. The reasons that my mom is the most important person in my life because she is always there for me, and she is a motivator. From these reasons who would you choose? Who would your person be? What would be your reasons be?

My mom is always there for me. She always helps me through the good and the bad times. She tries her best to get things that I really want or need. If it wasn't for her I don't know where I would be. She provides the food I eat, and the clothes on my back. She works really hard to support me, and my sisters.

My mom also is a motivator. She keeps me going no matter what. She helps me fulfill my potential by doing my best! She knows what I can do and she supports that. I want to be an artist and she supports me. She has plans for my artistic talent like art school to be even better in art.

That is why my mom is the most important person in my life she is the reason I am where I am today. If it wasn't for my mom who knows where I would be right now. She has some help with the bills but it is mostly her. She motivates me to fulfill my potential.

She has always been there for me through everything.

Izaiah Taylor, Grade 7
Mineral Springs Middle School, NC

My Pets

I love animals, so I have a few. I have three dogs and a hamster. They are very special to me.

My dogs' names are Borona, Twinkie, and Frida. Frida was my first dog ever. Frida is a Yorkie and Chihuahua mix. My dog Twinkie, I got after I got Frida, she is very playful. Twinkie is a Rat Terrier and Beagle mix. My dog Borona, I got last and she is a Chihuahua and Dachshund. When we first got her she thought Twinkie was her mom. She followed her everywhere and did everything Twinkie did. My hamster, Pixie, I got during the summer, when I first got her she would growl at my mom. My pets are always around me. I can't remember ever being mad at them. They do something bad and I can't look at them because I know I won't be mad for long. If I cry and have no person for comfort, I know I can go to the backyard or the hamster cage and a furry someone will be there making me feel better. I always feel loved when I'm around my pets because I know they love me and no matter what I do they will always love me. They don't judge me and we have a bond no one can break.

My pets are special to me and I love them as much as they love me. They are special and amazing; with them I'm never alone.

Karina Zuniga, Grade 8
Southwest Jr High School, AR

The Life and Diary of Anne Frank

Anne Frank's story, as revealed in her diary, is one of hope and optimism. The diary gives a first person account of the Holocaust and is one of very few published documents about hiding Jews. Even though Anne died during the Holocaust at Bergen-Belsen, her story lives on with others like Corrie ten Boom's.

Every day in the Secret Annex, the Franks, Van Daans, and Mr. Albert Dussel lived in fear of being discovered, but Anne seemed to always have some measure of hope. Her story is one of optimism in spite of fear in the midst of the Holocaust chaos.

Anne Frank received her diary almost immediately after her family moved into the Secret Annex. Anne wrote in the diary about eating rotten food until Miep Gies could bring them more food. Hearing the reports of Jews being found in hiding gave Anne the will to live.

Anne named her diary Kitty, because it was a friend to Anne during the war. Anne would express innermost thoughts and feelings as conversations that she could not tell to her father or Peter Van Daan, the people she talked to the most.

It is inspiring to study Anne Frank and her diary. Anne lived in hope while her fellow Annex occupants lived in fear. This young girl loved her diary and wrote openly about her experiences in the Holocaust. Anne talked through writing her innermost thoughts, leaving behind a voice which has never been silenced.

Mike Howard, Grade 9
Decatur Heritage Christian Academy, AL

My Name

My name. In Hebrew it means "God is my Judge." To me, it is a stolen identity. Standing in a crowd, I hear my name and turn, only to realize the call was not meant for me. It is like the crow, cawing repeatedly the same thing, but hardly ever intending that call for me.

It is the name of a book in the Bible. The Book of Daniel. The end of days. A sad subject. A subject of which does not describe me.

The sound of my name. It is like the wind whispering. A calming sound, yet it is so common. It is all around. Every day the wind, my name, blows as it will 'til the end of times.

It is, also, a loud name. The way it is pronounced. Danielle. It sounds like a yell. Loud and boisterous.

I dream of becoming something wonderful and my name being known everywhere. I am not sure what I will become. Maybe a singer, or an engineer, but it will be something wonderful.

I enjoy my name. I just wish that no one else on the earth had it. It would, then, be a name that describes me perfectly. A name that would describe me using only one word. Unique.

Danielle Kronmiller, Grade 7
La Salle Springs Middle School, MO

My Hero, My Mom

My hero is my mom she is so talented and so strong. My mom is the bravest person I know. After she and my dad got divorced she tried even harder to do her best and still will not settle for less than her best. Anytime something breaks it does not even cross her mind to call anyone to help because she has to do it herself.

Mom is so loving and even if things get rough or out of hand she is still so calm. While my mom was going back for her masters degree I knew it was stressful but she would not let you see her sweat. You knew it was hard and very nerve racking getting graded, going to school one night every week but when you asked her about her class she always said "it is fine," even if she was behind.

As my mom always says and shows me do not give up on your dreams because they are very important. My mom is the smartest, bravest, most talented person, and I love her very much. And as she constantly tells and shows me she loves me very much too.

That is why my wonderfully, beautiful, genius of a mom is my hero.

Bethany Buckner, Grade 7
Greenfield Jr/Sr High School, MO

The Terrific Touchdown

The crowd was on their toes. It was third down with ten yards to go and four minutes left in the fourth quarter. That Friday night was cool and the air was fresh. The teams were ready.

Will, who was the quarterback, and Stephen, who was the tight end, were in for the Rocket City Cowboys. Elizabeth, Stephen's sister, and I had butterflies because our brothers were in the game. Our moms were on the edge of their seats. When Will said, "hike," Stephen dashed off the line like a bolt of lightning. Looking for someone to throw to, Will spotted Stephen, who was wide open. Will launched the football. Stephen jumped up. He caught it with both hands. Then he ran into the end zone. The crowd cheered wildly. Did Stephen really make the touchdown? The referees raised both arms high and the touchdown was good.

Stephen and Will were extremely happy when the game was over. Their families were excited and ready to celebrate. The sisters and brothers were proud that their brothers' team won the game. The dads were also proud and talked about how Stephen and Will used to play in the front yard when they were five and six. All their fun in the yard had paid off in their big game. Now, their little brothers play in the yard and will someday be like Stephen and Will. They had a wonderful game. For many years, we have talked about that totally terrific touchdown.

Hannah Steward, Grade 7
Providence Classical School, AL

The Day of the Muddy Backyard

I'll never forget the day of the muddy backyard. It was a humid day the grass had not dried yet. Hurricane Wilma had just hit five days ago. The grass was full of mud.

My four and eight your old cousins had come over for lunch, after, we played a game of catch outside. It was my cousin Kianna and I against my brother Spencer and my cousin Kiki. I threw the ball over to them, Spencer and Kiki have always been competitive, they both started toward the falling ball. Kiki not noticing her slippers flying off kept running trying to deter my brother from getting the ball not knowing he was trying to do the same. All I could hear was the clamor those two were making.

When they had caught the ball both trying to pry it from the other with aspiration. When they finally settled the fight Spencer got to throw the ball first. As they were walking back to where they had started, Kiki picked one shoe up but could not find the other "My shoe" she yelled shockingly. Kianna and I rushed over to where she was standing there we found the shoe submerging into the mud. We started digging trying to retrieve the shoe. We dug for an hour but we lost it.

Perry Monteiro, Grade 7
Osceola Creek Middle School, FL

The Extravagant Winter Experience

Bursting with joy, I could tell it was wintertime because I looked outside my frosty window and saw hard, twinkling icicles hanging onto our old, battered house that made it look a cool, glittery white. Best of all, though, I had just awakened to the smell of my mom's buttery pancakes and her crispy bacon. I wandered to the kitchen, to be greeted by the glorious scent. At the table, I found my sister, Briana, eyeing the food hungrily. After breakfast, I looked out the window and saw children playing outside in the icy snow. I asked my mother if we could all go outside as a family. Of course she said yes. In a hurry, we put on our enormous coats, colorful gloves, hats, and scarves. We also put on our heavy boots.

Outside, I could feel the joy of the children as they were playing in the icy snow. My sister suggested that we build a massive snowman. After rolling up its huge body from the snow, I dashed inside to get a carrot for its nose, grapes for its eyes and mouth, and buttons for its body. We named the icy snowman "The Guardian." Out of the blue, my mischievous sister started a brutal snowball fight. After thirty minutes of throwing, hitting, and laughing, we decided to go into the warmth of our home.

After taking off our cold, wet, outer garments, our mom prepared us three steamy, marshmallow-filled mugs of hot chocolate. We sat and reminisced about all the fun we had during our time outdoors. In our haste to get warm, we didn't blow on the hot chocolate, and it singed the roof of our mouths. We laughed at ourselves and vowed that we would make more time to have fun together.

Braxston Jamal Miller, Grade 7
White Station Middle School, TN

My Best Friend

It all started when I was about four years old. I have always wanted a dog. My grandpa Cox has a Blue Heeler, so there was a chance I would get one soon! Then, one day, my dad told me she had a litter about six weeks ago, and they were ready to take home. I was so excited!

Then, we drove off to grandpa's house. Once we got there, I picked the one I wanted. It was a grey one with black and white spots. He was so adorable! When we got back home, I named him Max. Every day, when I got back from school, I played with him. We always raced, and of course, Max always won! It was so much fun!

Then, about one or two years later, my mom, dad, and I went to see our family. We took separate vehicles, so I rode with my mom, and my dad rode by himself. My dad went to my grandma Cox's house, and my mom and I went to my grandma and grandpa Stinnett's house. It was three hours away, so we stayed the whole weekend! Once we got home, my mom told me Max got hit by a car. I cried. So, about four months later, my dad went and got us another dog. It is a Catahula. Her name is Lacey.

Cassie Cox, Grade 7
Stroud Middle School, OK

My Favorite Teacher

Have you ever had a favorite teacher that you can depend on when you we're in school, or maybe even now, while you're still in school? We'll, I do, and her name is Ms. Hampton! She is wonderful, I mean, wonderful! Ms Hampton is pretty, outgoing, smart, and she has a lot of confidence in herself. I bet if you were in my seventh grade Language Arts class, you would love her too. Ms. Hampton is very hyper, and wild. She loves to have fun in class, but she still makes us work while we have fun.

Ms. Hampton carries herself respectfully, with confidence, and is an intelligent black woman. When she comes to school, she dresses appropriate, and within the school dress code. She teaches us in a way no other teacher does — we can relate to what she means and what she wants us to know and learn. When you look at her you see beauty and confidence. She is very respectful to us, she wouldn't say anything to us that we couldn't say to her, and I think that's really respectful of her.

When she teaches us, we have fun, and she makes us laugh a lot. We sing songs to help us learn and remember our vocabulary words. Ms. Hampton writes special chants for us when we are done with a unit in Language Arts as a review. Most of all, she teaches us what we need to know.

Out of all my years in Language Arts classes, Ms. Hampton's 5th period class has been the best ever. Ms. Hampton might not be walking down a runway, but in my book she is my Black-African American role model, and will always be.

Tyshayla Smith, Grade 7
Mineral Springs Middle School, NC

Macabbi Moments

In my life, there have been good, bad and ugly moments. For example, this August, I played basketball in Baltimore, Maryland. My teammates and I played 5 harsh games during the Macabbi Games, the annual Jewish Youth Olympics.

The good part of this experience was playing basketball, being with friends and going to the Orioles game. My friends and I stayed in a basement of a host family who were very nice. We played basketball against 5'8" to 6'4", 12-14 year old boys. Our team was about 5'2" except for two six footers. I like the fact that Jewish boys and girls from all over the country and Mexico came together to play. I was able to see my cousin Aaron, from Minnesota, who I don't often see. This experience was one in a lifetime.

The bad part was losing all five games. In one game, I scored 10 points, the most in a game, a good moment. Ugly moments were losing by more then 50 points in one game and during the playoff game; three 6'4" guys tripped me, one kicking me in the eye. I iced it but couldn't play, so I just cheered on my team. Sadly we lost, playing hard.

In my life, there have been good, bad and ugly moments. Even though there were sad moments in my trip, it was still great, one which I will always remember. I have learned to take the good with the bad and enjoy life every day!

Jeremy Terman, Grade 8
The Barstow School, MO

Richard Picciotto

Richard Picciotto. To many he is no one, but to others he is a hero. He answered the call about the September eleventh terrorist attack on the World Trade Center. He was helping to evacuate the citizens in the North Tower when he and some of his fellow firefighters heard and felt the South Tower collapse. He immediately realized that the North tower was not as sturdy as he thought. He made the call for all of the firefighters, rescue workers and any civilians that were left in the building to evacuate.

Despite his efforts, a few members of his team, himself included, and an elderly civilian woman ended up trapped in the ruins when the North tower fell. It was four hours until he finally made contact with a firefighter. Not long after he made contact with him, then he realized that there was a hole in the roof about four stories above him. He started climbing and led most of what was left of his crew out. The elderly woman and a few fire fighters stayed behind to be rescued three minutes later. Richard Picciotto wrote a book about what happened to him that day. The book is called *Last Man Down*. It is a tribute to the 343 firefighters and about 3,000 civilians that died because of the terrorist attack on September 11th, 2001.

Amanda Nault, Grade 9
Lincoln High School, AR

8 Seconds in Time

"Well I don't always ride that good, but I can usually get off pretty exciting or do something afterwards." He wouldn't know it, but this would be Lane Frost's last interview. Four days later on July 30, 1989 he would ride his last bull, Taking Care of Business. After a perfect eight seconds his dismount would land him in the mud, the bull turned and hit him twice and broke several ribs and severed a main artery. He died on the arena floor.

At the age of fifteen Lane was the bull riding champion of the Small Fry Rodeo Association. Then at sixteen he became the Oklahoma Youth Rodeo Champion, which he would hold for three years.

After he graduated in 1982, he joined the PRCA and rodeoed full-time. In 1987 Lane became the PRCA World Champion Bull Rider at the age of twenty-six. That same year he rode the bull Red Rock, which hadn't been ridden in three hundred and nine attempts. He would ride him four times successfully. Lane also competed in the Winter Olympics in Calgary, Alberta, Canada, which was the first exhibition rodeo in history.

Lane Frost died at the age of twenty-eight. He is buried by his friend and mentor, Freckles Brown, in Oilvet Cemetery in Hugo, Oklahoma.

As Oklahoma reaches its one-hundredth birthday we reflect on what is important in our history, even a sport like rodeoing, or just a cowboy with talent, we are reminded of our past.

Josh Thomas, Grade 8
Chelsea Jr High School, OK

A Few Days

My grandfather is very important to me. He is always there for me and gives me help if I need it. Whether that help is getting me out of a tight spot or just making me smile, he is there. As far back as I can remember he always been a likable guy. he is also very talkative, and he likes to makes jokes.

He has always enjoyed working with his hands. His work was carpentry and some welding. Everything he did, he did himself. He never made excuses and always finished what he started. For example, he always worked on his truck himself, and always got it fixed. That attitude inspired me to get into mechanics. He was always positive about what he was doing and let me help in whatever it was. Like when my brothers and I were little, he let us build a few chairs. It does not sound like it, but it was fun.

He is one of my closest family members, and I do not know how much longer he is going to be around. He was diagnosed with leukemia and has had to go to the hospital to get blood and shots. It is sort of depressing because some days he feels great and others he feels horrible. But the least I can do is just hope for a few more days to see my grandpa.

Dillon Feasel, Grade 8
Greenfield Jr/Sr High School, MO

A New Taste

Awwww, the sweet, fizzy delicious taste of Mountain Dew, my favorite drink. It all started four years ago at my friend Christopher Bastien's house.

It was just another eight year old day for me. It was a Sunday and there just so happened to be no school tomorrow. On Sundays I always had my Cub Scout meetings at Chris's house. The meeting was going very well and we got everything done. I was bored so I nagged and nagged for my Dad to let me stay over at his house until my dad snapped.

"Fine! You can. If you stop bothering me!" my dad said stopping the clamor. We drove home as fast as I could make my dad go. I packed some stuff and in a flash, I was out of there. Chris and I ran out, played some video games, and made jokes. Then Mr. Bastien (who we called Mr. B) walked out.

"Hey Hunter, have you ever tried this drink before?" Mr. Bastien asked referring to the Mountain Dew in his hand. A minute later he handed me some, I took a sip, and I was hooked! I drank it all night long and didn't go to sleep. All I remember after that was my mom picking me up, because I slept for the rest of the day.

Hunter Johnson, Grade 7
Osceola Creek Middle School, FL

A.M.B.

This year, we had an unfortunate event happen. On October 30, 2006, my sister called and told us that she was pregnant. I was going to have a niece! My sister was doing exceptional and she was excited that her stomach was getting considerably bigger. On January 31, 2007, she had her routine ultrasound. As she looked at the screen, they told her the news that exploded her heart.

The baby had Trisomy 18 and wasn't going to survive. It was killing her every day. Trisomy 18 is when you are born with too many chromosomes. It would be rare if she even made it through birth. My sister was so depressed and concerned, but we called her every day. The doctor talked to her and he said he was going to induce labor, and she reluctantly agreed.

On February 13, 2007, my sister went to the hospital and was emotionally shot. My grandmother went to her town to console her. That day after 22 hours of labor, the baby girl was born. She was named Amelia Marie Blackwell. She was 10 in. long and weighed 10.5 oz. When she was born she had already gone to heaven. My sister got to hold her and she cried. She now rests in a grave with my grandfather. This experience brought my family together and I realized that family was really meaningful. We try to not talk about Amelia, but no one will forget the baby born to heaven.

Rachel Green, Grade 7
Boyet Jr High School, LA

Volleyball the Game

Volleyball is a very interesting sport. You have to be in shape for it. You move your feet the most so you can get under the ball in time so it won't drop to the floor.

Volleyball is played all over the world. There are two different kinds of volleyball, there are Beach volleyball and gym volleyball. Beach volleyball is when you have two players on each team. It is harder because there is sand and it is harder to get under the ball, and there is not as many people to help cover the empty spaces. The other type of volleyball is gym volleyball which has six players on each side. This type of volleyball is much easier because there are more people covering you and you get to use knee pads to slide across the gym to get the ball faster and easier.

Volleyball is not a violent sport. It is actually more calm than most of your sports like football, soccer, and baseball. But it is a communication sport where if you have no communication you will run into each other and lose your game, but if you do have it, the game goes smoothly and you can control and know where the ball is going.

Katie Spendlove, Grade 8
Trinity Christian Academy, AL

Sheriff Harry Lee

Sheriff Harry Lee was born August 27, 1932 in a back room of his family's laundry business. Sheriff Harry Lee's family opened a restaurant called the House of Lee in 1959. He told his father he had decided to go attend law school and his father told him that was fine as long as he continued to work for the family's restaurant. Sheriff Harry Lee worked 72 hours a week at the family restaurant and managed to receive a law degree. He was also inducted into the Blue Key National Honor Fraternity.

Sheriff Harry Lee was a hard worker and Sheriff Harry Lee was elected sheriff for Jefferson Parish from 1979 until his death on October 1, 2007. He was seeking a seventh term and was diagnosed with leukemia, but he did not let that stop him from his hard work and dedication. Sheriff Harry Lee spoke his mind and did not care what anyone else thought. He always looked out for the best interest of the people who lived in Jefferson Parish.

I admire Sheriff Harry Lee for always standing up for what he believed in, whether people would be mad or not. He would make no excuses for the things he said. He was looking out to keep everyone safe. When I saw the news and coverage of his funeral I knew other people respected him just like I did. One of his quotes was, "Why be governor when I can be king," and that is fitting for the type of man he was. I never knew him personally, but I have learned a lot about him and I feel like I know him.

Matthew Leverette, Grade 7
St Rita School, LA

The Good Old Days

Did you know that Oklahoma is turning 100 years old this year? My grandpa, Joe Crutchfield, has lived in Oklahoma all his life. He is 71 years old, and has seen a lot in those years. He was born during the Great Depression. Times were very hard back then. There was no food to eat and no jobs to be had, to support their families.

He grew up in Inola, Oklahoma, with four brothers and sisters. He married a woman named Ann Steffen. They had three kids. One of them was named Wendy Crutchfield, which is my mom.

When my grandpa was a little boy, he and all his friends would go coon hunting in the bottoms. He said that they would stay down there for days at a time. Sometimes they would stay down there for days because they couldn't find their way back out.

He has told me a lot of stories. But I think my favorite is when he got his first car. It was a 1932 Model A Coupe. He said everyone had the same color of car: black. So my grandpa decided it was time for a change. So he painted his Model A a bright red with orange flames going down the side. And cut the exhausts really short so it would be really loud!

But remember that Oklahoma is turning 100 years old this year. So go out, have fun with your family, and celebrate Oklahoma Centennial!

Mason Hemphill, Grade 9
Chelsea Jr High School, OK

When I Eat a Moon Cake

Some myths have circulated about moon cakes, the small, doughy pastries we Chinese people eat. One of these odd myths is that they conceal swords. Moon cakes can, however, hold two eggs. The Chinese name for this type is *shuang huang*, which translates literally as "double yellow." Another type is the dark *dou sha*, bean paste, which is sweeter than the eggs.

We eat the moon cakes at the Mid-Autumn Festival, the Moon Festival, held at the Cordova Community Center every September. There are dances, delectable food, and games for all. When the performances are over, we head outside to light lanterns. We jostle each other due to the size of the central entrance. China is a very crowded country; we should be adroit at pushing through masses. Once we are outside, the bumping augments tenfold, for there are only about five people giving out the lanterns and candles. Lanterns aren't part of the traditional Mid-Autumn fare. However, the event was tried with great success one year and continued.

Whenever I eat a moon cake, I think of this Moon Festival. I think of the parties, the crowding, stomping flames of the lanterns, the fun of chasing my brother. Mostly I think of the lanterns. I think of toddlers, running around with their own brightly colored moons. I am closest to the lanterns. Even if I don't get one next year.

Daphne McKee, Grade 7
White Station Middle School, TN

State Championship

It was 25 to 32, it was hot and there was sweat running down my face. All I hear is hut so I run they give me the ball I run past the sixty-yard line to the fifty and then I get hit. I go down hard I'm hurt but I will not say anything, we are in the state championship with 2 minutes on the clock. We need a touchdown to tie the game then we can go into overtime.

I get on the line to go out for a pass, the quarterback throws it to me I catch it and I get tackled. We are on the thirty-five yard line my knee hurts badly so I go out for a play. They tape it up and tell me to get out there and score a touchdown. I go back up on the line with one minute and thirty seconds on the clock.

I go out for a pass and I catch it in the in-zone, the crowd goes wild but there is a flag on the play. Holding on the offense we go back to the forty yard line with ten seconds on the clock time for one last play, it is a sweep up the middle, hut I run as hard as I can I get hit I'm still up I get to the one yard line and I go down. Greenfield loses the state championship. Let's hope we do better next year.

Jake Freeman, Grade 8
Greenfield Jr/Sr High School, MO

Preserving Our Wildlife Habitats

Preserving our wildlife habitats has become very difficult throughout the years. We need to try to prevent all of the hazards that hurt the habitats. People, drought, and seasons are three of the main dangers that affect the wildlife habitats.

People are taking machinery into forests and clearing the trees. They are clearing some for development like housing. The trees being taken out are used for shelter by some animals. That causes the animals to find new homes or some die. The machinery and people also destroy some of the grass, which is used for food by most animals. That causes some animals to starve. The people's trash and their machinery's fumes pollute the environment and the animals that live in it.

Drought and the lack of rainfall cause plants not to grow. That means some might die. Drought can also cause fires, which burn the forest down. We need a food rescue source that can provide food for the animals. That will keep animals from starving.

Seasons or hunting seasons kill off many animals. People should not kill as many animals. They should not kill as many female animals so they can still reproduce. People should not keep all the fish and animals that they get. That would leave more food for the other animals.

Various things are starting to affect our wildlife habitats. People, drought, and seasons are making it hard for animals to survive. We are trying to develop new ways to preserve our wildlife habitats.

Brice Boatright, Grade 9

My Little Sister

My little sister Madilynn is very special. She is three years old. She will be four in November. Also me, my mom, and mostly everybody in my family calls her Maddie or Madster, which my grandma calls her Madster. It's really funny when she does.

Madilynn likes to do a lot of things like fish, draw, color, play with Barbies, watch princess movies, play dress-up, and all kinds of things. Maddie's favorite color of course is pink. Everything she wants she always want it pink and that's what's really funny about her.

I also babysit Madilynn on weekends when my mom is working. It's really fun because we do a lot of stuff together and almost all the days that I watched Maddie I've always gave her a bath. She's funny when she's in the bath. I have to admit there's one thing I can't stand when I'm babysitting. I always have to get up early and can't go back to sleep.

There have been days when Maddie has been really bad because Maddie isn't a perfect angel. She can be really bad when she wants to be and sometimes when she's bad and I yell at her I always feel bad and tell her I'm sorry and she says sorry too.

My sister and I are a pair. She's a great little sister even though she's really bad at times, but all three year olds are. As I told you we have a lot of fun together especially when I'm babysitting.

Alyssa Wills, Grade 8
Pigeon Forge Middle School, TN

The Man I Loved But Knew the Least*

Most people are extremely close to their grandparents. That is not the case for me. I got to visit my grandpa once every two months, if I was lucky. This year my grandfather passed after suffering a long while. I felt horrible, because I hadn't known him well. December 2006 my grandfather suffered a stroke, and lost movement in his right arm and leg. While he spent time in the hospital, I went on a (get to know my grandpa) journey.

December 2006 to early January 2007, I asked my mother everything about him. I even attempted to ask him questions in the hospital. Late January my pawpaw suffered through another stroke. This time he lost what I needed for him to have most, his ability to speak understandably. My time to ask him questions was gone. My chance for him to reminisce with me was then over.

Late January 2007 my papaw passed. I would never see him again, even to say hello. When I received the news, I started to remember the quirky things he did and bought for me and my sister. Then I also became thankful for all the time I spent with him. Then I realized I had known him, but I hadn't known him as much as I wanted to. Today and forever I will love the pawpaw I knew least.

Dynasty Allen, Grade 9
Baton Rouge Magnet High School, LA
*In loving memory of Clarence Rheams

A Time When I Never Gave Up

I have always been taught to never give up. I am going to tell you a story when I never gave up. I was getting ready for my mile run; I was going through my breathing exercises and the announcer said one minute until the mile run. So I went on the track we got ready in our places. The horn blew and we were off. I was in second place and we got halfway done and I started to slow down because I was getting tired I started to feel sick. The kid in first started to pull away and I just wanted to give up but everyone was cheering me on and coach said don't give up; I said to myself this is a big race and everyone is counting on me.

One lap to go the announcer said. I shot off like a rocket and started creeping up on the leader. We are coming down the backstretch now I am only a foot behind him. All of a sudden the crowd got real loud and cheered for their home team. We are side-by-side going in the last turn and I put everything I had in it and I pulled ahead just barely enough to win.

Everyone was congratulating me. The coach said good job. The announcer said I won by a half a second. Our team won 5 of the 6 events. This is my story of never giving up.

Charles Cooper, Grade 8
Greenfield Jr/Sr High School, MO

The Hungry Elephant

My mom always says, "If you go to the zoo don't sit by the elephants." There's a reason for that. It all started when I decided to go to the zoo. Everybody was busy except my mom. Therefore, she decided to take me to the zoo. We planned to leave the next morning. The next day, we were ready at 4:00 P.M.

We were at the zoo in Alexandria, Egypt. There, most people bring blankets and have a picnic on the floor. Well, that's what we did. We had a big blanket with a basket of food. We chose a great place to sit, by the elephants. We laid the blanket on the floor and put the basket on top of it. There were many people at the zoo, doing the same thing. My mom also brought coffee and tea because she knew I liked coffee, and she liked tea.

The elephants weren't stinky like they usually are. In Egypt, elephants are put in large cages. We sat by the biggest elephant because we thought he was the cutest. Anyway, we finally settled and sat down. My mom started eating a turkey sandwich, while I ate a cheese sandwich. After we ate, my mom had to go to the restroom. While she was gone, the huge elephant put his trunk out and reached for the tea.

I was so scared that I got up and went to tell one of the workers to stop the elephant. I was back to find my mother back. She wanted to know where I went so I told her, and I also told her what had happened. She was surprised, just as I was. I learned to never sit by the elephants again. Have you ever had a dangerous adventure at the zoo?

Alaa Elsayed, Grade 7
Haynes Academy for Advanced Studies, LA

Dogs, Dogs, Dogs Is All I see

There are many different breeds of dogs. Some of them are in my essay, like the Chocolate Lab, Golden Retriever, Dalmatian, and the Vizsla.

The best bred dog I think is the Chocolate Lab, because they are so hyper that only a really energetic person could effectively take care of them. Although I think dogs are the best pets, some people see it differently.

Another well-bred dog is the Golden Retriever. My first reason is that they're extremely smart. Another reason that a Golden Retriever is a good breed is because when the owner wants to go hunting the dog is very useful. The average life span is 10-12 years.

The Dalmatian is a good fire dog, because they have good noses and good eyesight. Another thing about the Dalmatian is their coats are for some reason spotted. The average life expectancy is 11-14 years.

The Vizsla is a wrinkly-looking dog. There are seven different recognized dogs in HPR (hunt, point, and retrieve.) There are two types of fur Vizslas can have, smooth and wire coats. Their life expectancy is 9-15 years.

I hope now you see that these are great dogs — the Dalmatian, Chocolate Lab, Golden Retriever, and the Vizsla.

Caleb Signorelli, Grade 7
Stroud Middle School, OK

Reunited

Reunited, and it feels so good! Have you ever felt this way? I have. One time in my life, I felt really happy, because I saw my two best friends after three summer months. We were reunited at sixth grade orientation. At orientation, my heart began to smile when I saw my two best friends, 'M.' and 'A.' We were so excited to be starting a whole new experience together. We learned various amounts of things. Afterwards, our parents agreed we could go someplace we wanted to go together. My mother drove us.

Out of all the places, we chose Chuck E. Cheese. Chuck E. Cheese is fun at any age. My mother dropped us off at Chuck's entrance. We were turned away by a person on staff, because he said one of us had to be eighteen or older. Who would have thought that three eleven year olds would have been turned away from a place whose slogan is "Where a kid can be a kid!?!"

Therefore, I called my mom and we then went to the mall. I had never been to the mall without parents. Freedom! We scoped out different shops and boys! Before the fun ended, we took a picture together from the photo booth.

Reuniting with 'M.' and 'A.' at orientation, spending a couple of hours at the mall, without parents, and even getting rejected from the kid friendly Chuck E. Cheese, made my life another day happier.

Kenthia Farmer, Grade 9

Injustice in Schools

School is not easy, for the simple fact that no student is given a fair chance. It should be easy for a teacher to treat every child equally, but as many know, they do not. Teachers pick their favorite students whether they're the smartest, sweetest, most shy, most popular, or even the most troubled. One thing, however, that they do not do is act as generous and "fun loving" with the other students in the current classroom. The children that occasionally get into trouble or act less interesting in class get treated much differently than those who don't.

Students are also guilty of this pitiful crime. They choose who they will bully or pick on according to race, sex, or intelligence. Most of these students that get made fun of are the ones who bullies know are afraid to stand up for themselves. Older students know how to take advantage of the younger kids around them. Children are children and they have no right to pick on, laugh at, or make rude comments toward each other. Everyone should have to face the facts: that teachers should stop picking on specific students and begin to favor each and every child, and that children should be less insecure and selfish, and worry about themselves, not the others around them. That is unjustifiable and now everyone can know it.

Tyler Rousseau, Grade 8
East Thibodaux Middle School, LA

Positive Influence in Bikini Bottom

Who lives in a pineapple under the sea? If you own a television, chances are you know the answer to that question — SpongeBob SquarePants, of course. But I bet you don't know how watching *SpongeBob* affects children.

In most of the episodes, SpongeBob goes on some sort of adventure or has a problem that he solves by being cheerful and trying his hardest. He is dedicated to his job at the Krusty Krab and works hard in boating school. He is a good friend to Patrick and Sandy and is an all around good person. In return, SpongeBob usually has fun and is happy. SpongeBob would see the glass as half full.

Squidward, on the other hand, is a grouchy whiner. He doesn't care about his job, he is selfish and self-centered, and is very rude to his neighbors and citizens of Bikini Bottom. He is vain, often referring to himself as the only cultured person in Bikini Bottom. He complains about basically everything, and in return, Squidward is miserable and would certainly see the glass as half empty.

SpongeBob is a positive influence on kids' lives because it teaches them that if you go through life happy, giving your best, and being positive, you will be happy and succeed. Squidward is a warning, that if you're grouchy, you will not be satisfied with your life, and people will generally not like you. *SpongeBob* may not be totally obvious with its message, but it does affect children who watch it.

Sarah Cobb, Grade 8
St Gerard Majella School, MO

Rachel's Challenge

Picking on other kids does not mean that you are the cool kid in school. It means that you are wanting to be a bully. The question now is, are you a bully in your school? If you are, then put caring about others in your vocabulary.

In the year 1999, there was a tragedy at Columbine High School. Last week our school went to an assembly called Rachel's Challenge. Rachel Scott was the first student to be shot at Columbine. The killers were two young boys that went to the school. Their aim was to kill five hundred students. They had even set two bombs in the cafeteria but, thank God they did not go off. If the bombs would have gone off, it would have killed more than thirteen students. Before the shooting Rachel had known she was going to die at a young age. Rachel had drawn a flower that had thirteen teardrops. A day after her death a guy called and told her father that he saw her eyes crying, and he saw thirteen teardrops.

Rachel was a good student who would stand up for people and would stand up against people bigger than her. All the bullies out there take this story and my advice, learn to be friendly. People who are not bullies watch around you for the kids who get bullied, and if you see someone getting hurt, go help them. Have good character!

Chelsey Martin, Grade 8
Greenfield Jr/Sr High School, MO

Friendship

A friend is someone who helps you get back on your feet before you hit the ground. Tells you the truth no matter how bad it hurts, and then helps the pain go away. Someone who helps make all your troubles disappear. A friend stands by your side when no one else does. Friends feel like your second family; they're your sisters and brothers.

A perfect example of a great friend is one of my best friends Alexa. Alexa is always ready to help in a time of need or just to help soften the blow of some random pain caused by anything. Alexa is the kind of person to tell you if your idea is stupid and then do it anyway because you thought of it. She'll do anything as long as it's with a friend. She just thinks being with friends makes everything better. Another fabulous example of a great friend is one of my other best friends Hannah. She is pretty much the same as Alexa only different. She speaks her mind and makes a friend wherever she goes. Hannah has a lot of friends so I consider myself lucky to be one of her best friends.

In all, I think being a friend means more than to just hang out and talk about nothing. I think being a good friend means really knowing that person. I think being a good friend could just be being there.

Elizabeth Hankins, Grade 8
Southwest Jr High School, AR

Fitness Woes of the United States

Being physically fit is becoming more and more critical because of the obesity of our younger generation. Sadly, the number of obese children is rapidly increasing, causing diseases such as diabetes. In addition to diabetes, children are also developing joint problems because their bones aren't strong enough to carry so much extra weight.

In particular, diabetes continues to become a bigger issue today due to the fact that kids don't feel the need to exercise. In fact, seven percent of the United States has diabetes. If kids exercised more, this percentage would gradually decrease. History of diabetes and obesity on both sides of my family causes me to make physical fitness a major priority in my life.

Also, in order for children to be physically fit, schools need to start making P.E. a requirement. In many schools, P.E. is not required. When parents work a lot, it's hard for them to have time for their kids to be involved in a sport outside of school, and many times fast food is the only thing they have time to eat. Therefore, schools should require some kind of physical activity to keep the children healthy and in shape. As a result, being physically fit is extremely important because it means that we would have a healthier society.

Kelsey Grace, Grade 8
Heritage Hall School, OK

My Friend Ella

Throughout life many experience hardships that turn into something good. Through my life I have been blessed by God not to go through many trials. My grandma has been ill ever since I was little and I have always worried about her. When I go through trials I quote Proverbs 3: 5-6 "Trust in the Lord with all your heart and lean not on your own understanding; in all your ways acknowledge him and he will make your path straight." Through illness and pain I know friendship can be built, and that is how I met Ella.

When people are ill their illness really affect the people who love them, but you always will have a friend to get you through the hard times. When I was in fifth grade I met a little girl named Ella. Ella's grandma had the same thing my grandma had, it was called Chronic Bronchitis. This disease affects the breathing process and makes it hard to breathe. Ella and I became good friends. Two months after I met her, Ella's grandma died. Ella was heartbroken and sad. I was there for her and a new friendship was formed.

Trials occurred in our life but something good came out of it. Ella's grandma was gone, but she had a new friend to help her through the hard times. I thank God every day for my family and friends.

Brandy Taliaferro, Grade 8
College Heights Christian School, MO

The Lost City of Atlantis

One of the greatest mysteries in this world is the legend of Atlantis. Sure one has seen the animated movie Atlantis, but is this lost city real? Let's go deeper and learn more.

The story takes place over 11,000 years ago. Atlantis was an island in the middle of the Atlantic ocean which was said to be a center of trade and commerce. It was ruled over by the god of sea, Poseidon. Poseidon fell in love with Cleito who later gave birth to five sets of twins. This paradise-like island was later corrupted by greed and power which led to punishment of the people. The gods finally decided to bury this island under sea.

For thousands of years, researchers such as Plato looked for evidences of this civilization. Since technology has improved, Robert Sarmast, a mythologist, claims Atlantis is located between south coast of the island of Cyprus and Syria because of remains on a strip of land under the sea. Robert Sarmast also said that Atlantis is a rectangular land mass lying 1.5 kilometers beneath sea level. Many well-built equipment such as sonar scanning are used to search this land mass. Surprisingly, many man-made structures are found. Although this discovery cannot proved to be Atlantis, many more researching is still going on today. Is legendary Atlantis real? We will soon find out in the near future.

Jin Jing, Grade 8
Appling County Middle School, GA

Walking Hand in Hand with God

I have experienced a great deal of life altering events in my fourteen years. However, I believe that my journey to finding God was the most significant. I grew up to a Pentecostal mother and a Muslim father. That proves that my parent's views towards religion were not compatible.

The Pentecostal beliefs that many people on my mother's side consider, did not fit my personality. My mother's Pentecostal family believes in speaking in tongues, as well as different physical characteristics. My father on the other hand is Muslim. The people of the Muslim religion pray five times a day, and it is mandatory that every Muslim visit the House of God, located in Mecca, Saudi Arabia. Since my parent's religions differed so much, religion is not mandatory in our household.

When I turned 12, I was invited to attend Healing Place Church. When I first went, I fell in love with my surroundings. I loved how the people were so friendly and how diverse they were. Over the weeks, my faith in God developed. I began attending church every Sunday, volunteered on many occasions, and became an active member of the youth group.

Finding my path to God has made me a new person. Not only is God, God, but he is what I call my best friend. God is the person that I can go to with all problems, and he is the most important person in my life.

Parissa Majlesein, Grade 9
Baton Rouge Magnet High School, LA

Stimulating the Young Mind and Body

Think about the youth of today. What are their favorite things to do? If they are typical, gadgets, technology and TV are central to their lives. Who doesn't enjoy the latest video game? Everyone knows how hard it is to turn off the TV, and it is impossible to drag kids from the computer. After all, from the mind of a teenager, spending hours on YouTube while 'IM-ing' their 'BFF-4eva' is a blast!

But where does exercise come into the picture? Often, it does not come into the picture at all. Today, kids are provided with a multitude of addictive devices that only require minimal movement and brain activity. We have to shine a more positive light on activities that stimulate both the mind and the body. Kids need to find a sport that they enjoy to a point of wanting to do it 'for fun' on a regular basis. We cannot allow our future generation to think of exercise as 'work.'

We as a society need to take a more active role in helping kids stay fit. The first step is simply turning off the gadgets! Once the Wii or computer is unplugged, we should encourage them to try any type of sport. If each of us attempts to better the mindset of youth towards exercise, we can have a lasting impression on the physical health and mental strength of kids around us.

Madison Chapman, Grade 8

Art and Literature

Instead of writing about how my wonderful family is important to me (like most people) I've decided to write about how art and literature are important to me.

First of all, expressing my feelings and talent through art is important to me because it makes me cheerful and content. Since first grade I have wanted to be an artist because art has always been incorporated in my life.

When writing, drawings, paintings or brainstorming I always try to use symbolism. To create this I use light and dark colors to express a mood or setting for the painting or story. To illustrate setting I could use the colors black and blue to signify something bad in the future, or I could use the color green in a painting to signify plentiful growth. Symbolism is important to me because when I write or paint it lets me create a meaning to be interpreted by myself or others. For example, in stories that I write I always try to create a purpose or lesson in the story.

Literature is important to me because it lets my imagination free into a book. Also, it shows me the culture of a place and time; literature is always a key importance to me because it helps me learn. Overall, literature and art are important to me because it lets me express my feelings and it fills my life with joy.

Hannah Moll, Grade 8
Heritage Hall School, OK

John Bulling: Soldier, Farmer, Grandfather

Many men have risked their lives for our country and our freedom. One man survived the conflict in the Korean War, my grandfather, John Bulling. He proudly served in the United States Marines. He was passionate about his duties. He continues to exhibit those qualities today.

John enlisted straight out of high school. He went through basic training and was sent to Korea. He was dropped by helicopter in the demilitarized zone. This zone was in between the U. S. and South Korean forces and the North Korean forces. He returned safely home and was sent to San Diego as a drill sergeant. He taught other Marines how to fight for three years. He returned home and attended Oklahoma State University. He completed college and started farming.

My grandfather, John, is now 73 years old and still very active on his farm. He is very intelligent and can strategize how to fix things. He is a great teacher and his experience is always helpful.

My grandfather loves his farm and owning it. He remembers that his service to our country helped allow us the freedom to own land. He loves to read war books.

We should be very proud of the men and women who serve this country. They are the reason we enjoy so many freedoms today. The next time you see a veteran or a current soldier, thank them and remember that you couldn't do what you do today without their service.

Bryce Bulling, Grade 8
Mulhall-Orlando High School, OK

Following Your Dreams

You have dreams don't you? Sure you do! Everybody has dreams. Whether it is about what you want to be when you grow up or who you want to marry someday. Dreams can be whatever you want them to be.

People have all kinds of different dreams. Some people dream about going to college and becoming a doctor so they can help others in need, or a lawyer and winning the big case, or even becoming a teacher to help kids learn everything they can. Your dreams can be far reaching or simple.

Other people have dreams of finding that one special person they want to spend the rest of their life with and starting a big family together. They dream of having the perfect life. Some people find that early, some find it later in their life. But they find it because it's what they want.

So no matter what your dream is, there is one thing you have to do to fulfill your dreams and that is to always believe that you have whatever it takes to make the dreams real.

So you see, everybody has a different dream and everyone has to work to make their dreams their reality. So keep dreaming big and never stop believing in yourself, so your dreams can come true.

Chelsea Waldrop, Grade 9
Rossville Christian Academy, TN

Does Hip-Hop Influence Society?

Does hip-hop influence society? I think society wouldn't be anything without hip-hop. You ask why? Hip-hop is a part of almost every human being's culture. We hear it on the radio; we watch videos and try to imitate what we see. Its music can be compared to a pet, it is always going to be loved. If we didn't have hip-hop in the black community, I feel that we would be stuck doing absolutely nothing because we have nothing to motivate us.

It tells us stories about how to change our lives and how we can succeed in life. TI makes it plain with "Big Things Poppin' and Little Things Stoppin'." The big things can be compared to my future, where little things are the roadblocks — the haters who quit. Hip-hop is the kind of music that you can listen to all day. Especially Kanye West's "Stronger."

Sometimes hip-hop may use profanity and some inappropriate lyrics, but they help us too. If I could marry hip-hop I would! I love it that much. Listening to hip-hop has inspired me to always believe in myself and never give up.

Some people don't like hip-hop. Hip-hop isn't just all about sex and profanity; it's about love and leadership. The luckiest celebrities are singers and rappers because they get to do something they love and they get to motivate other people and their lives — especially young people. Hip-hop should be a part of this society until this world ends.

Jaqueze Hudson, Grade 8
Turner Middle School, GA

Rose the Rooster

I am Katherine, KiKi, Kikialoo and Kikster. In Greek Katherine means pure. I must not be very pure because everyone calls me KiKi. Can you imagine an eighty-five year old struggling down the hall of an old folk's home named KiKi? Three of Henry the eighth's six wives were named Katherine. My name is spelled the same as one of the beheaded wives, Katherine Howard. KiKi has no translation what-so-ever. There was a Japanese movie called Kiki's Delivery Service about a witch named KiKi. The only other notable person who shares my name in the world is an anime witch. My friends call me Kikster. It sounds like a perky ladybug in a children's book. My parents named me after my great-great grandmother no one knows about. It's mysterious, but hollow. I like my middle name, Rose. I am named after Wilhelmina Rosalina Sinn, my Oma. Yes, I am glad I was not named Wilhelmina. My parents have a teaspoon of pity in their bones. I think she lived contently baking food with German music playing as the smells of dough permeated the kitchen. I think a different name lives within me. I was born in the Chinese year of the rooster. I am pecking the ground for food, and Cock-a-doodle-doing when the sun opens my beady eyes. I am a rooster. Rose the rooster will be my new name, and maybe now I will find some kind of peace.

Kiki Rogers, Grade 8
Baylor School, TN

Lake Incident

One weekend my dad, my sister and I went to the lake with a bunch of other people. When we got there we all got ready and we went to the boats. When we got to where we were going everybody jumped in. That day we swam, had lunch in the boats and went tubing. My sister, Elizabeth, and her friend, Autumn, were the first to ride the tube. They had a lot of fun.

The next day was our last day and we went out early. The group went to a spot and parked so everybody could swim. This day we took a big raft that looked like a banana. It could hold six people. Elizabeth, Autumn, Kevin and I went on the banana first. We were going fast and falling off a lot. When we were ready to go back we decided to do lots of turns on the way. Near the end, we went over our wake and my sister and Autumn hit heads and were knocked out. They were both floating in the water with their heads down. I picked up my sister's head to get it out of the water. When I reached for Autumn's head she picked it up herself. The driver turned the boat off and jumped in to help. Kevin and I were fine but a little scared. We spent the rest of the afternoon in the hospital and my sister ended up getting six stitches.

Jack Morgan, Grade 8
Heritage Hall School, OK

A Proud NASCAR Fan

Some consider me a "Jewish Redneck!" Becoming one was hard work and I don't mind being called one. I read, studied, watched a lot of television and I must admit it was WONDERFUL! Because of that, now I am a huge NASCAR fan. Some of my friends make fun of me mostly because they think only "rednecks" like NASCAR. But that's not true, even cool kids like me love the sport.

It all started in the 2nd grade when I had to do a book report. My teacher laid out the book choices on the table. Of course, I wanted a book on an athlete, and the only one left when I chose my book was one about a NASCAR driver. I knew absolutely nothing about NASCAR as I began reading the book. As I found myself becoming a fan of the sport. Five years later, I'm passionate about NASCAR. I am quite often called names, and I don't mind, because I am a NASCAR fan!

I know most people just don't understand the sport. They totally misunderstand it and don't get the sport's dreams. If they took the time to learn about it, they might actually find the sport interesting and fun!

As a commercial once said, "To some people NASCAR may not be a sport. They are right. It is a way of life." I couldn't agree more. I really love NASCAR, even if people ridicule me once in a while!

Daniel Barrach, Grade 7
White Station Middle School, TN

The Dogs in My Life

I've had dogs for my whole life. Three of them are German shepherds; Raven, Roxxy, and Brandy. I also have a wheaten terrier named Shammie. They are all very special to me.

Roxxy was the dog who I had since I was one year old, after Raven passed away. She was a German shepherd. Once, I came home from the neighbors, it was dark out, and the dogs were outside. Roxxy didn't realize it was me, so she almost attacked, until I spoke and she stopped. That proves how protective she was of my family! She just recently passed away six months ago.

Brandy is a German shepherd too. After Roxxy passed away, we rescued Brandy. Her owner was about to put Brandy to sleep, but the vet refused and put her in a German shepherd rescue center. My parents found her on the internet and surprised us a week after Roxxy passed. Brandy seems to have Roxxy's spirit within her because she does almost everything the same way as Roxxy.

Shammie is a wheaten terrier; she's four years old. She was a gift from my father when he went away for a week. When she was buddies with Roxxy, she was always tiring Roxxy out because Shammie was the puppy. *Now*, Brandy's the puppy and is tiring *Shammie* out! What goes around comes around!

They all love or loved to protect and care for us. They're important to me because they protect me and give me responsibility. I couldn't live without them!

Allison Schepers, Grade 7
Sebastian River Middle School, FL

Any Other Way

My cousin, Nick, is always in my thoughts, and he has diabetes. I remember when he was diagnosed he would cry at night and say "why me?" There were a lot of people trying to help him get used to testing himself, especially his two older brothers. With so many people at his side I believe that it changed the way he saw the world, because the next time I saw him he was smiling and saying "why NOT me?"

That is what I truly love about my cousin, because no matter what life throws at him he is able to turn around and look at it from a different angle. This attribute of his is so important to me that I would give anything to have the whole world to be able to look at things in a positive way like him. It makes life so much easier and we would be able to live it to its fullest. And if there were a place where nobody would have to worry, and people could just be friends, I would move there! But there is still so much that I have to do here, places to visit, and people I need to see. This world has so much to offer, and sometimes the world can be a mean and terrible monster. At times though, I swear, it has a more gentle side and it's at those moments where it's positively beautiful, and I would not have it any other way.

Kimberly Carrero, Grade 7
Bak Middle School of the Arts, FL

The Stare Down

It was around 7:00. You could see the sun in the distance. It had been a long day of wrestling then waiting, wrestling then waiting. I was down in Birmingham, Alabama at the Dixie Duals wrestling for Team Chattanooga. It was the second day of a long grueling tournament, and we made it to the semifinals. Our next team on the schedule was Team Alabama, a powerhouse. We warmed up on the sweaty mats by practicing our stand-ups and double legs like usual. We were ready. Each team lined up on either side of the mat and we began the match. As I waited to wrestle, my eyes locked in with my opponents, who was slumped in his chair getting mentally prepared. The thundering cheers of the wrestling moms and their cow bells didn't even cause a flinch in either of us. It was a dead stare down. We each sat there like stones. I kept thinking to myself, "Gah, he looks strong, and I wonder what move he will do first." We sat there staring, thinking the same thing about each other over and over until our time came to wrestle. In the end, the back and forth match fell his way and he walked away with the 2-3 victory. "You will learn from your mistakes," I heard coach Odis say as I walked off the mat. Lessons learned. I came, I sacrificed, and I excelled even with the harsh loss.

Matthew Cate, Grade 8
Baylor School, TN

Camp Longhorn

Getting a pretend little sis, mingling with new people, going fishing, and swimming a mile is part of camp excitement. Camp Longhorn holds many memories of insane activities I enjoy doing such as swinging off a fifteen-foot tower. Having a blast is what camp is all about. One of the reasons I love camp is that I get to meet interesting people from all over. Even though I only get to see them once a year, which seems like a long time, the girls I meet seem like my best friends. One of my fun camp friends, Paige, has an amazing personality and is always a jumpy. Together, we make up loony nicknames for each other and act crazy. If I went to school with her, I may get tired of all the nuttiness.

For three weeks we get to hang out and play all sorts of games like spoons, a card game, and have many great laughs. Not only do I have all of my cabin mates to hang out with but also my enthusiastic counselors. Some of the most peculiar stories are about our counselors. One time, we had a rather ecstatic counselor who always seemed thrilled about everything. In fact, when we bounced on the macroscopic blob, Anna, our counselor, would squirt us with ice-cold hose water. Even though we felt like we were in a freezer, it was loads of fun. Overall, camp is full of hilarious and memorable times.

Kristen Taylor, Grade 8
Heritage Hall School, OK

When My Dad Retired from the United States Navy

When my dad retired he was stationed at the Naval Station in Norfolk, VA. He had spent 24 years of his career in this location, which made it a good place for the ceremony.

The whole family attended the ceremony. At the retirement, everyone was in uniform and they were waiting for my dad. The Navy is like a big family because when it came time to give out the awards some of them were crying. They had four people march in front of my dad, two of them stopped, spread out a flag, and carefully started folding it. This is a Naval tradition and a show of appreciation for my dad's service to our country. The flag was flown first at the White House in Washington DC. When my dad received the flag he went over to my sister and gave it to her. He also had given my brother and me some of his uniform items. When they handed out awards my dad received a Commendation Medal and a letter from the president. My mother, brother, sister, and I received an award too. The award was to thank us for the sacrifice we made in supporting my dad and his job. After the retirement we said our good byes.

It was an extraordinary experience. It showed me how big and good of a family the Navy was. It was one of the best times I have ever had.

Preston Stickle, Grade 8
Albemarle School, NC

Writing Essays

Is there a certain subject or thing that you really hate doing in school? I do, and it's writing essays. I mean I just can't do them. One, I can never think of anything to write about, two, I have terrible handwriting and I can't spell, three, I'm just not good at them!

All right, let's get started, on the biggest reason I hate writing essays, and that is I can never think of anything to write. I mean it takes forever for me to think about anything halfway decent to write about, and when I do, half the time is up, so I don't have the time to write a good essay. Let's move on, shall we?

Like I said before, I have terrible handwriting and I can't spell to save my life. So when anyone reads it, it's hard to understand. I have tried time and time again to spell and write better, but it doesn't seem to work. Let's go on to my next reason.

Last but not least, my final reason. Even though I've tried to get better, I'm just terrible at writing essays! No matter what I do, my essays are never any good! I mean, I've tried everything, and it's never as good as I want it to be.

Like I said before, I hate to write essays because I can't think of anything to write, I can't spell, and it's never any good. That's why I hate to write essays.

Honre LeBar, Grade 8
Pigeon Forge Middle School, TN

My Middle School Experiences

It all started when I got off the bus at Harper-Archer Middle School. I went to my homeroom class and the teachers were walking in to meet me. I was surprised they knew me. That was because of my older brother Maximillian. They hoped I acted much better then he.

After a while, being in middle school changed my behavior. I stopped doing my homework and started skipping classes. When I got my first report card, I cried! I had never earned lower than a B. As the year progressed, I went back to the B's.

As I transitioned to the seventh grade, I moved to a new school, Turner Middle School. Eventually, I adopted new friends. I made better grades and got along with the teachers better. I wanted to maintain my B average. Currently I am an eighth grader. I have grown from what I used to be in sixth grade. I would never do some of the things I did then.

I need to focus on my work a lot more, in order to be ready for whatever high school has to offer. I think that moving to the ninth grade will help me realize that I don't have a lot of time before I will be getting out of school. Additionally, I have to focus on all my classes to be able to go to college. That is something I really want to do.

Alexis Thomas, Grade 8
Turner Middle School, GA

Being Drug Free

How will drugs help you in your future? They will not. Drugs are the worst thing that anyone could turn toward. They can have a major effect on a person's body physically, and mentally. People turn to drugs for many reasons. It may be hardships they face in everyday life. It may even be just so they can fit in. Whatever their reason may be, drugs cannot help anyone.

People, who turn to drugs because they have problems in their life, just use drugs as a comfort. I feel that in any situation, a person shouldn't turn to drugs as their shoulder to lean on. No matter what type of drug being used they all have a great affect. Drugs really change the way a person acts. Basically a person who does drugs as a relief or comfort should try other ways and learn how to stop.

Others may use drugs because that's what all their friends are doing. That is one of the worst excuses to ruin your body. No matter what your friends do, you should stand up for yourself and let them know what you do not want to do. Whatever words they may say, just walk away and be the more mature person. In my opinion using drugs because of peers is the worst way to start.

As stated before drugs are the worst thing to turn toward. They are really stupid. Hopefully one day drugs will be all the way out of society. They cause people to do crazy things and ruin the lives of others. Basically just remember, think positive, and never turn negative.

Ashley Tatum, Grade 9
Ridgeway High School, TN

My Mom in Vietnam

Have you ever wondered what life in Vietnam is like? I wasn't born there, but my parents were. I will tell you about the life of my mom. It all happened in Lang Cat in 1970, the day she was born, until 1985, the day she got a chance to get to freedom. Freedom was a place she had always dreamed of.

In Vietnam, she would brush her teeth with her finger because she had no toothbrush and toothpaste. The only way she got food was the food that she and her family planted in the garden such as potatoes, spinach, and rice. She only ate two meals a day. When she was thirsty, she got water from a well. She also used the water to wash herself.

She lived in a hut that she built, which means they had no electricity. She slept on four pieces of wood. She had one pair of pajamas and one pair of sandals which she got yearly. When she wanted to go somewhere, she had to walk because there was no transportation. You can see how poor she and her family were.

Her dad left Vietnam to go to America. He left five children, his wife, and his parents. Three years later, he sent a letter saying he was okay after the war. Then he sponsored eight people to go to America. My mom finally came to America in 1985 when she was fifteen years old.

Vy-Vien Nguyen, Grade 7
Boyet Jr High School, LA

The Nurse

In the 4th and 5th grade, one day out of the whole year we would reenact one of the battles from the Civil War. When I got to school that morning everybody was dressed like it was 1860, even the teachers. Girls were in dresses and bonnets; boys were in jeans with a gray or blue shirt, representing North or South. Once we got out there, all the tents were set up and the reenacting people, that were there to help us, were outside waiting. When we got to the tents, North went right and South went left. I went to my tent where the nurses and surgeons stayed for the day. I was a nurse. When they began having battles, people were pretending to die right and left. We had to take care of people from North and South. It was pretty hard work, because when people would get injured we would have to take them back to our tent on stretchers, and some of those boys weren't exactly light. When we got to the tent, we would have to bandage them up and then send them back out to battle. When the first half of the day was over it was time for lunch. We ate stuff that people ate in 1860. We ate biscuits, jerky, beans and cornbread. For the next half of the day we did the same thing. When 3:00 rolled around we were all tired, but we had a fun and awesome day.

Cayla Carlson, Grade 8
West Jr High School, MO

Don't Give Up When the Going Gets Tough

Don't give up, was what I was told to do when I was diagnosed with hypothyroidism at the age of twelve. Even though I was uninformed and terrified, I was determined to never give up hope.

It hit me one morning, like a ton of bricks that had just fallen on me when I woke up. My stomach, throat, nose, and head pain continued to get worse throughout the days and weeks. I felt sluggish; therefore, it was hard to continue my other activities. No doctor had been able to figure out what was going on. At last a doctor solved my problem when he took three blood tests. A specific test called Epstein Bar or a rare type of mono is what my sickness turned out to be. Along with finding the mono, the blood test detected a hereditary disease called hypothyroidism. This test told me that my thyroid wasn't functioning completely, and I was devastated. Because of my malfunctioning thyroid my attitude, mood, and energy level were changing every day. Thankfully my mother and I found a doctor in Tulsa, Oklahoma that would explain what to do and how to help.

Still today and for the rest of my life I will take a tiny pill to help my thyroid function completely. Even though this was a detrimental period in my life, I chose to never give up hope and faith.

Aubrey Marsellis, Grade 8
Southwest Jr High School, AR

A Fabulous Reference Tool

Among those books on my bookshelf, the most eye-catching one is a brick-shaped dictionary, which has become my lifelong friend, because it embraces so much treasure for me to dig through. My dictionary, *Webster's College Dictionary*, is a fabulous reference tool that includes thousands of very useful words, and their spellings, pronunciations, definitions, part of speech, and even sample sentences.

I have established a long-term relationship with my dictionary for the last six years, at the time I started grade school. As soon as I saw it, I knew that it would be my favorite book throughout my life. What triggered me to think this, was when school started, and I had to complete a science worksheet. I didn't understand some of the words, so I looked them up. I was hooked. Since then, I have been learning new words constantly.

Later, I had to make a hard decision. I felt that all the words in my former dictionary were not enough for me, and decided to move on. Despite the fact that pages were falling out, I kept the book that led me all the way through elementary school, because I didn't have the heart to throw it away. It was heartbreaking to know that I wouldn't be peering through it as I used to do. I bought a new dictionary, which I use to this very day. No matter what level dictionary I have, it will have the identical rank on my bookshelf.

Kevin Wang, Grade 7
White Station Middle School, TN

All About Me

My name is Taniquia Chonturrah Hudson. I was born on October 4, 1992 in Orlando, Florida. I have been living in Donalsonville, GA for the past 10 months. I enjoy living up here.

I love running track, playing basketball, and playing baseball. I'm an outgoing and respectful student with a positive attitude. I respect others even though they don't respect me half of the time. I am a Libra of course. I am a good cook and love to bake. When I was twelve years old I rode a dolphin. My favorite colors are blue, red, and black. My favorite foods are hot wings and cornbread. My favorite rap artists are Romeo, Nelly, Eva, and Kelly Rowland.

I have four brothers. I'm the only girl. When I was in elementary school, I was an AB honor roll student. I used to play football when I was about ten or eleven. When I played football my knee came out of socket. I love to draw and color.

Finally, I plan to graduate in 2011. This is my first year in high school. I plan to become a Nurse Practitioner. I know most of my family didn't graduate so that's not going to stop me from being what I want to, because I have faith in myself. I know I can be what I want to, because if I work hard at it I can be successful. I'm planning on going to college for four years to receive a bachelor's degree.

Taniquia Hudson, Grade 9
Seminole County Middle/High School, GA

Bubbles

The day started out like any other day; I came outside wearing my brand new scarf. My neighbor, Joy, ran outside too, and we developed a game that was new and exciting. Our new game, something like hide-and-seek, didn't have a name, but sounded like fun. While the person who was 'it' counted, the hider made a trail of bubbles as she ran to hide. The bubbles would help 'it' find the hider. I was going to hide first.

Joy started counting much too fast! With the bubbles container jiggling in my hand, I ran through a muddy patch in my yard, panting like a dog. The bubble container was shaking madly as I ran. Suddenly, I stepped on a rock. It slid underneath my foot, causing me to fall face forward. Hitting the ground, mud flew everywhere and I spilt the bubble juice in my hair and scarf.

I screamed as I scrambled to my feet. Joy was rushing toward me shouting, "What happened? Are you okay?" Tears poured down my face. "I got bubbles in my hair!" Joy looked and me for a second, and then burst out laughing. I glared at her, but she couldn't stop. My mom came to help me get cleaned up, but she started laughing too. I was angry for a few seconds, but as they helped me clean up, I couldn't help but giggle. All three of us laughed and laughed. Now I realize that this 'disaster' wasn't terrible, but fun!

Lily Gullion, Grade 7
St Mary's School, SC

Summer at the Beach

Sitting in the car and looking at the scenery of the Smokey Mountains was all right, but I had my mind set on seeing the ocean. I had only heard about how beautiful the ocean was in books and from friends, only now I was about to see this amazing sight in person. In a few hours I could be the one describing the waves crashing against the shore and the colorful sunset on the beach of South Carolina.

Pulling up to the condo, everything was really unique. South Carolina is nothing like Missouri. With the uncommon palm trees and sand everywhere, I was really looking forward to seeing the ocean and spending the next week there.

The next morning everyone was ready to go to the beach. When we arrived, I sprinted straight into the ocean, gaining speed when feeling the scorching sand on my feet. I quickly remembered that the ocean was full of salt when getting it in my mouth and eyes. The view was truly amazing, better than the ones in the books and magazines.

Getting back to the condo that night I was so exhausted that I feel asleep in no time. I couldn't wait for the next week ahead of me. I had so many other great things to experience. I will remember and cherish this day for the rest of my life and will always love the ocean. I couldn't wait to return home and tell all my friends how wonderful the ocean was.

Valerie Bell, Grade 9
West Jr High School, MO

Play Ball

Play ball yells the umpire. I stand on the mound getting the sign from the catcher. I wind up, I pitch, crack, base hit. The other team gets four runs off of me in the first inning. But I settle down only letting up one more run the rest of the game.

Now going into our teams last three outs. We are down three to five. The first batter strikes out. Next batter got walked. Then our third batter of the inning gets a base hit. Now runners at second and first. One of our best hitters comes up to the plate. He hits it high into the air but the outfielders catch it.

Finally it's my turn to bat. I stand up to the plate. I let the first one go by for a strike. The second pitch comes. I take a vicious swing but I miss. I am our last hope. The pitch comes, I swing, hit it. It travels far and high. It is going back to the fence and it goes over for a home run.

I run the bases, I round third base, my team all surrounded around home plate. I jump in the air and land on home plate and my team jumps up and down with excitement.

That was one of my best days ever. It was fun and exciting. I hit the game-winning home run.

Kyle Savage, Grade 8
Pigeon Forge Middle School, TN

The CIA Agent

I am a CIA agent. Well, not exactly. I am an agent of ethnicities, a *C*hinese *I*sraeli *A*merican, born in the United States to a Jewish mother and a Chinese father. Over the past twelve years of my life, I have learned as much as I could about my cultural background, because that is what is important to me.

I grew up in Memphis where I spent my elementary years in a Jewish school studying the beliefs and values of the Jewish religion. Also, every summer I take the long plane ride across the Pacific to China, where I pick up the language and habits of my father's side of the family. I like to think that when I am speaking Chinese or chanting a prayer from a Siddur, the Jewish prayer book, I am walking in the same footsteps that my ancestors walked before me. This is important to me, because we need to know where we came from in order to know where we are going.

Living with a combination of three completely different cultures has helped me understand that we are all the same, no matter which God you worship or which holidays your celebrate. Respect everyone, and you will be able to learn from them. That is why America, the melting pot of the world, is such a great place, because with so many blends of ethnicities and customs, one cannot help but become a better person.

Daniel Teitz Zuo, Grade 7
White Station Middle School, TN

JR Landry

In my opinion, JR's family is very important to him. He does his best in school. Also he has great friends. He is a very nice person.

In his life he has had a mom, a dad, a step-dad, and a sister. His mom means everything to him. Without her his life would be a wreck. His father in 2003 was killed by a bad motorcycle wreck. JR misses him so much. He wishes he could have just seen him one last time. Now he has a step-father. His name is Ray, he may not be perfect but JR still loves him. JR also has a sister. Her name is Cheyenne. She can be a little annoying sometimes but JR will always love her.

In school JR can be very smart. His report cards usually have A's, B's, and C's. He tries his hardest all the time. He does exceptionally well. He has never failed a grade and hopefully never will. His teachers are very strict; school can be very stressful.

JR's friends mean a lot to him. He has many friends. His best friends will stick with him through thick and thin. They even help him out in school. Sadly he moved to Florida from New Jersey. He left many friends behind. Now he has many new friends.

In conclusion I can say JR's family means the most to him. He takes his schoolwork seriously and he has awesome friends.

JR Landry, Grade 7
Sebastian River Middle School, FL

William Tilghman

1924, Cromwell, Oklahoma. A town of gambling and bootlegging. William Tilghman Jr. a legendary Marshall (now 70 years old) comes to town to clean it up. He died in less than a year of taking that post trying to disarm a crooked prohibition officer by the name of Wiley Lynn. Lynn got away but was killed years later in a gunfight with an officer by the name of Crockett Long. He was courageous, peaceful, and truthful.

Tilghman was known for his courage. Most officers of the time were corrupt because they were too afraid to stand up to the outlaws. He was one of the few who stood up and fought back. He never backed down not even when he had to face his fellow officer Wiley Lynn.

William was a very peaceful person. He hardly ever resorted to gunfight. When he could he always disarmed his criminals instead of shooting them. In all of his years as an officer he only killed 2 people. Sadly, his peacefulness is why he died.

He was also a very truthful person. When movies were beginning to be made that made outlaws seem heroic he made his own movie. The movie was about the fall of outlaws. He couldn't stand it when Hollywood made outlaws seem heroic.

That is why William "Bill" Tilghman is my hero. He was courageous, peaceful, and truthful.

Jason Austin, Grade 8
Mulhall-Orlando High School, OK

Rap Videos: Negative Effects on Teens

Just think, would you want your son growing up to disrespect women, use drugs and profanity, and ride on 22's? Well, this will happen if your son watches rap videos. I think watching rap videos has a negative effect on teens, because they glamorize drug use and they support making money in negative ways, and nudity.

Rappers glamorize drug use by selling snowman T-shirts in stores. They make it seem cool to sell or use drugs. On most videos, they talk about using drugs and alcohol. The "White Girl" video is an example of drug use, the video includes sniffing powder.

In videos they also support making money in negative ways, and nudity. They hustle for money. The women on the videos have on little to no clothes. The rappers disrespect women by using profanity towards them.

Rap videos are a bad influence on teens because they glamorize drugs, use profanity, they make money in negative ways, and they use nudity. If you don't want your son to be like rappers on videos that teens watch every day, stop your child now, before it's too late.

Bobby Williams, Grade 7
Mineral Springs Middle School, NC

My Dog

I have a pitbull. He is a brindle color. His name is Max. I also have a cat and my dog goes around chasing her all day. People may say pitbulls are mean and scary, well that may be true, but it all depends on how you raise them. My dog is definitely not mean. He may look mean but he's not. He is a very friendly dog. He is great with other animals too. My dog is crazy. He chases a flashlight. It is so funny. If he hears that sound of the flashlight turn on he freaks out. He is a mamma's boy. We have an electric fence around our yard so he does not get out and roam the neighborhood. The electric wire goes down to the ditch and my dog only goes half way down the yard, because he doesn't want to get shocked. My dog also knows a few tricks. One is sit. Another is lie down, roll over, paw, speak, and other paw. He listens very well. He loves my bed. So my mom has to put his bed in my room so he doesn't go on my bed. My dog is VERY protective. If you are just playing around with someone he will always protect you. He is a great dog. I came home from school and there he was lying on a big blue pillow. I love him and I'm glad to have him. He is like a best friend.

Victoria Card, Grade 7
Sebastian River Middle School, FL

Why I'm Glad My Life's a Musical

Music has always had a powerful influence on my life. While I cannot truthfully call myself a great musician, I am an admirer of those who are, and I strive to be in this category myself someday. I can honestly say that music is an inspiration, a release, an expression, and a definition of my life.

I am a strong believer in the healing qualities of music. I am convinced that God has ministered to me through song, without which, I could not have survived my father's death, my family's tumultuous disagreements, or the loss of my dearest and most greatly missed friend. In music, there is hope, energy, and life.

I cannot imagine a world without music. There would be a loss of art, of singing and dancing, of a form of praise, and of a way of communication. We could not understand the joy of listening to that force that makes us laugh and cry, remember and relive the best times of our lives. We'd never know the feeling of chills running along our spines as the orchestra pounds out those last few strains of our national anthem.

I am, and always will be, a lover of music. Nothing could never compare to the powerful melodies that are prayers to God, the creators of dreams, and the voices of our history. Music is more than just notes, chords, and scales. Music is a way of life.

Davina Van Essen, Grade 9
Trinity Christian Academy, AL

Football!

I believe that everyone in America knows what football is. Football is probably the greatest sport of all time. How do I know this? Because I play it. I practice the sport as much as possible. The sport is even more fun when you play it with your friends. Football can be enjoyed at home or on the field.

Football is about the greatest sport of all time. Why do you ask? For me, every second is filled with anticipation. The feel of the turf under your feet; the thrill of the long pass; the joy of scoring a touchdown. These all play a part in the football experience. Plus, it's fun knocking people over.

Playing football alone is boring. However, that's why there are friends. Not only do they make it more enjoyable, they also build self-confidence. Besides, who knows who could pop up during the game? It just keeps getting better after that.

If you can't make it to the home game, there's always TV. Whenever there is a game on TV, it's just as tense as any other game. You could have a tailgate party while watching the game. All in all, it's just plain fun.

So, as you probably already know, football is just plain fun. Friends just make it even better. That is what makes it about the greatest sport of all time. Some say that baseball is America's pastime. For me, it's football.

Patrick Conroy, Grade 8
Oakbrook Middle School, SC

Farming Effects on Human Environment

As we look back at our nation's history we notice that technology available now is much more fitting to our farming practices and environmental concerns. Waste control focuses on methods, odor, and effectiveness of these practices.

In Oklahoma State University's Swine Research Program, directed by Dr. Kim Brock, stands one of the most recent waste management systems. As he described to me, "In this system, the waste from our barns is pumped into a sewage tank, then the waste is separated, solids from liquids. The liquids are dispersed into a lagoon. In this specially designed lagoon is a two-layer filter. On the bottom layer is the liquid waste and is separated from the top layer by a plastic cover. The top layer is a pool of purified water. Every month or so, we run the clean water over into a second lagoon and keep the purification process going."

I realized what an innovative method they developed to decrease the odor by keeping a pool of water over the waste to keep gases and chemicals in the waste from being active in the atmosphere. OSU has installed a ventilation system that pulls the distasteful smell out of the building into a bed of straw. This method is to release a moderately cleaner smell.

I conclude that this method is a gateway of possibilities for the future in preserving our environment. It will remain effective.

Austin Kindschi, Grade 9
Mulhall-Orlando High School, OK

My First Long Course State Meet

It was my first time going to the Long Course State Meet at the University of South Carolina's swimming pool. I swam the 50 breast, 100 breast, 200 breast, 50 free, 100 free, 200 free, 400 free, and the 200 individual medley. Over the past year, I made the state cut in these events. During the summer, I practiced every morning and afternoon.

The meet was not exactly what I expected it to be. This meet was very hard for me. My coach, Tom Calloway had gotten cancer. The swim team was falling apart and most of my friends had already quit the swim team, Eastside Aquatic Club. Representing my team was Derek Williams and me, but not for long. Recently, Derek had broken his hand, and it was almost better but not quite. On Saturday, Derek swam the 400 individual medley, and he somehow broke his hand again. Derek went home, so it was just me. I got 2nd in 50 breast, 3rd in 100 breast, and 3rd in 200 breast.

In the other events, because I did not place in the top 10, I did not get a medal. I did my best for Coach Tom. I wanted to make it Coach Tom's best swim meet ever as this would be his last meet. I was very sad to see him leave. After the meet, he gave me a hug and said how proud he was of me. He had tears in his eyes.

Victoria De Maria, Grade 7
St Mary's School, SC

Baseball Heaven

Wham, the ball sails into the sky and finally over the wall into a kid's glove that only came to watch some dedicated people do their thing. Living in Saint Louis gives me the opportunity to visit one of the greatest ballparks in the country, Busch Stadium. Not only is it a great architectural design but in every home game it is filled with a sea of red. In this red is the throbbing Card's spirit brought by each spectator.

When the sun sets and the lights spill their glow is when it all starts. Before the game, the players fall into positions and a roar of cheers and whistles can be heard from blocks away. At the second inning, you do not even realize the peanuts are done and the nachos spilled into the aisle. All you are worried about is how your home team is doing or if Albert Pujols hit a homer yet to give a promising chance to take the Cubs out of the playoff opportunity. By the seventh, you are stuck in the baseball world and have forgotten all about what is happening outside the stadium's brick walls being led by the locally famous Stan Musial statue. End of the game, and you are full of Dip'n Dots and the wide variety of food the place offers. Time to pack up your foam finger, new shirt, and collector mug. All that money you thought would be a waste was worth every penny you spent.

Nick Ross, Grade 8
St Gerard Majella School, MO

The Sport I Admire the Most

The sport I admire the most is basketball. I like playing every sport, but basketball is my favorite. When playing basketball you need to have good sportsmanship. If you have played before, you should know it's not hard.

My first time playing basketball was last summer. I played with my friends and one of my teachers was my coach. I was the point guard, which I think is the best position. We were a good team, but we weren't the best. When we made it to the championship we lost, but I still think we could've won if our attitudes weren't so rude.

Our parents came out to support us, so that helped a little. When my mom came that's when I showed out, I was scoring back to back and I was playing good defense. My coach spent a lot of money just for us to play for an AAU team. Now he has everybody wanting to play for his or her school. I feel like an all-star when I play basketball.

You should always stay healthy while you are playing sports. You have to run and also do suicides so you should drink a lot of water or vitamin drinks. While I was playing basketball I had to exercise more than I usually do. I ate plenty of fruit. Now that I have started playing basketball, I will never quit.

Alisha Williams, Grade 8
Turner Middle School, GA

A Massacre Remembered

Imagine this scene from the Boston Massacre: you are standing among many people, and you are aware of two things. The despised Lobsterbacks, and the hate-filled aura of the mob. You're fighting for the Patriots. You scoop some snow up, fully aware of it having rocks. With a look of fury, you chuck it as hard as it will go. The yelling of the crowd drowns the noise; you hear a voice saying something, but you can only make out, "Fire!" Soon, the blast of the bloodybacks' bullets echoed through your ears. You realize that they had shot and wounded eleven; three of those are dead. Among them is a face you recognize only slightly — that of Crispus Attucks.

The Boston Massacre took place in Boston, Massachusetts (obviously), March 5, 1770. The three victims that were killed on the spot were Crispus Attucks, Samuel Gray, and James Coldwell. Two others died later. It was an important event in American history.

It was a good excuse for the Americans to turn against Britain. One man rose above the rest; his calls of justice were loud and clear. His name was Paul Revere.

At the court, with John Adams as lawyer defending the British soldiers, they had a fair trial. Two were accused of manslaughter; the rest were safe because they were defending themselves, and didn't shoot the crowd directly. However, most Americans called Adams a traitor. Either way, this event in history will be remembered well.

Daniella Gentile, Grade 7
Boyet Jr High School, LA

The History of Basketball

Do you like playing sports or at least heard about them? If you answered yes, you probably know a sport called basketball. Basketball is a very old and also popular sport. People play it all over the world as a career or just for fun.

Basketball was created in the year 1891 by a man named James Naismith. Naismith was a teacher at Springfield College when he created basketball. The idea came to him when he was teaching physical education classes during the winter. So the classes were getting boring and the students were too old to play kiddie games so he had to come up with an "athletic distraction" from the weather that wouldn't make the classes boring. In Naismith's mind he wanted a game of fitness, but not a too physical game. So, he came up with a soccer ball, two peach baskets that will sit 10 feet in the air, nine players on each team and some basic rules. When Naismith had the game and the rules down pat, he began explaining the game to his students and they loved it. With that happening, the students began spreading the word and basketball became so popular that everybody began to play it.

So, I will conclude that if you come up with a brilliant and exciting idea tell someone about it and you might be as famous as James Naismith. Always remember you can do anything if you put your mind to it.

Yvette Barron, Grade 8
Turner Middle School, GA

Growing Faith in the Lord

God is a very important aspect in my life. I try to grow through Him every day, and each day just gets better and better. Three important things that help me grow as a Christian is my church, my youth group, and my friendships with others.

When I go to church on Sundays, I try to accomplish one thing; have better faith in the Lord. In my opinion, it is important to grow as a Christian because it makes one become an all around happier, better person. Life is good, but it is better with God.

My youth group at church is an awesome place to learn about the Lord. We go to many youth rallies and get to meet other teenagers from other churches around the area. We also get to go to many places where we get to spread the word and share God's many blessings.

One major aspect that is really encouraging for me is all of the friendships I have made with other Christians. I have met so many amazing people through youth rallies and church trips. It is truly a blessing! Many of the friends I have made are so wonderful to be around and always teach me something new about Christ.

In conclusion, growing as a Christian is very important in my life. Through Christ, I am becoming a better person all around. The truest blessings in my life are church, my youth group, and all of my friendships.

Tori Bradley, Grade 9
Wilson School, AL

Why Friends Are Important

Friends are a thing that everyone should have in life. They are there for you when you need them. They make life easier and fun. Their houses save you from a boring weekend at home with your family.

Friends are there when their friends are going through a rough time. They will sit and talk about whatever is bothering them. Sometimes they even make fun of it. Finally, good friends stick up for you when you're not there or can't.

The people around you also determine how you feel. They make jokes to cheer you up. They know when the best thing to do for their friends is to keep their mouths shut. Finally, the best friends never leave or turn against you when others would.

No one wants to stay home all weekend with only their brothers and sisters to talk to. That's why they call their friends and ask to go over. Sitting over at someone else's house and making fun of what you could've been doing at home is more like what a weekend should be like. Staying up all night playing games is a lot more fun than listening to your siblings talking all night, trust me.

The friends you keep help you through whatever is going on. They make life easier and a lot more fun. They give you an escape from what could've been a long weekend at home. Friends make life worthwhile.

Samantha Lamon, Grade 8
Pigeon Forge Middle School, TN

Edisto Beach

Edisto Beach is my favorite vacation spot. It is replete with elegant houses, beautiful beaches, and all enhanced by the terrific Atlantic Ocean. However, those aren't the only things great about Edisto Beach.

Having fun at Edisto Beach is not naughty. You can rent bicycles, and tour the whole island. Before you do that, you can play a round of golf at the golf course. Edisto's beaches are full of fish. At the Marina, you can rent a boat and go fishing. If that is not enough, you can always go swimming in the ocean. Swimming in the non placid ocean, you can always have fun. However, you have to be careful. Watching out for sharks, you can still have fun.

Being one of the most beautiful beaches in South Carolina, Edisto Beach is a great place to relax, and a great place to nullify all your worries. You can relax on the abrasive sand on the beach and watch a magnificent sunset. Although you have to be careful because the sun can be noxious. All of this makes Edisto a great place to relax.

Edisto Island is a terrific place. One of the things that makes it so spectacular is that it doesn't have a lot of renown. All of these things are not counterfeit.

David Pollard, Grade 8
St Mary's School, SC

The Most Dangerous Pet

Pit bulls are dangerous animals. I don't think anyone should have them, because they turn on people. We've seen it on the news, and it is happening every day. Pit bulls turning on families and killing kids or hurting them severely. Did the adults in the family know they were going to attack? Usually, yes. They had seen it on the news or heard it from someone but thought it wouldn't happen to them.

Pit bulls should be outlawed is what I think. I think this because people are always thinking that it wouldn't happen to them, because they thought because they raised it ever since it was a puppy it would never attack them or their kids. That is the number one reason people have them. My family doesn't care because my brother and I have gotten attacked by one, and I had to get sixty stitches on my lip and up my cheek. She had that dog ever since it was a puppy, and I had been around it ever since I was at least four.

A better dog for a family with kids is a Labrador or a Golden Retriever, or maybe even a small dog not a pit bull. They will turn on you. It's in their blood. They're not a family dog. They're not a dog for anyone.

I'm telling you, for the sake of you and your kids, these dogs are vicious animals. They can't turn on you if you don't ever have it.

Abbey Pike, Grade 7
Stroud Middle School, OK

Inspire to Dance

"Dancing is like dreaming, but with your feet" — Constanze. Expressing yourself through dancing is very exhilarating because your movements can tell a story or show emotions that can make your audience want to take part in the fun. It can be very uplifting. There are three reasons why dancing is important to me. They are expressing yourself, fitness, and entertainment.

Initially, dancing lets you express yourself. "Dance to express, not to impress" — Unknown. Dancing makes you forget about everything else, and it makes you feel free by allowing your body to do as it wishes. It conveys a message and feelings through movements. Effectively, dancing can be a great way to stay fit. When you are participating in a dancing workout, it is a fun and exciting approach to staying healthy that doesn't seem like work anymore. Dancing can burn as many calories as walking or riding a bike. It can make you very flexible too. Finally, dancing is a method of entertaining your audience. No matter if the style is slow or fast, it has a way of mesmerizing the viewers. As a result, they will want to take part in the cheerful dancing.

In conclusion, dancing is important to me because you can have fun and be yourself. Expressing yourself, fitness, and entertaining your audience makes dancing very exciting and important. "Dance to inspire, and inspire to dance" — Unknown.

Kaitlyn Fulford, Grade 8
Home School, SC

Love of a Best Friend

Having a best friend is having everything you want in the world. I bet everyone in this world has someone they can call their best friend. I know I can. Having a best friend means the world to me. Having a person that believes in you, counts on you, and encourages you in the way you do them is creating a manmade miracle. I could stand before everyone in this world today and tell them about my best friend. He is just that great. As much as I hate to say it, I cannot stand in front of the 6 billion people that populate the world, and tell them about how much my best friend means. I can tell you though. I am proud to say that my best friend is one that is rare.

Frankie is my best friend. He's handsome and has these remarkable eyes. He's completely honest with you, and never tells you a false thing. His words can hurt but they aren't intentional. He won't judge you, but he will help to make you a better person. He loves me more than anyone ever has. I appreciate any kind of love but what he gives me is more than I could ever ask for. He gives me the love of a best friend. He makes me okay, he holds me, he tells me he loves me, and he makes me a better person. All by giving me, the love of a best friend.

Kayla Anderson, Grade 9
St Cloud High School, FL

Labrador Retrievers

The Labrador Retriever is a well-known dog. For many years, the lab has been a top dog for people with special needs. The lab originated from Canada and has moved its way into the hearts of many people across the world in places like Australia, Britain, and the United States. Labs have three colored coats: yellow, black, and chocolate.

I have a two year old lab named Angel. She is a white lab with a black nose; that is rare because labs have pink noses. She weighs about 70 pounds and is about two feet tall. Angel is registered in the American Kennel Club. One thing Angel loves is to play in the water, which is common for most retrievers.

It was not easy to train Angel. I trained Angel to sit, stay, fetch, and lay down. I am working on other tricks to teach her. When we got Angel we had to start house training her. We used puppy pads, treats, and many other things to get her to tell us when she wanted to go outside. Angel loved to sleep in the bed with me until she got too big. We plan to breed angel to another lab in the spring.

Angel and most other labs are great dogs and pets. If you are considering another dog, choose a lab. They are inexpensive, gentle, intelligent, energetic, and good natured. Love labs and they will love you back for a life time.

Chelsea Magrini, Grade 8
Albemarle School, NC

Acrobatics in a Vehicle

Trembling, I approached my first roller coaster ride at King's Island. It was a gargantuan, wooden-trestle roller coaster, called Son of Beast. My dad and I walked towards the ride. I was thinking, "Do you really want to ride Son of Beast?" The ride was ginormous! My dad saw me shaking and reassured me it would be a fun ride.

Finally, we climbed in, the bar came down, and we started moving. We went down a hill, around a curve and then slowed down. Looking ahead, the cars were ascending a huge hill. When we reached the top we dropped fast, down, down, down toward the ground. Right when I thought we'd hit the ground, there was a sharp turn and another hill. When we dropped, I didn't let go because I thought I was going to fall out of my seat. My heart was beating fast and my insides were trying to make an escape through my mouth. With increasing adrenaline, we went down, around and up another hill then the cars went in a corkscrew motion. I felt like a screw driver was drilling me into the ground. Then, abruptly, it ended.

Afterwards my legs felt like Jell-O. Exhilarated, we talked about the ride throughout the afternoon. As we left, I caught one last glimpse of King's Island. I vowed from now on, I'm going to ride roller coasters every chance I get.

Nicholas Poplos, Grade 7
White Station Middle School, TN

A Sting

It was a hot, summer day at my house. I was five years old then and was busy planting sunflower seeds in a small garden. These were my favorite flowers. My parents were helping me. I tired quickly in the hot sun and set my seeds on a bright yellow swing. This swing was meant for two people. The seats faced each other. The swing rocked a little when I put the seeds down.

I heard a sudden, angry sounding buzzing noise and felt something small land on my leg. I screamed and ran a small distance away from the swing. I hurriedly checked my leg and found nothing there. I walked over carefully and bumped the seat again, reaching to get my seeds. This time, a flash of pain entered my leg as I stumbled back, hearing the dreadful buzzing noise again. I screamed loudly and ran to my mother.

My mother lifted me up and took me inside the house to check what had caused me so much pain. My father stayed outside to take care of the insects that had stung me. When my mom sat me down to take a look at the damage, my injured leg revealed three large bumps. They were wasp stings. The bumps healed over a few days and the wasps were taken care of, but the fear of them is still in my mind.

Lindsay Mullen, Grade 9
Baton Rouge Magnet High School, LA

The Spread of Christianity

Christianity has made its mark upon the world. Bringing joy to those who want to obtain salvation. Youth groups and churches are doing everything they can to spread the word of our Lord Jesus Christ who died for our sins so that we may have eternal life with Him in Heaven. One of the many leading organizations around the world that resides in church is Royal Rangers. It teaches not only about Christ but how to survive in the wilderness. They help kids, and welcome you with open arms.

Often people ask what influenced Christianity, and why you choose to follow it. People follow Christ because they feel a belonging or they're trying to fill a void in their life which is ultimately Christ. Many people turn to drugs and everything else to solve their problems and fill that void. You may not think that Christ is real just because you can't see Him with your eyes, but oh is He real. He's watching over you making sure you're doing the right thing towards His commandments and not what the world says is right. The Lord once said, "Blessed are those who have not yet seen me and still believe that I am he, the son of man who has come into the world, to deliver it of its sins."

Christianity has been around for many years and still continues to save the ones who are in need of salvation. You may think you're alone in the world but you're not. Remember, if nobody else likes you, there's One who will love you and always have your back when you need Him the most. His name is Jesus Christ. He's the King of Kings and Lord of Lords. He's the Alpha and the Omega. The Beginning and the End.

Dante Bolds, Grade 9
Smiths Station High School, AL

Tips and Tricks for Volleyball

Before I started playing volleyball, I didn't really know what it was all about. From two years of practice I have discovered volleyball is a fun sport, yet aggressive and sometimes even confusing. Even though I have only played for a short amount of time, I have picked up on this so very fast. The purpose of volleyball is to pass it, set it, and spike it. This means that you need to pass the ball to the setter, then the setter should set a front row hitter, so that the front row hitter can attack the ball rapidly, aggressively, and very hard.

To start the ball game, you need to get your serve in. There are three ways you can serve: an underhand serve, an overhand serve, and a jump serve. They are all great ways to start the point. All of these aspects are important in volleyball, but the basics are the most important. Staying focused and passing correctly is the way to become a star. Work hard at this sport, because if you really like it you can become a great shining star. Then maybe, just maybe, you can get a volleyball scholarship.

Anna Denner, Grade 8
Heritage Hall School, OK

My Loving Sister

My sibling I would like to tell you about in my essay is my sister Ashley. I know most boys do not like having a little sister, but I do. She is a great person to me and others.

Ashley is a very caring person with a very tender heart. We have a poodle named Blackie, she feeds, walks, and plays with him every day. She helps me clean my room. I'm not saying that we always get along, sometimes she is mean to me. She likes to make everybody happy. She gives my parents and grandparents a lot of hugs and kisses and they love it.

Ashley makes good grades in school. She loves to do her homework and practice her cursive writing. Sometimes I hear her in her room teaching her dolls and stuffed animals about school and Bible. Which brings me to the best thing about my sister and that is what a good Christian she is and how that she does not like to miss a Sunday of church. She loves learning new Bible verses and Bible stories.

I hope that you now understand why I love my little sister and why she is such a good sister to me. I know that my family and I are very blessed that God gave us Ashley to love. When I say my prayers at night I always tell God "Thank you for Ashley."

Trent Townsend, Grade 7
Trinity Christian Academy, AL

A Double-Edged Sword

Have you ever wondered how the world will be fifty years from now? Do you ever stop to think how you can change the world? People say that if you want to be something, you can be it. Well, the future is when it will happen. But, the future plays out for better and for worse.

No matter what you do, nothing will end perfectly. We can make technologies that may end major problems like global warming, unsafe traveling, or fatalities on the battlefield, but it might not always end happily. Eventually, technology can fall into the hands of bad people. Transports can be taken by terrorists, along with weaponry, and other electronics that can be dangerous. The future can be one of peace or war, but it solely depends on how we live.

We can create a much brighter future, though, if we are willing to do something. People believe that we will find nonpolluting fuels, create hover cars, and that we will find cures for major diseases, such as cancer. We can if we are willing to work for it. With some research, we can cure cancer, have hovering vehicles, and even find fuels that do not cause pollution while keeping speed. But this will only happen if we try, if we are willing to do something about it. So, if we want the future to be a time where we can live in a better world, we will be willing to work for it.

Britton Black, Grade 8
Greenfield Jr/Sr High School, MO

The Harry Potter Series

When I read J.K. Rowling's Harry Potter series, I feel as if I'm being sucked into a whole new world where I can read for an eternity without any interruptions. As I read her works of art, I have my own personal movie playing inside of my head. In my pink, fuzzy chair I sit with my book and a nice, hot drink.

There is something magical and special about this series, for once I start reading these books, I never want to stop. I want to know what will happen to Harry if he is in a predicament, or how Lord Voldemort is getting stronger and attempting to kill Harry. My striving to keep on reading causes me to read at night when I should be sleeping. I know it is not good to get too little sleep, but when I reach the beginning of a chapter, I think, "Well, it's not too long! I think I'll just read one more chapter." This pattern continues on and on, turning into a routine, until I am sickly tired. Regretfully reaching this point, I finally retire from the amazing journey written on the pages within the book.

A great sorrow indeed when I finish the tale, but also very happy, for it means I am about to begin a new adventure. J.K. Rowling's Harry Potter series is a collection of books that never gets boring. I've read each one numerous times, yet I still enjoy them as if it were the first time. With me the wonderful series will stay, until my time in this world is over.

Marie Ponnath, Grade 7
White Station Middle School, TN

Why My Dad Is Important to Me

God's Fourth Commandment: Thou shall honor thy mother and father. Do you follow this commandment? My dad is important to me because he is very "Handy Dandy," he makes the right choice, and because my dad is always there for me.

What kind of dad do you have? Is it a dad that is "Handy Dandy," or "Give me the remote" kind of dad? My Dad is the kind of dad who is "Handy Dandy." In other words, he fixes objects that are broken. If I need help with a project he's right there to help me.

Unlike some other dads, my dad makes the right choice. For example, my dad got this huge job offer and he chose not to take the job because he would only be home on the weekends. He wanted to be with his family.

Instead of using my notes to study for science, I use my Dad. My stupendous Dad is a great source to study with. One day he helped me on cell division. I didn't know any of it. The test was the next day It turned out that I made a better grade than I would have made if my dad hadn't helped me. I thanked my dad for always being there for me.

My dad is extraordinarily important to me. I appreciate having a "Handy Dandy" dad that makes all the right choices and is always there for me. So, never forget to honor your father!

Allie Seale, Grade 7
Holy Ghost Catholic School, LA

Rodeo

My essay is about an adrenaline packed sport called rodeo. When you think of rodeo you assume it originated in the U.S. or Mexico, but actually it originated in Europe. Rodeo isn't like other sports that have a single event. Rodeo has many events, such as the most popular bull riding. Bull riding did indeed originate in Mexico. Team roping, barrel racing, bronc bustin', bull doggin', chute doggin', goat tying, are some of the events in rodeo today. There are different age division such as peewee ages 5-12, junior 13-15, senior 16-18, rookie anywhere from 13-21 depending on how good you do in the previous year, and the professional level, which you can achieve only after you have received your "rookie card."

There are many different associations to be in such as the PRCA, MJRC, AYRA, MFRA and many more. One of the most popular rodeos today is the Cheyenne Frontier Days often referred to as 'Daddy of Them All.' The rodeo originated in September of 1897 as a simple one day western celebration which has grown into a 2 week western festival. The festival includes carnivals, Indian villages, world-class concerts, parades, and a world famous rodeo. Today thousands of people attended this celebration each day.

My family has attended this rodeo several times since the summer of 1987. I had the chance to attend this celebration with my parents in 2005-2007. I can't wait to get our 2008 tickets. Cheyenne here I come!

Amy Friend, Grade 8
Greenfield Jr/Sr High School, MO

A Race Not to Remember

My family started taking me to NASCAR races when I was four. It was so much fun. We always pulled for Dale Earnhardt number 3 to win.

We used to go to Darlington, South Carolina, and Daytona, Florida. My brother and sister would go also. It was really great when Dale Earnhardt would win. Now we go to the Charlotte race in May. It is my favorite track, because it is at night, and the cars look different under the lights.

On the weekend of the Daytona race in February, 2001, racing took a tragic turn. My dad and I were on the 19th row, and my mom and nephew were sitting on the top row. It was a typical Daytona race; all of Dale Earnhardt's cars were in the top three, when toward the end of the race there was an accident with Tony Stewart. They red flagged the race. When the green flag came out and it was the last turn of the last lap, Sterling Marlin spun Dale Earnhardt out. Dale hit the wall and ended up on the grass, but it was too late; his seat belt came undone, and rumor has it that he broke his neck. Michael Waltrip won the race with Dale Jr. in second.

Nobody knew that the last turn of the last lap would be the last turn of Dale Earnhardt's life. Now we pull for Dale Earnhardt Jr. who is doing great.

Kathleen Brooks, Grade 8
Albemarle School, NC

The Rat Lady

One day during the summer while my mom was at school, my dad and I were making lunch. My dad and I decided to make hamburgers on the grill. In our backyard we had this huge tree about 100-150 feet tall and it was our fence line. Sometimes when the branch died it would fall into our neighbors' yard and Claudet hated when this happened. Well while we were cooking our lunch outside on the grill, a dead branch just so happened to fall in her yard. Then out of nowhere Claudet came rushing out yelling in her Chinese voice "NO! NO! NO! NO! STUPID TREE! YOU SO STUPID, ALL YOU DO IS PUT YA BRANCHES IN MY YARD!" Then from her yard something went flying into the air. At first I said "Daddy look it's flying squirrel!" Then we heard a "Splash!" The so called "squirrel" landed in our pool. We rushed over and came to find a dead rat floating belly side up in our pool.

After that incident every time a branch fell in her yard she would scream at us and throw her dead rats in our pool, and sometimes more than 1 rat would be thrown in our pool. Every time my dad would scoop them out and throw them in the trash. That's how Claudet got the interesting title "Rat Lady."

Jennifer Gianantonio, Grade 7
Osceola Creek Middle School, FL

My Future Career

Throughout my life, I have had numerous people ask me, "What do you want to be when you grow up?" I've always had one definite answer: a medical doctor. When I think about all the people in the world who have various diseases, some even incurable, I realize that they need my help.

Once, when I was a child, I entered a hospital to get my flu shot. The moment I stepped inside, I observed people lying in beds, having trouble breathing, or undergoing serious surgeries. My heart ached to see them suffer in pain. I knew that something had to be done.

At that time, my father applied for the residency match and wanted to find someone to practice for his interview. I was fortunate enough to act as a "professor" to interview him. Through several mock interviews, I gained some knowledge about the medical field. In the past three years as my father worked as a physician, I began to know what a physician's life is like. I saw how hard he worked, but how joyful he felt in his heart when he saved a patient's life.

From that time on, I was inspired by my father and choose to be a medical doctor as my future career. I cannot bear to think about people's loved ones at death's door. I understand that being a doctor requires hard work, perseverance, and intelligence, and I will try my best to achieve my goal.

Ellen Chai, Grade 7
White Station Middle School, TN

Softball

Softball, in my opinion, is a very fun, extraordinary sport. Softball takes a lot of dedication and concentration. Softball teaches you the importance of hard work and teamwork.

Softball has been played for many years and there are numerable great softball players. In a way softball is a girl-version of baseball. It takes a lot of concentration to time exactly when to swing at the ball. Also, you have to stay focused when deciding where to move to when trying to catch the ball. You need to be in good physical shape in order to play the wonderful sport because there is so much movement and reliance on your muscles for power. You must be dedicated for yourself and your teammates. The other members of the team rely on you to do your part and cover your area on the field.

This sport, in my opinion, is very fun and exciting. Softball teaches you good moral values also such as the following: hard work, dedication, team work and respect and honor as far as obeying your coach and the umpires.

Halie Cheatwood, Grade 8
Trinity Christian Academy, AL

Sweat and Pain Bond Friendships

A big part of summer is making new friends, and that's what happened while spending three weeks at Tulsa Ballet's Pointe to the Future Summer Intensive.

Although my fifth summer in Tulsa, I had never stayed in the dorms. Three weeks of freedom; I was ecstatic! I said good-bye to my mother and, after a few room mix-ups, my bunkmate and I were settled in our new home. Soon I would meet my new best friends, Troy and Sophia.

Tulsa Ballet's amazing reputation attracts students worldwide. Sophia Hernandez lives in Santa Monica, California. She couldn't believe Tulsa's July heat; I told her ballerinas were tough and could hand anything. She made fun of my accent; I laughed when she caught herself saying "ya'll." After a huge argument with our roommates, we were inseparable. It seemed Sophia and I had been friends forever.

I met Troy Herring at the studio. He lives in Owasso, Oklahoma, and regularly takes class at the Tulsa Ballet School. As a commuter student, we were only together during the day. At night we would talk on the phone — a lot — for hours. Being inseparable, our classmates called us "the love birds."

Our days were long and hard but we loved the routine, keeping each other gong with inside jokes and gossip around Epsom Salt foot soaks! There is nothing like sweat and pain to bond friendships, and that is that happened this summer. The last day at camp, saying good-bye to my friends, especially Troy and Sophia, was one of the most difficult experiences of my life. We still talk on the phone, but it's not the same. I really miss them.

Andrea Wolf, Grade 8
Heritage Hall School, OK

The Man Who Did It All

Imagine this, bullets flying through the air. Everyone yelling, but you're not able to hear a word. The clash of dirt and debris from buildings being shot into the air is tapping on your helmet. You look down to find bodies, and when you look up, you find clouds of smoke surrounding you and people that you don't recognize. This is how a man named James Robert Kalsu spent the last minutes of his life.

James Robert Kalsu was born on April 13, 1945. He grew up in Oklahoma and attended the University of Oklahoma where he was selected in an eighth-round draft by the Buffalo Bills. During the season of 1968, Kalsu played starting guard every game and was later elected the Bill's team rookie-of-the-year award. Wanting to satisfy his Reserve Officer Training Corps (ROTC) obligation, he was accepted into the army as a first lieutenant in 1969. Unfortunately, he died a year later in the Vietnam War.

Kalsu only had one child that he actually met. Her name is June Kalsu; she is 37 years old this year. On June 23, Mrs. Kalsu gave birth to James Kalsu's only son, which he has never met. His son's name is James Robert Kalsu Jr., to carry on his father's legacy.

Kalsu was the only recently active football player that died in the Vietnam War. Kalsu was remembered in many ways. A forward operating base in Iraq was named after him, and Del City High School's football stadium will always bear his name.

Shelby Miller, Grade 8
Chelsea Jr High School, OK

Football Is My Favorite Sport

Football is my favorite sport because I can have fun and play with my friends. I can enjoy myself on the field. I want to go to the NFL to play football. When I get to the NFL I can help out the team I play for. I can be a leader for that team.

We could go to the Super Bowl. Our best players can go to the Pro Bowl. We can be one of the best teams in the league. Once people see me play they can start looking at me play. People could buy jerseys from the store.

People could be ready for Sunday to come so they could come to the game or look at it on the television. Once people start looking at the games I would start a fan club. What will I do when I get to the NFL? When I get in the NFL I'm going to take care of my family. My family means a lot to me. I love my family and football. They both mean a lot to me.

In football you get to hit people. You get to do a lot in football; that's why I like it. I play football for my school. I play second-string quarterback, and on defense I play linebacker. I hope I make it in the NFL but if I don't I got a backup plan. You should always have a backup plan.

Sammy Evans, Grade 8
Turner Middle School, GA

The Horse Lady Who Hated Fireworks

I will always remember the time when we were all camping in Courtney's backyard. Courtney is my best friend. We weren't really camping we were just sleeping in a tent. We as in Courtney, Courtney's stepsister, and I.

It was such a blast but it got as hot as a sauna at night. We listened to music, took pictures, played board games, played card games, and shot off fireworks. This is where the funny part comes in.

After we completed playing a game of Doodle Cranium, we decided to shoot off some fireworks. Not necessarily me and Courtney, but her step-dad. It was about midnight and Brian shot of the first firework. BAM! Goes the second and not even after 30 seconds, the horse lady came out and started bellowing, "You hit my horse, don't shoot another one unless you want me to call the cops." So Brian of course, shoots another one. Courtney's mom, Beth, got so angry; she had to yell over to the horse lady "We're sorry, it won't happen again." The horse lady got so mad and frustrated, she stomped inside like a stampede of bulls and cows as fast as she could.

It turns out that she never called the cops.

Courtney Worthington, Grade 7

Bengal Tigers

The Bengal tiger lives in many different places such as India, Bangladesh, Nepal, and Burma. These animals live in mostly sanctuaries. There happens to be more Bengal tiger sub species than any other type of tiger. These tigers hunt for medium-sized animals such as badgers, deer, and also rabbits.

These male tigers get up to three meters long; the females get two point seven meters long. Since tigers hunt mostly at night their stripes help them hide in the shadows of tall grasses. The tiger eats up to 49 kilograms of meat in one serving, and they drag their prey to water to eat it. They are often seen wading in water or in shade cooling off.

Tigers are the largest member of the cat family. Over the last 100 years, the tiger population has reduced because of hunting and forest destruction. Tigers are hunted for body parts that are used in some Chinese medicines. Tigers live along aggressively scent-marked, large territories to keep their rivals away. Despite their fearsome reputation, they often avoid humans.

Females give birth from 2-6 tiger cubs; they raise them with little to no help from the father. The average life span is 8-10 years. A tiger's roar can be heard up to two miles away. Tigers also enjoy resting in tall, grassy meadows. The Bengal tigers are usually white with blue eyes; some call them albino. These tigers can weigh up to 500 pounds.

Hannah Nichols, Grade 7
Stroud Middle School, OK

Music's Influence on My Life

Imagine life without music. Isn't it hard? It sure is for me. People listen to music every day, like me, and with iTunes, the music industry has exploded with popularity.

I like to have music at my fingertips, which makes my iPod nano very handy. It has been only seven months, and I have over 200 songs on my iPod of varying genres, with my preferences being rock and alternative over country. Some very good artists, in my opinion, are Three Days Grace, Journey, Steve Miller Band, The Eagles, and Daft Punk.

My family, as well as video games and the radio, all play a role in the music I listen to. For example, one particular video game with rock music as its core is "Guitar Hero." It is responsible for many people to download the songs featured on the game from iTunes, and I have done that, too.

The iPod has altered the music industry. Ever since its release, it has been the major topic of discussion amongst my friends and I. It's very cool to see how much iPods have changed over such a short time, from the original iPod to the video iPod that can play movies and music videos.

Music has had a huge impact on my life, and I believe that it has changed my personality. Using my iPod has almost become an addiction, and I can't wait to see what technology has next for the musical world.

Joe Mungenast, Grade 8
St Gerard Majella School, MO

The Invention of the Automobile

There is no doubt that the automobile, or the car, is one of the most revolutionary inventions ever. Because before the car all they had was the horse pulled wagon. This had some disadvantages because the people in those times could not go very far because the horse got tired.

The earliest ancestor of the car was the Fardier, which was a three wheeled steam powered car that reached up to 2.3 miles per hour. The Fardier was built in 1771 by Nicolas Joseph Cugnot for the French minister of war. But this model never reached production because it went slower than a horse-and-buggy and was much harder to operate. Another French man was Amedee Bollee, who improved the car in 1873, but it was also slower that and horse pulled buggy and was much too complicated to operate.

The revolutionary vehicle was built in Germany in 1889 by Gottlieb Daimler and Wilhelm Maybach. This was powered by a 1.5 horse power, 2-cylinder engine it had a four-speed transmission, and traveled at 10 mph.

The first automobile that was manufactured in a great quantity was the 1901 Curved Dash Oldsmobile, which was built in the United States by Ransom E. Olds. Modern automobile mass production and its use of the modern day industrial assembly line thanks to Henry Ford, who was born in Detroit, Michigan. Who built his first gasoline-powered car in 1896. Thus, contributing to the invention of the car.

Michelle Jimenez, Grade 8
Ponce De Leon Middle School, FL

My Life

I was born September 5, 1993 at 7:00 a.m., at Bainbridge Hospital. My parents' names are Jennifer and Chris Morman. I have three brothers, but one died his name was Joshua. My other brothers stay with me. Their names are Wendell and Christopher. Wendell is 12 and loves to play football. Christopher is 9 and loves to play basketball.

Me, well right now I am trying to get over my cousin's death. I love him so much, but now he's gone. It's sad because when I was down he always made me laugh or smile. Marcus was lovable I'm really sad, but my grandma really makes me feel good. If she was to go I would have nothing to live for. I don't know but that is just how I feel about her.

I lost another person that was close to me. It was my grandma Annette. I loved her, but I did not get to know her as well as I wanted to. But all this stuff that has happened to me I always have a big smile on my face. I hate that they are gone 'cause I really loved them, but if you think about it they are in a better place, because they do not have to worry about sinning anymore.

Sorry that I bored you all with my life story, but I just want everyone to know me before they judge me. Like the saying goes never judge a fruit by its color.

Zagayvia Johnson, Grade 8
Seminole County Middle/High School, GA

My Dream

In my life I've had many dreams of what I want to do when I grow up. Like a police officer, astronaut, jet pilot, and many others. But there is one that almost all my life I wanted to be and that is an animal trainer. But not just any animal trainer, a killer whale trainer at Sea World.

From the age of about three, I loved water and any kind of animals, especially water animals, and wanted to do this. But when I was seven we moved up to Tennessee and I went on to look at other things to do when I grow up. But I never lost my love of the water and the animals that call it their home. But this past September I was reminded of my love for this animal and how amazing, beautiful, and wonderful these animals are and I will never forget it.

"Why a killer whale trainer?" you might ask. Because they are the most magnificent animals in the world, in my eyes. They are one of the world's top predators in the sea. But yet us and killer whales can love each other and trust each other in the water if we give them the right respect. What does it take to be a killer whale trainer? It takes a great love and respect for animals. You have to be a strong swimmer.

This is my dream of what I want to be when I grow up. And I believe that I can do it.

Rebekah Lindsay, Grade 8
Pigeon Forge Middle School, TN

Volleyball

All over the world over 80 million people play volleyball every week. It doesn't require any expensive and special training or equipment to play. All people can participate in the game.

In 1895, William G. Morgan was a fitness instructor at the Y.M.C.A. and wanted adults to get more exercise and have fun at the same time. He thought basketball was too rough for people who were out of shape. He decided since basketball used too much physical energy to create his own game. He borrowed a tennis net and strung it up so that it was at a height of 6.5 feet. He told them to hit the ball across the net to each other using only their hands and arms. He called the game "mintonette" because it reminded him of the game badmitten. Mintonette quickly became a popular game. A college professor visited the Y.M.C.A. one day to watch a mintonette match. He noticed how they constantly volleyed the ball back and forth. The professor suggested that they should change the name to volleyball.

Volleyball spread to athletic clubs and colleges. People everywhere loved to play. In 1928 the United States Volleyball Association organized rules and competitions. Clubs and tournaments were being held all over the world. This simple game became a highly competitive sport.

In 1964, men and women's volleyball were added to the Olympic summer games. Today, you can find people playing volleyball in a park, on the beach, or in a gymnasium. They may play on a competitive team or just for fun with friends. Volleyball is a sport people of all ages and fitness levels can enjoy.

Katie Henderson, Grade 8
Rhea Central Elementary School, TN

The Great Lego Boat Races

I will never forget the time my brothers and I had Lego boat races. These races were held in the curb on the sidewalk. Where we lived in Pembroke Pines, Town Gate in a small community called Cherry Bay, we were supposed to be watering the plants in front of our house. On the occasion when I had to go turn off the water my brother put down the hose in the curb. We noticed it had a powerful force and one of us decided to throw a boat in there and it took off like a rocket.

Off of this idea we held races my brothers always customizing their own "ships" to beat mine. Many attempts but they all ended in catastrophe. I was unbeatable but none of us cared it was hilariously fun. By the end of the day we knew how to place the hose, ships, and any accessory we set on them it was especially fun watching my brothers slaving over something to help them win. We all had fun in the end. It is something I will always remember from that house. Sometimes that's what I remember the house by, I must never forget.

Steffan Krolikowski, Grade 7
Osceola Creek Middle School, FL

The White Tiger

The white tiger is a very beautiful animal. That's why I'm writing my essay on them. Their eyes are normally blue, they have a pink nose, and a creamy white coat. Their stripes are a chocolate color. They have big, sharp claws, and thirty, 3 inch teeth. A male can weigh up to 570 pounds and grow as long as 125 inches. A female can weigh up to 355 pounds and grow up to 105 inches long. The tail of the white tiger can span out to 3-4 feet in length.

The white tiger's prey is deer, pigs, cattle, and wild horses. They can eat up to 40 pounds at one time but won't eat for almost a week afterwards. They live in mostly Southeastern Asia and Southern India. They live in an area of 10-30 square miles. Their main habitat is grasslands and forests which provides shelter.

Their life span in the wild is 10-15 years. In captivity, their life span is 20 years. When the cubs are born, they are completely white. The pregnancy lasts about six months. There are normally about 4-5 cubs at one time.

Jonny Walker, Grade 7
Stroud Middle School, OK

An American Savior

In America, in the 1900's, a devastating disease was going around. The disease was called polio and it struck quickly and suddenly, leaving terrible results in its tracks.

Jonas Salk was born in New York City and had a knack for medicine. While he was in college he got his degree in medicine and set off on his dream of setting up a university of medicine in Pittsburgh.

While he was setting up his university he got a call and was asked to help find a cure for the deadly disease. Many tried but he got there first. Not before long America jumped for joy because he had found a cure. It's this amazing feat that makes Jonas Salk live on in American history.

Jennings Newhouse, Grade 7
St Mary's School, SC

Alligator in the Pond

Once, on a hot summer morning, there was dew on the grass, and the sky was bright. When I woke up I ate my breakfast. Then when I went outside, I saw a small, dark green alligator with big yellowish eyes. It was about 3 feet long. So I said "Dad, Dad," and as soon as I said that he came sprinting to get to me. When he finally got to me I said that there was a baby alligator in our pond. So he went to the phone and called animal control. When they got here they didn't find any alligator, so they left. But after one day the alligator came back because we put fishes in our pond when we went fishing. So we decided to try to catch the alligator with a fishing pole, but that didn't work. So we called a different animal control and they used a big net and they finally caught the alligator and put it back in the canal.

Brent Mohammed, Grade 7
Osceola Creek Middle School, FL

Hawaii

Going to Maui and Kauai, Hawaii has been the quietest and loudest place I have ever been, on the beach and at a luau. I have been to Hawaii twice. Once when I was 6 years old and once when I was 8 years old.

The quietest place I have ever been is the beach. I sat in the soft sand building huge sandcastles all day with my cousin Kyle and my sister Kelsey. We swam, ran down the beach and searched for coral and seashells. Waves washed against the rocks and little kids played in the water with their floaties and balls.

As my cousin, my sister and I played, all I could think about was us. It was pretty quiet and it felt like we had the whole beach to ourselves.

The loudest place I have ever been is at the luau. There was singing, dancing, people who did tricks with flaming sticks and lots of other entertaining things. I even got to go up on stage and learn to hula. There were fruit, vegetables and meat to eat. Before the luau we saw a pig get roasted. All my family was there and Kyle, Kelsey and I ran through the tables looking for something to do. People were talking everywhere we went.

We partied until it was way after dark. We were at the beach almost every day of the week and had lots of leftovers from the luau. I hope to go there again.

Kayla Mueller, Grade 7
Excelsior Springs Middle School, MO

Why I Sing

I enjoy singing in the Mercer University Children's Choir because many people say we touch many hearts with our music. I joined on the second season of the choir's journey, we sang at many churches in Macon, GA. I enjoyed my first season of songs because the songs were about joy, happiness, friendship, and love.

At the Grand Opera House one of my favorite songs was included in the concert. We sang at many other churches during the spring. My favorite concert was our Christmas Concert. I really liked the Christmas songs we performed.

The following year on tour we sang the Star Spangled Banner and America the Beautiful for our congressman Jim Marshall in Washington, D.C. We went to a few nursing homes and a youth center.

All together during the tour we sang in the Carolinas, in Virginia, Maryland and Washington, D.C. and in Methodist and Baptist Churches as well as churches that choir members attended.

In addition, the reason I'm in the choir for this season is because I love to sing and I believe I have the heart of music, and music is a friend of mine.

Shelby Ashley, Grade 7
Ashley Home School, GA

The Fall and Rise of NYC

It was a very sad year. Way too many people died that year, but we still stood strong. Oh yes, we're still the land of the free and the home of the brave. That year was a year of mourning.

Overall there were more than 3,000 people who died and more who were hurt very badly on 9/11. Many family members were lost in that one tragedy. Sad, simply sad.

Surprisingly, the one thing that brought NY together was the one, the only, New York Yankees! After all of the Yankees' support, they were named America's team. Also, that year, the Yankees lost the World Series. That right there describes New York's rise and fall, baseball style.

During the World Series, there was another terrorist attack, but not like the one on 9/11. In the mail, there was a package sent to the mayor containing anthrax, a dangerous, powder drug that kills a lot of people. Luckily for him, he was not harmed during this deadly terrorist attack.

After the World Series, we eventually picked ourselves up and fought back. We thought of numerous ways to give back to the people by free food, free gifts, and stuff like that. We also started to clean up the mess at the site of the World Trade Center. While all this was going on, the President was deeply thinking of numerous ways to get back at those nasty, mean terrorists.

Josh Large, Grade 7
Excelsior Springs Middle School, MO

Spaghetti Warehouse

My stomach rumbled as I reached for the golden door knob. It hit me. The food was breathtaking, as the waiter walked us to our table. The mouthwatering aroma wrapped its arms around me and filled my body with warmth.

Finally the waiter came with some menus. It was so hard to choose what I wanted. Do I want alfredo, lasagna, or spaghetti? Spaghetti I thought. That sounded delicious. I could see it on the second page, as I stared at the menu. I could smell the garlic and the steaming sauces from other orders. The waiter walked by. I think we are ready to order.

After we ordered my mom and I went to the front to the picture booth they had. We looked into the black glass as the bright white light flashed. We made funny faces. We only took three pictures, but it took forever for them to develop. Then, my dad came and got us when our food was being served. I sat down at the table. My glass was three fourths full. "Waiter can you get me some more mango lemonade please!" The waiter took my glass; my fingers were still cold from the ice in the cup.

I looked at my food, it looked so good. As I dug in I savored the spaghetti. "Mmmmm" it tasted so good. I finished my meal not long after it was served. We were all done. I was stuffed. We all were. I told my mom that was the best food I ever had.

Autumn Williams, Grade 7
Chelsea Jr High School, OK

The Night of Flying Rolls

I remember once, last year around the summertime I had a very good friend who lived in Ft. Lauderdale, my old neighborhood. He had just moved away and I had really missed him and I had longed to see him again. So the following day my mother and my friend's mother had made arrangements to meet with my friend the next day. We were to drive up in the morning. So the rest of the day went by slowly and boring yet I couldn't say the same about that night. Well my friend's mother had a maid and we wanted to mess with her so we took a huge adult diaper and filled it with chocolate syrup and we tried to wake her up but that failed. So we tried a better plan we foxily snuck into the bathroom and took about 3 rolls then the fun began! We then snuck outside and we dished out some toilet paper to the whole neighborhood and when we were finished we had to throw the toilet paper all over our own house, so we didn't look suspicious. The next day we secretly scouted the area look at our former accomplishments. My parents never found out and I got to see my friend so it was a win, win situation, so I will never forget The Night of the Flying Rolls.

Dakota Allen, Grade 7
Osceola Creek Middle School, FL

Freedom

What is freedom? Freedom is not just liberty. It is the privilege of knowing your rights because you are free. It's a word of inspiration. It's the feeling that I get when I bend down to drink water from the fountain. It's freedom!!

Thanks to my African American heroes paving the way for my parents, my peers and myself, I am free to be anything that I want to be. As an African American female, I am entitled to an education. In a word, that information motivates me to take leadership in my education, and further my rights.

In conclusion, my rights will allow me to select my career and fulfill it in the best way possible. My goal is to graduate high school, and do at least four years of college, with a major in psychology. Then overall my main goal is to become a criminal profiler.

It came to my attention that I began being interested in fields such as criminal profiling when I realized my whole family is crazy, excluding myself of course. However, this career would help me to understand why they do the crazy things they do. Young people of today's society (our future) that don't take advantage of positive opportunities should be abashed within themselves.

In summary, it's time to take superiority of our freedom. They too can be what they want if they work to their full potential, and put their best foot forward.

Hermera Greene-Blanks, Grade 8
Turner Middle School, GA

Life of a Dolphin

Can you hear that splash? That's the dolphins jumping away! This story is about the life of a dolphin. What they do during the day, how and why they communicate, and also how they find food to survive in the waters.

Have you ever wondered what dolphins do during the day while we are in school? They are out finding food for their families. They also find different places to play or even hide from others. They play by seeing who can do the best stunts or swim the fastest. Dolphins are often attracted to humans, mostly while boating or scuba diving.

Dolphins communicate by making different noises or body movements. When dolphins make noises it can mean that something is wrong or it can be to say hello. Body movements can be a stunt to show affection for each other.

Dolphins are mammals, so they eat meat like mullet or chum. Dolphins find food while swimming or by hiding under the sand. When the right fish swims along, the dolphin munches away. They eat mullet and chum because that's what they were fed when they were young calves. As they get older they eat more and more. When food has been found it's not likely to be shared with others, especially sharks.

That's them…can't you hear them coming? I've got to see!

Victoria Fleet, Grade 7
Sebastian River Middle School, FL

Travel in History

It's amazing how travel can bring history alive. I enjoy both, so seeing the world is a great interest of mine. I recently had a chance to go to the countries of Greece and Turkey. I enjoyed the experience of my journey. While I was there, we boarded a small cruise ship and set sail to the most beautiful blue water I have seen and the ship navigated us slowly upon these amazing islands. We lived on this boat four days and stopped at two islands every day. To my surprise, I look at the history syllabus and find that we are going to study the Greek government this year and much of the governments were established with ideas from all the different island rulers. As I read about an island, I reflect on when I was looking over a valley and I wondered what the ruler felt 3,000 years ago. As I was reflecting on my trip, I remembered walking out of the airport in Istanbul, the largest city I have ever seen. This is the only city in the world that is on different continents. I went to the Spice Market where Asia and Europe meet. I remember the amazing smells of the spices as we walked through the market and thought we should get some. To bring this paper to a stop, I want to say the best way to learn is to witness, and that's what I did that trip.

Blaine Kennedy, Grade 8
Heritage Hall School, OK

It's a Killer Bee!

It's summer in New Orleans, Louisiana. You're mowing your front yard, with the engine roaring in the hot sun. Suddenly, you see a swarm of angry bees buzzing madly toward you! You start screaming, and you run into your house for safety.

Those were killer bees. A whole lot of things can set off the mad aggravation of a killer bee. For the scene I just portrayed, the roar of the engine and even the vibrations might have triggered an attack.

These bees will really kill you! Their venom from their hurtful stingers is the same as the regular bee, but they keep on stinging, for up to a quarter of a mile! Usually by then, all of those stingers and all of that venom has killed you.

The killer bee is actually a hybrid from the European honey bee and the African bee. The cruel temper of the African bee was passed on, instead of the sweet, gentle nature of the European bee. The hybrid was supposed to create more honey faster, but instead, things went terribly wrong. The bees somehow escaped from their quarantine and have spread rapidly.

Unfortunately for all of us in the United States, these bees are spreading rapidly and aren't stopping. They have mostly been seen in Texas, New Mexico, Arizona, Nevada, Southern California, and even now in New Orleans. If you see a hive in your area, LEAVE IT ALONE, or it just might be the last thing you do.

Alexis Abell, Grade 7
Boyet Jr High School, LA

Junior National Student Leadership Conference

An amazing event that I had was when I went on a trip to Washington, D.C. I was able to visit historical landmarks and meet new people. We were divided into groups, but two people from different groups had to stay in the same hotel room, probably to decrease the rivalries that would have come. While there, I met people from the west coast, Tornado Alley, and from really far up north. Each of the different groups had challenges, like building a bridge that could hold the most weight. For that challenge, there were teams within the groups, and my team's bridge held 37 lbs. The games I learned while I was there I used to stump my family once I got home, like alien numbers. In alien numbers, you take seven pens or pencils and arrange them into a shape or a figure. They you lean on your hands using your palms to support yourself. For example, if she shape was an "I" you would hold out 0 to 10 fingers on the ground. Some of the landmarks the groups visited were the Lincoln Memorial, the White House, and the Vietnam Memorial Wall. We also went to an obstacle course, where we climbed a large rock wall, but this one was shaped like an upside down pyramid, so there were ladders and ropes along the way up. It is one of the best memories I have.

Steven Ibold, Grade 8
James Weldon Johnson Middle School, FL

Depressed No More

S.E. Hinton was depressed all the time because her dad dies of a brain tumor. So her boyfriend made her write two pages every day. That was ancient history. Today, she is a world renowned writer.

Hinton was born is Tulsa, Oklahoma. She first began writing at Will Rogers High School. The Outsiders was her first book and she wrote it when she was 17 years old. This book was published by Viking in 1967 and sold as the second best novel ever.

She attended the University of Tulsa and earned her B.S. degree in 1970. In 1988 she was the recipient of the Margaret A. Edward's award, presented by Young Adult Library Association.

Next, she wrote Rumble Fish which was published in 1968. This didn't stop her, she confidently wrote *That Was Then Is Now* in 1971, *Tex* in 1979, and then her next piece of work was *Taming The Star Runner* in 1988. About all the books she wrote were in Tulsa Oklahoma. Being a writer all her life, she is no longer a depressed person, she is a confident person.

Dallas Baxter, Grade 8
Chelsea Jr High School, OK

Lemons Make Lemonade

Life is not easy: everyone experiences heartache and hardship at times. For me, these trials have often come in the form of my dad's health. He has struggled with many health issues the past several years, and has had multiple surgeries and visits to the hospital. Although this has been difficult for me, I am learning to see the positive side of the situation. I am turning the lemons in my life into lemonade.

Discovering how to turn sour things into something good isn't always easy. It can be a difficult process, requiring a complete change in attitude. It did not happen automatically for me; but as I endured the stress and worry caused by my dad's health, I began to see how it is possible. Instead of worrying about my problems, I began to seek ways to help others. I relied on God for my strength; and through my trials, I became a better person. Through difficult circumstances, I discovered how to find the positive in every situation.

Because of trials I have experienced, I am focusing on being optimistic. By concentrating on other's needs rather than my own, I can find positive aspects in a so-called negative situation. Through my dad's health issues, I have learned how much I love and appreciate him. In any situation I encounter, no matter how stressful it may be, I can always look for good in it. I have learned to turn the sour lemons life has given me into sweet-tasting lemonade.

Lindsey Conner, Grade 8
College Heights Christian School, MO

Positivity

Are you a positive thinker? Whatever your answer, thinking good thoughts can make all the difference in the world. People shouldn't put others down with negativity before they even know the outcome of something. Thinking positive can make for a happier person. Sometimes, positivity can even change what happens to a situation. Positive thinking can be powerful.

Nothing good can come out of putting someone down. By discouraging a person with negativity, they may actually start to believe what is being said. For example, someone may be in a contest, but people are putting them down. In the end, they win! Who looks ignorant now? Discouragement cannot lead to good.

Having a bad day? Just look for the positive. Even if a lot is going wrong, find something that's right and focus on that. If you are, it'll seem better. Some good things can come out of what looks like a bad situation. Let's picture this: You're playing soccer and the score is 8 to 10. It's nearing the end of the game. Your coach puts in a player who has completely convinced themselves your team is going to lose, and there is no hope left. The player has a bad attitude so they don't give their best. Your team loses. What would've happened if they had a positive attitude? Positivity can change a lot.

Being positive changes your whole life. Putting people down isn't nice and can hurt feelings. Focus on positive things and bad situations can seem better. Be positive and situations can change. In conclusion, I'm trying to say positivity is a powerful thing.

Marie Thurman, Grade 8
Pigeon Forge Middle School, TN

The Soggy Swamp

I have always been afraid of Freaky Forest, but one day, me and five of my friends decided to journey to the other side of the forest. Me, Monty, Luann, Zack, Courtney, and Josie, all decided that it was time to find out what was on the other side of that eerie forest. We told our parents that we were going to hang out at a friend's house, then we set out on our adventure.

After an hour of walking, it seemed as if we would never get to the other side of the forest, but after a few more hours, the trees started dispersing. With more animation, we walked faster, and broke through the last of the trees. At first sight, we all thought that we were dreaming. What lie before us was a swamp, a smelly, disgusting swamp. "This smells foul," said Zack. "Eww, gross," said Josie. I sighed with disappointment, and began walking back towards home. "That was so unfair. I thought something amazing was on the other side of the forest. Guess I was wrong," I said. Then we all heard a scream. Two screams, to be exact. We got really scared, and ran home as fast as we could. That will always be one of my favorite memories.

Jacqueline Provey, Grade 7
Osceola Creek Middle School, FL

Finding Yourself

When you were a young child you did not have the choice on whether you attended church or not. Your parents either took you, or they did not. It is not until you are older that you, as an individual, make the decision on whether you attend church or not. Religion is a wonderful thing to find and experience. Finding faith can help you feel more connected with life.

As a little girl, I did not attend church often enough. As I began to grow, I began to realize that I wanted to attend church and learn more about Christ. I began going to service every Sunday. I later started attending Sunday school as well. When I was about eight I decided that I wanted to become a member of the church. The next Sunday I had gotten saved. I was excited about it and could not wait until I could get baptized. There was only one big exception that I had; I wanted my dad to be there. When the time for my baptism finally came around, my grandpa had the privilege to baptize me. It seemed to me that I became a new person and I found myself. Now, because of that, I will never forget that day.

If you feel lost in this world, then you need to find yourself. If you believe in Christ, then you could start attending church. You would be surprised at what you find out about yourself.

Holly Benbrook, Grade 8
Greenfield Jr/Sr High School, MO

A New Beginning

A student in her last year of elementary school was about to receive an unexpected path to follow. She was to make decisions that would affect her very much for her entire life. Her relationship with God was about to begin at College Heights Christian School where she would learn to love Christ more every day and continue to grow in Him.

It started in the fifth grade. A few days before school ended, the entire class went to the public school they would be attending next fall. As they were walking in the hallways, the girl stopped and was thinking about what she hoped to pursue there. She had also thought about what God had planned for her in the future. The next week she visited a church, and it was also a school. As she was there she had a feeling in the school area of the church that God wanted her to be there. The girl's family sat at the dinner table and discussed how the girl wanted to attend College Heights Christian School. Instead of the public school, she attended College Heights and her relationship with God grew stronger every day.

Her relationship with God at College Heights has grown in many ways and her love for Christ keeps growing in her heart. The friends that God has blessed her with will always keep her on the right path. She loves College Heights Christian School and hopes to be successful in her choices in the future.

Shelby Norvell, Grade 8
College Heights Christian School, MO

A Backyard Adventure

It was a hot summer day in Lake Worth, Florida when a group of neighborhood kids got together. There was, what we called, a hill in my backyard stretching from the far left corner all the way to the center of the 2 acre haven. All of the kids on Mathis Street were going to come over to 1303, the last house on the left, to collect rattles from the tree. All of the younger kids cherished the tree and loved to make mud pies with seeds atop the wet dirt. Most of us were going behind the hill to find more precious rattles.

It was a windy day and the rattle tree's tiny seed pods shook until we thought they would fall to the ground. The younger ones stayed in the safety of the playground as we marched over to the hill's end. We reached the very corner of the yard; great bamboo trees creaked and swayed in the wind. A few of the kids seemed threatened by the trees and we just looked reassuringly back at them. Ralph and I ushered the kids along; we were the oldest and they always seemed to listen to us rather than each other. They looked up to us, I suppose.

After being smacked in the face with a palm frond on more than one occasion, we'd finally reached our destination. There must have been fifty rattles blanketing the ground. We were thrilled, and the little ones were every bit ecstatic.

Samantha Weigt, Grade 7
Osceola Creek Middle School, FL

My Bike

Hi do you have a bike? Well, I do and I ride it every day. I go to school on my bike every day. Some people ride the bus; some people get driven to school. Well, forget that! I ride my bike because I am healthy! My bike is a blue and black BMX bike with pegs.

I picked blue and black because it looked cool. The only reason I ride my bike to school is because I want to look cool. My brother will ride his bike to school but he only does it because he thinks he is cool. I go everywhere on my bike. I go to the store on my bike, I go to school on my bike, and I go to my Grandma's house. I do a lot of neat tricks on my bike.

Like, I will stand on my back pegs and hold my seat and twist my handlebars. Sometimes I will race my brother and of course, I lose. I also go to the park and ride down the hills. Sometimes I ramp off my homemade ramp. It is not really safe to jump off but I do it anyway.

When you ride your bike you have to have a helmet. I do not really care anyway. So I ride my bike without a helmet. I won't get hurt if I do not but any helmets a helmet. So be safe and wear a helmet!

Karston Rosenbaum, Grade 7
Greenfield Jr/Sr High School, MO

A Very Merry Christmas

My definition of a very merry Christmas is our family get-together on Christmas day. This day is not only just special; it is a day to fellowship with my family. There is joy, tears, memories and love at our get-together.

At our get-together, my family meets at my Granny's house. We exchange presents and stocking stuffers. It's not all about presents, it's about Jesus, fellowship, and love. It's Jesus whom we can thank for our family, presents, and tradition. One of our traditions is watching the Charlie Brown Christmas movie. We have watched this movie every Christmas Eve since I was five years old. My cousins Will and Drew also have a tradition of their own. It is called Christmas eve-eve-eve, three days before Christmas. Our meal we have on Christmas day is the greatest part to me. We have mashed potatoes, chicken, turkey, ham, etc. The best part is my Aunt Cheryl's prize winning corn. It is buttery enough, yet not real dry. The juice is what makes it so sweet. I also play a lot of football with my cousins.

Our Christmas traditions are really fun to do with my family. I always use this day to bond with my family.

Darian Patterson, Grade 7
Trinity Christian Academy, AL

Global Warming: Can We Undo This Mistake?

The founding fathers of America were remarkable people. They struggled with problems regarding Great Britain and they resolved these problems by having many brawls and combats during the American Revolution, but they soon managed to start a new nation with freedom, equality, and equal rights for all men of the Caucasian race.

Then, many of the Northerners realized there should be equality and human rights for all, and slavery was wrong. All men are equal in God's eyes. We then had the Civil War, a war fought over freedom and equal rights.

The United States led its people through a thriving industrial revolution, only this time they made a prodigious mistake. People started using factories powered by fossil fuels to make goods. This led to massive pollution. This is where global warming started to sprout. The atmosphere gradually started becoming thinner and thinner, and it kept in greenhouse gasses and CO_2.

All throughout the history of America, we undid our mistakes, through weapons and bloodshed. This blunder must be fought by cooperation.

The past generation was trying to make manufacturing easier and purchasing cheaper, but they also wasted our natural gasses, polluted the air, and the present generation are potentially continuing the errors of the past generation.

Will global warming come to a stop? The answer to this question is whatever our generation chooses it to be. So, if everyone puts in their cooperation we can make tomorrow's generation a clean and healthy environment.

Kimia Movahed, Grade 7
Arendell Parrott Academy, NC

Graduation Day

It was the day of fifth grade graduation and I was as happy as a kindergarten child is when it is time for school to start. I was leaving school after graduation, and it was just my mom and me. We had went to Olive Garden to eat. I walked inside dressed in my white shirt and khaki pants to the smell of fresh garlic bread filling the restaurant. As we were being seated, our waitress came up to us. She wore too much blush on her cheeks it looked like she had just came inside on a very cold day, so while she took our orders, I tried to hold in my laughter. After the waitress left our table, I said,

"Mom, she had on way too much make up."

My mom and I could hold our laughter no longer, so we let it rip. The whole restaurant heard us. I was embarrassed. Every time the waitress came to our table we had to hold in our laughter, but after she left we didn't laugh because we didn't want to embarrass ourselves. We had very good Italian food. After all my mom and I had a very good time without my sister to bug us and we had lots of fun.

AJ Morgan, Grade 7
Baylor School, TN

Bowling Requires Two Things…I Wonder What They Are

In bowling, there are two things that a lot of professional bowlers have that they see in a lot of children, preteens, and teenagers. Do you want to take a guess at what it is? If you guessed concentration and determination, then you take good guesses, because you got it right! Here are some examples of concentration and determination.

Concentration means you are on the lane, you know which mark you're going to throw the ball over, and you are not easily distracted. The teenager was on the lane ready to bowl, and the friend he decided to bring with him, took out his iPod, and put it on very high volume. Now, knowing a teenager, he probably would have said, "Hey man, what are you listening to, and why is the volume so loud?" He was so concentrated on the lane, that he didn't know that his friend's iPod was on until he finished bowling his frame! Now that is full concentration!

Determination means that you know one day, you are going to reach a goal you have set. I have set a goal to get a 250 game, or higher, in the fall league of bowling in Anniston, AL. To be able to reach this goal, I am going to have to practice, practice, and practice as much as I can.

I encourage you, the next time you go bowling, to try concentration, set a goal, and go back to that bowling alley. Also, you need to continue to practice as much as you can. I also would like for you to have determination and never quit. Don't let anything that anybody says about you or does to you get in the way of the goal you are trying to reach.

Joshua Caleb Green, Grade 7
Trinity Christian Academy, AL

Baseball

Baseball is America's favorite pastime. With thirty-two teams and one hundred and sixty two games, it is a season full of action. From opening day to game seven of the World Series, fans all over the United States pack the stadiums across the country to watch their favorite teams play their favorite sport. Many teams have a diverse background of players. Players with outstanding athletic talents come from around the globe to play baseball in the United States. Players from countries such as Japan, the United States, the Dominican Republic, Puerto Rico, and many others. Although baseball is played in nine innings and each team gets to hit and field, there is much more. Things like rivalries and pitching matchups are always fun to watch.

Me personally, I am a Cardinals fan, so I enjoy going to a Cardinal vs Cubs game. There's plenty of action, and if you get lucky, someone may get thrown out of the game or the benches may clear. So even if you don't enjoy baseball, you can still go to a game, and I guarantee you will have a great time. It may not be a memory that lasts forever, but you will still have fun.

Nick Yahl, Grade 8
St Gerard Majella School, MO

Girl Scouts

I like Girl Scouts because all the different things we do. Meeting new friends, going camping with your troop and other troops, singing songs and helping others.

Having all kinds of friends is really awesome. You make new and keep the old friends. Doing things with your friends that you meet. You can clean up the Earth with friends. Do community projects to help everything and everyone around you.

Going camping is really fun. Learning about nature. Seeing all the plants, flowers, and trees. Sleeping in tents is awesome, hearing all the big and little bugs, birds, and other animals. I like camping a lot, every time we go I don't want to leave.

Singing songs at camp, parades, meetings, and community service projects. We sing long and short, still and moving, and loud and soft songs. Singing at Girl Scouts is lots of fun. We have movements to some songs. Singing during projects like at the nursing homes and a whole lot of other projects we do for the community.

Girl scouting isn't just about friends, camping, and singing, it's about courage, confidence and character. Girl scouting isn't just for me, it's for everyone around the world, young or old, tall or short, any girl, anywhere. It's really fun to be in. Those reasons are just some of what I like about girl scouting. That's just the start.

JoAnn Ashbaugh, Grade 8
Pigeon Forge Middle School, TN

My Room

Do you know why rooms are so important to people? They create a sanctuary or a cave where you can hide out when you're upset. You can feel as though you're the only perfect person in the world. There are so many different types of rooms. Mine is my sanctuary and I love it for many reasons. I have furniture, technology, pictures, and lots of colors.

The furniture in my room is very soft. I have a chair that goes to my desk; it's soft and comfortable. It feels so smooth because it's made of wood. In my room I have a lamp desk. It has a steel base and colorful glass designs.

The technology in my room is up-to-date and working with speed. I have a radio clock that has an infrared light that is extremely bright. I also have a DELL computer; which I could not live without.

In my room I have a lot of colors like an extremely soft bed. It has yellow flower patterns and a soft pink monkey on it. It also has blue pillows that feel like your head is floating on a cloud. I have bright blue walls and a shiny white base. The wooden floor is so shiny and smooth you can skate on it.

In my room I have very creative pictures drawn by me and professional artists. I have a self portrait that was drawn in the Bahamas by a J.K. Roller. I also have a computer poster on the wall. It has bold black letters and lots of designs.

My room is as creative and as colorful as me. It's my sanctuary and my cave. I couldn't live without my privacy. That's why I and so many other people couldn't survive middle school life without our rooms.

Alexis Kaufman, Grade 7
Rosarian Academy, FL

Obesity

The world is becoming a very scary place; especially for kids under the age of 18. Some of the many problems that kids today face is obesity. It's hard enough to have deal with peer pressure, parents, and teachers, but now we have to deal with a rising uproar of obesity.

Obese counts have risen dramatically over the past few years. Presently, a shocking 19 percent of teenagers, under 18 are obese. This could lead to shorter life spans because children are more likely to develop diabetes and heart disease. In addition to the health side effects, children that are obese are more likely to get teased in school. This can lead to depression (psychiatric disorder showing symptoms such as persistent feelings of hopelessness, rejection). This is also damaging to kids' health. Watching what you eat and exercising are some things you can do to prevent or fight obesity.

In conclusion, obesity is a tough problem to face. It is also growing more and more common for kids to become obese. Do the smart thing and watch what you eat and exercise regularly.

Kylee Callais, Grade 9
Lafayette High School, LA

Backyard Tsunami

It was my 9th birthday and my friends Tori, Zoe, Meaghan, Morgan, and my sister Jamie and I were all in my above ground pool in the backyard. Hunter was supposed to be there but she was running late. Almost all of us had inner tubes around us except for Tori who was snorkeling underwater. We were making a wave pool by jumping up and down with inner tubes. Then, suddenly we all started to shift sideways a little; the pool burst open at one of the seams. Morgan, who was only 38 pounds, went flying across the yard about an acre with her inner tube, but the rest of us either just stood up or only traveled a little bit. It was hilarious, mostly because we all started screaming and the fact that Morgan went all the way across the yard and hit the shed. Afterward we went on the trampoline and were laughing about what had happened and making jokes. The neighbors that live behind us were also having a party, and when they saw what happened the started cracking up laughing! Around 7:00 Hunter came and asked "What happened to the pool?" And we replied, "Oh you should have been there." To this day, my friends and I will talk about it and laugh when it pops us in a conversation.

Kelsey Dalton, Grade 7
Osceola Creek Middle School, FL

One Nation with One Voice

Our nation can be easily influenced by the decisions that are made by the people within it. Our nation is greatly influenced by the decisions of the government leaders that are set over us. This is why the voice of the people needs to speak up for what they want and stand for.

As the tongue is the voice of the body, the people over every state are the voice for our nation. The only thing people do today is complain about taxes and other industries and how they do not like their governmental leaders. These problems could be stopped if people would step up and voice their opinions. It says in James that our tongue is so powerful that it can set fire the courses of nature. Why can't our tongues set our nation on fire? Things such as taxes, our future presidential elections, and the controversy over prayer in schools could be helped by voicing our opinions and getting something done. Voting for the right people that will be a good godly influence while in office is the main way our voices can be affective in a positive way. In the end, one nation without a voice will fade away and crumble.

In conclusion, our nation needs to have the freedom of free speech and press to be recognized. Without it, nothing can ever be done to benefit anyone. With one sound body and a clear edifying voice, our nation will be united once more.

Kendall Stewart, Grade 8
Trinity Christian Academy, AL

Wisdom

Allowing us to see the world and all that is in it through God's eyes is something very special that we receive from the Holy Spirit. This gift is called wisdom. As it helps us make good judgment, it also perfects the virtue of charity. Without wisdom, we would be lost in this world, making bad choices and stupid mistakes

Wisdom is acquired by the Holy Spirit and increased by prayer and reflection. By prayer for wisdom, you might be able to make the right choice. Also, talking to wise, elderly people about right and wrong things they have done in their life could help you make smart decisions. I have practiced wisdom by thinking before I acted and learning from my mistakes. If you just act before thinking about the consequences, you won't be able to acquire wisdom.

When leaders make decisions and we decide what we want to do with out life, wisdom becomes very important. Without it, we can't envision and understand that God is our everything and won't be able to know God's plan for everyone. At Baptism, we receive the gifts of the Holy Spirit, and they grow at Confirmation. It is important to me because it affects my decisions and those of all the people around me.

Amelia Feisal, Grade 8
St Mary's School, SC

Save the Dolphins!

Even though I had a choice of many topics, I chose to write on dolphins. I chose dolphins because they are my favorite animal. As a matter of fact dolphins' playful attitude and friendly appearance have made them popular in human culture. Dolphins suffer from a few natural enemies but the worst predator for dolphins are humans.

Dolphins are closely related to whales and porpoises. They are aquatic mammals found worldwide and are carnivores mostly eating squid and fish. They have few natural threats which are some species of sharks that are bull sharks, tiger sharks and great white sharks. Killer whales are also a natural predator. Parasites such as whale lice and barnacles are common around dolphins as well as diseases. Diseases that dolphins commonly get are respiratory, skin and digestive disease. Some of these diseases can be passed on to dolphins through human contact.

Humans play a big role in causing pollution's to the ocean. Pollution is responsible for forcing dolphins out of their natural habitat and having them come into contact with boats. Pesticides, heavy metals, plastics and other pollutants are the dangerous items that harm dolphins. In some areas of the world dolphins are viewed as food and game for hunting.

Dolphins are endangered in some parts of the world and the world needs to know these facts. We need to be more careful to recycle and throw away our trash in proper places. I feel by doing this, people can help save the dolphins!

Lori Williams, Grade 8
Home School, AL

Heroine of Horseshoe Falls

Would you risk your life for fame and fortune? Annie Taylor risked hers on the hope that she would live to tell the tale. Throughout her childhood, Annie was accustomed to the finer things of life. As an adult, she managed to maintain that lifestyle with an inheritance from her parents. By 1898, Annie had depleted her savings and was desperate for money. She decided to attempt the impossible.

Annie sought to achieve fame and fortune as the first person to go over Niagara Falls. On her 63rd birthday, she decided to plunge over Horseshoe Falls in a specially designed pickle barrel. At 4:05 p.m., on October 24, 1901, Annie climbed in her mattress padded vessel. Once the lid was nailed down, a bicycle pump was used to pressurize the inside of the barrel. Clutching her lucky heart-shaped pillow, Annie prayed every second as she drifted down the Niagara River in total darkness.

As the barrel plummeted over the thunderous falls, Annie fell unconscious. Nearby spectators saw the pickle barrel tumble over the fierce waterfall and surface in the dense mist at the bottom. The historic trip lasted eighteen minutes. Unbelievably, the pickle barrel was in one piece as it was retrieved from the water. Annie's fate was unknown until the lid was removed. She emerged with bruises and scratches, saying, "Nobody ought ever to do that again."

Annie Taylor received the fame she sought, but only for a few years. In 1921, she died penniless without ever achieving riches.

Mimi McCarthy, Grade 7
Arendell Parrott Academy, NC

A True Friend Named Mom

It takes a special person to be a true friend. This person is there whenever you are in need. They are there when you need someone to talk to and when you need a little love. That special person for me just happens to be my mom.

She has been there for me in both the good and the bad times. And yes, I have been in bad situations, but I have certainly learned from them. And if it were not for my mom, I probably would have not learned from my mistakes. I have learned from her and my experience that following your dreams is hard but with a little support, anything is possible. My mother is the one that supports me and tells me to use all that life has to offer, take it, and make something of it. And that is just what I plan to do.

I have always tried to make my mom proud of me, and I have succeeded in that! And I know that she will be proud of me no matter what. So when I decide to make my dreams a reality and graduate from high school and then go on and play professional ball somewhere, I know my best friend will be in the audience smiling and cheering me on. And I know she is happy for me because of all that I have accomplished. And in my eyes that is definitely a true friend!

Christina Thomas, Grade 8
Greenfield Jr/Sr High School, MO

Following Your Dreams

Since I was a little girl, I have always had big dreams. I intended on graduating from high school. I could see myself going to college. The job I admire involves children. Being a pediatrics nurse is where I see myself. So here is my start to follow my dreams.

At first, I didn't succeed at graduating from high school, but I am showing I can succeed in my education and "be all I can be." I am now in Gadsden Job Corps improving myself. I am going to make a difference. I will finish my dream.

Soon, I will be going to college to finish my nursing degree. I am almost finished with my trade since I only have 50% to go. When I complete this program, I will go back to Mobile to show all of my family who I really am.

Later on, I will get a job at the University of South Alabama Medical Center as an Echocardiogram Technical in the pediatric unit. After approximately two years, I am going to move away from home to get a job elsewhere.

Finally, I think if I complete this program, graduate college and get a job I will be able to take my family and myself on a vacation. I would rather take my family to a beautiful place like Hawaii. This is how I will follow my dreams.

Brittany Cole, Grade 9
Gadsden Job Corps Center, AL

One Terrible Day

This horrifying day is one I'll never forget. People don't believe me when I tell them this story. People think it's just a joke, but it's all true. Though I think it was a courageous act.

My house has an assortment of ducks. I'm not sure why, but my dad insists on having these ducks. These ducks are far but ordinary. They are truly evil. They poop on our porch in the backyard and tap on our doors all day and honk in the middle of the night. I believe that it's all on purpose.

I have never set foot in our backyard; I always thought that they would eat me alive. I was terrified of them, they hissed at me numerous times. I never liked them.

One day, our phone rang, it was my uncle. He requested to speak to my dad, who happened to be in the backyard. The ducks had surrounded the backdoor, blocking my way out. I had to get the phone to him, but how?

I grabbed a wire coat hanger from my closet, for protection. As I opened the old, squeaky door and the ducks rapidly raised their heads to me. They hissed and honked, and they flared their wings at me, and I think I saw some short, sharp, pointed teeth. I tried to keep them back with the hanger, but it failed. I quickly retreated and hopped in the den. I took a deep breath and never went out there again.

Ebony James, Grade 7
Osceola Creek Middle School, FL

My Favorite Teacher Is

My favorite teacher is Ms. Hampton, my seventh grade Language Arts teacher. Ms. Hampton is my favorite teacher, because she is a fun teacher, and she wants us to do our best. All these reasons are why Ms. Hampton is my favorite teacher.

One of the reasons why she is my favorite teacher is that she is a fun teacher. Ms. Hampton lets us talk in class, but we can't talk loudly. We have fun in class, but she knows when to learn, and get busy working. Ms. Hampton wants us to do our best in class, and pass all our tests. She has a special activity in class. She puts up a question of the month, and whoever finds and answers the question gets $25 dollars.

My last reason is that she wants us to do our best. She makes us find the main idea in reading passages, and teaches us how to use reading strategies. Ms. Hampton makes us put the story in sequence of events order, and she gets us ready for the Writing Test and the EOG, unlike other teachers.

My favorite teacher is Ms. Hampton. She is my seventh grade Language Arts teacher, and the best teacher. Ms. Hampton is a fun teacher, and she wants us to do our best. Now, what do you think of Ms. Hampton?

James Watkins, Grade 7
Mineral Springs Middle School, NC

Second by Second Our World Is Destroyed

Global warming is an expeditiously growing epidemic. "An increase of the earth's temperature by a few degrees resulting in an increase in the volume of water which contributes to sea-level rise." "A gradual warming of the Earth's atmosphere reportedly caused by the burning of fossil fuels and industrial pollutants." There are many meanings and explanations to this worldwide issue, but it began in eighteen eighty-four when Joseph Fourier discovered the greenhouse effect and the results it has on our planet.

In a simpler approach, global warming is caused by greenhouse gases, such as water vapor, carbon dioxide, nitrous oxide, and methane. When heat radiates off of our Earth, the greenhouse gases prevent it from escaping, therefore heating our earth more than needed. Causes of greenhouse gases are carbon fuels in car engines, emissions from coal-powered plants, deforestation, and other pollutants.

As you read, effects of global warming are occurring now. Due to the increase of temperature, polar ice caps are melting, making sea levels rise that will possibly flood low-lying coastal areas. Also due to the rise in warmth, Montana's Glacier National Park went from one hundred and fifty glaciers to twenty-seven in just ninety-seven years. Soil in areas has become too dry to support vegetation growth and development. The United Nations' Intergovernmental Panel on Climate Change reports "Eleven of the past twelve years are among the dozen warmest since 1850." As time progresses, the list of consequences will escalate.

Horace Matthews, Grade 8
Wacoochee Jr High School, AL

The NFL Star

I once went to a Monday night football game and it seemed like it was a big game on Sunday. Everyone was yelling and I walked across the field and it felt so good to do that; it was awesome. The fans were so happy because the star player from college #25 a rookie had become a NFL star and he had great speed and he was just awesome. They got ready to kick it off and I hurried and ran to my seat. The fans were waiting to holler out loud so they kicked it. They took the ball to the 60 yard line.

We were ready to see him play and they handed it off to him to the left side. He was breaking tackles and running by everybody. It was amazing he scored on the first play and that is an athlete. He played very good that game and ran all the time he was a good player.

When the game was over I went home and dreamed about him and how he scored on the first play in the NFL. I asked my dad the next morning could I play recreational football and he said yeah and I was happy for him to say that.

Finally, we had games on Saturdays and practiced on Mondays. I played tailback and it was game time and I was ready and they handed it off to me and I ran it to the end zone just like him.

Javaris Virgin, Grade 8
Seminole County Middle/High School, GA

An Oklahoma Icon

"I never met a man I didn't like," said Will Rogers a man who was born in 1879, on a ranch owned by his family in present day Oologah, Oklahoma. Although he didn't know it then as a baby he would become one of the most famous Oklahomans ever known.

An average man in size and stature he was not different in appearance than any other man really. While his stature was normal his voice brought him out he was known for speeches and hilarious jokes. A humble family man he was funny and down to earth. Will was a roper which is to be expected since he grew up on a ranch. He was taught to rope by a freed slave. One of his many tricks went like this: one rope went around the horse's neck and then the other rope went around the rider's body and the final rope gathered up all four legs of the horse.

Will Roger had a great life that was until one flight going to Alaska in 1935 in which the plane crashed killing both Will Rogers and the pilot. After the crash the whole world grieved his death most of all his family. "If you live life right death is a joke as far as fear is concerned," quoted Will Rogers. I believe everyone thinks he lived right.

In my mind William Penn Adair Rogers is one of the best influences a boy can have. Will Rogers 1879-1935.

Levi Morrison, Grade 9
Chelsea Jr High School, OK

Will Rogers

Who is Will Rogers? He's a famous roper. William Penn Adair Rogers was born in 1879, and he grew up on his family's ranch in the Cherokee nation, later known as Oologah.

Rogers was soon taught by a freed slave how to use a lasso to work Texas longhorn cattle on the family's ranch. Rogers got better and was listed in the *Guinness Book of World Records* for throwing three lassos at once. One rope caught the horse's neck and the other rope would hoop around the rider. The third rope would swoop under the horse to loop all four legs.

Rogers dropped out of school after 10th grade to become a cowboy in a cattle drive. Later he became the star of Broadway shows and 71 movies during the 1920s and 1930s. He was a popular radio broadcaster. He wrote 4000 syndicated newspapers and also six books. Rogers traveled a lot, mostly by airplane.

Will Rogers was always a humble man to his wife and his children. He was always there to help people in need. That was the kind of person Will Rogers was.

Will Rogers died on a flight to Alaska with his friend. The world was united the morning of the crash and sad. Nobody will ever forget Will Rogers.

William Konnoff, Grade 8
Chelsea Jr High School, OK

Cuba

Today I am going to be telling you about a very important place to me. That place is Cuba! Cuba is where my father's family is from. I am going to write about the government, culture, and family history.

In Cuba the laws are very strict. There is not as much freedom in Cuba as there is here. Cuba is a communist country run by a dictator. Cuba is a country that lives on their own. They closed the doors to the United States and a lot of other countries.

The culture in Cuba is Hispanic. People work very hard and take pride in their work. The number one sport in Cuba is baseball. Their food preferences are white rice, beans, fried bananas, and pork. Cuba is a very tropical island and they show it through their music and dancing.

My dad was born in Cuba. He left and came to the United States at the age of 7. In order to leave Cuba my grandfather had to ask permission to leave Cuba and they granted him that permission. He had to quit his job and go cut sugar cane for 2 years and be away from his family. It was a sacrifice he made. I still have my great-grandmother that lives there and other relatives. I hope one day that Cuba will become a free country and I can go visit my family.

Raymond Rodriguez, Grade 7
Sebastian River Middle School, FL

How Baseball Was Invented
and How It Changed Over Time

Here's something to think about. You know that baseball is a popular sport in the United States. It is usually referred to as America's pastime, but do you know how the game got started?

Baseball was invented in America in 1845. But even before that, as early as the 1600's, people in England played a similar game called rounder. The players on the other team tried to tag the runner by throwing the ball at him and hitting him with it. Ouch! This painful practice was called soaking the runner.

Late, in the 1700's men in the American colonies played town ball. Any young colonist who came to town for a meeting was allowed to play. Sometimes each team had as many as 25 players. And all had to come to bat before the other team got a chance to hit. That would take a while!

As time went on, the popularity grew and grew. One man who loved to play the game was Alexander Cartwright. He used to play town ball every Sunday on a field in New York City. He was the inventor of a new type of town ball.

One Sunday in 1845, Cartwright came to the game with a piece of paper with some new rules he had made up. He had also drawn a field shaped like a diamond, and called his new game baseball. Batters would now use bats instead of paddles. Wow! The game has really changed over the years.

Alex Carnoali, Grade 7
Incarnate Word Elementary School, MO

Choices! Choices! Choices!

Should I wear jeans or shorts? Should I have sausage or bacon? Every day people in the world are faced with these types of choices, whether they are easy or hard, good or bad. Those minute decisions may not affect their lives dramatically, but some can have major side-effects, such as deciding whether or not to make fun of someone, if you are going to steal that knickknack you cannot afford, or if you are going to cheat on your next test. It is important to know that all choices you make in life can lead you down various paths which may be good or bad.

If you still doubt that the choices you make are important here is an instance in which the decision you chose is critical. Perhaps you are out with your friends one day and someone asks if you want to try some alcohol. Freeze! You have two choices, one being you accept their offer or two you decline. Each decision has a different outcome. In scenario one, if you accept, you could become addicted to alcohol and your grades could decline, which may result in you not graduating from high school or even going to college. One the other hand, if you chose to reject their offer you will most likely stay focused in school and will not run the risk of underage drinking or addiction. So, from now on always remember to choose carefully, no matter what the situation.

Rachel Ghazarian, Grade 8
St Gerard Majella School, MO

The Angels That Watched My Grandpa

In mid-February of 2007, my grandpa was in the hospital. When he was there, he and some of my aunts experienced something that words cannot describe. One day while lying there, my aunts asked him what he was looking at on the ceiling. He told them he was seeing people who had passed away in our family and he saw a big house and asked who built it. My aunts looked at each other with questions going through their minds, but said nothing. Finally my aunt said, "God built that house and he wants you to go live in it with Him." Grandpa asked why he did not see my grandma. My aunt responded, "She will be up there with you soon. She is coming."

One night my family and I went up to see my grandpa. He was unconscious but still alive. His body was running off of nerves. When he opened his eyes and started coughing, I broke down. I did not like seeing him suffer like that.

When my grandpa died February 17, 2007 it was very hard for me to face the fact that he was really gone. My grandpa was watched by angels that kept him here for as long as they wanted. When I faced that fact, it made me feel a lot better that he was gone. He had suffered for the longest time and angels decided it was time for him to live in peace.

Ashtin Truesdale, Grade 8
Albemarle School, NC

Reliving the Moments

Continually glancing at the turning wheel, I anticipated the car pulling up to the Northwest Airlines terminal at the airport. I remember especially the tight security and having to witness my sister's dad actually having to remove his shoes so the police officers could make sure that he didn't have any weapons under his foot. But I was not allowing such a small interruption to overrule the uncontrollable pounding heartbeat of excitement throughout my body.

Heading for Disney World on the plane, we were treated as royalty by the flight attendants who catered to our every need. Once in Florida, I thought I was in the Promised Land when the wooden, hand-carved doors opened to show the most amazing replica of Africa in one hotel resort. The scrumptious African buffet, the patio view of the calm, rare animals grazing in the grass, and the friendly employees were only the beginning of the wonderful world of Disney!

Not only were we astonished by the numerous parks in Disney World, but it was the adrenaline-rushing thrill rides that caught our eye! I definitely enjoyed the 3-D movies and junk food. Unfortunately, they all tired us out, so we packed our bags and headed for Memphis. Thankfully, we got back home before Hurricane Charley hit Florida, home of the famous and well-known Walt Disney World.

Jessica M. Shotwell, Grade 7
White Station Middle School, TN

What Is Wisdom?

What is wisdom? Some people say wisdom is intelligence, but wisdom is more than the ability to learn things, or being intelligent. Wisdom is making right choices using your intelligence. Wisdom is a knowledge that God alone gives you. If one has wisdom, that means one has the ability to know the difference between right and wrong. One man had great wisdom. He was the wisest man that ever lived. His name was Solomon. Solomon was a young king, and he knew he couldn't rule without God's help. God asked him what he needed to become a great king. He told God that he needed wisdom and understanding. He didn't ask for earthly things as in silver and gold, but wisdom. Many people would have desired riches rather than wisdom, but because of Solomon's choice, God gave him not only wisdom, but great riches also. As you can see from this example, wisdom is only given from God. Knowledge is to know certain facts, but wisdom is to know how to use those facts for good purposes. A wise person will obey the Lord and prepare for Jesus' coming, but the unwise cares only for what the day brings. We should all act as the wise man and be observant of the signs of the time.

Ibawolatei Iyegba, Grade 7
Home School, AL

Family Ties

Family — just saying the word ignites a fuzzy comforting glow throughout my body. The sense of belonging, loving, and being loved by another is a lifelong experience that I hope all creatures have the opportunity to live through. God blessed me with a family that is proud of who I am, supportive of my endeavors, has been the guiding light of my past and continues to illuminate my future.

It is mind-boggling to me how my family is such a unique mix of funniness, seriousness, intelligence, strength, sensibility, generosity, trust, and above all — love. We pull together like a Chinese finger trap — the harder someone tries to pry us apart, the closer and more inseparable we become.

My mother, Sylvia, father, Lloyd, and sister, Emily, as well as our extended family, are people who never fail to astonish me with their ever-growing love for one another, and unbelievable generosity. Having a strong and stable relationship with your family, I believe, is among the most important aspects of living. The unmistakable comfort of knowing that someone will always be there to catch you if you fall is such a powerful feeling. It is as if there is a plush, squishy mattress that moves with you, subtly protecting you, but always there.

Trying to live my life without these irreplaceable people in it would be like asking an ant to lift a thousand pounds — it would never be possible.

Nicole Granet, Grade 8
Bak Middle School of the Arts, FL

Never Be Forgotten

September 11, 2001 four planes were hijacked. Two planes hit the twin towers of the World Trade Center. Another plane hit the Pentagon. The fourth plane was retaken by the passengers and crashed. September 11th is also known as the day the United States once again became united.

Tuesday morning September 11, 2001 American Airlines Flight 11 was flown into the north tower of the World Trade Center. Everyone thought it was accidental, until 9:02 a.m. when United Airlines Flight 175 flew into the south tower. This was no accident. America was under attack.

Thirty-five minutes after the south tower was hit American Airlines Flight 77 flew into the west side of the Pentagon. People were horrified. Loved ones of the passengers on United Airlines Flight 93 received calls. The calls stated that Flight 93 had also been hijacked.

The passengers on Flight 93 fought back, and regained control of the plane. They crashed in a field near Shanksville Pennsylvania. Those forty-five brave people died including four terrorists. Certainly those 41 passengers are heroes.

September 11, 2001 thousands of innocent people were murdered because of four planes that were hijacked. The World Trade Center burnt to the ground. The headquarters for America's military operations was crashed into. One of the hijacked planes they regained control and crashed. Many brave men and women died. In other words the victims and this day will never be forgotten.

Carolina Moralejo, Grade 8
Pigeon Forge Middle School, TN

The Greatest Car on Earth

The 1968 Corvette is one of the fastest cars on Earth. You know the third generation of co-arted in 1968. The Corvette's top speed is 126 miles per hour.

There are different types of Corvettes. The one that I'm researching is the Mako Shark 2. The Mako Shark 2 was displayed in the New York International Auto Show in April 1965. The manufacturers problem was the engine cooling. Back then, cooling was barely sufficient for big block engines with air conditioning. The 327 cubic-inch, 300 horsepower engine was offered as standard equipment.

The power glide automatic transmission was no longer offered. As its replacement, a three speed Turbo Hydra-matic was offered. That improved performance and fuel efficiency. The car's concept claim to fame was its influence on the resigned Corvette of 1968. The Mako Shark 2 was debuted in 1965 as a show car. The Chevrolet company actually created two of them — only one of which was fully functional.

The non-running show car sported some interesting, futuristic details, such as square-section side pipes and a squared-off steering wheel. While the functioning version didn't have these features, it did not have a retractable rear spoiler, and a square section bumper that could extend for added protection. The Mako Shark 2 was powered by a 427 Mark 4 engine which became available on production Corvette models. The Mako Shark 2 can beat almost any car in a race.

Mathew Schwab, Grade 7
Stroud Middle School, OK

My Favorite Place

A place is a particular area or space. There are an endless number of different places in the world, some of which I have been to and others that I daydream about. Some of my least favorite places are the dentist's office, hospitals, and mortuaries. These places are never fun. They usually do not make me feel happy. I dread the thought of going to these places. Some places I like better are sport stadiums, airports, amusement parks, and big cities. All of these places give me the feeling of happiness. They give me a spark of excitement. I look forward to going to these places with great anticipation.

Of all the places that I have been in my thirteen years life, my favorite place is my room. It is a place where I always feel at home. My room is a comfortable living space where I feel safe and secure from the troubles of the outside world. It is all about me in my room. My favorite things surround me wherever I look, and these things make me feel happy. It is the one place on this large planet that I can call my very own. Each day of my life begins and ends in this place. It is a place that I know will always be waiting for me no matter what happens. My room is my favorite place.

Andrew Graneto, Grade 8
Incarnate Word Catholic Elementary School, MO

Querencia

Two years ago, the option to join the track team hung in my mind. I hadn't ever been in a race before. People had always told me that I was fast, and asked me if I was on a track team. I hadn't. Fairyland school didn't have any sports teams what-so-ever. The first day, I remembered feeling very nervous, walking shakily to the track. As I ascended the hill, the black track emerged. Wrapping around the football field, the seven lanes stood ever prominent, in my watchful eyes. I saw people sprinting down the first two lanes. I jogged anxiously towards my destination. My turn was next. I was up against a huge eighth grader with enormous feet. I knew for sure I was already done for. He loomed over me as I dug the starting block's sharp metal teeth into the rugged track, and was ready to go. POW! The gun fired and we sprang off the blocks. Wind whipping in my face, my legs strained with every ounce of my strength. I plucked up the courage and looked to see him just ahead of me and realized that I was not going to lose horribly, and that this track was my querencia.

Eric Daniel, Grade 8
Baylor School, TN

4-wheelin'

Four-wheeling with my cousin and myself is fun. One time, my cousin and I were racing up through the holler at my papaw's house in Virginia. It was fun until he flew ahead of me and put dirt in my face and my mouth. Then my cousin Billy and I went up to the gas well. After that, we went to my Uncle Don's house.

Four-wheeling is fun. I remember that every time that I went to my papaw's house during the winter, my papaw and I would go up the holler with our four-wheelers and go huntin'. We don't always kill anything but we do have a lot of fun going. Then the next day I usually ride with my uncle and my cousin and we go anywhere until lunchtime.

Four-wheelers are hard to fix because there are so many things in the engine just like a car. But when you get used to fixing it, it gets easier. Just like last week I couldn't get it started and I saw that the spark plug was wore out, so I had to go to Advance Auto to get a new one and I put it in and it started.

Four-wheeling can be fun for all ages. Kids can ride with family members riding four-wheelers until they reach age 5 then they can ride by themselves with a 50 cc. I ride a 250 cc and they go fast. Now you try 4-wheeling.

Austin Bateman, Grade 8
Pigeon Forge Middle School, TN

My Bicycle Accident

One bright, sunny, day, this past summer in Stockholm, New Jersey my cousins and I were having a terrific time playing outside. We were engaged in a variety of different sports such as: soccer, football, and basketball. Just when we all thought we were all exhausted, we decided to go inside. My cousin suggested, "Try riding our bikes uphill and then downhill." This took about five minutes to unanimously decide that we should venture this great feat.

We got on our bikes, and pedaled uphill. Being a very hot afternoon we were almost exhausted and sweat was dripping from our faces. Now for the best part, pedaling down the hill. My cousins and I had a little pow wow and decided that we should be very cautious while going downhill. At first we started of at a slow pace, but then I noticed that I was going faster than a cheetah. Everything was going smoothly until I spotted a car coming in my direction. I tried to apply my brakes, but I couldn't, my bicycle became unbalanced and it caused me to flip off my bike. I rolled over several times downhill hitting my ankle on rocks and pebbles. I finally landed in the middle of the street with a messed up ankle. I was in excruciating pain.

I was rushed to a nearby hospital where they operated on my ankle immediately. It was a success. Now, I keep telling my story to my friends and warning them about the dangers of going downhill.

Nevin Alummoottil, Grade 8
Williams IB Middle School, FL

Art and Science: The Sport

The student I was fencing had much to learn, and I was told not to make his sabre spar easy. Looking through the screen of my mask, I saw the student dressed in an armor of white fabric moving towards me. He swung his sword confidently down at my head. Expertly, I brought my blade horizontal above my head defending the attack. I followed this by up curving my sword down across his stomach.

Obviously the student had never learned the art of fencing. Like a paintbrush my sabre moved masterfully into defensive parries and swiftly into strikes. Because I landed one hard against his chest, the apprentice fell straight to the ground. I helped him up, for I knew now he hadn't studied the science of fencing.

I told the student that bended knees give a better center of gravity for more balance and improved movement. Continuing, he started to defend more attacks. He moved his blade to parry mine, gestured upwards to deceive me, and ducked down to avoid a high slash.

Finally, the beginner parried an attack with the same horizontal block I had used. The student attempted the identical downward strike. Time seemed to freeze. I leaned back and looked to see the tip of his sword swish millimeters away from my body. My opponent's and my eyes met. I smiled as I tried to dink the top of his mask. Like a flash, he beat my sabre away and, for the first time, landed a hit. I laughed aloud, and congratulated myself. I had taught the art and science of fencing.

Caleb Pepperman, Grade 7
White Station Middle School, TN

My First Dirt Bike and Four Wheeler

Have you ever ridden on a dirt bike or four wheeler before? If you haven't, then your in for a treat. If you have, you know exactly what I am talking about. Dirt bikes and four wheelers are fun! They can be very dangerous because you could flip it or fall off of it. I have done some very silly things on them like riding wheelies on the road.

I have also jumped at big places such as a place in my community called Buckles Berry. It is a park for dirt bikes and four wheelers. You do nothing but ride, jump things, go four wheeling and anything else that you can think of doing. You only have to pay a couple of dollars to get in the park and you can ride all day long. Many people get hurt out there, especially at Buckles Berry. When I pulled up at the entrance one time, there was a truck coming our way and they asked if we had a cell phone they could use because the passenger was bleeding. He flipped his four wheeler on a jump. So that is an example of how dirt bikes and four wheelers can be dangerous.

Dylan Hunnings, Grade 8
E B Frink Middle School, NC

The Best Father in the World

My father is the best father in the world. One reason he is the best, is he would do anything for me. Another reason is he loves me very much, and I love him. If I am in a cranky mood my dad loves me and tries to make me feel better. And the third reason is he trusts me, and listens to me when I have to talk about something.

My dad's name is Arlis Hester, he is forty years old. He will do anything for me. When I say I am hungry, he gets me food. And when I say I am sick, he gets me medicine. He would risk his life for me. I think he is very nice. He is very caring. Every weekend he takes me to my mom's house. He will do whatever makes me happy. I love my dad, he is a very considerate guy. When I am upset and mad at him he tries to make things better. Sometimes he gets mad at me too. But we get over whatever we are mad about. I will always love my dad. When I have to talk about something, he is there to listen to me. My dad trusts me when I tell him something serious.

Overall, my dad is the best dad in the world. Because he will do whatever he has to do, to make me happy.

Elaina Hester, Grade 7
Greenfield Jr/Sr High School, MO

Halloween

Halloween is one of the oldest holidays still celebrated. It is also one of the most popular next to Christmas. Although many people celebrate Halloween they celebrate it without knowing it's origins. The history and facts of Halloween are what make it very interesting. So in this essay I will tell you a brief history of Halloween.

Halloween first originated with the Celtics who lived around 2,000 years ago. They celebrated a festival called Samhain. Their new year was November first. They thought that the day before this, the void between the dead and the living became blurred. On the night of October 31st they celebrated Samhain, it was believed that then the ghosts of the dead entered their world. They thought that the presence of the dead made it easier for the druids, the Celtic priests, to make predictions which were very important to the Celtics to help them through the harsh winter.

Later when the Roman Empire took over the Celtics they continued a ritual similar to Samhain called Feralia, when the Romans commended the crossing of the dead. Later when Christianity spread towards the Roman Empire the Pope made the day after Samhain All Saints Day or All Hallows. The day before All Hallows was called All Hallows Eve. The day after All Saints Day was later called All Souls Day. All Souls Day was celebrated similarly to Samhain. There would be big bonfires and people would dress up as saints, angels, and devils.

Giovanni Gabriele, Grade 7

A Global Garden

When you look around at the world, what do you want to see? Do you want to see a world whose air is black with exhaust? Do you want to see a world that has no animals, no beauty? As humans, we need to be aware of how our lifestyle affects our planet. As humans, it's our responsibility to care for our beautiful, but neglected, earth garden.

A thriving garden is full of life. But global warming threatens the precious balance plants and animals need. Polar bears have drowned because of large expanses of iceless water. Early springs hatch caterpillars sooner than normal, leaving birds with no food. Beautiful plants that are accustomed to cooler weather wither and die in the heat.

Extreme weather changes affect our garden as well. The more polar ice melts, the more heavy and damaging storms originate over open water. Also, the hottest ten years on record were all in the past thirty years. Heat dries and cracks our soil, and kills living things. If this continues, can you imagine what life might be like in the future?

But don't give up hope. Many little things we do can cut down on pollution, and therefore global warming. Plant a tree, wash your clothes in cold water, recycle more, conserve electricity. We can make a difference. We can make our garden beautiful once again.

Hannah Jeffress, Grade 7
Home School, TN

More Than Just a Sport

Every day after school and the usual routine of homework, I spend time at Dance Dynamics, my dance studio. Putting hours into hard work, I always leave sweating. It's not easy to be a dancer, but I couldn't live without it because it improves so many parts of my life.

Dancing keeps me in shape. I am physically fit and strong and have become more flexible since I started at age four. Also, dance teaches me balance, posture, muscle control and most of all, self-confidence.

Interestingly, dancing also keeps my mind in shape. Learning new steps and leaps as well as complete dance routines forces me to think. Yearly, I have performed at least four, and sometimes six, dances at my competitions and recitals. Dance has disciplined me to learn and taught me the value of practice.

Most of all, dancing keeps me happy. Because of the studio's location, I meet girls of varying ages and from many parts of the city. This makes each day exciting because there is always something new to share.

My feelings of excitement and pride when I'm on stage make all the work and time worthwhile. The best feeling comes when I receive applause and even trophies for my performances. Knowing that I have reached a goal and succeeded keeps me dancing each new season.

Catherine Moore, Grade 7
White Station Middle School, TN

Fun with Granddaddy!*

Boom! Boom! His yawns sounded like cannons. I swiftly snuck across the room to my unknowing target. I picked out my weapon and started my torture. I carefully pinned and brushed not wanting to dismay my captive. Yawn! I quickly ducked down out slightly out of sight to watch my plan come to action. "What the?!" the sleepy man groaned in disbelief. He got up out of his recliner and scuffled over to the mirror to examine every pin, bow, clip, and scunci I had garnished in his silver kissed hair what was left of it. He smiled slightly and I couldn't help but laugh at the sight of his hip new hairdo that I had taken the pleasure to do out of the kindness of my 5 year old heart. He rushed over to my hideout that I was currently occupying and picked me up. Being the venturesome little child I was I always was looking for new ways to mess with my granddaddy. That one time that I spruced him up would to no knowledge of mine become a tradition. My granddaddy was very close to my heart. He was my idol. He died in April of '06 but I will always remember the fun times me and my granddaddy had shared over the years forever.

Tori Owen, Grade 7
Osceola Creek Middle School, FL
*Dedicated to Charles George Owen 1919-2006.

What Does It Take to Be a Hero?

Merriam Webster dictionary defines a hero as a person who is admired for his or her achievements and noble qualities; one that shows great courage, or has great strength or ability.

There are many types of heroes. People may think of military, a sports player, a religious person, a political figure, a musician, someone who stands strong for human right and dignity, or someone working for world peace and nonviolence. My favorite is the everyday hero. People who do what needs to be done. Think of health care workers, emergency workers, teachers and volunteers.

My personal heroes are Helen Keller, Ann Frank, Dr. Martin Luther King Jr., and Emilia Earhart. These people made sacrifices, made positive impacts on the world, and stepped up and showed what they believed in. A hero is someone who faces odds, but does what he or she has to do for the greater good of mankind, and has the courage to move forward. All it could take to be a hero is one simple moment in time that makes a difference.

Look inside yourself. Fight for what you believe in! Don't be afraid to do what is right. Be educated so that you can do better. Be patient and kind. Do not judge. Love unconditionally. One person can make a difference, and that person could be you!

Caitlyn Spencer, Grade 7
Harrison Jr High School, AR

September 11

On September 11, groups of terrorists hijacked two American aircraft holding 40 to 60 people, and flew into the World Trade Towers; thus killing nearly 3,000 innocent people. We knew then, our border was not secure.

These terrorists were able to learn how to fly an aircraft by attending air flight classes in America on American soil. But, we didn't even know. That goes to show that we have weak national security. They were easily able to enter the United States.

After 9/11, the government decided to declare war on Iraq. We then sent troops to Iraq, Afghanistan, and surrounding countries to find the terrorist leader and cells. Then violence broke out and there are many American casualties. We captured Saddam Hussein and executed him for killing thousands of innocent people. Now we have another terrorist leader, Osama bin Laden.

We have learned that our borders are not secure. But the government says we're safer than we were. We have also learned that because it is still easy to enter the United States, there are terrorist cells all over America.

Now we know we should be more cautious in the future to prevent another severe event. I think I speak for everyone when I say, we need a new and better plan.

James Bissonnette, Grade 7
Sebastian River Middle School, FL

Birthday

Birthday parties are supposed to be happy times when a singular person is made special and give gifts. Now, when two separate children of incredibly different tastes are celebrated on the same day, at the same party, things become a little hectic. I was there, on the sidelines, when a five year old, male LSU fan and his one year old 'flowers, pink, and Barbies' girly-girl of a sister tried to get all the attention.

Little did they know that they would not be the life of the party.

They had a piñata. 'Oh, joys of joys,' something to do. I was first after the little kids.

Now, they decided that I was a 'big kid' and thusly needed to have my eyes covered while trying to hit the piñata. I did not like that plan and protested. I told that I would hit someone; I told them! Did they listen? I do not believe they did.

So, I stood with a wooden baseball bat, eyes covered, and swung. Nothing, I tried again. Still nothing. I tried for a third time. I hit something.

Then I heard, "Oh, my God, is she all right?"

I took the blind fold off and looked down. Oh, no, that was bad.

I had hit Garrett's grandmother. I had knocked her out. I became the life of the party.

Alexis Martin, Grade 7
Alexandria Middle Magnet School, LA

Tennis Popularity

Studies indicate that tennis popularity has decreased since the 70's. However, 700,000 individuals are involved in the United States Tennis Association and even more throughout the world! The USTA, as it's called, encourages participation and interest in tennis.

Players of all levels can participate in camps, lessons, and tournaments all over the country. In camps, dedicated instructors teach technique and strategy of the game. Tournaments are available for varying levels of players, ranging from beginner to national. When the tournament is over, you can look up your results on the Internet and receive a weekly ranking in your district; this encourages players to compete at a high level of intensity.

In addition to the USTA's commitment to tennis, professionals have contributed to promoting the sport. Roger Federer, Novak Djokovic, Rafael Nadal, and Andy Roddick — some of the best pros — dedicate much of their time making tennis ads for popular brands such as Nike and Lacoste. Many of these pros also donate their time and money to charitable organizations, which greatly benefits the community. For example, Andre Agassi, a former number one player in the world, runs a charity named after him in Las Vegas that was created to help provide an education to at-risk boys and girls.

Even though tennis is not considered a popular sport in America, its fan base is increasing every year and it may some day become a premiere sport.

Jonathan Borsky, Grade 8
Heritage Hall School, OK

La Donna

My mother is truly the definition of a role model. My mom has definitely changed my life forever and for always. She has always been there, right behind me, pushing me in the right direction. She is my world.

She has been through so much in her life. She has stayed strong through it all. How she does it I have no idea. As I have grown up I feel closer to her than ever before.

I hope that as I get older I possess at least half the qualities that she has. She is my life. If she wasn't here with me every day, I don't know I would do. She is my rock. Whenever I'm having a bad day she makes it better.

My mom is the only one in this world I can trust. I don't have to worry about her leaving me, or choosing friends over me. She will always be there right behind me.

My mom is my strength. She can get me through everything. I'm always here for her too.

I know she needs me just as much as I need her. Yes, we fight. It's usually about stupid things, but we always break through it all and in the end we will always love each other. I am her Nicole and she is my La Donna.

Nicole Harris, Grade 9
Countryside High School, FL

The Runaway Go-Cart

One sunny morning after fighting with my brother about what we were going to do, we finally decided that we were going to ride our new and beautiful go-cart. I was only five at the time so my older brother got to drive. We had a route that we went through. I had on my pink sunglasses, and my brother had on his slick black glasses. We were all ready to go. After we had went around my yard a few times, my brother got bored and decided that we would go somewhere new. As we started driving I saw his eyes become blank with emotion, as he started to loose control of the go-cart. We drifted into a new trail, and on our way we hit a tree. I jumped out as soon as it happened.

Neither of us was hurt, but the gas peddle was stuck. The go-cart went crazy, as my dad tried to chase it down. As it was going around it seemed to chase me down and run me over. I got up weeping, as I ran into the garage. My dad had finally caught the go-cart, and came to check on me. He told me to sit down, and show him my back. It had tire prints on it. While I was sitting I leaned back and hit the plastic rack leaning on the wall. On top of the plastic rack was a leaf blower and it fell right on my head. Ouch!

Olivia Bialczak, Grade 7
Osceola Creek Middle School, FL

911

It was a beautiful day in Baton Rouge, Louisiana. There were no clouds in the sky, and an occasional light breeze. My third grade class had just come back from recess. Then things started to change. I couldn't understand what was happening. We entered class quietly, with lack of understanding.

My teacher turned on the TV to show us what had recently happened. It was showing a replay of planes crashing into tall buildings. I looked at the TV very sadly. Then, I understood. I could only cry. I felt a mixed feeling of sadness and anger. I asked myself, "Why did those people do that, and how could someone have done such a thing?" My mind began to spin a thousand miles a minute asking questions. Then I thought of my mama. I wondered if she was okay? I feared that the terrorist might attempt to destroy the governmental building where my mama worked, or the plant that's only neighborhoods away from my house. "What about my daddy?" I wondered.

When I got home, I made sure that everything was the way my family had left it. Everything was the same, but the way I felt. I was sad for the kids who had seen their parents for the last time that morning before they had to head out to school. I felt sad for the people who promised to take their children to the park, the mall, or the movies, but didn't.

Darriel Nettles, Grade 9
Baton Rouge Magnet High School, LA

All About Me

My name is Jennifer Genovese and I am 12 years old. My birthday is June 20, 1995. I am in seventh grade.

I live with my mom, my sister, my two cats, and one dog. I do not live with my dad because my parents are divorced. My younger sister is 10, and my older sister is 21 years old. My older sister has two baby boys; one is 19 months and the other is only one week old.

My mom, my younger sister, and I have moved 10 different times. I have gone to 5 different schools. After a little while I got used to moving so much. Even though it is not fun to move so much I am ok with it.

Although I have broken three bones, and that hurts a lot, the most painful thing I have ever had to deal with was when I was hospitalized with IGA nephropathy. IGA nephropathy is a very, very bad kidney problem, and it can make your kidneys bleed.

So now in order to get better I have to take a lot of medicine. One kind makes me gain a lot of extra weight. So whenever I get sad my mom tells me to be happy because I could have died.

So that concludes my life so far. I have two sisters, three pets, and my kidneys are still working.

Jennifer Genovese, Grade 7
Sebastian River Middle School, FL

My Dream

I have loved to dance ever since I was little. I love the stage, the lights, the audience, but there is one friend I love more. Bowing deeply, I waved to the audience with a smile; inwardly I began to cry, "What is happening?" I ran off the stage, trying to forget my prayer with God the night before. "Sarah, you'll have to stop dancing." A few nights before, all I could think about was living, dancing, and breathing ballet. Now…my dreams are gone.

A few hours later, I entered my room, sadly setting down my costumes and make-up; I was soon weeping. It was useless to keep the tears from streaming down my face. I fell onto my bed guiltily.

"Father, I don't want to be disobedient. I'm just confused. You said to delight in You and You'll give me the desires of my heart. Jesus, isn't that dancing? Lord, I'm delighted to be in You; I love You, and pray, and…" I stopped, knowing He wanted me to listen.

"Sarah, I have huge plans for you, dreams that you do not know. Trust in me."

I stopped crying and realized maybe ballet wasn't my purpose in life. My purpose was to praise Him. I now smiled and wiped away my tears, as I exited my room.

I then looked back, and realized how God had turned this outcome into something good. I heard a still small voice, "I love you."

Sarah Buford, Grade 8
College Heights Christian School, MO

True Friends

Friendship is a bond between two people. It's caring for another person, and wanting the best for them. You never use a person, because that's not true friendship; you need to take time to get to know a person and not just to use them for their things or to make yourself look better.

There are tons of ways to practice friendship. First you need to find something to appreciate about everyone. Next you need to be nice to everyone even if you don't like them. Finally you need to include everyone not just reject the people you don't like or think aren't cool. While I do try to be nice to everyone there are people who really annoy me to whom I should try to be nicer to.

God want us to have friends. Having friends makes us happier and more like God. God wants everyone to be happy and like Him. So with friends we can cheer each other up and bring out the best in each other. I enjoy being with all my friends and I love having fun, but I should stop more often and make sure my friends are having fun or if they want to do something else, because that builds stronger relationships with each other if we're all having fun.

Symmes Culbertson, Grade 7
St Mary's School, SC

Dubble Bubble

All of my life I have been chewing the delicious Dubble Bubble bubble gum. I've always loved it as a kid and never really cared about the history of it. Then, I asked myself, "How did Dubble Bubble ever begin?"

It all started in 1928, by a man named Walter Diemer. He liked to experiment with recipes in his spare time. While experimenting, he stumbled upon a unique recipe that was delicious. Before he died, he explained, "It was really all an accident!"

On the inside of each wrapper, was a comic strip. In 1930, the first Double Bubble comic strips featured the twin brothers Dub and Bub. In 1937, the gum went on the markets. They were a huge hit! In 1950, Dub and Bub were replaced. Pud was the new main character for the comic strip. Pud is still the main character for Double Bubble today!

In 1945, Dubble Bubble came out with grape and apple flavors! Since then, they have come out with many other flavors. The greatest change of Dubble Bubble since the original making of it is the various flavors it has. As people continued to love Dubble Bubble, in 1999, they created Dubble Bubble gumballs!

Ever since the creation of it, Dubble Bubble has been loved around the world. It is sold in 50 countries. I'm sure it will be around for many more years to come too.

Lauren Brandon, Grade 7
Incarnate Word Catholic Elementary School, MO

Page 269

The Worst Morning Ever

It all started one rainy, cold, cloudy day. I was on my way to my neighbor's house, so we could walk to school together. I knocked once. No answer. So, I knocked once more. This time there was an answer. It was Sevinah. "Hold on," she whispered. She closed the door. I sat down on her porch and waited for her to come back outside. When she came back out she said, "I think something is wrong with my mom, she is pale, will you come look at her?"

I followed her into the house. She went straight to the kitchen. She looked at me and asked, "Is she ok?"

I looked at her and said, "Get the neighbor."

She ran out the door. About a minute later the door opened and there was a grown woman behind her. They both ran to the kitchen where I was. The grown woman checked her pulse and started crying. She told us to get the phone out of her house and call 911.

We hurried out of the house. We ran into her house and got the phone that was laying on the table. I dialed 911 and handed the phone to the grown woman. "We need an ambulance right away, my neighbor is lying on the kitchen floor not awake." We waited for 30 minutes. Finally, they showed up.

Amanda Hunter, Grade 7
Stroud Middle School, OK

The More Friends the Better

Tears shed every day at Turner Falls youth camp, because in the month of May 2007 over 100 people a day got saved.

The thing I miss most about youth camp is my friends, youth service, games, and late night, two of the friends I made are, Jake and Hunter. They live in Mannford, Oklahoma, which is about an hour and 30 minutes away from where my friend and I live. We hung out with them most of the time at youth camp. Our church competed every day in dodge ball, volleyball, soccer, basketball, and tug-a-war against all different kinds of churches. We also had a thing called Mud Mountain which is just an enormous mountain of mud. We had to do relay races in it. It was awesome but really gross because when you got out you were covered with mud from head to toe. After playing in the mud everyone took showers and got ready for dinner and service. We all headed to dinner, then after eating and cleaning up the cafeteria everyone headed out to the tabernacle for service, we had a hilarious speaker. Then we had something called late night, which is when you get to stay up really late at night and play games and do whatever you want. After a whole week of fun and staying at youth camp. It was time to say goodbye to all our friends. And the year this happened it was the Oklahoma Centennial.

Katrina Sears, Grade 7
Chelsea Jr High School, OK

The First Day of School

Sometimes we argue. Sometimes I get so angry at him that my blood boils. But if I think about it, my dad has definitely had the most impact in my life. Since I was two he's cared for me all by himself. When I was about one, my parents went through a divorce. Now my dad has taken care of me ever since.

When I was still about two years old he would always feed me, teach me new things, and even play sports with me. But when I think of my dad one memory sticks in my head.

It was the first day of school, and I had butterflies in my stomach. But as we arrived and came out of the car, we both looked around. All the other kids were with their moms, and the moms crying all over them. We looked at each other, and laughed. Right then all my butterflies were gone.

And even now he still does so much for me. He takes me to school at six-thirty and goes to work until six P.M. even after that he still takes me to football practice and cooks dinner. He literally works from seven to ten at night, every day of the week.

There are so many more things I can think of saying, but to list them would take an eternity. So now if I even get angry at my dad, I'll just think of that first day of school.

Darian Johnson, Grade 9
Countryside High School, FL

Being an American

Being an American means more than just living in a free country. It also means enjoying security, freedom, and liberty more than any other country. Many factors define a country: the people, the culture, and the religions. Without these, a nation would not exist. These support what the American flag represents, freedom. And with that freedom comes responsibilities, respect, and privileges. When most people go about their everyday lives doing their everyday things, they normally don't think about their responsibilities. Instead, they take living in America for granted.

When we give our nation respect, it gives us many privileges. And that is where freedom comes in. It is very easy for people born into modern society to take rights and privileges for granted, but was not for our ancestors. We have the privilege to live on a beautiful planet with many freedoms and opportunities and can interact in a society with people of many ancestries. America was created by immigrants wanting to better themselves. We have been born in a country where we can have a voice in deciding how our country is run. This is truly a privilege that is not accepted in many other parts of the world.

Being an American means loving our country and constantly trying to make it better. A quote taken from Daniel Webster states that, "God grants liberty only to those who love it, and are always ready to guard and defend it."

Kami Nelson, Grade 8
Hale High School, MO

Family Vacation

On our three hour trip to Sevier County I wonder what our new cabin would look like. I imagined a log house with two rooms that had spider webs in corners, but it turned out, I was wrong. I walk into the cabin, amazing. The first thing I see when I walk in the cabin is a white kitchen with an island counter, past the kitchen is a beautiful living room. The living room has a large fireplace, a wide screen TV, and a coffee table with a fake bear that held it up. On both sides of the living room are master bedrooms with a jacuzzi tub each. My favorite place was downstairs though. Downstairs are two connecting rooms with two beds in each. Once you exit one of the rooms there is a pool table and a high table with chairs. When I go out of the glass doors there is a hot tub with a wonderful view of the white frosted mountains.

Then, after our family got settled in, I set off for the hot tub. The water was steaming so I had to slip in very carefully.

Another day went by and so on. Finally, it was our last day. Just to make the day great, it started too snow. That day went by fast and the car ride home came quick. Once we get home I was already wishing that we could go back for another week of fun and family games.

Ryann Satterfield, Grade 7
Baylor School, TN

Annual Family Reunion

Once a year we go to Myrtle Beach, South Carolina. My grandparents, aunts and uncles and cousins all come. I remember waking up at 7:00 A.M. We finished getting packed and loaded up the car. Then we were on our way. We always stop at one specific gas station on the way up there, Pilot gas station.

When we get there we eat dinner. After we get back from dinner we walk along the beach. I take off my shoes and feel the sand squishing between my toes and can smell the salt. Then I walk in the water. It is really cold but you quickly forget about it when you watch the sun set. Then we walk back and go to bed exhausted from our long drive.

The next day I wake up to bacon and eggs cooking. I quickly eat so we can go to the beach but first have to put on lots of sunscreen.

When we get to the beach we quickly find a place to sit then get in the water. We stay at the beach until lunchtime. Then we go to the pool and float around the lazy river. That repeats for the next two days.

On Wednesday we go to a Pelicans minor league baseball game, and on Thursday we go on a sunset cruise. We occasionally see dolphins. Then on Friday we say good-bye to the beach. Everyone is sad but also happy because we got to see our family.

Sarah Oliver, Grade 7
Trickum Middle School, GA

Hands

My father has always had meaty hands with long, double-jointed fingers. He can bend his finger into a 'J' shape. His hands are good for checking heart rates with his stethoscope, and for examining the cuts and bruises my sister and I collect. He wears a colossal college ring. He enjoys laying his hand rather forcefully on my head. My mother has long hands but skinny fingers, good for laying her hand on my shoulder when I feel sad. Her hands maneuver the frying pan with precision, cooking up fried okra and love. Her hands are not pinioned by the stereotypes that women are supposed to live up to. She is a walking Women's Rights Movement. Her long nails are never painted; she's not that kind of person. Her index finger is a wand. Spell after spell she casts on my sister and me. As zombies, we must obey. My sister's hands are long and have skinny fingers, too. They are perfect for playing the piano and clarinet, just like her mom's. Often, my sister's fingernails are painted because she is a look-at-me kind of person. And my hands, my hands, are small and not very muscular. Despite this, they are good for writing, building things, and paying close attention to detail. They are gentle, not aggressive. My hands are also good for helping people with chores and homework. Without hands, nobody would ever accomplish anything. Hands are what make humans human.

Cory Walker, Grade 7
Baylor School, TN

What's the Meaning of Juneteenth?

Juneteenth is the oldest known celebration commemorating the ending of slavery in the United States. Dating back to 1865, it was June 19th that the Union soldiers, led by General Gordan Granger, landed on Galveston, Texas with the news that the war had ended and the enslaved were now free. The reactions to the news went from pure shock to jubilation. Many of the now free slaves left even if there was nowhere to go for them, but leaving the plantations would be the first thing to celebrate their freedom. North was a great resort but most wanted to be with family in other southern states. The celebration of June 19th was coined "Juneteenth" and grew with more participation from descendants. I think of Juneteenth as a day where we celebrate the ending of slavery in the United States.

I believe the meaning of Juneteenth is a day where honor and respect is paid for the sufferings of slavery. I like to think of Juneteenth as a day where we commit to each other the needed support as one happy family. It is a day where we all take one step together, to better realize the energy wasted on racism. Juneteenth always focuses on education and self-improvement. I see now where we still have to do and know that as a 13 year old, we have to educate the masses so they will understand the importance of Juneteenth.

M'ary Miller, Grade 8
Heritage Hall School, OK

Nature, What Makes Earth Great

Nature is an amazing part of the world we live in. I think we should appreciate it and realize just how much we might not have if there were not any trees, rivers, or any of our other natural resources. Trees are one of the main reasons we can live on Earth by producing oxygen and providing us with fruits like apples, pears, and oranges. Rivers are also important because they are where we get our drinking water. Mountains provide protection from harsh winds, and snow melts in the spring to create runoff water. All of these resources are important parts of nature and are important for us to have to survive.

Even though people we know need nature's natural resources to survive, some people still waste and destroy the resources that make this place a livable environment. People can recycle things like paper and plastic. Recycling paper and reusing it can save thousands of the oxygen-producing trees that we need to survive. Recycling plastic can prevent it from ending up in landfills where it takes a long time to decompose. The more we recycle these natural resources, the less pollution future generations have to deal with. Nature is something that will always be a very important part of my life.

Jacob Hoog, Grade 8
St Gerard Majella School, MO

A Chain Reaction

"I have this theory that if one person can go out of their way to show compassion then it will start a chain reaction of the same." This was written by Rachel Scott. She was the first person to be shot and killed at one of the worst school shootings. That place was at Columbine High School, when two boys chose to watch violent movies and stuff. They decided to put a propane bottle (bomb) in a backpack in the cafeteria; then come in and shoot at the bottle and kill many students. When they shot at it, it didn't go off so they shot at students with guns. The two boys killed twelve students and one very brave teacher.

I agree with Rachel's theory. I believe if one person would go out of the way to show kindness, it would start a chain reaction. Rachel's challenge has five steps. They are eliminate prejudice, dare to dream, choose your influence, use kind words, and start a chain reaction. Rachel's challenge has influenced me to be nice, and not look at someone and say "they look dorky." I am also setting goals for myself.

Rachel's family is now going to schools and sharing Rachel's story with students. Rachel drew eyes with thirteen tears and the tears were growing a rose. Rachel always told her friends that she was going to die young. She also said that she was going to touch millions of people's hearts. I believe she has.

Emily Daniel, Grade 8
Greenfield Jr/Sr High School, MO

S.O.S.

S.O.S. Few know what it is and what you do. This past summer I got the chance to go to Bing Hampton and help restore an old man's house. It was fun but also great to help someone else. Even though we never got to meet the owner it was still nice to say, by the end of this week I fixed that house.

S.O.S. is an amazing place and activity. S.O.S. stands for Service Over Self and that is just what you do. You get assigned a group and a house. I was lucky to get in the group with the contractor and to be in a loving group. We also had to stay on schedule. Here is our schedule: Wake up, get dressed, go downstairs, goof around, then go to the work site. They make you a lunch and you stay there until 5:00 p.m., then girls got in the shower and after the girls then the guys went. Lights went out at 10:30.

I made a lot of new friends there. The staff is nice. For the first time in a long time I felt good about doing something.

S.O.S. will change your perception on life and the world.

Emily Hoover, Grade 7
White Station Middle School, TN

To Serve or Not to Serve

Successfully serving in tennis is a challenging task. For two years, I ha been banging the ball against the side of the garage by my yard. Although that exercise was preparing me for rallying, my obligation to serve the ball had not occurred to me. When students signed up for spring sports last year, of course, I chose tennis, believing I might have some of the necessary skills.

After the first week, I realized the serving technique would become an important element for securing my desired team position. Facing this challenge led to a feeling of discouragement. For most of the season, I had failed to hit my serve within the required boundary. Other than my pathetic serve, I was progressing well in tennis; this kept me going.

After lots of embarrassment and lost matches, I realized that if I wanted to conquer serving, acquiring that one skill — the serve — would take lots of extra practice. And that's exactly what I did: I practiced obsessively night after night until I achieved my goal.

During our match a few weeks later, my doubles partner was so surprised when I had hit all but one of my serves within the lines! Prior to this, I had caused my partner and myself to lose quite a few matches. How pleased we both were about my new skill! Having gone through the ups and downs, being determined, and setting goals, I now maintain more confidence about not giving up on anything.

Madeline Perry, Grade 8
Heritage Hall School, OK

The Battle for Moscow

The Battle of Moscow, Russia's Capitol, was one of the most important battles of WWII. Hitler believed that if this battle was won it would cut off supplies going through Russia. This battle was a turning point in the war. It was the first time since the battle of Rostov, that the Germans had to make a full retreat.

Hitler had this attack planned out very well. He was going to surround the Capitol with panzers and then move in and attack. Hitler wanted to have a victory here because the casualties could be up to a 1000 deaths in this one place alone. Hitler expressed, in his diaries, how he wanted to win this battle. Hitler wrote, "The surrender of Moscow will not be accepted." Hitler emphasized this to his generals, so they knew how much he wanted to destroy Moscow.

Even though Hitler had a great plan to take Moscow, the Russian defense was ready. They weren't going to let Hitler kill all the people who lived there without a fight. The Russians did have some challenges to overcome before they could claim victory. First, they found it difficult to communicate with their defensive lines, and second, they frequently had to put up with air and artillery raids.

It was a brutal battle for both sides, but in the end, Russia was able to keep their State Capitol. It does make you wonder if the German's had won, how it may have changed the course of WWII.

Joey Kallial, Grade 7
Incarnate Word Catholic Elementary School, MO

Home Away from Home

As I opened the door the familiar scent of yellowed paper finds its way into my nose. Being the only person allowed in the restricted section of the Collinsville library is the best thing in the world. I flop down in one of the big high backed chairs and settle into *The Egyptian Book of the Dead*.

The Collinsville library is my home away from home. The staff there includes Ina the librarian, and Dylan the cataloger. They are my second family. As I walk in I'm usually greeted by, "Hi Jake read any good books lately?" As a regular at the library I know where all the different kinds of books are. I even help fix the computers when they're broken or glitched. It even gets me into all the fancy book clubs! When I'm sad I hop onto my bike and slowly ride down Main Street. I take in all the sights and smells, as I pass the Silver Dollar Café, I smell friend chicken. Tempting, but my sights are on the library.

As I arrive I find my friends bikes already there, Tyler and Pao. I walk through the front door and catch the elevator. I find Tyler on the computer playing Runescape, and Pao in the back reading X-men comics. I quickly decide to read comics with Pao, reading soon turns into a conversation. This is my favorite place because it turns 100 with Oklahoma.

Jake Mickelson, Grade 7
Chelsea Jr High School, OK

School, It's There Like It or Not!

Everybody has their pros and cons about school. It's hard to say what exactly the pros and cons are because everyone's opinion is different. So, I'm going by the one opinion I know, mine!

Friends, tests, homework, dress codes, all of these things are experienced during the school year. Tests can be a good thing in some cases. For instance, if you fail you know what you need to work on. Tests can also be bad because of all the stress. Homework is good because it helps prepare you for stressful tests. Although it's good in some cases, it can also be troublesome. When teachers give you too much work, you end up being stuck at home worrying about getting it done. Dress codes are not my favorite thing but they can also be very helpful. The good thing about dress codes is it's harder for people to judge you based on the kinds of clothes you wear because they are wearing the same thing. For instance, certain dress codes require clothing that you can't find in the average store. Despite the ups and downs of school, there is always one thing that will stay with you and that is your friends. They are always there for you regardless of the circumstances. Keep them close, and never let them go.

In conclusion, schools have the good and the bad. Through it all, friends are there, and school is a good experience if you look at it the right way.

Nance L. Clevenger, Grade 8
Trinity Christian Academy, AL

People Are Most Important

When people ask me who the most important person is in my life I do not answer because that person is actually people. My family is the most important thing in the world to me. I would give anyone who would dare hold my family for ransom all the money in the world not to hurt or to kill my family.

I would not let anything happen to them because they are my ahona. Ahona means family. Family means no one gets left behind or forgotten.

But my family is not the only thing that is important to me, my friends are important to me as well. Even if they get mad at me they are still my friends and they are still important to me. When I say they are important to me I mean I would give my life for them just to spend time with them. I mean they are more than just my friends they are like family to me and I love them like family very, very much. As of now I have a friend that is mad at me and I wish I knew why she is mad at me because maybe I can fix it. But although she is mad at me or even if they all are mad at me they are still important to me.

April Boothe, Grade 7
Greenfield Jr/Sr High School, MO

What Families Are for

My family is very important to me. We love each other unconditionally no matter the circumstances. Your family is the best thing anyone could ever ask for. My mom, brother, sister, and grandparents motivate me to strive for my goals, help me to make the right decisions, and are always there for me when I need them most.

First of all my family motivates me to strive for my goals because they want me to be successful in life. When I was first learning how to do a back hand spring in cheerleading, they were there to cheer me on and encourage me to do the best that I possibly could. Thanks to that support I know I can do four in a row. Next, they help me to make the right decisions in life. When I have an obstacle in everyday life they help me to work it out with the best outcome. That's what keeps me safe and learning all the time. Finally, my family is always there and going to be there for me when I need them the most. I love to know that someone will always help me through the good times and the bad. I always have my family right beside me to love and to care for. That's the greatest feeling in the world!

In conclusion, family means everything to me and I will continue to love and respect each and every one of them just as they do me.

Kelsie Carmean, Grade 8
Southwest Jr High School, AR

A Miracle of the Heart

My cousin, Emry, was born with a heart defect. She had a hole in her heart that made her condition life threatening. Everyone was praying constantly because we all wanted our new baby to be healthy. But we hoped everything would turn out great because God works all miracles.

The doctors said that my new cousin was very strong and my cousins would be able to take her home, but they had to watch her very closely. He also said that she would have to have surgery on her heart when she was twenty pounds. We all knew something was to be done, but at the same time, we wanted our new baby to be all right and healthy.

We were all waiting for the day to come when my cousin turned twenty pounds. When she finally did, my cousins drove up to Little Rock, Arkansas to the hospital. We were all praying that God would work a miracle for this less than a year old baby girl. And He did. The doctors said that my cousin was very strong and that she would probably have to have surgery again later on in her life.

My cousin, Emry, and her family were very brave. I am happy that we still have her with us today. She is now two years old and is a daredevil. I am glad that we all have God in our lives and that He worked this wonderful miracle.

Katy Kaminsky, Grade 8
College Heights Christian School, MO

Rejoice in Suffering

A trial that I go through every day is my brittle bone disease, Osteogenesis Imperfecta. When I was born, I had 11 broken bones. Immediately, the doctors knew something was wrong. I was diagnosed with Osteogenesis Imperfecta. At thirteen, I've had over seventy fractures, mostly in my legs. Currently, I've had thirteen surgeries to put rods in my legs. All the time spent recovering made my muscles weak; therefore, I cannot walk without the assistance of a walker. Despite all the trials I have been through, I believe that God has given me this disease for a reason, as part of His plan.

Through having this disease, I have been blessed with the opportunity to share God's word with many people. I have spoken at schools, churches, and I have even taught a vacation bible school lesson, all because of my bone disease. I've touched many people's lives through my disease, and I try to show people that God can use anyone, no matter who you are. Even though I cannot walk, I can still help people come to know God.

So, despite the pain and suffering I have to go through, I trust in God's plan for my life, and I am not going to let anything keep me from sharing His word.

Jacob Everett, Grade 8
College Heights Christian School, MO

The Discovery of Artimus

One afternoon my family decided to take a curious visit to the SPCA. When we arrived, we went straight for the dogs and darted in all directions for our favorites. Mom and I were toying with a fuzzy black dog when we saw Dad beckoning us over to a dog he had noticed. It was a white dog labeled Artimus dappled with a million amber-brown specks.

An employee approached us, noticing our fondness of this dog, and kindly offered for us to take Artimus on a walk down the hill. We happily obliged and trooped out the kennel door, dog in tow. I was spacing out when I felt a heavy weight thrust upon me, and I turned my head. I was currently gazing into the heart-melting brown eyes of the dog presently hugging me.

I gently nudged her off of me, and we headed back up the hill to the kennel doors. Mom and Dad explained to the employee waiting at the door for us that they already owned a dog but were interested in taking this one home. She informed us that we needed to bring our other dog to meet Artimus and see how they got along.

We led our energetic dog to Artimus and left the two canines to their sniffing as we eyed them apprehensively. There seemed to have been an unspoken agreement between the two because a heartbeat later they were sitting side-by-side like best buds.

"She's going home," Dad said with a smile.

Claudia Rutkowski, Grade 7
Our Lady of Lourdes Elementary School, NC

The Sound of Freedom

There were so many soldiers who fought for the freedom of the thirteen colonies from Great Britain. However, not all of them are known as the traditional soldiers with their muskets on the battlefield. Some of them, such as Thomas Paine, spread the message through writings, such as *Common Sense* and *The American Crisis*. These writings produced a lot of different opinions in the colonies, among both Loyalists and Patriots. Of course, there were also many soldiers on the battlefield; most with little or no experience. Some of these soldiers were deceiving, such as Deborah Sampson, a female soldier going undiscovered for a year and a half. There were also dangers amongst the barracks. Spies and traitors were hard to differentiate from the other soldiers in camp. One such Patriot spy was Nathan Hale. Hale worked as a spy for the Continental Army for a few months and was one of the first to be executed in the fight for Liberty. His last words were "I only regret that I have but one life to lose for my country." All in all, there was an enormous sacrifice for the freedom of our country from Great Britain. Many lives were lost, and many have been lost since then to maintain peace and order in the United States, as well as give all people of the United States their basic rights — life, liberty, and the pursuit of happiness.

Jyoti Lodha, Grade 9

No More Drugs

In my community, there are too many drugs being used. When I go to school, I see people selling marijuana on the corner. This persistent use of drugs must stop. Drugs are not healthy for our bodies. Drugs keep us from getting jobs and going on with our lives. Drugs infect our minds with filth and ignorance. People who do drugs do them because they refuse to do something with their lives. I think drugs are a waste of time. If the wrong person gets their hands on them it could be pernicious. Parents who do drugs and leave them in the reach of their children are not decent parents.

I think that community should help to get rid of these illegal substances by stopping the usage of them. I think people who sell drugs should stop soliciting them to young adults and find something better to do with their lives, like getting a job. Drugs pollute the air and make it a non-healthy breathing source. Drugs are putting all children in danger of getting lung cancer. Drug users are not good exemplars. We have to be good role-models and stop the solicitation and usage of drugs. Parents should also talk to their children about drugs because if they're using them they're putting not only themselves in danger but others too. By getting rid of drugs we are creating a better environment for ourselves and the children as well.

Bobbie Parham, Grade 8
Turner Middle School, GA

The War That Shouldn't Have Been Started!

The Iraq War is going on its fifth year with about four million of the six million veterans still alive. When are our troops coming home? Five thousand seven hundred troops will be home for Christmas. Some say the troops will never come home if they're waiting for the terror to end, but if they do, then the ones that do survive will leave pieces of them behind and wish they could leave some of their memories too.

Why are we still at war with Iraq? The U.S. elected to go to war in Iraq on March 19th, 2003 to try to get rid of the terrorists. Why was Iraq targeted? Iraq was targeted because that is where the longtime leader, Saddam Hussein, lived. Saddam, a much feared man in the entire world, especially in his own country, led a dictatorship. President Bush strongly believes that we need to stay in Iraq to help the new government.

Like the other people, I think it is time to bring them home. Look at how many people have died, and there are moms, dads, brothers, and sisters that are not getting to see their little ones grow and hear their first words and all the things parents go *crazy* about. I do not know about you, but I know what it feels like to have people in your family leave to Iraq because that is where my brother is going, I know how much pain it can cause to know that they might never come back.

Faith Robertson, Grade 7
Stroud Middle School, OK

I Wonder What It Is Like

Waking up early, seeing the sun shine through your window. You see pinks, yellows, and oranges all colliding throughout your bedroom, making you feel like you are in a rainbow. Hearing the sounds of your mom cooking breakfast for you. Getting dressed and going outside to see the beautiful leaves rustling on the ground. The smell of fresh air running over your face, like chilly air on a snowy day.

Last night the wind blew and I thought a storm was coming, but actually all it did was blow all the leaves off the trees. So, since it is Saturday and I don't have school today my mom asked met to rake the leaves. I do not really want to, but I guess I will do it anyway. I go to the shed, grab a rake, and go to the biggest oak tree in our yard. After a while of just standing there I start raking. While I am raking the colorful leaves I start thinking about things like, what is heaven like and how did God create such a wonderful Earth.

What is it like up in heaven? I have always pictured it with a field of gold lilies and a castle. That castle is sitting there waiting to be filled. The sky is full of what I would call cotton candy clouds. You can do whatever you want to do in what most people call, "Heaven."

Sometime I just sit and think, "I wonder what it is like!"

Mackenzie Coffey, Grade 8
Greenfield Jr/Sr High School, MO

The Most Important Person in My Life

The most important person in my life is my mom, LeAnna Phibbs. My mom is always there for me, and thinks about others before herself. Who else would I choose?

My mom is always there for me for different things. She has been to all of my plays, all of my graduations, and all of my award ceremonies. She is also a good source of advice about pretty much anything. She is very good about calming me down, when I am angry. My mom has taught me a bunch of things like teaching me to walk, talk, potty train, tie my shoes, read, write, and use my manners; these are a few of the billions of things my mom has taught me.

She always thinks about others before herself; she takes me places that probably don't even benefit her. My mom also feeds me healthy foods that are good for me. She is always buying me stuff that I want, and tries to get it for me eventually, if she can't right on the spot. She is also working at the school so that she is always fully involved with all parts of my life and education.

So you see, I appreciate my mom very much, and that is why I think she is the most important person in my life. I don't take it for granted at all! I love my mom!

Mathieson Phibbs, Grade 7
Mineral Springs Middle School, NC

The Freedom Riders: Their Journey

When Martin Luther King, Jr., in the 1960s, spoke out against racism in America, most of the nation recognized its error and was willing to change. Since the settlement of the United States, the southern states had supported segregation and were much more reluctant to change. One specific group of people, however, made a stand for what they believed in and demonstrated to the South that everyone is equal in God's eyes.

According to a law in the South, black citizens were supposed to sit in the back of public buses while white Americans were allowed to sit in the front. Many people began speaking out against this law, but the South stayed set in its ways.

The Freedom Riders, a group of black and white citizens, decided to stage a protest by one group sitting in the back of a Greyhound bus and the other in the back of a Trailways bus. As the Greyhound bus pulled into Anniston, Alabama, an angry mob formed and shook the bus and slashed the tires. Shortly after leaving, the bus was forced to stop and the mob mercilessly beat the Riders as they fled. Many more of these incidents occurred during their long, trying journey.

Although the South may have felt like they had won the battle, the rest of the country became aware of the segregation and the conflict was eventually won. Because of their bravery and courage, the Freedom Riders played a huge role in the Civil Rights Movement of the 1960s.

Taylor Elkins, Grade 8
Providence Classical School, AL

Football Rivals

It was a sunny, warm Sunday afternoon. However, there was tension in the air which could be felt like a thick woolly gray blanket covering the field. Our flag football team was getting ready to play our biggest rivals from West Orange. As the game started and we ran out onto the field, the roar of the crowd was so loud it shook the ground as if an earthquake was happening. We scored first. I was thrilled! My blood was pumping through my veins like water in a fire hose. Then the other team got the ball. Their quarterback threw the football so fast that it flew by my head faster than I could blink. Luckily, the receiver didn't catch it. From then on, I was ready for the ball. We scored seven points, and they scored seven points. It was on and off, neck to neck. It came down to the last play, and the score was tied at 21. With only five seconds left on the clock, our quarterback threw to a receiver deep in the end zone. It was a perfect pass. Just as the receiver was about to catch it, a defender came across the field as fast as lightning and intercepted the ball as it touched the receiver's fingertips. He ran it back the length of the field for a touchdown. That was the end of the game, but there's always next season.

Zechariah Musselman, Grade 9
Champion Preparatory Academy, FL

The Wise Man

I remember a while back when me and my grandpa first went fishing together. I was about the age of six at that time. When we got to the lake, I was anxious to catch a fish. My grandpa just laughed at me because I kept catching turtles! Eventually he helped me and I caught a small, sleek bass.

With a lean, muscular build, my grandpa looks as though he could take an ox down. He's got dark, shaggy hair. He's always wearing jeans and either a tank top or short-sleeved shirt.

For me, the best thing about him is when he's got something that needs to be done, he does it without hesitation. I remember that he used to work out in a shop outside, and creating furniture that I always thought was beautiful. He'd work out there for hours just to get a fraction of the work done. He also has that Oklahoma spirit.

A long while back when my grandpa wasn't as aged as he is now, he used to take me fishing whenever possible. He was always showing me the ropes and teaching me nifty tricks. He's always encouraged me to do my best and never give up.

If I were to decide who to guide me and encourage me, it would be him. He will continue to encourage me for as long as he lives throughout the rest of his years. He will never be replaced by anyone else.

Mikyle Betche, Grade 8
Chelsea Jr High School, OK

Looking Through My Eyes

Blood leaking from every soul,
The heart burning as if of coal.
Peace is something they will never learn,
Hope is something they will always yearn.

This land I love has become a place of hate. Innocent women and children are dying unceasingly. Amidst the pain and suffering, one looming question remains, "Will this misery ever come to an end?"

My name is Iraq — that's strong and true. My tears are shedding from the sight of the world. I was a glory for all creations; I was a dream for all nations. My land is very ancient with dear memories of great discoveries and people. Before, Iraq was a beautiful place of peace and harmony. Now, look at what we have done to it! It's a terrible, hostile place! No one wants to visit or return out of fear.

What began as Operation Iraqi Freedom, led by America, has resulted in a senseless civil war. Everyone has begun to believe that his or her own religious group is best. There are many different groups of Christians and Jews, but they have learned to live in peace. Now, it's our turn to learn.

When I return to my country, my dream is to promote peace and to encourage everyone to settle disputes by talking instead of fighting. We all deserve to live in a world of peace, and someday that will happen.

Shilan Hameed, Grade 7
Islamic Academy of Alabama, AL

The Importance of Community Service

Community service is a great opportunity to help others, to help your community, or to just improve something. Giving your personal time to be a part of an effort to help is what community service is ALL about. I enjoy community service because it provides me with a sense of accomplishment and achievement. It also helps me in the long run; I can put community service on applications for jobs or colleges in the future. I am fortunate enough to have plenty of opportunities for community service where I live. Some of the simplest ideas that I may come up with can be helpful to numerous people.

If someone is not a "people person," then they can help in another way. Animals shelters are a great option for community service. Even cleaning up in the neighborhood. One of my favorite choices is helping in libraries. Sorting, shelving, and checking books helps not only the librarian out, but the people who are looking to read those books.

Some other options are baby-sitting, care taking, baking for a nonprofit bake sale, raking leaves for a neighbor who is unable to, snow-shoveling for someone, and cleaning for an elderly person. If you want to help someone who really needs it, or you feel the need to get out in the community and do something, then you are ready for community service!

Alisha Potter, Grade 9
Harding University High School, NC

Ballerina

Maria Tallchief was born in Fairfax, Oklahoma. It is a small town near Missouri border. It was considered Indian land, but as we know it has changed since then. Her father was Joseph Tallcheif. He was a member of the Osage Indian tribe. Her mother was Ruth Mary Porter, of Scottish-Irish descent. Later, her family lived in California, where she developed an increasing talent in ballet. Maria's sister and other prima ballerinas emerged from Oklahoma.

Maria Tallchief was a famous dancer. She took ballet classes before the age of seven. Maria also played the piano and took piano lessons. She was committed to what she wanted to do. When Maria was in high school she was chosen for a solo part in *Chopin Concerto*. She was also in a Judy Garland movie and danced. Later after working very hard to get where she was she joined the New York City Ballet.

"It is my hope that in the 21st century, people with special skills will recognize that if they mentor children and young adults, they will be making an enormous contribution in assuring a better society," said Maria. She has been honored with many awards and honorary degrees.

A man named Walter Terry wrote of a 1954 performance, "Maria Tallchief, as the Sugar Plum fairy, is herself a creature of magic, dancing the seemingly impossible with effortless beauty of movement, electrifying us with her brilliance, enchanting us with radiance of being."

Megan Patterson, Grade 8
Chelsea Jr High School, OK

When I Was Young

Billy Joe Brown was born September 29, 1940 in Chelsea at a hospital ran by Dr. Jeannings. When he was young he went to Chelsea schools. At that time, the Dollar General Store was the local basketball gym. He attended McIntosh, Longfellow, and Chelsea High School.

When he was a junior in high school he dropped out and joined the Navy. At first he was stationed in San Diego, California for two years as part of the Navy. While in Florida he took two tours of duty in Cuba. When he got discharged from the Navy he came home to the United States and went to work at the West Coast on the Alaskan Pipeline in Washington and Oregon, where he met his wife Rae. They have been married 47 years and have three children.

They moved to California for 35 years and owned a trucking and a custom drapery business. In 1993 they moved back to Chelsea, Oklahoma, his hometown. He then went to work for Rogers County District 1. To this day he is proud to be a Cherokee Indian from the state of Oklahoma which is celebrating its 100th birthday.

Jane Kramer, Grade 8
Chelsea Jr High School, OK

Page 277

My Dream

As a child, I've never thought of having a dream, until I hit the age of ten. I started to watch animation movies and I liked it. For the past few years I was inspired to draw, but I never liked my own drawing. My creations didn't look like anything else out there so I gave up for a while.

Then my sister, a wise person, told me that no matter how hard or different my work is to keep on trying. Practice is all it takes. She has helped me to become a better artist. I have realized that it is my dream to become an artist.

People have always asked "Why do you want to become an artist?" Well, I want people to see the beauty of a drawing and understand it. I also want to express my thoughts and feelings when I draw a picture. The best part about being an artist is creating something that does not really exist. I use my imagination to draw and it helps me think about more ideas and be a better dreamer. My dream is what created my imagination, thoughts, feelings, and what made me keep the courage to continue dreaming.

When I accomplish my dream my parents will be proud of me. I will be proud of myself; accomplishing such a dream is special. It will be the greatest time in my life if I get to realize my dream.

Sandy Lor, Grade 9
Mount Airy High School, NC

American Idol Country Pop Singer

During 2004 Carrie auditioned for *American Idol*. She was always placed second place. Eventually, Carrie Underwood and Bo Bice made it through finals and on May 25, 2005, Carrie was crowned the winner. Simon Cowell predicted that Carrie would not only win, but will outsell all the previous Idol winners. Carrie Underwood became a country pop singer. She had won the fourth season of *American Idol*. Carrie was the first *American Idol* winner of all three major music awards in the same awards show.

Carrie Marie Underwood was born in Checotah, Oklahoma, on March 10, 1983. She grew up on her parents' farm. Carrie has two older sisters, Shanna and Stephanie Underwood. She is the third youngest daughter of Stephan and Carole Underwood. She is a kind and loving person. She's openhearted to others, and has a great sense of humor. Carrie has long blonde hair, and brown eyes, and she's really beautiful. Carrie Underwood's personal interests are her skilled guitar talents. Carrie is also a vegetarian, she stopped consuming beef at the age of 13. Also she has supports that Humane Society of the United States, and has done a lot of public service announcements for the organization. Carrie Underwood is a beautiful singer and has made the state of Oklahoma very proud.

Arika Lee, Grade 8
Chelsea Jr High School, OK

Preacher Roe: When Baseball Was Still a Game

Many kids today probably have never heard of Preacher Roe, but if you ever go to the Baseball Hall of Fame, you will see his name and number amongst the greatest players ever. He played baseball when it was still just a game.

Preacher was born in a simple town called Ash Flat, Arkansas on February 26, 1916. His real name was Elwin C. Roe, and he grew up to live the American dream.

At age 23, Preacher was recruited for the St. Louis Cardinals by Frank Rickey to play in the minors. In 1944, he started his major league career for Pittsburgh. However, in 1948, it was the beginning of a whole new season in Preacher's life. He started playing for the Brooklyn Dodgers, and the very next year, he played in his first of three World Series. In game two of the 1949 World Series, Preacher pitched a shut-out game against the Yankees' legendary "Murderers' Row." Then three years later, he played in the 1952 World Series and later on played in the 1953 World Series.

Preacher never had anything bad to say about the sport when asked about his career in later years. To him, it was an honor to play with legendary players like Jackie Robinson and Roy Campanella and to pitch against the all-time greatest hitter Stan Musial. According to Preacher, baseball was nothing but good to him, and he played not for money but for the love of the game.

Alexander Lee Miller, Grade 7
Stroud Middle School, OK

From High School to the Bigs

Have you ever heard of a Super Bowl MVP named Troy Aikman? He grew up in Henryetta, Oklahoma. He went to college at Oklahoma University his freshman year, but got hurt and was not going to play in his sophomore year so he wisely transferred to University of California at Los Angeles.

Troy Aikman stood out in college, winning four awards in 1988 including first team All-American, finished third in the Heisman voting, won the O'brien award, and ranked fourth in the nation in passer rating. Troy Aikman finished his two years at UCLA with 406 completions, 627 attempts, 5298 yards passing, 64.8% completion rating, 41 touchdowns, and 17 interceptions. Then he went on to the National Football League, to play for the Dallas Cowboys. Troy Aikman has played with a lot of talented teammates including Emmitt Smith. You may even know Troy Aikman from his famous quote when he won the Super Bowl, "I'm going to Disneyland!"

He is one of my favorite football players to ever play in the NFL because he is still nice and kind to the competition, he is often found consulting with other players after the game and congratulating them on being a part of a great game win or lose.

Austin Gill, Grade 8
Chelsea Jr High School, OK

Look Towards Life

As I stared down at the ground which seemed to be a mile away, I realized how far up I was. I was about to jump, but inside I was still hoping someone would talk me out of it. This was the first time I had ever dared to try a zip-line. I closed my eyes and stepped off into the unknown. As I soared through the air, I knew I would gladly volunteer to do it again.

This experience has given me confidence to take a leap into what I have not ever before experienced. Even though it may be frightening, I find it can be fun and exciting to try new things. Last year, I went out of state to a week long missions camp 500 miles from home. While at missions camp, I helped a group of inner city kids and slept in a college dorm, but the fact that I was so far away from home was the scariest thing of all. The experience was new for me, but I was glad I decided to go.

In the future, I will strive to experience new opportunities, knowing they may benefit me. When something new presents itself, I will think of the zip-line and the missions trip and remember the exhilaration that came from each. Every inexperienced incident will come to me as a challenge, something waiting to be accomplished, something that will help me later on in life.

Shawn Wu, Grade 7
White Station Middle School, TN

Acceptance

When you walk into a restaurant, do you ever notice someone may be a little different? Maybe it might be someone with a disability. Some may stare or feel terribly sympathetic towards that person, but they are people just like you and me. Just because they are having a hard time in class or are just in their own world does not mean we can look down on them. They are our equal. Rather than staring, try to understand what it's like for a change. They should not have to adjust to society.

I have a younger sister with Down syndrome. She may struggle in school or have a hard time learning the sports drill, but I believe we should make it easier on her socially. She should not fear failing, being judged, or being ridiculed just because that is who she is. She should not be made fun of because she loves a certain dance move, and she deserves to make friends normally not because she has Downs. When she becomes an adult, there should be no job discrimination just because she cannot learn a task as fast.

There are great organizations and programs that are helping people with disabilities to fit into society across the United States. I believe we should lend a hand or at least try to understand.

Abby Stewart, Grade 8
St Gerard Majella School, MO

The Wonderful Gift of Wisdom

Wisdom is the gift that allows us to see the world and all that is in it through God's eyes. To have wisdom you must be baptized because you receive the Holy Spirit at Baptism. All smart people do not necessarily possess wisdom, but most people that possess wisdom are smart because they were seeing the world as God sees it.

I practice wisdom by praying before meals and before I get out of bed and when I go to bed at night. I am baptized so I have received wisdom and soon I will be confirmed which lets me exploit wisdom more fully. These will all help me become close to God and help me become a wiser person.

Wisdom is important in my life because it is a tool I was given by God, so I want to make him proud and use every bit of it. If at baptism, God gives you Wisdom, why wouldn't you do your best to use it? I want to fulfill this virtue to get closer with God and make him proud. I am not going to waste my gift that I received at Baptism from God through the Holy Spirit. Wisdom is important because it comes from God and makes me a better person.

Emily Spitzmiller, Grade 8
St Mary's School, SC

The Greatest Winter Sport on the Planet

Snowboarding is a very fun and addictive winter sport. It is a combination of surfing and skateboarding where the rider travels downhill on a board made of fiberglass, laminated plastic, wood, and aluminum. Along with a board, the rider must wear proper equipment, clothing, and eye protection. The rider must be physically fit to snowboard. This includes eating right, strong ankles and leg muscles, good balance, and the ability to react quickly. Snowboarding can be hazardous if abused, and lessons are a requirement before snowboarding.

Snowboarding was first established by Sherman Poppen and originally designed for his children. Poppen nailed two planks together for his children to slide downhill. The first true pioneers of snowboarding, Dimitrije Milovich or Jake Burton (founder of Burton Snowboards from Londonderry, Vermont), came up with new designs for snowboards and other equipment that we now know today.

Snowboarding is extremely hazardous if abused or done improperly. Thirty-five to forty snowboarders die every year because of improper technique, falling down, or just abusing the way they snowboard. Helmets, wrist guards, knee pads, and goggles must be worn when snowboarding to prevent being injured.

Snowboarding is very fun and safe (if done responsibly). It has become the favorite sport of many winter athletes, and competitions are held every winter. Many snowboarders are recognized for their talents.

Taylor Andrews, Grade 7
Stroud Middle School, OK

Summer Fun

This past summer was one of the most memorable summers of my life. Summer should never end because old friends remain and new friends are gained. Hanging with friends and taking vacations with the family were my summer activities.

A typical summer day for me is sleeping late and awaking to my phone buzzing. After my brutal awakening, I eat breakfast and then venture outside to start my day. My street is always alive with kids to hang with. After a tiring game of football, we adjourn to someone's house to play Xbox 360. One of our favorite awesome games we play is Halo. Eventually, we get bored and go see a movie. My friends and I always seem to find a place to spend the night no matter the occasion, even though our mothers aren't so willing.

Whether a vacation is at the beach, at a lake, or in the mountains, I always enjoy them. I prefer wake boarding in the cool, crisp, water early in the morning when the sun is rising at Lake Tenkiller. When I am in the mountains, I love the scent of fresh pine trees and to hear the swaying of the tree branches. Listening to waves crash against the shore soothes me at the beach. These are some of the peaceful noises and sites I remember each summer. Summertime fades away but I know it will always return!

Coalson Hagan, Grade 8
Heritage Hall School, OK

My Life Story

My name is Larry Henderson and my life revolves around sports. The hardest part is that I'm not real good at them. My father Larry Henderson Sr., by the way I forgot to mention that I am a Junior.

He was always in books and was never good at any sports either. That's what my family tells me. He died when I was five years old. I think my half sister was two or going on two. They tell me don't let his death stop one from doing what I want to do in life. The fact is that it's very hard to do that sometimes. Because I think about him all day every day, everything's hard.

Another reason my life is hard because of the responsibilities I have at my home. My mom is a single parent and works very hard to have the stuff I and my little brother's need to have. That leaves me to watch them five days out of the week. She works from seven in the morning 'til seven in the evening. So I get up in the mornings to get my little brother dressed. After school I make sure that somebody's at home to watch them 'cause I have football practice. But when mother needs something done football comes last. Like if she tell me she needs me to get groceries I go straight home, get the car and go get groceries.

She tells me that she wouldn't know what to do without me and that I'm her angel.

Larry James Henderson Jr., Grade 8
Seminole County Middle/High School, GA

Ripped Pants

One steaming, hot afternoon Pierce, Jessica and I all decided to hang out. We met up by the clubhouse we had built a few weeks before. We walked around the block until one of us had an idea.

"Let's play tag!"

Pierce sat there as if we had two heads, but we decided to play. To see who it was, we had to use our only method, which was rock, paper, scissors, and SHOOT! I was not it, nor Jessica, but Pierce. We ran while Pierce counted lurking for a spot to hide. Jessica had picked the shed and I had picked the woods.

Jessica and I had waited for about 30 seconds 'til we heard, "READY OR NOT, HERE I COME!" We became so anticipated I could hear Jessica breathing, because the shed and the woods were very close. Then at that very second I tugged on my pants, but they were STUCK. Stuck on the tree, I tugged, tried to lift up, but no use. I just had to do it, RIP MY PANTS. I hauled out of the yard as fast as I could, and grabbed the remaining part of my pants. I got home, put some pants on, and stayed home for a day or week. Who was counting? I stayed until the news passed over, but I guess it never did because Pierce said, "Hey I saw you," and he giggled.

Kayla Deeren, Grade 7
Osceola Creek Middle School, FL

Singing

Many people have told me that I have a naturally higher register, much to my surprise, but I've had trouble learning how to use it. I sing the lower notes down in my chest. To hit the higher notes I have to switch into my head voice. What usually happens to me is I get nervous and the note gets caught in my throat. My throat can't sustain that high note and my voice cracks. I've improved since I have started taking lessons, but I'm still far from perfect.

Most to singing, like any other form of performing, is confidence. If you were to walk into an audition and sing, act, and dance with confidence you would really stand out to that director because they know they can ask you to do anything without worrying about your insecurities. If you seem nervous and timid they will be a little more wary of casting you. You have to be willing to step out of your shell and really perform with character and energy. Confidence when I sing is most likely what needs the most work. I've always been comfortable acting and dancing in front of a packed audience, but singing is not the same. I'm trying to start small and work my way up to more people with more difficult songs. It's going to take a lot of singing and time, but it's worth it if it will help me grow as a performer.

Alex Davies, Grade 8
Heritage Hall School, OK

Roller Coaster Tycoon

Roller Coaster Tycoon in one of the best games ever. There are many tricks, though. You need to know how to organize your park. You need to have some staff, too. Lastly, you need to know how much to charge the people. These three things are the keys to success.

You need to know how to organize your park. You need the right amount of rides. They all need to be in the right places. If they are all squished together, there will be no room to walk. Last, there has to be both roller coasters and kiddie rides.

You need staff to keep your park in tip-top shape. You will need handymen, mechanics, security guards and entertainers. You can't have too many of each though. Then your park would be overflowing. Also, you need to set them in certain places. You do this by clicking the footprints.

Last, you need to know how much to charge for everything. At first, entry tickets should start at $1, but go up. Also, never charge more than $.30 a ride except on the Log Flume. Last, you never go over $55 for entry tickets. If you do, no one will come.

In conclusion, there are many tricks to *Roller Coaster Tycoon*. How to organize your park is a huge help. Just the right amount of staff is also important. Also, never charge too much for anything. With all of this knowledge, your park will be a huge success.

Robby Kinsley, Grade 7
Sebastian River Middle School, FL

My Life

I was born in Colquitt, Georgia on July 28, 1994. My mother's name is Beverly; she's an LPN at the Donalsonville Hospital. My father's name is Henry; he's a mechanic at Mike's Auto Sales. He has fourteen kids, and my mom has four. I don't know all my brothers and sisters, but I know some of them. My brother Allen is good at sports; he's 6'1" and only fourteen. Johnny is 18 and he's just as short as me. Everlyn stays on the phone all day. I have a dog named Dj.

I am a tomboy so I can be pretty rough. I became a tomboy because I used to play with Allen all the time. He was my best friend. Once I was at Allen's football game and I was playing on the swing and I jumped off and turned around and it hit me on the head.

I have two best friends named Zaqayvia and Marquitta. Zaqayvia talks a lot so there is always something new she's telling me. Marquitta is always laughing and has a smile on her face. I love them both. I love to read, so I will always have a book with me.

After I finish college and get a job, I want to get a big house. I am an artist. I really like to draw, but just for fun. I like to bake too. I have everything a kid could want, and a bright future ahead of me, so I wouldn't change it.

Bridgett Glenn, Grade 8
Seminole County Middle/High School, GA

My Guitar

My guitar is a very special object to me. It's what I use to make my music; my passion. The day I got it was like no other. I was hoping to get it for Christmas, but did not. So I thought, "Okay, maybe I'll get it for my birthday." On my birthday, after I got home from school, my mom told my dad to go get that 'thing' out of his truck. I'd already seen the big box through the window, so I had an idea of what it was. After I opened it, sure enough, a black Talman TCY10 was staring back at me. I was so excited! The thing I'd dreamt of for months was finally in my hands. When I play it, I have a rush of joy. The acoustics are amazing. I've never heard a guitar with such a beautiful sound. I feel like this guitar is the key to my success. In between practice sessions I gawk at its distinction. Just looking at it is a sight to see. The marvel is black with white trimming. It's shaped like an electric guitar, with the feeling of an acoustic. I've always imagined myself up on stage, playing the guitar. If I had to think of one thing wrong with it, I couldn't. Because of its merit, it's perfect for me. When it comes down to it, there's only one thing to say: I'm in love with my guitar.

Brandon Rambo, Grade 7
White Station Middle School, TN

Otto Flasch

My Oklahoma hero is my great-grandfather, Otto Flasch. Otto was born on January 3, 1909 on a farm near Pleasant Valley, Oklahoma (near Coyle, Oklahoma). He had perseverance, he was strong, and he was kind to everyone. He lived to be 97 years old when he died on July 29, 2006. In that time, he led a great life and set an excellent example to live by.

Grandpa was a person of great physical and mental strength. He farmed wheat all of his life. When he farmed, he would work a long 48 hour shift on a tractor. He was also strong because even in his old age, he could still drive a four-wheeler.

Grandpa was the kindest person I knew. In all the years I knew him, I never heard him say a curse word. He never talked bad about anyone behind their back. He did anything he could to help our church. He was generous and he gave away all of his extra crops that he didn't need.

Grandpa had great perseverance. He never gave up when the doctors found out that he had diabetes. He was still happy when he knew that he could never walk again. He always looked for the good in things when things seemed to go wrong for him.

My grandpa was the greatest person I knew. People might think that it's strange to look up to my grandpa, but he really was the greatest person I knew.

Joseph Beck, Grade 8
Mulhall-Orlando High School, OK

Never too Old!

The crowd roars, as a Hall of Famer, Troy Kenneth Aikman achieves the goal of being the third all-time touchdown passes against the Buffalo Bills in 1990.

Troy has a commanding presence on the field with him being 6'4 and weighing in at 220 pounds. His blonde hair barely hangs out of his mask.

Before playing with the Dallas Cowboys, he was a star for his high school team, the Henryetta Knights. Then, after graduating he got a diploma at Oklahoma University. While there, he fractured his arm. He got replaced by the second string quarterback. So he decided to go to UCLA.

His first year there, he decided to sit out a season and then start fresh the next year. His third year there he got drafted to the pros. There he went and played for the Dallas Cowboys.

Troy achieved a lot of goals that he never thought he could. He had the most touchdown passes, the most consecutive completions and so much more. Troy Aikman is one of the most famous athletes from Oklahoma.

Now Aikman is moving on with his life and spending more time with his family. Aikman will always remember the fun and the excitement he spent through his football years.

Destany Wooten, Grade 8
Chelsea Jr High School, OK

The Game

I finally got to the game. It was Tuesday, September 25, 2007. My baseball team was playing at Cal Ripken on Field Two. We were looking to improve our record to two and one.

We started the game and I was placed behind the plate at catcher. Our team had a loss when our starter had been hurt and now was unable to play. We had only nine players but we were forced to go on.

We started the game at 6:00 PM. As the game progressed, I realized that our pitcher was struggling to throw strikes, but by the time he calmed down, the other team had scored two runs. After struggles at the plate, my team finally scored in the fourth inning.

We came out to the field with a one run deficit in the top of the fifth inning. To our detriment, we gave up two runs, but finally ended the inning. After the next inning, it was the bottom of the sixth and we were down three runs. Although we yelled and cheered, we couldn't will our team to victory.

The game had ended and our team was in great disarray. We had lost the game four to one. I was very disappointed because I had gone zero for two with two pop outs. After the coach gave us a talk, we left. The game was over, nothing left to do.

Jonny Corin, Grade 7
Goldie Feldman Academy, FL

That's Life

I was in a mood, and it wasn't just any mood. I wanted to do something spontaneous and independent. Really, I was supposed to be getting ready for bed, yet a scrumptious brownie was jostling through the jumble of thoughts in my mind, becoming so vivid, I could taste its sweet flavour on my tongue. Jump-started, my imagination took flight. *I could make a brownie with 20 layers!!* I thought. However, the recipe demanded I stick with only five.

Furrowing my brow and scrutinizing the complex recipe, I felt a great weight upon my shoulders. Baking has been a way of life for generations in my family; this had to be good. Adrenaline coursing through my veins, I assured myself that with my baking acumen, and with all the delicious things I had made, what could go wrong?

After two days of baking toil, however, I had made the most disgusting, the driest, and the *worst* brownies I have and hopefully will ever make. The results had nothing to do with my mixing, stirring, melting, or spreading. The culprit here was simply a bad recipe.

One may think I went home a sad girl, but really, I think this is an amusing tale of life's true colours. Setting foot into uncharted territory has its risks. But being able to laugh off failure and keep trying is a skill I value in myself. When I fall off the bike I have to get right back on again. That's what life's about, isn't it?

Natalia Lutterman, Grade 7
White Station Middle School, TN

How Youth Force Changed My Life

When I signed up for our church mission trip called Youth Force, I only wanted to go because I thought it would be fun. We got to go to Clinton for a week working on houses and hanging with our friends. However, once I arrived at the house we were going to fix and met the owner, I realized there was much, much more to this trip than just having fun. Our home owner was in her late 80s, early 90s, whose husband had died. She lived in a small home shared occasionally by her sister. Her garage door was falling apart, her favorite porch swing was broken, and her fences along with her porch were rotting. Apart from that, her yard was a mess and very trashy. After each work day and after we had taken our showers, we returned to the church and hung out before dinner. Each night we had worship, in which at the end, each church had a banner, and on it, we wrote how we saw God that day. I hadn't realized it, but I had seen God a lot during that week, and it took that God sighting banner each night to show that. When the week was over, our homeowner came out, saw what we did and cried. It was then that I realized that even the littlest things that we did for her meant a lot. I think that not only did she get something out of this, but so did I.

Jake Odgers, Grade 8
Heritage Hall School, OK

Mookie

They had come back. They had always been there, just hidden and forgotten. Then one day they began to eat away at her soul once again.

On the back porch of her home, she laid resting on a soft, warm blanket. Panting, her body swollen with fluid, she listened to the cricket chirps whistling through the night. Her mother and her sister rested by her side fighting the sensation to cry, for they knew that this would be their last time with her. The air was thick with sorrow. She lay with a heavy heart; she knew that it was time for her to go.

She slowly started towards the back yard, her head hung low. Her sister sat up and started to follow behind her, but the gentle dame turned around and stopped to look at her. They stood face to face and stared into each other's eyes. She touched her sister's nose with hers, as if to say "good-bye," and she proceeded into the caliginous garden. She found a dark, soft patch of grass and laid herself down to sleep. Her breaths got softer and softer, until she finally took her last breath.

She was my dog Mookie. Mookie was a very calm and loving dog, but she was also an old dog with heart worms. She died on September 12, 2006. Although she is gone, the memory of Mookie still lingers on today.

Kierra Male, Grade 8
Oakbrook Middle School, SC

Following Your Dreams

There are many dreams that never come true. There are also dreams that mean so much to people that they put forth every single day trying to make it real. I, myself, am a dream follower. I have dreams that I want to do and I do my best to pursue them. People who think negative and don't believe their dream will come true, are what I like to call, give-uppers. Quitters think that their dreams don't matter. They just give themselves the worst possible reason why their dream isn't going to come true. Some people have so many dreams that they want to come true, but when they don't come true because it's too late, they start doubting what they are able to do. If you are very serious about a dream, you should give it time to come true and work your way up to that dream. Your dream isn't going to come true if you don't work for it. Many of life's greatest heroes came from following their dreams. They have dreams, stick to them, follow them, and succeed in life. Dreams aren't just a thought that can be erased at any time. They create your future, and it's what makes life important. It's the key to designing the importance of your future.

You need your dreams for a good future. You need your future for a good life.

Brianna Irby, Grade 7
Greenhill Elementary School, MS

Life

Life as we know is changing. People's ideas are changing. Our beliefs are changing. In all, some change is good. Some is bad. It depends really on your perspective. But life in general should be valued and enjoyed. We must respect ours and others' lives. I think we should live our lives to the fullest extent but, we must not damage anything else because there are others who will come after us. I believe God put us on this Earth because he believes we can do good for it. We should fulfill God's wish because there are many ways we can. Now I'm not just talking about recycling and all. I'm talking about being a good person. Not PERFECT but good!

If we could just take five minutes each day to smile at someone or just sit down and talk, that could be the key to stopping them from running into a building with a gun and killing everybody. Just the small things in life could make a big impact. Life is so short, so why waste it? As I said earlier we must live life but, we must live it good. Now the thing I don't understand is how could someone just take their life or someone else's? NOTHING in life could EVER be that bad! Another thing is if something in life seems bad there is someone worse off than you. Life is a very, very precious gift. Don't waste it.

Kelly Onstad, Grade 7

I Love Lucy

In life a person will face an assortment of trials and pain…but during these time it's nice to have a person, who will always love and support you; a person who will tell you, "Don't worry Chibee."

The most influential person to me is my five year old sister, Lucy. She has such a quirky, fun-loving little personality. She has auburn hair with a slight curl, big brown eyes and a stunning smile.

Since she was a little baby, she always had trouble pronouncing my name and so she called me Chibee. Now at age five my nickname is Chibee.

My sister and I have always been too close for words. We are not the type of siblings that quarrel, or fight. We are the type that has a secret handshake that really has no meaning. Sometimes we play cowgirl and horse…she is the cowgirl; I am the horse.

When she is scared, I sing her favorite song, "Gospel Train." One day she boldly decided she's not going to school because she feared the fire drill, I helped her forget about her fear.

Lucy is also there for me, too in her own special way. When I am in a fight with my friends, Lucy is still my very best buddy. She always comes and greets me when I get home from school and it is always the highlight of my day. I love my sister more than anything; she is my friend, my teacher and my little cowgirl.

Christopher VanDemark, Grade 9
Countryside High School, FL

The War in Iraq

When fighting in a war, what does a belligerent country gain? The country *loses* the support and trust of other nations. Other resources lost include people and money. Did you know that the cost of the war in Iraq is about $453.8 billion dollars and rising every second? Also since the capture of Saddam (12/13/03) the total amount of casualties in Iraq ranges from 3000 to 3500.

The entire mission of the war in Iraq is to 'support' and 'stabilize' the Iraqi government. Nearly 12 million Iraqi's cast their ballots for a unified and democratic nation, but yet in 2006, the opposite happened. The violence in Iraq overwhelmed the political gains the Iraqi government made. Al Qaeda terrorists and Sunni insurgents realized the threat Iraq's elections posed for their cause, and responded malicious acts of murder aimed at innocent Iraqi citizens.

We are fighting in Iraq to give peace to innocent citizens, but how much will *peace* cost? Our soldiers are fighting in foreign lands so Americans can be free in our home country. The war on terror, as it is called, has sparked the steepest increases in extra military funding in two decades. Since our country has declared war, the government has approved about $110 billion additional funding. Around 4000 casualties have occurred in Iraq since the war began in 2003. So I ask you again, what does a belligerent country gain in a war? The country gains security and freedom, but tragic losses also occur.

Nicholas L. Tennant, Grade 7
North Iredell Middle School, NC

My Inspiring Friendship

To most people, friendship is a safety net that you know you have, but before you know it, that safety net slips right out from under you. Getting the news that your friend you've known for your whole life is moving is like a big slap in the face. Not only does it hurt, but it can leave a scar on your heart forever. Even though you know you'll stay in touch, it still doesn't patch up that big hole that is left.

My friends inspire me to be the best that I can be and strive to do better every day. This one friend in particular is especially inspiring. She has been with me through the ups and downs of our lives. She know when to say something and when to just stay silent. If you truly care, you will not walk in front of or behind me, but just walk beside me and be my friend. This special girl has walked beside me ever since we first met, even though we didn't know it.

Even though it's hard to manage when you lose special people, we know we'll make it out all right in the end. True friends will the good of each other and will always help you out. So if I ever feel discouraged, I always know that my friends will try their best to be there for me and I will do the best I can to be there for them.

Katherine Reynolds, Grade 7
St Mary's School, SC

Baseballs and Forest Don't Mix

"Hit it out of the field, Sammy!" Gloria shrilled at the nervous, wobbly-kneed child in the baking sun, ready to hit the ball. "No, no! The other way," Ashley ushered her teammate to sprint in the correct direction. It was two against four. One pitching with three in the outfield; one on second base and another up to bat. Dogs were yapping and barking as excitement crackled in the air like lightning. As I readied my pitch cheers and screams were thrown my way in a gust of breath. I swung that ball like there was no tomorrow. Sam socked the ball with all her might and it soared through the air then, THUD! It hit the ground when it landed in a mass of pines and brambles. Luckily, my faithful dog Dexter, charged into the undergrowth with a rustle. That's when the yelps and cries of pain shot out from the trees, tearing at my heart. Dexter had stumbled into a raccoon's den. I tried to dash toward the towering forest but I was held back by my mother. Soon, what felt like forever, a black mane of torn fur and scratched muzzle and pelt limped out of the bushes. A triumphant shine in his eyes as he lumbered forward, head held high, the baseball a trophy for his deed. After some shots, ointments, and a little TLC he was back on the field ready to face whatever came out of the unforgiving tangle of shrubs.

Courtney McGowan, Grade 7
Osceola Creek Middle School, FL

What Makes Me Unique?

My voice, my smile, my ears, my style. All of these things make me unique. Think about it, if I looked and acted like you, would I be unique? No, not at all.

My name is Danielle Maxine Parker. The name sounds pretty boring right? Yeah, it does. But the girl behind the name is far from it. My loud and boisterous personality makes you think I'm loud, obnoxious, and self-centered. Actually, I'm far from it. Unique, funny, fun, silly, caring, athletic, outspoken, and crazy. Yes, I know it's a lot, but that's me. Danielle Maxine, only one me.

If everyone tried to be somebody else, what would the world be like? There would be mass chaos in people bickering about who is who. A grotesque image flashes in my mind just thinking about it. How can we prevent this? Look yourself in the mirror, and say, "I am unique and special in my own way." Just as I do to embrace me in all my uniqueness.

So again, back to what I was saying, what makes me unique? The fact that I love myself, and declare it every morning, afternoon, and night, and THAT MAKES ME UNIQUE! Danielle Maxine, yup that's me, and that's all I can be, and that's me.

Danielle Parker, Grade 9
Overton High School, TN

Videogames and Books

Have you ever visited far off kingdoms or traveled atop a vicious dragon while enemies close in around you? I have with two very simple things. Books and videogames are a great source of fun and cure of boredom. Sometimes when I am really bored, I visit several different places in a matter of minutes. Without books and videogames, my life would not be as fun or as eventful so maybe you will change your attitude toward them if you do not want a boring life.

Books and videogames, there are so many good things to say about them I do not know where to begin. How about this, you are standing outside the stronghold of an evil king. Thousands of men in shining steel armor are standing around you. Suddenly from above you hear an order given; then a hailstorm of arrows and the battle begins. This is not a real book phrase or a part of any particular videogame, but it gives you are pretty good idea about what you can experience.

So as you can see, books and videogames take you to far and exciting worlds, if you take the time to use them. This is one of the many reasons they are important to me. See, not only are both of them great sources of fun, but you can learn at the same time.

Parker Pearce, Grade 7
Greenfield Jr/Sr High School, MO

The First Robotics Program

The First Robotics Program is a wonderful opportunity for kids to get involved with science and technology. It was founded by Dean Kamen, who was responsible for the Segway. The program is offered for kids aging from seven to eighteen, and is divided into four leagues.

For ages ten to fourteen the FFL (First LEGO League) is offered. In this league the teams build and program a robot using LEGO brand software, motors and pieces. They are given a theme each year and an eight by four game mat on which challenges made of LEGOs are placed. They then program the robot they build to complete these challenges. The teams do a presentation on the current theme as well, which means that they do a power point or skit and present it to a panel of judges. They are also judged on the technical aspects of their robots. This means that local engineers look at the robots and see just how much the teams actually know about the mechanics of their bot. All teams compete in regional tournaments. There is only one winner, but there are other awards as well, like the best presentation, and best programming strategy, team spirit, things like that. But what all teams compete for is the coveted Directors Award. The teams that win this award then proceed to the World Festival in Atlanta Georgia against teams from other countries. The tournaments are run exactly the same, but on a much larger scale.

Michael Bush, Grade 9
West Jr High School, MO

Use Your Super Hero Power

Do you remember that Skittles commercial? The people are always sitting at the top of a rainbow eating Skittles. Why can't you do that, too? Everyone has seen the commercials where you can change your whole room with the press of a button. Why can't that happen? Anything can happen, if you can believe.

Imagination is the key to making things happen. If you want to sit on a rainbow, why not! Changing your room with a button, no problem! When you use your imagination, anything is possible. To tell you the truth, while this is being written, I am sliding down a rainbow reading a book.

For those of you who think imagination is overrated or not cool, I have some news for you. Imagination is about having fun. If it is not cool, then I guess you're no fun. Every once and a while it is fun to try something new. Try imagining yourself riding a bull, or fighting a giant dragon, or climbing a mountain with no gear but suction cups.

No matter where you are, imagination is there. Even for some jobs, you are required to use your imagination. For example, if you want to design houses, you need imagination to make your dream house come to life.

Using your imagination is your super power. It is much better than any super hero's power because imagination is real, and it always will be.

Amanda Schmelzle, Grade 8
St Gerard Majella School, MO

P.A.T.

My two best friends and I are extremely close. We call ourselves P.A.T., for Paige, Audrey, and Taylor. We will be best friends forever and ever. All three of us are unique and we know how to enjoy ourselves.

We love to do so many strange things. Reciting lines from Napoleon Dynamite is part of our everyday lives. In fact, Paige and I made our own remix of that movie. Taylor and I are easily entertained. Locking ourselves in the bathroom and acting like we are going to battle, is just one of the incredibly odd things we do. Just recently we learned how to three-way our phones. Now we are always talking even if we are not together. Our parents were not exactly thrilled with that discovery. We like all the same things. Sports, food, and sleepovers are some of our favorites. We laugh and giggle more than anyone could imagine possible. For Halloween we are planning to be nuns. As you can see we are not your normal trio.

I have amazing friends. Whether it is talking on the phone for hours or making our own version of awesome movies, my two best friends and I always know how to have fun. I love being a part of P.A.T.!

Audrey LaSalle, Grade 7
Greenfield Jr/Sr High School, MO

Safe Haven

A sanctuary is rare. Everyone needs a place to get away from the daily troubles of life. The heavens begin to sing every Friday as the doors to the University of Memphis open. As fast as cheetahs, people file in to prepare for the five hours ahead. Why are they here? To play chess of course!

My friends and I wait for this time; finally, it's here, six forty-five. When I sit at the board, all my troubles seem to fade away. As the game goes by, all I see are the board, pieces, and my opponent pulling his hair out in frustration. As time flies, the clock strikes ten. Faces are sagging and pieces dropping. Now eleven o'clock, my adversary and I are neck to neck, eye to eye. As the tension gets to him, he careens off to get a glass of water. I make my move and see him gallivanting back to the table. Time is thinning, and we are both playing in rapid succession. Mistakes are being made, but not caught. The final blow is yet to come.

Finally the clock strikes twelve. The time has come. With a smirk I play my move and say checkmate. After a collision of hands and murmurs of good game, I exit the chess dimension. Now as you can clearly see, the game of chess is important to me. For most a sanctuary comes once a year, but for me, once a week.

Jason A. Gupta, Grade 7
White Station Middle School, TN

Importance of Literature

Studying literature is important because we need to know our history in order to survive. There are many reasons for studying literature. The main reason is so that we can have knowledge of our past and learn from the mistakes of others and in result, have a better future. Another reason about the importance of studying literature is that it tells you about time periods that we didn't live in so we have a chance to see what it was like to live at that time.

Learning about our history to have a better future is important in many ways. Reading about mistakes that happened in the past will really help to improve our lives. Even if things went well at times, there is always room for improvement.

Our history is very important to learn. But, most people haven't lived for two hundred years or more. So, we must rely on literature to teach us about the past and learn what it was like to live a long time ago. If we don't know what it was like to live a long time ago, then we will never know what went wrong.

As you can see, studying literature is very important, and should still be taught, read, and learned a long time from now. I am very thankful I have the opportunity to study literature and I will keep reading so I will obtain knowledge and be successful in the future.

Nicole Carlson, Grade 8
Heritage Hall School, OK

My Family

My family is the most important thing to me. They love me, they take care of me and they keep a close eye on me. They are the most important thing out of millions of other stuff like game systems, video games, television, and even amusement parks such as Disney World, Universal Studios, Islands of Adventure and Bush Gardens. Compare all this stuff to your family. Do amusement parks feed you, does television watch you, did video games take care of you? The only people that ever did anything for you was all from your family.

Everything in the world has a purpose; amusement parks are to have fun, video games are for playing when there's nothing to do, and getting money is for buying stuff you need. And the purpose for your family is to love you and take care of you. I can't believe some people actually worship money. Also I've seen my friends they stay on their video games playing *Halo 3* for a whole day. Besides everything you get is from your family like video games, television, going to amusement parks, and getting food. If your family struggles to take care of you and you don't care about them you go up to your parents and you give them the best day they ever had ok. And you treat them with respect, because the only reason any person is here are because of their parents.

Abdul El-Noursi, Grade 7
Kernan Middle School, FL

Thrills and Chills

Do you ever have that excited feeling that almost makes you sick? Well that is the feeling that I get when I was at the Tulsa State Fair, especially right before I get on a gigantic frightening ride. Don't get me wrong, I love gigantic frightening rides, it's just that I always get butterflies in my stomach.

Like this one time when I rode this ride that takes you to the top and drops you. It is so freaky. However, after you get off you are ready to do it again, but I was shaking like a leaf. I looked over at my grannie and she was laughing. So then, I started laughing even though it was not that funny. Anyway, back to my story.

After, that we got something to eat, I love to eat the fair's baked potatoes. They are so yummy especially with sour cream, butter, shredded cheese and chopped up lettuce, it makes my mouth water just thinking about it.

Of course, my grannie had to look in the exhibit buildings so we looked for about thirty minutes, after that we went back outside to go ride. We rode a few rides then my grannie had twenty tickets and sold them for ten dollars. Just because she said it was time to head home.

The Tulsa State Fair was amazing. In addition, I miss the thrills and chills and I will never forget the baked potatoes.

Emma Pilkington, Grade 7
Chelsea Jr High School, OK

A Goal and a Dream Are Different

A goal is something you set and can achieve. Often a dream is very far-fetched and may never be reachable. Let's say you had a dream that you were the king/queen of England, that would never happen. If your gal was to go to college and become a physician, that could happen if you tried really hard to do so. Dreams are often what people do when they don't set goals. They should stop dreaming about what could be. Next time you catch yourself dreaming, stop and think of a goal you can set for yourself and follow that goal. You may find that it will help you in your future. I used to dream all the time and my dreams were never answered; as I got older, I set a goal to make good grades in school so I would graduate. Ever since then, I have been making great grades and I love the feeling of reaching my goal. I have even set a new goal to go to college and become a veterinarian. As you can see, I easily could have dreamt this, but I would not have expected myself to accomplish this on my own. I would have expected my dream to just happen, and let's face it, that would never happen. A goal is different from a dream.

Kayla Burlette, Grade 9
Grandview Alternative School, MO

Why Music Is Important to the World

There is one main thing that can shape the way the world runs. Although seemingly impossible, that thing is music. Music is the universal language, the same no matter where you are. Everyone understands it, and it's the only way for efficient conversation from one nation to another.

At times, music is a very controversial subject. The message that songs put across can possibly affect the world in a negative way. Songs that degrade any race, sex, nation, and so forth can actually make people feel that they are less than what they are. People need to stop making bad songs altogether. They need to put the hope, inspiration, and good times back into their lyrics.

Music is a great way to learn. You get better in math, science, and history with learning music. You can also get a better understanding of the rest of the world. Interests in music help you learn more about a person, too. Those interests can lead to friendships and companionships or just build them up even more.

The universal language can either make or break the world; lift or destroy your spirits. Although sometimes negative, music has an overall good effect on people. It changes the way you view the rest of the world and helps you understand that everyone is the same. No one is better than anyone else, we just all have different ways of expressing ourselves. Music is the only way of showing that, the only way that everyone will understand.

Courtney Cosby, Grade 9
Overton High School, TN

Becoming the Best You Can Be a Dancer's Life…

Many believe that when you are younger and beginning in the world of dance you should stick with teachers with similar teaching techniques. I believe if you have the chance you should explore what new teachers offer. Although moving out of your comfort zone may be challenging, a good dance class can be like a good meal, nutrition for the mind and body.

No matter who is teaching your class there are several helpful things that can get you ready for your classes. Beginning with being prepared, taking a few minutes before class to focus and relax your mind, also to stretch and warm up your body. Allow yourself to adjust to the class and the teacher. Pay close attention to the teacher's movements and steps. This will give you the confidence and a positive attitude about yourself. Make sure you enjoy your classes. Sometimes performers tend to focus on the final performance and miss out on their class time. While nobody wants to fall flat and make mistakes, you should always be open to try new things. Always set yourself goals, and try to stick with them. This will give you confidence onstage and off.

Although a lot of work, labor, aches, and sweat go into becoming a dancer, love and dedication always overrides any physical problems. Remember each time you walk into a dance class, you dance because it brings you pure joy and every movement is thrilling. A dancer's life is short, enjoy it now.

Haley Boatright, Grade 8
Southwest Jr High School, AR

The Love of Life

What's important to me? If I had to choose just one thing, it would be life. People say that money is the source of all happiness. It's not. Money is actually partly made of cotton. All of the plants, animals, and humans contain life.

Life is what we are. We are life. Animals eat plants, and other animals eat the animals that eat plants. Life fuels itself. Without life there wouldn't be anything. Not even death which claims the lives of everything living eventually.

Without life, we wouldn't be able to talk to friends or enjoy a weekend with our family. People say that life is pretty much just a bunch of chemical reactions, but it's more than that. I doubt that chemical reactions tell me how to think. That is our soul, the essence of life which death has no claim to. Our soul is immortal.

That is what I think is important. The instinct to hold on to life is burned deep into the hearts of every living being. That is what they talk about when they say, "the will to survive." For humans it's made us capable of advanced thought. For other animals it has honed their hunting or foraging skills to something more than we could ever have. Life is the basis of the universe.

Emily Campbell, Grade 7
Boyet Jr High School, LA

Marvelous Animals

There are three kinds of monkeys in this essay. One is the chimpanzee, a very smart creature with black fur, which eats leaves, nuts, fruit, and meat. Sometimes when a chimp can't crack a nut it gets a big rock or log and slams it on the nut, but young chimps aren't strong enough, so they have mom do it until they are. Baby chimps weigh 30-50 pounds; adult chimps weight 100-150 pounds.

The second kind of monkey is the gorilla, a very large creature, which also has black fur. The king of gorillas is the silver back which is like a president to the gorillas. Gorillas eat nuts and fruits and pretty much anything they can find. Baby gorillas weigh 60-100 pounds; adult gorillas weigh 450-500 pounds.

The third animal is the spider monkey. The spider monkey's scientific name is Ateles Geoffroy. Spider monkeys have brown bodies and dark limbs. Their hands and feet are black in color. The spider monkey usually has a tail longer than its own body. When the spider monkey is on the lookout, it stands on its two hind legs. The spider monkey is hanging by its tail 70% of its lifetime. The spider monkey rarely comes down to the forest floor. Spider monkeys live in the evergreen forests. The spider monkey is going extinct because of the human lifestyle of cutting down trees.

Nicky Renfrow, Grade 7
Stroud Middle School, OK

Attitude Worth Knowing

Whenever I'm having a gloomy or dreary day, my brotherly friend, Joseph, is always there to make me laugh my head off and forget about my dilemmas. Being one-in-a-million, his bubbly and priceless personality makes me enjoy every moment that we share together. Joe is an absolute burst of confetti among the bland world that makes me wonder why everyone else can't have a fraction of his personality. He is the one that pops out amid his large family, and greets everyone with a warm and inviting smile. It's people like Joe that make Earth seem so lively and amusing.

Being genial and cordial is so unimaginably essential to me that I consistently think, why can't everyone be so carefree and good-natured? The world can be so lifeless that it must be diverse enough to have a community with at least one person that can make things interesting, and once in a while, goofy. Even with just a sweet smile or joke, it is enough to keep any situation colorful and vibrant.

Such a boisterous and cheerful charisma is authentic and extremely genuine to me, which is why I cherish every person around me with that much enthusiasm. I know, because a person with such an animated personality only comes rarely in a lifetime. Therefore, I will always acknowledge people like that, because they are like a comet…coming unpredictably in and out of our lives.

Sarika Bhageratty, Grade 7
Bak Middle School of the Arts, FL

Friends

I love friends! To me that's how I make it through life. They keep you busy so you're not bored, or you can talk to them on the phone, and you can always trust them with real juicy secrets. When we spend time together I'm never down I'm very thrilled. I don't see what would happen if I didn't have them.

I am always with a friend. Whether it's one or twenty we are together forever. We are always having fun even if we're out in a hail storm, even if it is raining hail the size of mini vans. My friends and I like to spend the night together, that is a big part. That is the main part why I like friends.

Have you ever had a secret you had to tell someone, but if you told your parents you would get in trouble? I can tell my friends anything and they won't tell a soul. On some things I trust them more than my parents. As you see you can tell friends are very valuable.

The phone is a great way to communicate. As soon as I get home I call a friend. I could talk for hours! It is way better to talk in person than on the phone.

Can you see friends are important? If you have a friend you should be able to talk, or tell them secrets, or they should never keep you bored! I think if you can't do that stuff they are not good friends. That is three reasons they are important to me.

Sara Thomas, Grade 8
Pigeon Forge Middle School, TN

Having Your Dad as a Coach

This year and last year I have had my dad as a coach. Since he is my dad, he has to be harder on me than anyone else, but it doesn't really bother me as much. For example, a kid on our team does something wrong he gets in trouble, but if I did the same thing it would have been a lot worse. My dad isn't always mean, most of the time he is funny and nice. In spite of him being a little harder on me, he can help me if I am doing something wrong, or don't know what to do in a situation. He always makes things fun, unfortunately this year he isn't coaching 8th grade basketball. Just in case you are wondering what sports he coaches, he coaches: football, basketball, and track.

Most of the kids including me that have passed through when my dad was coaching like him the most of any coach. Coach Gaddis has been coaching at heritage hall since 1996. In addition to him being popular he also has great strategy. Another tough thing about having your dad as a coach you can't call him dad or something like that. This was hard for me to do most of last year. Lastly I would just like to say that I am lucky to have my dad as a coach, and this year especially I won't forget that.

Brent Gaddis II, Grade 8
Heritage Hall School, OK

My Grandpa and Pawpaw

This story is about my grandpa and pawpaw.

My pawpaw was on a Navy tug boat in the Bikini Islands in the Pacific Ocean. He was there for the atomic bomb testing. My pawpaw had to clean the boat because the chemicals from the atomic bombs fell on the boat.

My grandpa joined the Marines, when he was 17. He had already left for San Diego when his class received their diplomas.

He went to the Philippine Islands. The day after Pearl Harbor was bombed, the Philippines were attacked. Four months after fighting, they were captured by the Japanese. He traveled by a hell ship to a prison camp. Many men died on these ships. In the prison camp, he worked in coal mines. Over 3 1/2 years, he was tortured and starved. When he was rescued, he weighed 80 pounds. All this time, his parents didn't know if he was dead or alive.

I am proud of my grandpa and pawpaw for what they have done. They were so nice; you would never know they went through all of this. My grandpa received a lot of medals, but not the Purple Heart. My mom is trying to have my grandpa honored with the Purple Heart. The D-day Museum is going to be showing some of his things that we donated after he died in 2001. I am looking forward to seeing his things displayed there.

Gina Bouis, Grade 7
St Rita School, LA

An Angel Is Born

In 1938, a baby girl named Mary Frankie Adeline Beede was born in Leonard, Oklahoma. She had six brothers and sisters. She had a very close relationship with her family including her parents. She married Robert Cox in 1963, in Bixby, Oklahoma. They were married for 42 years. As my grandma, I loved her. She was very kind, always willing to help anyone in need and making a friend out of everyone she met. She was smart, by telling me when I was scared of tornadoes that there was nothing to be scared of and that nothing was going to happen to me. She was right.

She was also very beautiful. She had four children. The oldest is my father, Mike Cox, he has three children. Next is my uncle, Ronnie Cox, he also has three children. The only girl and third child is my aunt, Bobbie Jo Tilley, she has two daughters. The youngest is my other uncle, Marty Cox, so far he has two children. She and my grandpa were rarely found at home. They were either at work, a family member's house, or a friend's house. My grandparents spent most of their time as a married couple in each other's company. If they were not traveling to California to visit us, they could be found painting someone's house. My grandma Mary died January 15, 2006. If she were alive today and had made it to Oklahoma's Centennial she would be 68 years old.

Mikey Cox, Grade 8
Chelsea Jr High School, OK

I Dare You

Have you ever strived to do something outrageous, something no one else would ever do? Well, then you must be pretty brave. A lot of people think being brave is amazing, and that is all they would ever want to be, but it doesn't have to be that way.

Being brave is great, but staying cautious is equally as great. You don't always have to go out on a limb and be the daredevil in the group, but stepping outside your shell is a good thing, as well. Do not think you have to be willing to do anything because that is definitely not the case. I think it's healthy for people to go out on a limb once in a while, but you never have to do anything you don't want to.

I learned in a program called D.A.R.E. to just say no, and that is okay. Never let anyone pressure you into something you don't want to do. The next time you see someone who you think you want to be like, don't. Be happy with who you are, and never let anyone pressure you into thinking differently because you are the best you can be and, most importantly, who you want to be.

Kristina Glassl, Grade 8
St Gerard Majella School, MO

Jack Zellner, an Intelligent Oklahoman

Jack Zellner is a tall, well-built man; he is tan with a well-shaven face. Jack has emerald green eyes with flecks of red and gold. Jack has dimples that dance across his face when he laughs. The most memorable, admirable thing about him is he always looks at the bright side of things. Jack is also a Cherokee Indian. He has an Indian card and has the Indian nose.

As a young adult Jack's role model was Jacques Cousteau. Every Sunday he would eagerly await the adventures of Jacques Cousteau, a famous French diver, on television. Later Jack would get a lifetime scuba divers license because of Jacques Cousteau's show's impact on his life.

Jack graduated valedictorian of Spartan. After college he did masonry and built houses. One of his fondest dreams he thought would never come true was being a father. Now he is a father of four. Jack Zellner is my father, my inspiration, and most of all, my reason to write.

His sarcasticness and positive outlook reflect a wonderful life because he always kept his chin up. One of his quotes is "I spent a great deal of my life running away from home and the farm life. Now I am only a mile away from where I started!"

On Thursday Oct. 4th, 2007 I went to the fair with my dad, Jack Zellner, and we celebrated Oklahoma's one hundredth birthday. May your fields prosper on the fertile land you graciously behold! Happy birthday, Oklahoma!

Casey Harman, Grade 8
Chelsea Jr High School, OK

Swim Swim Swim

Over this past summer I have done many physical activities, but my favorite activity had to have been swimming. Many people say that I am the best swimmer on our team, but I don't like it when people brag about me in front of other people. Also during the summer, as you can imagine, I had competitions. I always gave 100% effort, but the same girl on a different team kept beating me in freestyle, so my mom (who is the coach) told me to work harder at that stroke, and eventually you will beat her.

It was now nearing the end of the summer, and our last swim competition was nearing. So those last few days, I worked harder than anyone on my team. Finally the last competition came and I felt like I was prepared to win! So I stepped up to the block, and was feeling confident. Then the timer suddenly blew his whistle, and I took off into the water. I felt like a fish, and my stroke was perfect. I could see the girl out of the corner of my eye, so I began to kick my legs harder, and move my arms faster, and gradually, I came ahead of her and ended up winning the race, but not by much. I finally felt like I was the greatest swimmer on the team. From that swim competition on, I have never let that girl beat me again.

Berkley Petersen, Grade 8
Heritage Hall School, OK

My Life

Hi, my name is Michael Flournoy. The topic I chose was my life. The reason I chose that topic was because I always wanted to write about things that happened in my life. So let me start telling you about some crazy things that happened in my memorable life.

One thing that happened in my life was that one of my grandmothers died, September the tenth, two thousand and seven. It was hard realizing that she was gone, but I knew she went to a better place. It took me almost three days until my mind was where it needed to be. My life has been changed since then. I went to her funeral September the fourteenth, two thousand and seven. I was surprised about how many people showed up.

A second thing that happened in my life was when I turned thirteen. I was so excited I had become a teenager. My family threw me a party at my aunt and uncle's house. Almost all of my family came. That was the best birthday I've had yet.

The last thing I am going to tell you about, which happened in my life was when my mother had my little brother, November the ninth, two thousand and six. I went wild when my mom told me I was going to have a little brother or sister those were some memorable things that happened in my life.

Michael Flournoy, Grade 8
Turner Middle School, GA

Daring to Try

My lungs feel like they are exploding as I gasp for air, pumping my arms, flying down the soccer field, racing my opponent. Suddenly, a player comes out of nowhere and swiftly takes the ball from me and runs down towards the opposite end of the field.

Someone yells from the sidelines, "Good try" and somewhere inside me, that makes me enraged because I only tried, I did not succeed.

But, somewhere else in side me it makes me feel excellent because I know that I gave it my all; tried my best. Trying your best is what it's all about, right? Sometimes, trying your best isn't just it. Sometimes, you have to give it will power. You have to be daring to try.

You may be wondering why "daring to try" is so important. I believe that if you dare to try things in your life, instead of laying back and giving up in advance, you will become deeply successful in the long run. If you decide not to try, you won't have a pleasing consequence. Bad results could lead to more and more important things which could drastically affect the daily aspects of your life.

Just remember to always "dare to try." And don't forget! I promise you, your life will improve if you undertake it. Maybe the outcome will surprise you.

Jenna Freeman, Grade 7
Trickum Middle School, GA

Football

Football is my favorite sport to play. Football is a fun sport to play because it is a contact sport. My favorite sport is football.

Football is my kind of sport. I like football because you get to tackle people, run the ball, catch the ball, and kick the ball. When you tackle people you wrap your arms around them like you are giving them a big hug. When you run the ball you have to get your butt down low and hold on to the ball. The quarterback is the person who throws the ball. The person who catches the ball is the wide receiver he puts his hands up and catches the ball. The kicker is, well you probably know what he does, he or she kicks the ball. I also like this sport because you get to use your brain. What do I mean about this? I mean that it is a mental sport. You have to use your brain to find the open field. That is why I like football.

Football is an enjoyable sport to play. It is a sport that you can hit people. Suppose you got mad you can hit someone and you aren't as mad. It is an enjoyable sport because you get to run the ball and catch it. That is why football is an enjoyable sport to play.

My favorite sport is football. A fun sport to play is football. The best sport is football.

Tyler Boyd, Grade 7
Greenfield Jr/Sr High School, MO

Friendship

One day in the park in my neighborhood late in the day, I sat down at the bench for a while just thinking. I looked down and saw my shadow and felt as if a friend was with me. When the sun went down my shadow was gone and I felt a sense of loneliness, I got up and as I walked home, I realized that friends are important whether you see them five minutes a day or twenty-four hours a day, or whether you argue with them about dumb things or you agree on everything and get along perfectly. Friends help you when you need their help. They cheer you up when you're feeling down and blue. With no friends I wouldn't have someone like James who calls the night before the weekend is over to ask what was the homework over the weekend, or Austin to tell hilarious jokes with and weird out my other friends. So, what I learned was that, friends are something you should cherish and try to get more of rather than get less because the more friends you have, the more people you have to make your world bright and happy.

Francisco Gonzalez, Grade 8
Eagles Landing Middle School, FL

Doors

Doors are secret passageways that are begging to be opened by a person who understands the risks and consequences upon opening it. These opportunities are perhaps the reason why people keep going on instead of halting in despair.

Although some of these openings reveal bad things, they end up teaching you a valuable lesson in a mysterious way. Opening your kitchen door to find your dad burning dinner, you realize that he isn't a very good cook. The point is that you always gain knowledge and information from these experience.

Even the good doors have virtues to be taught. Let's say that you opened a door and find Regis Philburn there saying that you just won a million dollars; thus teaching you to have confidence and pride in what you do.

This delicate balance of confidence and fear is never perfect in a person. Some fear the unknown things in life and are too scared to do anything while others have too much confidence and pride and try to do everything. For those filled with confidence, they need to take a step back and see what they have really done with their life. The fearful ones need to learn how to take a chance and go out of their box.

Doors have potentials that are waiting to be discovered. They broaden your perspective of reality in a gently way. Next time a situation comes along, make the best decision for you, and don't let anyone interfere with your choice.

Meredith Cox, Grade 7
St Mary's School, SC

Follow the Leader???

Why do pilot whales become stranded on the beach? The answer lies in one whale whom all the other whales in the pod follow. That lead whale sometimes becomes disoriented and leads his pod into danger. This is usually caused by a disease that affects the ear of the leader.

Look at pilot whales in comparison to humans. In human society there are leaders and followers also. When the leader messes up the followers will join him in disaster. As you can see, there are many varieties of behavior in social groups.

Humans have difficulties to overcome, much like the pilot whales. The whales become stranded on a beach which creates a huge dilemma for them. There are some social groups that can be led by leaders that have no ability to discern correct behavior. For example, the followers of Adolf Hitler.

Whales lose their ability due to certain diseases that infect them. Some humans are similar. They can be affected by a disease or a substance that distorts their judgment. Mental illness or substance abuse could be factors. Also, greed for wealth or power may also contribute.

Pilot whales become stranded due to the fact that they follow a leader. Some humans also follow a leader that may lead them into disaster. This may be caused by many factors. You may conclude that all social groups have some portion of population that cannot make decisions. So they gravitate toward someone who may or may not lead them correctly.

Trenton Smith, Grade 8
Pigeon Forge Middle School, TN

The Lollar Clan

Family is something that has always been a very important part of my life. In the sports that I play there has always been a place where my family has been watching and caring for me like a hawk to her chicks. My family will always have a spot in my heart.

Whether it is baseball, football, basketball, or even soccer my family is there. Ever since I could play sports my dad has been there to show me the way. When I play football my grandpa is always yelling and the loudest one there. On the other hand my grandma is always cheering me on, but sometimes she can be a little gushy. My dad is the one that is always yelling to me to step up, or what I am doing wrong. After the game no matter what, they are always the first ones to tell me "good job." My grandma always has to take me to practice at six o'clock in the morning. During sports my family is there at all times.

In my life my family comes first. When you see your family all the time, I think you kind of start to take them for granted. Some kids never get to see their family. If my family was not there to watch me play sports I do not know what I would do.

Cole Lollar, Grade 7
Greenfield Jr/Sr High School, MO

Untitled Slang

The English language, along with our culture and society, has evolved over time. We have added slang words to our language and now almost every word has a double meaning. We have disposed of "Shall I compare thee to a summer's day?" and gone to more simple terms such as "I think you are pretty." What happened to the magnificent language that is now in the back corner of the library? You can't compare any present day writer's masterpieces to the one of William Shakespeare's sonnets. Clichés are no longer part of our language. Now conversations are filled with movie references and swearing. As well as losing the colorful adjective that used to be a part of English, children have taken it upon themselves to say everything as bluntly as possible. Feelings are of no importance to teenagers anymore. They say everything that's on their mind, no matter how rude it sounds. Just 100 years ago, it was unheard of for a girl to say "blast," and now there isn't one minute throughout the day that someone in a high school doesn't swear. It is incredible that most students cannot understand the Constitution or the Declaration of Independence. Will there come a time that our children struggle to understand *Pride and Prejudice* because slang has overtaken the English language? Eventually everything will become "American" and English will be long forgotten; forever subdued to untitled slang.

Colleen Roetemeyer, Grade 8
West Jr High School, MO

The Field Is My Life

It's fourth quarter. We're down by five, they kick the ball to me there is no blocking up front. Then, I spin, juke, and hurdle players. There is nothing but 40 yards of beautiful green grass, my heart is pounding as fast as a drummer beating his drums. Wow! A 95 yard touchdown the crowd is roaring like the roar of a fierce lion.

I love playing football, because there is the feeling of getting tackled and you always think am I going to break it. Then again, you have to think about how bad the grass is going to taste. It's like eating some leaves that have been stepped on a lot.

I'll always love the feel of giving someone a big hit in the heat of the lights. It's the best feeling in the world to be able to run the football. It's like getting your first present on Christmas Day. Football is unlike any other sport, because you can do it just for fun and you can do it to take your anger out on someone.

Since my fifth grade year I've playing tackle football and I've loved it ever since. I'll never forget the time I dove over the pylon for the win and it got called back. There is always the feeling when you leave the game that you wanted to redo a play or tackle you wanted to make so much. This is my life and I love it — this is football.

Kennedy Lockhart, Grade 7
Chelsea Jr High School, OK

Horses

Today, horses are used for many different purposes. Some of the riding styles include English and Western. They are the main riding styles but there are many more! There's so much you can learn about horses including their breeds, colors, saddles, types of jumps, types of courses, the types of bridles, also types of riding.

The most important part of a horse is their care. You must pay very close attention to your horse whether they're riding or they're just in their stall. Before you're about to ride, you must do various things to make sure that the horse isn't hurt or in pain. This includes brushing, picking their hooves to look for rocks and much more! Then, after saddling, you get the correct size of girth and buckle it to the side of the horse. It must be as tight as possible or you won't have any control. There's much more to horse care!

When you're tacking your horse, there are very many different tackle items you must apply on the horse. The English style has two stirrups, of course, and a leather material. Here's some example: English saddle, D-Ring bit, a bridle, stirrups, and horse shoes. These all are essential to a successful ride.

Horses are very important to many and people enjoy riding them. Whether you're walking, trotting, cantering, or even galloping you will feel a great sense of freedom and will have a great time!

Rachel Volmert, Grade 7
Incarnate Word Catholic Elementary School, MO

My Favorite Uncle

I am writing about my favorite uncle, Uncle Merdi. He was so cool and funny. I always enjoyed being around him. So now you can see my uncle is awesome.

Uncle Merdi was so cool. He lived in Mississippi and so the very little times I got to see him, I cherished. He is the best uncle ever. Besides that I love my uncle.

He was always so funny. My dad told me that when him and Merdi went golfing one day that he scared two younger guys. The younger guys told uncle Merdi to keep his eye on the golf ball, so since he had cancer in his eye, he had to have a glass eyeball, so he took it out and put it on the ball and said "is that good enough?" In other words he had a great sense of humor.

Being around him was probably the funnest times. I always had so much fun around him. But since he died of cancer only just a year ago, I can't stop thinking about him. He always was a great, happy person.

So you see why he is awesome, why he was so cool and funny, and why I enjoyed being around him. Last you see why he is still and will always be my favorite uncle.

Stefani Stephens, Grade 8
Pigeon Forge Middle School, TN

Younger Brothers and Sisters: The Positive Side

What do you think of when you hear 'younger brothers and sisters'? Do those words make you shudder? Do you think of selfish, annoying kids who seem to get all of the attention? Well, believe it or not, that's not always true. A younger sibling can be a burden, but they can also be a blessing. Sometimes, we just need to stop and think on the positive side.

There are many great things about younger siblings that we, many times, fail to realize. First of all, they can be fun. When your friends aren't around and you don't know what to do, your siblings can almost always find ways to amuse you. When you play with them, not only are you having a good time, but you're also bonding with them. Second, you can gain a lot of respect from younger brothers and sisters. Few things are more uplifting than to hear them "brag" about you. You are their role model and it is important to try to set a good example for them. Lastly, you can learn from your siblings. If you watch closely, you may find them copying your habits — both good and bad. When they get on your nerves, your character is tested. There are may more reasons to be grateful for younger brothers and sisters. Take time to thank God for them and learn to think on the positive side.

Piper Danay Smith, Grade 8
Blue Ridge Christian School, MO

Unknown Intellectuals

Zachariah Razi (864-925), do you know who he is? Most people have no idea. Razi was a Persian man who discovered two very important medical related things in our society during the eight-hundreds and even today. Smallpox was a wide spread disease in the world and especially in Europe during the eight-hundreds. After studying the symptoms of smallpox for many years, he discovered the cure; this was the end of suffering from smallpox for the world and especially for Europe. Unfortunately, most people do not recognize the works of this great physician, scientist, and philosopher.

Another magnificent man was Abu Ali Sina (976-1037), one of the most important philosophers of Asia and Europe; Sina was also a Persian. Most importantly he wrote in his philosophies, "One must combine the ideas of the past with the ideas of today to create a successful and open-minded society." After his teachings had a booming affect in the Middle East, Europeans of Spain and Sicily translated his teachings into Latin for the whole European world to read. Concluding was the great Renaissance period of Europe; the time of Michelangelo, Leonardo DaVinci, Albrecht Durer, and many more. Abu Ali Sina lit the fire of the Renaissance period in the Middle East and in Europe which both still influence us today. Behind every great idea is a mind which created it.

Aurian Khajehnouri, Grade 8
Heritage Hall School, OK

Erin Go Bragh!

When most people think of Ireland, they think of leprechauns, step dancing, fiddlers on every corner, and rain. But there's much more to it than that. For me, the Irish culture is a big part of my life, and Saint Louis Irish Arts is what began that part of my life.

When I was eight years old, I began class at Irish Arts. I was always excited to learn a new song or dance step to show my friends at school. As the years went on, I became more and more dedicated to my passion.

My friends didn't understand why I wanted to go to a four-hour class every Tuesday night, or why I wanted to miss a trip to the mall to go to a performance, but it's not something that can really be explained. It is just a feeling that tells me this is what I should be doing, and it's what I want to do my entire life.

After five years of hard work at Saint Louis Irish Arts, I had made many new friends, made it into the Senior Group — a group of the best musicians at Irish Arts, been on two CDs, performed at one hundred locations, gone on a two-week trip to Ireland, but most importantly, gained a sense of family. We were all brothers and sisters, and it's one of the best feelings in the world.

I love Irish Arts, and I say Erin go Bragh — Ireland forever!

Maria Orr, Grade 8
St Gerard Majella School, MO

Deer Hunting

Deer hunting with my dad is a great experience. He takes me out before the first day of deer season to scout around the hunting grounds to see where the deer have been scraping on trees or leaving a trail or marking their territory. So when that is all taken care of, we will go out in the morning and get in our tree stand or just set up a blind and stay on the ground. The coolest part about being in the woods is no one is there to bother you.

But sometimes it can get a little boring just sitting there for the whole morning. That is what hunting is all about. When me and my dad hear animals, it sometimes feels like a deer is close by. But when a deer really does show up, I am so surprised, and my dad calms me down. Then I get my gun out, line up the deer with my gun's scope, then take down the deer.

Then, after a long morning, we bag up the deer, take it to a man that will butcher it, then he calls you to tell you that the deer is cut up and packaged. Finally, you eat the deer for Sunday night dinner and, to top it all off, we watch Sunday night football. So hunting can be a hobby for the whole family.

Austin Emery, Grade 7
Greenfield Jr/Sr High School, MO

The Indian Way

India is the world's largest democracy. India lies in South Asia, usually referred to as the subcontinent. India is a very diverse land from marsh and thick rainforest in the South to the Himalayas in the North.

India was settled by the early Aryan tribes around 1500 B.C. Later on, the Gupta Dynasty, was referred to as India's Golden Years. The Taj Mahal was built during this period by the Mughals. Later on, the British established the East India Company in Calcutta. Led by Mohandas Gandhi, India fought its way to a peaceful independence.

The capital of India is New Delhi. India is the second largest population in the world. India is also the fourth largest economy. Three-fifths of Indian workers are farmers. India is quickly becoming one of the world's richest countries. Exports include tea, rice, gold, iron, wheat, cotton, textiles, and petroleum. India is culturally diverse. The main religion is Hinduism, which is 80% of India's population. The second religion is Islam (14%). Other major religions include Buddhism, Christianity, Judaism, and Sikhism. Many Indians live abroad. The fourth largest amount of immigrants to America are Indians.

India has had some political problems over the years. After having gained independence in 1947, India has had a problem with its neighbor, Pakistan. Many violent disputes have occurred between the two countries. The major dispute is over who claims Kashmir. Kashmir has always belonged to India, but because the majority of the population is Muslim, there are disputes to which country Kashmir should belong.

Akanksh Ramanand, Grade 9
McKinley Sr High School, LA

Famous

"I never met a man I didn't like." That was a quote by Will Rogers, a famous cowboy from Oklahoma. However, he wasn't just a cowboy; he also was an actor, a trick roper, an author, and a radio commentator.

I think it would have been cool to see how he lived when he wasn't famous. It would have been cool to see some of the tricks he could do with his rope. He could throw two different ropes at once. One would catch the guy and one would catch his horse.

I would like to sit down and talk to him about what it would be like to be him. What it was like to grow up in Oolagah, Oklahoma. What it was like doing the different things he did.

I wonder what Will Rogers would think about the Oklahoma centennial and I'd like to ask him what he'd be doing today. But no matter what, he was famous then and he is still just as famous and cool today.

Colton Mixson, Grade 8
Chelsea Jr High School, OK

One Event That Turned World War II

The Battle of Kursk, also called Operation Citadel, took place from July 4 through August 23, 1943. It was the last major offensive campaign attempted by Nazi Germany. It was also the last German offensive in the east. The purpose for Germany was to make a breakthrough into the Soviet Union. The Soviets planned a defensive strategy that would not allow the Germans to break through.

The Germans began this battle with 2,700 tanks, 800,000 infantry, and 2,000 aircraft. Germany had 500,000 troops dead, wounded, or captured. They also lost 900 tanks and 200 aircraft. The Soviet Union army had 3,600 tanks, 1,300,000 infantry, and 2,400 aircraft. The Soviet infantry losses were 607,737 dead, wounded, or captured. The Soviet Union lost 1,500 tanks and 1,000 aircraft.

This was considered a big risk for Nazi Germany. They took a huge chance by committing so many resources to one campaign. The sub-battle at Prokhorovka still is the largest armored conflict and costliest loss of aircraft to date. The defensive stance of the Soviets frustrated the Germans. This allowed the Soviet Union to use counteroffensives to wear down the Germans.

The Germans never again were in an offensive position during World War II on the eastern front. The risk taken by the Germans was too great. Counterattacks that retook Orel, Belgorod, and Kharkov pushed Germany back. The Soviets were now on the offensive.

Dalton Gooch, Grade 7
Stroud Middle School, OK

Those Memorable Days

Some of my best memories from childhood were in my elementary school. I think one of the main reasons I liked school then was because of all of the nice teachers I had. They really paid attention to how much I learned, always helped me when I didn't understand something, and encouraged me to think of high goals. Of my days in elementary school, I think the biggest thing I remember about being in elementary school would have to be the teachers. I say this because when teachers get to know the students well, then the students put their trust into that teacher and its almost like having a family member in school that you respect. In a way, the student tries to get respect back from the teacher for putting effort into the class. The teachers also gave info sheets sometimes that we would have to fill out (like our birthday or favorite hobby, color, pastime) and share with other students. If I ever become a teacher, I would try to figure out what my student's interests and dislikes are so I could be more than just a teacher, I would try to be a friend they could trust. That's why out of all the things in my elementary school, I remember my teachers the most.

Sereno Adams, Grade 9
West Jr High School, MO

Middle School Stress

Life in middle school is stressful. Take our lunch schedule, for example. We get thirty minutes to get in line, get our food, eat, go to our lockers, and get to the next class on time. By the time you get to your table in the cafeteria, you don't have enough time to eat your lunch. You eat as much food as you can, clean off your tray, and rush off to your locker. Once you get your books out of the locker for the next two periods, you're late for your next class…again. An hour for lunch to enjoy our food and talk with our friends would make lunch an enjoyable experience.

Trips to the locker are also stressful. There are rows of lockers and too many kids at the same time, trying to get in and out. Then to open the lockers, you have to start at "0," spin the tumbler three times, get to the first number of the combination, spin it counter clockwise once to your second number, then spin it clockwise to the third number. If you make a mistake, you're dead. You have to start all over again. Then you're in a panic…the bell is about to ring. Easier combination locks and lockers with more space between each locker would make middle school so much more enjoyable and less stressful.

Stress free lunches and locker visits would make me much happier to be in middle school.

Aakash Kumar, Grade 7
White Station Middle School, TN

What My Family Means to Me

My family means a lot to me. I do not know what I'd do without them. My mother is special because she raised my sisters, my brothers, and me. My mother was a single parent, she did everything by herself. Before I was born my mom lived in some broke down apartment. My mother moved with my auntie after I was born.

When it come to problems my family always finds a way to seek the problem out. When one of my family members have some ups and downs we are always there to help. It's hard sometimes, because my mom has bills to pay and she needs help. To me it's very hard because a year ago my mother found that she was a diabetic. Every day I have to make sure she takes the medicine. Most of the time she forgets.

My sisters and my brothers mean a lot to me too. When I need somebody to talk to I can go and talk to one of them. If I need somewhere to go my sister will take me. The only thing wrong with my brothers is that they are too protective. They like to ask my friends a lot of questions. Things like that make me mad.

My family is special. I still love them when they make me mad, or get me in trouble. I would be nothing without them. My family is a big part of my life.

Erica Luckett, Grade 8
Turner Middle School, GA

My Home

Hey, I'm a person who moves a lot, you want to know why my Columbus home meant the most to me? I had a somewhat diverse neighborhood, and there were lots of things to do around the county. One family in my neighbor hood was very sports-minded and about 70% baseballish, and 30% footballish. I admired them very much, because they did lots of family oriented things that most people wouldn't think of as family oriented things, such as making festive crafts and having pictures of their distant relatives on their refrigerator. One of the houses across from them was a fine, classy African-American woman who loved artwork and who you could smell Christmas cookie dough from twenty feet away from her.

Then next to her was a group of South Korean immigrants in which the mom worked at Lazarus and then switched to Lord and Taylor. The son was an academic FREAK; sometimes he'd reject invitations to my house because of homework (Come on). In addition to all the good neighbors, Columbus has a GREAT Ohio State football team, restaurants, and a very satisfying rec-center to swim and shoot hoops in, and much, much more!!!!

Marshall Farrell, Grade 8
Baylor School, TN

My Favorite NFL Football Players

My favorite football players of the NFL are: Reggie Bush, Adrian Peterson, Darrent Williams, Michael Vick, and Terrell Owens.

Reggie Bush's college year was pretty good, but they had to face the Texas Longhorns in the Rose Bowl. USC lost 41-43, but Reggie Bush did get the Heisman that same year they lost. Reggie Bush's rookie year in the big leagues was an all right year; he played in the playoffs too.

Adrian Peterson, his past college year he was probably the best in the nation; he was fast and always found someway to get around the other team to score. Now his rookie year in the pros, which is this year, he made his first touchdown with a one-handed grab from a bad pass and dove into the end zone.

Michael Vick, he went to college at Virginia Tech so did his little brother Marcus Vick. Now Michael has got himself in a bit of trouble this past year. He was caught fighting pit bulls for money. That is wrong, but I do still like him even though that's wrong.

Darrent Williams, he went to college at OSU until he got drafted into the NFL by the Denver Broncos. He played there for two years; he was the cornerback until one game on New Year's Eve against the San Francisco 49ers. Denver beats the 49ers, and Darrent Williams and a couple of teammates went to celebrate, and he was shot in a drive-by shooting. He was a very good player and person.

Greg Banta, Grade 7
Stroud Middle School, OK

Harold Roe Bartle

Harold Roe Bartle was born June 25, 1901, and lived a long, successful life until his death on May 9, 1974. Bartle was born in Virginia and moved frequently in the U.S. Honest and dynamic describe this intelligent man, who had a booming voice and a deep desire to help the young in their journey through youth. Bartle was very interested and involved in scouting. He started his professional scouting career at the age of 21 as a Scout Executive for the Cheyenne Council in Wyoming. While working with the American Indians, he received the nickname "The Chief." During his time of employment in scouting, he founded the tribe of Mic-O-Say to recognize boys who have shown dedication in scouting.

Another of Harold Roe Bartle's great accomplishments was serving as mayor of Kansas City for two terms. His only campaign promise stated, "I will take my honor, integrity and ability to City Hall and nothing else." Mr. Bartle could have served as mayor Kansas City for three terms but asked to not be re-elected. Another notable accomplishment was a negotiation with Lamar Hunt that brought Mr. Hunt's NFL team from Dallas to Kansas City. Lamar Hunt renamed the team "The Chiefs" to recognize and honor Mr. Bartle.

The longest lasting legacy that Harold Roe Bartle left with us, that will be continuously reinforced and forever remembered, was his leap into American Humanics. Mr. Bartle is considered the founder of American Humanics. Mr. Bartle noted that many adults did not have the knowledge and preparation to run a nonprofit organization. Having observed this, Mr. Bartle supported the making of a course that taught students everything they needed to know for running a nonprofit organization. Harold Roe Bartle showed leadership to many people around the country.

Kate Sims, Grade 8

Derek Jeter

Derek Jeter is my hero. I love to watch him on TV. He is the best. He always is willing to go the extra mile to win the game. That's a main part for why the Yankees are so good. He is a good sport about everything. He never yells at the umpire to say the call was wrong. I can tell he is always thinking about the game and knows what's going on.

Derek and I both have the same birthday. As a kid, Derek wanted to play for the Yankees, and my dream is to also one day play for the Yankees. His came true on May 29,1995, that was his first game wearing number two. If you ever watch him in person he is so cool. Derek is just like me smaller and he does not want to hit 756 home runs. He wants to get on base so he can score 756 times. I think that he is just the best guy alive and I idol him. He shows respect to everyone and is a great team player, he is not all about himself, so that's why Derek Jeter is my hero.

Jordan Carter, Grade 8
Leesville Road Middle School, NC

The Value of Family

Nothing is better than spending precious time with my family. Every summer my mom, dad, brother, and I visit my mother's family in Tela, Honduras. Tela is a pristine beach in northern Honduras with crystal clear water. Everybody wakes up very early in the morning to swim and jump waves in the salty ocean water. Eventually, the children tire of the ocean, and play in the soft, wet, white sand, and take turns digging an enormous hole. When it is deep enough, one of us climbs into the hole and is buried up to the neck. We all laugh and eventually, the sand is washed away into the vast ocean.

La Tigra is a cloud-capped mountain just outside Tegucigalpa, Honduras, and known as a family friendly place where my cousins and I like to play, go on long hikes, and eat a delicious picnic. Some of our favorite outdoor games are tag, hide-and-seek, and water balloon fights. When our bellies start to rumble, we sit on the grass and eat chicken, grilled corn, tortillas, and beans. During our picnic, we usually talk about where we will hike. Most of the time, we decide on a lengthy trail covered with green rain forest vegetation.

Whether spending time in the cool ocean breeze or a cloud-capped rain forest, the true value of family is time spent with loved ones, regardless of the location.

Vera Gardner, Grade 7
White Station Middle School, TN

Why My Mom Is So Special

My mom is the most important person in my life. If someone was to take her away I don't know what I would do. I always wonder about that. I think, "What would I do if I was separated from her?" You're about to find out why I think about that.

Everyone thinks that their mom is the best. Well, my mom is the best. She takes care of me, and makes sure that I'm safe. She doesn't let me roam around wherever and whenever I want. She makes sure that she knows where I am, and I also have a curfew. Most people think it's weird that I'm 'protected' this much. It's not weird, it's love.

Another thing that I love about my mom is that she's strong-willed. If there's something that she wants to do, she's going to do it. Being strong-willed is helpful in life. That's why my mom is so successful. I hope to be strong-willed like her.

There are many things that I'll do to become like my mom. When I grow up, I want my daughter to admire me as I admire my mom. I pray that someday that will happen.

I would like to write a long essay, but there are no words to describe how special my mom is. I love her so much, and she loves me! That's why my mom is so special!

Terri Smith, Grade 7
Boyet Jr High School, LA

My Background Country, Cuba

My essay is going to be on my background country, which is Cuba. I feel a lot for this country. One of the reasons I love Cuba is the food. Another reason I like Cuba is the climate. The last reason I LOVE CUBA, and especially NOT the least, is family.

My first reason I love Cuba is the food. If you have never tasted Cuban food you should because it is very tasteful. There is one dish called picadello. It's ground beef with many spices. You eat it with white rice. Furthermore, that is one of the reasons I love Cuba!

The second reason I like Cuba is the climate. The island is a tropical paradise. There are many different types of trees. It rains a lot and since it is in the Caribbean the beaches are magnificent. The wonderful climate is what attracts many tourists. It is hot but a slight breeze runs through the air at night.

Equally important is my last reason, my family. My mother and father were born in Cuba. My mother still has some family, including her parents over in Cuba. I really enjoy going to visit them. That is my last but most important reason why I like Cuba.

Now you have seen my three reasons for liking Cuba. Number one was the food. The next was the wonderful climate. Third, but most important was my family. I LOVE CUBA!!!!!!!!!!

Lizette Aparicio, Grade 8
Pigeon Forge Middle School, TN

Having Faith

Faith is a big word for someone to use. There are a lot of people that have faith in something. It could be themselves, another person, Christ, etc…Having faith means you believe and try your hardest not to let it down. Faith and believing mean almost the same thing. For instance, everyone has their own faith or what they believe in. Having faith is what guides you through life. Without having faith you'd probably let yourself go. For instance, like not caring how you look or what people think of you and your family background. Even though some people don't have faith, faith should be in everyone: gothics, normals, Christians, etc…

Queen Latifah had faith in being a rapper or an actress and what do you know, she's both! I also have faith in being a basketball player and playing in the WNBA, but I have to put forth the effort in doing so. Just by having faith isn't going to get you, me or anyone else, anywhere we want to go. We have to work hard for it. When you have faith in something, you do whatever it takes to get where or what you want. If you just pray for something it might get done, but you have to want/need it and be sure that it will be done. In order for you to receive, you have to do something about it. What do you have faith in?

Angelica Davison, Grade 8
Greenhill Elementary School, MS

My Life Savors in All Flavors and Colors

My favorite life savors are cherry, orange, and grape. These tie into what I value because cherry means God, orange means my family, and grape means my friends. God has been important since I gave up sin. My family has been important since the day I was born. My friends are one of a kind. There are many reasons why the flavors of my life are important; let me tell you more about each delectable delight.

First, God is important because He centers my life. If it wasn't for Him I don't know what I would do. He is most important in my life. Next, my family, they are the second most important thing in my life. They are definitely one of a kind. They love and care for me and on a bad day they can really make you feel good. My friends are the third most important thing in my life. They help me through the bad times and make the good times great. Especially, my good friend Bethany (Berty). Even though we've only known each other for a few weeks she is one of those people you will never forget. I don't know how I could get through the day without her cheerful laugh and her caring heart.

Hopefully you can see why these things are important to the flavors of my life. I don't know how I would get through life without my three life savors orange, cherry, and grape! What are your flavors?

Dominique Bonilla, Grade 8
Southwest Jr High School, AR

My Grandpa

My mom said, "There goes Grandpa again riding his lawnmower doing nothing." My grandpa mows all the time. Sometimes he rides down to my uncle's house just to be riding. It is about one mile away.

He also likes to play cards. He goes in his room sits at his desk, and then opens his desk drawer and pulls out his cards. I'm not sure what he plays, but he is always in there. Sometimes I go in his room and he starts telling me stories about when he was little.

My grandpa was in the military. He doesn't tell us anything about it, but my aunt tells me that he really didn't like it. He did it, to take care of my grandma and his kids.

He's really funny. He always uses a strong choice of words with my aunt, and my aunt's boyfriend. All of his stories are funny, he always tells me about when he was little.

He always wears jeans. I have never seen him wear shorts. He cuts his hair so short, that he is almost bald. He has never had long hair that I know of. Every time I see him he is wearing a cowboy shirt. I'm guessing that he has at least a hundred of them. I don't know if he knows that this is Oklahoma's 100th birthday, but knowing him I'm sure he does. He probably even has a story to go along with it.

Kyle Mitchell, Grade 8
Chelsea Jr High School, OK

My Hero

My mother is my friend, my role model, and my hero. I think that a hero is a person who exhibits most, if not all, of the character traits a hero should. My mother thinks of others before she thinks of herself. In addition to being kind and caring, she is an individual and thoughtful. She always listens to what I have to say and can always make me smile when I'm feeling down.

When I need advice, I can always feel free to go to her. My mom is the type of person that you could go to for advice and leave with an honest, straightforward answer. My mom never looks at a person's past, but will always try to improve their future. Since my mom is a bail bondsman; she gets people out of jail and gives them a second chance at life. She gives and gives but never looks to receive.

She doesn't have super powers, but it is safe to say that she is a super mom! Aside from raising my brother and me, she has a job, goes to school, and even helps take care of my dog. My mom doesn't wear a cape or run around in tights, but she is my hero. She is the Superwoman in my life.

Michael Lawrence, Grade 8
Leesville Road Middle School, NC

The Most Important Person in My Life

Who is the most important person in your life? Well, mine is my mom. Her name is Elsy Martinez. She is always there for me when I need her. She never gives up on me.

She is always there for me. She buys clothes, and food for me. When I'm sad, she's the only one I talk to, and makes me happy. When our family is apart, she always tries to keep us together like letting some of our family sleepover or talk about what could have happened if we never got in an argument.

My mom never gives up on me. Even if I made her mad she will always love me. If I don't understand something, she explains to me how to do it. She always gives me advice. If I do something bad, she will ground me, and she will tell me the reasons why she did.

This is why my mom is the most important person in my life. She is always there for me. She never ever gives up on me. Do you have an important person in your life? Well, you should think about who it is. If I cry about pain, she would know what to do. Whenever I come home with an attitude, she asks me what's wrong, and I can tell her.

I'm so thankful that my grandparents had my mom. Sometimes, I think that God made me a guardian angel for my mom, because anything she needs I can do it, or if she needs to talk to me she can. My mom is the only person I can really talk to about anything. That's why I love my mom so much. So, in just four little words, I love my mother.

Sabrina Martinez, Grade 7
Mineral Springs Middle School, NC

Leaves of Fall

Their usual dull green has faded, replaced by brilliant colors. The flaming red, orange, and bright yellow I came to know are omnipresent. I watch as they're carried by the wind, carefree. Minds clouded with dreams, fantasies, and perhaps mischief. Landing in a pool, they lay on their back, floating across the crystal water. Occasionally, they glance at their growing shadows as the sun travels its daily journey. In the muddy water, left by last night's rain, I see them prance; playing for a while, but then getting a mischievous twinkle in the eyes. Trailing them, they lead me to my neighbor's yard. I peer over the fence wondering what's going on. A snicker escapes my chapped lips. They are playing an endless game of tag, a game which the neighbor will never win. Finally, the neighbor gives up and storms into the house. Following are frustrated screams. Boredom comes, so hastily they find more entertainment. The new game seems to involve the sidewalk and skipping. Watching carefully I see that they are avoiding the cracks. "When will they ever get tired?" I wondered. my question is soon answered. In the sky, night stars appear and the moon's silly grin. I hear the wind give a sigh and then no more. The once lively, funny, little devils start looking limp and weak. They fall to the ground staying motionless for hours. I hope for some action, but none appears. I walk home with a sad expression. In a whisper I tell myself, "Nothing lasts forever."

Holly Liu, Grade 7
White Station Middle School, TN

Outdoors

Hunting is where you get a bow or gun and go somewhere and sit for a while and shoot animals. Some people that live in the country drive around in their truck and look for deer from the side of the road and shoot it. Now, I am pretty sure that is illegal to do. The way I go hunting is you get a gun, then go in the middle of the woods and set up your tree stand. You have to be real patient, sometimes you have to wait hours before you get to shoot at something.

Fishing is where you get a fishing pole and some hooks of any kind. Then, you throw the rooster tail out and reel it in slowly. In a boat you don't have to reel it in when the boat is moving it causes it to spin by itself. One time my uncle, my brother and I went fishing at Douglas Lake, we went early in the afternoon which we probably should've went way earlier than that. My brother and I started having a competition on who can catch the most catfish. We both caught one but his was bigger. I almost got a bigger one than his, but the hook only caught its fin or tail.

I don't really go hiking, but I have gone hiking before. I've gone hiking somewhere in Alabama. I've seen a lot of animals when I went hiking. When I went there were people mountain climbing a cliff. I had a lot of fun.

Shawn Shaver, Grade 8
Pigeon Forge Middle School, TN

Gifted A.K.A. Nerd

Being classified as gifted is a stereotypical thought, because we are said to be nerds. I would say that gifted kids are just like honors kids, except the way we think, which, I guess, is why we are considered gifted.

In sixth grade some of the kids were adversaries. I personally didn't like being embroiled in these discords, so I would just watch. I thought it seemed funny watching all these belligerent kids argue. Mrs. Gunter, our teacher, went through strife when we were in sixth grade.

Seventh grade was almost like sixth grade, but a little better. We still basically had the same students, Danielle, Patrick, and Nolan. We got a new kid named Hayden. There would be some skirmishes, but no all out wars. These little battles would start over miscellaneous comments, but they were all ugly. Luckily, everyone did mature to some extent as the year went on. We did haggle with Mrs. Gunter on some things, but in the end, she always won.

Now we are in eighth grade. My gifted class is still the same, meaning the people. Everyone's attitude has changed though. We can now come to a consensus on some things. We have done some communal projects, and they did not turn out as a disaster. The boys, they are a different story, but overall we are just a throng of nerds. I guess that is what you call it.

Brittany Partain, Grade 8
Alexandria Middle Magnet School, LA

OU vs. Texas

It's that time of year, when orange and red clash together for the biggest war of the football season. Early the morning before, cars pull out of their garages and start the three hour drive. Anticipating, children wait to get out and stretch their legs. Finally they arrive, children happily ask their parents, "When do we go to the fair?" Dragging by, the day passes oh so slowly even though they are having fun. Darkness starts to fall; the pale moon reaches out to the children and makes them sleepy. Night, a happy reminder to all that OU, Texas is coming.

Brightly, the sun peeks through the windows and excited eyes open. Everyone rolls out of their beds and into their cars. Longhorns and Sooners plague the State Fair Grounds waiting for kickoff. The air is filled with chants and yells for and against the two teams. Now the time has come, people rapidly filter into the stadium to find their seats. The blazing sun beats down upon the anxious crowd. At the peak of the stadium you can see who is for which team. Red, orange and white shirts surround you. Later someone will walk out with his or her heads hung low and drowned by chants of the other team.

Blaire Reynolds, Grade 8
Heritage Hall School, OK

My Dreamland

Have you ever imagined that you were in another world away from all potential dangers? Have you ever pretended that you had a friend that stood up for you when you were being bullied? If you have, you've been to your own little, personal world, your imagination.

My imagination is a place for me to travel to when I'm happy, disappointed, thinking, or curious. I believe my imagination is what makes me a very unique individual. I imagine things that are out of this world! If I created the same things as everyone else, I'd be one dull person.

I don't need a map or a GPS to go to my secret hideaway. I don't have to perform any complicated techniques. I only have to close my eyes, drive down Unique Street, and stop at Imagination Lane. I'm finally there to create new and amazing ideas!

My secret hideaway is a place to take a rest from all of the worries and troubles in my life. No one can ever stop me from inventing ideas in my merryland. I can do whatever I want to in my imagination. It's my world!

Kristen Black, Grade 7
Greenhill Elementary School, MS

Football

To start why football is so awesome, you have to know some rules. One football field measures 120 yards by 53 yards and one foot. At each end there are goal posts. Each team has 11 players. Each team will try to get the ball into the opposing team's end zone.

People who watch football can be crazier than anything. They shave their heads, paint themselves with team colors, and also wear mascots on their heads.

The main position in football is the quarterback, who plays on the offensive line. He is the brain of the team. The offensive line's goal is to move the ball down the field. The offensive team has to move the ball 10 yards in four tries, called downs.

When you make a touchdown, this is worth six points. Kicking a field goal is worth 3 points. The extra point conversion is worth 2 points. The extra kick after a touchdown is 1 point.

Many kids start playing flag football at an early age, around 5 years old. The good ones end up playing in college. The superior players end up in the NFL making a lot of money. The NFL only has 32 teams with only 22 starting players. The teams are named after birds or cats with many different logos.

Football started in America as rugby and has grown since then. This sport is a very physical and mental sport, which only the strong survive. America has grown to love this sport and waits patiently every August for the season to start. I love football. GO PITTSBURGH STEELERS!!!!!!!!!!!!!!!

Keenan Petersen, Grade 7
Sebastian River Middle School, FL

Nature versus Nurture

When you are born, your first childhood experience is getting to know your parents. Once you are old enough to understand what is going on around you, you start becoming more familiar with your surroundings and your community. Therefore, your community plays a big part in raising you!

An African proverb says, "It takes two parents to produce a child, but an entire village to raise the child." The community, or the "village," influences how you think, and who you will become as you grow up. My community is culturally diverse. By culturally diverse, I mean people who speak different languages, eat different foods, listen to different music, and view the world from different perspectives. Seeing so many differences around me has taught me not to judge people by preconceived notions. I know this, all thanks to my community!

If you look at life in terms of "nature versus nurture," I can say that my parents have done a great job in raising me. In addition, my community has helped me was well. I am who I am today because of my surroundings. Because of my community's cultural diversity, I have learned not to judge others.

So, now I pass the baton to you. How has *your* community played a part in raising you and who you will become today?

Antonina Vargas, Grade 7
Nautilus Middle School, FL

Running the Distance

Sports brings joy to a lot of people in the world and when you read about all the negative things in sports sometimes you need a story like this. Dick Hoyt was the father to Rick Hoyt. When Rick was born he was strangled by his umbilical cord. The doctors said there was no brain activity and he would be a vegetable for the rest of his life. The doctors said he should be put in an institution. The Hoyts didn't want to see their son there. Dick said Rick would follow them around the room when he was two.

Tufts University made Rick a computer with a mouse that was put by his head and he would click it with his head and a letter would show up. His first words were "Go Bruins" after the college they were by.

He went to a marathon when he was 15 with his dad and he clicked out "Dad, I want to do that."

Yeah right. He'd fall over when he ran a mile now his son wants to push him for five. He went into his first marathon and his dad was about to pass out. Rick clicked out to his dad "Dad when we were running it felt like I wasn't disabled anymore." That changed Dick's life.

Dick and Rick have run 212 triathlons and twenty-four Boston Marathons now. When Rick was interviewed he said, "I wish I could push my dad instead of him pushing me."

Evan Belk, Grade 8
College Heights Christian School, MO

Words

Words are powerful beings, to be revered and feared. Were it not the words of Shakespeare that made him immortal? Were it not Niccolo Machiavelli's words that instilled fear and ruthlessness into the very souls of future monarchs and their subjects? These conglomerations of letters have caused havoc among the ranks as citizens braced themselves for Orson Welles' reports of alien warfare to come true. Such is their valor as Socrates refuses to flee his dear Athens and instead chooses to drink the hemlock and forfeit his life. If these words are so powerful, should we not use them wisely? Many students think about that as they rush to finish that horrid essay they had for homework. Let responsible adults chew on this as they soak in the latest celebrity gossip. Every word written or spoken should be for a purpose noble in virtues. As was the Declaration of Independence, or the endearing words of Martin Luther King, Jr. as he inspired hope in the hearts of millions. If a pen is mightier than the sword, then the word speaks louder than deeds. May these words on this paper prove meaningful and worthwhile. For every writer of words has a dream that their words will thrive through the ages.

Juliette Holthaus, Grade 8
James Weldon Johnson Middle School, FL

You Never Know What You Have Until It Is Gone

"What's wrong sissy?" my two-year-old brother asked without the understanding of the situation unfolding in front of us. I tried to stop my lip from quivering and stay strong for my brother, but it wasn't easy.

On August 4, 2005, my grandfather passed away. He was always the kind of guy that came to all my sporting events and supported me. He loved to be around my brothers and I even though he was a quiet man. When we were at our grandparent's house, I would usually sit in the kitchen and talk to my grandmother about recent happenings in our lives while my grandfather and brothers flipped on the Cardinals game in the living room. When it came time to leave, I would give my grandmother a hug and a kiss but just give my grandfather a hug.

When I would call their house about once a week, my grandfather was always the first to the phone. We never really talked about much. He usually asked me how I was doing and I would return the question. Then he would pass the phone off to my grandmother and we would have a more in-depth conversation.

Those are just some small examples of where I could have done more to enjoy my grandfather's presence while he was still here. In the end, it is the small things that mean the most.

Alexis Reilly, Grade 8
St Gerard Majella School, MO

Nature's Aquarium

Imagine swimming with beautiful colored fish with shimmering scales of different colors and other fish that look rather odd but yet fascinating. Well anything is possible of course.

As I inhale the warm, salty breeze of the Caribbean ocean through my snorkel, my eyes scan over the extraordinary looking fish that fly under water beneath me. Some with yellow and blue with white fins and others with flat heads and huge eyes, but all God's wonderful creations.

Fast as lightning, the little water animals scatter into their homes under and inside the hollow rocks that lay on the ground of the talcum powder feel of the ocean floor. A barracuda comes closer and closer looking for its next meal. I gasp for air as my back becomes frozen with fear. As I put my royal blue snorkel back on, I see the long wolf like fish striking for a fish, but missed, phew! Gazing in the water, my cousin sees a moving object going the opposite way. "Look Ana, look!" she yells with excitement. A baby manta a ray, sand colored with random dots of red and black.

Once I lay my head back on the salty water again, I spot two chunks of sand moving one bigger than the other. What's this, I ask myself. A baby flounder and its mother! Before I saw them move their thin tortilla like bodies to the reef, my eyes caught sight of something else, all the fish were staring at me! Once I shooed them away, my mother called me to tell me to head back to the hotel.

Although I didn't go to an aquarium, I still entertained myself with the wonders of the underwater world. You don't have to go far to enlighten your day.

Ana Taylor, Grade 7
St Mary's School, SC

A Part of Church

Being involved in church is a very important part of my life. Being Catholic, there is a large amount of stewardship involved in the church. Every Sunday I go to church, and I wouldn't miss it for anything! Then on Wednesdays I go to Religious Education class to learn more about my faith. I have many friends at my church, and I believe that when we all participate together it really gets you into things. My church is not only about stewardship and helping with the poor, but also as growing as a community closer to God by his word.

When I go to church I feel as if I am part of a huge family. That is the way a church is supposed to be. My friends at church are a very important part of my life. I can talk to them about anything, and I know that they will understand. When you are involved with the community, you feel like you are really benefiting people's lives through your doings. My church brings family and friends together to worship God for all he has done, and will do for us in the future.

Neely Zorio, Grade 8
Heritage Hall School, OK

Fears No More!

When I was a little girl I had always been afraid of heights; I could never put my finger on it, but they terrified me. A few years ago my parents took me and my sister on a cruise in the Bahamas. My dad had decided to go parasailing but didn't want to go alone, he also has a fear of heights, so he convinced me to go with him. I asked if I was allowed to ride on the boat but the guide said I had to go in the air to ride.

It is my turn I get into the harness and they hooked me to the cable, I was so terrified my knees were shaking and I had given myself hick-ups. The boat takes off and I'm suspended in the air, I shut my eyes and gripped the cables slowly but steadily the sound of the boat disappeared. When the sound was completely gone I opened my eyes and saw blue, the crystal blue ocean had blended in to the sky and the only thing differing them were the few soft white clouds, it was breath taking. I feel myself relaxing and letting go there is no sound just the faintest whisper of the wind. I realized something that day height is only a variable; the brilliant Franklin Roosevelt once said "We have nothing to fear but fear itself." This was lesson I had never understood until that day I tried something new.

Morgan Rund, Grade 8
Heritage Hall School, OK

Memories

Memories are something that you can't store in a box, or save in case of a fire. Your baby brother can't rip them up or you can't say, "My dog chewed them up." Your memories are something special that you always have no matter what, if you are sad, you can think of happy memories that will brighten your day, and will never disappear.

Everybody has different memories; nobody has the exact same as you. You can laugh, cry, smile, or sing the blues with memories. You never have to share them with anybody, and if you do I'm sure they have memories just as embarrassing as those when you feel like you want to rip your hair out and scream.

We have billions of memories from squishing bugs and eating them from when you were two, to just one second ago when you were reading this. When you get old and your children have children, you can sit your grandchild up on your lap and tell them all of the exciting, and surprising memories that you had when you were young.

As I say again, your memories can be sad, happy, angry, etc, but you can never replace them with any possession not even the finest gold. You can't sell them but only remember them in times of need. Everybody has them, so you can never say "She's so lucky that she got to go there," because you can always remember those good or sad times called memories.

MaryJohn Long, Grade 7
St Mary's School, SC

About My Life

My name is Brandon Bryant and I'm 13 years old. My mother's name is Ozzie Bryant and she is thirty. My sister's name is Amber and she is 8 years old; my other sister's name is Tylin and she is 7 years old, and my brother's name is Tyler and he is 7 years old.

My role model is my mother because she is an angel to me. She has nice manners and she is a very hart given person to me. I love my mother to death and she loves me too. Sometimes when my mother gets home from work and she is tired, then I go help her with anything she needs to help her out. My mother is a hard working single mother. I try to help my mother when I can. But she understands, because I have to go to band practice every day, then come home and do my homework.

We all are hard workers in our house. On the weekend I don't have a free time, because I have this weekend job with my uncle to help my mother around the house to get us some clothes and something to eat. I love my mother to death and she will do anything for us. She will get us anything we want that's why I always help and love my mother.

Brandon Bryant, Grade 8
Seminole County Middle/High School, GA

Clouds of My Mind

From the age of one day to thirteen-years-old, I have looked at these marvelous shifting wisps in the sky. Always they are changing, splitting up, coming together, and turning into different pictures, all while drifting in the wind.

Thundering can cause misery and woe with the power of fear or by making the small sparks, lighting the flame that can destroy anyone's dreams and memories. But, to me, they are the beautiful pictures in my mind.

Everyone always sees their own ideas plastered upon the big blue canvas of the sky. Watching the blue, I see a rabbit and hare racing on top of a dragon underneath a feather. In the sky, that is what I see, but five minutes later I see a completely different picture on top of the mind's easel called the sky.

My mind has many colors, but when the sky paints, it is deprived of everyday hues and can only use white, gray, and black. But with the day's best friend, the sun, the sky and it's pictures can be lifted from their bond of neutral colors, transforming into a whole new image with orange, yellow, red, and purple.

I am amazed at these wonderful prospects of the Earth's water cycle every day. I wish that I could be as free as them, no troubles, traveling the world, and flying around all while brightening people's days. If only I could be a cloud in the wind...

Matt Riddle, Grade 7
White Station Middle School, TN

Drifting Off

Lying down at the end of the day in my soft bed, I sigh with relief that the day is finally over. I love the sensation of wrapping up my tired body in the smooth sheets and sinking into the soft, cushy mattress. In the summer I enjoy the cool crispness of the cotton sheet when I first lie down. In the winter my mom puts flannel sheets on my bed. I like the warm, soft feeling of the flannel. The stillness, with the occasional subdued sound, is pure bliss to me. On moonlit nights the light streams into my room through the slits in my blinds, creating places of light and shadow. On overcast nights I enjoy the absolute darkness of my room.

Sometimes, I think of how lucky I am to have the only upstairs bedroom, which makes the sounds of cars less loud and the sound of rain more pronounced and relaxing. In this period between lying down and falling asleep, I like to think of the things I accomplished that day. Also, I find that this is when I think of interesting or funny things I want to tell someone. Most days are exhausting and I fall sleep quickly, but some nights I like to lie awake and daydream. Hearing my parents talk or just more around downstairs is a very pacifying experience. Lying there, thinking about nothing, I am astonished to see that night turned into day without me even knowing I had fallen asleep.

Harry Tronsor, Grade 7
White Station Middle School, TN

A Special Someone

Caring, kind, thoughtful — these words describe a great friend. My best friend is exactly like that. People like her don't come around too often. Her name is Madison.

I met Madison in 5th grade, during P.E. Everyone had to get a partner. Neither of us could find one, so we became partners. After that, we started to hang out with each other. We share many interests. Both of us like to read, swim, and play video games. Also, we are both quiet. Madison and I spent a lot of time together. First, we were acquaintances, then friends, and now we're best friends.

We always have a good time together. Once, I visited Madison's relatives with her. I got to meet her baby cousin, and go on a boat ride. After that, we fed the geese that were swimming nearby. I will never forget that day.

Everything was fine until one day at recess. I ran to greet her. Usually she does too, with a smile on her face. This time was different. Madison was standing far away, looking sad. When I reached her, she explained she had to move. Her dad's job got transferred to Alabama because of Hurricane Katrina. We both were very sad. I cried the rest of the day.

Even though Madison is far away, we still keep in touch. We call each other, and sometimes visit. The point is, you never know how much you like someone until they're gone.

Audrey Gurnik, Grade 7
Boyet Jr High School, LA

Pride

Pride, in my experience, is a powerful, corruptive thing. It turns friend against friend, brother against brother, sister against sister. Let me show you where I am coming from.

I know someone (for obvious reasons, I will not give the name) who is unbelievably arrogant. One consequence of pride I have noticed in this case is that said person has no real friends. He might think he does, but in reality, he does not. The reason no one likes him is because while he might not say, "I'm better than you," he puts people down. Therefore, no one wants to be his friend. However, that's not the only consequence of being arrogant.

The second consequence of pride is failure. Most people are familiar with the famous proverb, "Pride cometh before a fall." You could also say: eventually, your head gets so swelled your neck breaks. Do not misunderstand me. I am not saying we should not trust our abilities, but always believing we are right is stupid. We will be wrong sometimes. The way I figure, we are all homo sapiens, and we are going to make mistakes. If our noses are up too high, we will trip, no matter how smart we are. Arrogance actually makes you stupider, I have found.

Do not get me wrong here. I am not saying pride is a bad thing. I keep just enough knowledge of my talents so that I will never have a low self-esteem. Too much pride will lead you right off a cliff. Just like a lot of things in life, pride is best served in moderation.

Emily Farmer, Grade 8
Leesville Road Middle School, NC

Never Give Up

Giving up always means you're a quitter. You should never give up. One time my brother and I went down to my grandma's house. She bought us a couple of ramps for Christmas. We brought our bikes to her house and we started ramping. Well, my brother would wreck every time he ramped. So he decided to give up. I said, "You can't give up, if you give up you will be a quitter." He said that he would rather be a quitter than wreck every time he ramps. So he went inside and I kept working on my ramping.

About the same time I landed my signature move, which is a barspin 360, my brother comes out with his bike and starts ramping again. I told him he could not use my ramp because he gave up on it earlier. He said, "No matter, I have my own ramp."

Then he decided to ramp into a stream. When he used my ramp to do it, I pulled it away at the last second. It may sound harsh but it was worth it. When I started to laugh because he was covered in mud, he chased me for the rest of the day. If you give up, you will ALWAYS be a quitter.

Michael Bennett, Grade 7
Greenfield Jr/Sr High School, MO

My Grandfather

My grandfather has always been one of the biggest heroes in my life. His life has not been very easy and he has always handled it correctly as a good Christian. He has taught me a lot of important things in life whether it was how to run a successful business or how to do the right thing. His teachings and qualities resulted from a successful background. Growing up on a farm taught him many things. My grandfather has worked hard his whole life, has a lot of money, and never cheated his way to it.

He is a very hardworking man. This quality has been proven many times in his past jobs. His modesty is extremely great. He does not care if he is given a lower job than everyone else. He just does his best at it and works his way up. Strict and hard do not describe his personality in any way. He is a well rounded person but only in good qualities. His friendliness earned him a good name to his associates and this name helped him start a business that is now a success.

He has a very good name to all that know him. He never cheats a friend, never makes enemies, and is active in his church. He has had the greatest influence in my life besides my mother. I am very grateful he is my grandfather.

Christopher Messer, Grade 8
St Mary's School, SC

My Favorite Place in Oklahoma

One of my favorite places in Oklahoma is Turner Falls. Turner Falls is located in the Arbuckle Mountains, in south central Oklahoma, just north of Ardmore, Oklahoma.

My favorite place is the waterfall. It is the largest waterfall in Oklahoma. It stands seventy-seven feet tall. It runs off into a little swimming hole, which gets really deep. It's a whole lot of fun.

When you first get there, driving down the road there is big walls of rocks that are all different colors. It looks so cool. You should check it out someday.

When you get into the park there's a strip of food places such as an ice cream shop. A grilled food place and a lot of other shops too. Also there is a gift shop with a lot of cool stuff.

Farther down the road in the park, there is Honey Creek, it's really long. It starts at the waterfall and ends somewhere up in the mountains. Further down the river there is another waterfall that goes into a swimming pool called Blue Hole.

Off of the river are lots of hiking trails, with a lot of caves, such as, the Crystal, and Outlaw caves. You can have a lot fun exploring the Arbuckle Mountains. They have horseback riding and some pretty nice cabins.

Before you leave, check out the Blue Hole. It has a sandy beach, two really cool slides, and a diving board. It is a lot of fun visiting Turner Falls.

Chris Bucher, Grade 7
Chelsea Jr High School, OK

Challenging Events in My Life

Personally in my life there have been many challenging events that have affected me. One of these challenges was my mom breaking her ankle. Laurie, my mom, is usually quick on her feet but now even a few months after the incident it can be straining on her to do things physically; that really affects me too. She is the one that brings me the occasional forgotten football jersey and lunch, but recently that has been tough on her. Psychologically that was a challenge too, when my mom broke her ankle there was no help, it was just me and her. I had to lift her into the car and call my father. That really affected me, seeing a parent in so much pain and knowing at the moment you couldn't help her.

Now onto a more cheerful note, basketball is a huge challenge for me too. You have to sacrifice a lot of your time in playing this particular sport. Going on my 8th year of playing basketball tells you how much I love the sport. There are many things I have to work on in playing basketball. For example, ball handling is probably the hardest and most important skill you have to be good at in basketball. That's something I had started practicing since day one and I'm still improving at it too. Those are the events in my life that are the most challenging things that I have had to overcome.

Devin Totoro, Grade 8
Heritage Hall School, OK

Friendship

Who do you call when you're angry? Sad? Even happy? Friends are there when you need them the most. Friendship is like a growing plant. You want a true friend you can trust and look up to. As a result, many people think they found the right friends, and end up changing them.

It's amazing how when you need your friends, they're there for you. They always say the right things at the right times. It's like we share a brain. They know when you're frustrated, sad, and happy. Furthermore, you need a friend that will be there for you.

A plant is much like friendship. You need to nourish your plant so it can grow. Just like plants, you need to nourish your friendship. If you don't your friendship will die away. For example, if your friend is everything but nice to you and you're rotten to them, you won't be friends much longer.

Everyone needs a friend they can trust and look up to. Just like a role model, and if you couldn't trust your friend who could you trust? Someone to tell everything to. Maybe about nothing at all. Just realize, you need to be a good friend, too, or you won't be trusted.

Everyone talks to their friends when they're in need. Your friend always gives you a push when you need it. Always remember to nurture your friendships. Pick friends who you can trust and look up to. In addition, I think I did pretty good choosing my friends!

Lynsey Ramsey, Grade 8
Pigeon Forge Middle School, TN

Trips

Since I was a baby, I've been going on family trips. They might not be to Hawaii, but they are still fun.

One year I went to Washington, DC. It was so much fun and I got to spend a lot of time with my family while I was there. We went to the White House and Capitol building. We also went to the Holocaust Museum. I was upset when we had to leave for home.

In the fourth grade, I got to go to Disney World. It was the best amusement park I've ever been to.

Every summer I go to Florida to visit my grandparents, aunts, and uncles. It is so much fun going to the beach and just taking a break from Greenville for a while.

We also go to Myrtle Beach every January or February. It isn't crowded like it is in the summer. You can relax and there isn't as much noise.

Those are just a few of the places I've been over the years. Do you know what the best thing about these trips is? It's being with my family.

Jessica Scovel, Grade 7
St Mary's School, SC

The History of Halloween

Halloween is an ancient harvest festival. It started in Celtic Ireland in 5 B.C., which was 2,000 years ago. It was originally celebrated on November 1st. It was the end of summer and started a dark, cold winter.

The celebration was called Samhain. They thought on October 31st the ghosts of the dead came back to Earth. They thought this was a night some people predicted about the future. They would build bonfires where they would burn crops and animals as sacrifices to the Celtic gods. They would wear costumes made of animal heads and skins.

When the Romans conquered, they celebrated a goddess named Pomona which was fruit trees. It's believed this is why we bob for apples. During the 1800s, Christianity reigned in the Celtic area, and in the 7th century, a Pope designated November 1st All Saints Day to try and not focus on the dead and make it a church holiday. That's where we get All-Hallows Day.

Now, I am going to tell you some fun and interesting facts. The United States began officially celebrating Halloween in 1921 in Atoka, Minnesota. There are 36.1 million trick-or-treaters, mostly between the ages of 5-13 in the United States. One point one billion pounds of pumpkins are also sold around Halloween time in the U.S. We also eat about 26 pounds of candy a person in a year; most believe the largest portion is eaten around Halloween, which is not hard to believe for me. So, I hope you learned a thing or two about Halloween.

Alexis Herr, Grade 7
Stroud Middle School, OK

U.S.A. Invading

"RPG (Rocket Propelled Grenade) round coming in! Open fire!" These might be some words you would hear if you were part of the invasion of Iraq.

Though I strongly disagree, the United States of America, United Kingdom, Australia, Poland, and Denmark invaded Iraq during March of 2003. Using weapons like the Blackhawk Helicopters, M-1 Abram tanks, Challenger 2 tanks, F-15 Strike Eagle fighter jet, and KC-135 Stratotanker bomber, these countries tried to stop terrorism in Iraq.

Staying awake for 72 hours at a time, people fought and some even died. Iraq set oil fires and heavily fired RPG rounds at our tanks, but we stood strong.

Though we are still fighting today, terrorism in Iraq has decreased, but many good men were lost. Iraq has used car bombs, guns, oil well fires, and much more to destroy us. So far they have done a good job, but we are doing better.

I think we should have left Iraq alone and let them attack. From my view, we had no reason to invade them. All I heard was that their government was messed up, and we got involved, losing many good men. Iraq lost more people than we did, and war kills not only men, but our souls, especially those who lost loved ones.

And so that concludes my essay. Sorry to all the people who lost family and friends.

David Wagnon, Grade 7
Stroud Middle School, OK

Friends

I do not think that I could live without my dearest friends. They are always there for me when I need them. It is really good when you have a lot of different kinds of friends with all different personalities. I have friends who are quiet and compassionate. I always go to them when I am sad. I also have friends who are outgoing. They are always there for me when I want to talk with somebody. I have had many experiences where I was sad because something bad happened, and my friends immediately knew that something was wrong and came and talked to me.

It is also important that we are good friends to each other and do not leave anyone out. We need to think of how we would feel if we were the person that was being left out of a game or conversation. How would you feel? I would feel really bad. We need to make sure that every person has friends like we do.

Everyone should have friends within their families. Some of my best friends are in my family. We do a lot of things together. The best example of a friend is Jesus. He is with us all the time. He said, "Greater love has no one than this, than to lay down one's life for his friends."

I am so glad that God made friends for me to have! I could not live without them!

Elizabeth Cummings, Grade 7
Providence Classical School, AL

A Gift

This story is about a gift that I received that meant the world to me.

"Come on," my brother yelled. We were headed to our mom's house. My mom lives a distance away. All of a sudden we came upon this huge hill while riding our bikes. Josh got up the courage to try and climb the hill. At first he was doing well, until his bike got a flat tire. He ended up hiding the bike in a bush and pulling me up the hill.

When we arrived, Mom was smiling and said, "I have a surprise." She went into the next room and brought out a Cocker Spaniel. Josh stood still and finally got out the words, "Where's my present?" Mom looked and said, "The dog is for both of you." "I'm not a dog person," he moaned. "I'm sorry I didn't know besides you should be grateful." They both turned to look at me, I was showering the dog with hugs. "What are you going to name her," mom announced. "Awl! I think I'm going to name her Angel or Baby, since she's so small." As Josh left the room he turned and said, "Thanks" with a scowl. This present has made me so happy, I love it!

Renecia Hines, Grade 8
Turner Middle School, GA

Cabin Builder

My goal in life is to become a cabin builder. All my life I've build things and done carpentry. I started when I was ten years old and I have continued my success with it. One reason I want to become a cabin builder is that I know a lot about building. You also make good money doing it too. The power tools are awesome and with this job you need them.

The first reason I want to become a cabin builder is that I know a lot of things about building. I've helped build houses, churches, and a lot of other things too. My granddaddy bought a log cabin that wasn't finished and I helped him complete it.

This job also makes good money. I want a job that makes good money. When I get older I want to go to football games, NASCAR races, and have a lot of other things. All of this involves money. I'll also have to take care of my parents and grandparents.

This job isn't just for the money, it's for the power tools. At the age of ten years old I got a miter saw and other tools. This past summer I cut my finger on a table saw but it didn't stop me from using it. Power tools are fun, you just have to be careful with them.

I hope that I can achieve my goal. With all my experience I think I can. The money I make I will be able to buy more power tools. Maybe I won't hurt myself with them.

Hunter Bonner, Grade 8
Pigeon Forge Middle School, TN

Preventing Pollution

Pollution is a big problem of today all over the globe. Most of the pollution, however, can be prevented. Many of the things humans do that cause pollution, we do not have to do. The main sources of pollution are people, industries, and vehicles.

The first source of pollution is people. There are many ways we can prevent pollution. One is to stop wasting food and throwing away things we can recycle. We should save and recycle things such as plastic and clothes. One very important thing is to not dump chemical toxins and waste in the lakes and oceans.

The next source is industries. Industries cause a huge amount of pollution. They release millions of pounds of harmful emissions through smokestacks and leaking pipes daily. To prevent this, industries should find a cleaner burning fuel than coal to make their product. Industries can also limit the number of stages in production of their product.

The third source of pollution is vehicles. To reduce the amount of emissions you can use oxygenated fuels. Another way to reduce emissions is to drive at medium speed. This will release fewer emissions and improve your gas mileage. You can carpool and find ways to drive fewer miles, and walk or ride a bicycle for short errands.

In conclusion, you can see that many things cause pollution. Much of the pollution can be prevented if people work together to stop it.

Tiffany Woolery, Grade 9
Mulhall-Orlando High School, OK

Doctors Are My Heroes

Doctors are my heroes and I admire them with all my heart. You might be wondering why they are. Well, first of all they save many lives including mine. I was 15 months old when they found out that I had Wilm's tumor, a cancer in the kidney. I had to go through many treatments such as chemotherapy. They took out my right kidney that had cancer. Now thanks to them I survived. I also admire them for their determination in new ways of finding cures, saving lives, and preventing diseases by making vaccines. I would consider them to be my role models like my parents. My dad's a doctor of physical therapy, and my mom's a physical therapist as well. I plan to attend Harvard Medical School to get my degree in medicine. I'm also planning to become a pediatrician like those at St. Jude's Research Hospital, the doctors that saved my life. In believing in myself, the strength of God within me, and chasing my goals in life, I know that I can achieve my pursuit of happiness. That is why I think doctors are my heroes.

Elizabeth Catapang, Grade 7
Immaculate Conception School, MO

My Brother Luke

My little brother completely changed my life when he was born. I am the oldest of five kids; my brother is the youngest. Luke is ten years younger than I am, but he did change my life.

There has always been a special bond between Luke and I because by the time that he was born I was a pro at taking care of babies. By the time that Luke was five months old he had said his first word, my name. This was new, because most learn Mama or Dada first, but not Luke. His first word was Alex. Another reason that Luke completely changed my life, was that he was different from the others. Luke has loved the camera, and to smile all his life. Luke always wants someone to take his picture, no matter what he's doing. The only thing I dreaded when Luke was born was that we were going to have to move, which would mean a different school. I hate change, whatever type. This was different though; I liked it. Now here I am today and loving the change that my little brother Luke brought when he was born.

As you can see my little brother changed my life in a way that I never imagined. Luke means so much to me for he is one of the reasons I am who I am today.

Alex Sharum, Grade 8
Southwest Jr High School, AR

White-Tail Deer

The white-tail deer is a medium sized deer found throughout most of the continental United States, southern Canada, Mexico, Central America and northern portions of South America as far south as Peru.

White-tail deer are generalist and can adapt to a wide variety of habitats. Although most often thought of as forest animals depending on relativity small openings and edges, white-tail deer can equally adapt themselves to life in more open savanna and even sage communities as in Texas and in the Venezuelan llanos region.

Females enter the breeding period normally in late October or early November. Females give birth to one, two, or even possibly three spotted young, known as fawns in mid to late spring, generally in May or June. Fawns lose their spots during the first summer and will weigh from 44 to 77 pounds by the first winter. Male fawns tend to be slightly larger and heavier than females.

White-tails communicate in many different ways including sound, scent, and marking. All white-tail deer are capable of producing audible noises, unique to each animal. Fawns release a high pitched squeal known as a bleat, to call out to their mothers. Does also beat as well as grunt. Grunting produces a low, guttural sound that will attract attention of any other deer in the area. Both sides and bucks snort, a sound that often signals danger. Those are just a few of the many interesting facts about the white-tail deer.

Kyle Hurst, Grade 9
Trinity Christian Academy, AL

Soccer Skills = Life Skills

Soccer is the world's favorite sport. Soccer is important because it teaches values. Important life lessons soccer teaches are the value of hard work, confidence, and teamwork.

For me, the happiest moment in soccer is scoring. Scoring makes me feel pride in my work. It's the end result of hours of practice. It also feels good to win an aerial challenge over a bigger player. Working to overcome obstacles in soccer helps me see I can overcome obstacles in other areas of life. One way to apply this lesson is through academics. A student who isn't the smartest in the class can overcome that by working hard. Getting good grades and getting into a good college is the equivalent of scoring a goal in soccer.

Running past players and taking the ball from players makes me feel confident. After a good play, I play even better. This shows that it's good to have confidence and that trait will pay off. If a person is confident during a test he will probably do well.

In soccer it's also important to be a team player. Success in life also requires teamwork. For example, if a student wants to get smarter, the student must work with the teacher. The teacher cannot help the student unless the student cooperates.

Soccer is the most popular sport because it teaches the most about life. Soccer teaches the value of hard work, confidence, and teamwork. This is why soccer is so loved.

Wesley Eads, Grade 8
Oakbrook Middle School, SC

My Favorite Sport

My favorite sport is football. Out of all the sports I have played, football to me is the best sport. It's my favorite sport because it's what I love to do on my spare time. This sport is fun to me because I like contact and football is a contact sport.

Football is an easy sport if you pay attention and listen. Sometimes you lose sometimes you win, but it feels better to win than lose any day. Football is a fun game if you understand the rules. Once you learn the rules, you can play all day.

If you play football you have to have a good attitude, unlike me I don't like to lose. I get really mad and sometimes want to quit. You will have to be a team player to play because you can't play by yourself.

When you play football you're going to want a good coach. If you have a good attitude you will go a long way and win a lot of games. The coach will encourage you to have a good attitude winning or losing your games.

Jeffery Cash, Grade 8
Turner Middle School, GA

Reading Magic

Today's society is more involved in electronics than into books. They think it takes them too long. Most people think reading isn't cool. I am not one of those people.

Most people have probably heard the saying "Reading is magic." To me, it really is. When I open a new book, the smooth crackling of pages and its sweet smell invite me to jump into the story within. I don't read about the characters' problems. I am the character. I am inside the story, watching, and trying to find the answers that the characters and I seek.

When I read, I can go to places I've never even dreamed of — China, Africa, England, Fantasyland. I can fly with dragons, swim with mermaids, and journey for answers. I fight alongside the characters and share their feelings.

I shudder to see people misuse or damage books, but in truth it doesn't harm the story at all. Reading is magic to some people and not to others. Books to me are held above any other form of entertainment. There are people who view books as just what they are — a bunch of papers. There are others who are open to them, but it doesn't hold the same happiness. And there are very few people like me, who disappear into the story and read so intently that the words flow together into sounds, feelings, pictures, and places — and create Reading Magic.

Dahlia Ghabour, Grade 8
Brandon Academy, FL

The Extinction of the Polar Bear

The polar bear is a beautiful animal. Sadly, there are not many left due to global warming. The global warming melts more than 23,000 square miles a year. The ice is melting in the main habitat of the bear, therefore, the bear has no place to live. The bears hunt on the ice mostly. Sometimes you can see them sitting by an air hole waiting for a seal to come up. These great mammals have thrived for many years; now they're on the verge of extinction.

The polar bear is just one of hundreds of animals about to become extinct. The tiger, for example, is almost extinct because humans are cutting down the forest where they live, and farmers are shooting them in fear that they will kill farm animals. Like the polar bear, these great creatures don't deserve to die. We should be ashamed because we're what's causing it through pollution and other things such as carbon dioxide.

I wish all creatures could live together in peace. Look at how bad pollution is now; if we do not act fast, just think of how many more animals will become extinct. We need to step up and throw things away where they belong. I mean just drive down the highway and look at the filth. So next time you see a piece of trash, pick it up. It may not look like it, but it makes a difference.

Ryan Mathews, Grade 7
Stroud Middle School, OK

Gary's R-E-S-P-E-C-T

R-E-S-P-E-C-T! Find out what it means to me! This is one of the songs my brother would just burst out singing, even if we were in Walmart.

Gary was tall and had black hair with orange dye streaked through it. He was tan, and he liked to wear shirts with funny words on them. He had brown eyes, a big smile, small ears, and a pointy nose.

For me, the best thing about him was he was not a quitter. If someone told him to do something, he never backed down. He had a great sense of humor, and was fun to talk to. On August 14, 2007, he had a serious wreck and was life-flighted to St. Johns Hospital.

Before the accident, Gary would always e-mail Carrie Underwood. Gary was an all-time Carrie Underwood and an Oklahoma Sooners fan. His whole room is Carrie Underwood, and Oklahoma.

He loved to bowl with all of us at the bowling alley in Claremore. He worked there before he graduated. After he graduated, he starting working at American Airlines. He worked on the computers. My brother is a very good person. He brings everyone together as a family, and is fun to have around.

My brother Gary died August 21, 2007, at St. Johns in Tulsa. We had his funeral that Friday in Claremore. It is hard for our family to go on, but we are hanging in there. I know he is gone, but to me he is still in my heart.

Kimberly Autry, Grade 8
Chelsea Jr High School, OK

The Gleaming Day

Ahh! I reached my most favorite and peaceful place, my deer stand. As I walked up to the door I undo the latch and gently opened the squeaky camouflaged door. I carefully put my gun down against the creased wall and took off my orange coat. Then opened the windows for the magnificent breeze of the scented flowers.

Yellow, white, and purple flowers fill the wooded area. Each one as bright and scented as the next. As I waited peacefully, blue jays and robins flew around and young brown squirrels played tag from branch to branch in the old pecan tree. Then, the most beautiful brown buck jumped the stretched tight brown barbed wire fence to graze in the colorful field.

While I sat there and watched the buck, a momma and her spotted baby jumped the fence and started eating the bright colored flowers. The baby looked up and jumped and hopped around chasing butterflies like Bambi.

Forty-five minutes later, the deer jumped the fence and wandered away. So I got up and headed back to the house when then I smelled the sweet aroma of pancakes for breakfast.

Terri Boland, Grade 7
Chelsea Jr High School, OK

The Deaf Boy's Life

If you want to know about a deaf boy's life, you're fixing to find out. I had two favorite teachers. Their names were Mrs. Burr and Mrs. Cochran. I had a pretty cool class. It was sign language class.

I had a cool friend in this class. His name is Jake. He's hard of hearing like me. I wear two blue hearing aids. They were $3,000 each. I'm supposed to get two new ones. They are red, white, pink, and blue. Pretty cool hearing aids I think.

Claremore, Oklahoma taught me sign language. From day one to the end of the next two years, they taught me sign language. I learned 3,000 words in one year. Amazing, huh? I loved it.

I would have love to have stayed for two more years, but my mom wanted to move to Chelsea, Oklahoma really bad. So, here I am in Chelsea. However, I'll never forget my years of learning sign language.

The playground there is pretty awesome. They have a soccer field, giant slides, swings, and tire swings. They had a ton of dandelions in the field. Jake and I loved to roll in them. I love Claremore. Well, that's the life of the deaf boy.

Seth Francis, Grade 7
Chelsea Jr High School, OK

Never Give Up

My mother Patricia always liked to run around with her friends, drive fast and act crazy. She never worried about wearing her seat belt or paying attention to her driving until one night, my mom was driving to town. She was going way too fast around a corner. She lost control of the vehicle and flipped the truck four times throwing her out of the driver's side window. When the truck finally stopped, my mother had been pinned underneath the truck and had to stay that way until the fire department used the Jaws of Life to get the truck off her. The doctor told my grandmother to call the rest of the family in because my mother would not make it through the night. The next day, the doctor told my mom that she wouldn't be able to walk or have children.

Patricia was 17 years old. She had a very small frame and weighed 120 pounds. She always liked to be around children and always wanted to have kids of her own, be able to run and do athletic things.

The best thing about my mother is she never gave up when the outcome looked grim. She just kept trying and proved the doctor wrong. After two months in tractions she stood up and walked. Before the accident my mother didn't wear a seat belt and drove carelessly. This has taught me a lesson for life. That lesson is that it isn't ok to be careless and never give up.

Arizona Tatum, Grade 9
Chelsea Jr High School, OK

Plaid

You're about to read how I received a kitten, what it was like living with her, and how hard it was saying good-bye. I hope you'll be regaled while reading this.

The last week of summer, my neighbor, Chasen, took a free kitten without asking. The poor kitten was covered in fleas, so Chasen, my mom, and I gave her a flea bath. We spent two hours cleaning her. When Chasen's mom arrived, she answered no. My mom said we could keep her until we found a home.

Before Chasen left he named her Plaid because the markings on her head looked like a plaid pattern. She was a calico with an orange, black, and white fluffy tail. Her body was white except her tail and above her eyes. We kept Plaid in the laundry room because I have two dogs and two cats. Whenever she was alone she'd audibly meow. If someone was with her, she'd stop. So I took a sleeping bag and slept in the laundry room. It wasn't the best sleep, but it was worth it. Soon, she got used to my pets and hung around the house.

A month later, my mom found a home. When Plaid left, I tried so hard not to cry. It was a long, sorrowful good-bye. After she left, I cried for a long time.

Today, I've been missing her for three weeks. I still wish I could keep her. As my mom said, it was for the best.

Kasey Lentini, Grade 7
Sebastian River Middle School, FL

The Beach and Its Wildlife

Have you ever been to a beach? If so, you know how fun it is relaxing, reading a good book, and playing in the water, but have you ever thought about what really happens to those soda rings you leave on the beach and take for granted they will be buried? Guess what, they do not.

Most of the time trash is thrown away, but when it is left out, animals can harm themselves. Seagulls eat that stale bread thrown out to them, but that is edible. Occasionally they will eat a plastic wrapper left from that tuna fish sandwich you ate and choke and die. Baby turtles will get their head stuck in that plastic ring you get with every six-pack of soda. Eventually they grow up, and the plastic cuts off the turtle's breathing, and it is now dead.

Off the beach, manatees, stingrays, and dolphins are being hit and badly hurt by boats and wave runners. Other times, pollutants dumped overboard just plain poison the fish and kill them. Part of our ecosystem is dying because of our recklessness on the beach and in the waters, and we need to stop it.

Companies have for the most part eliminated the plastic soda rings, but by doing our part by recycling and throwing away trash and by not polluting the environment, we can protect the ecosystem and save our world for another day.

Jack Mimlitz, Grade 8
St Gerard Majella School, MO

Becoming an Officer

I would like to begin by saying that I respect all kinds of police officers, sheriffs and any type of law enforcement officer. I am mainly saying that because I am looking forward to becoming a law enforcement officer some day in the future. Also, these people help us to obey the laws of the Constitution.

My dad used to be a traffic officer. He worked at the Miami International Airport for 22 years. Now he is retired but he still encourages me in the field of law enforcement.

When I turn 14 in the fall, I can be active in a program called Teen court. It is for teenagers who have committed small crimes. I can learn to be a court officer such as a bailiff. Your peers judge you and punish you. I want to help offenders be given a second chance. I can also see if there are any crimes being committed in my neighborhood.

When I turn 15 I will be able to be a Police Explorer. It is a program offered by the Boy Scouts. The program helps to prepare teenagers who want to become law enforcement officers. I can help in parades or clerk in an office and assist at special events.

Now, I am doing my part by helping young children respect law enforcement officers. I made a puppet stage and puppets. I am going to local libraries, schools and parks to celebrate Law Month. My puppet shows are about police officers being your friends. The children can also learn about safety, dialing 911 in an emergency and to not talk or take anything from strangers.

Brad Allen, Grade 8
Florida International Academy, FL

California Vacation

On a nice hot summer day my family and I went to the airport for an exciting vacation to California. Instead of staying at a fancy hotel we all went to our uncle's house that used to live next to a famous celebrity named Blink 182. The next day we all went to the beach, and while we were surfing surprisingly, a dolphin swam right next to me. At first I thought it was a shark, but when I realized it was just a dolphin I felt much better. Later that day we all went to an ecstatic restaurant; while we were eating the waiter put the food down and spilled lots of sauce all over my shirt. Further on we all went to Beverly Hills and Los Angeles and saw many famous celebrities. To sum up the last few days we went to California Adventures and rode massive amounts of exciting rides. The best was the ride called California Soaring. It was amazing. The reason why I wrote this essay is because I learned that vacations can really bond your family. When we came home our whole family thought that this would be a vacation that we all would never forget.

Colton Kerr, Grade 8
Heritage Hall School, OK

A Real Friend

Do you know the saying about friends being your emotional safety net? Well my best friend Sarah was an actual safety net for me!

While we were on our Peace River Trip, my seven classmates and I had to climb a tree. We were standing in no particular order when our teacher, Mrs. Klein, told us, "Without talking, arrange yourselves in alphabetical order, by middle names." We were getting pretty comfortable with the idea and then she said, "If anyone says anything you have to start from the beginning." We were all thinking to ourselves, "What are you crazy!"

After many tries we were finally one move away from conquering our goal. It was up to Sarah and I. We had to maneuver ourselves on a branch that probably spanned about twelve inches. Sarah started shaking, which made me start to shake. Then my friend Maddy grabbed onto us to help stop the movement on the branch. Then Sarah lost her balance and started to fall off the branch. Out of nowhere her hand came up and grabbed my shirt. As I was falling I was thinking to myself how hard that dirty ground was going to be on my back. I was thinking whether to fall on my left shoulder or my right. I was closing my eyes, ready to brace myself for that hard ground and then I heard an "ouch!" It wasn't the ground; it was my best friend Sarah!

Jessica Zimmerman, Grade 8
Goldie Feldman Academy, FL

The Great Gift of Wisdom

Wisdom is a gift of the Holy Spirit that allows us to see the world through God's eyes. Wisdom is sometimes found in children, and you do not have to be brilliant to have the gift of wisdom. St. Thomas Aquinas believed that wisdom perfected the virtue of charity and that all sources of wisdom come through the Holy Spirit. Along with many virtues, Wisdom is truly a gift, given freely by God.

Wisdom is given to us at Baptism and is increased through Confirmation. All leaders need wisdom. Teachers, presidents, the Pope, students, priests, and deacons all need wisdom to make the correct decisions. Wisdom was practiced during the life of St. Cecelia. On the other hand, Wisdom was not practiced when Peter told Jesus how to be the king.

The overall effect of wisdom is that if used correctly, you will get to heaven. Also, you will acquire the decision-making skill. In many circumstances, I will be faced with making decisions and I hope that I make the correct one. The effects of not practicing wisdom are leading down the wrong road and eventually drifting from God. But remember, with God all things are possible!

Madison Vick, Grade 8
St Mary's School, SC

The Sale

Me and my friend Tyler loved the band AC-DC. We would always listen to their songs when we were together.

AC-DC has been a band for a long time, even before me and Tyler were even born. But still, we loved to listen to their songs.

Tyler, one day, called me and said, "Oh my goodness AC-DC isn't playing any more gigs and isn't making any more CDs!" At that time, I thought it was the end of the world. I had to check this out for myself, so I went on-line and I Googled and Googled 'til I found the truth. What Tyler said was true! They were retiring, and they weren't making any more CDs. I couldn't believe it, to me at the time, they were the best classic rock band that there was! Right then I probably felt every emotion there was, so immediately I called Tyler back and, pretty much for the whole night, talked about why AC-DC would retire other than the reason that they were an older band.

I was still in shock for the next few days, and so was Tyler. But one day after my guitar lessons, I was waiting on my Mom to pick me up and I looked around the store a little bit, and as I was looking at the CDs they had, I saw a ton of AC-DC albums and they were on sale! I couldn't believe it!

In the end, everything turned out good.

Kolby Schneider, Grade 8
College Heights Christian School, MO

The Hunt

Last winter I went to Indiana on a hunting trip with my dad. I honestly will say that Indiana is the prettiest place I have seen so far in my life. After an eight hour drive, we arrive. The first thing we have to do is unpack all of our gear and supplies. We load our tree stands onto the golf cart, to make it easier to carry to the fields. My dad and I had put up all of the stands except for mine, just then I spotted the perfect place. A wonderful spot overlooking the corner of a corn field and soybean field and it was loaded with hardwoods. I knew this was the spot I would kill my deer. After putting up my stand, we headed to the house to rest up for the early morning. My dad said we were getting up early, but I hardly remember sleeping at all. I was too excited. Before the sun was up we were dressed in our camo best and boots and headed to the woods. I took a seat in my stand and waited, and as all hunters know, is the most important part. Quite a few hours later I heard the crackle of the leaves and looked up and there was a huge seven pointer right in front of me. I slowly raised my muzzleloader and BOOM! I hit it; it dropped where it stood. After getting my dad to help load the big buck and haul him to the house, I was still excited.

My dad and I already have our next trip to Indiana planned for this year, and I can't wait!

Prestan Kittle, Grade 9
Sylvania School, AL

My Life as a Teenager

My life as a teenager is really great. I have a lot of great friends, and I have the best mother ever. My most important thing I want to do as a teenager is just to live my life as a teenage drama queen. I like to go shopping as a girl and be myself 'cause there is a lot of things to do as a teenage girl. I sometimes think that I am not fitting in with other girls that are my age, but sometimes it is best to be yourself.

I like to go to parties with friend and have fun, but my most important thing my mom told me to do as a kid, teen, and an adult is to give respect even if they don't give it to you back. As a teenage girl I just want everything to be okay 'cause I know that I am not perfect and nobody else is perfect.

Finally, I like to chat with boys on Myspace and anywhere else 'cause that is sometimes what teen girls do. I love to listen to all kinds of music that is interesting to me like gospel and R&B. My hero I look up to is my mom. She is great 'cause she always does for me and my sister and I know that she will always love and care for me, so that's my way of saying I love my mother and that's my hero.

Tonavius Marshall, Grade 8
Seminole County Middle/High School, GA

A Friend for Life

The time I spend with my older sister Lucy is extraordinarily valuable. Because she is only 19 months older than me, Lucy has experienced many of the frustrations and dilemmas that I am currently going through, and she remembers clearly and recognizes my pain. Unlike many of my friends, Lucy is sensitive and rarely acts silly when I reveal my secrets and problems. Although my mother is important to me too, my sister appreciates my feelings in a way my mother cannot. More important, my sister doesn't judge me or consider me too young or insignificant.

Giver is one of Lucy's other roles. She values my opinions and gives me the opportunity to listen to her predicaments and guide her through her problems and hurts. She has faith in me. At a time when I am going through so many changes and new experiences, Lucy's faith in me gives me confidence and security.

Nonetheless, Lucy has her faults. Some nights my sister seems as if she would much rather be somewhere else with someone else. Moments like these hurt me deeply because I love her so much and hate being left out. Lucy is going through many changes as well. When she does something disappointing, it is especially painful, as if my good "twin" has gone and been replaced with a stranger. Luckily, our bond is strong, and we forgive each other easily. For this, she will always be my best friend, and I will admire her forever.

Zoe Harrison, Grade 7
White Station Middle School, TN

Ryan

The most important person is my cousin. Ryan is seven years old. Sometimes he is a handful and other times he is not that bad. My mom thinks he is always a handful, but she still loves him. He has two brothers and one sister. Their names are Dusty, Wyatt, and Athena. His mom's name is Amy and his dad's name is Wes. He lives in Lockwood.

He does not live in a normal house. His house is an old building. His mom drives a van and his dad drives a pickup truck. He lives in a very evil town called Lockwood. I call Lockwood evil because of the cops that live and work there. Ryan's mom, dad, brothers, and sister love living in Lockwood. I do have to admit that Lockwood is not that bad. My mom and dad drive to Lockwood's grocery store to get more food.

Ryan's sister Athena is actually called Froggy. One of Ryan's brothers is Dusty I call him Dusty Dog. The other brother's name is Wyatt but we call him Cowboy. My cousin is the most important person. My cousin Ryan is not a bad kid at all. His mom brings him almost every weekend saying that Ryan has been doing bad things, when Ryan has not been doing any thing bad at all.

Zachary Wright, Grade 7
Greenfield Jr/Sr High School, MO

Hank Aaron

Crack!!! Another home run by Hank Aaron. Hank Aaron was one of the greatest baseball players our world has ever seen. Hank Aaron wasn't only inducted into the Cooperstown Hall of Fame, but held the home run record for a long period of time. Hank Aaron faced many rough times in his baseball career.

First, Hank Aaron was inducted into the Cooperstown Hall of Fame. Hank Aaron was inducted for the many records he set over his career such as 2,297 RBI's. Hank Aaron achieved the greatest achievement in baseball. His home run record of 755 home runs was the biggest record in baseball.

Second, Hank Aaron has set many high records in his time. He played for the Milwaukee Braves from 1954-1965; he played for the Atlanta Braves from 1966-1974, and played for the Milwaukee Braves from 1975-1976. During this time he had a batting average of .332 and an NL MVP award. Hank Aaron set many records during his career.

Thirdly, Hank Aaron faced many death threats, racist letters and threats against him and his family. During this time Hank Aaron still stayed mentally strong and physically strong. He let his bat do the talking for him. Hank Aaron made it through all those tough years and kept a cool head.

In conclusion, Hank Aaron was one of the greatest baseball players of all time. Hank Aaron fought through all the hard times to play the game he loved. Hank Aaron played some good baseball.

Anthony Civita, Grade 7
Sebastian River Middle School, FL

Exchange Student

Two years ago, my parents got a phone call asking if our family would like to host an international student. My parents were not real thrilled about it, but my sister and I were. Our family discussed the issue and came to the conclusion that we would make an attempt at it. In less than two weeks, a nineteen-year old Mexican man moved in with our family. It was a little awkward at first, but when we got to understand his lifestyle and wonderful sense of humor, we had a great year with him.

Learning his Mexican culture was the best part. His family sent us gifts from Mexico that were always very unique and had a classic part of Mexican history to be told about it. His Mexican cooking was very delicious! My sister and I had fun helping him cook the cultural meals. He would talk about his family and friends, and how much he had always wanted to be educated in America. We had the opportunity of traveling with him and showing him different places in America. Our family took the time to show him some different American and other cultural food during his stay.

He became very popular in school and at church. He became a Christian in our home shortly after he arrived. Some of the greatest memories of my life took place in that one year with him. The experience of having a "brother" for the first time was fun, educational, and unforgettable.

Megan Wilson, Grade 8
College Heights Christian School, MO

Why I Am an American Patriot!

What do I mean by patriotism? I speculate to suggest that what I mean is a sense of faithful loyalty… a patriotism which is not sudden, abrupt outbursts of passion, but should be the imperturbable and steady devotion of a lifetime. Charles Chesterton stated, "My country, right or wrong, and it is like saying, my mother drunk or sober." I agree, don't you?

In a wonderful speech that touched many hearts, John F. Kennedy stated, "Ask not what your country can do for you, but what you can do for your country." Now that I am older, I see a major problem in our nation. We rely on our country when our country needs to rely on us. *Democracy* means that *we* select and determine what happens to our country and who our government is. Voting is a good example. As a patriot, you should do something for your country today, tomorrow might be too late.

"In God We Trust" we often declare, yet we give it no meaning. Our founding fathers would be very disappointed in today's nation. America was founded on God. We have given up on God, and we haven't realized that we don't care. He has enriched our country with everything we want and need. We should give him *ALL* honor and glory for it. Reword "In God We Trust," form it say "In God I Trust." Be a patriot, if not for me, for your country, for yourself!

Hannah West, Grade 8
Clara Jr High School, MS

Lost But Never Forgotten

Leaving with no say, she left me. Who? My mom. Wondering every day what it would be like if she was still here. Going through life with trials and tribulations. Burning in my heart. Why me? Thinking back when we were a 'true' family, life was normal. She was my best friend. In my mind, Nigela (Mom) and I had a non-ending thought. Every time we would ride in the car, I would ask her many questions. I cannot do that anymore. Living in my house is like coming home for no reason. I do not like to be at home because it feels dull and empty without her.

Basically, that is why I love school so passionately because she loved education. She had many degrees and she also wanted to be a doctor. Well, I do also. We are and were so alike. I remember when we used to do countless things together. I am a different person now. It is like a piece of me has gone missing. Because she has done many great things, I can look back and do the same without her. One day my being will be a testimony to how I made it without my mom. I will always consider and value her. She may be gone, but she is never forgotten.

Chase Moore, Grade 7
White Station Middle School, TN

Music in My Life

Music has really changed my life. It has become my passion, love, and life. I don't know what I would do without it.

A talented lead guitarist inspired me to learn how to play. One day in October 2005, I received my first, acoustic, blue guitar.

I couldn't put the thing down! My mom was so amazed that she signed me up for lessons! I started right away in November with a great teacher named Bill. I have a blast taking lessons with him.

Then on Christmas day, I woke to find a shiny, new, metallic blue electric guitar! I started to play it immediately! I didn't even want to open the rest of the gifts! I just loved it!

As I continued to take lessons, I became even better. I went from doing basic chords, to doing power chords. My parents were amazed. It made me feel good about myself.

I continued for another year still learning. It was amazing how many songs I could play! I was so grateful I had found my talent.

So I am grateful for the gift that I have been given. It has helped me realize that sports are not everything. I now have the ability to feel that I am good at something. I am very happy about this great gift to play music.

I hope that this story of passion will inspire others who may feel the same way. Just find your talent. It's out there.

Sam Koltun, Grade 7
Incarnate Word Catholic Elementary School, MO

How to Play Fantasy Football

Today, I will tell you how to play Fantasy Football. It is a fun way to keep up with professional football. One of the first things you must do is select from several of the internet websites that offer free Fantasy Football Leagues, such as ESPN.com, NFL.com, or CBS.com. Let's say you decide to play fantasy football through ESPN.com, you begin by clicking "Fantasy." You then click on "Football" and press "Join League."

Once you have chosen a league, you have to worry about which players you want to pick or draft. To win at Fantasy Football your team must accumulate or score the most points by the end of the season. Therefore, it is important to draft a set of players that will hopefully earn the most points. For example, if you choose Larry Johnson as your running-back and he scores in next Monday night's game, you earn a certain amount of points.

The day of the Fantasy draft, you should be prepared with a list of the players you hope to acquire. You are required to pick two running-backs, 2 wide-receivers, one quarterback, one kicker, one tight-end, and one team's defense. You will also need to be prepared to select a "Bench," which are your backup players in case of injury. If you just started following sports, Sports Illustrated or ESPN's websites list their top players.

After your draft is over, you can kick back and watch the games and see how your team does. Have fun!

Jay Cohlmia, Grade 8
Heritage Hall School, OK

Broken Arm!

When I was five years old, I broke my arm. I remember I was watching TV and for some reason I started running up and down the couch. I tripped and fell off. I remember lying there on the floor looking at my left arm. My arm looked like it had been twisted all the way around. My mom and dad came running in and my dad said we had to go to the hospital. We got in the car and my dad was holding me and asked if I could move it. Then I tried to move it, it felt like I didn't even have an arm. It felt like nothing was there it was hurting so badly.

When we got to the hospital, we had to wait about an hour for the doctor to look at my arm. When he finally took me back to get x-rays, we could see that it was broken. The two bones twisted over each other. We had to wait until the next morning because I had eaten earlier and they could not do the surgery. All night my arm hurt so badly but the next morning they took me in for surgery. I remember them saying count back from 100 I only got to 99, and then I fell asleep. The surgery went fine. I was really happy to hear it. I know now to never do that again. I guess running on the couch is not a good idea.

Ashlyn Baker, Grade 8
Eagles Landing Middle School, FL

Good Friends

What are the requirements for being a good friend? First, you have to be trusting. Secondly, you have to be there for your friend. Also, you have to stick up for them. And you have to be honest.

I don't know about everyone else, but I love to be in the know. If you have a friend that doesn't trust you with secrets, you feel like you're in the dark. Trust is *very* important. And when you do trust your friends, it gives you something to talk about.

Going through hard times? That's what good friends are for, to get you through them. When your friend has your back, it makes you feel so special. It's even better when you have their back, too.

I hate seeing people get insulted, and nobody stand up for them. If their friends were loyal enough, they should be right there insulting the bully back. That is a very big characteristic of a good friend.

Well, now that you know what a good friend is, let's review. You have to trust your friend first of all. You have to have their back. And, you need to stand up for them. Now, go out there and be the good friend you're meant to be.

Callie Smith, Grade 8
Pigeon Forge Middle School, TN

A Clutch Kicker

The kick is up and it's good! Who would have thought that a kid from a small town of around 250 people would grow up to play professional football for the Seattle Seahawks?

Josh Brown was born in Tulsa, Oklahoma on April 29, 1979. When he was in the 8th grade, he moved to Foyil, Oklahoma. He grew up in a small town, right off of Highway 66 playing football and other sports, just like me. In high school, he was a state high jump champion. In football, he was a running back, punter, kicker, kick returner, punt returner, and safety.

After high school, Josh went to the University of Nebraska to kick for the Cornhuskers. While there, Brown hit a regular season career long of 48 yards. He also made 104 point after touches (PATs) in a row.

After graduating from Nebraska with a communications degree, he was drafted by the Seattle Seahawks. Since 2003, Josh has been playing for the Seahawks and has a career long of 58 yards. He is considered one of the best clutch kickers in the National Football League. He earned that title by hitting four game-winning field goals in the final minutes of games.

Seeing him on television makes young people realize they can reach their dreams. He makes over a million dollars a year doing what he loves to do.

Caleb Captain, Grade 8
Chelsea Jr High School, OK

Ocean

You see miles beyond miles of water. The sunlight flashing on the sea shooting up into your eyes. The sparkling water crashes down on the shore as if it were a huge monster tearing apart a city. Below lies dark creatures that could rip you apart in seconds. At the same time what lies above are beautiful things from big to small. The ocean seems as if it could swallow you whole. With its huge glaring eyes staring you down and you find a shiver throughout your body, with a rush of fear. But at the same time you wish you could give it a big hug for what an impact its done for you. You see dolphins jumping out of the water and starfish stuck to rocks. For you jump into it and feel a warm sensation move through your hair as you get it wet. The water shoots by your skin as you dive under. The moans of fish swimming frantically beside you. Salty water plunges into your mouth as you open it. A taste of nastiness creeps down your throat. The ocean is a large place to get lost in wonderful things.

Dakota Barker, Grade 9
West Jr High School, MO

The Fighting Cancer

According to Wikipedia, cancer is "any various malignant neoplasm marked by the proliferation of anaplastic cells that tend to invade surrounding tissue and metastasize the new body sites." Cancer is a group of diseases in which cells are *aggressive* (grow and divide without respect to normal limits), *invasive* (invade and destroy adjacent tissues), and/or *metastasis* (spread to other locations in the body). These three malignant properties of cancers differentiate them from benign tumors which are self-limited in their growth and do not invade or metastasize (although some benign tumor types are capable of becoming malignant). Cancer may affect people at all ages, even fetuses, but risk for the more common varieties tends to increase with age. Cancer causes about 13% of all deaths. Apart from people, forms of cancer may affect animals and plants.

In today's world, cancer is a very serious disease. There are many different types of cancer. A lot of people die every day from this horrendous disease. Unfortunately, there is no cure for cancer. Hopefully, there will be soon! Cancer does not have an age limit; it is found in young and old. Anyone can get cancer anytime or anywhere in their body. Cancer is also a disease that can be hereditary.

According to Wikipedia, heredity is "the transfer of characteristics from parents to offspring through their genes, or the transfer of a title, style, or social status through the social convention known as inheritance (for example, a Hereditary Title may be passed down according to relevant customs and/or laws)."

Julia Conner, Grade 7
Stroud Middle School, OK

Mr. Rogers

If you have never seen an episode of Mr. Roger's Neighborhood, I think you should. He talks about, and does very good things. Mr. Rogers is a great television show.

One morning I was going through the channels trying to find something to watch. I didn't see anything that I wanted to see. However, I came to a show where a man was singing. I was just going to see what it was, but before I knew it I had watched the whole episode. After he had changed his jacket and shoes, Mr. Mcfeely stopped by with a speedy delivery. Mr. Rogers had asked him to bring by a video about how crayons were made. They showed how to draw nice pictures with crayons. They also talk about what would happen if you draw on something that you shouldn't. The video showed how the crayons were molded, wrapped, and put into boxes. After we watched the film, Mr. Mcfeely had to go. Although they both agreed it was a good video. Listening to what Mr. Rogers says is great.

Mr. Rogers never has a bad thing to say. He is as nice as pie. Before we have to leave, he goes into his kitchen and feeds his fish. In summary, he sings one last song. Then we have to say goodbye for the day. Through he promises that he will be back when the day is new. Mr. Rogers is the best show on TV.

Paige Hargis, Grade 7
Greenfield Jr/Sr High School, MO

A Tragic Death

My grandma Kay was always my hero. She was the light in my eye and the sunshine in my day. Then, when I was in second grade she came down with leukemia. When my grandma was diagnosed with leukemia I remember my family being under a lot of stress, especially my mom who was very close to her. It was tragic and no one wanted to go through it, but we all had to be strong.

Once my grandma started chemotherapy she looked miserable. She looked like she would have rather died than been put through all the pain. She shaved her head as soon as she started balding from the medicine, knowing it would happen anyway. Everyone felt horrible for what was happening, but they know all they could do is pray.

Although everyone tried they just couldn't keep her here. One night my parents got a phone call telling us she went to a better place. My parents took me and my brother to the truck I was scared because I wasn't quite sure what was happening. They took us to her house and put us back to sleep. The next morning they told us she was gone.

I cried a lot and missed several days of school. It was very depressing and no one wanted it to happen, but they knew that she wasn't suffering anymore. To this day I still miss and love my grandma and would give anything to have her here with me.

Jordan Masters, Grade 8
Mayflower Middle School, AR

My Friend's Bar Mitzvah

On March 24th, I went to my friend, Greg's, Bar Mitzvah and had a great time. Before the service started, we had to wait for all the guests to arrive. As soon as I entered the sanctuary, I observed all the things in the room, like the beautiful stained glass and the big ark. On the top of the ark were gold Hebrew letters going down the ark's sides. Then we listened and watched the service. After Greg read his Torah portion, he recited his speech and thanked everyone who had done something to help him. After the service ended, it was time for his party. At the party there were a lot of games like DDR, basketball, and arcade games. While the kids were playing in the lobby, the adults had their own room. That room had different kinds of food including a sushi bar.

Now while all of this was going on, I compared my friend's Bar Mitzvah to my upcoming one. First of all, I noticed that he read all of the Hebrew way too fast and it was hard to understand. I realized that I'll have to speak very slowly for people to understand what I am saying. Then I noticed that even though he was speaking into the microphone, Greg wasn't projecting his voice, so I couldn't hear him very well. My observations will prepare me for my Bar Mitzvah and I know I'll do better than him.

Ryan Price, Grade 8
Eagles Landing Middle School, FL

First Flight

The first time I jumped while I was horseback riding I fell. It was not the normal kind of flop off of the horse, it was the kind where one's foot gets caught in the stirrup and lose your balance kind of fall. Let me take you back to that lovely evening in the middle of August. It was nearly dusk, and I was cantering astride Skipper. We were flying over the jumps; the wind was streaming our hair out behind us. We were a glorious sight to behold.

It all started when we landed after the 4' 5" jump, Skipper had landed all wrong and his stride was off. I could tell he had hurt himself and as I tried to stop him, he just started going faster. As we approached the 5' jump he started to gallop, we were midair when I realized that I had lost my stirrup. I started to freak out and Skipper sensed my fear. He twisted around to make sure that I was okay. Then it happened; I felt myself slipping. As Skipper landed, I fell. I landed on a rock and started to cry.

My trainer rushed over to make sure I was okay. After I assured her that I was okay, she went to make sure Skipper was not injured. He was still in one piece!

Skipper escaped with a sprained tendon, and I with a bruised tailbone.

Morgan Schott, Grade 9
Baton Rouge Magnet High School, LA

Why I Like Halloween

Why I like Halloween. Because it's a season where you get to dress up as something you're not. Anything you want to be. You also get a lot of candy. Too much actually. Then you and your friends can go together and have a blast walking up and down the parkway.

The first reason I like Halloween is because you get to dress up as something you aren't or want to be. It's a good way to express yourself. Most people dress up as a scary movie character or a funny creature. It's whatever you want.

Also you get a lot of candy. I mean a lot. So much you want to eat candy for a year. It's great, but it's kinda embarrassing to walk up to random people and ask for candy by saying "Trick or Treat." Sometimes your bucket or bag will break then you have to carry it in your shirt.

Another exciting thing about Halloween is getting to walk on the parkway either in Pigeon Forge or Gatlinburg. You can stay out pretty much all night. Just you and your friends having a blast with candy and dressed up. Then you just hang out and finish all your candy.

Those are three reasons why I like Halloween. Because you get to dress up, you get to have a lot of candy, and you also get to hang out with your friends. I love Halloween.

Destiny Mason, Grade 8
Pigeon Forge Middle School, TN

The Hindenburg

The greatest zeppelin that was ever built was the famous Hindenburg. It was so enormous that it was called "The Titanic of the Sky." At 803 feet long and 242 tons of hydrogen, it was larger than a football field. On March 4, 1936, this beauty took flight for the first time in Frankfurt, Germany. It continued its service of traveling from Europe to the United States in 1936 to 1937.

In the beginning of May, 1937 on a regular trip across the Atlantic Ocean the Hindenburg was scheduled to land in New Jersey at a naval air base. The Hindenburg's tail suddenly burst into flames during landing. The flames spread quickly as hydrogen is highly flammable. Ninety-seven people were onboard, including passengers and crew members. As the zeppelin caught fire, many people were frightened so they jumped to the grassy air base below. In 34 seconds, the whole craft was engulfed in flames.

Thirty-five people were killed that day in the tragic accident. Some people think that lightning struck the aircraft and others assume that German Nazi groups sabotaged it with a bomb. Recently, scientists studying what was left of the Hindenburg found out what really started the fire. The fabric was found to be the culprit because it was flammable and caught on fire with a small spark. Even if modern airplanes took over today's air travel, the Hindenburg has helped us look to the future of zeppelin travel.

Daniel Strohmetz, Grade 8
Oglethorpe Charter School, GA

Come Soar with Me

Have you ever gone places you've never been before? Not physically, I mean, mentally. A whole new world that you can make as real or crazy as you'd like? If so, you have imagination. There are many types of imagination such as the one I just described to you, but you can have imagination just by opening a book.

The first type of imagination is the kind you make up by yourself. Surely you remember when you were a kid playing with dolls or (so the boys won't yell at me) "action figures." Of course you do. Most of the time you didn't pretend your doll was in the real world. It was usually in a magical land or an army camp in the sky. You get the drift. Although sometimes the drift is gotten when you open a book.

You don't have to have creative thoughts by imagining that you're a princess. As soon as you open a good novel you can feel your mind going to that place in the book. For example, if you are reading *The Chronicles of Narnia*, you are instantly taken into Narnia. That does show imagination though it's mostly by the writer.

So here's my point. Imagination can come in all shapes and sizes, so be on the lookout for an opportunity to use yours. You never know when you'll pass something by. So pick up that book or doll and let your imagination soar.

Jenna Grant, Grade 7
Boyet Jr High School, LA

Fashionable Fur

Bears, tigers, and foxes. All animals with beautiful fur. But should we be wearing it? Soft, scarlet coats. But is it worth it? I think wearing real animal fur is wrong. We shouldn't be killing animals for unneeded clothes, using them for fashion, and taking their fur. I think it's wrong and it should be stopped.

People pace about the cold, crisp air, wearing fur coats and hats. It is not right. Real fur is wrong. There is no reason to be killing animals for their fur when there are so many other materials to make jackets out of. Their death is unnecessary.

Fashion. It is mainly for fashion. People walk around with dead animals on their backs for fashion thinking it's cool and stylish, but there is nothing pretty about killing animals. Seriously, animals are dying for our sense of clothing craze. They obviously have no say in using their skin for coats. We pretty much rip the fur off their back, sew it into something trendy, and sell it to people who want to show it off. Well I am not amazed or jealous. If we need to kill innocent animals for fur, there is something wrong.

Basically, I think we should stop wearing animal fur. It is wrong. We only use it for surplus clothing and vogue, and animals have no preference. If we have no good reason we shouldn't do it. It seriously needs to stop.

Rio Jacobbe, Grade 7
Bak Middle School of the Arts, FL

Reasons to Visit Europe

My family recently visited Europe and came up with great things to do there. The first reason being the shopping. In most European cities, you will find fantastic upscale shops and even some flagship stores. Milan would be the best city for you if you are looking for flagship. The stores in Milan included Versace, Giorgio Armani, Dolce & Gabbana, Louis Vuitton, Gucci, and Burberry.

Another great reason to visit Europe are the amazing sights. The most beautiful city we visited was Como, Italy, home of Lake Como; it was the most beautiful thing I have ever seen. We took an evening boat ride around the coastline of Lake Como and saw George Clooney's home, which is actually a point consisting of several homes. He and several other men were on his boat dock and waved to us. It is interesting to be in Lake Como and know that just over the other side of the mountains is Lake Lugano, so if you were to draw line over the mountain, one side would be in Italy, and the other in Switzerland. We saw bridges and architecture that were from the 1500's. There were many fishing villages and cosmopolitan cities based on the coast with large casinos.

A last reason is the European travel. We traveled throughout Europe by train which was unbelievable. You would be surrounded by mountains and everywhere you looked were waterfalls coming from the tops. It was by far the most interesting experience in my life.

Allison Hall, Grade 8
Heritage Hall School, OK

Personality

A personality is the emotion and behavioral characteristics of a person. Which means the way a person acts or feels. When you meet someone new, do you want them to be your friend because of their looks, or how smart they are, how they treat people, or their personality? The one thing we need to do is think about our personality too. We need to have our personality acceptable to God. Mainly, we need our personality to be in a Godly Manner, and then it will be acceptable to others.

Another question to ask yourself is; do you ever wonder what people say about you or the way you act toward people? Which really means your personality can also help in the way you handle things and the way you do things. All these things are the things people see when they look at you. So if you think your personality needs a little help you should ask someone "Do I have a great personality?" Everyone needs a little help in this situation, so the moral of my story is that we need to work on our personality and make it acceptable to God and others.

Me'Kayla Canady-McGee, Grade 8
Blue Ridge Christian School, MO

Vick Is Getting into Deeper Trouble

With his football world crashing around him, Michael Vick apparently did something to take the edge off the stress. He smoked some weed. Now, I'm willing to bet more people knew about Vick's alleged marijuana use than his dogfighting escapades while he was playing for the Atlanta Falcons, but that's a story for another time.

In the last few days, the word on the legal front was that Vick might be sentenced to a lot less than 18 months by U.S. District Judge Henry Hudson after his guilty plea for bankrolling a dogfighting operation. Now that he was tested positive for marijuana use — the sample was taken a week after the start of the NFL season — who knows if this could alter Judge Hudson's stance toward Vick?

Granted drug use is illegal, but I doubt that many of Vick's fans believe this latest offense is any big deal. The NFL, however, has higher standards for its employees. Once Vick was indicted, the NFL commissioner Roger Goodell placed the Falcon quarterback on indefinite suspension. Of course, one has to figure that Vick wasn't playing in the 2008 season at all given that he'll most likely be serving a prison sentence.

However, from the very beginning, the speculation has been rampant that the government would suspend Vick for one more season once he left federal prison stemming from his involvement in illegal betting. And this test definitely means the league will tack on a minimum of another four games lost to his career.

J.T. Freeman, Grade 7
Stroud Middle School, OK

Why Can't We All Just Be Happy?

Here recently, I have noticed that so many people in our society just act like nothing is ever good enough for them. They complain and complain, when other people, who have half the things, if even that, compared to these people, think everything is going just great! I think there are several reasons why people are like this, but the reason I think most about it is that some people let drama get to their heads and people want to be better than everyone else.

First of all, I think people let drama go to their head. For example, "Oh my goodness! That girl just said my shirt is ugly! Hide me!" Yet the girl beside her, in a secondhand flannel shirt is saying, "Hey isn't this shirt so cool? I bought it last night for $3!" The difference in these two girls, is that one wants to be better than she can be all the time, when the other is perfectly fine not having quite as much, and she would probably be okay with having less.

In conclusion, people should learn to be happy with what they have. Especially if they have more than most, and those who are all about themselves, should spend some time worrying about other things, like how to help those with less than them.

Charley Cochran, Grade 8
Rhea Central Elementary School, TN

Woodland Hills Mall

Have you ever gotten lost in the Woodland Hills Mall in Tulsa, Oklahoma? Well guess what I did when I was six years old. I was scared to death. I was screaming for my mom and dad. I was crying and everybody was looking at me running.

They have stores and all kinds of stuff. Well I'm going to start with sports there. I love to go to the sport stuff because I'm a sports fan. They have air soft guns, hunting stuff, fishing stuff and all kinds of sporting goods.

They have restaurants like Chick-Fillet, Chinese, pizza, and corndogs. My favorite food there is Chick-Fillet. It is the best. I love their chicken and French fries.

Back to the stores, I like American Eagle. Their clothes and shoes are very nice. I got a lot of clothes from American Eagle. You should go there. I also like Pac Sun because they have hats, shoes and other stuff. They also have awesome clothes and sweatshirts. Well they have a JC Penny and Payless. "JC Penny is a good place to shop," said my mom. I really like to hang out with my mom a lot. That's why I like Woodland Hills Mall.

Alex Mariezcurrena, Grade 7
Chelsea Jr High School, OK

Football: A Way of Life

One of my best friends, Arizona, is always up to play football. For Arizona, football is a way of life.

When the football lights come on, he's ready to play. He's more pumped than anyone I've ever seen. Just the way the football field looks makes him happy. You can always tell when Arizona is ready to play though. The look in his eyes can explain everything.

Arizona is five-eight and weighs about 180 pounds. His size, along with his short blonde hair makes him look very strong. He likes to wear sleeveless Under Armour shirts to show off his muscles. It makes him look pretty cool.

For me, the best thing about Arizona is that he never gives up. Even in the worst of situations; he tries he to make the best of them. He always knows what to say and when to say it. Although no one knows, Arizona is really sweet and has a big heart.

He has taught me many things throughout the years that we've known each other. One thing is that you can never look at life without open arms. Second, is that you should never look at the bad things in life. Only the good things. And no matter what, everything always works out.

I can't wait to see what else Arizona teaches me throughout my life. He is an inspiration to me. He's my hero. I know that Arizona is someone I can count on forever. I love him and he is my best friend.

Shelby Prather, Grade 8
Chelsea Jr High School, OK

Political Pretense

If you have ever watched *An Inconvenient Truth* you will immediately understand hypocrisy. The 100 minute documentary is contradictory despite its statistics. Throughout the film, there are constant shots of Mr. Gore in a car on a computer; he is not speaking, but those scenes represent a dramatic effect. The laptop uses energy, the car uses energy, the camera uses energy and editing these unnecessary moments into a film uses energy. I am not saying that Mr. Gore's statistics on global warming are inaccurate and I am not stating that they are accurate; only thirteen years old, I don't have the information to make a judgment on scientific topics. What I *am* saying is that it doesn't seem right to tell us the statistics (right or wrong) without giving us a solution. It doesn't seem right to tell us to cut back on energy use, then throw in bits and pieces of unnecessary biographical information and shots of people on computers in moving cars which all uses energy.

An Inconvenient Truth is just one example and global warming is just one topic. All across the country, politicians are too preoccupied with their parties to focus and solve the real issues. If they would give us a solution and personally contribute themselves, we might actually accomplish the goal.

Especially now, politicians need to forget about politics. We need to see them doing what they say they will do. We need them to live by their word. We don't need political pretense.

Jacqueline Frenkel, Grade 8
Brandon Academy, FL

Eyes

In my family, everyone has different eyes. My mom's are like a horse's mane, you can see the brown and each individual line looks like a strand of hair. My dad's are a greenish brown when he is dirty and sweaty because of working outside. They are bluish-green when he is happy like a lake. My eyes. My eyes are the green of the Incredible Hulk. The darkness is a black hole that even Columbus could not explore. The eye lashes flap and play sweet smooth music like the mockingbird's. My eyes are a brown dove that flies freely over the sky until September. My eyes are also two white magicians on the wrestling mats. I look at the enemies' faces and go for their legs and then look at their wrists and grab the ankles.

My eyes talk to me: they see through scopes, see baseballs while batting, and tell me who my friends are and who they aren't. Men have strong, rough-and-ready, eyes, while women have sympathetic beautiful-as-the-sunset eyes. They are the thumb print of your face, your vision, and contain the insights that guide your brain.

Spencer Craig, Grade 8
Baylor School, TN

Moving to Florida from New York

I moved from New York to Florida. I lived on Long Island in Inwood for 9 years. Then I moved to Cedarhurst, 5 minutes away. I lived in Cedarhurst for 2 years, renting a house. First we were going to move to North Carolina, but we didn't. We moved to Florida.

It took us two days because we stopped at a hotel and slept overnight. My aunt came too. On the day we left I went to my friend's house. We left at 7 p.m. We rented a 26-foot Penske truck. Me and my dad rode in the truck and my mom, brother, and aunt drove the car.

We got to the hotel at 3:00 in the morning. We left at 9:00 a.m. On our way down here we stopped in South of the Border in Dillon, South Carolina. I got a key chain. My dad got stickers. My mom got a coffee mug. We stopped at a gas station in South of the Border and got drinks, and my brother got firecrackers.

On our way there we made a lot of stops because we had to go the bathroom, or eat, or just stretch. I slept half of the way. We also brought 2 fish down.

Yeah! We finally got here at 4 a.m. I went out to see the pool, and my brother pushed me in with all my clothes on, and my money, gum, and my cell phone in my pocket! That was our trip to Florida.

Jesse DiSabato, Grade 7
Sebastian River Middle School, FL

Markelle's Strength

Strength, what is strength? Is strength only how much muscle you have, or is it much more? Can you have strength or belief in something without being able to measure it or see it? Well, I think you can have strength in something much more than your power. My strength is in God. Markelle is a woman fighting cancer with strength in God.

Markelle's life is as rough as anyone who is fighting cancer. Markelle has to rely on God. She knows the only way she can fight and win this battle of cancer is to have her strength in God. I have known Markelle for a long time now. She is a wonderful woman, with two children and a husband. She loves God and receives her strength through him. Markelle is doing great now through the power of prayer. Markelle has now gone two months without chemotherapy. She is doing incredibly well. Markelle trusted and put all her strength in God and is now doing better than she could have hoped.

Markelle's cancer has truly taught me a lot about God and the power of prayer. My friends, my church, my school, and I all prayed for Markelle for the past two years. She has gone through an incredibly long journey through this course of cancer. She relied and trusted God. He gave her all the strength she needed to make it through this rough time. God rewarded Markelle with life, because she trusted in Him.

Olivia Massey, Grade 8
College Heights Christian School, MO

The Window of Peace

Have you ever looked out your window and saw or heard something that made you feel passionate about something? I feel that way every time I return home after a busy day and look out the window of my room.

I see a small circular path near the street, shaded by magnificent, tall trees overlooking the house. Bushes grow along the path, covering the ground with bright, red berries. Grass grows abundantly in the middle, crowding around clumps of clover, fallen twigs, leaves, and seeds. This creates a very peaceful and serene environment in my mind.

In the circular path, there are small children from the neighborhood riding their bikes, laughing as they race each other. In the middle are kids running around, chasing each other for fun, but no matter what they are doing, they are all smiling, laughing, and chatting as they have fun with each other.

It pleases me to know that everyone can get along so well like that. They don't ever fight or tease each other just because of their differences. The children aren't prejudiced by where they came from; instead, they enjoy the mix of many cultures. They are all best friends and care for each other like a family. It is hard to think that such young children could be setting an example for all of us, but it is true. If they can be so peaceful, loving, and caring, why can't the rest of the world do the same?

Tiange Zhan, Grade 7
White Station Middle School, TN

Obesity in Children

Over the years kids in America have become fatter. I think the reasons for this are that parents aren't at home as much, poor food choices, and kids are not as active.

In the past not many moms worked, instead they would do household chores like cooking and cleaning. But now many more moms also have jobs, leaving the kids at home with no supervision of what they do. Many kids don't know how to cook, so they eat snack foods that are normally not healthy.

Now that we have at least one or two cars per family, on average kids don't get much exercise. In the past kids always walked to school. Now there're buses, and parents can drive them. There are also video games and the Internet which make kids not want to go out and play.

The last reason I think kids are fatter is food choices. People have busy schedules now so they eat fast food and often make poor choices. Also most of the time kids won't eat anything but what they want, which isn't always healthy. I think if Americans would eat healthy foods and exercise we wouldn't be so overweight!

Haley Becker, Grade 8
Immaculate Conception School, MO

Lane Frost

This is a story of the real 1986 World Champion Bull Rider, Lane Frost. Lane was a man that everyone liked. He persevered with courage and a good attitude. All his friends said he was a good man.

One reason why I chose Lane Frost was that he never gave up. At one rodeo, he was injured and the second day he rode and got a 92 point ride. In his marriage, he and his wife Kelly were going to get divorced, but he worked hard enough that he saved it.

How would you like to ride bulls that are two thousand plus pounds? Well Lane Did! He was in a seven matched up contest with Red Rock. He ended up riding him three of the seven rides. The loan, for the land he was going to start a bull riding school on, was approved on the day of Lane's funeral.

One of Lane's best qualities was his good attitude. Even after a bad ride, he had a smile on his face. At rodeos, you could find him behind the chutes showing kids the best technique for riding bulls. Lane was always glad to do his share and more of work. He believed that you could make mistakes and rise above them to get your life back on track.

He was a good example for kids and adults. he died doing what he loved to do. That is why Lane Frost is my "Oklahoma Hero."

Payton Alley, Grade 8
Mulhall-Orlando High School, OK

Kinder Transport

Kinder transport is about kids in World War II. World War II was very tragic, horrifying and devastating. Kinder means child or children and Transport means to take a large amount of something and move from one place to another. Imagine you're back at home in your bed sleeping. Your father is downstairs reading the newspaper, while your mother is in the kitchen baking cookies. Then suddenly a bomb hits the house across the street shattering people and glass. Your father yells up the stairs "AIR RAID!" You wake up terrified, grab your robe and run downstairs out the back door, into the safety shelter. World War II has begun.

The next day the whole block is destroyed and your house in one of few that did not get destroyed. Your friend is coming to live with you because her house got bombed. People all over the place are talking about something called Kinder Transport and your mother signs you up. You don't know if you will ever see your family again.

One month later, three bombings have happened again and it's time to load up on the Kinder Transport train. Bunches of kids are there and the station is full of mothers crying and kids saying goodbye. You turn around and see your mother is crying and then you realize what's going on. You hug her and tell her everything is going to be fine, climb aboard and the journey begins!

Leah Cashman, Grade 7

A Series of Mysteries

As I open the well-worn pages of my book, I go back in time almost eight years. I travel to a place where cell phones don't exist and River Heights is the rage. In that little town I follow around a famous girl detective. We're always equipped with a trusty flashlight and a handy magnifying glass in the glove box of the sporty blue roadster. Always timelessly dressed in classic fashions, we are on the lookout for someone who needs our help. We will search for anything from old clocks to dancing puppets. I travel with her as she searches mysterious bungalows, dusty hidden staircases, and haunted showboats. Kidnapping is no big deal, for we always manage to escape. Whether it is jumping off of moving trains or escaping in a rickety old rowboat, the criminals never hold us captive for long.

It is hard to get jealous when she relies on her chums Bess and George to help her solve the case, given that she has known them since 1929. If the cousins can't make it, Helen Corning is always glad to lend a hand. We might not be popular with circus ring masters, but Police Chief McGinnis loves our extraordinary crime solving ability. Therefore, he asks us to help with some of his most perplexing cases.

Suddenly my mom calls me, bringing me back to the present. Finally I put he Nancy Drew book on the shelf and smile, knowing I can go back tomorrow.

Mara Scarbrough, Grade 7
White Station Middle School, TN

An Unknown Hero

As the EP-3E ARIES II airplane looked as if it was going to crash, a steady hand held the wheel and ended up saving his crew of 20. When Shane Osborn was a young man he always dreamed of being a pilot. At age 13 he became part of the part of the Civil Air Patrol, and his career only got better. Years later, on April 1, 2001 Shane became mission commander for their weather observation missions. At first it looked like a textbook mission until a Chinese F8-II fighter crashed into the wing after a lot of harassment. The nose of the plane was severed from flying debris and it was all Osborn could do to keep the plane going straight.

For the longest 33 minutes of Osborn's life he held the plane steady and landed the plane safely on the Communist Chinese island of Hainan. For eleven days Osborn and his crew were questioned about the crash by Chinese officials who tried, unsuccessfully, to put the blame on Shane and his crew. The determination of the crew was amazing as they held their ground against night and day interrogations. For their bravery all 21 crew members received medals for their performance, and Shane received the Distinguished Flying Cross, which is the highest honor for airmanship. Lt. Shane Osborn was a man whom we should all take after because of his courage, dignity, and leadership, he helped others in a way nobody else could making him a hero.

Tyler Griggs, Grade 8
West Jr High School, MO

Bravery

Not being afraid is not bravery. Bravery is being afraid but overcoming that fear. My grandmother had cancer and was afraid, but she overcame it. She overcame her fear by not slumping down in self-pity and crying about it. She went to the doctor and had chemotherapy and surgery. Now she has a pouch on her side called a colostomy, where she has to go to the bathroom. Yes, it may seem a little strange but that is what the cancer did to her. She showed bravery by living through it and staying the same throughout it.

Just being scared is not bravery either. When my grandmother was younger, about eleven or twelve years old she was lying in bed when she heard a panther scream. A panther scream sounds like a woman's scream, only it sends a shiver down your spine. When she heard this she got scared and hid under her covers. Well, her dog got scared too. It was outside, saw a window open, and jumped through into my grandmother's room. The dog then decided the next safest place was my grandmother's bed and jumped in. She thought the dog was the panther and screamed until her dad came in, saw what was happening, and started laughing. Neither my grandmother nor her dog showed bravery. Bravery is doing the right thing even when you are afraid to do it. Overcome your fear. Be brave!

Jonathan Munton, Grade 8
Greenfield Jr/Sr High School, MO

God Is Good

There was an event in my life that was bad, but God turned it into a blessed time. My grandpa was diagnosed with cancer and the doctor said that he was only going to live for six more months. The worst part of this was that my grandpa wasn't saved. Six months seemed like such a short time. I didn't want my grandpa to die and go to Hell, and I wondered how God might work this out.

Soon we saw how the Lord was going to make this sad situation positive. We knew a pastor that lived near my grandparents. Our pastor friend began to visit my grandpa and grandma. My grandparents really liked this pastor. My aunt met him too and he spent a lot of time with them. After a couple months, not only did my grandpa get saved but so did my grandma and my aunt and my uncle and my cousins. God had worked it out that my whole family in St. Louis got saved!

All this time I worried about my grandpa's salvation, and in a moment's time God blessed my entire family. It was an amazing event that seemed like a modern day miracle to me. God had this whole thing planned from the start. He made an awful thing into a sweet memory.

Annie Bridgford, Grade 8
College Heights Christian School, MO

Disneyworld

Last year me and my family took a trip to Disneyworld. We stayed at the best hotel. We went to all the parks and rode a lot of rides. We saw a lot of characters and got their autographs. It was a really fun trip and one day we're going back.

We stayed at the Pop Century Hotel. The hotel pools were really fun. We had three rooms that were right beside each other. The hotel is really big and has many rooms. The hotel was really fun and we're going to stay at it again.

We went to all the parks, which were fun. We rode a lot of rides, but we didn't ride all of them. My favorite ride was the Tower of Terror. I was scared at first, but then I got on it. As you can see, we had a lot of fun riding most of the rides.

We saw a lot of characters and we got their autographs. At Magic Kingdom we saw some of the characters. On the last day we finally saw Mickey and Minnie Mouse. We also got to see many others. We didn't get to see all of them, but we got to see most of them.

Brittany Metcalf, Grade 8
Pigeon Forge Middle School, TN

A Peaceful Place

I moved to Chelsea when I was just over a year old. So I basically grew up in Chelsea. I started school here when I was five. I liked my kindergarten teacher Mrs. Hays, and I thought Mrs. Belles was nice too. This is a quiet town and my mom says that if we lived anywhere else I would not be able to ride around the way I do. My most favorite teacher was Mrs. Pack. She was my teacher for third grade. She moved away at the end of my school year. After that I started school at Art Goad. I liked some of my teachers, but not all of them. Every year in Chelsea we have the Jamboree. There are rides and food and I have lots of fun. The Hurricane is my favorite ride and I love the games. I always want to bring home some prizes and stuff. The food is good, giant corn dogs and fresh lemonade taste so good! I just want to stay here forever. And the best thing about Chelsea is that it's home. No other place on Earth is the same, no people nicer, no streets as familiar, no places as comfortable. These are just a few of the reasons that Chelsea is my favorite place in Oklahoma!

Scott Barrows, Grade 7

Football

My first football game was when I played for LaGrange Bulldogs when we played against Pink Hill. Even though we lost that game we came close that game. But when we played against Banks we beat them so bad. And then we went on to a 10-2 record. And my second year I played football was when I played for Banks, but when I played for Banks we were the worst team because we lost all our games but one because we tied up 0 to 0 on our first game we played. Now I am on my third year playing football. I play football for the Frink Caveliers and I am in 8th grade and I am starting on defense as a cornerback. And now we are on our fourth game, we are going to play against Woodington and we hope to beat Woodington so our record can be 2 and 2 because we play against them on a Thursday. And then our last game will be against a hard team so we will have to practice hard if we want to beat that team.

Tyler Clark, Grade 8
E B Frink Middle School, NC

Index